WITHDRAWN

SOCIETY IN CHANGE
STUDIES IN HONOR OF BÉLA K. KIRÁLY

Edited by

Steven Bela Vardy
and
Agnes Huszar Vardy

East European Monographs, Boulder
Distributed by Columbia University Press, New York
1983

EAST EUROPEAN MONOGRAPHS, NO. CXXXII

SOCIETY IN CHANGE: STUDIES IN HONOR OF BÉLA K. KIRÁLY

Advisory Editorial Board:

Istvan Deak
Columbia University

János Decsy
Greater Hartford Community
College

Stephen Fischer-Galati
University of Colorado

Joseph Held
Rutgers University

Robert L. Hess, President
Brooklyn College
City University of New York

Peter Pastor
Montclair State College

Hans L. Trefousse
Brooklyn College
City University of New York

Copyright © 1983 by Steven Bela Vardy
Library of Congress Catalog Card Number: 82-83524
ISBN: 0-88033-21-X
Printed in the United States of America

General Béla K. Király

FINANCIAL CONTRIBUTORS

Fund Raising Committee

János Decsy, Chairman   Agnes Huszar Vardy
Peter Pastor   Steven Bela Vardy

* * * * * * * * * * *

Stephen G. Baracsi, Providence, Rhode Island
Raymond F. Damato, Manchester, Connecticut
Orest T. Dubno, Hartford, Connecticut
Neil M. Ellis, Manchester, Connecticut
Mr. & Mrs. Joseph F. Gately, Bolton, Connecticut
Miklos Gellert, West Hartford, Connecticut
Michael B. Lynch, Manchester, Connecticut
Arpad Merva, Providence, Rhode Island
Mr. & Mrs. Elemer Nyarady, Bolton, Connecticut
John E. Parmelee, Warwick, Rhode Island
Joseph Sanady, West Hartford, Connecticut
Istvan Simon, Woodland, California
Dr. & Mrs. Balazs B. Somogyi, Southington, Connecticut
Sandor Taraszovics, Washington, D.C.
Leslie Szilagyi, Hartford, Connecticut
Ludis Upenieks, Manchester, Connecticut
Mr. & Mrs. Arpad M. Vajda, Essex Jct., Vermont
Mr. & Mrs. J. Michael Zabkar, Jr., Andover, Connecticut

CONTENTS

Foreword ix
The Hon. Christopher J. Dodd, United States Senate
Editors' Preface xi

I. BÉLA K. KIRÁLY

1. Béla K. Király, the Man and the Historian 3
   S. B. Vardy, *Duquesne University*
   Agnes Huszar Vardy, *Robert Morris College*
2. Béla K. Király's Bibliography 15
   S. B. Vardy and Agnes Huszar Vardy

II. SIEGES, WARS, MILITARY THEORIES AND MILITARY ALLIANCES

3. The Defense of Nándorfehérvár (Belgrade) in 1456:
   A Discussion of Controversial Issues 25
   Joseph Held, *Rutgers University*
4. The Economic Policy of "Kriegsraison" in Germany
   during the Thirty Years War 39
   Gerhard Benecke, *University of Kent, England*
5. Clausewitz: The Forerunner of Mathematical Praxeology 53
   Géza Perjés, *Hungarian Academy of Sciences*
6. Combat Organization and Command Style as Command
   Problems in the "Honvéd" Army: December 1848-April 1849 75
   Zoltán Kramár, *Central Washington University*
7. Hungary and the Common Army in the Austro-Hungarian
   Monarchy 89
   Gábor Vermes, *Rutgers University at Newark*

8. Limits of War Planning: Roosevelt and "RAINBOW 5" 103
   Mark M. Lowenthal, *Library of Congress*
9. Power and Politics: The Military and Communist Power within the Warsaw Pact 123
   Ivan Volgyes, *University of Nebraska*
   Hans Brisch, *University of Nebraska*

III. ETHNICITY, IMMIGRATION AND DOMESTIC POLITICS IN AMERICA

10. The New Anti-Semanticism: Ethnicity and Nationalism 153
    Louis L. Snyder, *City College–City University of New York*
11. Haraszthy: A Hungarian Pioneer in the American West 169
    Mario D. Fenyő, *University of Calabar, Nigeria*
12. The Great Economic Immigration from Hungary: 1880-1920 189
    S. B. Vardy, *Duquesne University*
13. Significance and Possibilities for Existence of a National Minority: The Romanian Subculture in the USA–Theory and Perspectives 217
    Stephen Fischer-Galati, *University of Colorado*
14. America through Hungarian Eyes: Images and Impressions of American Civilization as Reflected in Recent Hungarian Writings on the United States 231
    Ivan Sanders, *Suffolk County Community College*
15. Abraham Lincoln versus Andrew Johnson: Two Approaches to Reconstruction 251
    Hans L. Trefousse, *Brooklyn College*

IV. CENTRAL EUROPEAN AND BALKAN SOCIAL AND POLITICAL DEVELOPMENTS

16. The Seven Hungarian Counties in Medieval Transylvania 273
    Imre Boba, *University of Washington*
17. Delinquent Lords and Forsaken Serfs: Thoughts on War and Society during the Crisis of Feudalism 291
    János M. Bak, *University of British Columbia*

18. Seventeenth-Century Bulgarian "Pomaks:" Forced or
    Voluntary Converts to Islam? 305
    Dennis P. Hupchik, University of Pittsburgh
19. Budapest: A Dominant Capital in a Dominant Country? 315
    Istvan Deak, *Columbia University*
20. God's Vineyard: Excerpts from a Political Autobiography ... 327
    Tamás Aczél, *University of Massachusetts*
21. Peasants in Two Political Systems: An Austrian and a
    Hungarian Village Compared 349
    Michael Sozan, *Slippery Rock State College*

V. CENTRAL EUROPEAN AND BALKAN CULTURAL DEVELOPMENTS

22. The Problems of Hungarian University Foundations
    in the Middle Ages 371
    L. S. Domonkos, *Youngstown State University*
23. Hungarian Historiography and European Currents of Thought
    from the Late Baroque to Early Romanticism, 1700-1830 ... 391
    Thomas Szendrey, *Gannon University*
24. Venelin and Bulgarian Origins 413
    James F. Clarke, *University of Pittsburgh*
25. The Evaluation of Leopold II in Hungarian Historiography .. 435
    Peter F. Sugar, *University of Washington*
26. The Turks and Ottoman Civilization in Jókai's "Historical
    Novels" and Short Stories 449
    Agnes Huszar Vardy, *Robert Morris College*
27. The Hungarian Poets' Task: The Historic and Historical
    Mission of Hungarian Poetry through Five Centuries 471
    Louis J. Elteto, *Portland State University*
28. "Die Frau ohne Schatten:" Opera as Conservative Allegory .. 489
    Paula Sutter Fichtner, *Brooklyn College*
29. Vilfredo Pareto's Love/Hate Relationship to Italy and His
    Transition from Economics to Sociology 501
    Frank J. Coppa, *St. John's University, Jamaica*

INTER-NATIONALITY RELATIONS IN THE DANUBE VALLEY

30. Hungary in the Habsburg Monarchy: From Independence Struggle to Hegemony 523
    Stephen Borsody, *Chatham College*
31. Central European Federalism in the Thought of Oscar Jászi and his Successors 539
    N. F. Dreisziger, *Royal Military College of Canada*
32. Socialist Patriotism and National Minorities: A Comparison of the Yugoslav and Romanian Theory and Practice 557
    Andrew Ludanyi, *Ohio Northern University*
33. Patterns of Minority Life: Recent Hungarian Literary Reports in Romania 585
    Károly Nagy, *Middlesex County College and Rutgers University*

VII. INTER-STATE RELATIONS IN CENTRAL AND EASTERN EUROPE

34. Andrássy's Views on Austria-Hungary's Foreign Policy toward Russia 599
    János Decsy, *Greater Hartford Community College*
35. Mihaly Károlyi and his Views on Hungary-Russian Ties 613
    Peter Pastor, *Montclair State College*
36. Goering's Italian Exile: 1924-1925 623
    Michael Palumbo, *Brooklyn, New York*
37. Hitler and the Statesmen of East Central Europe: 1939-1945 641
    György Ránki, *Indiana University and Hungarian Academy of Sciences*

Contributors 673

FOREWORD

I feel honored by the request of the editors to open this volume with my thoughts about Béla Király—soldier, revolutionary, scholar.

When I stood on the Senate floor a few months ago, speaking to commemorate the Hungarian Revolution of a quarter century before, my motivation was twofold. I wanted to pay tribute to those who, in 1956, gave their lives for the freedom of all of us, but I also wanted to honor the living heroes of that historic struggle, some of whom I am fortunate to count among my friends.

Although in the lifetime of my generation, America waged three wars and faced other serious challenges, we were spared of a war being fought on American soil. The generation of Béla Király was not as fortunate in Hungary. The ravaging of two world wars and a savagely suppressed revolution, Nazi German and Communist Soviet occupations have shattered the political and social system of the country again and again, profoundly altering the way of life of the inhabitants. In other words, during a generation, history rudely and repeatedly intruded on everyone's life.

Béla Király was not contented to be a passive witness to these upheavals, a mere pawn of history. As a soldier, rising to the rank of general—and when necessity arose, as a revolutionary, member of Imre Nagy's revolutionary government—he was always with the bravest of the brave, facing ultimate danger against overwhelming odds. He was active as an anti-Nazi and later as an anti-Communist. Imprisoned on the false charge of being an American spy he spent years on death-row. He escaped his second death sentence only by his timely flight to the West, after the Red Army descending on revolutionary Hungary made further resistance virtually suicidal.

I have known Béla Király since my childhood, inheriting his friendship from my father, and as a child, I was certainly impressed by the heroic deeds of this larger-than-life real general. Now, however, when I try to take a measure of him, after a second life as an American educator, professor of history, his scholarly side impresses me just as much. Driven by the same urge to do what is right he became one of our most eminent scholars of East European and military history. Class after class of American students benefited from the wisdom of this man who was not only chronicler, but also a maker of history.

With all his warrior past, Béla Király remains a modest, serene man of profound wisdom and balanced views. As a foe of both totalitarian scourges of this century he has been a moderate and a humanist as an American as well. He has been a tremendous gain for his new homeland and his advice has often been sought by our Presidents as well as our military.

Rumors of his retirement are greatly exaggerated. I do not believe for a moment that he will be content just to rest and that we have heard the last of him. Since this volume honors him on the occasion of at least his formal retirement, I want to thank him for all the experience, wisdom and humanity that he brought for us with him, and that he distributed so generously. I hope these thoughts about him that I included in this Foreward will serve as a token of my deep respect and warm friendship.

CHRISTOPHER J. DODD
United States Senator

EDITORS' PREFACE

This collection of essays encompasses a broad spectrum of European and American history—with particular emphasis on the military, social, cultural and inter-nationality relations of the peoples of East Central Europe and their immigration and fortunes in the United States.

Chronologically the spread is equally wide, stretching over a whole millennium of history. Yet, these essays may also be viewed as constituting an organic whole. They are bound together by the personality of Béla K. Király, whose scholarly interest has ranged over much of the fields and topics covered by his friends' and colleagues' essays contained in this volume.

When originally conceived in the fall of 1981, we were thinking only of a dozen or so closely interrelated essays in military history. Soon, however, we were forced to conclude that Béla K. Király's popularity made our goal unrealistic. So many of his friends volunteered to contribute to this volume that we were compelled to broaden its scope considerably. In addition to seven essays in military history, we have added contributions in five other categories. These include six essays on ethnicity, immigration and domestic American politics, six essays on Central and Southeast European social and political developments, eight essays on the cultural development of the same region, and four essays each on the inter-nationality and inter-state relationships in Central and Eastern Europe.

We have also compiled a list of Béla K. Király's publications, and prepared an assessment of his achievements as a historian. Whether we have succeeded or not in this portrayal, is for the readers to decide.

As the enclosed essays were authored by thirty-six contributors in four distinct fields from about half a dozen countries, the views represented here are also far from uniform. While we did engage in a certain degree of editing, we did not—nor could we have—altered the scholarly, aesthetic or politico-ideological views of the individual authors. Those views are their own, and do not necessarily reflect the views of any of the co-authors, nor of the two editors.

Our greatest difficulty in editing these studies was to create some degree of uniformity in the use of geographical, national and institutional terms, and in the system of documentation. Here we have achieved only modest results. Stylistic changes—which at times included the removal of strong or emotionally-charged adjectives—were somewhat easier; although in the case of translated studies this work was often most gruelling. We also tried to standardize spelling—except in the case of English and Canadian authors, where the British spelling was retained.

This work could not have come about without the close cooperation of some of Béla Király's closest friends and admirers, more specifically Professors János Decsy, Stephen Fischer-Galati, Hans Trefousse and Peter Pastor—all of whom are also members of the Advisory Editorial Board, along with Professors Istvan Deak, Joseph Held and Robert L. Hess.

We are particularly grateful to Senator Christopher J. Dodd for his introduction to this volume; to President Robert L. Hess of Brooklyn College who has faithfully supported Professor Király in his many endeavors; to Professors János Decsy and Peter Pastor who were the driving force behind this undertaking and who—under Professor Decsy's chairmanship—carried out the necessary fund drive; and to all of Professor Király's friends whose financial contributions have made the publication of this work possible.

S. B. Vardy and Agnes Huszar Vardy
Pittsburgh, Pennsylvania
Fall 1982

I

BÉLA K. KIRÁLY

S. B. Vardy and Agnes Huszar Vardy

BÉLA K. KIRÁLY:
THE MAN AND THE HISTORIAN

The roots of Hungarian historiography reach back to the medieval chronicles of the eleventh to the thirteenth centuries, but the rise of critical historical writing in Hungary is only a nineteenth-century phenomenon.[1] Similarly, historical works on Hungary and the Hungarians by foreigners have their roots in the Middle Ages—predating even the birth of Hungarian historiography.[2] Large-scale research on Hungarian history abroad, however, is really the product of the post-World War II period. This is so, partially because of Hungary's new position as a western frontierland of Eastern Europe (for a thousand years before 1945 it was the other way around), and perhaps even more importantly, because of the presence throughout the world of a great number of historians of Hungarian birth or with Hungarian roots. The latter phenomenon became especially pronounced in the course of the past quarter century since the Hungarian Revolution of 1956, which saw the emigration of many historians and prospective historians from Hungary, as well as the rise of a whole generation of Western-educated historians with Hungarian roots, or at least with considerable interest in Hungary. The result was the unusual flowering of Hungarian historical studies in the West, which phenomenon was also aided in recent years by the increasing contacts with Hungary and the Hungarian scholarly world.[3]

Among the historians who made this flowering possible—especially as it relates to the United States and the English-speaking world—none is more distinguished than Béla K. Király, a former general of the Hungarian Army, and currently a highly respected Professor of Military History at the City University of New York (Brooklyn College and the Graduate School).

General Béla K. Király—who has just arrived at the major milestone of seven decades of human life—is indeed a man of many accomplishments in at least two distinct fields: military leadership and historical research. Compelled by circumstances to change careers in mid-life, he became a distinguished scholar-historian after an equally distinguished career as one of Hungary's brilliant young military leaders.

Born on April 14, 1912 in the small Transdanubian city of Kaposvár, Béla Király grew up with the intention of becoming a veterinarian. The thought of a military career never came to him until he was offered his home county's much-coveted scholarship to the Ludovika Military Academy (Hungary's West Point). Graduating in 1935, within five years he was already a captain and assigned to the Hungarian General Staff's War Academy (1940-1942) with brilliant career possibilities. After receiving his second degree in 1942, Király was attached to the Ministry of Defense, where—with the exception of three separate stretches spent on the eastern front—he remained until 1945.[4]

Following Ferenc Szálasi's coup d'état (October 15, 1944), which placed the national socialist Arrow Cross Party into power, Király immediately joined the opposition. After the war, he continued to serve in Hungary's new armed forces right up to his arrest in 1951. In 1948 he became the deputy commander, and in 1949 the commander of the Hungarian infantry; while in the following year he was named the superintendent of the War Academy.

In 1951 Király fell victim to Hungary's "Stalinist purges" directed by Mátyás Rákosi. He was condemned to death as an "American spy," but his sentence was commuted to life imprisonment. After five years of incarceration he was freed in September of 1956, largely as a result of the "liberating winds" that heralded the coming of the revolution. Soon after regaining his freedom, Király joined the ranks of Imre Nagy's immediate supporters, and as such he also became embroiled in the revolution. During Nagy's short tenure in office, Király was elected commander-in-chief of the reestablished Hungarian National Guard, and almost immediately was also appointed the military commander of Budapest.

After the defeat of the revolution in November 1956, Király left Hungary for the United States, where he became involved in emigré politics, and also founded the Hungarian Freedom Fighters (National Guard) Federation. His political activities took him to many countries and most continents. But while so engaged, he also sensed the increasing futility of such activities and began to search for a way out. Instead of simply lamenting the past—as is customary among ex-politicians and ex-military leaders in immigration—Király decided to begin a new life and a new career by retraining himself as a professional historian.

Enrolling at Columbia University, Béla Király continued his studies in East European and in military history. He received his M.A. in 1959, and his Ph.D. in 1966. In the meanwhile he joined the faculty of CUNY's Brooklyn College (1964), where in 1969 he became a full professor, and in 1973 the Chairman of the East European Section of the Graduate School's Center for European Studies. Two years later Béla Király was also appointed the Director of the University's Program on War and Society in Change, while in 1981 he became the editor-in-chief of the Atlantic Studies on Society in Change, distributed by Columbia University Press. During the late 1960s and early 1970s, he also served as Visiting Professor both at St. John's University (1968-1970), as well as at Columbia University (1970-1973).

* * * * *

Those who study the integration of immigrants into American society tell us that beyond a certain age, the process of adaptation and assimilation is very difficult. This same phenomenon was expressed by the mid-nineteenth-century Hungarian poet, Mihály Tompa (1817-1868), as follows:

". . .anguish and slow death is the fate of a tree
that's planted all mature to lands beyond the sea."[5]

Tompa wrote his "Letter to a Self-Exiled Friend" [*"Levél egy kibujdosott barátom után"*] to his fellow poet Frigyes Kerényi (1822-1852), after the latter's emigration to America following the defeat of the Hungarian Revolution of 1848-1849.[6] And Tompa's assessment proved to be prophetic, for Kerényi was never able to fit into the New World. He wasted away, gradually losing his sanity, and then dying alone and forlorn somewhere on the great American prairie, while on his way from Iowa to Texas. True, very few of the transplanted immigrants ended up like Kerényi. Yet, most of the adults among them had considerable adjustment problems, and relatively few of the non-technical intelligentsia were able to create new careers commensurate with their skills, education and past experiences. And this holds particularly true for those who were military officers, state and local administrators, lawyers, or intellectuals connected with one of the humanistic disciplines.[7]

Not so Béla Király. Unlike most of his fellow military officers, he refused to spend his time simply bemoaning the past, but went ahead to put his talents and experience to work. And in carrying out his goals, he may have been the only Hungarian ex-general who was even willing to become a student again. He had been a most capable and successful military officer in Hungary, and he proved to be an equally competent and successful scholar-historian in the United States.

* * * * *

In the course of the past two decades since becoming a professional historian, Béla Király had authored three books and over fifty research articles and chapters, while at the same time also editing or co-editing nearly a dozen volumes. His writings have appeared in over half a dozen countries in seven different languages, including English, French, German, Hungarian, Japanese, Spanish and Swedish. This is a prodigious achievement indeed, particularly if we consider that Király began his publishing activities only after his fiftieth birthday. And he is still going strong, both as an author, as well as an editor and organizer of Hungarian-related historical research in the United States.

Topically Béla Király's scholarly works can be divided into half a dozen categories, three of which—the Hungarian Revolution of 1956, enlightened despotism, and Ferenc Deák and Hungarian liberalism—are anchored into his three authored books.

Of these three topics, the one closest to Király's heart is the Hungarian Revolution of 1956, in which he himself has played a significant role. It is the subject of several of his earliest English language studies, as well as of his latest book entitled *The First War between Socialist States* [*Az első háború szocialista országok között,* 1981].[8] As is natural and expected, this work is not really the history of the Revolution of 1956, but an account of General Király's personal role therein. Although not all of his writings on the revolution are so personal in nature, they all carry the touch of a prominent participant in this momentous event. And this also holds true to some degree for Király's account of "Hungary's Army under the Soviets" —a study that also appeared in German and in Japanese.[9] In light of his personal involvement in Hungary's military leadership both before and during the Revolution of 1956, Béla Király's studies on this question will undoubtedly be read and used for a long time, not only as scholarly treatments of Hungary's military development during the 1940s and 1950s, but also as primary sources for at least some aspects of the events of those years.[10]

Although events connected with 1956 and with Hungary's postwar military development are closest to Béla Király's heart, the topic which first made him into a recognized scholar–historian in the United States was his study of the period of enlightened despotism in Hungary. Originally written as his doctoral dissertation at Columbia University (1966),[11] this work was published in 1969 under the title: *Hungary in the Late Eighteenth Century: The Decline of Enlightened Despotism.*[12] In this volume Király gave a detailed examination of late-eighteenth-century Hungary's complex social and governmental structure, and also analyzed the "reactionary alliance between the Hungarian estates and the Habsburg dynasty" that replaced the socially much more progressive Josephinean Age.[13] Most contemporary reviewers praised Király's above work as an example of excellent scholarship, and most predicted that it would stand the test of time and become the standard English language work on late-eighteenth-century Hungary for a long time to come.[14] After the passage of nearly a decade and a half this projection proved to be correct. It is now even more evident that Király's work will continue to remain the standard handbook on this topic for many more years.

As a by-product of this major work, Király also published a number of related shorter studies. These include his description of Hungary's peasant movements of 1790,[15] a similar description of the Prussian involvement in Poland and its relationship to the Hungarian "feudal revolt" of 1790,[16] his analysis of the military and nationalistic aspects of that feudal revolt,[17] his study of the impact of the Napoleonic ideas on Hungary,[18] as well as his analyses of Hungarian-Polish relations at the time of the Polish partitions and the November Insurrection of 1830.[19]

Perhaps as a natural extension of his study of late-eighteenth century Hungarian society and political developments, Király soon turned his attention to the period of the Hungarian Reform, and more specifically to the personality of Ferenc Deák (1803-1876).[20] Although not as well-known and not as conspicuous as either Count István Széchenyi (1791-1860) or Lajos Kossuth (1802-1894),[21] Deák—the primary architect of the Austro-Hungarian Compromise of 1867—may have been "the only Hungarian statesman of the past century and a half or two centuries who managed to achieve his goals."[22] In preparing his biography of Deák for Twayne Publishers' "World Leaders Series," Király was compelled to work within certain constraints of space and scholarship. Even so he produced a well-documented, balanced, reliable and—most importantly—readable account of Deák's life and achievements, which had filled a significant gap in American historical scholarship on nineteenth-century Hungary. Moreover, similarly to his earlier efforts, his study of Deák's life and nineteenth-century Hungarian political developments also resulted in the publication of several related articles. Included among these are his studies on Deák's views on serfdom,[23] his radicalism,[24] his role in pre-revolutionary Hungary,[25] his activities as a social reformer during the revolution,[26] as well as his views on Hungarian nationalism.[27]

Béla Király's historical research on eighteenth and nineteenth-century social and political developments in conjunction with the preparation of the above-mentioned two volumes and numerous related articles also turned his attention to the so-called "peasant question," which was the most acute of Hungary's social problems throughout the modern period right up to our own age. Some of the results of his aroused interest were incorporated in his cited volumes and several of his mentioned essays. But this interest also found expression in such other major articles as those concerning neo-serfdom in Hungary,[28] Maria Theresa's serf reforms,[29] serf emancipation in East Central Europe,[30] and various peasant movements in nineteenth and twentieth-century Hungary.[31]

While concentrating on the peasant question, Király also wrote scholarly assessments about a number of other related social and political issues. These include articles on the Transylvanian conception of liberty,[32] Hungarian-Turkish relations at the time of Prince Ferenc Rákóczi II's exile,[33] Reformation in Hungary,[34] the role of the Catholic Church in eighteenth-century Hungary,[35] Hungarian attitudes toward the Polish question in the eighteenth and nineteenth centuries,[36] Hungarian views on nineteenth-century America,[37] Oscar Jászi and his views concerning Danubian Europe,[38] Paul Teleki and Hungarian Revisionism,[39] and international polycentrism[40] —all published in respectable journals and books, some of the latter having been edited by Király himself.

While engaged in researching, writing and publishing the above books and dozens of articles, in 1975 Béla Király also initiated the monograph series entitled "Brooklyn College Studies on Society in Change."[41] This was soon followed by the sub-series "War and Society in East Central Europe," the first volume of which appeared in 1979.[42] In addition to serving as editor-in-chief of both of these series, Király also edited or co-edited nearly a dozen of these volumes.[43] Furthermore, he contributed to most of these volumes significant chapters on various aspects of Hungarian and European military history, from the Middle Ages to our own period. These included his study on the mounted knights and the first standing armies,[44] his essays on eighteenth and nineteenth-century European warfare,[45] his assessments of the military operations and peacemaking during and after World War I,[46] as well as about two dozen articles and chapters on the military aspects of the Hungarian Revolution of 1956 and the period that preceded it.[47]

* * * * * *

All in all, in the course of the past quarter of a century Béla Király has been a most productive scholar. The topics of his books and research titles encompass a wide range of the history of Hungary and of East Central Europe. And he is still going strong: writing, publishing and editing in his chosen fields. What he has done is truly enviable. Yet, his role in Hungarian and East Central European studies in the United States goes far beyond the broad scope outlined by the spectrum of his publications. He is one of the top organizers of the historical studies in his area of specialization. As one of the founders of the American Association for the Study of Hungarian History (1970),[48] he was instrumental in bringing order and direction into the ranks of the American researchers of Hungarian history. Also, as the past president of the AASHH (1980-1981), he was likewise responsible for injecting new vigor into this important organization. Moreover, the annual conferences that he organizes in conjunction with CUNY's Program on War and Society in East Central Europe serve as magnets for many of the top scholars in the field, including dozens of fellow historians and social scientists from Hungary. As a matter of fact, next to the pioneering Hungarian Studies Program (since 1979, Hungarian Chair) at Indiana University,[49] currently Béla Király's War and Society Conferences at Brooklyn College are among the most significant—if not the most important—forums of scholarly exchanges between American and Hungarian historians and scholars in the related disciplines.[50]

In light of the above, we are convinced that Béla K. Király's impact on American historical scholarship on Hungary and to a lesser degree on East Central Europe, is a most significant one. It is perhaps much more significant than one can perceive today without the appropriate historical distance and perspective. While our assessment concerning specific areas of his impact may perhaps be altered or amended in the future, few would question that his contributions to historical scholarship and his role as an organizer of Hungarian historical studies in the United States will always stand as guiding lights and reliable cornerstones of the discipline of history.

NOTES

1. On the development of Hungarian historiography see S. B. Vardy, *Modern Hungarian Historiography* (Boulder: East European Quarterly, Distributed by Columbia University Press, 1966); and C. A. Macartney, *The Medieval Hungarian Historians* (Cambridge: The University Press, 1953).

2. Concerning the earliest historical reports on the Magyars see György Győrffy, ed., *A magyarok elődeiről és a honfoglalásról: Kortársak és krónikások híradásai* [Concerning the Magyar Ancestors and the Conquest: Reports by Contemporaries and by Chroniclers] (Budapest: Gondolat Kiadó, 1975). See also István Dienes, *The Hungarians Cross the Carpathians* (Budapest: Corvina Press, 1972).

3. Cf. S. B. Vardy, "Hungarian Studies at American and Canadian Universities," *Canadian-American Review of Hungarian Studies,* II, 2 (Fall, 1975), pp. 91-121; and S. B. Vardy and Agnes Huszar Vardy, "Research in Hungarian-American History and Culture," in *The Folk Arts of Hungary,* eds. Walter W. Kolar and Agnes Huszar Vardy (Pittsburgh: Duquesne University Tamburitzans Institute of Folk Arts, 1981), pp. 67-124, reprinted as *Duquesne University Studies in History,* No. 11.

4. Concerning Béla Király's life and career see *Contemporary Authors*

(Detroit: Gale Research Co., 1976), LXI-XXIV, p. 301; Péter Gosztonyi, "Király Béla köszöntése" [Homage to Béla Király], *Irodalmi Ujság* [Literary Gazette] (Paris), XXXIII, 2 (1982), p. 5; and Király's own summary of his life, "Király Béla–Király Béláról" [Béla Király on Béla Király], in No. 3 of his *Works*, pp. 87-88. (Henceforth reference to Király's publications will be as *Works*, with the appropriate number, as found in his appended bibliography.)

5. Our translation. Tompa's original lines read as follows: "Mert hosszú hervadás emészti azt a fát,/Melyet nagy korában tesznek más földbe át." Cf. *Magyar versek könyve* [The Book of Hungarian Verse], ed. János Horváth (Budapest: A Magyar Szemle Társaság Kiadása, 1942), p. 464.

6. Concerning Kerényi see Lajos Biró, "A honvágy halottja" [The Victim of Homesickness], *Pásztortűz*, II (1922), pp. 695-697; and Géza Kende, *Magyarok Amerikában. Az amerikai magyarság története* [Hungarians in America. The History of Hungarian Americans] (2 vols., Cleveland: A Szabadság Kiadása, 1927), I, pp. 190-194.

7. For an unusually interesting portrayal of the inability or near-inability of the non-technical intelligentsia to adjust to the conditions in the New World see Kázmér Nagy, *Elveszett alkotmány. Vázlat az 1944 és 1964 közötti magyar politikai emigráció kialakulásáról* [The Lost Constitution. Sketches Concerning the Development of the Hungarian Political Emigration between 1944 and 1964] (Munich: Auróra Könyvek, 1974); and the much expanded and rewritten second edition of this work (London: Szerző Kiadása, 1982). See also S. B. Vardy, "Hungarians in America's Ethnic Politics," in *America's Ethnic Politics*, eds. Joseph S. Roucek and Bernard Eisenberg (Westport, Ct: Greenwood Press, 1982), pp. 171-196.

8. *Works*, no. 3. For a review of this work see Gyula Schöpflin, "Könyvek ötvenhatról" [Books about Fifty-Six], *Irodalmi Ujság*, XXXII, 3 (1982), p. 21.

9. *Works*, nos. 39-43.

10. *Works*, nos. 13, 19, 21, 34-38, 44-48, 50-54, 59-61, 68-69, 73.

11. *1790: Society in Royal Hungary* (Ph.D. Dissertation, Columbia University, New York, 1966), 475 pp.

12. *Works*, no. 1.

13. See S. B. Vardy's review of this work in *The Catholic Historical Review*, LIX, 3 (October 1973), pp. 468-469.

14. See also George Barany's review in the *American Historical Review*, LXXV, 4 (April 1970), pp. 1157-1158; Marian A. Low's review in the *Slavic Review*, XXXIII, 1 (March 1974), pp. 168-169; Paul Bődy's review in *East European Quarterly*, IV, 1 (March 1970), pp. 112-113; and Laszlo Deme's review in *East Central Europe*, I, 1 (1974), pp. 95-98.
15. *Works*, no. 55.
16. *Works*, no. 56.
17. *Works*, no. 58.
18. *Works*, no. 15.
19. *Works*, nos. 62, 64.
20. *Works*, no. 2.
21. On these two prominent Hungarian statesmen see George Barany, *Stephen Széchenyi and the Awakening of Hungarian Nationalism, 1790-1841* (Princeton: Princeton University Press, 1968); and Istvan Deak, *The Lawful Revolution: Louis Kossuth and the Hungarians, 1848-1849* (New York: Columbia University Press, 1979).
22. Stated by Imre Kovács in his review article on Király's book, "Akinek sikerült a terve" [He Who Succeeded in his Plans], *Új Látóhatár* [New Horizon] (Munich), XIV, 4 (September 20, 1975), pp. 366-369. See also the relevant reviews by S. B. Vardy in *Canadian-American Slavic Studies*, XI, 4 (Winter 1977), pp. 477-478; Peter F. Sugar, *Slavic Review*, XXXVI, 1 (March 1977), pp. 145-146; and Thomas Spira, *East European Quarterly*, XI, 4 (Winter 1977), pp. 505-507.
23. *Works*, no. 63.
24. *Works*, no. 66.
25. *Works*, no. 71.
26. *Works*, no. 72.
27. *Works*, no. 28.
28. *Works*, no. 67.
29. *Works*, no. 74.
30. *Works*, no. 65.
31. *Works*, nos. 22, 26, 27.
32. *Works*, no. 33.
33. *Works*, no. 24.
34. *Works*, nos. 16, 17.
35. *Works*, no. 23.
36. *Works*, nos. 56, 62, 64, 70.

37. *Works*, no. 20.
38. *Works*, no. 49.
39. *Works*, no. 14.
40. *Works*, no. 57.
41. In addition to the nine volumes under Király's edited works (nos. 4-12), this series includes over a dozen other volumes both on European and American topics.
42. Four volumes of this projected ten-volume sub-series have already appeared in print (nos. 9-12).
43. Király's edited volumes are listed under nos. 4-12 of his *Works*, with several others in the process of publication or preparation.
44. *Works*, no. 30.
45. *Works*, nos. 25, 29.
46. *Works*, nos. 18, 31, 32.
47. See note 10.
48. The American Association for the Study of Hungarian History (AASHH) was founded at the December 1970 Convention of the American Historical Association. The three founders were Béla K. Király, Peter F. Sugar and S. B. Vardy (one of the authors of this study). They were soon joined by Peter Pastor, who served as the AASHH's first Secretary. For this reason the information given by Péter Gosztonyi concerning this matter in his otherwise valuable study on recent Hungarian historical research abroad is completely misleading. He fails to mention anyone of the founders. Cf. Péter Gosztonyi, *A 20. századi magyar történelemkutatás nyugaton* [Twentieth-Century Hungarian Historical Research in the West] (Zürich: SMIKK, 1979), 16 pp.; the reference is to p. 13. This work is reprinted from *Magyar Mérleg II: Nyugati magyar kulturális élet a II. világháború után, 1945-1979* [Hungarian Scale II: Hungarian Cultural Life in the West after World War II, 1945-1979], ed. Éva Saáry (Zürich: Svájci Magyar Irodalmi ás Képzőművészeti Kör, 1979).
49. On the Hungarian Studies Center at Indiana University see Denis Sinor, "Uralic and Altaic Studies," *The Review* (Indiana University), 9 (Fall 1967), pp. 1-8; Béla Várdy, "Magyarságtudomány az észak-amerikai egyetemeken és főiskolákon" [Hungarian Studies at North American Colleges and Universities], in *A XII. Magyar Találkozó Krónikája* [Proceedings of the Twelfth Hungarian Congress], eds. János Nádas and Ferenc Somogyi (Cleveland: Árpád Könyvkiadó, 1973), pp. 102-132; S. B. Vardy,

"Hungarian Studies," pp. 91-121; *Hungarian Studies Newsletter* (New Brunswick, NJ), 21 (Autumn 1979), p. 1; and György Ránki, "Megkezdi munkáját a bloomingtoni magyar tanszék" [The Hungarian Chair at Bloomington Begins its Work], *Magyar Hírek* [Hungarian News] (Budapest), XXXIV, 1 (January 10, 1981), p. 4.

50. In the past, other significant forums included Columbia University, and more specifically, its Uralic Studies Program directed by János Lotz, as well as its Institute on East Central Europe directed by Istvan Deak. This also holds true for Rutgers University where Joseph Held has been active for many years. More recently Pittsburgh, and more specifically the Duquesne University History Forum, directed by S.B. Vardy has also become an important forum of exchange. Concerning the Pittsburgh program see : Ágnes Huszár Várdy and Béla Várdy, "Magyar kultúrmunka Pittsburgh-ben" [Hungarian Cultural Activities in Pittsburgh], *Magyar Hírek*, XIV, 1 (January 10, 1981), pp. 12-13; and Ágnes Huszár Várdy, "Magyarságtudomány Pittsburghben: eredmények és lehetőségek" [Hungarian Studies in Pittsburgh: Results and Possibilities], in *Nyelvünk és Kultúránk '81: A IV. Anyanyelvi Konferencia tanácskozásainak összefoglalása* [Our Language and Culture '81: Summary of the Deliberations of the Fourth Mother Language Conference] (Pécs, 1981), pp. 292-298.

S. B. Vardy and Agnes Huszar Vardy

BÉLA K. KIRÁLY'S BIBLIOGRAPHY

I. Authored Books

1. *Hungary in the Late Eighteenth Century: The Decline of Enlightened Despotism* [East Central European Studies of Columbia University] (New York: Columbia University Press, 1969), 295 pp.
2. *Ferenc Deák* [Twayne's World Leaders Series] (Boston: Twayne Publishers, 1975), 243 pp.
3. *Az első háború a szocialista országok között. Személyes visszaemlékezések az 1956-os magyar forradalomra* [The First War Between Socialist States: Personal Reminiscences about the Hungarian Revolution of 1956] (New Brunswick, NJ: Magyar Öregdiák Szövetség Bessenyei György Kör, 1981), 88 pp.

II. Edited Books

4. *Tolerance and Movements of Religious Dissent in Eastern Europe*, ed. Béla K. Király (Boulder: East European Quarterly, Distributed by Columbia University Press, 1975), 227 pp. (Vol. I of Brooklyn College Studies on Society in Change = BCSSC; Vol. 13 of East European Monographs = EEM).
5. *The Habsburg Empire in World War I*, eds. Robert A. Kann, Béla K. Király and Paula S. Fichtner (Boulder: East European Quarterly, Distributed by Columbia University Press, 1976), 247 pp. (Vol. 2 of BCSSC; Vol. 23 of EEM).

6. *The Hungarian Revolution of 1956 in Retrospect*, eds. Béla K. Király and Paul Jónás (Boulder: East European Quarterly, Distributed by Columbia University Press, 1976), 213 pp. (Vol. 6 of BCSSC; Vol. 40 of EEM).
7. *East Central European Perception of Early America*, eds. Béla K. Király and George Barany (Lisse, The Netherlands: Peter de Ridder Press, 1977), 144 pp. (Vol. 5 of BCSSC).
8. *The Mutual Effects of the Islamic and Judeo-Christian Worlds: The East European Pattern*, eds. Abraham Ascher, Tibor Halasi-Kun and Béla K. Király (New York: Brooklyn College Press, Distributed by Columbia University Press, 1979), 314 pp. (Vol. 3 of BCSSC.)
9. *War and Society in East Central Europe.* Vol. I. *Special Topics and Generalizations of the Eighteenth and Nineteenth Centuries*, eds. Béla K. Király and Gunther E. Rothenberg (New York: Brooklyn College Press, Distributed by Columbia University Press, 1979), 461 pp. (Vol. 10 of BCSSC.)
10. *War and Society in East Central Europe.* Vol. II. *Pre-Revolutionary Eighteenth Century*, eds. Béla K. Király, Gunther Rothenberg and Peter F. Sugar (New York: Brooklyn College Press, Distributed by Columbia University Press, 1982), 566 pp. (Vol. 11 of BCSSC.)
11. *War and Society in East Central Europe.* Vol. III. *From Hunyadi to Rákóczi. War and Society in Late Medieval and Early Modern Hungary*, eds. Janos M. Bak and Béla K. Király (New York: Brooklyn College Press, Distributed by Columbia University Press, 1982), 543 pp. (Vol. 12 of BCSSC.)
12. *War and Society in East Central Europe.* Vol. VI. *Total War and Peacemaking: Essays on the Treaty of Trianon*, eds. Béla K. Király, Peter Pastor and Ivan Sanders (New York: Brooklyn College Press, Distributed by Columbia University Press, 1982), 679 pp. (Vol. 15 of BCSSC.)

III. Chapters in Books

13. "Les problemes du commandement militaire et la Garde Nationale dans la revolution hongroise," in Péter Gosztonyi, ed., *Histoire du soulevement hongroise 1956* (Paris: Editions Horvath, 1966), pp. 274-299.

14. "Paul Teleki the Theoretician of Hungarian Revisionism," in Paul Teleki, *The Evolution of Hungary and its Place in European History*, 2nd ed. [Central and East European Series, No. 20] (Gulf Breeze, Florida: Academic International Press, 1975), pp. xix-xliv.
15. "Napoleon's Proclamation of 1809 and its Hungarian Echo," in Stanley B. Winters and Joseph Held, eds., *Intellectual and Social Developments in the Habsburg Empire from Maria Theresa to the First World War: Essays Dedicated to Robert Kann* (Boulder: East European Quarterly, Distributed by Columbia University Press, 1975), pp. 31-54.
16. "Protestantism and Hungary between the Revolution and the *Ausgleich*," in Király, *Tolerance* (No. 4), pp. 65-88.
17. "The Sublime Porte, Vienna, Transylvania and the Dissemination of Reformation in Royal Hungary," in ibid., pp. 199-222.
18. "Elements of Limited and Total Warfare," in Kann-Király-Fichtner, *The Habsburg Empire* (No. 5), pp. 135-158.
19. "The Military Aspects [of the Revolution of 1956]," in Király-Jónás, *The Hungarian Revolution* (No. 6), pp. 57-71.
20. "Béla Széchenyi's American Tour," in Király-Barany, *East Central European Perceptions* (No. 7), pp. 73-87.
21. "La premiere guerre entre etats socialistes," in Pierre Kende and Krzysztof Pomian, eds., *1956 Varsovie-Budapest. La deuxieme revolution d'octobre* (Paris: Editions du Seuil, 1978), pp. 40-48.
22. "Democratic Peasant Movements in Hungary in the 20th Century," in Heinz Gollwitzer, ed., *Europäische Bauernparteien im 20. Jahrhundert* (Stuttgart: Gustav Fischer Verlag, 1978).
23. "The Hungarian Church," in William J. Callahan and David Higgs, eds., *Church and Society in Catholic Europe of the Eighteenth Century* (Cambridge: Cambridge University Press, 1979), pp. 106-121.
24. "The Sublime Porte and Ferenc II. Rákóczi's Hungary. An Episode in Islamic-Christian Relations," in Király-Ascher-Halasi-Kun, *The Mutual Effects* (No. 8), pp. 242-276.
25. "War and Society in Western and East Central Europe during the 18th and 19th Centuries: Similarities and Contrasts," in Király-Rothenberg, *War and Society*, I (No. 9), pp. 1-33.
26. "Peasant Movements in the 19th Century," in Joseph Held, ed., *The Modernization of Agriculture: Rural Transformation in Hungary,*

1848-1975 (Boulder: East European Quarterly, Distributed by Columbia University Press, 1980), pp. 131-167.
27. "Peasant Movements in the 20th Century," in ibid., pp. 319-350.
28. "The Springboard of Ferenc Deák's Liberal Nationalism: The Emancipation of Hungary's Serfs," in Michael Palumbo and William O. Shanahan, eds., *Nationalism. Essays in Honor of Louis Synder* (Westport, CT: Greenwood Press, 1981), pp. 131-140.
29. "Eighteenth-Century Warfare in East Central Europe," in Király-Rothenberg-Sugar, *War and Society,* II (No. 10), pp. 1-25.
30. "From the Mounted Knights to the Standing Armies of Absolute Kings," in Bak-Király, *War and Society,* III (No. 11), pp. 23-58.
31. "World War I and East Central Europe," in Samuel R. Williamson, Jr. and Peter Pastor, eds. *War and Society in East Central Europe.* Vol. V. *World War I and East Central Europe: Case Studies on War Aims and Prisoners of War* (New York: Brooklyn College Press, Distributed by Columbia University Press, 1982), p. 264.
32. "Total War and Peacemaking," in Király-Pastor-Sanders, *War and Society,* VI (No. 12), pp. 15-21.
33. "Transylvanian Concept of Liberty and its Effects on Royal Hungary during the 17th and 18th Centuries," in John Cadzow, Andrew Ludanyi and Louis J. Elteto, eds., *Transylvania: The Roots of Ethnic Conflict* (Kent, OH: Kent State University Press, 1983), in press.

IV. Articles in Scholarly Journals

34. "Újonc kiképzés" [Recruit Training], *Honvéd* [Homeguard] (Budapest), I, no. 3 (March 1949), pp. 16-24.
35. "A pancélelhárításról" [On Antitank Warfare], *Honvéd,* I, no. 6 (June 1949), pp. 26-39.
36. "Az újonc kiképzésről" [On Recruit Training], *Honvéd,* I, nos. 9-10 (October-November 1949), pp. 36-41.
37. "A sztálini hadsereg. A szovjet gyalogság" [The Stalinist Armed Forces: The Soviet Infantry], *Honvéd,* I, no. 12 (December 1949), pp. 80-92.
38. "How Russian Trickery Throttled Revolt," *Life* (February 18, 1957), pp. 119-127.
39. "Hungary's Army under the Soviets," *East Europe,* VII, no. 3 (March 1959), pp. 3-14.

40. "Hungary's Army: Its Part in the Revolt," *East Europe*, VII, no. 6 (June 1959), pp. 24-36.
41. "Honvéds unter Sowjetbefehl: Persönliche Erlebnisse eines hohen ungarisches Offiziers," *Hinter dem Eisernen Vorhang* (Munich), IV, no. 5 (May 1958), pp. 1-14.
42. "Honvéds unter Sowjetbefehl: Die Rolle der ungarischen Armee in Volksaufstand," *Hinter dem Eisernen Vorhang*, IV, no. 7 (July 1958), pp. 20-32.
43. "Hungary's Army under the Soviets," in *Hungary's Army under the Soviet-Economic Co-operation in the Soviet Bloc*, by General Béla Király and East European Experts (Tokyo: Japan Institute of Foreign Affairs, Inc., 1958), pp. 1-96. (In Japanese.)
44. "Asi se traiciono a Hungaria: Algunos aspectos militares de la revolution hungara," *Manual de Informaciones* (Rio Bamba, Argentina), II, nos. 4-5 (1959), pp. 107-112.
45. "Általános leszerelés vagy disengagement?" [General Disarmament or Disengagement?], *Uj Látóhatár* [New Horizon] (Munich), XI (1960), pp. 66-69.
46. "The Hungarian Revolution of 1956," with Árpád F. Kovács, *Thought Patterns* (St. John's University, New York), VII (1960), pp. 69-100.
47. "The Partisan: Comments on Guerilla Warfare Readiness in a Soviet Satellite Country," Office of the Secretary of Defense's Publication, Washington, D.C. (March 22, 1961).
48. "The Tide Turns," *Military Review* (Fort Leavenworth, KA), XLII, no. 12 (December 1962), pp. 80-84; and its Spanish version, "Los tiempos cambian," ibid., pp. 84-88.
49. "The Danubian Problem in Oscar Jászi's Political Thought," *The Hungarian Quarterly* (New York), V, nos. 1-2 (April-June 1965), pp. 120-134.
50. "Two Misconceptions about the Hungarian Revolution," *Scope: A Journal of the Social Sciences* (New York University), III, no. 1 (1966), pp. 18-31.
51. "The Organization of National Defense during the Hungarian Revolution," *The Central European Federalist* (Jackson Heights, NY), XIV, no. 1 (July 1966), pp. 12-22.
52. "A honvédelem problémái a forradalomban" [The Problems of

National Defense in the Revolution], *Új Látóhatár*, XVII (1966), pp. 421-434.
53. "Millenium and Decennium," *The Central European Federalist*, XIV, no. 1 (July 1966), pp. 3-5.
54. "Le discourse," *La Voix Internationale de la Resistance* (Brussels), IX (November-December 1966), pp. 12-13.
55. "Peasant Movements in Hungary in 1790," *Südost-Forschungen* (Munich), XXVI (1967), pp. 140-156.
56. "Prussian Diplomatic Adventure with Poland and the Feudal Revolt in Hungary in 1790," *The Polish Review* (New York), XII, no. 1 (Winter 1967), pp. 3-11.
57. "International and Domestic Polycentrism," *The Central European Federalist*, XV, no. 1 (June 1967), pp. 1-4.
58. "Paramilitary, Military and Proto-Nationalistic Aspects of the Feudal Revolt in Hungary," *Canadian-Slavic Studies* (Montreal), XII, no. 2 (Fall 1968), pp. 342-353.
59. "Budapest 1956-Prague 1968: Parallels and Constrasts," *Problems of Communism* (Washington, D.C.), XVIII, nos. 4-5 (July-October 1969), pp. 52-60.
60. "The Hungarian Revolution" [Two Record Albums] (New York: Produced by H. Roach, 1969).
61. "Why the Soviets Need the Warsaw Pact?" *East Europe*, XVIII, no. 4 (April 1969), pp. 8-18.
62. "The November Insurrection and the Hungarians," *Antemurale* (Rome), XIV (1970), pp. 229-252.
63. "The Young Ferenc Deák and the Problem of the Serfs, 1824-36," *Südost-Forschungen*, XXIX (1970), pp. 91-127.
64. "Galicia: The Hungarians and the Poles between the Partitions and the November Insurrection," *The Polish Review*, XV, no. 3 (Summer 1970), pp. 19-31.
65. "The Emancipation of the Serfs in East Central Europe," *Antemurale*, XV (1971), pp. 63-85.
66. "The Radical Liberal Phase of Ferenc Deák's Career," *Südost-Forschungen*, XXXIV (1975), pp. 195-210.
67. "Neo-Serfdom in Hungary," *Slavic Review*, XXXIV, no. 2 (June 1975), pp. 269-278.
68. "The First War between Socialist States: Military Aspects of the

Hungarian Revolution," *Canadian-American Review of Hungarian Studies* (Kingston, Ontario), III, no. 2 (Fall 1976), pp. 115-123.
69. "Budapest Twenty Years Ago," *The New York Times* (October 23, 1976).
70. "The Hungarian Democrats and the Polish Question during the Nineteenth Century," *The Polish Review*, XXII, no. 1 (1977), pp. 1-20.
71. "Ferenc Deák during the Vormärz Era," *Austrian History Yearbook*, XII-XIII (1978), pp. 13-25.
72. "Ferenc Deák the Social Reformer in the Revolution of 1848-1849," *East European Quarterly*, XIV, no. 4 (Winter 1980), pp. 411-421.
73. "Den sovjetiska interventionen Ungern 1956. Det forsta kriget mellan socialistiska stater," *Osteuropa*, VI, no. 2 (1979), pp. 15-18.
74. "Maria Theresa's Hungarian Serf Reforms," *Topic 34* (Washington and Jefferson College, Washington, PA), XXXIV (1980), pp. 43-55.

II

SIEGES, WARS, MILITARY THEORIES AND MILITARY ALLIANCES

Joseph Held

THE DEFENSE OF NÁNDORFEHÉRVÁR (BELGRADE)* IN 1456: A DISCUSSION OF CONTROVERSIAL ISSUES

The siege of Belgrade by Mehemed II the Conqueror in the summer of 1456 aroused considerable contemporary attention and has remained an event of great interest to historians ever since. Coming within three years of the conquest of Constantinople, this fortress-city was the key to further Osmanli expansion into Central Europe.[1] Its fall could have opened the gates for the Osmanli to the European heartland and this would certainly have changed the history of the world.

Given the abundance of sources of the siege, one would expect few outstanding problems and controversies to remain for later historians to explore. But this is not so; as in the case of other historical turning points, the siege of Belgrade continues to generate conflicting interpretations. This paper will not attempt another detailed study of this event; rather, it will be devoted to the examination of some of these controversial issues. They will include the debate about the size of the participating armies, the roles of Hunyadi and Capistrano in the defense, and the activities, or rather inactivity, of the barons of the Kingdom of Hungary. A fourth issue

---

* We intend to use the current name of this great city in all of our subsequent discussions.

the role of the peasants in the siege, has been dealt with elsewhere,[2] and will, therefore, be omitted from this paper.

One of the continuing controversies concerns the size of the participating armies. Only estimates of these armies were ever given by the participants, and most estimates served propaganda purposes. If a gigantic army was unsuccessful, the valor and prestige of its opponent would be greatly enhanced, and this was not missed by the antagonists in question.

There can be no doubt that the Ottoman army arrived at Belgrade in full strength. Preparations for the campaign began already in the fall of 1455. The call for troops went out to all parts of the Ottoman Empire, and the various contigents were assembled on the plains between Constantinople (by then Istanbul) and Edirne (Adrianople). However, when the army began to move in the early summer of 1456, it did not march in one large mass. The troops were divided into two major and possibly several smaller groups. In Franz Babinger's phrase, they "gradually moved from the south towards Belgrade in dense swarms."[3] Since no opposition was expected by the peoples in the Balkans, the Ottoman groups did not have to be concentrated and could, thus, follow different routes.

Western estimates of the Ottoman army varied from 150,000 to 400,000 soldiers.[4] But it seems that even the lowest number may have been too high. Professor Norman Tobias discussed this issue in a lecture delivered in May 1980, at the 16th Annual Conference of Medieval Studies at Kalamazoo, Michigan, and he was kind enough to let me peruse his manuscript. Although his study examined the movement of Arab armies before the first siege of Constantinople in the early eighth century, his findings are relevant for most armies in the pre-modern age. According to his findings, the maximum number of soldiers who could march into battle in the southern fringes of Europe could not exceed 60-70,000. This was not so much the consequence of limitations on provisions that an army could carry along its route of march, or acquire through purchases or requisitioning from the population it encountered, although all of these factors had to be considered. The major problem was finding enough drinking water for men and animals. Thus, the movement of armies of even that size had to be planned to follow the course of rivers or larger streams where their drinking water could be secured. This was a task for which the answer in the Balkans would have been the Danube River. But to

The Siege of Belgrade

follow the river would have meant for Mehemed II, a long detour and waste of precious time.

One way out of this dilemma was, as the Sultan must clearly have seen it, to send the army in smaller groups along different routes. Thus, it has been estimated that he himself moved with about 60,000 men along the north slopes of the Balkan Mountains, while another large part of the army, containing perhaps 20,000 soldiers took the southern route. But the army must have moved in smaller groups than those reported; even so, they must have moved at a few days' intervals, in order not to overtax the water supplies. Besides making provisioning the troops easier, this order of march also secured the eastern flank of the Ottoman army against surprise attack from the direction of Wallachia or Transylvania, and helped to keep its opponents in suspense about its main thrust.

We must also consider the fact that armies, (and the Ottomans were no exception to this rule), drew to themselves all sorts of camp followers. There is, of course, no way to learn the exact size of such groups, but a purely speculative estimate of about twenty percent may seem plausible. An army of this size needed all sorts of auxiliaries, including wagon and pack-animal drivers, feltschers and barbers, musicians and soothsayers, personal servants for the leaders and bodyguards, water carriers and repairmen, whores and their procurers, adding perhaps another ten percent to its numbers. If Mehemed II had 70,000 men, then we may count less than 50,000 fighters in the ranks. This was still a formidable force, probably the largest single army that could be assembled in contemporary Europe, even if its size fell short of the estimates of frightened Westerners.

A letter by Bernhard van Kraiburg, Chancellor to the Archbishop of Salzburg (dated Vienna, 25 August 1456), shows our estimate to be close to the probable size of the Ottoman army. Kraiburg reported the account of a "reliable eyewitness" (probably one of the participating soldiers of the Viennese contingent)[5] according to which about 100,000 Turks came to Belgrade. They had twenty-one ships carrying provisions for the army on the Danube. The dead came to about 4-5,000 men on both sides. Hunyadi's troops, including the mercenaries recruited for the defense, amounted to about 16,000 men, half of whom took part in the fighting. The Christian forces numbered about 70,000 men, but most of them remained only spectators to the siege. Only thirteen cannons were captured from the Ottomans, including one of large size.[6]

Even this report must be considered exaggerated. If 100,000 Ottoman soldiers came to Belgrade, and the opposing forces amounted to 16,000 men, then 4-5,000 dead appear to be a small number indeed. On the other hand, the number of ships mentioned by Kraiburg's informant seems to represent an underestimation. It is possible that the "reliable eyewitness" reported only the larger vessels, discounting barges of which there may have been a larger number present.[7]

This leads us to the issue of the size of the defending army. If the Western participants overestimated the size of the Ottoman army, they would naturally present a smaller number of their own forces than was actually the case in order to emphasize their own valor (or the miraculous nature of the victory). It is very unlikely that the fortress itself was defended by more than 16,000 soldiers. Eyewitnesses reported that Hunyadi had reinforced the defenders before the arrival of the Osmanli by about 5,000 of his own men, placing his brother-in-law, Mihály Szilágyi, in command. In addition, Hunyadi probably had another 5,000 soldiers available in his own *banderium* that accompanied him to Belgrade. We know that at least another *banderium,* that of János Koroghy (or Korogyi) was present, (Koroghy was *bán* of Macsó [or Mačva] at that time), and perhaps parts of the private armies of László Kanizsai, Sebestyén Rozgonyi and Joan Bastida. There were no troops sent by Western monarchs or princes, nor was the Pope or the Italian city states interested enough in the defense of Belgrade to send their own contingents. Giovanni de Capistrano recruited crusaders for the defense with great zeal indeed, but he began the recruitment campaign too late. (He was too busy with "saving" heretics, including Djuradj Branković, the aging Serbian Despot!)[8] It seems that large numbers of these crusaders arrived late at Belgrade, some of them even coming long after the siege was over.[9]

One of the problems in this may be in trying to establish the size of each *banderium* at Belgrade. There was no standard size for these formations, the number of their soldiers depending upon the wealth and influence of the owner. Moreover, these private armies fluctuated in size, depending upon the need or the occasion on which they were to fight. Now, we know that Hunyadi spent 32,000 gold florins in gathering his *banderium* for the long campaign (which included mercenaries) in 1443, and twice this amount for the campaign that ended in Varna in 1444.[10] We do not know how much he spent before the siege of Belgrade, but even if he spent the maximum amount, let us say the equivalent of the money he used for the campaign of 1444, and if the salary of an armored cavalryman was 8-10 florins a month, he could have had little more than 6,000 mercenary soldiers in his *banderium*. To this we must add the number of his *familiares* who served him on a contractual basis. Even so, unless Hunyadi received help from the special tax offered by the Diet on this occasion, of which there is no proof, his private army must certainly have consisted of less than 10,000 men.[11]

Another problem is presented by the estimated number of crusaders recruited by Capistrano and his fellow friars. Although a small number would enhance the valor of the victorious troops, it would certainly reflect badly upon the charisma and suggestive power of Capistrano. The Franciscans mentioned 30,000 soldiers that they recruited for the defense of Belgrade. But in fact no one ever provided an accurate account of these recruits. In any case, Kraiburg's report makes it clear that no matter how many of the crusaders were present at Belgrade, only 8,000 of them participated directly in the battle. However, it would be wrong to underestimate the effectiveness of this peasant army. Two independent sources which, although they do not give an estimate of the size of this mob, permit us to evaluate their actual contribution to the defense. Mihály Szilágyi, the commander of the fortress before the arrival of Hunyadi, declared that he never believed that there were so many men in Hungary available for war until he saw their multitudes swarming over the river banks,[12] and Joannes Thuróczi, the chronicler of the Hunyadi-era, stated with glee that the haughty Sultan who intended to eat his supper in peace in Buda two months after he conquered Belgrade, was driven away in shame by these simple peasants.[13]

The solution to the discrepancy between the various estimates of the size of the crusading army may be in the fact that the crusaders also arrived at Belgrade in swarms (as reported by the eyewitnesses) and continued to arrive both during and even after the siege. Long after it was all over, in November 1456, when King László V (Ladislas Posthumus) gathered enough courage to inspect the battered remnants of the battlements of Belgrade, he was accompanied by a large retinue of German crusaders who were still coming in droves to "defend" Belgrade.[14] All in all, it is most likely that less than the reported 70,000 men were involved in the siege on both sides, of whom perhaps 45-50,000 were Ottoman soldiers and less than 16,000 were the defenders.

It should not surprise us that nearly everyone on the victors' side, especially János Hunyadi and the friars, should claim a decisive role in the battle for the fortress. This was especially true for the participating Franciscans who were already building up a case for the beatification of Capistrano. That the crusaders had played a great role indeed, came in handy for this purpose. Capistrano's undoubted courage gave credence to some of the stories surrounding his activities. But what the records actually indicate is that all those present were called upon by circumstances to do their very best which sometimes came to efforts that appeared near the superhuman.

Capistrano's role has often been evaluated by historians mainly on the basis of his previous actions, especially as a papal inquisitor of heretics, and this is wrong. As such, he was appointed in 1451. He was certainly not interested in endearing himself to liberal-minded historians of any age. Besides, his fellow friars were not bashful in providing fanciful descriptions of the old man's behavior and its effects on the enemy during the siege.[15]

Capistrano was certainly no prancing youngster; he was 71 years old in 1456. In 1455, he was invited to the Kingdom of Hungary by the king, in order to convert heretics (mostly Hussites and Orthodox Christians).[16] He pursued his task with great zeal and vigor indeed, belying his age. Cardinal Juan de Carvajal, the papal legate to Austria, Bohemia and Hungary whose major task was the supervision of recruitment of crusaders for an anti-Ottoman campaign, had a difficult time in convincing Capistrano to help him in this effort.[17]

It was not until February 1456, that Capistrano finally embarked on a recruiting campaign. Once he did so, he vigorously pursued his new task and he was successful. Although he could not speak Hungarian, his interpreters succeeded in conveying his enthusiasm to his listeners. Frail and old as he was, he travelled all over Hungary (no mean feat, given the generally poor roads and means of travel) in his pursuit of volunteers. He did augment Hunyadi's army with recruits probably getting most of his soldiers from the threatened districts of Hungary in the south. These must have included Serbs, many of whom were refugees from Turkish-occupied Serbia, a great many Hungarians and even some Greeks. (The city of Belgrade had a large Greek population). But crusaders also came from Germany, Bohemia, and Austria. What was most remarkable about them was their discipline, reflecting the strictness of the friars' own discipline. It was also possible that it was a sign of the popularity of the anti-Ottoman cause.[18]

Capistrano himself directly participated in the defense. He certainly was not strong enough to fight, but his presence must have been inspiring. At first, he commanded the crusaders' camp at Szalánkemén, then moved into the fortress with Hunyadi. In the final battle, begun against Hunyadi's orders by the crusaders, Capistrano seems to have played a major role. Although his fellow friars, Tagliacozzo and Nicholas de Fara, were not modest in describing Capistrano's share in the ensuing victory, their words do ring true when shorn of the alleged appearance of fiery angels over Capistrano's head as he supposedly marched against the Ottoman lines.[19] This was obviously a fragment of their overwrought imagination, and certainly did not help their cause with later historians.

In any case, it appears from all the evidence that Capistrano was physically able to do most of what seems factual in the friars' reports, and he was not too feeble to shuttle between the fortress and the crusaders' camp. He definitely showed courage and determination during the siege. It is another matter entirely that he was not the one who singlehandedly saved Belgrade as his supporters had claimed.[20]

That role must be assigned to Hunyadi. Although there is no space here to describe his activities in detail before the siege, it seems safe to say that he prepared the fortress as well as he could and provided it with a reliable, tough commander before his arrival, Mihály Szilágyi. He was an exceptionally able soldier who, in another age, would have been recognized as an equal of Hunyadi. He certainly was the right person in an emergency. But it was Hunyadi whose organization of the defense, bold actions in breaking the naval blockade, effective instructions during the siege to the defenders made him *the* hero of Belgrade. It was true that Hunyadi entered the last battle only after the crusaders had already succeeded in breaching the Ottoman lines. It is also true that the crusaders acted by disobeying his order not to leave the demolished ramparts. But without Hunyadi's last charge the crusaders would have been massacred by the Ottoman cavalry and the battle would have been irretrievably lost. Hunyadi was, therefore, the decisive person in the siege without whom Belgrade would have fallen to the Osmanli.

This brings us to the last issue of our discussion, namely, the behavior of Hungarian aristocrats during the siege of Belgrade. Almost all contemporaries, as well as later historians, agreed that the aristocrats were conspicuous by their absence. Hunyadi in a letter sent to King László V stated that only (János) Korogyi was present at the siege.[21] But this may not have been the entire truth. Antonio Bonfini mentioned that László Kanizsai was there,[22] and Joannes Thuróczi stated that Ujlaki was also present.[23] Hunyadi's word would seem to be decisive here but for one fact; he failed to mention Capistrano in his letter to the king. But even if Bonfini and Thuróczi were right (and they might have mentioned Kanizsai and Ujlaki only in order to curry favor with their families), this would still mean that very few of the 50-60 families comprising the Hungarian aristocracy at that time wanted anything to do with the siege.[24] What was even more interesting was the absence of any help from King László V, who had the most to lose if the Ottomans succeeded in taking the fortress. The young King of the Hungarians had shown remarkable lack of courage as he fled Buda when news of the Ottoman troop movements towards Belgrade was received.[25] Could this mean that the aristocrats lacked the courage to face the Ottoman enemy? Perhaps.

But what historians have failed to stress in the past was the equally remarkable absence of the lesser nobility from Belgrade. To place this issue into its proper perspective, we maintain that the nobility as a whole, including the aristocracy, did not understand the extent of the Ottoman danger. With the exception of a few lords, (mostly those whose estates were directly threatened by the Ottoman raids) the nobility remained aloof from the struggle. This was not the result of cowardice or a conspiracy against Hunyadi (although at least three historians writing in widely separated periods steadfastly maintained the opposite),[26] but the consequence of internal conditions in the Kingdom of Hungary.

First of all, most aristocratic families, including the Hunyadis, were deeply involved in the struggle for power during the interregnum following the death of King Sigismund in 1437. In this struggle momentary advantage was gained by Hunyadi by his judicious use of force and diplomacy. Hunyadi's struggle with the Ottomans must, therefore, be viewed in this context. This struggle meant, in the eyes of Hunyadi's aristocratic opponents, first of all the defense of the properties of the Hunyadi family. Only secondarily was it considered the defense of the realm. Moreover, it may have appeared to many of the aristocrats that Hunyadi had taken upon himself the traditional role of the king whose duty it was to defend the country against external enemies. We must remember that Hunyadi did maintain control over the royal revenues even after King László V came of age and he was no longer regent.[27] If Hunyadi appeared to have placed the interests of the realm above his personal interests (and this was by no means as clear as later historians would like us to believe) this may have been considered by many of his contemporaries as a foolish and unnatural thing to do. This is, of course, not an apology for the behavior of the Hungarian aristocrats. But the simplistic arguments of the recent past will not do,[28] since they reflect a projection of current thinking about patriotism and nationalism into the distant past.

As for the lesser nobility, they stayed away from Belgrade because nobody asked them to come.[29] By Hungarian law, the king had the right to call for a *generalis exercitus* or mobilization of the lesser nobility and selected members of the peasantry, in times of emergency. This he did not do. Hunyadi did what he could within his own jurisdiction, calling on the Székelys (Szeklers) and Saxons of Transylvania to join him at Belgrade.[30] We do not know if they obliged. But we do know that, according to King Sigismund's report in 1435, the lesser nobility as a whole was so impoverished, that they did not have the necessary means to go to war. Their conditions had not changed significantly in the twenty-one years after that assessment, and this could explain the king's missed call to arms.

We are fully aware of the tentative nature of all of our arguments in this paper. Nevertheless, they might stimulate further research that can benefit us all in our journey into History.

NOTES

1. So the Ottoman historians maintained at the time. Cf. Tursun bey in József Thúry, *Török történetírók. Török-magyarkori történelmi emlékek* [Turkish Historians. Historical Monuments of the Turkish-Hungarian Times] (4 vols., Budapest, 1896), I, 77. See also the renegade Greek historian, Kritobulos, *II. Mehemed élete* [The Life of Mehemed II], Vol. XXII of *Monumenta Hungariae Historica* (Budapest, 1875), 140-41. That they were quite right was shown after the fall of the city in 1521. Within a few short years thereafter the Ottomans destroyed the Hungarian army at Mohács (1526), reached the city of Vienna (1529), and took possession

of the city of Buda (1541), establishing control over the central Danubian Basin for a century and a half.

2. In my article, "Peasants in Arms, 1437-1438 and 1456," in János M. Bak and Béla K. Király, eds., *From Hunyadi to Rákóczi. War and Society in Late Medieval and Early Modern Hungary* (Brooklyn College Press, East European Monographs, No. 104, 1982), pp. 81-102.

3. Franz Babinger, *Mehemed der Eroberer und seine Zeit* (München, 1953), p. 153.

4. Mehemed II's administrative and military reforms included the reorganization of the court and army. In 1456, this army was reported to have included 12,000 janissaries and 8,000 cavalrymen. The number of sipahis was said to be 80,000, and there was a reserve of 40,000 men. Nicolai Jorga, *Geschichte des Osmanischen Reiches* (2 vols., Gotha, 1901), II, 7. However, although the entire army of the Empire was mobilized in 1546, a good part of it was sent as a diversion against the Albanian Skander Bey in order to keep him away from Belgrade. Cf. *Történelmi Tár* [Historical Repository], XXIV, (1901), pp. 193-94.

5. There were several hundred Viennese volunteers fighting at Belgrade. Cf. A. L. G. Muratori, *Scriptores Rerum Italiacarum* (28 vols., Milan, 1723-1751), XXIII, 59. One of these was Johannes Goldener who may have been the "reliable eyewitness" of Kraiburg. See Thomas Ebendorffer von Haselbach, "Chronicon Austriacum," in Hyeronimus Pez, *Scriptores Rerum Austriacarum* (Lippsiae, 1721-1745), II, 880. See also József Teleki, *Hunyadiak kora Magyarországon* [The Age of the Hunyadis in Hungary] (12 vols., Pest, 1852-1857), II, p. 437.

6. Ebendorffer, "Chronicon . . . ," p. 880.

7. Even in this case there were large discrepancies among various reports. For instance, Giovanni da Tagliacozzo, one of the participating friars, reported 200 Ottoman vessels of which 64 were said to have been seagoing galleys. Cf. A. R. P. Luca Wadding Hiberno, *Annales Minorum seu Trium Ordinum A. S. Francisco Institutorum* (Florence, 1932 ed.), XII, 401. Another friar, Nicholas da Fara, supported this claim in Stephanus Katona, *Historia critica regum Hungariae* (42 vols., Pest, 1779-1817), XIII, 1067-70. Hunyadi himself wrote to Emperor Frederick III after the siege that his troops captured 20 large vessels; Haus- Hof- und Staatsarchiv (Wien), *Handschrift Blau,* No. 8. See also Teleki, *Hunyadiak . . .* , II, 412-4. The problem may have been in the varied sizes of the

Ottoman ships; some of the smaller ones may or may not have been counted by the observers.
    8. See *Történelmi Tár* XXIV, (1901), 187-8. Capistrano's Hungarian hagiographer, Ödön Bölcskey, described his activities in an uncritical but very thorough manner in *Kapisztránói szent János élete és kora* [The Life and Times of Saint John of Capistrano] (3 vols., Budapest, 1931), see II, 200. See also Béla Petkó, "Kapisztrán János levelezése a magyarokkal" [The Correspondence of John of Capistrano with the Hungarians] *Történelmi Tár*, XXIV, (1901), 161-222, 185-86.
    9. For a questionable, if entertaining, explanation see Lajos Elekes, *Hunyadi* (Budapest, 1952), 447-9. According to this author, the reason for the slow arrival of crusaders at Belgrade was a conspiracy against Hunyadi by the Hungarian lords and the king who did not want him to emerge victorious from the struggle. A more likely explanation may be found in a letter of the papal legate to Hungary, Juan de Carvajal, the Cardinal of Sancto Angeli, dated June 14, 1456 at Buda. The legate notified Capistrano that a great many crusaders were gathering in Germany, but they were delayed in their start to Hungary since they had as yet no leader. In Petkó, "Kapisztrán . . . ," 214-15.
    10. Teleki, *Hunyadiak . . .* , I, 316. See also, *Historia critica. . .* , XIII, 1067-71, and Georgius Fejér, *Codex Diplomaticus Hungariae ecclesiasticus ac civilis* (42 vols., Buda, 1829-1844), Volume IX: *Supplementa Genus, incunabula ac virtus Joannis de Hunyad,* 71-5.
    11. The Ottoman historian Seadeddin noted that Hunyadi sent 5,000 men into the fortress of Belgrade before the siege began. Cf. Thúry, *Török. . .* , I, 153. This would correspond to the description of the capacity of the fort as given by Bertrandon de la Brocquiere in *Ouvrage extrait d'un manuscrit de la bibliothek nationale par le grand d'Aussy* (Memoires de l'Institut national; Sciences, morales, politiques, Paris, 1896), XII, 96. In addition, Hunyadi recruited Hungarian, Czech and Polish mercenaries. Elekes, *Hunyadi,* 450-1, and Teleki, *Hunyadiak. . .* , II, 423, stated that Hunyadi had about 10,000 soldiers which, together with those in the fortress, would have brought Hunyadi's army up to 15,000 men.
    12. Teleki, *Hunyadiak . . .* , II, 423.
    13. Joannes de Thurócz, "Chronica Hungarorum," in Joannis Georgius Schwandtner, *Scriptores Rerum Hungaricarum veteres ac genuini. . .* (3 vols., Vindobonae, 1746-1748), I, 273. See also Teleki, *Hunyadiak . . .* , II, 412.

14. Teleki, *Hunyadiak* . . . , II, 417.

15. See Tagliacozzo's fantasies about Capistrano shooting lightening bolts at the Ottomans from his face, and the "molten lead" that allegedly fell from the sky on the infidel. Cf. Bölcskey, *Kapisztránói* . . . , II, 337. Fara's statement about flying angels accompanying Capistrano in his march against the Ottoman lines in the last battle is worth equal attention. Ibid., 338. See an equally prejudiced account, this time in the opposite direction, by Elekes, *Hunyadi* . . . , 471.

16. *Történelmi Tár*, XXIV, (1901), 187-88.

17. Elekes in *Hunyadi*, 445-6, argues that the hesitation of Capistrano to begin the recruitment campaign and his conflict with Cardinal Carvajal over this issue originated from their differing viewpoints. According to Elekes, Carvajal was intent, first of all, on furthering papal interests; these would have been enhanced by a crusade, since it would have expanded papal control over areas where the Orthodox religion was predominant. Capistrano, on the other hand, was intent on extending the control of his own order, the Franciscans, and in this endeavor a crusade played only a minor part. Such an interpretation is, of course, a bit more simplistic than what reality had been in 1456.

18. The composition of the crusaders' army had never been in question. Its soldiers were "unarmed peasants, blacksmiths, taylors, carters, craftsmen of all sorts and students. . . ." Ebendorffer in Pez, *Scriptores*. . ., II, 880; "only craftsmen and other poor people were there. . . ." *Történelmi Tár*, IX (1886), 65-6; "mostly a mass of peasants was recruited . . . ." Thuróczi in Schwandter, I, 167; "agriculturists, ploughmen and men of the hoe. . . ." Fara in Katona, *Historica critica* . . . , XIII, 1097; "they were heavily recruited in southern Hungary. . . ." *Történelmi Tár*, XXIV (1901), 215-16; "they included Greeks from Belgrade . . . ." Tagliacozzo in Wadding, *Annales* . . . , XII, 401; they were extremely well disciplined, Bölcskey, *Kapisztránói* . . . , II, 306-7.

19. See note 15. Also, Wadding, *Annales* . . . , XII, 400, and Katona, *Historia critica* . . . , XIII, 1090.

20. Erik Fügedi in his "Kapisztránói János csodái. A jegyzőkönyvek társadalom-történeti tanulsági" [The Miracles of John of Capistrano. The Sociohistorical Lessons of the Records], *Századok* (Budapest), CXI (1977), 871, analyzed the travels of Capistrano between May 30, 1455 and July 2, 1456. According to my calculations based on Fügedi's study, he traveled

nearly 600 kilometers during that year on bad roads. This feat should put to rest once and for all any questions about Capistrano's physical stamina at the age of seventy years.

21. Fejér, *Supplementa Genus* . . . , 223-5.

22. Antonius Bonfini, *Rerum Hungaricarum decades* . . . . (Pozsony, 1744 ed.), decas 3, liber 5.

23. Thuróczi in Schwandtner, I, 167.

24. Against Elekes's explanation, according to which Hunyadi was the subject of a conspiracy on the part of the king and the nobles (noted above), (in *Hunyadi*, 441) there stand two unexplained facts: one is embodied in a royal patent confirming all of Hunyadi's possessions before the battle, in Teleki, *Hunyadiak* . . . , II, 405. The other fact is represented by the renewal of a league between Hunyadi and the Count of Cilli, his major opponent, an alliance guaranteed by the king, Hunyadi's close friend and ally, János Vitéz de Zredna, and the aristocrats László Garai, Miklós Ujlaki and Mihály Pálóczi, ibid., II, 402-3.

25. Katona, *Historia critica*. . . , XIII, 1059; the papal legate reported that the king went on a short hunt with his entourage and never returned to Buda. See also, Teleki, *Hunyadiak* . . . , II, 409-10.

26. Elekes, quoted above; also, Thuróczi in Schwandter, I, 168; Bonfini in *Rerum Hungaricarum* . . . , decas 3, liber 6.

27. Teleki, *Hunyadiak* . . . , II, 330.

28. See Elekes, *Hunyadi*, note 24 above.

29. Only Elekes maintains that the king did call upon the lesser nobles to mobilize against the Ottomans in April 1456. But even if this were the case, the nobility could not have known where to go; the real intentions of the Sultan were not known even to Hunyadi until Belgrade was surrounded by the Ottoman host. Under such conditions, it was illusory to expect the lesser nobles to gather for defense.

30. Hunyadi's letters to the Saxons in Teleki, *Hunyadiak* . . . , X, 525, 526, 528.

Gerhard Benecke

THE ECONOMIC POLICY OF "KRIEGSRAISON" IN GERMANY DURING THE THIRTY YEARS' WAR

> You may read in many places that the raping of women in time of war is permissible, and in many others that it is not permissible. (Hugo Grotius, 1587-1645)
>
> A soldier entering a private house in enemy territory, so Pierino Belli (1502-1575) stated, was allowed to take anything there. (F. Redlich: De praeda militari. Looting and Booty. Wiesbaden, 1956, pp. 4, 20, 37.)

It is unlikely that there will be agreement about the economic effects and social consequences of the alternating hot and cold wars that ravaged Germanic Central Europe during the three decades before 1648. Evidence is too fragmented for satisfactory quantification. Local and regional studies we do have in increasing number, but they present even greater historiographical problems than the facts would themselves warrant. Over the last hundred years the Gustav Freytag school of war-horrors called forth its opposite extreme with the post Second World War interpretations of S. H. Steinberg and R. R. Ergang. There is no generally accepted view on whether the various territorial and regional German economies were well or badly run as a whole before the start of the wars, and whether the war years made the situation as regards prices, wages, production and trade better, worse or just stagnant. No satisfactory explanation has been offered for a generally rapid recovery during the immediate years of peace in the 1650s.[1]

Why is this the case? The problem is largely due to the way in which the archives have been read, simply by expecting them to tell us too much, too quickly. We must return to the question of how economic and fiscal records were created, reflecting upon motives and necessities also as regards what they could not possibly have been expected to cover, whilst at the same time appreciating that they lay bare the limited possibilities of local control in the hands of the administrators in each territory, locality or *Amt* with its parishes, villages, markets and urban centers. Given the ever-present threat and actual reality of the military system with its wearisome round of billet and campaign from winter to summer; with its brutal discipline enshrined in corrupt legal practices and arbitrary taxation; cornerning of the market by requistioning others' property, we are faced with a new type of mundane executive, political leadership. Above it all was the *Amtmann,* the local territorial official, who exercised prerogative rule to suspend law and custom and keep village and market alive. Somewhat as happened in the Second World War where the unsung heroes on the British home-front were the air-raid warden and the shopkeeper who mediated between supply and demand with and without ration-coupons, so Thirty Year War Germany created a coterie of *Feldschreiber* (local company and regimental paymasters) and civilian *Amtmänner* in life-saving liaison to apportion, collect and account for the massive amounts of illegal taxes and supplies requied to keep the troops in such a way as to prevent regular large-scale mutinies that would have destroyed massively the productive power of peasant agriculture, urban handicraft and essential local communications between barns, mills, bakeries and markets.[2]

It all depended on the everyday military system of billet and *Ordinanz.* Yet we now need to know more about how the archives of *Urbar* and *Weistum* estate and village management, of *Landschatz, Kopfsteuer* and other taxation and accountancy were affected by the vicissitudes of that capricious military system with its arbitrary war-levies called *Kriegskontribution.* We also require more studies into *Amtmänner* records of local political control in order to assess developments from the 1620s through to the 1640s. Despite religious differences and dynastic jealousies these records began to show how the territories of the Holy Roman

Empire kept themselves afloat sufficiently to survive major foreign and civil hostilities in such a way as to allow a reconstitution of their co-federal constitutional system of *Reich* institutions with all the complexities of the fragmented aristocratic, theocratic, feudal social system so very peculiar to early modern Central Europe.

Only by finding out how wartime worked for most Germans from day to day will it be possible to comprehend socio-economic effects on population, production, communication and marketing. The sources should more circumspectly make plain the immediacy of that sense of "loss" which caused nineteenth and twentieth century historians to claim variously that the war years saw a reduction of the overall population from sixteen to four millions, or merely by five percent, whatever the original prewar total may have amounted to. Such crudities remain in modified form in G. Franz: *Der dreissigjährige Krieg und das deutsche Volk* (Jena, 1940), the standard work of demography which makes no attempt to come to grips with the tortuousness of the sources before using them at second hand to modify population loss down to at least about one-third of the whole in town and country.

Why were there not more massacres, mutinies and atrocities of the sort made scandalous at Magdeburg (1631), Eger (1634) and Breisach (1638)? The answer is provided by the overall success with which military and civilian authorities learned to cooperate with each other at the local level. It was extremely rare for a soldier to meet his opposite number in battle. Whilst only some thirty-three significant battles were fought across the whole of Germany during the Thirty Years' War, they probably incurred a high destruction rate of one in four, plus firepower that was deadly at over one in seven. This was estimated to have been a threefold increase over sixteenth century battlefield casualty rates. Main battle areas stretched from Mecklenburg and Pomerania on the Baltic through to Brandenburg in a three-pronged, fork-like movement down to Silesia in the southeast; Saxony, Bohemia, Moravia and Austria to the south; and above all through Thuringia, Anhalt, Upper Palatinate, Franconia, Palatinate, Swabia, Württemberg, Upper Rhineland and into Alsace to the southwest. It is along this fork that we can discern most of the death and destruction to which the inhabitants of German territories were subjected. Yet despite the military campaigning, war was much more of an organizational problem for civil government.[3] Soldiers were on the whole prevented from going on strike, running amok and deserting for lack of pay and keep. Like townsmen and villagers, they were reasonably well disciplined through the courts once a battlefront had settled into camp routine. *Kleinkrieg*, the brawling and mauling of soldiers and peasants turned bandit, was no worse than it had always been, as, for example, after the Peasants War of 1525, and after the War of Emperor Charles V against the Protestants of the Schmalkaldic League, 1546-52. The only problem was that in the first half of the seventeenth century such warfare extended over a wider geographic area, and it lasted sporadically for a much longer period of time.

The real killers were lack of hygiene, dislocation and short-term emigration, overcrowding in forts, disruption of market supply and lack of clean water.[4] A new word to describe this crept into the German language at that time. It was the verb "exilieren."[5] A series of plagues swept over all the battlefronts in the later 1630s. Death, hunger and epidemics may have affected one in four of the population. According to Habsburg imperial assessors, who naturally exaggerated in order to obtain for their own side a greater amount of tax-relief in lieu of compensation, the Swedes and their allies were said to have damaged 2,000 manor houses, 18,000 villages, and 1,500 towns, which especially included barns, workshops, crops, cattle, woods and gardens during their eighteen years involvement. The Swedes used methods of intimidation somewhat cynically called safe conduct, *salva guardia*, which broke down since their regimental commanders were logistically totally incapable of doing anything else but live off the German land and seek non-Swedish subsidies for their war effort. Within days of his landings in Pomerania, King Gustavus Adolphus's army had become a band of international freebooters enriching themselves in the name of Swedish security and Protestant satisfaction. With Dutch help they masterminded north German territorical economies, above all their armaments industries through control of the strategic metals, copper, bullion and coinage. Swedish-Dutch-controlled North Germany was forced into using a copper coinage, and taken off the silver standard. By 1632 inter-German trade between Swedish and Imperialist areas began to be affected, but we need to know much more about fiscal policies as worked out by Friedrich Bothe from the pre-First World War Frankfurt archives to supplement more recent work on Swedish war finance.[6]

Like Mansfeld, Tilly, Wallenstein, Gustavus Adolphus, Wrangel, Bernard of Saxe-Weimar, so also all the smaller commanders and captains in the field could survive only as long as they adapted themselves to day-by-day economic cooperation with the local civilian population. They used systems whereby local civilian officials, *Amtmänner,* and urban and rural mayors provided their soldiers with daily rations and shelter in return for involuntary protection. The troops of friendly rulers were generally no better and no worse than those of the enemy. All used the system called *Ordinanz,* which had been promulgated in 1625 from Halberstadt in its classic form by Wallenstein during his First Generalship under Emperor Ferdinand II. Gross pay was calculated from the full, nominal troop strengths in horses, cavalrymen and footsoldiers, plus daily disbursement from supply depots stocked on a weekly and monthly basis by local civil authorities, requisitioning what was needed in money and in kind from their taxable subjects. This process superceded regular channels of collecting rents and produce, and of normally recorded estate management and accounting, as peacetime payments of land tax were suspended, or as they merely collapsed under the strain and weight of new, *ad hoc* systems of tribute-barter-tribute with the troops and their *Feldschreiber.*

Calculating drastic demographic and economic effects from the chaotically reduced numbers of entries, listing the heads of formerly taxpaying peasant households in the estate registers of individual German territorial state archives, has been up to now the method of assessing population loss cumulatively. But the poorly kept tax registers of the 1620s, 1630s and 1640s can only now tell us that a new, illegal but practical, emergency economic system was being operated in order to enable town and village Germany to survive through to peacetime in the 1650s, when once again land tax and excise, *Urbar-Cataster* estate management, village *Weistum* and town charter regulations were reinstated with amazing rapidity in order to pay the heaviest burden of *Reich* tax ever levied in demobilizing Swedes and Imperialists alike. It could not have been achieved, had the mass of land-tax payers lost from the wartime registers not remained at least in the near vicinity of their homes, ready once more to take over their farms and businesses under peacetime, treasury *Amtmann* control. Of course there were failures as in parts of Württemberg, and losses as in parts of Mecklenburg, but fiscal administration became universally chaotic, and its superficial records cannot be used to calculate population loss as has been done to date.[7]

In her memoirs a south German nun, Clara Staiger, looked back on the war years, and saw the whole thing as a twenty-year struggle against the Swedes, who stayed in occupation of her local town of Greding in the Bishopric of Eichstätt until November 1649.[8] For her, these war years were a perpetual coming and going: a "dreadful unrest, fleeing and seeking refuge." She bemoaned the fact that

> Peace negotiations lasted many years but were never properly concluded, for the demands of the enemy and the amount of war tax were so great in damaging all land and people that no debts, whether rents or interests, were paid.

Her other real complaint was that in wartime she was forced to purchase grain at higher prices from more distant cities, at a time when communications were more insecure. Yet when the Swedish General Horn billeted a regiment of one thousand dragoons on her local market town of Herrieden at an equivalent weekly cost to her nunnery of half a *Reichstaler* per cavalrymen in fodder, cereals, meat, fish, beer and wine, local organizations stood up to the challenge at a mere twelve hours' advance notice. Indeed Herrieden could have coped with its new wartime "tribute-barter-tribute" system, whereby civilian marketfolk became suttlers, and the whole place was turned into a military camp. However, its very success attracted attack and counterattack from rival detachments of Swedes and imperialists in the vicinity. In the siege of April 2, 1633 there were civilian casualties, which led to the creation of an annual memorial service in the parish church at which 152 names of the native, non-combatant dead were read out. We have their names to date, as if we were dealing with any parish memorial from the Second World War of our own twentieth century. But such information is rare from the Thirty Years' War era: more common is general complaint against property damage in order to obtain tax concession of one form or another. At least in Herrieden the war tax system by 1640 was firmly back in the hands of local civilian officials, who were feeding troops from whichever side as their "guests." Their rate of *serviz* gave a cavalryman from a half to a whole *Reichstaler* of keep on a mutually agreed price tariff. By comparison, officers' wives received the

Economic Policy of "Kriegsraison"

equivalent of six to seven *Reichstalers*. Herrieden survived by adapting to the new economic system which suspended all normal, peacetime rents, taxes and interest payments. It was the *Kriegsraison* of local wartime until the troops had been demobilized in 1649-51. What the Thirty Years' War pioneered at local level was an economic system of suttling, price fixing and camp control which allowed soldier and civilian to survive, first under direct field army supervision in the 1620s, and then increasingly under local civilian administrative control in liaison with regimental officers in the 1630s and 1640s. That system was best implemented at local *Amt* or *Kreis* level with military cereal depots established under the youthful Great Elector of Brandenburg in the 1640s. It led a way towards the standing armies and subsidies of eighteenth-century Prussian militarism. It had all started with the Habsburg Generalissimo, Wallenstein, billeting his troops on Hohenzollern towns and villages in the later 1620s.[9]

Wallenstein's principle was not to cheat the soldier with unexpected docking of pay. The declared aims of his *Ordinanzen*, military-economic regulations, however much they were later revised, were "that the troopers shall indeed have every month their fully monthly pay in money handed over to them." With this policy Wallenstein had little difficulty in attracting men to his colors. At least for the first few weeks of mustering, he overpaid field officers and men. In 1625 he outbid by fivefold the rates of pay offered by Tilly, his ally in the Bavarian-run Catholic League army. That was soon modified to a threefold lead in pay for a regimental commander, levelling down to a fifty percent increase for subalterns, and a ten percent rise for footsoldiers and cavalrymen. Regimental pay officially ranged from three hundred talers a month down to fifteen. It speeded up the transfer of money economy generally in Germany, at a time when a ploughman handled perhaps thirty to fifty talers a year, and a craftsmen, shopkeeper, priest-clergyman, and local *Amtmann* managed on a hundred to two hundred talers a year. Troops were outrageously expensive. Their power of military destructiveness was dwarfed against their economic cost. In the outcome, the German economy overheated in an unconstructive orgy of overspending.[10]

By the late 1620s, however, rates of pay and supply had settled down, and they remained fairly constant for the rest of the war years. In Wallenstein's revised *Ordinanz* of November 1629, a regimental commander had his pay officially reduced to two hundred *Reichstalers* a month. Civilians were allowed to choose whether to supply the army with victuals *or* money, rather than victuals *and* money, once billets had been apportioned to a locality. For each billet of one footsoldier, called a *Platz* (place), the rate was two pounds of bread, two pounds of meat, two tankards of beer a day, or its equivalent in money at local market rates. A corporal was allowed two *Plätze*, and so on, up the scale of command. To the average soldier in camp, this basic billet was worth twenty to twenty-four *kreuzers* a day (at four *pfennigs* to the *kreuzer*). The soldier was served by an elaborate network of licensed suttlers, called *Marketender*, who were mainly stall-holders, integrating the narrower military into the wider civilian economic system. It brought military discipline via its most sensible channel, namely economic regulation based on what a local market could stand in the short, medium and ultimately long-term. Such a system was not created overnight, nor was it successful at-a-stroke. Sensible price fixing in camp was a laborious and never-ending task. It ultimately subordinated the military to the civilian authorities.[11]

In 1631, prices and wages in the Saxon army gave a common soldier on twenty *kreuzers* a day purchasing power equivalent to nearly thirty-three pounds of rye bread, or twenty tankards of beer, or four pounds of Dutch cheese, or forty eggs, or eight pounds of beef. Eighteen years later a Swedish dragoon waiting for demobilization at Ulm received twenty-four *kreuzers* a day. He had to feed his horse at eighteen *pfennigs* a day, and so he was marginally worse off than the Saxon soldier (not accounting for regional price fluctuations).[12] How effectively were these legal rates of military pay and prices operated? We do not as yet really know. The answer lies in finding and systematically examining military field-treasury accounts together with military legal records. So far, only the work of Fritz Redlich has come near to achieving this. We still have a long way to go before knowing to what extent the ordinary soldier was accommodated to this *ad hoc* economic system in the 1630s and 1640s, and to what extent his overwhelming presence produced short-term mutations in that system.

A soldier was still responsible for his own equipment. He bought what he needed from licensed peddlars and stall-holders. As salesmen overcharged and soldiers reacted violently, so the military policeman, or *Profos*, became the key figure in camp. He started to enforce the small print of the *Ordinanz* by policing the camp market, its licensed butchers bakers and tapsters. These people comprised the core of the *Tross,* camp following. Camp followers could outnumber combatants by as much as four-to-one. They made an army possible, just like shopkeepers make a town a reality.[13]

How did suttlers, military policemen and regimental accountants liaise with local civilians? It all depended on the skill of the latter in providing a quality of traditional leadership that was sufficiently businesslike, flexible and imaginative to suspend the rules of peacetime interest rates, rents, mortgages and land and excise taxes. The hopelessly inefficient Pomeranian territorial administration, with local officials, who had not even kept proper accounts before Wallenstein's and Arnim's troops occupied their towns and villages, were incapable of providing the supplies agreed under the *Ordinanz* of November 11, 1627.[14] Field officers retaliated by resorting to the age-old Germanic system of *Einlieger-Schmähung-Fehde,* that is, using violent self-help to collect debts by damaging all sectors of the economy. It was something that the overall *Reich* legal system had been trying to stamp out ever since the Golden Bull of 1356, the Imperial Land Peace of 1495, and the *Reichskreis* policing arrangements at regional level since the sixteenth century. By contrast with Pomerania, the administration of the County of Lippe in eastern Westphalia was much more aware of ruthlessly having to humor and buy off men and officers in billet and on routemarch between nearby battlefronts. The effects of the wars need still to be assessed from the archives produced by local civilian leaders, with their successful economic counter-policies, for the German territorial system in the Holy Roman Empire did survive to go from strength to strength under Emperor Leopold I in the second half of the seventeenth century.[15]

Whilst regimental commanders were loosely held responsible to their generals and political overlords, civilian mayors and *Amtmänner* were far more strictly controlled by having their accounts scrutinised in territorial rulers' treasury committees, and by territorial Estates' parliamentary commissions before each subsequent round of tax grant. When troops had to be kept fed, speed was of the essence. Daily reports of this process show how wartime Germany survived. Despite the voluminous presence of such records in most of the myriad town and state archives of territorial Germany, these *Meldungen* have not been evaluated systematically by economic historians. Only Ingomar Bog's brilliant thesis from 1952 can be said to have attempted this task, but only at the level of one rural locality.[16] This thesis gave the most exact picture of the economic effects of the Thirty Years' War on the German people, for it provides the detailed facts behind the economic policy of German *Kriegsraison* without any macro-economic oversimplification and guesswork.

The place is wartime Franconia, where local *Amt* officials are supervising 461 households, comprising the agricultural estate of Monastery Heilsbronn, including 183 full peasant tenures, 33 half-tenures, 212 cottage plots, fields, meadows, woods, 33 mills, smithies, herdsmen's and craftsmen's homes, under the Lutheran condominium of the Margrave of Ansbach and the Imperial City of Nuremberg, pitted against a variety of allied Imperialist and allied Swedish troop incursions all through the war years from the 1620s onwards. It documents the process, whereby, in order to survive economically, peasants handed over all aspects of local public life and administration to expert civil servants in the fiscal and judicial field. In the latters' regular accounts we find the estate paying footsoldiers at actual rates of fifteen to twenty *kreuzers* a day, whilst its ploughhands netted eight *kreuzers* a day. When the price of a horse rose to 100 florins in the 1630s, local estate officials arranged for their peasants to return to ploughing with oxen, costing no more than 60 florins a pair. They calculated seed corn to harvest yields as fluctuating around an estimated norm of one-to-four. Even so, the records continue to show that conflicts between tenants and officials over tithes tended to strangle production and sour local social relations in the long run in a far worse manner than did troop incursions. But in Heilsbronn wartime destroyed economically weak and inefficient agribusiness. By the end of the war it was estimated that between 500 florins and 1200 florins was needed to repair a derelict mill or a full peasant holding. That compared with an estimated annual cash need to run such a unit of up to 500 florins in *Handlohn* a year. The cost of a tenancy was equally very reasonable. Farm prices in rural Franconia started at about 250 florins for a smallholding. With a soldiers' rate of pay at 60 florins to 90 florins a year, compared with that of a ploughman at 30 florins to 45 florins a year, there was no shortage of young men to try their hand at camp life for a few years. Since the capital cost of refurbishing a farm was hardly more than its ordinary running cost, movement between soldiering and farming was relatively easy and economically advantageous for younger members of a well-organized family. Equally, the soldier avoided paying land tax, which, by contrast, was taken from the peasants, and their laborers and domestic servants, and then diverted towards paying for the soldier, rather than for the land lord and mortgage creditor. Peasants on the Heilsbronn estate paid a composite property tax of 12½ percent all through the war years. Base rates for nominal assessments tended rapidly to move out of step with actual market values at times of emergency:

> Only he who survived the years of Wallenstein's camp with his ready cash intact, could see his family and cattle through the subsequent years of coming and going between farmsteads and fortress, which was very costly, until hard-learned experience under competent civil servants had developed cheaper, more effective forms of self-protection and defense.[17]

The communication network from *Amtmann* to *Amtmann* coordinated practical economies with the mentality of *Kriegsraison* at village and market level. By the Spring of 1645 Heilsbronn estate officials were receiving daily written reports of local troop movements and demands via their own postal system. A typical week's reporting ran as follows:

> 9 April 1645—by messenger, letter from the Mayor of Rothenburg to Vogt Schenk at Neuhof. An area up to four and five German miles from the town is free of Weimar and French troops. They are heading for the Danube.

> 13 April. Messenger from Court to Benedikt Krebs. 4000 Hessians are converging on Rothenburg. 46 riders billeted on Eyb. God help the poor country!

> 14 April. Reporter from Ansbach. One regiment of French marching on Rothenburg; Bavarians on Leutershausen.

> 15 April. Messenger from Rothenburg on his way through to Nuremberg. Hessians and French want to join forces near Rothenburg.

> 16 April. Christoph Keck reports via messenger. Rioting near Neuenmünster and Gunzenhausen.

> 17 April. Messenger from Schwabach. Nothing new.[18]

Once village Germany had become this well organized internally, the chaos of the Thirty Years War definitely had been overcome internally. For most people the cost was probably more psychological rather than directly economic. Politics became paternalistic as never before. The territorial state sent its experts to operate prerogative jurisdiction in the villages, whilst the traditional class structure was reimposed more absolutely, and it muzzled the new economic forces of freer local trade and manufacture with gild-mercantilist restrictions. The real socio-economic casualty was the common man's spirit of self-government and self-confidence at local, community levels of practical politics in town and country.

NOTES

1. G. Freytag, *Pictures of German Life*, translated by G. Malcolm (London, 1862), II. S. H. Steinberg, *The 'Thirty Years War' and the Conflict for European Hegemony, 1600-60*, (London, 1966). R. R. Ergang, *The Myth of the All-destructive Fury of the Thirty Years War* (Pocono Pines, 1956). The best survey is H. Langer, "Neue Forschungen zur Geschichte des dreissigjährigen Krieges," *Zeitschrift für Geschichtswissenschaft*, 16 (1968), pp. 931-50. For selected documents and further bibliography, see G. Benecke, ed., *Germany in the Thirty Years War* (London, 1978).

2. G. Benecke, "Labour Relations and Peasant Society in Northwest Germany c. 1600," *History*, 58 (1973), pp. 350-51. G. Benecke, "The Problems of Death and Destruction in Germany During the Thirty Years' War. New Evidence from the Middle Weser Front," *European Studies Review*, 2 (1972), pp. 239-253.

3. Well outlined in M. van Creveld, *Supplying War. Logistics from Wallenstein to Patton* (Cambridge, 1977), pp. 1-39.

4. E. Woelkens, *Pest und Ruhr im 16. und 17. Jahrhundert* (Uelzen, 1954) is a usefully detailed study of a locality in Lower Saxony. See also G. Lammert, *Geschichte der Seuchen, Hungers- und Kriegsnoth*, reprint (Niederwallhof, 1971).

5. "Nachdem ich endlich wieder zu einem Bauern gekommen war..., der...zu Hofstett ebenfalls *exilierte.*" Taken from the diary of a prominent Lutheran pastor fleeing from Catholic troops in Württemberg after the Swedish Allied debacle outside Nördlingen in late 1634. P. Antony, ed., *Johann Valentin Andreä* (Heidenheim, 1970), p. 82.

6. H. Langer, *Hortus Bellicus. Der Dreissigjährige Krieg. Eine Kulturgeschichte*, (Leipzig, 1978; English translation, 1980), who tends to take inflated figures at face-value here. F. Bothe, *Gustav Adolfs und seines Kanzlers wirtschaftspolitische Absichten auf Deutschland* (Frankfurt-am-Main, 1910) is a pioneering study. See also R. Nordlund, *Krig på avveckling. Sverige och tyska kriget 1633* (Uppsala, 1974); and J. F. Jameson, "Willem Usselinx, Founder of the Dutch and Swedish West India Companies," *Papers of the American Historical Association*, 1887.

7. M. Ritter, "Das Kontributionssystem Wallensteins," *Historische Zeitschrift*, 54 (1903), pp. 193-249; F. Redlich, "Contributions in the Thirty Years' War," *Economic History Review*, second series, 12 (1959-60), pp. 247-54; F. Redlich, "Military Entrepreneurship and the Credit System in the 16th and 17th Centuries," *Kyklos*, 10 (1957), pp. 186-93.

8. The following is from J. Schlecht, ed., *Eichstätt im Schwedenkriege. Tagebuch der Augustinernonne Clara Staiger, Priorin des Klosters Mariastein, über die Kriegsjahre 1631-50* (Eichstätt, 1889).

9. F. Schroer, *Das Havelland im Dreissigjährigen Krieg* (Cologne, 1966), Cf. A. Gindely, *Waldstein während seines ersten Generalats 1625-30* (2 volumes, Prague, 1886).

10. Ritter, loc. cit., pp. 225-27. See I. Bog, *Die Bäuerliche Wirtschaft im Zeitalter des Dreissigjährigen Krieges* (Coburg, 1952).

11. H. Branig, "Die Besetzung Pommerns durch Wallenstein während des Dreissigjährigen Krieges," *Baltische Studien*, 64 (1978), pp. 31-40; F. Redlich, "Der Marketender," *Vierteljahrschrift für Wirtschafts- und Sozialgeschichte*, 41-2 (1954-55), pp. 227-52.

12. Langer, *Hortus Bellicus*, op. cit., pp. 92-3.

13. Ibid., pp. 97, 157; and the articles of Redlich, cited above.

14. Reprinted by Branig, loc. cit.

15. *Schmähschriften* and allied legal materials reproduced in G. Benecke, "Northwest Germany, Lippe and the Empire in Early Modern Times," St. Andrews University Thesis, 1970, vols. 2 and 3; also Benecke, ed., *Germany in the Thirty Years War*, documents 13, 14, 55-7.

16. Bog, op. cit., and for the following information, especially pp. 16-23, 36-8, 41-4, 98-166, 154.

17. Translated from ibid., p. 44. See G. Zillhardt, ed., *Der Dreissigjährige Krieg in Zeitgenössischer Darstellung. Hans Heberles 'Zeytregister' (1618-72)* (Ulm, 1975).

18. Translated from Bog, op. cit., pp. 145-49.

Géza Perjés

CLAUSEWITZ: A FORERUNNER OF MATHEMATICAL PRAXEOLOGY

> "Research tries to define the different patterns of military behavior, including the decision-making process, the ideologies, attitudes and actions...."
> (Program on Society in Change. War and Society in East Central Europe.)

Seventeenth and eighteenth century pioneers of the calculation of probability thought to possess a means by which they could facilitate the decision of people made in "uncertainty" and determine the rules of rational human behavior.[1] On the basis of the results achieved by the thinkers of the above two centuries, Condorcet elaborated his "social mathematics," the essence of which he summarized as follows:

> In short, without the application of rigorous methods of calculation and of the science of combinations, one would soon come to the limit beyond which all progress becomes impossible, and the advance of the moral and political sciences [as that of the physical sciences] would soon be halted.[2]

On the basis of these foundations developed the decision and game theory of our day, the operation research, informatics, cybernetics and, in general, the behavioral sciences based on the theory of probability. We cover all these disciplines by the collective term: "mathematical praxeology."

This new tendency of thinking completely escaped Germany. As an example, the examination of human practice is totally missing from Kant's philosophy.[3] Consequently, when Clausewitz set out to investigate military praxis, he could not get any assistance from Kant[4] and needed to resort to the scientific results of the scholars in the field of the theory of probability.

The author of the present paper has already pointed out over a decade ago (in a lecture delivered in the Section on Military History at the International Congress of Historians held in Moscow in 1970) that the theory of probability plays a central role in Clausewitz's system of ideas.[5] His research since that time has further confirmed him in this conviction.[6] The present paper summarizes the results of this research, although only to a degree permitted by the limits made available to us.

The Role of Probability in Clausewitz's System of Ideas

In the interpretation of Clausewitz's thoughts much confusion and misunderstandings have resulted from his frequent use of concepts such as "absolute war," "ideal war," and "abstract war." An "absolute war" is the war that ought to occur according to the philosophical concepts of war, in which "the natural aim of the military operations is the enemy's overthrow, and the strict adherence to the logic of the concept can, in the last analysis, admit of no other."[7] If we adhere to the concept of absolute war, "our theory will everywhere approximate to logical necessity, and will tend to be clear and unambiguous."[8]

> Theory has the duty to give priority to the absolute form of war and to make that form a general point of reference, so that he who wants to learn from theory becomes accustomed to keeping that point in view constantly.[9] . . . In fact the very campaigns of 1805, 1806 and 1809, and those that followed are the ones that make it easier for us to grasp the concept of modern, absolute war in all its devastating power.[10]

Further examples could also be enumerated.

We are, however, convinced that the concept of absolute war that causes so much confusion, can be quite safely left out of consideration from Clausewitz's conception. The validity of this concept is suspended by Clausewitz himself in Chapter 1, Book I of his work *On War*, i.e., in the very chapter which he considered the only ready, completed, and definitively formulated part of his work.[11] Let us, therefore, examine this chapter.

He begins his analysis by stating that war, in its philosophical sense, is the unlimited application of violence; consequently, it goes to the extremes. For several reasons, however, these extremes cannot be imagined: First, because war is not an isolated act, but is the result of the political relations that dominated the preceding peace period; second, because it does not consist of one, but of several subsequent acts; and third, because its process is influenced by the political objectives which we want to achieve in the peace treaty.[12] But it is just these three conditions which never coincide in reality, thus "the probabilities replace the extreme," as well as the absolute. "Once the extreme is no longer feared or aimed at, it becomes a matter of judgement what degree of effort should be made; and this can only be based on the phenomena of the real world and the *laws of probability*."[13] In war, however, the opponents facing each other are not abstract concepts, but "actual states and governments." Consequently, "from the enemy's character, from his institutions, the state of his affairs and his general situation, each side, using the *laws of probability*, forms an estimate of his opponent's likely course and acts accordingly."[14]

To all this come "the frequent periods of inaction," which

> *remove war still further from the realm of the absolute and make it even more a matter of assessing probabilities.* The slower the progress and the more frequent the interruption of military action, the easier it is to retrieve a mistake, the bolder will be the general's assessments, and the more likely he will be to avoid theoretical extremes and to base his plans on probability and inference.[15]

It is in this way that Clausewitz arrives at the definition of "real war," by which he invalidates the concept of "absolute war":

As a total phenomenon, its dominant tendencies always make war a remarkable trinity—composed of primordial violence, hatred, and enmity, which are regarded as a blind natural force; of the play of chance and probability within which the creative spirit is free to roam; and of its element of subordination, as an instrument of policy, which makes it subject to reason alone.[16]

There are several other places which could be quoted, where the probability character of war is emphasized by Clausewitz. Thus, the reference made by him to probability is not by chance, and it is not used by him in the everyday sense characteristic of Germany[17] at that time, but rather in the sense used by English, French and Swiss probabilistic thinkers. For Clausewitz, in this way war becomes a stochastic process, and a military decision a deliberation of probabilities.[18]

By all this we do not want to say that Clausewitz saw things exactly the way present researchers of war gaming do, nor as researchers of "automated troop leading systems."[19] Moreover, we are not quite sure that he would have completely understood Condorcet's work and the probability calculations applied therein.[20]

At the same time, it cannot be left out of consideration that, living in Germany, it was hard for him to get away from Kant's influence. And this is so even though no two things are more incompatible than Kant's idealistic philosophy and probabilistically-based social mathematics. For this reason Clausewitz cannot apply Kant's concept of causal law based on the physics of Newton,[21] and he comes to the strange conclusion that the concept of law is inapplicable in war both from the point of view of connaissance and from that of action.[22] This, by the way, is in sharp contrast to his statements made elsewhere; among others to those where —as it was seen—he speaks about the "laws of probability."

Knowing this, it must still not be forgotten that people always make their decisions on the basis of deliberation of probabilities, without having the slightest idea of probability. The peasant inferring from the distribution of good and bad yielding years, to the expectable crop, the international tradesman sailing on dangerous oceans, the banker speculating on future booms, all make their prognoses in "uncertainty" i.e., on the basis of unconscious deliberation of the probabilities. This was even more so in the case of military leaders who—contrary to the peasants, the tradesmen and the bankers—could never confine themselves to the passive consideration of probabilities, but strove to influence them by actions. Thus, when Clausewitz referred constantly to the role of moral, spiritual and intellectual factors, he did so because he knew very well from his own experiences that the uncertainties of war, resulting from lack of information, danger, exhaustion, frictions and weather can in fact be diminished by courage, resolution, and, naturally, by thorough technical knowledge. Or to put it into the language of our days: in the mathematical model of war, the effect of the residual part can be decreased by the bold and shrewd management of the determined part. This was known intuitively to the great poet and politician of seventeenth-century Hungary, Count Miklós Zrínyi; and Montecuccoli also saw things this way.[23]

The Roots of Modern Game Theory in Clausewitz's Work

If we examine the concepts, methods and rules of decision and game theory, we may be surprised to experience how many of them were anticipated by Clausewitz.[24]

It is well known that the theory of probability in the seventeenth and eighteenth centuries gained much stimulus from various games of hazard, and that the game theory itself owes its very name to the latter. Clausewitz saw a great resemblance between war and a game of cards. Following his description of the probability character of war, he writes: "In the whole range of human activities, war most closely resembles a game of cards."[25]

Game theory differentiates among several types of games. One of them is the zero-sum game, in which one player's gains are always equal to the other player's losses. Clausewitz also saw things this way, although he called contradicting interests "polarity"[26] and then defined them as follows: "By thinking that the interests of the two commanders are opposed in equal measure to each other, we have assumed a genuine *polarity* .... In a battle each side aims at victory; that is a case of true polarity, since the victory of one side excludes the victory of the other."[27]

If we think of the fact that in a zero-sum game the gains and losses of the opposing players are both recorded in the payment matrix, then this statement of Clausewitz deserves special attention:

> A may not feel strong enough to attack B, which does not, however, mean that B is strong enough to attack A. The additional strength of the defensive is not only lost when the offensive is assumed but is transferred to the opponent. Expressed in algebraic terms, the difference between $A + B$ and $A - B$ equals $2B$.[28]

Even if he does not use the expression "utility" coined by Daniel Bernoulli, which plays such a most important role in game theory, when speaking about the "value" and the "price" of some military action, Clausewitz has this expression in mind. It is not the absolute value of the alternative resulting from a decision that is expressed in the term "utility," but rather its subjective significance. This importance is interrelated with the scale of values, level of demands, motives and momentary requirements of the individual.[29] In Clausewitz's opinion there are no aims of absolute value in war, and the relative value of individual aims is determined by politics. We would say today that the utility scale of war can be determined if we take as a starting point the political aim. This is deduced by him in a very interesting way in Chapter 1 of his work, after having rejected the absolute concept of war. In other words, if war does not follow its laws striving at extremes, which can be deduced from its philosophical concept, then "the political objective...comes to the fore again."[30] The smaller the political sacrifice that we demanded from our opponent, the smaller will be his military efforts; wherefore our own efforts will also be naturally more modest: "The political objective—the original motive for the war—will thus determine both the military objective to be reached and the amount of effort it requires."[31] Naturally, a political goal *in itself* cannot determine the magnitude of the military efforts, because at different times and under different conditions the same political goal may have quite different *values*. Thus, there is no unambiguous determined interrelationship between the political and military aims of a war. There are cases when the political and the military aims are identical, e.g., when all we want is to occupy a province, and our military operations are adjusted to this aim. It may, however, occur that the value of the political aim is so small that some military "equivalent" has to be sought in its place, which then can be offered as an "object of exchange" during the peace negotiations. This is the case, for example, when we occupy a province only to renounce it later in exchange for the fulfillment of our political claims. Finally, it may also happen that the military "equivalent" needs to be much greater than the political aim.[32]

The utility-oriented thinking of Clausewitz manifests itself also in his much misunderstood concept of total "annihilation."[33] Among others, he deals with the question of annihilation in the chapter entitled: "Purpose and Means in War." In the course of history many peace settlements were concluded which had not been preceded by the complete defeat of either one of the combatants. The reason for this is that generally two other circumstances may also compel the weaker opponent to conclude peace: "The first is the improbability of victory; the second is its unacceptable cost."[34]

As we have seen, war "is bound to move from the strict law of inherent necessity toward probabilities." And if this is the case, then it is understandable that "an analysis of probabilities may lead to peace itself" when the motives of war are faint.

> When the motives and tensions of war are slight, we can imagine that the very faintest prospect of defeat might be enough to cause one side to yield. If from the very start the other side feels that this is probable, it will obviously concentrate on bringing about *this probability* rather than take the long way round and totally defeat the enemy.[35]

The other reason opponents might conclude peace without an annihilating blow by one side to the other, is the high price of annihilation, which also hides great dangers:

> That the method of destruction cannot fail to be expensive is understandable; other things being equal, the more intent we are on destroying the enemy's forces, the greater our own efforts must be. The danger of this method is that the greater the success we seek, the greater will be the damage if we fail.[36]

A very useful analytical means of game theory is the "game tree" or "labyrinth" in which the probable steps of the opponents are graphically illustrated.[37] Clausewitz makes several such analyses, although only verbally. Whatever he describes, however, could be illustrated without difficulty with the help of a game tree. From this point of view, the most interesting is his analysis of the campaign of 1797 found in the chapter entitled: "Critical Analysis." Here he examines, at first from the point of view of Napoleon operating in Italy, and then from that of the French Government, how the Austrian Government could have reacted to certain individual actions.

In Clausewitz's work we encounter at every turn the "uncertainties" of war, which he considers exactly the same way as the probabilistic thinkers of the seventeenth and the eighteenth centuries did. Moreover, similarly to these thinkers, he also speaks of several degrees of uncertainty. The modern decision and game theory deals also with the decisions made in different situations of uncertainty, although it uses different terminology. According to some authors there are two, in the opinion of others there are three situations of decision in the games:[38]

a. *decision under risk*—when the probability of the realization of the chosen alternative is known;
b. *decision under uncertainty*—when a part or all of the probabilities are unknown;
c. *decision under risk and uncertainty*—when the probability of the realization of the individual alternatives is known within certain limits only.

As already mentioned, this decision situation is treated only by a few of the authors.

It is mostly case "c" to which Clausewitz's "Method" can be applied, which is defined as follows:

> *Method*... or *mode of procedure* is a constantly recurring procedure that has been selected from several possibilities. It becomes routine when action is prescribed by method rather than by general principles or individual regulation. It must necessarily assume that all cases to which a routine is applied will be essentially alike. Since this will not be entirely so, it is important that it be true of at least *as many as possible*. In other words, methodical procedure should be designed to meet the most probable cases. Routine is not based on definite individual premises, but rather on the *average probability* of analogous cases. Its aim is to postulate an average truth, which, when applied evenly and constantly, will soon acquire some of the nature of a mechanical skill, which eventually does the right thing almost automatically.[39]

What is this "average probability of analogous cases?" The expression "average probability" [*probabilité average*] is used also by Condorcet, although not in the most appropriate way.[40] It may, however, be assumed that Condorcet—and perhaps, following him, also Clausewitz—wanted to express by this the "Modulus" of De Moivre, which is a part of the normal distribution curve delineated by two standard deviations, where 68 percent of the cases are to be found.[41] We think that this is the way that "average probability," as used by Clausewitz, should be interrupted; all the more so, as he understood this to apply to the "most probable cases," which might not be all identical, but "as many as possible" are considered.

How should all this be interpreted? The answer can be gained from those acts of war, to which these methods can be applied; and these are as follows: the general disposition of the army, the standard order of battle, and the system of advanced guards and outposts.[42]

The essence of this can be most easily understood from the method of the system of advanced guards and outposts. The quartering of an army of 100,000 requires an area of 255 square kilometers (km^2). Considering the territory to be a circle, its radius is approximately 9 km and its circumference 57km.[43] How can we ensure the nightly rest and security of this quartered army? Naturally, in a way that the enemy should not be in a position to carry out a surprise attack from any direction. At first glance we might think that the advanced guards and outposts should be equally distributed alongside the circumference of the circle formed by the units of the army. Casting a closer glance at the situation, however, it turns out that this would be a wrong approach. Let us start from that point of the circle which is farthest from the enemy, i.e., the rear of the army. If the enemy wanted to attack at this point, then it would have to circle the whole army. This means that it would have to cover at least the distance amounting to half of the circumference of the above circle, i.e. 27-28 kms. But his possibility can be excluded, because such a distance cannot be covered by the opponent enemy during a single night.

Consequently, the probability of the enemy's attack from the rear is almost equal to zero. If the enemy chose to attack from the flank, it would have to cover a distance of only 13-14 kms., i.e., the length of a quarter of that circle. Yes, but they would have to march on untrodden ways, and—on top of all this—in the middle of the night. Thus the probability of a side attack is also very small. Advancing on the circumference of the circle, the probability of the attack increases, the greatest danger being at that point of the circle which is nearest to the enemy. Therefore, this is just the place, or to be more exact, the very short segment to the right and to the left from this point of the circle, where 70 to 80 percent of the advanced guards and the outposts are placed. This means that the probability of the enemy's attack in this place is estimated to be 70 to 80 percent. We do not think that anyone has carried out the aforementioned calculations before. But we are certain that ever since people have made wars, on the basis of their earlier experiences and on the subjective consideration of probabilities, they have set up their security detachments in this way. This is how "the method of the system of advanced guards and outposts" was born.

Clausewitz on the Nature of Military Decision-Making

The title of Book I of Clausewitz's *On War* is *On the Nature of War*. This book comprises chapters with the following titles: "On Danger in War," "On Physical Effort in War," "Intelligence in War," and "Friction in War." In the closing chapter of Book I the following may be read:

> We have identified danger, physical exertion, intelligence, and friction as the elements that coalesce to form the atmosphere of war, and turn it into a medium that impedes activity.[44]

This atmosphere of war is the cause of the fact that "everything in war is very simple, but the simplest thing is difficult."[45]

For Clausewitz the most important and most interesting question of first priority was precisely the problem of how to make the right decision in this atmosphere of war so much burdened with a great number of uncertainties, spiritual and physical afflictions. It is without any doubt that his acquaintance with the theory of probability was of great assistance to him. Yet, the most significant factor was still his very thorough technical knowledge and his inclination to introspection. We have the feeling that the decisions he made in war games, and especially those he made in war, he replayed again and again subsequently in his brain. He simulated them, and it is in this way that he came to conclusions concerning the nature, structure and dynamics of the decision process, several of which would be still valid among the results of the behavioral sciences of our days.

Behavioral sciences differentiate between two types of decision processes or decision behaviors: the routine and the creative decision processes, i.e., the habitual behavior and the genuine decision making.[46]

The function of the routine decision process of habitual behavior is double: it ensures our rapid and appropriate action in certain situations, and frees us from being compelled to devote intellectual energy to the solution of certain problems. In other words, it helps to relieve our minds.[47] So much is this the case that we would be completely unable to make creative decisions if we did not possess a sufficient repertory "of the patterns of habitual behavior."[48]

Let us return to Clausewitz's concept of methods. He writes that methods "are the best of the general forms, short cuts, and options that may be substituted for individual decisions."[49] Isn't this identical with the concept of habitual behavior in modern behavioral sciences?

At the same time, the application of methods offers security to the military leaders in the drift of wars.

> The frequent application of routine [method] in war will also appear essential and inevitable when we consider how often action is based on pure conjecture or takes place in complete ignorance.... Even if we did know all the circumstances, their implications and complexities would not permit us to take the necessary steps to deal with them. Therefore, our measures must always be determined by a limited number of possibilities. We have to remember the countless minor factors implicit in every case. The only possible way of dealing with them is to treat each case as implying all the others, and base our dispositions on the general and the probable.[50]

It is in this way that man may become "omniscient" both in war and also among the uncertainties of everyday life.[51]

Routine behavior has a very important role also in the operation of organizations.[52] There are certain routines which belong to the role played in the organization. These routines determine the behavior of the individuals, and the possessor of power may provoke from his subordinates by appropriate stimuli, attitudes and actions that stem from their own roles and are in accord with the given situation. This ensures the expedient operation of the organization. Clausewitz formulates his views very similarly:

> We have to remember that as the number of officers increases steadily in the lower ranks, the less the trust that can be placed on their true insight and mature judgement. Officers whom one should not

> expect to have any greater understanding than regulations and experience can give them have to be helped along by routine methods. . . . These will steady their judgements, and also guard them against eccentric and mistaken schemes.[53]

The formal deployment of the army with the help of methods constitutes the foundation of a commander's "internal model" or "image"[54] on the basis of which he forms a mental image of the given situation, which subsequently determines to a large degree his creative decisions: "A standard order of battle or system of advance guards and outposts are methods by which a general may be fettering not only his subordinates but, in certain cases, also himself."[55]

According to modern military psychology, the "estimate of the situation and the decision-making" is a creative intellectual process, which brings about a theoretically new and therefore unknown result.[56] In the time of Clausewitz, creative ability was attributed to genius.[57] But at that time the concept of genius was interpreted differently in England and France than in Germany. In the first two of these countries, this concept was extended to the sciences, politics and war; whereas in the latter, it was applied only to the arts. Thus, when Clausewitz speaks of "military genius," then he basically deviates from the concept of the German philosophers, and first of all naturally from that of Kant. At the same time, however, he does not take over in its entirety the English and French concepts of genius either. Nor does he apply it to military genius, because he does not restrict its creative activity to the intellect, but includes into it other psychological factors as well, among them personal character. His definition is as follows:

> But we cannot restrict our discussion to *genius* proper, as a superlative degree of talent, for this concept lacks measurable limits. What we must do is to survey all those gifts of mind and temperament that in combination bear on military activity. These, taken together constitute the *essence of military genius*. We have said *in combination,* since it is precisely the essence of military genius that it does not consist in a single appropriate gift—courage, for example—while other qualities of mind or temperament are wanting or are not suited to war. Genius consists of *a harmonious combination of elements,* in which one or another ability may predominate, but none may be in conflict with the rest.[58]

This is really a very circumspect, sophisticated and realistic definition of military genius, since a mathematical or musical genius may quite easily exist without courage, steadfastness or strong will that can overcome physical fatigues, but a military genius cannot do so.

How does this military genius operate and how does it facilitate decision-making in war? He does so with the help of the "tact of the judgement" *(Takt des Urtheils)*. We could not find out whether this expression was created by Clausewitz himself, or did he borrow it from someone else. This, however, is not so important. Much more important is that it is not Kant's "faculty of judgement" *(Urtheilskraft)* that he is using, because that would be far removed from the idea he has in mind.[59]

Clausewitz nowhere defines the concept "tact of judgement," but from the way he uses it, one can deduce what he means by it. In one of his "Notes" written in 1830, we can read the following:

> The theory of major operations [strategy, as it is called] presents extraordinary difficulties, and it is fair to say that very few people have clear ideas about its details—that is, ideas which logically derive from basic necessities. Most men merely act on instinct [*Takt des Urtheils*], and the amount of success they achieve depends on the amount of talent they were born with.
>
> All great commanders have acted on instinct [*Takt*], and the fact that their instinct was always sound is partly the measure of their innate greatness and genius. So far as action is concerned this will always be the case and nothing more is needed.[60]

In the chapter on "Military Genius" Clausewitz writes: "War is the realm of uncertainty; three quarters of the factors on which action in war is based are wrapped in a fog of greater or lesser uncertainty. A sensitive and discriminating judgement is called for; a skilled intelligence to scent out the truth."[61]

Writing on the frictions of war he states that they cannot be learned in theory; but even if it were possible, we would still miss "the practice of judgement which is called tact.... As with a man of the world instinct [*Takt des Urtheils*] becomes almost habit so that he always acts, speaks, and moves appropriately, so only the experienced officer will make the right decision."[62]

A special chapter is devoted to courage, which,

governed by superior intellect, is the mark of a hero. This kind of boldness does not consist of defying the natural order of things and in crudely offending the laws of probability; it is rather a matter of energetically supporting that higher form of analysis by which a genius arrives at a decision; rapid, only partly consciously weighing the possibilities.[63]

When examining the military efforts necessary for the achievement of a political aim, Clausewitz writes the following:

At this point, then, intellectual activity leaves the field of the exact sciences of logic and mathematics. It then becomes an art in the broadest meaning of the term—the faculty of using judgement [$T.d.U.$] to detect the most important and decisive elements in the vast array of facts and situations. Undoubtedly this power of judgement [$T.d.U.$] consists to a greater or lesser degree in the intuitive comparison of all the factors and attendant circumstances; what is remote and secondary is at once dismissed, while the most pressing and important points are identified with greater speed than could be done by strictly logical deduction.[64]

As is evident, Clausewitz has touched here on the essence of the discoursive and intuitive thinking, and did so in a manner still acceptable to us today.

The number of quotations could be further increased, which would all prove that Clausewitz considered the "tact of judgement" to be the ability that facilitates most the decision-making of a genius. And if the expression itself is obscure—perhaps even mysterious—Clausewitz can be excused for it, all the more as he characterizes by it the "creative" decision-making process, the nature of which is still obscure to us.[65]

Today we are living in the midst of a "Clausewitz renaissance." We are convinced, however, that this renaissance cannot be complete if researchers disregard—unfortunately most of them do so—his magnificant achievements in the field of mathematical praxeology. This is all the more so, as rational military behavior is merely a part of the general, rational human behavior. Consequently, all that was described by Clausewitz in this field is of great importance, not only from the vantage point of military science, but also from that of the behavorial sciences in general.

NOTES AND ABBREVIATIONS

OW = Clausewitz von, C., *On War.* Edited and translated by M. Howard and P. Paret. Introductory essays by P. Paret, M. Howard and B. Brodie, with commentary by B. Brodie. Princeton, 1976.

VK = Clausewitz von, C., *Vom Krieg.* 18. Auflage. Mit erweiterter historisch-kritischer Würdigung von W. Hahlweg. Bonn, 1972.

Note: For specific bibliographical information on cited works, see the separate bibliography below.

1. Concerning seventeenth and eighteenth century history of probability theory, see the works of Baker, Coumet, David, Jordán, Guilbaud, Pearson and Rényi in the bibliography.
2. Quoted by Baker, 333.
3. See Hermann's introductory study in Kant, 1966, 27.
4. It is presumed that Clausewitz was familiar with Kant's writings on the basis of the Kant-vulgarizer, Kiesewetter. Cf. Paret, 69.
5. Perjés, 1972.
6. Perjés, 1982.
7. *OW*, 579; *VK*, 952.
8. *OW*, 580; *VK*, 954.
9. *OW*, 581; *VK*, 955.
10. *OW*, 584; *VK*, 959.
11. *OW*, 70; *VK*, 181.
12. *OW*, 78; *VK*, 195-196.
13. *OW*, 80; *VK*, 199.
14. Ibid.
15. *OW*, 85; *VK*, 207.
16. *OW*, 89; *VK*, 212-213.
17. Kiesewetter: "Eine Meinung [Muthmassung], die allein subjektive Gruende gar deine objektiven Gruende hat, ist eine *Chimaere, Hirngespinst.* Sie ist ein blosses Spiel der Einbildungskraft, das weder Erfahrung noch Vernunft unterstuetzt. . . . Was meiner Meinung nach wahr ist, muss, wenn es nicht alle Gruende fuer sich hat, wenigstens mehr Gruende *feur* als *wider* sich haben. Dasjenige, was mehr Gruende fuer als wider hat, ist *wahrscheinlich. Wahrscheinlichkeit* ist also das Fuerwahrhalten aus Gruenden;

wobei man sich aber bewusst ist, dass die Gruende unzureichend sind, sich von der Sache gewiss zu machen."—This is naturally a precise definition, but much more is contained in the following sentences written by Arbuthnot in 1692 on the human practices and the rational human behavior: "I believe the Calculation of the Quantity of Probability might be . . . applied to a great many Events which are accidental, besides those of Games; only these Cases would be infinitely more confused, as depending on Chances which the most part of Men are ignorant of; . . . all the Politics in the World are nothing else but a kind of Analysis of the Quantity of Probability in casual Events, and a good Politician signifies no more but one who is dexterous at such Calculations." Quoted by Pearson, 140.

18. We think completely justified Aron's reflection on whether Clausewitz considered the laws of war as laws of necessity or laws of probability. Finally, he states: "les lois nécessaires n'appartient pas au monde réel mais au monde idéel, celui des concepts. Toutes les conclusions praxéologiques déduites de l'univers conceptuel se trouvent du même coup condamnées *selon la logique de la pensée finale* de Clausewitz, dès lors qu'elles ne se fondent pas sur les données et les probabilités du monde réel." Aron, I, 297.

19. See for example the works of Bondarenko and Volkov, Brewer and Shubik, and that of Wilson.

20. Presumably Clausewitz had studied Condorcet's posthumous work entitled: *Elements du calcul des probabilités, et son application aux jeux de hazard, à la loterie, et aux jugements des hommes.* The work was published in 1805 and Clausewitz arrived in France in 1806, as the adjutant of the Prussian Archduke Augustine, who was interned there by Napoleon for security reasons. Clausewitz went back to Prussia only in the fall of 1807. In Berlin, he devoted much of his free time to the study of mathematics, in which he achieved excellent results also at the Prussian School of General Staff. As we learn from his letters written to his bride, he eased his strong homesickness and lovesickness with the "opium of mathematics." In one of his letters he writes with great enthusiasm that he deals with a branch of mathematics which hides prognostical possibilities. It is quite evident that he was referring to the probability calculation with which he became acquainted probably from Condorcet's cited work. The letter in question was published by Schwartz, I, 250-251.

21. For the critic of Kant's causal regularity see Reichenbach, 211, 266-267.
22. *OW*, 152; *VK*, 306-307.
23. Perjés, 1972, 124.
24. For the game theory see the works by Harsányi, Junne, Rapoport and Thomas.
25. *OW*, 86; *VK*, 208.
26. That with the concept of polarity Clausewitz basically anticipated the "zero-sum game" concept has been recognized both by Rapoport and by Aron. Cf. Rapoport, 1979, 74 and 76; and Aron, I, 115, 187 and 232.
27. *OW*, 83; *VK*, 204.
28. *OW*, 217-218; *VK*, 409.
29. For the utility theory see Rapoport, 1974; Harsányi, 1977; and Junne.
30. *OW*, 80; *VK*, 200.
31. *OW*, 81; *VK*, 201.
32. *OW*, 81 and 551; and *VK*, 201 and 914. The translators of *OW* avoid the expression "equivalent." On the basis of what was said, this does not seem to be justified.
33. In this question the number of misunderstandings is almost infinite. In the large scale of opinions the two extremes are represented by Schlieffen and Liddel Hart. Wallach and Liddel Hart.
34. *OW*, 91; *VK*, 216.
35. Ibid.
36. *OW*, 97; *VK*, 227.
37. For the "game tree" Rapoport, 1974, 141. Kirsch, II, 150.
38. Harsányi, 1977, 628-629; Thomas, I, 105-107.
39. *OW*, 151; *VK*, 306.
40. Baker, 185.
41. Pearson, 159-160.
42. *OW*, 154; *VK*, 309.
43. *OW*, 328; *VK*, 571. One Prussian mile is equivalent to 8.5 kilometers or 5.3 English miles.
44. *OW*, 122; *VK*, 265.
45. *OW*, 119; *VK*, 261.
46. Kirsch, I, 65; II, 133 and 141; Thomas, I, 67, 143 and 238.
47. Kardos, 280.

48. Kirsch, I, 75.
49. *OW,* 153; *VK,* 308.
50. Ibid.
51. Rapoport very wittily clarifies the essence: "Wherever combinations or permutations of things must be counted, fantastically large numbers are bound to occur. This should not be of itself a major concern to the theoretician. The vastness of the numbers of combinations does not prevent him from calculating by relatively simple means the probabilities of combinations which are of interest. In poker, for example, it is a simple matter to compute the occurrence probabilities of flushes, straights, pairs, etc., and also the probabilities of filling these combinations, given the card on hand. There are situations where "omniscience" means nothing more impressive than a knowledge of such probabilities, and "rationality" means simply taking these probabilities into account when making choices." Cf. Rapoport, 1974, 110-111. Montecuccoli, who must have been informed of the probability theory of his age, writes the following: "He who wants to consider everything, will not do anything, but he who takes into account a few things only, will be mistaken." It is not possible—he goes on—to get acquainted with all things in their details, but even if we know them, it would be impossible to take into account all of them, since: "Ten words can be combined in so many ways... that millions of groupings could be achieved." Montecuccoli includes here in the text a combinatory example. "From the extremely few and the extremely many," says Montecuccoli, "a limited number of useful and to the situation appropriate things have to be selected...; and it is only after this that the suitable theses of the arts of war can be applied. Cf. Montecuccoli, Libr. I, Cap. 46. It is for this reason that "patterns of recognition" and "muddling through" have still considerable significance in the research concerning the mental process of finding solutions to problems. No man, and not even a computer can take all possible circumstances into consideration. Cf. Kirsch, I, 88; II, 61.
52. Kirsch, III, 52, 107 and 195.
53. *OW,* 153; *VK,* 308-309.
54. For the internal model see Bondarenko, 76-77, 128ff.; Kirsch, I, 63, 76; Thomas, I, 29, 55ff.
55. *OW,* 154; *VK,* 309-310. From this point of view it is most interesting what Clausewitz has to say on "meeting engagement" in his work

entitled: *Leitfaden der Taktik der Gefechtslehre.* According to him, in this type of battle "the general disposition of the army, the order of battle, and elementary tactics substitute for the actual plan of battle as stereotypical dispositions with certain modifications required by the field." Cf. *VK,* 1170. This is exactly what he means also when he writes: "The commander takes as a basis alternately the 'tact of judgement,' the rules and the crutch of established routine [method]." Cf. *OW,* 213; *VK,* 401.

56. Bondarenko, 57, 79, 232; Thomas, I, 143, 202.
57. *Historisches Wörterbuch der Philosophie:* title "Genius."
58. *OW,* 100; *VK,* 231-232.
59. Kant describes "Urtheilskraft" as follows: "Urtheilskraft überhaupt ist das Vermögen, das Besondere also enthalten unter dem Allgemeinen zu denken. Ist das Allgemeine [die Regel, das Prinzip, das Gesetz] gegeben, so ist die Urtheilskraft, welche das Besondere darunter subsumiert, [auch wenn sie als transcendentale Urtheilskraft a priori die Bedingungen angibt, welchen gemäss allein unter jenem Allgemeinen subsumiert werden kann] bestimmend. Ist aber nur das Besondere gegeben, wozu sie das Allgemeine finden soll, so ist die Urtheilskraft bloss *reflectierend.*" Cf. Kant, 1913, "Einleitung," xxvi, 179. The term "Takt des Urtheils" cannot be at all identified with Kant's "Urtheilskraft," as has been suggested by Hahlweg and Aron. Cf. Hahlweg, in *VK,* 18-19; and Aron, I, 368. However special expression the "Takt des Urtheils" may be, we are convinced that it should be considered as a term of Clausewitz. For this very reason we would have considered it much better for the translator of *OW* to use this expression in the English text. It is another question whether the "tact of judgement" used by us is the proper expression, but we do not think that "intuition," "skilled intelligence," "instinct," etc., are appropriate. Quoting the *OW,* naturally, we could not change the text deliberately, therefore, we inserted the expression "Takt des Urtheils" i.e., the abbreviation "T.d.U." after the expression used by the translators. When this solution cannot be applied, we quote the German text in its original in the footnote.
60. *OW,* 70-71; *VK,* 182.
61. *OW,* 101; *VK,* 233. The second sentence in the German original is as follows: "Hier ist es also zuerst, wo ein feiner, durchdringender Verstand in Anspruch genommen wird, um mit dem Takte seines Urtheils die Wahrheit herausfühlen."

62. *OW*, 120; *VK*, 263-264. The following English translation: "development of instinct and tact will still need" was retranslated by us as follows: "the practice of the judgement which we call experience." In the German original: "so wurde jene Übung des Urtheils immer noch fehlen, die mann Takt nennt. . . ."

63. *OW*, 192; *VK*, 369. The second part of the sentence in the original German text is as follows: "den das Genie, der Takt des Urtheils in Blitzschnelle und nur halb bewusst durchlaufen hat, wenn er seine Wahl trifft."

64. *OW*, 585; *VK*, 961.

65. Kirsch, II, 202.

BIBLIOGRAPHY

Aron, R., *Penser la guerre, Clausewitz*, 2 vols. Paris, 1976.

Baker, K. M., *Condorcet. From Natural Philosophy to Social Mathematics.* Chicago-London, 1975.

Bondarenko, V. M.–Volkov, A. F., *A csapatvezetés automatizálása* [The Automatization of Military Leadership]. Translated from the Russian original. Budapest, 1980.

Brewer, G. D.–Shubik, M., *The War Game. A Critique of Military Problem Solving.* London, 1979.

Brooks, F., "The Stochastics Properties of Large Battle Models," *Operations Research*, September-October, 1966.

Clausewitz, C., *Vom Kriege*, 18. Aufl. Bonn, 1972.

Clausewitz, C., *On War.* Princeton, 1976.

Coumet, E., "La théorie de hasard est-elle née pas hasard?" *Annales, économies, sociétés,, civilisations*, Mai-Juin, 1970.

David, F., *Games, Gods and Gambling. The Origins and History of Statistical Ideas from the Earliest Times to the Newtonian Era.* London, 1962.

Guilbaud, G. T., *Éléments de la théorie mathématique des jeux.* Paris, 1968.

Harsányi, C. J., "Rational Choice Models of Political Behavior vs. Functional and Conformist Theories," *World Politics*, 1969/4.

Harsányi, C. J., "Morality and the Theory of Rational Behavior," *Social Research*, 1977/4.

Hermann, I., *Kant teológiája* [Kant's Theology]. 2nd ed. Budapest, 1979.

Historisches Wörterbuch der Philosophie. Herausgegeben von J. Ritter. Basel-Stuttgart, 1974.

Jordán, K., *Fejezetek a klasszikus valószínűségszámításból* [Chapters from Classical Probability Calculations]. Budapest, 1956.

Junne, G., *Spieltheorie in der internationalen Politik. Die beschränkte Rationalität strategischen Denkens.* Düsseldorf, 1972.

Kant, I., *Az itéleterő kritikája* [The Critique of the Tact of Judgement]. 2nd ed. Translated and edited by I. Hermann. Budapest, 1966.

Kant, I., *Kritik des Urtheilskraft.* (*Kants Werke,* Band V.) Berlin, 1913.

Kardos, L., *Általános pszichológia* [General Psychology]. Budapest, 1964.

Kiesewetter, J. G. E., *Grundriss einer allgemeinen Logik nach Kantischen Grundsätzen.* 2 vols. Leipzig, 1825.

Liddel Hart, B. H., *Strategy,* New York, 1954.

Montecuccoli, R., *Trattato della guerra col Turco.* Edited by Grassi. Milano, 1832.

Paret, P., *Clausewitz and the State.* New York, 1976.

Pearson, K., *The History of Statistics in the 17th and 18th Centuries. Lectures Given by K. Pearson at the University College London.* Edited by E. S. Pearson. London, 1978.

Perjés, Géza, "Clausewitz magyar fordítása" [The Hungarian Translation of Clausewitz], *Hadtörténelmi Közlemények* [Military History Review], 1966/1.

Perjés, Géza, "Histoire militaire et psychologie," *Revue Internationale d'Histoire Militaire Compareé,* 1970.

Perjés, Géza, "Szerencse, valószínűség és hadvezéri szemmérték. Katonai döntés és a valószínűség Montecuccolitól és Zrínyitől Clausewitzig" [Chance, Probability and Guess Work in Military Leadership. Military Decision and Probability from Montecuccoli and Zrinyi to Clausewitz], in *A Magyar Tudományos Akadémia II. Osztályának Közleményei* [Proceedings of Section II of the Hungarian Academy of Sciences], 1971.

Perjés, Géza, "Militärgeschichte und Militärpsychologie," in *Geschichte und Militärgeschichte. Wege der Forschung.* Herausgegeben von U. von Gersdorff. Frankfurt am Main, 1974.

Perjés, Géza, "Zrinyi Miklós a haditudományi író" [Miklós Zrínyi, Author of Studies in the Military Sciences], and "Vitéz Hadnagy. Bevezetés"

[Introduction to the "Brave Lieutenant"], both in *Zrínyi Miklós hadtudományi munkái* [Miklós Zrinyi's Studies in Military History]. Budapest, 1957; 2nd ed., 1976.

Perjés, Géza, *Clausewitz*. In manuscript. To be published by Magvető Publishers, Budapest.

Prohorov, A., "Prinzipien der Truppenführung und Forderungen der Kybernetik," *Militärwesen,* 1968/10.

Rapoport, A., *Fights, Games, and Debates.* Ann Arbor, Michigan, 1974.

Rapoport, A., Introduction to C. von Clausewitz's *On War.* London, 1979.

Reichenbach, H., *Gesammelte Werke in 9 Bänden.* Herausgegeben von A. Kamlach und M. Reichenbach, Band I: *Der Aufstieg der wissenschaftlichen Philosophie.* Braunschweig, 1977.

Rényi, G., *Valószínűségszámítás* [Probability Calculations]. Budapest, 1954.

Schwartz, K., *Leben des Generals von Carl von Clausewitz und der Frau von Clausewitz.* 2 vols. Berlin, 1878.

Sziperski, N.-Winand, U., *Entscheidungstheorie. Eine Einführung unter besonderer Berücksichtigung spieltheoritischen Konzepte.* Stuttgart, 1974.

Thimm, W., "Betrachtungen zum militärischen Chance-Risiko-Problem," Militärwesen, 1969/6.

Weiss, H. K., "Combat Models and Historical Data: The U. S. Civil War," *Operations Research,* September-October, 1966.

Wilson, A., *War Gaming.* London, 1970.

Zoltán Kramár

COMBAT ORGANIZATION AND COMMAND STYLE AS COMMAND PROBLEMS IN THE *HONVÉD* ARMY, DECEMBER 1848-APRIL 1849

Over the past one hundred and thirty years, the Hungarian War of Independence has been analyzed at great length and in considerable detail. The resultant literature, on the *Honvéd* Army and its operations alone, is rather impressive in quantity. That the conclusions of five generations of historians studying the same set of phenomena will at least in part be contradictory is of course hardly surprising. But leaving our conflicting political points of view and ideological controversies aside, we must admit that we do have at least a fair amount of "objective," or better perhaps, "technical" understanding of the conflict.

Among many other data apropos to the subject, we know, for example, which units of the Imperial-Royal Army were and remained, at the disposal of the Batthány Government and then of its successor, the National Committee of Defense. We know how these formations were successfully integrated into the newly created *Honvéd* Army. We know in what ways the combat organization of this new army differed from that of the Austrian forces. We also understand that this new combat organization demanded the development of its own tactics and, above all, needed a matching command style, very much different from that practiced by most Austrian commanders. In more recent times, contemporary Hungarian historians have done yeoman work in tracing the national composition and social stratification of both the rank and file as well as those of the officer corps. We certainly know a lot about the top commanders. But here, perhaps, we had laid too much stress on their intramural jealousies, conflicts and bickerings. And when it comes to their largely dysfunctional relations with Kossuth, who as president of the National Defense Committee, in a sense, filled the position of a civilian-political commander-in-chief, the emphasis is once again too much on the problem of conflicting political attitudes, loyalties and ambitions.

To put it briefly and in somewhat different terms, current wisdom in Hungary seems to have it that Kossuth never quite managed to get a proper grip on the *Honvéd* Army. The reason for that seems to be that too many of the key commanders were reluctant, if not downright disloyal, servants of the revolution.

Far be it for me to dispute the validity of this interpretation of the data. That the problem of command at the highest level, that is, at the point of contact between the army and the civilian government leadership, was never solved is all too obvious. But to assume that the failure to solve it was due largely to the lack of revolutionary consciousness on the part of the officer corps, or alternatively, to the inflated pride and near pathological ambitions of certain high commanders, is to do less than optimum service to historical understanding.

The purpose of this brief study, therefore, is a modest attempt to sketch the outlines of a possible complementary explanation. Admittedly, the latter is based upon a number of assumptions. I assume that my perception of the components of this command problem is at least approximately correct. I further assume that these components, that is, the *Honvéd* Army's combat organization, a command style appropriate to that organization, and Kossuth's own personal leadership style partake of the nature of objective constants. If my assumptions are correct then the command problem was indeed insoluble. And finally, while personality clashes and conflicting political attitudes and ambitions clearly aggravated the problem, the problem, at its core, was and remained systemic.

* * * * *

The *Honvéd* Army, being forged in the heat of the 1848 events, was initially a "many splendored thing." It contained formations of the professional, standing Imperial-Royal Army,[1] growing masses of untrained and underequipped National Guardsmen and an increasing number of *Honvéd* battalions.[2] After the introduction of conscription in September 1848, the number of *Honvéd* battalions rapidly grew and soon constituted the dominant element in the army.[3]

While there were plenty of enthusiastic volunteers—thousands upon thousands flocked to the standards—the embryonic army lacked unity[4] as well as uniformity in a number of essential ways.

To begin with the mundane, it lacked uniforms in sufficient quantity; it was short on standardized weapons; this was particularly true of the artillery. Woefully lacking were experienced officers, especially those of higher rank. As far as the political attitude of the officer corps was concerned, it covered a rather broad range, but perhaps with a rather heavy concentration around the loyalist-constitutionalist position. Certainly, from a purely revolutionary, not to speak of a republican point of view, the professional officers were and remained suspect. Finally, unity of command at the highest operational level was nonexistent. For all that, the task of organization was energetically tackled and it was tackled along thoroughly professional lines.[5]

I suspect that the unavailability of sufficient numbers of senior field grade officers made the regimental organization—traditional with the standing armies of Europe—rather impractical. Instead, making a virtue out of necessity, the Defense Ministry turned the infantry battalion into the basic maneuver formation of the new army. Next, several battalions were brigaded with appropriate cavalry and artillery units. Typically, two such brigades would then be pulled together into a division. Finally, two or more divisions would form an army corps.[6]

Until January-February 1849, when the attempt was made to establish a field army command structure, these self-contained army corps fought separately with minimum "formal" and usually even less "effective" central coordination. One of them, General Görgey's Army Corps of the Upper Danube, became famous, or perhaps notorious, for its totally independent operations.

While this army was obviously a product of the revolution, it was not what might be called a typically revolutionary army. This was largely due to its top commanders, who, with a very few exceptions, were all officers with professional line experience. While making necessary concessions to the prevailing extraordinary circumstances, they nevertheless tended to follow accustomed standard operating procedures, insisting, for instance, on an iron discipline with all the outward manifestations such discipline implies.[7] At the same time it would be a mistake to consider the *Honvéd* Army merely as an underequipped, small scale version of its Austrian opponent. In fact, it was groping for and gradually finding its own identity.

With its battalion-centered combat organization, led by its inspired young commanders, who had been professionally trained, but were not yet ossified by years of stultifying garrison duty, this army was turning into a quick moving, supple, highly maneuverable and flexible force. These characteristics are, of course, best demonstrated by the army's new, evolving tactics. The commanders, from company level to corps, seemed to have instinctively and almost simultaneously recognized the impracticability of attack by dense infantry formations in the face of concentrated artillery and musket fire. Thus the assault formations were loosened up considerably, minimizing thereby the effect of the opponent's superior firepower. Then again, there was never enough time to train the men in the intricate, time consuming ritual of volley fire. Instead, the commanders recognized that the explosive energy, the exuberant offensive spirit of the rank and file would find optimum release in a crescendo of psychologically terrifying bayonet charges.[8]

In fact, what we see is the skillful adaptation of small unit tactics to medium and large size field forces. In other words, we see top commanders handling brigades and divisions as if they were companies and battalions.

This highly mobile warfare then developed its own ethos within the army, characterized by a sustained, more intimate contact between officers and men. A solid and effective communal spirit evolved within battalions, where the rank and file knew each other and their officers as well.[9] While orders were considered sacred and were expected to be carried out punctiliously and with dispatch, the officers lived, ate and slept with their men sharing with them dangers and discomforts alike.[10] To be sure, this almost ideal relationship between leaders and led was not only an automatic product of the new combat organization and its very own *modus operandi*. On occasion it was consciously reinforced, even demanded by the political leadership.[11] To that extent at least, the *Honvéd* Army did owe its ethos to the general revolutionary spirit then prevailing in the country. But it is equally clear that the commander's personality, and hence his command style, i.e., the manner in which he chose to exercise his legal authority, had a much more decisive effect upon his men than it ever could have had upon the units of the Austrian Army. It is thus advisable to consider, at least in summary fashion, those qualities and characteristics of the top *Honvéd* commanders, which seemed to be most influential in shaping the fighting spirit of the troops.

As already mentioned repeatedly, the characteristic of the corps commanders that strikes the observer right away was their relative youth. With the exception of the 57 year old General Louis [Lajos] Aulich and the 54 year old Polish General Joseph Bem, the corps commanders were surprisingly young. General George [György] Klapka was 29, General Arthur Görgey was barely 30.

With the exception of the radical revolutionary politician, General Maurice [Móric] Perczel, they all had company grade, line experience in a standing army, most usually the Austrian.[12]

They were all talented leaders; Görgey was brilliant. They all had great physical courage; General John [János] Damjanich had it to the point of recklessness.[13] They also tended to be hypersensitive; in the cases of the Generals Klapka and Perczel, to the point of vanity.[14] They were charismatic, strong willed, jealous of their authority and fiercely independent-minded; in the case of Görgey to the point of repeated insubordination.[15]

Their command style was direct, "up-front"; while they demanded unconditional obedience, they took care of their men's needs. Their troops in turn repaid them with absolute loyalty and in the case of Bem, Klapka, Damjanich and Perczel, with affection that bordered on veneration. Even the personally cold and remote Görgey was the object of admiration and profound respect.

Thus, by the beginning of February 1849, it may be said that the new *Honvéd* Army, having successfully developed and integrated its new combat organization with matching tactics, ethos and command style, has become a respectable fighting force. What prevented it from becoming a truly formidable one, was the intractable problem of the high command.

As noted above, until early February 1849, the seven army corps (Corps VIII and IX were fortress garrisons), in the absence of a field army command structure, operated by and large independently of each other.

The corps commanders, who visibly enjoyed their operational independence, were, in theory at least, subordinated to the Minister of War. The incumbent, General Lázár Mészáros, had moved to his high administrative position directly from a regimental command.[16] Unusually learned for one of his profession in that age,[17] he was a more than competent administrator.[18] He might have had an even more positive effect on the war effort, had he been permitted more latitude of action. But as minister, he acted mainly as a conduit for that avalanche of exhortatory letters, advisory memoranda and just plain orders directed at the several corps commanders by the President of the National Defense Committee, Louis Kossuth.[19]

Louis Kossuth was a charismatic revolutionary leader of the first rank, and a genuine statesman. Unfortunately, he was also too much akin to those latter-day political chief executives who, in time of war, have a disconcerting habit of suddenly discovering in themselves strategic abilities of the highest order. Not only did Kossuth deal with grand strategy, which was his *ex officio* right and responsibility, he had the disturbing and at times demoralizing tendency of interfering in ongoing operations on the campaign-strategic and even tactical levels. It is small wonder that some of the young corps commanders soon lost patience with his often professionally unsound and sometimes contradictory orders, which then too often led to friction and a frittering away of sorely needed energy and mental concentration on matters merely tangential to the waging of war.

While most of the top commanders had their share of personal problems with Kossuth, no one had as many as Görgey.

There is no need in this brief study to review the "Görgey Question," one of the great ongoing controversies in modern Hungarian historiography.[20] Still, certain incidents of Görgey's running "feud" with Kossuth must be mentioned because only through them can the nature of the command problem be properly illustrated. Beginning with two givens, first, it must be emphasized that Kossuth tended to suspect and mistrust all officers who had once served under the Imperial standards.[21] Second, beyond the ideological pros and cons of the Görgey controversy,[22] one cannot avoid the fact that had it been not for Görgey, a significant number of the professional officers would early on have abandoned the struggle. As has been so well put: "Imperial-Royal officers who would not serve Kossuth, the civilian and the revolutionary, obeyed Görgey, the soldier and the constitutionalist."[23]

Soon after Kossuth appointed Görgey to the command of the Army Corps of the Upper Danube, mentor and protege clashed over the utilization of irregular formations and over the debated introduction of guerrilla warfare.[24] Görgey, the professional, had nothing but contempt for the former and saw in the post-Schwechat period no practical way of waging the latter. By the same token, Kossuth, the revolutionary leader, was clearly more comfortable with citizen forces not under the command of politically suspect professionals. At the same time one cannot but wonder to what extent Kossuth had at the time been under the strategic influence of General Joseph Bem. With one revolution already under his belt, the experienced Polish soldier had some rather definite ideas on how irregular bands, waging guerrilla war could aid in the overall struggle for liberation and independence.[25] In the end, nothing came of Kossuth's plans for partisan warfare, but the disagreement left a residue of frustration and diminished trust in both men for each other, that boded ill for the future.

The second round of conflict between Kossuth and Görgey broke out over the question of the proper response to the Austrian invasion of Hungary in early December 1848. Both agreed of course that withdrawal at this time was unavoidable. It was rather over the nature of the retreat that they came to disagree. Görgey aimed for a well-ordered, smoothly-executed withdrawal. Accomplishing that without serious losses in the circumstances, would actually be a moral as well as a strategic victory of sorts. Kossuth, on the other hand, wanted a fighting withdrawal in which the *Honvéd* forces would every so often stop and offer battle to the pursuers. He hoped thus to gain at least one or two small, tactical victories which then could be used to bolster the sagging national morale.

Up to this point there is surely nothing out of the ordinary in this disagreement. It is yet another example of the traditional conflict between the political leader and his field commander: between a Lincoln and a McClellan; between Churchill and Montgomery. What is unusual is the manner in which Kossuth triggered the conflict and that brings us to his own command style.

Effective commanders will usually strive to give simple and, above all, unambiguous orders. Beyond that, they will, as a matter of course, accept the responsibility for such negative effects as the carrying out of their orders may entail. On both these counts Kossuth had a habit of falling short of the ideal. For example, on January 1, 1849, he ordered Görgey to stand and fight a "decisive battle" west of the capital, but in such a fashion that neither Budapest nor his own hopelessly outnumbered army be serious endangered. Thereupon he and the government transferred themselves beyond the Tisza River to Debrecen. It seems that this order, this pathetic attempt to square the circle, was not at all unusual for Kossuth. If anything it was rather typical of him.[26] It is no wonder that the coldly calculating Görgey, that supreme rationalist, refused to obey the order, looked with contempt at the fleeing civilian government, then took the first opportunity to take his corps beyond the range of government "interference."

Before he did that, however, he laid down the principles which motivated and guided him and his corps in this war. The Manifesto of Vác, published January 5, 1849, was in one sense Görgey's public declaration of insubordination to the post-Batthány Revolutionary Government. But in another, and I believe, in a more important sense, it was a challenge to Kossuth to gain control over the army, if he could.

Görgey-baiters, as may be expected, have always had a field day with the Manifesto of Vác. To those who have judged him a traitor, his road of treason, which ultimately led him to Világos, began at Vác.[27] Without going into lengthy details, or entering the debate itself, let me make the simple observation that in political matters, Görgey was a constitutionalist. He fought because the Kingdom of Hungary had been assaulted and because the Austrian Government had violated Hungary's age-old constitution. No one today accuses Francis Deák, the great constitutionalist jurist, of having been a traitor. It appears to me that the major difference between Deák and Görgey in this matter was rooted in the fact that the former was a lawyer and the latter was a soldier. In this growing constitutional crisis the point was finally reached where the lawyer had to stand aside, while the soldier could still resist.

Far more important to me than any argument about Görgey's possibly self-serving motivations and Machiavellian calculations, stands the fact that he was a constitutionalist. The Manifesto was an impeccably constitutionalist document. Most importantly, he and his Manifesto fully reflected the constitutionalist attitude of a great majority of his regular officers. That is why they followed him. They knew that Görgey would fight the invaders of Hungary, but would not fight merely for a republic.

The *Honvéd* Army, or at least Görgey's corps at this time, was not a republican institution. It is doubtful whether it was even a revolutionary institution; it certainly wasn't that in any Jacobian sense. In the meantime, however, the attempt was made to establish a field army command.

By late January 1849, the military situation had stabilized along the main defense line of the Tisza River. The time appeared ripe for a major coordinated counteroffensive by the *Honvéds*. For this purpose, however, it was essential that the several independent corps, available for the offensive, be integrated into an appropriate field army structure. This in turn necessitated the appointment of a field army commander.

The two men, who most clearly qualified for this position, Kossuth could not or would not consider seriously. Apparently, General Bem's presence in Transylvania continued to be essential. As for Görgey, Kossuth judged him politically quite unreliable. In this dilemma Kossuth turned to his agent and recruiter in France, Count László Teleki, through whom he secured the services of a Polish emigré, Major General Henryk Dembinski [Dembinszky], one of the heroes of the 1831 Polish uprising.[28]

In the event, Kossuth's choice was a very bad mistake. Though his accumulated laurels were genuine enough, in Hungary, Dembinski gave the impression of a man, who in the words of Istvan Deak, "...was conceited, dull, sensitive and quarrelsome."[29] He was also ignorant of the terrain, of the character of the forces he was about to lead into battle and of the abilities and shortcomings of his corps commanders, not to speak of those of his opponents. Furthermore, his command style was not only incompatible with the spirit of the *Honvéd* Army, it was quite unsuitable for an army commander.

A modern study on the art of command discusses leadership in terms of these truisms: "It is incumbent upon the senior to understand and respect his subordinates. But this is not enough. Unless the subordinates respect the senior, trust him and understand his intentions and efforts, the senior-subordinate relationship suffers."[30] These hoary commonplaces were clearly quite alien to Dembinski. He was profoundly suspicious, secretive, remote and sarcastic.[31]

To be sure and to be fair, Dembinski received some very unsound advice from Kossuth. Before they ever met, Kossuth wrote him "...don't listen to anyone. After mature consideration do what you think is right, and defeat the enemy somewhere."[32] Dembinski had his first interview with Kossuth on January 20, 1848. It was a long one.[33] Soon Kossuth was speaking of Görgey in terms so damaging to the latter that one should really not be surprised at Dembinski's angry and raw conduct when he and Görgey first met.[34] On February 3, 1849, Kossuth once more advised his faithful Pole to be extremely tight with information concerning his operational plans.[35] Dembinski apparently took these counsels as encouragement to deal with his subordinate generals as with so many junior company grade officers. In his memoires he complains that his generals ". . . insisted on knowing in the minutest detail, the reasons behind my orders."[36] At a critical juncture in his Hungarian career, he flatly refused to call a war council, saying that ". . . only that general calls a council of war who cannot counsel himself. . . ."[37] He not only did not counsel with his corps commanders, he routinely by-passed them in giving direct orders to divisions.[38]

I am not trying to be hard on Dembinski. For once, he obviously was in over his head. He was a foreigner, made leader of a team, whose members he did not know and who were constantly being undercut by Kossuth, the man who hired him and to whom he felt responsible. Additionally, his subordinates' conduct had not always been exemplary either, so there was provocation for his own unfortunate reactions. In the final analysis, however, one must conclude, kindly and with charity, that Dembinski may have been a heroic divisional commander in the past, a commander of a field army he was not, and most certainly not of one consisting of *Honvéd* units. The complete lack of trust and candor which surrounded him like some evil mist, and above all, his inability to develop easy and smooth communications with his subordinates, rendered his position untenable.

After the ineptly conducted Battle of Kápolna, fought on February 26-27, the *Honvéd* Field Army withdrew behind the Tisza line. There, at Tiszafüred, on March 3-4, the corps commanders, with Görgey as their spokesman, refused further obedience to Dembinski.

The question of Görgey's culpability in engineering this "Generals' Mutiny" is irrelevant to this brief study. What is central to its theme is the way Kossuth handled the situation. His first impulse was to have Görgey courtmartialled. Five days later he decorated "the traitor" for heroic leadership in Debrecen.[39] What happened between the 4th and the 9th of March is that Kossuth had a chance to take the pulse of the army, gauge the temperature in camp, and contemplate the deep disunity prevailing within the National Defense Committee. And so, he ultimately decided to legitimize, *ex post facto,* Dembinski's removal from his command.

With this action, Kossuth, among several other things, demonstrated his impotence in the face of a united officer corps. That the problem of the army command was not necessarily and certainly not exclusively the product of the Görgey-Dembinski clash, but that it might have been systemic in origin, seems to be evidenced by the fate of Dembinski's successor. While Kossuth felt obliged to accept the result of the Tiszafüred coup, when it came to replacing Dembinski with Görgey, he dug his heels in. Instead, he appointed General Vetter, Chief of the Central General Staff, as commander of the *Honvéd* Field Army.

Major General Anton [Antal] Vetter von Doggenfeld was a most competent staff officer cursed with a disagreeable disposition. Today, no doubt, he would be accused of "being deficient in interpersonal skills." He was also chronically ailing. Shortly after his appointment, General Vetter had occasion to address the senior commanding officers of III Corps. In the presence of the corps commanders, General Damjanich, Vetter apparently made several belittling, besmirching, in short, insulting statements. As a result, after the meeting, there was an exceptionally violent verbal confrontation between the two generals, which for Vetter, had certain physiologically incapacitating consequences.[40] It was at this point that Kossuth, most reluctantly, appointed Görgey, but only as Deputy Army Commander.

Thus finally, and for the first time, the *Honvéd* Field Army found a leader whose command style was a perfect match to its combat organization, its tactics and its ethos. The subsequent series of victories which swept the country clean of the Austrian forces, seems to be a not unnatural consequence of this happy match. Alas, unlike Alexander the Great, Görgey was not invulnerable, and this ideal partnership did not last beyond the spring. When later, he had a second chance to lead the army he had helped to create, circumstances were tragically different. Then, the most he could do was to avoid further futile bloodshed. And that he did, even at the cost of his name, his reputation and his honor.

* * * * *

In conclusion, I must repeat, that Kossuth's failure to control the *Honvéd* Army—not that it would have made any difference to the outcome of the war—cannot be definitively explained in subjective ideological terms. Ultimately he could not control it because it was not given him to control it. The *Honvéd* Army was an army *sui generis*. It had its own internal arrangements, its own tactics, its own esprit, and it responded optimally to a commander whose style of leadership matched its unique characteristics. Kossuth's command style not only did not match them, it was incompatible with them. To be sure, the army could have been controlled, but not by Kossuth; and Kossuth might have been able to control an army, but not this *Honvéd* Army. As long as both remained fundamentally unchanged, the command problem at the highest level could not be solved.

NOTES

1. István Deák, *The Lawful Revolution: Louis Kossuth and the Hungarians, 1848-1849* (New York: Columbia University Press, 1979), p. 194.
2. Ibid., p. 195; Aladár Urbán, "The Hungarian Army of 1848-49," in Béla K. Király and Günther E. Rothenberg, eds., *War and Society in East Central Europe*, I (New York: Brooklyn College Press, 1979), p. 97.
3. Deák, op. cit., p. 195.
4. Ferenc Eckhárt, *1848. A Szabadság Éve* [1848. The Year of Liberty] (Budapest: Káldor György Könyvkiadó vállalat, 1948), pp. 167-168.
5. See Görgey's memorandum on army organization, addressed to the National Defense Committee, dated November 11, 1848. Arthur Görgey, *Mein Leben und Wirken in Ungarn in den Jahren 1848 und 1849* (Leipzig: F. A. Brockhaus, 1852), p. 100.
6. István Nemeskürthy, *"Kik érted haltak, szent világszabadság." A negyvennyolcas honvéd katonaforradalmárai* ["Who Died for You, Sacred World Liberty." The Honvéd Soldier Revolutionaries of 1848] (Budapest: Magvető Könyvkiadó, 1977), pp. 338-339.
7. Ibid., p. 317.
8. Ibid., p. 320.
9. Ibid., p. 318.
10. Ibid., pp. 325-326.
11. See Government Commissioner Bertalan Szemere's letter to corps commander, Colonel George Klapka, dated January 14, 1849, cited in George Klapka, *Emlékeimből* [From My Reminiscences] (Budapest: Franklin Társulat, 1886), pp. 73-76.

12. Nemeskürthy, op. cit., p. 318.
13. György Gracza, *Az 1848-49-iki Magyar Szabadságharcz Története* [The History of the Hungarian War of Independence, 1848-49] (5 vols., Budapest: Lampel Róbert Kiadása, 1894-1898), II, p. 90.
14. For Klapka see his *Reminiscenses,* pp. 96-97; for Perczel see Alfonz F. Danzer, *Dembinski Magyarországon: A vesér hátrahagyott kézirataiból* [Dembinski in Hungary: From the General's Unpublished Manuscripts] (Budapest: Az Atheneum Tulajdona, 1874), pp. 55-57.
15. Deak, op. cit., p. 185. Görgey's attitude toward his political superiors reminds one of General MacArthur, whose career, according to Janowitz "...was based on a flouting of authority, although he demanded strict obedience from his subordinates. MacArthur resisted...authority when it involved an affront to his honor and, by implication, to his fighting spirit." Morris Janowitz, *The Professional Soldier, a Social and Political Portrait* (London: Collier-Macmillan Ltd., 1960), p. 156.
16. As Colonel, Mészáros was commander of the 5th Imperial-Royal Hussars.
17. Mészáros was a member of the Hungarian Academy of Sciences.
18. Nemeskürthy, op. cit., p. 338.
19. For Kossuth's preferred *modus operandi* both in general, as well as with particular reference to the Ministry of Defense, see Deák, op. cit., pp. 197, 224-226.
20. The most recent, as well as the most judicious summary of this controversy is by Deak, op. cit., pp. 182-187.
21. Nemeskürthy, p. 253.
22. Typical of the nineteenth-century nationalist historians is Gracza, op. cit., III, pp. 74-77. For the Marxists, paradigmatic are George Spira, *A Magyar Forradalom 1848-1849-ben* [The Hungarian Revolution in 1848-49] (Budapest: Gondolat, 1959), pp. 359-360; Erik Molnár, ed., *Magyarország Története* [The History of Hungary] (2 vols., Budapest: Gondolat Könyvkiadó, 1964), I, p. 525.
23. Deak, op. cit., p. 186.
24. Eckhart, op. cit., p. 182; Görgey, op. cit., pp. 105-106, 110-111.
25. Emanuel Halicz, *Partizan Warfare in 19th Century Poland: The Development of a Concept* (Odense University Press, 1975), pp. 103-104; 109; 115; 118-119.
26. Deak, op. cit., p. 232.

27. István Görgey, Sr., *1848 és 1849-ből. Élmények és benyomások. Okiratok és ezek magyarázata. Tanulmányok és történelmi kritika* [From 1848 and 1849. Experiences and Impressions. Documents and their Explanations. Studies and an Historical Critique] (Budapest: Franklin Társulat, 1885), I, p. 129.
28. Zoltán Horváth, *Teleki László, 1810-1861* (2 vols., Budapest: Akadémiai Kiadó, 1964), I, p. 260.
29. Deák, op. cit., p. 240.
30. Col. Samuel H. Hays and Lt. Col. William N. Thomas, eds., *Taking Command: The Art and Science of Military Leadership* (Harrisburg, PA: Stackpole Books, 1967), p. 192.
31. Reading, for instance, the memoires of Görgey and Klapka, on the one hand, and those of Dembinski, on the other, one soon becomes aware on both sides of a large number of irritating and cumulatively demoralizing incidents.
32. Kossuth to Dembinski, January 12, 1849, quoted by Danzer, op. cit., pp. 96-97.
33. Ibid., p. 344.
34. Arthur Görgey, op. cit., pp. 214-215.
35. Danzer, op. cit., pp. 71-72.
36. Ibid., p. 95.
37. Ibid., p. 173.
38. Ibid., p. 95.
39. Dénes Pap, *Okmánytár Magyarország függeltenségi harczának történetéhez, 1848-1849* [Documentary Selection for the History of Hungary's War of Independence, 1848-1849] (Pest: Heckenast Gusztáv, 1869), II, p. 356, doc. no. 431.
40. Klapka, op. cit., pp. 119-120.

Gábor Vermes

HUNGARY AND THE COMMON ARMY IN THE AUSTRO-HUNGARIAN MONARCHY

The 1867 Compromise between Austria and Hungary, in view of the circumstances and lack of other viable options, was possibly the only solution to a political impasse. Although the political and economic arrangements growing out of this partnership were cumbersome, it is difficult to see what other forms of cooperation could have simultaneously satisfied the Habsburg dynasty, Austrian public opinion, the *Reichsrat*, and, finally, a most volatile Hungarian public. When judging these complicated arrangements, therefore, it is necessary to remember that their aim was the fulfillment of various demands made by these constituencies, and not the efficiency or effectiveness of the new Austro-Hungarian Monarchy.

For example, the Delegations sent out by the *Reichsrat* and the Hungarian Parliament held sessions alternately in Vienna and Budapest. Since these Delegations alone were empowered to question Ministers for Joint Affairs and to discuss matters pertinent to both halves of the Monarchy, it would have made sense for them to meet together. However, particularly the Hungarian Delegation would have considered such a suggestion an infringement upon the sovereignty of their country. Consequently, the Delegations met separately, and instead of engaging in a healthy dialogue, they were prone to hurl insults at each other from a distance. This arrangement, like others, reflected not the ideal, but merely the possible degree of cooperation which, in light of still smoldering mutual resentments and sensitivities, was often the sole alternative to having no solution at all.

Military affairs constituted the only area in which parity between the two halves of the Monarchy was observed in a relatively insignificant manner. The establishment of the Hungarian *Honvéd* and the Austrian *Landwehr* amounted to little, especially during the early years of Dualism. In comparison, the Common Army remained essentially unified, essentially German, and bound by its loyalty to Francis Joseph alone. This example of the Common Army demonstrated that 1867 was rooted as much in sober judgement as in emotional impulse. Delegations held their sessions separately because of jealously guarded national prerogatives, but this separatism was not extended to the army, because it was feared that fragmentation in that area would undermine the very foundations upon which the Monarchy rested. Selectively applied parity, however, created a source of chronic instability.

Czechs and South Slavs envied the Hungarian position within the Monarchy, a position that they aspired to reach, thus providing the foundations for plans to transform the Monarchy along trialistic or federalistic lines. In fact, Austro-Hungarian Dualism proved the essential failure of a federal solution in the Monarchy. Austria-Hungary was, after all, the federal union of two states. Total equality between them notwithstanding, there could be only one capital where the ministries for joint affairs were established; there could be only one foreign service, and, last but not least, only one army with a single language of command. Federalism can work only where either common historic tradition, as in Switzerland, or the same with the added strength of a common language as in the United States, encourages the relatively smooth coexistence and division of functions between the constituent parts and the whole. These prerequisites were missing in Austro-Hungarian Dualism, a marriage of convenience born of necessity rather than the outgrowth of longstanding historical trends, and the situation would not have improved by elevating more nations to the mirage of equal partnership.

The Compromise conformed best at the time to the intentions of the enfranchised liberal public's majority in both Austria and Hungary. On the Hungarian side, political expediency and the desire to preserve the liberal heritage merged to prop up a constitutional arrangement that seemed to guarantee Hungary's survival in the eyes of contemporaries. "If the Monarchy would disintegrate," said the principal Hungarian architect of the Compromise, Ferenc Deák, in 1867:

Hungary could enter into alliance with its smaller neighbors or could become totally independent. But the former would lead to frictions in the area of territorial integrity, while the latter would be good only if we were to have the power and the strength that such an independence requires.... Once we were a large state, but can we stand on our own now, wedged between the Russians and the Germans? ... [No,] we cannot survive without powerful support.[1]

This line of thinking regarded the Compromise as the cornerstone and supreme guarantee of national security. Mutual defense had become, in Deák's words, "an obligation," an indispensable tool incorporated into the settlement, benefitting the country without jeopardizing its constitutional freedoms.[2] Throughout the dualistic period of Hungarian history from 1867 to 1918, politicians faithful to the 1867 Compromise kept emphasizing the inherent logic and rationality of a common army, based on the jointly shared obligation of mutual defense. Count Gyula Andrássy, Jr., the son of Deák's closest associate, devoted an entire book to the defense of the Compromise, which was published in 1896.[3] Andrássy asserted that should a war break out, the Common Army would protect the restored constitutionalism and territorial integrity of Hungary exactly the same way as the best Hungarian patriots had done in the past, frequently paying for the defense of those objectives with their blood and lives. Such being the case, he argued, it did not matter at all that soldiers responded to the command "vorwärts marschiert" instead of "előre." Furthermore, Andrássy added, it was beyond doubt that Austria and Hungary would fight a future war together, and on purely strategic grounds, the most expedient and serviceable tool of mutual defense had to be a common army under unified command.

The writer and journalist Kornél Ábrányi followed closely in Andrássy's footsteps. Admittedly, Ábrányi argued, the Common Army did not correspond to the "national ideal," but it was not obstructing the realization of that ideal. On the contrary, the Common Army was the country's defensive shield against "the subversive activities of the ethnic minorities, pan-Slav aspirations, and the continuous expansion of the Russian Empire." Even the German character of the Common Army should be considered an asset, since it represented a stumbling block to "Slav hegemony and federalism."[4]

Another pro-Compromise, popularly known as 67-er, argument emphasized Hungary's obligation within the constellation of the great powers of Europe. "It is our duty," said Baron Géza Fejérváry, the Hungarian Minister of Defense, in an 1886 session of the Upper House, "to guarantee the great power status of the Monarchy, along with the prestige of our country, through the expansion of the armed forces, so that we should not fall behind the other great powers of Europe." This precaution was felt to be necessary because, already at that date, the coming of a future major war was anxiously contemplated. "We must be prepared and ready ourselves for war while there is still peace," exclaimed the rising young star of the ruling Liberal Party, István Tisza, in an 1889 parliamentary speech, adding that "should a war break out, then we can all agree that it would not be child's play, but could easily develop into a life-and-death struggle for the Hungarian nation."[5]

These rational arguments failed to appease the Hungarian opponents of the Compromise, popularly known as the 48-ers, who kept alive the *gravamina* (grievance) mentality deeply rooted in the Hungarian political tradition, as a defensive shield against real and imagined assaults on the part of foreign aggressors. A touchy obsession with matters of national prestige and the need to compensate for a perceived underdog status vis-à-vis Austria persisted in Hungarian political circles. Paradoxically, the reality that the Hungarians, alone among all the other nations of the Monarchy, had reached an equal status with the Germans of Austria inflamed, rather than diminished, this traditional mentality. The 48-ers pointed to the apparent discrepancy between official claims of achieved parity and Austria's alleged continued domination over Hungary.

The Common Army's lack of Hungarian character, and indeed its mere existence, were thought to bolster this domination. To the opponents of the Compromise, the external trappings of independence were vastly more important than substantial guarantees for its preservation. In a sense, this view reflected a different kind of logic, that of national dynamics, striving for the fullest representation of independent institutions and symbols as the indispensable attributes of national sovereignty. Certainly, the attempt to substitute purely Hungarian institutions and symbols for joint ones had a corrosive effect on Dualism. But the result was predetermined by the ill-adjusted accommodation of a nation, imbued with the inflated notions of a romantic nationalism, to a rational but artificial construct, the 1867 Austro-Hungarian Compromise.

In addition, the desire for an independent Hungarian army coincided with the emphasis on the Magyar character of the Hungarian state. The 48-ers in particular assumed that, as long as non-Magyar recruits from Hungary had to serve in an army where dynastically-oriented loyalty prevailed over nationalistic prerogatives, Magyar supremacy could never be fully secured in the country.

Of all matters under joint control, military affairs most strongly attracted the Hungarian public's attention. Vienna was the Monarchy's undisputed capital, but Budapest was gradually moving closer in terms of size, cultural life, and urban amenities. Although the lack of an independent Hungarian customs area was good material for nationalist propaganda, it was in fact an advantage to some Hungarians while damaging the interests of others. Apart from certain periods, most Hungarians demonstrated no particular interest in foreign affairs. The Army, on the other hand, was everywhere. Its garrisons were scattered throughout Hungary, a conspicuous reminder of incomplete independence, and in the 48-ers' judgement, the sad truth behind the glittering facade.

Skepticism about the need for a unified army was a consistent argument in the 48-ers' arsenal. Gábor Várady, in an 1868 session of the Hungarian Delegation, expressed his doubts about the assumed damage that the Army would suffer should one of its flanks go to battle with the cry, "For Country and Emperor!", while another would do likewise but shouting, "For Country and King!" Várady thought that such diversity would reinforce rather than diminish, the Army's *élan*. Kálmán Thaly reminded his parliamentary colleagues that the winners of the Crimean War had listened to commands in four languages and the losers had heard commands in only one.[6]

These comments missed the point, because unity had less to do with strategic considerations than with the fact that only an army placed above the growing divisiveness of ethnic animosities in a multinational Empire could present a force of necessary cohesion. The Hungarian sociologist and politician, Oszkár Jászi, no friend of the Habsburgs, nevertheless admitted that an army torn by conflicting national loyalties would have "broken the Monarchy to pieces under sanguinary civil wars." Although the Monarchy possessed a German character at the top and in its joint institutions, Jászi correctly perceived that dynastic efforts did not reflect a Germanizing tendency, nor a nationalistic point of view, but a desire to assure the interests and unity of the Habsburg Empire.[7] Francis Joseph never budged from this iron rule, understandably so from his point of view, and hints that a relaxation of centralistic control over the Army should be allowed made no impact on a ruler who regarded himself as the trustee of a supranational dynastic heritage.

However, it was precisely this dynastic heritage which filled the 48-ers with bitterness. After all, conflicts in history frequently carry the weight of a long list of complaints, accumulated through centuries, with the most recent grievances as the latest in a progression. "What connects us to the [Common] Army?," asked Károly Eötvös rhetorically. "The memory of painful conflicts. What the Army regards as its glory is sadness and mourning to us; what we cherish as our national honor is insurrection, rebellion to the Army." Lajos Mocsáry considered the Common Army an army of occupation which had brought to Hungary only "executioners, Caraffas, and Haynaus" in the past, a reference to Generals Caraffa and Haynau, brutal commanders of the Austrian armies in Hungary during the late seventeenth and mid-nineteenth centuries respectively. Mocsáry then gleefully noted the record number of battles lost by the Habsburg Empire. Kálmán Thaly actually took the trouble to list these battles from the time of Napoleon, concluding with the observation that the tradition of muddling through remained firm in the Common Army, along with the love of routine and formalities, so stifling to the human spirit. Gábor Ugron called the Army "a spoiled child," and Baron Dezső Prónay characterized it as "an alien wedge."[8]

There was undeniably a great deal of truth in this last observation, which represents the brief summary of opinions held by many Hungarians. Even if the bulk of the Army's rank and file were drawn from the country's population, a majority of the professional officer corps belonged to that supranational caste, whose home was the Army and who did not necessarily feel any more emotional attachment to Hungary than to Bosnia, Moravia, Bukovina, or Galicia. Isolated from the rest of society, living within the confines of their own rather narrow world, the officers placed loyalty to the Emperor high on their list of priorities, in contrast to national preferences. In a rare outburst, General Gregor Grivičić delivered a passionate speech before the Hungarian Delegation in 1868, calling the soldiers of the Habsburg Army patriots of the Monarchy, admonishing the delegates to respect the soldiers' feelings, and expressing the hope for a uniform patriotism among the peoples of the Habsburg Empire. Such a blatantly centralistic view enraged the Hungarians present at the meeting, including the 67-ers, because it clearly contradicted the Magyar commitment to constitutionally sanctioned national prerogatives. Upon their pressure, General Grivičić was replaced as the representative of the Austrian Minister of War at the Delegation by a less abrasive and possibly less candid army major.[9]

Around the same time, military circles in Vienna, with Archduke Albrecht at their head, were adamantly opposed to any division in the Army along national lines, which in 1868 meant granting Hungary the right to form its own small auxiliary army. Colonel Friedrich Beck, chief of Francis Joseph's military chancery, considered such a division the greatest danger for the Monarchy. In his judgement, the Hungarian Government was loyal, but he wondered what would happen if extremists were to seize power in Hungary and if eventually the Czechs and the Poles were to pose similar demands. Indeed, it had taken the brilliant and forceful diplomacy of the Hungarian Prime Minister, Count Gyula Andrássy, Sr., to extract the desired concession of a separate home guard, the *Honvéd*, along with its Austrian counterpart, the *Landwehr*.[10]

However, both in size and combat capability, the Common Army remained the dominant force.[11] To a large segment of the Hungarian public, the officers of this Army were foreigners, and the tension between them and the public transcended the customary rift between civilians and soldiers.

Incidents, fully exploited by the 48-er press, were numerous. For example, in 1879 in Eger, Lieutenant Colonel Seemann had a Hungarian flag thrown out of a military ceremony with the exclamation, "Away with that old rag!" In 1880, Miklós Bartha, the 48-er journalist and member of Parliament, was physically assaulted by two officers because Bartha was unwilling to fight a duel over certain articles that the officers had found offensive; no punishment was meted out to the officers. In 1886, General Janszky laid a wreath on the grave of General Hentzi, who had fallen during the siege of Buda in 1849 as the commanding general of the Austrian garrison defending the fortress against the besieging Hungarians. Against virulent attacks in the Hungarian Parliament, Archduke Albrecht, Inspector General of the Army, defended General Janszky, whereupon troops had to be called out to stop demonstrations in the streets of Budapest. General Janszky was subsequently promoted and transferred, while his superior, who had approved the Hungarian Government's position of censuring Janszky's tactlessness, was pensioned off.[12]

For all their protestations and rhetoric, however, the 48-ers regarded the idea of an independent Hungarian army as a remote objective, along with the concept of a truly independent Hungary with only the person of the Emperor/King in common with Austria. They were compelled to adopt this position because they recognized the insurmountable hurdles confronting a possible realization of their program. The stubborn adherence to the status quo on the part of Francis Joseph and the military leadership was undoubtedly counted among the major obstacles. In the meantime, the appeal of national exclusivity was making steady inroads into the 67-er ranks, who had appeared to stand only on the platform of pragmatic logic and cold rationalism.

An intermediate position between the 48-ers and the 67-ers evolved on the issue of the army. People holding this centrist view, while wishing to retain the Common Army, advocated a more emphatic Hungarian presence there. They advocated the extended use of Magyar as the language of command and as one of the languages of instruction in military schools, a growing role for Hungarian officers, and increased use of Hungarian symbols. Not even Dezső Szilágyi, the 67-er stalwart of orthodox liberalism, remained entirely immune to the lure of such enticing political eclecticism. In a parlimentary speech on January 23, 1889, Szilágyi demanded reforms that would satisfy national sentiments while leaving the essential unity and organization of the Common Army intact.[13]

But it was Count Albert Apponyi who came to represent best this centrist point of view. After the mid-1880s, Apponyi began to believe in the inevitability of the trend toward a fuller national existence, which he regarded as an elementary "biological force."[14] While for some time he retained part of the level-headed defense of the Compromise and did not go over to the 48-ers until 1905, he deluded himself into believing that somehow an accommodation between Hungarian *Realpolitik*, as represented by the 67-ers, and the popular, emotionally charged demands of the 48-ers, could be struck. He convinced himself that, once Hungary had succeeded in acquiring certain important requisites of a national existence, his fellow Magyar patriots would cease to raise their sights higher, the "biological force" would vanish, and harmony between his nation and the dynasty would be restored.

Standing between dreamers and realists, Apponyi personified the illassorted hybridity of the Hungarian political center. He could see that remaining satisfied with achieved gains did not conform to popular sentiments, but he wished to gratify these sentiments only to the degree that they did not endanger the achieved gains. Such a balancing act would have rendered lesser politicians ludicrous, but Apponyi mastered contradictions with unparalleled rhetorical brilliance.

The momentum of this centrist position was such that, by 1905, even Count Andrássy, author of the book dedicated to the defense of the Compromise, came to adopt it, as did Baron Dezső Bánffy, who had been the 67-er Prime Minister of Hungary between 1895 and 1899. In actuality, even the 48-ers had no choice but to pursue this centrist policy, because the realization of an independent Hungarian army was beyond hope. However, such relative moderation did not lessen tensions, which became particularly acute at times when the Hungarian Parliament was called upon to vote for the defense budget.

In January of 1903, Baron Fejérváry, the Hungarian Minister of Defense, introduced requests to sanction a rather modest increase in the contingent of recruits. The 48-ers countered these requests with proposals that approximated demands for an independent Hungarian army. Their favorite parliamentary weapon was filibustering, and consequently the budget was not passed. Prime Minister Kálmán Széll tried to wear down the opposition with passive resistance, but this tactic failed and he was compelled to resign in June.

The King's choice fell on Count Károly Khuen-Héderváry, the Ban of Croatia during the previous two decades. Reputed to be an energetic and skillful administrator, he struck a deal with the 48-ers, but the deal fell through and filibustering was resumed. The situation was further complicated by Francis Joseph's order of the day, issued during military maneuvers at Chlopy in Galicia, on September 17, 1903. This order stressed the unity of the Army in a manner offensive to Hungarian national sensitivities. Khuen-Héderváry's skill, so superbly successful in Zagreb, failed him on the unfamiliar terrain in Budapest, and he resigned at the end of September.

Seeking to break the deadlock, the ruling Liberal Party leadership was forming "a committee of nine" to hammer out a number of symbolic and instructional modifications aimed at heightening the Hungarian presence within the Common Army. These proposals, moderate in relation to the 48-er demands, met with the King's resolute objections. Finally, Count Tisza succeeded in persuading the committee to modify some points in its proposal. A compromise agreement with Francis Joseph was then reached, and Tisza became Prime Minister in November 1903.

Contrary to Tisza's own hopes, he suffered rather than benefitted from the lull in the Monarchy's foreign policy around the turn of the century, when Austria-Hungary's chief adversary, Russia, had turned its attention to the Far East. The 48-ers saw no need of bolstering the Monarchy's defenses, which Tisza regarded as a shortsighted view with possibly fatal consequences. Ironically, his staunch defense of the 67-er position was not universally appreciated in Vienna. Archduke Francis Ferdinand in particular found Tisza even more troublesome than the 48-ers, because he rightly feared that the energetic Tisza would be the most dangerous enemy of his centralistic "Great Austria" plans, to be implemented upon his ascension to the throne. Francis Ferdinand was committed to the eventual destruction of what he considered Hungarian nationalistic recalcitrance, including the 67-er variety which defended Hungarian constitutional prerogatives while supporting the association with Austria. High-ranking officers of the Army, infuriated by Hungarian separatist demands, were prone to share the Archduke's opinion. When, during the January 1904 session of the Delegations, Minister of War General Heinrich Ritter von Pitreich pursued a conciliatory line based on the resolutions proposed by the "committee of nine," some other generals branded him a "Heeresverderber," a spoiler of the Army. Not surprisingly, he was relieved from his position in September 1906, upon the Archduke's insistence.[15]

Relations further deteriorated following the disastrous electoral loss of Tisza's Liberal Party in January 1905. Apponyi joined the 48-ers, and even Andrássy refused to dissociate himself from military separatism and to form a government on the basis of Francis Joseph's renewed acceptance of the points proposed by the "committee of nine" in 1903. The King, supported by the government, political parties, and the public at large in Austria, was adamant about not giving fuller concessions. In fact, it was in April 1905 that the general staff developed a secret plan under the code name, "Fall U," for a "modified general mobilization" and the subsequent military occupation of Hungary.[16]

Luckily for both halves of the Monarchy, a confrontation was avoided by the readiness of the 48-er leadership to drop their military demands in return for an end to an unconstitutional regime and Francis Joseph's willingness to appoint a coalition government with the 48-ers as dominant partners. Although frictions between Budapest and Vienna continued, this coalition ruled until 1910, proving that the 48-ers' rhetoric was far more extreme than their actions in power. At the end, they recoiled from following through with their army program, which would have precipitated a confrontation and put Hungary into a vulnerable military position.

Once out of power again, however, the 48-ers could afford the luxury of obstructing plans to augment the Monarchy's military power. A new army law was passed in the Hungarian Parliament in June 1912 only through a legislative *coup* by the Speaker, Count István Tisza, who excluded opposition members from voting by force. While his law raised the number of recruits in successive stages, its immediate impact was slight, and the delay contributed to the Austro-Hungarian Army's undermanned and underequipped condition at the outbreak of World War I.

After a period of "sacred unity," old resentments and prejudices flared up again, with even greater bitterness since the stakes were higher. Already in the spring of 1915, the 48-er leader, Count Mihály Károlyi, strongly protested the inclusion of Hungarian troops into "alien units." At the same time, Nándor Urmánczy demanded the termination of alleged persecution of Hungarian soldiers by the Army. "We have to put a stop," Urmánczy said, "to the outrages committed by Czech sergeants, non-Magyar lieutenants, captains, and idiotic generals in persecuting Hungarian boys with impunity and earning some merit this way."[17]

This chauvinistic outburst revealed the fundamental incompatibility between dynastic centralism and integral nationalism, which weakened the Common Army throughout its existence. Political speeches notwithstanding, peoples of the Monarchy did fight side by side during the war, but at the end, the Common Army's disintegration along national lines preceded the collapse of the Monarchy as a whole.

NOTES

1. *Deák Ferenc emlékezete. Gondolatok* [Ferenc Deák's Memory. Thoughts] (Budapest: Ráth Mór, 1889), pp. 297-298, 345.

2. Ibid., p. 286; Béla K. Király, *Ferenc Deák* (Boston: Twayne Publishers, 1975), p. 182.

3. Gróf Gyula Andrássy, *Az 1867-iki kiegyezésről* [On the 1867 Compromise] (Budapest: Franklin Társulat, 1896), pp. 253-262.

4. Kornél Ábrányi, *Nemzeti ideál* [The National Ideal] (Budapest: Légrády Testvérek, 1898), pp. 350-351, 356.

5. Hungary, Parliament, *Proceedings* (Upper House), 1884-86, vol. 2, p. 206. May 22, 1886; József Kun Barabási, ed., *Gróf Tisza István parlamenti beszédei* [The Parliamentary Speeches of Count István Tisza] (4 vols., Budapest: Akadémiai Kiadó, 1930-37), I (1930), p. 22.

6. *A közös ügyek tárgyalására a Magyar Orzággyűlés által kiküldött bizottság naplója* [Proceedings of the Delegation Authorized by the Hungarian Parliament to Discuss Joint Affairs] (Vienna: Cs. Kir. Állami Nyomda, 1868), p. 111. March 10, 1886; Hungary, Parliament, *Proceedings* (Chamber of Deputies), 1885-86, vol. 11, p. 321. May 5, 1886.

7. Oscar Jászi, *The Dissolution of the Habsburg Monarchy* (Chicago: The University of Chicago Press, 1961), pp. 143, 137.

8. Károly Eötvös, *Harc a nemzeti hadseregért* [Struggle for a National Army] (Budapest: Révai Testvérek, 1906), p. 35; Lajos Mocsáry, *A közösügyi rendszer zárszámadása* [The Final Reckoning of Dualism] (Budapest: Franklin Társulat, 1902), pp. 63-64; Hungary, Parliament, *Proceedings* (Chamber of Deputies), 1885-86, Vol. 11, pp. 316-17. May 5, 1885; Ibid., p. 371. May 7, 1886; Hungary, Parliament, *Proceedings* (Upper House), 1884-86, vol. 2, p. 208. May 22, 1886.

9. *A közös ügyek tárgyalására kiküldött bizottság naplója*, pp. 155-57.

10. István Berkó, ed., *A Magyar Királyi Honvédség története, 1868-1918* [The History of the Hungarian Royal Honvéds, 1868-1918], (Budapest: Magyar Királyi Hadtörténelmi Levéltár, 1928), pp. 16-17; Gunther E. Rothenberg, *The Army of Francis Joseph* (West Lafayette: Purdue University Press, 1976), pp. 76-77.

11. According to Austria-Hungary's new Defense Law, carried into effect in 1869, the Common Army was to have a war strength of 800,000 men and the *Honvéd* and *Landwehr* 100,000 each for the first ten years. C. A. Macartney, *The Habsburg Empire 1790-1918* (New York: The Macmillan Company, 1969), p. 564. The *Honvéd* did not acquire artillery until 1912. Berkó, *A Magyar Királyi Honvédség*, p. 97.

12. Gusztáv Grátz, *A dualizmus kora, 1867-1918* [The Age of Dualism, 1867-1918] (2 vols., Budapest: Magyar Szemle Társaság, 1934), I, pp. 244-45.
13. Gyula Fayer and Béla Vikár, eds., *Szilágyi Dezső beszédei* [The Speeches of Dezső Szilágyi] (4 vols., Budapest: Atheneum, 1906-13), IV, pp. 96-97.
14. Count Albert Apponyi, *Emlékirataim. Ötven év* [Memoirs. Fifty Years] (Budapest: Pantheon, 1929), pp. 30, 32, 148.
15. Theodor von Sosnosky, *Franz Ferdinand. Der Erzherzog Thronfolger. Ein Lebensbild* (Munich and Berlin: R. Oldenbourg, 1929), p. 66; Rothenberg, *The Army of Francis Joseph*, pp. 133, 137.
16. Rothenberg, *The Army of Francis Joseph*, p. 134.
17. Mihály Károlyi, *Az új Magyarországért. Válogatott írások és beszédek 1908-1919* [For a New Hungary. Selected Writings and Speeches] (Budapest: Magvető Könyvkiadó, 1968), p. 71; Antal Balla, ed., *A Magyar Országgyűlés története, 1867-1927* [The History of the Hungarian Parliament, 1867-1918] (Budapest: Légrády Nyomda és Könyvkiadó, 1927), p. 371.

Mark M. Lowenthal

THE LIMITS OF WAR PLANNING: ROOSEVELT AND "RAINBOW 5"

All nations have plans for war, regardless of their size, military potency, international position, foreign policy or geography. It is a simple act of prudence, a limited national life insurance policy "just in case" the worst happens. Within that generalization, however, there is a broad range of possibilities, going from limited and strictly defensive contingency plans across a wide spectrum of defensive and offensive choices to openly aggressive plans. Moreover, a nation may have several types available at any one time. Yet for each plan, planner or planning staff the basic requirements are the same: a calculation of the likely circumstances at the moment of conflict, the opposing forces involved, and the best military course to achieve whatever policy ends are understood to be the final goal.

Two of these three basic ingredients—likely initial circumstances and the final goal—derive, at least in theory, from the political goals for which the war is being fought. The clearer the political goal, the greater clarity the planners can bring to their task. If the planners have done their jobs well the proper plan can be put into motion, hopefully increasing the chances for success based on reasonable expectations of at least preliminary phases of action. Of course, once operations commence numerous extraneous factors intrude—weather, chance, execution, and the independent will of the enemy. History offers numerous examples of successful prewar planning and of detailed plans which went awry. Moltke's campaign against France in 1870 and his nephew's rape of the Schlieffen Plan are but two opposites within one staff group against the same target, and with roughly the same goal albeit in very different circumstances.

But in the absence of known political goals planners have but two choices, neither of them enviable. They may either make assumptions (or educated guesses) as to the likely goals, or simply take their plans as far as they dare in the absence of these goals.

Such a choice faced United States military planners from 1939 to 1941. While much has been written about the result of the efforts, RAINBOW 5, which has been lauded as the proper framework for the successful prosecution of the war, the shortcomings inherent in this plan have been glossed over. In essence, RAINBOW 5 was but a skeleton without muscle or sinew, a strategic concept without operational underpinnings.

The significance of these limitations were perhaps most apparent during the four days of December 7-11, 1941, when the United States had the wrong war in the wrong theater, at least according to RAINBOW 5. The reasons for these limitations bear examination.

Roosevelt and the Evolution of RAINBOW 5

The RAINBOW plans, the basic US strategic planning documents from 1939 to 1941, evolved from the earlier color-code plans, individual contingency plans in which each case received a different color code, Japan being ORANGE, Cuba—TAN, Britain—RED, and so on. By 1937 only ORANGE seemed relevant in terms of likely enemies or threats, and by 1939, when RAINBOW planning began, it was apparent that Germany too required attention.[1]

The RAINBOW planning process took place under twin handicaps. The first was the rush of events, commencing with the war in Europe and accelerating rapidly with the German *Blitzkrieg* in Western Europe in May and June 1940, which created increasingly gloomy circumstances amidst growing recognition of US inadequacies. The second was the absence of political guidance from President Franklin Roosevelt. Working together, these two factors had opposing effects. Events drove the planners and their plans, but without political guidance the planners and plans could only go so far and no further.

The Limits of War Planning

Working amidst a vastly changed international environment the US planners developed the RAINBOW series by June 1939. There were five variations:

RAINBOW 1: US defending Western Hemisphere (north of 10° south latitude) alone.

RAINBOW 2: war in concert with Britain and France. Allies responsible for Europe, US to defend Western Hemisphere and responsible for the Pacific, including the defeat of enemy forces there.

RAINBOW 3: US acting alone, defending Western Hemisphere and projecting forces to control Western Pacific.

RAINBOW 4: US acting alone, defending entire Western Hemisphere and projecting forces into Eastern Atlantic.

RAINBOW 5: war in concert with Britain and France. Defense of Western Hemisphere, and projection of US forces to Eastern Atlantic and to Europe and/or Africa to defeat Germany and Italy.[2]

Each plan had the common goal of defending the Western Hemisphere, a minimal necessity for the defense of the United States proper. With the exception of RAINBOW 3, which was consciously presented as a Pacific alternative, each plan gave primacy to Europe. Also, RAINBOW 2 and 5 assumed war in cooperation with Britain and France, a result of initial staff talks with Britain.[3] Another interesting underlying concept was that a violation of the Monroe Doctrine by the Fascist powers would be the likely *casus belli*.[4] Here, indeed, the military and the President diverged, as Roosevelt had spent much time making the doctrine multilateral and a symbol of hemispheric solidarity. While the military's interpretation of the Monroe Doctrine was not wholly incompatible with this diplomatic effort, it still represented a more traditional unilateral interpretation of US hemispheric interests.

After these general guidelines were adopted the plans had to be fleshed out. RAINBOW 1 was given top priority, as its concept of Hemispheric Defense was basic to all of the plans, and it also represented the defense of the United States and its immediate interests. Work on the plan proceeded swiftly. The Joint Planners submitted RAINBOW 1 to the Joint Board on July 27, 1939; the Secretaries of War and of the Navy approved it on August 14, 1939. President Roosevelt approved the plan verbally to Captain Daniel J. Callaghan, his naval aide, on October 14, 1939.[5]

The details of the plan offer some insight into the breadth and limits of US strategic thinking at that time. First, the Western Hemisphere as defined in RAINBOW 1 included Hawaii, Wake Island, American Samoa and the Atlantic Ocean as far east as 30° West Longitude, thus encompassing most of Greenland and virtually extending to the Azores. The plan presumed the neutrality (but sympathy) of Britain and France and the Latin American countries. Hostilities were envisioned as including Navy action to secure the Western Hemisphere, and possible expeditionary forces in case of enemy lodgements.[6]

The political premises of the plan, especially the neutrality of Britain and France, were necessarily speculative. In part the exclusion of Britain and France as active US allies was valid, as RAINBOW 1 represented the most basic plan for the defense of US interests only, and not those of Britain and France. Yet it would have been difficult to envision how the Axis could threaten the Western Hemisphere, Britain and France being neutral, unless the Joint Planners, the Joint Board and their civilian superiors presumed a continuation, if not an acceleration, of the Allies' policy of appeasement. But RAINBOW 1 also suggested that the US secure the use of limited base facilities in British colonies in the Caribbean. How this would be negotiated with a power standing neutral in an Axis-US struggle remained unexplained. The inconsistencies within these political premises underscore just how limited a plan RAINBOW 1 actually was.

By the time Roosevelt approved RAINBOW 1 war in Europe had broken out, effectively removing the questionable political premises of that plan, but also necessitating an extension of the entire war planning process. But the war in Europe settled into its "phoney" lull after the elimination of Poland, and so US planners then gave priority to RAINBOW 2 (US responsible for the Pacific; Britain and France responsible for the Atlantic), a likely scenario under the prevailing circumstances. This responded to the perception of the Joint Board and the Joint Planning Committee that the Pacific area remained the most threatened under current conditions. After the completion of RAINBOW 2, priority went to RAINBOW 3 (US acting alone, forces into the Western Pacific), and then to RAINBOW 5 (US allied with Britain and France, forces into the Eastern Atlantic and Europe/Africa). RAINBOW 4 (US acting alone, forces into the Eastern Atlantic) had the last priority.[7]

The Limits of War Planning

The initial German offensive against Denmark and Norway in April 1940, seemingly undermined some of the premises in RAINBOW 2 and 3, the two plans having immediate priority, which saw the United States concentrating on the Pacific. While the Allies were still very much in the war, Hitler's Scandinavian thrust raised new issues for Hemispheric Defense, especially as Greenland was still a Danish colony and was considered by US planners to be within the Western Hemisphere as defined in RAINBOW 1 (30° West Longitude).

It should also be noted that all of this planning activity between October 1939 and April 1940 took place without reference to the President. Although none of the plans except RAINBOW 1 had reached a state where Presidential approval was required, the Joint Planners and the Joint Board were now proceeding according to their best estimates as to likely circumstances. While their concepts did not represent improbable or unacceptable circumstances, neither did they necessarily reflect Roosevelt's own preferences, nor did he try to make these clear, hoping instead to play some vague role in containing the war via the ill-conceived mission of Sumner Welles to Europe in February and March 1940.[8]

With the Scandinavian campaign US planners shifted their attention to RAINBOW 5, a sudden reorientation back to Europe, and a plan far beyond current US capabilities.[9] Whatever damage was done to planning assumptions and scheduling by events in Denmark and Norway, however, was minor compared to the effects of the German *Blitzkrieg* across the Low Countries and into France.

Army Chief of Staff General George C. Marshall, using a memorandum entitled "National Strategic Decisions," drafted by the Army War Plans Division which he had personally revised, urged that the United States concentrate on Hemispheric Defense, given its current limited capabilities. Roosevelt agreed, although he took no action in response to Marshall's request for some necessary policy planning.[10] While Roosevelt accepted the premises of the memorandum, including the acceptance of losses beyond 180° West Longitude, he replied with concerns of his own, namely possible aid to the Brazilian Government against Axis-inspired revolts. This led to the contingency plan archly named POT OF GOLD, calling for an expeditionary force of 100,000. This figure was also above current capabilities but reflected the alarm which had begun to infect planning.[11]

In late May 1940, with France near collapse and Britain's future uncertain, RAINBOW 4 suddenly moved from last priority to center stage.

Now it was presumed that the United States alone would face the Axis, with the Allies defeated and their fleets in enemy hands; Axis troops would be in Iceland and Western Africa; there would be Axis agitation in Brazil, Peru, Mexico and the European colonies; and Japan would be moving freely about the Far East. The date that the Allied fleets were lost was seen as the key factor, with perhaps six months being necessary before they were operational by the Axis.[12]

The final goals of RAINBOW 4 (US forces into the Eastern Atlantic) was still beyond current US capabilities (then 249,991 enlisted men), ultimately requiring 297,000 men. To a certain extent, therefore, this plan represented more of an interim guideline for the continued build-up and rearmament of the armed forces in response to the new military situation. Much would depend on the date of the Allied surrender and the disposition of their fleets. Nonetheless, the quick work done on RAINBOW 4 showed how much necessary preparation had already been done on the RAINBOW series, as well as the maturation of the US staffs in their ability to respond quickly to a suddenly changed situation.

The two Service Secretaries approved RAINBOW 4 on June 13, 1940; President Roosevelt did so on August 14, 1940. Ironically, on the same day that the Secretaries approved the plan, Roosevelt offered the military one of those rare glimpses into his own strategic thinking. The President offered the military an hypothesis of the global situation at the end of 1940, asking them to evaluate it. This hypothesis was strikingly more optimistic than the RAINBOW 4 premises, assuming that Britain and the Empire would still be intact; France would be occupied but still resisting Germany, perhaps from North Africa; the US Navy and Allied fleets would hold the Persian Gulf, Red Sea and the Eastern Atlantic, and perhaps the Western Mediterranean; the Allies would still hold the Near East; and US naval and air units would be active in the war.[13]

Here was a sharp divergence in mental outlooks between the President and the military. The capitulation of France on June 17, 1940 undid much of Roosevelt's hypothesis, and he did give formal approval to the gloomier RAINBOW 4 in mid-August 1940, the last plan he formally endorsed up to December 1941. This approval, however, represented less than a meeting of minds over likely premises for war planning, despite the efforts of the military to discern the President's wishes or intentions. Throughout 1940 the military tried to elicit or prod the President into

The Limits of War Planning

making firm policy decisions upon which they could base their plans. First there was the June 24, 1940 memorandum "Basis for Immediate Decisions Concerning the National Defense," in which Marshall and Chief of Naval Operations Admiral Harold Stark urged a concentration on Hemispheric Defense, and a curtailment of aid to Britain.[14] Then, in the famous Stark Memorandum of November 12, 1940, the Navy chief offered four strategies to fulfill US goals, arguing that Plan D, an offensive in the Atlantic with Britain against Germany, and a defensive in the Pacific was the best option.[15]

However, none of these efforts resulted in any futher definition of policy. Roosevelt revised the June 24, 1940 memorandum so that the Pacific Fleet could remain at Hawaii to deter Japan, and so that aid to Britain could continue. The Stark Memorandum got lost in the lengthy vertical processes of the Joint Board apparatus, and was overtaken by events, primarily planning for the ABC conference with the British staffs in early 1941.[16]

In the absence of further direction from above the planners worked according to their own best judgements. By the end of November 1940 emphasis had shifted to **RAINBOW 3** (US acting alone, defending Western Hemisphere and projecting forces into the Western Pacific). This did not represent a sudden change in strategic thinking, but rather was a fallback position should Stark's Plan D run into trouble. The Army was suspicious of the Navy's motives in going on with **RAINBOW 3**, fearing that this meant a return to the old Pacific emphasis they had fought against for so long. In truth, both services did prefer **RAINBOW 5**, which was the embodiment of Stark Plan D, but old hostilities brought out latent suspicions.[17]

Roosevelt gave his military advisors another indication of his thinking at a meeting on January 16, 1941, in preparation for the upcoming talks with the British staff. Although the military had accepted as early as September 1940 that the US would eventually have to participate in the war, this was no longer the case for the President, who had withdrawn from the assumption implicit in his June 13, 1940 hypothesis. In the January 16, 1941 discussions Roosevelt emphasized those methods which could bolster the British and divert Japan without resulting in US entry. Indeed, in revising Marshall's and Stark's opening remarks for the conference, Roosevelt changed the phrase "decide to resort to war" to "should the United States be compelled to resort to war," a subtle but significant difference. Further, the President mandated that the two powers be called associates, not allies.[18] In the end Roosevelt had not given his subordinates instructions so much as he had given intimations of the limits of policy.

Despite some awkwardness and some very deep disagreements, especially over the relative importance of the Far East, the ABC talks resulted in final agreement with the British on the need to defeat Germany first, although how this was to be accomplished remained vague.[19] Nonetheless, ABC-1, as the final report was called, did provide the basis for the next step in US war planning, RAINBOW 5, although this step was taken on the basis of Roosevelt's having *not disapproved* ABC-1, rather than on his having approved it.[20]

RAINBOW 5 was completed on May 14, 1941 and approved by the Secretaries of the Navy and of War in May and June 1941, respectively. RAINBOW 5 represented the strategy urged by Stark and generally agreed to in ABC-1: a war between the United States, Britain and other states against a combination of the Axis powers. The primary strategic objective was the defeat of Germany and its allies, with the Atlantic/European area being seen as "the decisive theater." If Japan entered the war, the Associated Powers would go on the defensive in the Far East.[21] RAINBOW 5 concerned itself with the opening phase of the war, largely meaning the preservation of the status quo as far as possible until sufficient forces could be built up for the successful prosecution of the war. This plan remained the basic military strategy for the United States until the US entered the war and beyond, although through the remainder of 1941 it did not necessarily represent Roosevelt's preferred outcome. Instead, he continued to concentrate on aid to Britain and then to the Soviet Union as well after the German invasion began in June 1941, and on the continued deterrence of Japan. Here, at least, the President and the military were in accord, viewing Japan as a secondary concern compared to Germany.

Roosevelt did not blind himself to the possibilities outlined in RAINBOW 5, but he did little to given them political meaning. Typical of this was his July 9, 1941 request to Secretary of War Henry Stimson and Secretary of the Navy Frank Knox that an examination be made of "the overall production requirements required to defeat our enemies."[22]

The tone of Roosevelt's commitment remained hypothetical. His main concern was current production problems and necessary future production levels without any inference that the United States would enter the war. Roosevelt left the assumptions and premises of this Victory Program to the planners. As one historian noted, Roosevelt was more concerned with the show window than with the stockroom, with the appearance of preparedness rather than its reality.[23]

Roosevelt's attitude made it difficult to foresee how the United States would enter the war. His changes in the ABC instructions had made it plain that he assumed that war would result from enemy action. Roosevelt had suggested as much in conversations in March 1941, although as confrontations began in earnest in the Atlantic in the autumn of 1941, the President refused to use them as a means of entering the war.[24] Some greater provocation seemed necessary.

In the Pacific, meanwhile, avoidance of conflict was the main purpose of US political and military moves taken with regard to Japan, including the Hull-Nomura talks, the planned deployment of B-17s, and the fleet deterrent at Pearl Harbor. There was the general expectation that Japan would not be so foolish as to provoke war with the United States. This "mirror-imaging," as intelligence analysts term such self-deceptive thinking, at least fit in with the concepts of ABC-1 and RAINBOW 5. However, it also created a blindspot which could seriously undermine the planning premises of RAINBOW 5, which foresaw no increase in US forces in the Pacific, with British forces going to the Far East as they were relieved by US forces in the Atlantic and Mediterranean.

Roosevelt himself undid much of this Pacific premise in the final days of peace, apparently without the knowledge of his chief civilian or military advisers. Japanese expeditionary forces moving south of Formosa, destination unknown, were the main focus of attention. At a meeting of the War Council (Roosevelt, Secretary of State Cordell Hull, Stimson, Knox, Marshall and Stark) on November 28, 1941, it was assumed that if Thailand were invaded, thus posing a threat to Malaya, Britain would fight (a point which the British Chiefs of Staff did not accept), and in that case the United States would have to fight as well.[25] However, this decision, which was crucial to British plans, as they had resolved not to move without assured US military support, was not conveyed to London, nor would Hull respond to a direct inquiry along these lines from Lord Halifax, the British Ambassador.[26]

It was not until December 1, 1941 that Roosevelt informed Halifax of the conclusions of the War Council three days earlier. Indeed, Roosevelt went further, promising United States support should Britain counter Japan on the Isthmus of Kra in Thailand. This news brought tremendous relief in London, although Churchill still did not want Britain's Pacific policy to get out in front of that of the United States.[27] Several issues arise from this US offer. First, in the period between the decision (November 28) and the notification to Britain (December 2, when Halifax's telegram arrived in London), five days had been lost. During this time Japan had made its final decision to go to war (December 1).[28] Although it is unlikely that a public declaration of US support for Britain in the Far East (regardless of such a declaration's political feasibility for Roosevelt) would have deterred Japan, given the concept and scope of Japanese military plans, the effects of such a declaration remain open to speculation. Second, it is not clear that any of the US leaders considered what the US could actually do to carry out the War Council's decision. US forces in the areas certainly were not adequate to undertake major operations against Japan. Indeed, throughout this period the military continued to ask Hull to prolong negotiations as long as possible, until planned reinforcements could be brought to the Pacific.[29]

Roosevelt's pledge to Britain, which was reconfirmed on December 4 and again on December 5,[30] represents one further problem. The President's advisers, with the probable exception of confidant Harry Hopkins, evidently did not know about these assurances to Britain.[31] Such secrecy further underscores the divergence between these assurances by the President and concrete US plans.

A second prewar anomaly in US plans was the actual implementation of RAINBOW 5. At a War Department meeting on December 9, 1941 Brigadier General Leonard Gerow, Acting Assistant Chief of Staff, War Plans Division, stated that RAINBOW 5 "has already been in effect for some time against the Axis in the Atlantic."[32] The tasks for the Atlantic under RAINBOW 5 were general enough, largely a continued build-up of Hemispheric Defense to ward off Axis aggression, and naval operations against the Axis in the Western Atlantic. However, it is noteworthy that this phase of US war plans was considered to be in operation not only in advance of war with Germany and Italy (December 11), but also in advance of the Japanese attack (December 7). This points up once again a divergence between policy and military activity. In the continued absence of firm policy guidance the military took those steps which were

The Limits of War Planning   113

deemed necessary either to safeguard US interests or to carry out known or presumed policies. Thus, Roosevelt's willingness to confront German naval forces in the Atlantic was translated into a limited implementation of RAINBOW 5, although the President himself was now shying away from the consequences of these incidents. In a curious cycle of cause and effect, Roosevelt's limited but provocative naval moves, without any firm political goal, led to naval clashes and the necessity of implementing a war plan totally without any concept of a likely *casus belli*.

Thus, on the eve of war US plans consisted of very general agreements about the strategic direction that operations would take. The premise was war with the European Axis, with Japan hopefully being kept at bay, or at most being met with defensive action, although Roosevelt had pledged support to Britain should there be any further Japanese aggression. The exact nature of the circumstances under which the United States would enter the war remained unknown, being almost wholly up to the President's interpretation of enemy actions, barring a direct attack. This strategic blindness proved to be of lesser concern than might have been the case, as RAINBOW 5 for the Altantic was already in operation.

The Wrong War

At 1:40 p.m. on December 7, 1941 Secretary of the Navy Knox telephoned the President to report that an air raid was in progress at Pearl Harbor. Fifty minutes later the Navy Department informed the War Department. The United States was at war, but in the Pacific against Japan.

A War Department G-2 (Intelligence) summary for that date captures some of the immediate confusion which descended on responsible officials. Radio reports announcing a naval battle off Hawaii and Japanese paratroopers near Honolulu were duly monitored and logged in, as was the report of one Japanese carrier being sunk off Hawaii and another off the coast of Latin America. Only the report of Japanese landings on Oahu has a denial written next to it in the log.[33]

A number of officials felt that the Japanese attack meant the United States should be at war with the entire Axis. This was certainly the feeling at the War Department, and Secretary of State Hull told Lord Halifax that German and Italian declarations were expected. However, Hull's comments hit upon the central point. Roosevelt still was unwilling to move first. He would wait for Hitler to act.[34]

The military had already begun to respond to events. On December 7 all senior Army commanders were ordered to carry out RAINBOW 5 tasks "in so far as they pertain to Japan." As noted, these tasks were vague and mandated little beyond taking whatever action was possible against enemy forces and communications. The full magnitude of the situation became more evident at the meeting of the Joint Board on December 8, 1941. The Navy members announced that their losses at Pearl Harbor precluded their carrying out tasks assigned in the war plan, and that revised tasks were being established. It was also noted that renewed Japanese attacks and further US losses might result in the loss of Hawaii, but that ships were being transferred from the Atlantic. The unknown location of at least five Japanese aircraft carriers caused some concern, leading to fears of renewed attacks on Hawaii or even operations against the West Coast.[35]

Deliberations of the Joint Board on December 9, 1941 again reflect the concern with defending Hawaii against further attack, air defense of vital points within the United States, and the need to transfer units from the Atlantic to the Pacific. That same day, in the meeting of the Army's high command noted earlier, General Gerow announced the "full" implementation of RAINBOW 5 against the Axis, and that it had already been in operation in the Atlantic. On December 10, 1941 the Joint Board again considered reinforcements for Hawaii, and two new subjects, the situation in the Philippines, and the rumored release of French naval units to Germany by the Vichy Government, which was of special concern given the presence of the aircraft carrier *Bearn* at Martinique.[36]

Only on December 11, 1941 does the tone of the Joint Board meetings begin to change, showing some sense of doing more than reacting spasmodically to the rush of events. The defense of Hawaii remained the major concern, followed by command arrangements in Panama. But the Board also considered the attitude of the Soviet Union toward Japan, and consideration of President Roosevelt's request to examine the seizure of the Azores and the general problem to be taken into account in that proposed action.[37]

But the Joint Board only reflects the military reaction at the highest level, one where some sense of deliberation can perhaps be expected. An examination of War Department "operational decisions and actions" offers a slightly different view. Here one can see the details of the Army beginning to respond to the demands of the war in terms of manpower and materiel. Once again the main concerns are the rapid movement of forces to Hawaii and the Pacific, the air defense of the United States, and moves intended to enhance Hemispheric Defense. Three items tend to stand out from this pattern. The first is the concern, again, with keeping the *Bearn* at Martinique. The second is the proposal to induce the Soviet Union to carry out air attacks against the Japanese Home Islands. The third is a proposal that the State Department ask Brazil for permission to station one company of marines at each of three cities, Belem, Natal, and Recife.[38] While this last item fits in with the concerns over Hemispheric Defense, it also is the sole reflection of immediate concern with a German-based threat, in the wide arc stretching from Vichy-controlled territory in Western Africa to the eastern "bulge" of Brazil.

Once again, amidst these detailed decisions, there is the note that with some minor exceptions, RAINBOW 5 has been put into operation. However, the general terms of the war plans and the details of men and materiel being moved to the Pacific are contradictory. Several factors can explain this. The first is that the terms of RAINBOW 5 were so general that the movements to the Pacific did not represent any grave disruption. Should this have continued, especially without a state of war against Germany, then the basic premise of RAINBOW 5, the Europe-first strategy, would have been undone. Second, it is possible that these moves were seen as being only temporary expedients, which they were; and that once the Pacific situation stabilized the necessary readjustments would be made. However, the question of war with Germany looms over this explanation as well, dependent as it is on time to react first in the Pacific.

A third and final view of US staff reactions can be seen in the Army's G-2 chronology for the period December 7-11, 1941, which faithfully logged in all reports concerning relevant events. In the Pacific there were two reports of enemy paratroops at Hawaii; a report of a Japanese landing, later denied; reports of Japanese carriers sunk off Hawaii and Latin America; and a report of a Japanese attack on Hawaii on December 8. The chronology logs in several reports of impending enemy air raids on the West and East Coasts, as well as reports about the impending movements of the *Bearn*. Finally, on the European theater, there are numerous reports about an imminent declaration of war by Germany, as well as subsequent retractions and clarifications until the declaration did come on December 11, 1941.[39]

The pattern that emerges from these varied activities and reports is that of the celebrated "fog of war" descending with a vengeance. Yet, to the credit of the staffs, the keynote of their activities is not panic, but rather alarm, which is understandable under the circumstances. But there is also very little reflection, also understandable, as to what these events and actions mean.

More surprisingly, initially, is the faithfulness with which they adhered to the broader concepts of RAINBOW 5. The attack on Pearl Harbor undercut all of the plan's premises, and Roosevelt's unwillingness to move against the European Axis compounded the inappropriateness of the plan. Yet RAINBOW 5 went forward. At least two explanations are possible, both of which are plausible. First, there was little alternative to RAINBOW 5 in terms of available plans to guide the continuing military build-up. Certainly neither RAINBOW 2 (Allies responsible for Europe, the US for the Pacific) nor RAINBOW 3 (US alone, forces into the Western Pacific) had any relevance to the current situation. Moreover, as the US staffs had concluded—similarly to their British counterparts—that Germany could not be defeated without US intervention, and as Germany's defeat was seen as the main goal, only some sort of adherence to RAINBOW 5 could achieve that end. Thus, at one level, adherence to RAINBOW 5 was an act both of daring and of maintenance of aim by the US staffs.

But at another level, the second interpretation intrudes, one that has been glossed over in past analyses of RAINBOW 5. The plan, in fact the entire RAINBOW series, was in essence a barebones guide for the build-up of US forces to achieve a certain distant strategic objective, but without any detail at all as to how or where, and without any clue as to how or why the United States would enter the war. Ultimately, the RAINBOW series represented plans with very basic beginnings and very long-range ends without any connecting middle. The United States entered the war with a plan saying "What," but with little answer as to "How" or "Why."

Conclusion

Except for the nation with an overtly aggressive design, or the one facing a proximate and perhaps repetitive threat, it is difficult for a nation to foresee the exact circumstances under which war will arise. Certainly

The Limits of War Planning

the knowledge that war against a specific foe is possible, is a sufficient basis to being war planning. Indeed, a plan with inherent flexibility as to the events beyond the onset of the war should be the goal, for the fog of war and the independent will of the enemy can wreak havoc upon too detailed a plan. At the same time this should not be flexibility by default, but rather by design. Such was not entirely the case with RAINBOW 5.

Franklin Roosevelt was an active albeit distant and elusive participant in the war planning process. But the role he chose to play was more negative than positive, in that he mainly set limits beyond which plans could not go. This had a vastly different effect than would have been the case had Roosevelt expressed the political limits he was willing to allow, and had he attempted to frame the political and security purposes for which the war would be fought. That he did not stemmed from several sources. Initially, his fear of the isolationists was a primary factor, although this concern probably outlived his foes' political potency. Second was a deep abhorrence of war. But once President Roosevelt decided that the Axis represented a definite and fundamental threat to the United States, he still sought indirect means of stemming them. The eventual failure to better define policy, and thus war plans, resulted from Roosevelt's own reluctance to admit that, past a certain point, the United States had little choice but to enter the war. All else followed from the President's unwillingness to grapple with this fact.

The effects of Roosevelt's unwillingness to accept the necessity for US entry into the war were more far-reaching than just the frustrations posed for military planners, or for the inherent limits this reluctance created in RAINBOW 5. It also put the United States at a serious disadvantage vis-à-vis Britain in deciding upon the operational steps necessary to achieve the final strategic goal. Moreover, it denied both US civil and military planners the opportunity to pose the more important question: What sort of a peace do we want, in what sort of a post-war world? The initial limits imposed on war planning by President Roosevelt also postponed any inquiry into this most basic question for any nation facing the prospect of war.

NOTES

1. For greater detail on the earlier history of these plans see Louis

Morton's two articles, "War Plan ORANGE: Evolution of a Strategy," *World Politics,* XI (January 1959): 221-50, and "Germany First: The Basic Concept of Allied Strategy in World War II," in Kent Roberts Greenfield, ed., *Command Decisions* (Washington, D.C.: Office of the Chief of Military History, 1960), pp. 12-20.

2. J. B. No. 325 (Serial 642): "RAINBOW Nos. 1, 2, 3, 4 and 5," Record Group [RG] 225, National Archives, Washington [hereafter cited as NARS].

3. These were the talks conducted by Captain Royal Ingersoll with members of the Admiralty in London, in January 1938. See Lawrence Pratt, "The Anglo-American Naval Conversations on the Far East of January 1938," *International Affairs,* XLVII (October 1971): 745-63.

4. J. B. No. 301: Minutes, 1939-1940: Joint Board Meeting, November 9, 1938, RG 225, NARS.

5. J. B. No. 325 (Serial 642-1): "RAINBOW No. 1," RG 225, NARS.

6. Ibid.

7. See the two draft manuscripts of Tracy B. Kittredge, *Evolution of Global Strategy* (Washington, D.C.: Historical Section, Joint Chiefs of Staff, n.d.), Chap. VIII, pp. 110-11; and *United States-British Naval Cooperation, 1940-1942,* Vol. I, Section II, Part D, pp. 153-54.

8. Mark M. Lowenthal, "Roosevelt and the Coming of the War: The Search for United States Policy, 1937-42," *Journal of Contemporary History,* 16 (July 1981): 419-20.

9. Ray S. Cline, *Washington Command Post: The Operations Division* (Washington, D.C.: Office of the Chief of Military History, 1951), p. 57. RAINBOW 1 called for the use of 177,800 men beyond the US; RAINBOW 5 called for 445,300. The legally authorized limit for the Army in the spring of 1940 was 280,000. See J. B. No. 325 (Serials No. 642-1, 642-5): "RAINBOW 1" and "RAINBOW 5," RG 225, NARS. On May 10, 1940 Army Chief of Staff General George C. Marshall estimated he could then field 80,000 men against a German attack. See Morgenthau Presidential Diaries, May 10, 1940, Henry M. Morgenthau, Jr. Papers, Roosevelt Library, Hyde Park, NY [hereafter cited as FDRL].

10. WPD 4175-7: "National Strategic Decisions," Memorandum by Army War Plans Division, May 22, 1940; WPD 4175-20: Memoranda by Major M. Ridgway and General G. Marshall, both May 23, 1940, RG 165/281, NARS.

11. Mark S. Watson, *Chief of Staff: Prewar Plans and Preparations* (Washington, D.C.: Office of the Chief of Military History, 1950), pp. 95-96, 106; Stetson Conn and Byron Fairchild, *The Framework of Hemispheric Defense* (Washington, D.C.: Office of the Chief of Military History, 1960), pp. 33-34, 273-74.

12. J. B. No. 325 (Serial 642-4): "RAINBOW No. 4," May 31, 1940, RG 225, NARS.

13. WPD 4199-1: OP-12-CTB: Memorandum, Captain R. S. Crenshaw to Admiral H. Stark, June 29, 1940, RG 165/281, NARS.

14. WPD 4250-3: "Basis for Immediate Decisions Concerning the National Defense," Memorandum, Stark and Marshall to Roosevelt, June 22, 1940, RG 165/281, NARS. The final version, dated June 24, embodied changes made by Roosevelt on that date.

15. Memorandum, Stark to Knox, November 4, 1940, PSF, Box 3, Departmental Correspondent: Navy Department, November-December 1940, FDRL. See also Mark M. Lowenthal, "The Stark Memorandum and the American National Security Policy Process," in Robert William Love, Jr., ed., *Changing Interpretations and New Sources in Naval History* (New York: Garland Publishing Inc., 1980), pp. 352-59.

16. On the June 24 memorandum see n. 14; on the fate of the Stark Memorandum see J. B. No. 325 (Serial 670): "National Defense Policy for U.S.," Memorandum Stark to Colonel W. P. Scobey, February 18, 1941, RG 225, NARS.

17. WPD 4175-15: Memorandum, Stark to Marshall, November 22, 1940, and WPD 4175-5: "Tentative Draft, Navy Basic War Plan—RAINBOW No. 3," Memorandum, General Gerow to Marshall, November 27, 1940, both in RG 165/281, NARS. "Tentative Draft, Navy Basic War Plan—RAINBOW No. 3," Memorandum, Marshall to Stark, November 29, 1940; Serial 047112: "RAINBOW Nos. 3 and 5," Memorandum, Stark to Marshall, November 29, 1940; and "RAINBOW Nos. 3 and 5," Memorandum, Marshall to Stark, December 2, 1940, all in RG 165/12, Box 7: OCS 16374-57, NARS. On the earlier Army-Navy dispute over Pacific strategy see the articles by Louis Morton cited in n. 1.

18. On the military's acceptance of US entry into the war see Minutes of the Standing Liaison Committee 1938-1943: Meeting, September 23, 1940, RG 353, NARS. WPD 4175-18: "White House Conference of January 16, 1941," Memorandum, Marshall to Gerow, January 17, 1941, RG

165/281, NARS. Roosevelt's changes are in Memorandum, Roosevelt to Knox, January 26, 1941, PSF, Box 64: Departmental Correspondence: Navy Department, January-June 1941, FDRL. For an overall analysis of Roosevelt's thinking at this time see Lowenthal, "Roosevelt and the Coming of the War," pp. 420-30.

19. "ABC-1," March 27, 1941, CAB 99/5 Public Record Office, London [hereafter cited as PRO]. This file also includes the conference minutes in their most useable form. For a summary of the talks see Maurice Matloff and Edwin M. Snell, *Strategic Planning for Coalition Warfare, 1941-1942* (Washington, D.C.: Office of the Chief of Military History, 1953), pp. 32-43.

20. Ibid., pp. 46-47.

21. J. B. No. 325 (Serial 642-5): "RAINBOW No. 5 (Revised)," November 19, 1941, RG 225, NARS.

22. Letters, Roosevelt to Knox and Stimson, July 9, 1941, PSF, Boxes 66 and 86, respectively, Departmental Correspondence, FDRL. The texts of the letters are identical.

23. William R. Emerson, "FDR," in Ernest R. May, ed., *The Ultimate Decision: The President as Commander-in-Chief* (New York: George Braziller, Inc., 1960), p. 142.

24. Harold L. Ickes, *The Secret Diary of Harold L. Ickes* (New York: Simon and Schuster, Inc., 1954), III, pp. 466-70. See Roosevelt's public statements in Samuel I. Rosenman, ed., *The Public Papers and Addresses of Franklin D. Roosevelt* (New York: The Macmillan Company, 1950), X, pp. 438-44, 462-64.

25. Henry L. Stimson Diary (mircofilm edition), November 28, 1941. For British views on the Isthmus of Kra see COS (41) 39th Meeting (O): Chiefs of Staff Meeting, Confidential Annex, December 1, 1941, CAB 79/86, PRO.

26. COS (41) 39th Meeting (O), cited in n. 25; Telegram No. 5493, Halifax to Foreign Office, November 30, 1941, FO 371/27913, PRO.

27. Telegram No. 5519, Halifax to Foreign Office, December 1, 1941, FO 371/27913, PRO; DO (41) 71st Meeting: Defence Committee Meeting, December 3, 1941, CAB 69/2, PRO.

28. Nobutaka Ike, ed., *Japan's Decision for War: Records of the 1941 Policy Conferences* (Stanford: Stanford University Press, 1967), pp. 262-83.

29. The Army wanted three more weeks, the Navy three more months. They had initially requested six months in February 1941. See Adolf A. Berle, Jr., *Navigating the Rapids, 1918-1971: From the Papers of Adolf A. Berle,* ed., Beatrice B. Berle and Travis B. Jacobs (New York: Harcourt Brace Jovanovich, 1973), p. 379.

30. W. M. 124 (41): War Cabinet Meeting, December 4, 1941, CAB 65/24, PRO; Telegram No. 5603, Halifax to Foreign Office, December 5, 1941, CAB 21/1029, PRO.

31. U.S. Congress, Joint Committee on the Investigation of the Pearl Harbor Attack, *Pearl Harbor Attack,* 79th. Cong., 2d sess., 1946, II, 454 (Hull); V, 2331-34 (Stark); X, 4802-03 (Admiral Hart).

32. Chief of Staff, Notes on Conferences: "Conference in General Bryden's Office," December 9, 1941, RG 165/30, NARS.

33. Far East Branch Subject File (1926-1946): "Chronology on December 7, 1941," Memorandum, G-2 Intelligence Division to General Miles, December 7, 1941, RG 165, NARS.

34. Stimson Diary, December 7, 1941; Cordell Hull, *The Memoirs of Cordell Hull* (New York: The MacMillan Company, 1948), II, 1099-1100; Ickes, *Secret Diary,* III, p. 664; Telegram No. 5668, Halifax to Foreign Office, December 7, 1941, Paper F 13339/86/23, FO 371/27914, PRO.

35. AG 381 (11-27-41)-(12-10-41): "Far Eastern Situation," Memorandum, Gerow to Adjutant General, December 7, 1941, RG 407/360, NARS; J. B. No. 301: Joint Board Meeting, December 8, 1941, RG 225, NARS.

36. Ibid., Joint Board Meetings, December 9 and 10, 1941.

37. Ibid., Joint Board Meeting, December 11, 1941.

38. Plans and Operations Division Subject File (1941-47): "Daily Summary, War Department Operational Decisions and Actions," RG 165, NARS.

39. "G-2 Chronology," in file cited in n. 33.

Ivan Volgyes and Hans Brisch

POWER AND POLITICS:
THE MILITARY AND COMMUNIST POWER
WITHIN THE WARSAW PACT*

The purpose of this study is to discuss the role of the military in the politics of the European communist states since the assumption of communist power in the region. It will focus on three distinct problems of analyzing communist civil-military relations in communist states: the peculiarities of communist civil-military relations, specifically regarding the involvement of the armed forces in politics under communist rule; the historical development of the armed forces of the WTO and the role the Warsaw Pact has played in world politics during the last three decades; and the question of political reliability of the military in Eastern Europe. In its final section, the paper will also offer some concluding remarks evaluating the question of military involvement in the affairs of the communist states of the region.

This study regards Eastern Europe as a political region, rather than a geographical, social or ideological force. Although, as will be seen below, we do not regard the region as a "cohesive" unit, the fact that these states are tied together by a variety of supranational contacts and contracts—from the Warsaw Pact and Comecon, on the one hand, all the way to a network of Soviet-East German or Soviet-Hungarian Friendship Societies, on the other hand—renders a comprehensive evaluation of the area as a political unit possible. For this reason, of course, Yugoslavia and Albania, with their minimal or few similar ties to the USSR and other communist powers of the region, will be excluded from our examination.

Generalizations, or "models" as social scientists are wont to say, are rarely the most valuable tools when studying as complex a region as Eastern Europe. The area under examination includes regimes that are now extremely liberal, as well as those that are exceedingly dictatorial. These political configurations, of course, always determine the role that may rightfully be played by the military in the political life of the region. Moreover, the political weights of the militaries involved are also at variance, since the Soviet Union places different values on the importance of these sub-apparats. The importance of the Polish or East German militaries, as far as the USSR's over-all strategy vis-à-vis NATO is concerned, differs substantially from those of the Hungarian or Romanian military establishments. Nonetheless, it is clear that there are many aspects of commonality that exist in regard to the basic roles of the military in political affairs. Thus our treatment of the military in the region, with important exceptions that will be noted, will be based on generalizable phenomena that can be observed region-wide.

Peculiarities of Communist Civil-Military Relations in Eastern Europe

The armed forces of the communist states of Europe, at first glance, fulfill certain obvious and traditional roles played by armed forces everywhere: they provide the backbone of domestic defense for the regime against enemies from the outside and the inside. There is nothing peculiar about such a role; the army of every state and every nation fulfills these same functions.[1] Moreover, the army in the states under consideration, as elsewhere, are convincing interest groups constraining the regimes' ability to advance in areas other than military might. They tend, as do most military establishments, to agitate for an increase in military might and to ally themselves with the "steel and coal" complexes for ever greater strengthening of the "commanding heights" of industry.[2] Furthermore, just as in many other developing states, these armies are also purposive social instruments whose roles in the transformation or maintenance of social equilibrium are major factors in the strength of the nation.[3] In all these traditional contributions, the armies of Eastern Europe fulfill accepted patterns that are replicated in just about every society.

There are, however, certain things that are peculiar in the nature of communist states and which differentiate the relationship of the military and the polity in these systems.

The first aspect of these peculiarities lies in the nature of the allocation of power in communist states.[4] Although in many states—except in the so-called party-army or army-dominated states—the military and its powers are curtailed by "civilian" considerations, in communist states the role of the military, like the role of other instruments, is subordinated to the commumist party in all its manifestations. Much has been said about the subordination of the military to the party through such traditional methods as the use of political officers, the main administration within the party apparat, or through the double informing activities of the ever-present political spies. At this stage, perhaps, we should merely try to conceptualize this relationship as functionally determined, rather than engaging in futile controversy over the party-army relationship.[5]

The concept of functional determination allows us to view the party-army relationship in a variegated light.[6] In communist polities, to use somewhat outmoded systems analysis terminology, the party controls the output, the input, and the feedback mechanisms of society. The party, in other words, determines the bases on which decisions are made, makes the decisions, and then manufactures support for them. With respect to the army, however, the party has always had, and during the last four decades certainly enlarged, a somewhat different role: it allows—and with some notable exceptions has always allowed—the army to play a role in the input process. It is safe today to say that the input processes have been more open to army demands than to any other apparatus, with the possible exception of the political police organs. It is also clear that as the modernization of the technical levels of the armed forces has increased, the input has become ever greater; complexity has demanded technical expertise and secrecy, and the party has found itself ever more reliant on the army which—when the chips were down—on the input level it had to trust.[7]

Remarkably, as the Soviet polity developed, the party also had to open up, to some extent, even the feedback loop of support to "spontaneous" expressions as well. There, the army had been genuinely involved in expressing support of or opposition to certain measures instituted by the party that affected the performance of the military as a whole. For example, such "minor" controversies as the percentage of recruit training time devoted to political instruction or the use of conscripts in the physical aspects of "building socialism," have certainly been clear instances where genuine feedback, though channeled, was used as the basis for altering decisions already set.

It is also true, however, that the output process of decision-making have remained closed to the army and have been monopolized by the party apparat. The centralism of that process is well known and there is no doubt that once decisions are rendered the army must accept them. And yet, even this process has been refined and tuned during the last decades, and today there are two mechanisms that make the process of subordination more palatable to the army as a whole.

The first of these mechanisms relates to the role of the leading personalities of the military complex. The party has been exceedingly careful that military leaders be promoted not merely for their technical knowledge, but also on the basis of their party loyalty. Consequently, a military decision-maker, regardless of rank, is not placed in his position of authority because of his abilities, but because of his party connections. That is, the system rewards loyalties *coupled* with military ability. Though this can be said to be true in any sphere of communist power relationships, it is especially evident in Soviet and East European military-party power relationships. "Mistakes" will, of course, occur—a Marshal Zhukov, a General Moczar or a Colonel Maléter may step forward in periods of stress—but the party has been remarkably successful in judging its military cadres.[8]

The second mechanism of output "subordination-pallatibility" refers to the peculiar nature of the alliance system within which multinational units are integrated. Here the independent decision-making within national units regarding the military is subordinated not merely to national desiderata, but also to crosscutting cleavages within the alliance system.[9] In other words, local decision-making regarding what percentage of the national budget can be devoted to the armed forces is only one element of the process. The military leadership often receives additional "funds" or "equipment," "training" or "exercise support" from the Warsaw Pact, more specifically from the USSR. Conversely, national-level decisions regarding the percentage of allocations for defense or army-related activities are frequently set at the Party level rather than at the domestic level. In a sense, of course, this duality creates tensions within the domestic decision-making system—e.g., Romania, East Germany, or Hungary—but it does lend a certain level of responsibility to the leaders of the armed forces that they would otherwise not possess.

A second aspect of this peculiarity lies in the fact that the armed forces, in general, are supposed to have grown out of the population and represent the widest strata in the common national effort to defend the socialist fatherland(s). However, from the outset of the existence of communist power, a not too irrational fear of Bonapartism has plagued the communist leaders.[10] Trotsky's power as the head of the Red Army, Tukhachevsky's and Zhukov's power combined with their powerful personalities capable of acting against the party "proper"—e.g., against its leadership—were viewed with alarm that was greater than necessary from the perspective of rationality. Nonetheless, while this somewhat irrational fear of Bonapartism is based on the mistaken reading of incidents in European history from which incorrect "laws" were deduced, it has led to the peculiarity that the party created two instruments that are the *duopolists* of power simultaneously: the army on the one hand, and the political police on the other. For example, the KGB and its separate organizations are expected to act as checks on the power of the military and, in the service of their mission to the party, they are certainly expected to exercise at least a coequal function in system and subsystem maintenance activities.[11]

Some, of course, would argue that this twin role is not unique; Hitler's Germany was also characterized by similar dualities.[12] What is distinctive in the Soviet and East European cases is that the KBG and its various local counterparts have been successfully penetrated and to a great extent *control* to date the various armies, and retain a cross-national network of control than is truly integrated under Soviet direction to a far greater extent that that in existence among the communist armies in general.[13]

A third important aspect of the peculiarity of the communist alliance system stems from the nature of ideology. Marxism, before the establishment of the Soviet state—and internationally before the establishment of the communist states of the region—was a prescriptive ideology. From 1917 and 1945, respectively, it has become descriptive, a tortuous zig-zag of "meaningless" phrases in search of justification for the existence and exercise of power. As the doctrine acquired body and the system territory, and as communist encirclement replaced enforced isolation, the presence of the new "fraternal" states had to be justified in ideology as well.[14] The cautious justification of instilling "socialist patriotism" in the citizenry of the member-states of the alliance systems, as this ideology developed "creatively," comes dangerously close to uncorking the specter of nationalism and that of the common enemy. Aside from the perspective of Bulgaria, such a possibility is not viewed by the USSR as beneficial to its own existence. Consequently, the USSR and the ruling parties have utilized two major and more controllable issues in order to insure mastering the military subsystem: fostering cynicism on the one hand, and instilling certain "socialist" values on the other.[15]

The fostering of cynical attitudes is unique to Soviet-type systems only insofar as the scope of cynicism is concerned. In other systems cynicism is an accepted part of the operation of society. Due to the all-comprehensive nature of communist ideology, however, cynicism—the operationalized concept of cognitive dissonance—is mandated for a whole array of human activities. It is, of course, true that for the efficient operation of the communist system one must drift away from the prescriptive ideology that lies, grossly misunderstood, in the nineteenth century. As the system develops, cyncism, fostered by reality and prophecies that are unfulfillable, must be stressed over idealism and, indeed, becomes necessary for survival and system maintenance. What *is* unique, however, is that the adoption of cynicism becomes expected in all forms of socio-political existence and behavior must conform to values already set in advance.

A concomitant desire of instilling certain values through the process of socialization as a long-term goal, however, must reinforce the instilling of cynicism mentioned above. As far as the USSR is concerned, it is obvious that its leaders care very little about a whole array of value-socialization that takes place internally. They do not care if internal systems propagate a wide array of values with differing emphasis in each of these states. The parameters of tolerance relate to two values only: the unquestioned control of the society by the party, and the non-existence of unbridled anti-Soviet nationalism. The *necessitas sine quo non*, therefore, that the Soviet elite must instill in the members of the alliance system lies in the socializing of *attitudes that require the army to follow orders of the party and not act against the USSR on the one hand, and to be prepared to fight "traditional enemies" other than the Russians, on the other.* The USSR does not care if a political system in the Warsaw Pact stresses Stalinism or democracy, liberalism or centralism, private farming or state control, private initiative and profit or total socialist control. It only cares that the values of the allies not propel them toward loosening the reins held by the party or turning them away from the existing military-political alliance system. Consequently, with the help of the party and the KGB, and through the benefits, training, and elite status extended to the military, the system must insure the loyalty and reliability of the professional armed forces.

The Warsaw Pact: Systematic Peculiarities

Excellent past studies have dealt with various aspects of the Warsaw Pact as a military alliance. Both classified and unclassified studies in the United States and in the countries of the region have done an admirable job describing the physical dimensions of this impressive alliance system.[16] Based on these studies, intelligent observers can delineate the physical size, organization, and even performance of the Pact. Suffice it to say, here, that the Warsaw Pact is primarily composed of armies of communist states whose *physical locus* is Eastern Europe, whose deployment as a force in action has only taken place in intra-systemic conflict, and whose development and deployment have been generally in accordance with the desires of the major actor of the alliance, the USSR.

Herein lies the first major conceptual problem in the discussion of the alliance system: whether one can regard this system as a "genuine" alliance, or one that is "imposed upon" the participating states. It certainly should be noted that the very size of the USSR makes its weight in the system so great as to raise serious questions about the importance of such tiny allies as Bulgaria or Hungary. At the same time, the dominance of the USSR and the distribution of military global tasks among the various armies of the Pact—for example, the assignation of global political police training tasks to the East German army and the UB—raises the point that it is a specific type of an alliance system with variegated missions.

History, of course, is limited in its ability to provide predictive values. It is contradictory at best, and descriptive analyses of past events are useful only as visits of condolence. For history tells us that the size of a preponderant ally renders its miniscule partners' role so subordinate that the "true" nature of an alliance becomes obsolete.[17] Although it assures us that such aberrations as the "tail wagging the dog" are possible, compatible size remains one of the operational concepts for "genuine" alliance systems. Yet the history of this alliance system shows remarkable divergences of opinion on various issues, regardless of actual size. Witness, for example, the vehemence of demand on the part of such states as Germany and Czechoslovakia for a speedy occupation of Hungary in 1956, far ahead of Soviet shifts in the policy toward occupation. This contrasts with the divergent attitudes of the variously-sized allies in 1968.

The genuinesess of the alliance system has also been questioned since it is viewed as imposed upon the member states. Certainly there is a great deal of proof that the Soviet forces, even after thirty-five years of presence in the region, are viewed as occupiers. The events of 1956, 1968 and 1981 are outstanding examples of this point, although in the case of Czechoslavakia the true animosity toward the USSR only occurred *after* August 21, 1968. Some elements of the support for the alliance—aside from that of sheer imposition—have, however, come from within the native military establishments and from the officer corps that has lived a continuous existence for more than a quarter of a century. The reason for their support of the system is relatively simple. They have been told that the only options to their participation would be: (1) retaliation by an angry populace; (b) at best, a neutralization and abolition of the army as a potential defender of the historic nation; and (c) a corresponding end to their power, prestige, and livelihood. Although we will be dealing with this subject later, it is safe to conclude that the vast majority of the professional members of the armed forces prefer their present existence to an uncertain future.

It would be, certainly, unfair for us not to mention some aspects of the Warsaw Pact that are more positive from the communist perspective than the views implied above. Undoubtedly, from time immemorial there has been a broad spectrum in which "alliances" tended to work. Notwithstanding Machiavelli's advice to his Prince, alliances have frequently been unipolar and concentrated around a particular actor.[18] Preponderent German or US strength did not and have not brought NATO or the Axis alliances into question as to their genuineness. What brings the Warsaw Pact into question is the political reality of imposed rule upon Eastern Europe and *not* the nature of the military alliance that stemmed from the political imposition of occupation by the USSR. Nonetheless, we must mention that the USSR itself, in general, has been averse to the institutionalization of that alliance system; informal arrangements are more subject to manipulation by the dominant power. In this sense (though probably only in this sense) the Warsaw Pact can be and should be viewed as a "victory" for the non-Soviet actors of the system.[19] Curiously, there are other aspects of the Warsaw Pact that are "peculiar" though not necessarily counterproductive from the systemic perspective. One of these is the fact that the presence of the alliance system helps psychologically to mitigate the feeling of "loneliness" as the "whipping boy of history," experienced and deep-down admitted by the USSR. It is a symbolic function, to be sure, but to be able to refer to an action undertaken by the "communist alliance system," or the "Warsaw Pact," is preferable to acting alone. Hence, unlike in 1956 in Hungary, the invasion of Czechoslovakia in 1968 was undertaken by the Warsaw Pact —even if Romania did not participate and Hungarian participation had to be coerced from Kádár by very real Soviet pressure on the Hungarian leader who wished to avoid being labeled as an "invader" by the Czechoslovak population.[20] In fact, there is a great deal of evidence that Bulgaria, East Germany, and Poland had agitated *for* intervention *before* the Soviet Politburo had been prepared to do so.[21]

Moreover, it is important to recall that the Warsaw Pact also can be regarded as a genuine system because of the great deal of mutuality of interaction that takes place every day. As mentioned above, the military in each of the member states derives not merely prestige, but real, significant benefits from the system. From plush officers clubs and special stores, these benefits range to include the possession and use of the most modern military hardware glittering to awe foreigners *as well as* the domestic environment. The more modern and extensive the hardware, the greater the prestige of the domestic controllers of the use of violence. Conversely, the lack of such hardware—for example, anti-aircraft or modern missile systems—implies a lack of prestige in intra-alliance scheme. In this respect, the USSR is regarded by the military elite as the source of benefits and the source of tension as well: one gets from the USSR as it gives, and complains about the USSR not giving as much modern equipment to its allies as it gives to some nonmember states in military aid.

Lest we forget, this alliance system is also an important contributor to the physical prowess and economic health of at least some of the member states. The allocation of responsibilities for military production—

small arms, artillery, tanks, etc:—within the Pact has increased the economic capabilities of such states as East Germany and Czechoslovakia significantly. The net export of arms produced in some of these states brings a hard currency influx or other external trade benefits. But there is one more export item that is as important as the hardware export: the export of military personnel. East Germany's "traditional" role of supplying the developing states with security training personnel and apparatus, for example, in some parts of the world is certainly for more ubiquitous today than the role of the United States had been in previous times. Moreover, it must be mentioned that the role played by the East German security forces makes CIA training of the SAVAK look like a child's play in the international setting.

In short then, the system that exists in Eastern Europe is an alliance based on two contradictory elements: (1) an imposed rule by a great power that determines both the political context of the domestic environment and the limits of its change on the one hand, and (2) a system of mutualities and mutual benefits of military-economic relations on the other hand. The stresses and tensions existing between these not very creative contradictions provide the dynamics upon which the alliance system must operate.

The Evolution of the Warsaw Treaty Organization: The Historical Process

Let us now try to reconstruct the changing historical processes that have been responsible for the alteration of the goals of the Warsaw Pact. It would be simplistic and not very useful to say that these changes have always been the *results* of changing Soviet strategies related to the differences in the course of the pursuit of Soviet policies. At the same time, it should not be denied that they were not *related to* or *connected with* these alterations, but not in the ways Soviet strategists and ideologues would like to see. In a sense, as the Pact matured one could detect two sets of evolving differences: (1) between the individual armies and the parties that ran them, on the one hand, and the USSR on the other hand; and (2) the Pact as a whole and Soviet desiderata.[22] A brief survey of the last three decades serves, here, as a useful guide to bolster our line of reasoning.

The implications of the last sentence should serve as a takeoff point to guide our tortuous path to the truth. The last "three decades," of course, is an imprecise statement since *theoretically* the Warsaw Treaty Organization [WTO] came into being only in 1955 with the original goal of providing a common defense against the imperialist.[23] Informally, the Warsaw Pact as a defensive organization had come into being much earlier. There were various manifestations of this: the primitive form of cooperation against Fascism; a common and coordinated organization among Polish troops under Soviet command; organizations of Bulgarian and Romanian troops after their defection from the German cause and their switch to the Allies in August and September 1944, respectively, and among the various Czech and Slovak "volunteer units" operating along with the Soviet Army as it advanced west.[24] The cooperation referred to here was enormously strengthened by the Sovietization of all the armies that took place beginning in 1948-1949 and by the creation of an East German fighting force in 1949. Although these military alliances were informal and deliberately vague in order to give maximum latitude to Soviet control and influence, the new "people's armies" had shown a not too surprising proclivity toward an identity of views and policies.

These common views were especially strong concerning the native-military perception of a threat from the West. That threat existed in the perfectly understandable fear of the renewal of German power. The awesome destructive potential of Germany and its ability to wreak havoc upon Eastern Europe was shown in two preceding World Wars. This was coupled with the near omnipotence of the United States. Indeed, it is a real tribute to American performance that the Eastern European communist states, including the USSR, have always exhibited a much deserved inferiority complex vis-à-vis the United States. There was a widespread perception that power of this sort could once again affect adversely the lives of the inhabitants of the power-vacuum known as Eastern Europe.

This fear of the allies, both in the beginning years of the Cold War and after, was not just a fear for the nation. One could, of course, attribute it to that, admitting some national decency to policy-makers who could otherwise be simply labelled as mere Soviet stooges. Rather, it was a fear for themselves personally; a fear for both what *would* happen if the Soviets lost and their satraps had to retreat with them back to the land where so many of them spent years filled with terror, a land from where even the hell of the Spanish Civil War was a land of blessed dignity and quietude. But an even greater fear had also gripped these men: the fear of losing and having to face personal retribution from within the nations upon whose military thrones they now sat, ensconced there by the bayonets of a Red Army that was clearly viewed in 1949 as an *occupying* force by most of the people of the region. It was these fears that compelled the military and political elites to band together with the USSR in a common defense against real and perceived threats from the West and in *this* sense the Warsaw Pact has been in existence since at least six to seven years before its official inauguration.[25]

These fears were reinforced by (1) American political developments and growing commitment to the Cold War, (2) the establishment of NATO, a formal alliance aimed at containing perceived Soviet aggression, and (3) the subsequent creation of the strategy of encirclement through such organizations as NATO, CENTO, SEATO and ANZUS. As the Cold War matured and as the USSR tried to maintan its position in Eastern Europe, it had to commit all its efforts to the maintenance of its systemic powers. The death of Stalin and the revolts and riots in East Germany, Czechoslovakia, Hungary, and Poland, kept the Soviets hopping from one trouble spot to the other. They therefore had little opportunity for mischiefmaking that really threatened the West in the early years of the existence of the WTO. It is true that the doctrine of strategic encroachment—the acquisition of bases and allies on a global scale with the purpose of countering the policy of encirclement—had already been developed in Soviet military thinking. *Practically,* however, it could not be implemented as long as the West stood firm, had the strategic, material, and tactical capabilities, and the desire to oppose Soviet aggression or encroachment wherever it took place.

All of this, of course, began to change with the common possession of thermonuclear weapons and with the adoption of a "more reasonable" Western attitude toward the USSR. These views as they appeared in the West—noting that many of us whose perceptions are rather hardline today were supporters of these attitudes in and around 1960—felt that the theory of "containment" and the Dullesian hardline policies placed the USSR in a position that was "unfair"; that given enough leeway and incentives, the USSR could become a stable and status quo power with whom agreements for the maintenance of peace and spheres of influence could be made if reasonable men sat together and negotiated in good faith. Fueled by the tragedy of 1956, the sudden break in NATO unity at Suez in the same year, and by the spirit of accommodation that led Eisenhower to Geneva, Nixon to Moscow, and Kennedy to Vienna, a new era began whose main motto was detente by many other names. This policy of noncontainment has been in force since the advent of the Kennedy administration. It has had various ups and downs, notably the Cuban Missile Crisis and the war in Vietnam. But the lessons drawn from Cuba and Vietnam by the USSR—e.g., the necessity of an enormous military machine that can never again be humbled, on the one hand, and the defeat that *can* indeed be inflicted upon the United States and its allies with relative ease and by a minimal commitment of men and prestige on the part of the USSR, on the other—were unfortunately not lessons that had served either American strategic or domestic interests.

The strategies of "globalism," the penetration of the Third World, and the use of proxies, had all been tested during these years. These followed to perfection Soviet expansionist opportunism—the hotel hallway effect that John Lawrence suggested—as a tactic aimed at the strategy of expanding Soviet influence. It is worthwhile to repeat that at the root of the decrease in American belligerence toward the USSR and its goals lay a conviction that "peaceful coexistence" and the subsequent policy of detente marked an essential end to major conflict between the two superpowers. Unheeded and unappreciated was the constant Soviet disclaimer that detente and peaceful coexistence did not mean an end to "ideological struggle" and the termination of Soviet assistance to "national liberation movements." The elixir of a peaceful world, especially in the post-Vietnam years, was too strong and prevented the United States from reevaluating a USSR policy that had become one of global range during these very years.

The global strategy of the USSR was a natural consequence of the fact that it faced less and less *real* threats from NATO. The major goals of the USSR toward Western Europe—that of a neutralization, the division of the alliance system through the encouragement of splits within, and the potential Finlandization of the area—were assisted by a variety of factors. These included: decreasing Western defense expenditures; social turmoil and welfare-state policies that sapped defense; a morale and drug problem within the manpower of the armies; squabbles between NATO arms manufacturers; and, not the least, the switch in recruitment strategies within the US Army, a change with potentially the most damaging results. This relative demobilization on the part of NATO by 1975 created an imbalance that led to the conventional arms superiority of the Warsaw Pact in many different theaters, both on land and sea.[26]

All this is perhaps, only too well known. Nevertheless, it is worthwhile to restress these points, for the policies referred to above have also led to some serious mistakes on the part of the USSR and its allies. The mistakes and miscalculations are well known: the failure of Soviet-Chinese policies; the instability of some of its allies; its inability to maintain some alliances in peripheral areas, the underestimation of Western resolve and interests in other areas; and the miscalculation concerning Western and Third World responses to the Polish and Afghanistan situations and the consequent doubt cast on Soviet "intentions" by those who were previously willing to view these intentions as serving the interest of "peace for mankind."

It is at this pont, sufficient to say that both the few failures and the relative abundance of successes—in short the very historical development processes—have had unintended effects in creating stresses within the Warsaw Pact *qua* an alliance system. These stresses have been responsible for a major change in the nature of the alliance system, from its totally subservient role to one where major cleavages are exhibited.

These miscalculations on the part of the USSR also resulted in specific strains in intra-systemic levels. The Soviet leadership, always mindful of the fact that its alliance system is based on the use of force and the presence of overwhelming numbers of Soviet troops in Eastern Europe, has had to reexamine the capabilities and intentions of its own allies in Eastern Europe. In addition, they have also had to find an answer to the question of how "reliable" the Eastern European armies really are, and to what extent the USSR can trust them both as internal defenders of a system and as potential allies in external conflicts.

The Reliability of the Major Actors

Let us now turn to the equally complex subject of the reliability of the various armed forces and the impact of that reliability upon the differentiation between the two tiers of the Warsaw Treaty Organization. The definitional problems and the genesis of evaluation procedures designed for the concept of reliability have already been dealt with in a study produced for the Department of Defense in 1981.[27] In evaluating the readiness of the armed forces of Eastern Europe we need to concern ourselves with four different sets of reliability issues: internal defensive; internal offensive; external defensive, and external offensive. We also have to test whether the regional variable is indeed independent of these categories.[28]

The first category, internal defensive reliability, refers to the ability and willingness of the armed forces, led by the professional army core, to come to the aid of the respective regimes should they be in trouble with their population over their own policies, or those of their allies. Although, as mentioned above, past history is far from an accurate guide as to the future behavior of any actor on the historical stage, past actions do provide at least the basis of such an evaluation. Looking at the regional disparity in behavior we find that the northern sector has experienced some major problems in the past.

In Czechoslovakia in 1953 the Czech Army would not come to the assistance of the regime; Soviet troops had to be called in.[29] In 1967, just before the Dubček group gained power, there was an attempt by the army to come to the aid of the leadership through some sort of show of strength. That action was either bungled or aborted, and the beleaguered Novotny had to bear the scorn of the Prague Spring all by himself.[30] But the record is equally dismal as far as the Czech reformers and their links to the army is concerned. In 1968, for example, "no orders" were given for the army to participate in defending the government, and the army sat in its barracks watching the Warsaw Pact forces dismantle the liberal regime of Alexander Dubček. Even this behavior, however, is more confusing than comforting for the government leadership, since immediately after the invasion 57.8% of all officers refused to sign an oath of loyalty demanded by the new regime.[31]

Thus, as far as the Czechoslovak Armed Forces are concerned, we may quite safely conclude that its internal defensive reliability is low. Perhaps a "plague on all your houses" mentality and "playing it safe" attitudes compel the army not to choose to become the arbiter of domestic political life.

Neither does East Germany provide us with a shining example of a totally loyal socialist army that will in all instances, come to the aid of a beleaguered leadership. In 1953 (the only time when the internal defensive reliability of the East German army has actually been tested) the Berlin garrison simply refused to leave its barracks and fire on the rioting East Berliners.[32] Soviet groups had to be called in by a shaking Ulbricht. While this particular event certainly does not offer incontestable proof for a lack of internal defensive reliability on the part of the present army, the continuous defections of soldiers and pilots from the East German Armed Forces, against sometimes improbable odds, raise at least some questions concerning the grand statements concerning the "absolute" reliability of the East Germany Army.

Poland and the Polish Army have always figured prominently in Soviet scenarios of problems within the Pact. The internal political defensive reliability of the Polish troops has always posed a mixed-bag of historically unpredictable behavior. In the past the Polish Army usually defended the regime. For example in 1970 it assisted in putting down the riots. But firing on civilians was regarded by many a Polish officer as an act of shame.[33] The army also had shown some "misfunctions". In Gdansk in 1970, in Lodz and Warsaw in 1976, the army refused to leave the barracks and fire on demonstrators, forcing the regime to rely on security forces of the UB and ZOMO to quell these revolts. And not even the Jaruzelski coup in December, 1981, may be regarded as a clear indication of the internal reliability of the army. While the troops did obey Jaruzelski's command, a great many questions were raised. One of these was whether that command was issued in the name of a communist regime (the party's name was not mentioned once in the proclamation of martial law!), or in the name of a commander-in-chief who simply used the army to seize power, just as Pilsudski did in 1926.

Thus, as far as the internal defensive reliability of the northern tier armies is concerned, their records (drawn from the history of the last three-four decades) are at best mixed. As defenders of the system or the current leadership, these armies have a rather poor record. Unlike the security forces—which are deliberately kept separate and treated with deference as the privileged enforcers of the regimes' polities—the regular armies are far from being as reliable as communist leaders would like them to be.

Is the southern tier any better off in this respect? Bulgaria seems to provide the most clear-cut case. Here the army has not been asked to come to the aid of the regime (except when it had to squash its own comrades in arms in 1965) and there seems to be no real issue over which they should have been called out.[34] Unlike in Bulgaria, the army was called out to defend the Hungarian communist regimes in 1956, but with a few exceptions, it chose to sit out the revolt.[35] The mere fact that over eighty percent of the army's officers, even under a threat of dismissal and probable retribution, refused to sign the loyalty oath in 1957 indicates that the internal defensive reliability of the army should be seriously questioned.[36] The Romanian Army provides us with an equally interesting perspective. The deliberate discrimination against the professional army and the military's interests in doctrine, equipment and control make it unlikely that they will be great defenders of the regime should any anti-Ceausescu activities erupt.

It does seem certain, therefore, that in the southern theater internal defensive reliabilities are equally questionable. However, we must exclude the security forces from this general statement. With the exception of Hungary where these forces are part of the general army structure, the security police remain the most reliable supporters of the respective regimes. Would the picture be different, or even any more "coherent" if we examined the internal offensive activities of the armies in question? Coup attempts by the military against these regimes (or against the system) have been few and far between, and available information about them is generally quite fragmentary. The best documented of these coups was the one performed by the armed force in Poland in 1981. Whether this was a coup against the party is not certain, but it definitely was a classic army coup against a system that was "unable" to keep "order," and was hesitant and compromising. It is sad to admit that the system was far more liberal than the army leadership was content on seeing. It was, of course, a pro-Moscow coup in one sense, and a conservative one. Regardless of the excuses that were raised (that it was necessary for the national salvation, that it was really an act by the security forces, and that the army "really saved the nation from extinction"), it was a successful coup that wrested power from the communist party, albeit temporarily, and imposed the will and administration of the army even over the party apparat.

The Polish coup, of course, was not the only army coup against a communist party-leadership. In 1967 a half-hearted attempt was made in Prague by General Jan Šeja and his supporters. In 1971, an attempt by General Ion Serb occurred in Romania, and in 1965 obscure coup preparations were undertaken by General Ivan Todorov-Gorunya in Bulgaria. These cases may all be considered military coups of varying importance.[37] They took place in the north as well as in the south; some were pro-Moscow. But the Bulgarian attempt was probably more pro-nationalistic than all but the Polish coup. Whether they have occurred in the northern or southern theater seems to matter very little.

In turning to the external reliability of the armed forces, we come to the question that Soviet planners must continually wrestle with. How trustworthy are these armies of the north or south when coming into contact with external forces? The trouble is that so far the only enemies the communist armies have faced were their "fraternal allies" and not the West. In this respect, however, the USSR can draw some comfort from the fact that in previous confrontations involving Soviet troops, only the Hungarians opposed the Russians with arms in 1956, and even in this case the army generally remained neutral. And yet can the USSR always count on the fraternal armies to be at least neutral? This was clearly not the case in 1956 and in 1976 when the potential for a Soviet-Polish armed and organized conflict was an obvious possibility. Nor was this the case in 1980-1981 when a direct Soviet invasion of Poland would surely have resulted in at least sub-division level opposition in which the Soviet Army's losses would have been considerable. Moreover, these considerations also exist in the southern tier, where the Romanian Army (regardless of its resentment of Ceausescu and his ilk) still would be quite willing to act as a defensive force against any "fraternal assistance."

As far as Western invasion forces are concerned, however, these armies seem to be quite reliable. Regardless of their location in the southern or northern theater, the armies would probably be willing to defend their "historic homeland" against any Western army attacking them. These attitudes would likely change very rapidly in both theaters should such an "attack" be the result of a failed Soviet/WTO attempt to conquer Western Europe. In such a case the NATO forces could be regarded as potentially victorious "liberators" from Soviet domination. As time-tested practices in the region indicate, glaring and sudden "shifts" in allegiance would be quite commonplace, regardless of the theater locus. Finally, as far as the external offensive reliability of the member states of the WTO is concerned, at the beginning of a general conflict with NATO, the USSR could probably count on successful and loyal performance by the armies of the northern sphere.[38] Lacking any alternatives for non-participation, and sandwiched between Soviet forces, the Warsaw Pact armies (especially in an initially successful first strike phase) would perform well and fulfill their assigned missions. The distances of modern fighting obliterate the necessity of "seeing" brother shooting brother in Germany, or Czech and Polish soldiers shooting American "friends" in plain sight. The front lines would stretch toward the West and heady feelings and giddy expectations of quick victories would add to the reliability of these forces.

The southern tier provides us with somewhat different perspectives.[39] While Bulgaria could be counted upon to take revenge for five-hundred years of occupation by the Turks, Romania's doctrinal opposition of engaging in wars on other than Romanian territories renders the southern tier far weaker than the northern theater. Moreover, the miserable conditions of the Romanian Army, most notably its antiquated equipment and its defensive training missions and orientation, would compel the Soviet leadership to seriously ask: "Do we really want them on our side in any major conflict?"

Nor is the situation in Hungary totally acceptable from a Soviet point of view. The brevity of Hungarian military training and the strongly anti-Russian attitudes found in many sectors of society, including the military, are not exactly plusses for the Soviet sector commandants.[40] And while it is possible that, since they are sandwiched between Soviet forces, the Hungarians would have no choice but to go along with the Soviet program and participate in their missions of heading faithfully toward Ljubljana-Trieste-Rijeka, they would constantly have to be reminded of the overwhelming force of the Soviet Army at their back. In this respect as well, regarding the offensive reliability of the WTO armies, there appears to be a major difference between the northern and southern theaters.

Summary

From its very inception the Warsaw Pact armies have, of course, been instruments of Soviet goals and purposes. Founded under the aegis of Soviet power, these armies have never been regarded as the sole defenders of the nation's independence or only protectors of the frontiers of the states of Eastern Europe. Indeed, what has been peculiar about all of these armies is that they have always had to act as if their role of defending the frontiers from the USSR simply has not existed at all. Ultimately, since the Warsaw Pact armies have only been utilized in intra-systemic confrontations, the very legitimacy of the army as an instrument of national goals and national purposes, has been reduced to a hollow shell. Especially in places such as Hungary, East Germany, Czechoslovakia and, more recently, Poland, the activities of the armies have destroyed the national consensus that the army is a representative of the historic nation and a defender of the people against tyranny and foreign occupation. The result of the events of the last four decades is that the people of Eastern Europe regard their armies as extensions of the party; faithful servants in the administration of party-rule over them. The lack of legitimacy that the party possesses is thus reflected in a lack of legitimacy for the army as well.

Having earned the scorn of the population as the "enforcers" of policies whose interests appear occasionally to be distinctly contrary to those of the population at large, does the military at least have the trust of the party and the USSR? The answer here is also negative, for neither the party nor the Soviet military can trust the armies in all instances either in external or internal affairs. While it is clear that in some cases the armies would be reliable and trustworthy, in other scenarios they would be a shaky ally at best.

Can polities that are based on such problematical balances survive and indeed progress throughout long historical periods, or is it likely that the equilibrium would eventually be destroyed, for instance in Romania as it had happened in Poland in 1981? Once again we have no crystal ball, but historical experience does seem to indicate that the equilibrium that exists between the party and the military need not be stable and static. Parameter values of a dynamic balance, however, do seem to exist. At the bottom line these parameters are defined by the Soviet High Command, not merely in terms of the domestic policies these nations may pursue, but also regarding the extent to which the Eastern European armies may or may not play independent roles in the life of their respective nations. Sad as this evaluation may be to the pride of the armies in Eastern Europe, its reality cannot be challenged by anyone familiar with party-military relations within the Warsaw Pact countries.

NOTES

*This paper is based on several earlier studies from which material has been drawn extensively. The most significant ideas of this study have been discussed in Ivan Volgyes, "The Warsaw Treaty Organization in the 1980s: Can Internal Differences Be Managed?" in Frank Margiotta, ed., *The 1980s: Decade of Confrontation* (Washington: National Defense University, 1981), pp. 189-217, and Ivan Volgyes, "The Relevance of Regional Differences in the Warsaw Pact Hierarchy," paper prepared for the Conference on the Warsaw Pact in the 1980s (Cornell University, May 13-15, 1982).

1. J.C.M. Baynes, *The Soldier in Modern Society* (London, 1972).
2. F.D. Freeman, "The Army as a Social Structure," *Social Forces*, 27 (1948-1949); Vernon V. Aspaturian, "The Soviet Military Industrial Complex: Does It Exist?" *Journal of International Affairs*, Spring-Summer, 1972.
3. Samuel Huntington, *The Soldier and the State: Theory and Politics of Civil-Military Relations* (Cambridge: Harvard University Press, 1957).
4. Dale Herspring and Ivan Volgyes, *Civil-Military Relations in Communist States* (Boulder, Colo.: Westview Press, 1978).
5. David E. Albright, "A Comparative Conceptualization of Civil-Military Relations," *World Politics*, July, 1980, pp. 553-576.
6. Timothy Colton, *Commissars, Commanders and Civilian Authority: The Structure of Soviet Military Politics* (Cambridge: Harvard University Press, 1979); Michael Deane, *Political Control of the Soviet Armed Forces* (New York: Crane, Russak, 1977); Raymond A. Garthoff, "The Marshals and the Party: Soviet Civil-Military Relations in the Postwar Period," in Harry Coles, ed., *Total War and Cold War: Problems in Civilian Control of the Military* (Columbus, Ohio: Ohio State University Press, 1962); Roman Kolkowicz, *The Soviet Military and the Communist Party* (Princeton: Princeton University Press, 1962); William E. Odom, *The*

Soviet Volunteers: Modernization and Bureaucracy in a Public Mass Organization (Princeton, N.J.: Princeton University Press, 1973); and Edward Warner, *Military in Contemporary Soviet Politics* (New York: Praeger, 1977).

7. Zbigniew Brzezinski, *Political Controls in the Soviet Army* (New York: Columbia, 1954); Dale Herspring, *East German Civil-Military Relations (1949-1972)* (New York: Praeger, 1973); and "Technology and the Changing Political Officer in the Armed Forces: The Polish and East German Cases," *Studies in Comparative Communism*, Autumn, 1977, by the same author; and David Holloway, *Technology, Management and the Soviet Military Establishment* (London: Institute for Strategic Studies, 1971).

8. Timothy Colton, "The Zhukov Affair Reconsidered," *Soviet Studies*, April, 1977.

9. Lawrence Caldwell, "The Warsaw Pact: Directions of Change," *Problems of Communism*, Sept.-Oct, 1975; Walter Clemens, "The Changing Warsaw Pact," *East Europe*, June, 1968; Curt Gasteyger, "Probleme und Reformen des Warschauer Paktes," *Europa Archiv*, January 10, 1967; Patricia Haigh, *The World Today*, April, 1968; and Hans Von Krannhals, "Command Integration within the Warsaw Pact," *Military Review*, May, 1961.

10. Needless to say, the fear of Bonapartism or Praetorianism has not been confined to the communist militaries. For a few classical studies dealing with the topic, see S.E. Finer, *The Man on Horseback* (London: Pall Mall Press, 1962); and Samuel Huntington's numerous works including, *Changing Patterns in Military Politics* (New York: Glencoe, 1962); and *Political Order in Changing Societies* (New Haven: Yale University Press, 1968), especially Chap. 4.

11. John Barron, *The KGB* (New York: Reader Digest, 1974); Frederick G. Barghoorn, "The Security Police," in *Interest Groups in Soviet Politics* (Princeton: Princeton University Press, 1971); Robert Conquest, *The Soviet Police System* (New York: Praeger, 1968); Peter Deriabin, *Watchdogs of Terror* (New Rochelle, N.Y.: Arlington House, 1972); and Simon Wolin and Robert M. Slusser, *The Soviet Secret Police* (New York: Praeger, 1957).

12. Bracher, Sauer and Schultz, *Die Nationalsozialistische Machtbegreifung* (Kohls: West-Deutsches Verlag, 1960).

13. Kent Brown, "Coalition Politics and Soviet Influence in Eastern Europe," in Jan F. Triska and Paul Cocks, eds., *Political Development in Eastern Europe* (New York: Praeger, 1977).
14. Colonel General P.I. Efimova, *Boevoi Soiuz Bratskikh Armii* [Military Union of Brotherly Armies] (Moscow: Voennisdat, 1974) contains a good statement of these changes.
15. Ivan Volgyes, "The Military as an Agent of Political Socialization," in Herspring and Volgyes, *Civil-Military Relations in Communist Systems*, and Herspring and Volgyes, "The Military as an Agent of Political Socialization of Eastern Europe," *Armed Forces and Society*, February, 1977.
16. Aside from the works already quoted above, see Peter Gosztony, *Zur Geschichte der europäischen Volksarmeen* (Bonn: Hohwacht, 1977); Walter C. Clemens, "The Future of the Warsaw Pact," *Orbis*, Winter, 1968; Michael Csizmás, "Das militärische Bundnissystem in Osteuropa," *Allgemeine Schweizerische Militarzeitschrift*, October-November, 1967; Michael Garder, "Der Warschauer Pakt," *Europa Archiv*, December 25, 1966; and in French "Le Potential Militaire des Satellites de l'URSS," *Revue Militaire Generale*, June, 1965; Guedon, "Le Service Militaire dans les Pays du Bloc Sovietique," *Revue de Defense Nationale*, April, 1964; Eugen Hinterhoff, "Die Potentiale des Warschauer Paktes," *Aussenpolitik*, August, 1965; and, by the same author, "The Warsaw Pact," *Military Review*, June, 1962; Béla Király, "Why the Soviets Need the Warsaw Pact," *East Europe*, April, 1969; Roman Kolkowicz, "Spezifischer Funktionswandel des Warschauer Paktes," *Aussenpolitik*, January, 1969; and by the same author, "The Warsaw Pact: Entangling Alliance," *Survey*, Winter-Spring, 1969; Andrzej Korbonski, "The Warsaw Pact," *International Conciliation*, May, 1969; Malcolm Mackintosh, "The Warsaw Pact Today," *Survival*, May-June, 1974; J. Pergent, "Le Pacte de Varsovie et l'Inventaire des Forces de l'Est," *Est et Ouest*, July, 1967; Robin Remington, *The Warsaw Pact* (Cambridge, Mass.: MIT Press, 1971); and, by the same author, "The Warsaw Pact: Communist Coalition Politics in Action," *Yearbook of World Affairs*, 1972; Col. Paul R. Shirk, "The Warsaw Treaty Organization," *Military Review*, May, 1969; Richard F. Staar, "The East European Alliance," *U.S. Naval Institute Proceedings*, September, 1964; Thaddeus von Paschta, "Das System der sowjetischen Militarberater in den Satellitenstaaten," *Wehrkunde*, September, 1962;

and Fritz Wiener, *Die Armeen der Warschauer Pakt-Staaten: Organisation, Taktik, Waffen und Gerate* (Wien, 1974).

17. For a good statement on the problem, see Robert O. Keohane, "Lilliputian's Dilemmas: Small States in International Politics," *International Organization*, Summer, 1969.

18. On the general topic of alliances as "genuine" systems, see for some of the following recent studies: J. Basso, "La cooperation internationale," *Annuaire du Tiers Monde*, 1(1975), pp. 447-462; S.J. Brams and J.G. Hellman, "When to Join a Coalition, and with How Many Others, Depends on What You Expect the Outcome to Be," *Public Choice*, 17 (Spring 1974), pp. 11-25; W. Von Bredow, "Intersystemare Kooperation und Abrüstung" (Cooperation Among Systems and Disarmament), *Blätter für deutsche und internationale Politik*, 19, 1 (1974), pp. 17-32; Theodore Caplow, "A Theory of Coalitions in the Triad," *American Sociological Review*, 21 (1956), pp. 489-493; Theodore Caplow, "Further Development of a Theory of Coalitions in the Triad," *American Journal of Sociology*, 64 (1959), pp. 488-493; H.R. Day, "The Resource Comparison Model of Coalition Formation," *Cornell Journal of Social Relations*, 10, 2 (Fall 1975), pp. 209-221; R. Gordon Cassidy and Edwin Neave, "Dynamics of Coalition Formation: Prescription Versus Reality," *Theory and Division*, 8, 2 (April 1977), pp. 159-171; Jeff Chertkoff, "The Effects of Probability of Future Success on Coalition Formation," *Journal of Experimental and Social Psychology*, 2, 3, (July 1966) 265-277; Terry L. Deibel, "A Guide to International Divorce," *Foreign Policy*, 30 (Spring 78), pp. 17-35; V. Dimitrijevic, "International Relations and the Existence of Regions," *International Problems* (Belgrade) 14 (1973), pp. 81-83; and R.A. Kann, "Alliances versus Ententes," *World Politics*, 28, 4 (July 1976), pp. 611-621.

19. For a good statement of the topic, see Frigyes Puja, "Miért van szükség a varsói szerződésre?" [Why is There a Need for the Warsaw Pact?] (Budapest: Zrinyi, 1970).

20. Jiri Valenta, *Soviet Intervention in Czechoslovakia* (Baltimore: The Johns Hopkins University Press, 1979), p. 96.

21. Erwin Weit, *At the Red Summit* (New York: Macmillan, 1973), p. 201.

22. For a Soviet view see I.I. Lakubovskii, *Boevoe sodruzhestvo bratskii narodov i armii* [Fighting Alliance of Brotherly People and Armies]

(Moscow: Voennizdat, 1975).
23. V.G. Kulikov, ed., *Varshavskii dogovor—soiuz vo im'ia mira i sotsializ'ma* [The Warsaw Pact—Alliance in the Name of Peace and Socialism] (Moscow: Voennizdat, 1980). For a Hungarian view see László Serfőző, *Barátok, fegyvertársak* [Friends, Comrades in Arms] (Budapest: Zrinyi, 1976); Rezső Dondó, *Védőpajzsunk* (Budapest: Zrinyi, 1980); and *A varsói szerződés szervezete. 1955-1975* [The Organization of the Warsaw Pract, 1955-1975] (Budapest: Kossuth and Zrinyi, 1976). For a Polish view see Marian Jurek and Edward Skrzypowski, *Tarcza pokoju* [The Defense of Peace] (Warsaw: Wydawnictwo Ministerswa Obriny Narodowej, 1975). For an East German collection see *Zeittafel zur Militärgeschichte der Deutschen Demokratischen Republic: 1949 bis 1969* (East Berlin: Militärverlag, 1969).
24. Zoltán Vas, *Viszontagságos életem* [My Life of Vicissitudes] (Budapest: Magvető, 1980), pp. 209-210.
25. A.V. Antosiak, et al., eds., *Zarozhdenie narodnikh armii straruchastnits varshavskogo dogovora, 1941-1949* [The Origins of the People's Armies of the Countries Participating in the Warsaw Pact] (Moscow: Voennizdat, 1975); R. Wustner, "Die Polnische Armee," *Militärwesen,* 9 (1973), p. 13; Michael Checinski, "Polnischen Armee und Offiziere in der Organisation des Warschauer Paktes," *Osteuropa,* 10 (1980), pp. 1110 ff.; and Herspring, *East German Civil-Military Relations,* pp. 43-55.
26. John Collins, et al., *United States/Soviet Military Balance* (Washington: Government Printing Office, 1976).
27. Ivan Volgyes, *The Political Reliability of the Warsaw Pact Armies: The Southern Tier* (Washington: Department of Defense Contract, 1981 to be published by Duke University Press, 1982), pp. 1-15.
28. For the development and explanation on the categorization see Dale R. Herspring and Ivan Volgyes, "Political Reliability in the Eastern European Warsaw Pact Armies," *Armed Forces and Society* (Winter, 1980), pp. 170-196.
29. A. Ross Johnson, "Soviet-East European Military Relations: An Overview," in Herspring and Volgyes, eds., *Civil-Military Relations in Communist Systems* (Boulder, Colo.: Westview, 1978), p. 46.
30. Robert W. Dean in his "The Political Consolidation of the Czechoslovak Army," RFE, 4/29/71 offers an evaluation different from H. Gordon Skilling, *Czechoslovakia's Interrupted Revolution* (Princeton:

Princeton University Press, 1976), or Galia Golan, *Reform Rule in Czechoslovakia* (Cambridge: Cambridge University Press, 1973).

31. Golan, *Reform Rule in Czechoslovakia*, pp. 16, 20.

32. Heinz Godau, *Verführter, Verführer* (Köln: Markus, 1965), pp. 78-84; and Heinz Lippmann, *Honecker* (New York: Macmillan, 1972), pp. 152-158.

33. For an evaluation of these events see Michael Costello, "The Party and the Military in Poland," RFE, 4/26/1971, and Johnson et al., *East European Military Establishments: The Warsaw Pact Northern Tier* (Santa Monica: RAND, 1980), pp. 58-63.

34. For the original reports on the coup see *Christian Science Monitor*, 8/9/1965; *New York Times*, 7/3/1965; *Christian Science Monitor*, 6/25/1965; *London Times*, 6/21/1965; *Süddeutsche Zeitung*, 6/21/1965; *New York Times*, 6/21/1965; *Unita*, 6/21/1965; *Die Presse*, 6/8/1965; *Süddeutsche Zeitung*, 6/5 and 6/7/1965; *Daily Telegraph*, 5/25/1965; *Vorwaerts*, 5/19/1965; *Washington Star*, 5/18/1965; *Daily Telegraph*, 5/13/1965; *Frankfurter Rundschau*, 5/6/1965; *Süddeutsche Zeitung*, 5/5/1965; *New York Times*, 5/3/1965; *Christ und Welt*, 4/30/1965; *Rheinischer Merkur*, 4/30/1965; *Süddeutsche Zeitung*, 4/30/1965; *Münchener Merkur*, 4/30/1965; *New York Times*, 4/29/1965; etc. First report on the coup came on April 15, 1965, a week after the coup attempts on April 7, 1965. The report was filed by UPI. For an extensive treatment see J.F. Brown, *Bulgaria Under Communist Rule* (New York: Praeger, 1970), pp. 173-187.

35. For the most extensive treatment see Béla Király, "Hungary's Army: Its Part in the Revolt," *East Europe*, 6(1958); Péter Gosztonyi, "A magyar néphadsereg a forradalomban" [The Hungarian People's Army in the Revolution], in *Magyar változások, 1948-1978* [Hungarian Changes, 1948-1978] (Vienna: Integration, 1979); Zoltán Sztáray, "A néphadsereg és a forradalom" [The People's Army and the Revolution], *Új Látóhatár* [New Horizon], 5 (1961); for a communist evaluation see "A Magyar Néphadsereg szerepe az ellenforradalom időszakában és harca a munkás-paraszt hatalom védelméért" [The Role of the People's Army in the Period of the Counterrevolution, and its Struggle in the Defense of the Power of the Workers and Peasants], *Katonai Szemle* [Military Review], 2 (1957).

36. Ferenc Váli, *Rift and Revolution in Hungary*, (Cambridge: Harvard University Press, 1961), p. 434.

37. The best summary remains Walter Bacon's account in his "The Military and the Party in Romania," in Herspring and Volgyes, *Civil-Military Relations*, pp. 165-180.

38. These views are best summed up by Johnson, *et al.*, *East European Military Establishments: The Warsaw Pact Northern Tier*.

39. For a summary of these views see Volgyes, *The Political Reliability of the Warsaw Pact Armies: The Southern Tier* (Washington: Department of Defense Contract, 1981 to be published by Duke University Press, 1982).

40. In fact, the Hungarian and the Romanian armies have the shortest prescription time among members of the Pact; in 1981 it was 18 months.

III

ETHNICITY, IMMIGRATION AND DOMESTIC POLITICS IN AMERICA

Louis L. Snyder

THE NEW ANTI-SEMANTICISM: ETHNICITY AND NATIONALISM

For all those who have the privilege of knowing him, Professor Béla K. Király presents the ideal combination of gentleman and scholar. One can testify to his unfailing courtesy, his careful consideration for others, and the humanitarianism and sense of decency that motivate his life. As a distinguished and prolific scholar, he always has shown respect for accuracy in the printed word. In his published work he invariably uses terms that are clear-cut and acceptable by his colleagues. Above all, he avoids indulging in vague and shadowy generalizations in which specific meaning is violated.

It is in this sense that this study is devoted to a recent trend in historical scholarship that is proceeding rapidly beyond the boundaries of acceptable semanticism. It is concerned with nationalism, a subject on which Professor Király is an outstanding authority and for which he has received international recognition. The concept of nationalism is inchoate, filled with conflicting definitions, approaches, and explanations. It is suffused with inconsistencies, contradictions, and paradoxes. There is already enough frustration in the field without adding more complexities. Yet this has been done in recent years by the continuing confusion of nationalism with ethnicity.

Before proceeding with the heart of the argument, a few observations should be made about the meaning of words, or more properly the discipline of semantics.

The extreme importance of the meaning of words was recognized as early as the fifth century B.C. by Socrates. Believing that he had a divine mission to counter ignorance and convict "the god of falsehood," the Greek philosopher, probably in part to avoid the tongue of his temperamental wife Xanthippe, came daily to the market place in Athens to speak to the people he saw there. He became annoyed by loose usage of such terms as "soul," "love," "truth," and "faith." Using his own method of "examination in arguments," he questioned systematically the fundamental assumptions from which discussions of morality and conduct arose. He made himself unpopular among his fellow citizens by insisting vehemently on a strict definition of terms. He understood that words are the most important means of communication for human beings and that misunderstandings could cause grievous harm. If one thing was said and another understood, there was much ground for mischief in human relations.

This necessity for clarity of meaning is just as important today as it was in the market place of fifth-century B.C. Athens. It is especially of significance in defining the modern "isms"—nationalism, capitalism, socialism, communism, *et al.* The term nationalism, for example, has become enmeshed in semantic difficulties because of its many conflicting interpretations, so much so that it is difficult to arrive at any acceptable definition.[1]

The problem is that we are living in an age of semantic confusion. Twentieth-century anti-semanticism received a tremendous boost with the ideology of Lenin and his followers in the Soviet Union. Lenin rewrote the dictionary to suit his own philosophy. He introduced a new definition of morality by insisting that moral is that which acts to the advantage of the working class. It is morally acceptable to use illegitimate methods and hide the truth (euphemism for plain lying) as long as it is in the interest of the proletariat.[2]

With this standard as a guide, Soviet ideologists presented their own version of meaning, that kind of doublespeak described by George Orwell in *Nineteen Eight-Four*. This kind of semantic onslaught is revealed in distortion of the word "democracy." Democracy has a specific meaning—

from the Greek *dēmokratia,* from *dēmos,* the people, plus *kratein,* to rule. It is the opposite of dictatorship. But communists blandly appropriate the word for their own use and trumpet it to the world in their own version—the "German Democratic Republic of East Germany" and the like. By communist logic a party and party-leader dictatorship is presented as a "democratic society."

Similarly, communists project their own definition of imperialism. In the mid-twentieth century, at a time when Britain, France, Holland, Portugal, and Italy were liquidating their colonial holdings, and at a time when the Soviet Union was constructing a global imperialism of its own, the Kremlin with an innocent face continued to denounce Western imperialism. Meanwhile, the USSR was sending Cuban mercenaries into weakened African countries, probing wherever there was a political vacuum in order to extend Soviet power. At the time of the December 1981 crisis in Poland, Vladimir Bolshakov published a 23,000-word article in *Pravda (Truth)* charging that events in Poland over the previous seventeen months were due to "the old plans of imperialism for the restoration of capitalism in Poland, for wresting the country out of the socialist community, above all from the Warsaw treaty organization.[3] At the same time, the Kremlin officially condemned the United States for "interfering" in the internal affairs of Poland when Russian soldiers were reported to be wearing Polish uniforms in satellite Poland.

In other words, by Soviet definition, the Western retreat from nineteenth-century imperialism was still orthodox imperialism, while the new Russian imperialism was merely "liberation." That is why Western historians at international conferences shake their heads in disbelief when their Russian peers make mincemeat of accepted definitions. It is difficult to take the Russian semantic revolution seriously.

* * * * *

Unfortunately, one cannot absolve Western scholars from anti-semanticism, although their confusion of terms, unlike that of the Soviets, seems to be unwitting and unconscious. In recent years there has grown a sizeable literature revolving around the term "ethnic" and such corollary terms as "ethnic groups," "ethnicity," "ethnonationalism," and "ethnopolitics."

Use of the basic term "ethnic" is well nigh universal from the daily press to scholarly tomes. We shall see that little distinction is made between racial and cultural connotations of the term. When the television personality John Belushi died tragically in Hollywood on March 5, 1982, apparaently from an overdose of heroin and cocaine, the New York *Post* reported: "Why did Belushi stand out? His girth, his grossness. The ethnicity of his characters."[4] The comedian was known for his portrayal of comic characters of varied nationalities which were given an ethnic connotation. The press furthermore called Belushi an "ethnic Albanian" because he was born in Chicago on January 24, 1949, "the son of an Albanian American restaurateur." Now by no stretch of the imagination can an American whose parents were Albanain be classified as "ethnically" Albanian. The juxtaposition of nationalities has nothing to do with "racial" background. Belushi was not an Albanian-American by "race."

This kind of confusion is not limited to the popular press. It exists also in the scholarly world. The prestigious Belknap Press of Harvard University Press published the *Harvard Encylopedia of American Ethnic Groups* (Cambridge, MA, 1980), under the editorship of Stephan Thernstrom, and produced cooperatively by many scholars and experts. It provides essays on over one hundred "ethnic groups" in the United States, ranging from Acadians to Zoroastrians. A typical section on the Mexicans consists of twenty-two large double-columned pages on historical background, immigration, the Mexican-American experience, Chicano culture, and bibliography. The book was awarded the Waldo G. Leland Prize by The American Historical Association in 1981 in its search "for broadly conceived works dealing lucidly and authoritatively with important subjects of interest to a substantial number of informed readers." "These works should combine sound and original scholarship, graceful presentation, and practical usefulness, and they should provide valuable information not readily available elsewhere."

It is a strange phenomenon when outstanding scholars are said to contribute lucidity and sound original scholarship in an encyclopedia listing Acadians, Zoroastrians, and Mexican-Americans among more than one hundred "ethnic groups." There is, as we shall see, a major difference between the rich mixture of cultures in the United States and so-called ethnicity.

Added to this encyclopedia is a stream of studies devoted to variations of the ethnic approach. An example is Joseph Rothschild's *Ethnopolitics:*

A Conceptual Framework (Columbia University Press, 1981), which attempts to provide a conceptual framework for understanding how "political entrepreneurs" mobilize ethnicity for political purposes, for "political legitimation or delegitimation of systems, states, regimes and governments." Rothschild traces the development of nationalism in the nineteenth century, the era of the emergence of the large nation-state, through the twentieth century, when a reverse process set in with "the burgeoning pressures of political ethnic assertiveness" in all types of states, including modern and developing, capitalist, communist, and socialist. The accent of the study is on ethnicity, its structure, leadership and dynamics. In emphasizing the relationship of nationalism to ethnicity, the author enters a realm of problemical definitions. He is not alone among scholars who have done the same thing.

*****

Let us proceed to fundamentals. It is scarcely necessary to say that the meaning of words is essential to the understanding of any historical movement or of the formulation of any ideology. The term "ethnic" originally had two basic meanings in *Webster's International Dictionary of the English Language:*

> 1. Pertaining to the Gentiles, or to nations not converted to Christianity; heathen; pagan—opposed to *Jewish* and *Christian*.
> 2. Relating to community of physical and mental traits in races, or designating groups of races of mankind discriminated on the basis of common customs and characters. [For two additional meanings see footnote 6 of this chapter.]

We may disregard the first meaning (heathen, pagan) as obsolete. But the second definition is vital and as basic presents the theme of this argument. It refers specifically to "races," "groups of races," and "physical and mental traits in races." In other words, by common usage the earlier definition, referring to "nations not converted to Christianity," has been dropped in favor of that meaning devoted to "races of mankind."

This is where the trouble starts—and the reader is urged to keep this definition in mind whenever he sees the term "ethnic" and its corollaries. Over the course of the years "ethnic" has been used loosely and interchangeably with "racial" and as such has become significant in elaborating the many myths connected with race. The result is compounded confusion, for as soon as we enter the area of race we fall into linguistic quicksands. There is little clarity in use of the terms, "ethnic," "ethnical," "ethnicism," "ethnocentric," and "ethnocracy," all of which have been identified weakly with "nations." There is an uncomfortable synonym connotation for "race" here and as such there are recurring difficulties in transmission of meaning.

Indeed, certain varied compound versions of "ethnic" are acceptable linguistically as long as they are restricted to the racial sense. Thus, ethnography is that branch of anthropology which treats historically the origin and filiation of distinct races. Ethnology is the science which divides mankind into races and discusses their beginnings, distribution, and relation as well as the peculiarities that characterize them. Ethnology and ethnography are often confused, but the latter is properly restricted to the purely descriptive treatment of races, while the former is concerned with their comparative study and analytical classification. There is also the discipline of ethnogeny concerned primarily with the genesis and evolution of races. Ethnopsychology examines the psychology of races.

There is no end to extension of the term "ethnic" into new and innovative fields, a development which makes for even more confusion. Thus, *Time* in 1982 published an article in its "Behavior" section an "Ethnotherapy," or "Therapy for Ethnics," a discussion of how troubled adults seek treatment with their own kind. Among the "ethnics" *Time* includes Jews, Italians, and Blacks. The theme was expressed by clinical psychologist Judith Weinstein Klein: "All ethnic minorities have to deal with self-hate and feelings of inadequacy as members of the American culture."[5] There is no indication in the article that, of the three groups treated, only Blacks can be identified as a race—the Jews are specifically a religion and Italian-Americans a nationality.

The basic fact is that by definition, the terms "ethnic" and its variations—from ethnology to ethnotherapy—are concerned with races. An example is the work of Franz Boas (1852-1942), the distinguished American anthropologist, who did pioneer work on the racial characteristics of Eskimos. A prodigiously productive scholar, he contributed much to statistical physical anthropology, descriptive and theoretical linguistics, and folklore and myths as ethnographic tools. But note that he restricted his work mostly to specific *racial* types—the ethnology of Eskimos and American Indians.

* * * * *

At the root of the linguistic problem is the tendency in recent years to remove "ethnic" from its racial sense and use it as a cultural term.[6] This source of confusion is a classic case in violation of semantic standards. Early definitions linked ethnic groups directly with race. Later, the word "ethnic" was tied up with a sense of group identity based on cultural similarities. Like Topsy, the error "just growed."

The moment the term "ethnic" is removed from its racial sphere to the field of culture we enter the realm of the obscure. For example, the hybrid term "ethnonationalism" immediately confuses race with nation, but the terms are by no means interchangeable. Obscurants cannot have it both ways linguistically. They cannot use "ethnic" as connected with "race" and also as a word with purely a cultural meaning. Yet, over the course of decades, scholars, who should have known better, persisted in confusing race with nation. The new literature on ethnicity adds mystery instead of enlightenment. Historians, sociologists, and anthropologists have gone ahead to investigate ethnicity, forgetting that they have appropriated what is essentially a biological term and use it weakly in a social sense. They speak lightly of "ethnicity" or "ethnic culture" when they mean linguistic, territorial, or religious cultural manifestations. By confusing two different images—racialist and culturalist—they contribute to a complicated conceptual muddle.

The excuse given invariably is that usage tends to change language. Perhaps so, but definitely not when scientific conclusions are violated. It is wrong to appropriate a term having a distinctive meaning in matters of race and give it a cultural connotation. We do not measure culture by race—that is the mistake of the new ethnicists. Cultural qualities must be sought in a people's nationalism, mini-nationalism, or macro-nationalism. Such peoples are united not by racial but by national consciousness. The two should not be confused.

The point might be raised here that if use of "ethnic" and its corollaries in a cultural sense is so widespread, then why raise a molehill to a mountain by objecting to it? The answer lies in the Socratic view of the problem of meaning. It is wrong to subject language to hazy concepts merely because lazy reporters and equally careless scholars consistently confuse race with nationality.

* * * * *

Because "ethnic" relates to community of physical and mental traits in races, let us turn briefly to race. Few subjects are so permeated with myth and fallacy. In 1939 and again in 1962 the present author attempted to clarify the haziness surrounding the subjects of race and racialism, especially because of the confusion of "nation" with "race."[7] It would be satisfying to report that these inquiries had some effect, but unfortunately they did not in any way solve the continuing dilemma.

Here, too, we are faced with semantic perplexity. Some otherwise highly intelligent minds have contributed to this confusion thrice confounded. Winston Churchill, undoubtedly motivated by patriotism, insisted on using the term "race" in an improper sense as a cultural community. Throughout his career he referred to the accomplishments of "the British race," which has never existed beyond his fertile imagination. His last book, an abridgement of his *History of the English-Speaking Peoples* (1956-1958), appeared some months before his death (1965) under the title of *The Island Race*. Here the famous statesman was using the word in its Victorian meaning (Englishmen at that time generally criticized the cultural values of other communities). Churchill was a magnificent war leader with a golden tongue, but he must be given poor marks as a lexical specialist or a logical linguist. We shall see in a moment just what the British "race" means.

There are, indeed, certain conclusions about race which have scientific validity and which should be kept in mind when considering the meaning of "ethnic" and its corollaries. They are presented here in brief form:

1. Race is a biological or anthropological term referring to species of human beings based on such characteristics as skin color, hair texture, stature, and other physical or inherited characteristics. Scientists generally speak of five human races—white, black, red, brown, and yellow, with varied sub-races falling within these groups. Note that the term denotes a *common biological descent,* not common cultural characteristics. The terms "black race" or "ethnic Blacks" are commonly and correctly used.

2. There is no such thing as a *pure* race. Over the course of centuries the races have intermingled and the process of mixing continues. Hitler's concept of a "pure Aryan race" was a simple fraud—Aryan or Indo-European are linguistic not racial terms. Churchill's Englishman by race was a man of many strains.

The great stateman would have been enlightened had he read and absorbed the following judgment by Karl Pearson, British eugenist, who gave a devastating description of the "pure-blooded Englishman":

> We are accustomed to speak of a typical Englishman. For example, Charles Darwin; we think of his mind as a typical English mind, working in the typical English manner, yet when we come to study his pedigree we seek in vain for 'purity of race.'
>
> He is descended in four different lines from Irish kinglets; he is descended in as many lines from Scottish and Pictish kings. He has Manx blood. He claims descent in as many lines from Alfred the Great, and so links up with Anglo-Saxon blood, but he links up also in several lines with Charlemagne and his Carlovingians. He sprang also from the Saxon Emperor of Germany as well as from Barbarossa and the Hohenstaufens. He has Norwegian blood and much Norman blood. He has descent from the Dukes of Bavaria, of Saxony, of Flanders, the Prince of Savoy, and Kings of Italy. He has the blood in his veins of Franks, Alemans, Merovingians, Burgundians, and Longobards. He sprang in direct descent from the Hun rulers of Hungary and Greek Emperors of Constantinople. If I recollect rightly, Ivan the Terrible provides a Russian link. There is probably not one of the races of Europe concerned in folk-wanderings which has not a share in the ancestry of Charles Darwin.[8]

There is no scientific basis for the existence of pure races anywhere. In recorded history the peoples of the world have become so intermingled biologically that there is little possibility of the existence of a pure race. The only people who today might with some justification be called a *nearly pure race* are the African pygmies, but even here there is no satisfactory proof. Every people of which we have a record has been a hybrid group. Purity of race is nothing but a myth.

3. There is no such thing as a "superior" race. The fact that every civilized group of which we have a record has been a hybrid group disposes effectively of the theory that cross-bred peoples are inferior to so-called pure-bred ones. The idea that any one race—white, black or red—is inherently and biologically superior in meeting the challenges of its environment is merely wishful thinking. The growth of civilization has proceeded with serene indifference to racial lines. The assertion that only the white race is capable of founding and sustaining culture cannot be demonstrated historically. The white race came into civilization rather late at a time

when Chinese culture had progressed well beyond its European counterpart. All groups who have had the opportunity to acquire civilization have not only acquired it but added to its content. No one race has an exclusive claim to represent the final stage in human evolution. There is especially no valid claim for superiority of any one single race.

4. Race should not be confused with nation or nationality. There is no such thing as a British race, Churchill to the contrary, any more than there is an American race. Loose usage of the terms race and nation as synonymous is responsible for much of the confusion surrounding both words. In popular thinking race and nation are often identified as one and the same thing. The reason is that most people find it difficult to conceive of a close social unity without a physical bond and cannot think of a common mentality without common blood. The idea of solidarity between members of a nation takes on the implication of a real relationship between members of a family.

The term *nation* belongs properly within the sphere of the social sciences, while *race* should be reserved for the natural sciences. Nation designates historical and social characterisitcs that can be altered by society, while race refers to hereditary, biological traits not easily changed by education or assimilation. There never has been a German, French, or Italian race, but there are German, French, and Italian nations.

A nation, then, is not the physical fact of one blood, but the mental fact of one tradition. Race refers to a common physical type, nation to a common mental content. Race is a natural fact, nation is an artificial structure set up by the thoughts, feeling, and will of the human mind.

5. Race should not be confused with culture. Race is essentially a matter of heredity, while culture is one of tradition. Race is concerned with the inheritance of bodily characteristics, while culture is concerned with what is transmitted through social organization. Culture refers to a whole structure of beliefs, knowledge, and literature, of concepts, sentiments, and institutions carried from one generation to another through the vehicle of language.

Even this brief treatment indicates the disorder, nebulosity, and lack of precision surrounding the entire idea of race. The best possible procedure for social scientists is to avoid use of the term "race" altogether and leave it to the biologists. There are far too many strands of confusion here.

All these obstacles to meaning are repeated when the word "ethnic" is used as a synonym for "race." We often hear the terms "ethnic Italians," "ethnic Poles," and "ethnic Germans" in the United States, all living in the conglomerate American melting pot.[9] Yet this practice merely adds to the confusion already surrounding the subject of race. Why add to the muddle of meaning?

* * * * *

Much difficulty has been caused by the application of the term "ethnic" and its variations to the field of nationalism. Even without the term "ethnic," nationalism is already suffused with so many inconsistencies, contradictions, and paradoxes that there is small room for enlightenment when the myths of ethnicity are added to it. The basic problem consists in the false identification of race with nation.

The word "ethnonationalism" was first used by Walter Connor in 1973 in an article in which he described "internal discord predicated upon ethnic diversity."[10] He defined an ethnic group as "a basic human category (i.e., not a sub-group), characterized by unity of race and culture."[11]

If by the suffix "ethno-" Connor means "national," then we have a redundant "national nationalism." If he means "racial," then we are caught in the quicksands of race. If an ethnic group, as noted by Connor, really is characterized by unity of race and culture, then its use must be confined to the broad category of races and not to Albanians, Mexican-Americans, or Scots. Undoubtedly, Connor was using the term in a broad sense to indicate shared culture, language, and traditions, but there is no reason for extending what is essentially a racial term into a cultural term. It cannot be stressed too often—it is dangerous anti-semanticism to confuse biological race with cultural attributes of a nation. Georgi Pasquali, an Italian journalist, became annoyed when he came across the confusion again and again. His criticism took a highly satirical vein: "I prefer the word *nation* when I speak of human beings, and the word *races* when I speak of Pekinese, racing horses, chickens, and Yorkshire swine."

Two years later Nathan Glazer and Daniel P. Moynihan introduced the term "ethnicity," which was destined to win universal usage.[12] Until this time the word "ethnicity" did not appear in any general dictionaries nor was it mentioned in any social science encyclopedia or guides. There were, indeed, references to "ethnic," "ethnic groups," "ethnic identification," and "ethnic communities," but not to "ethnicity." The new word caught on quickly and began to appear again and again especially in studies on nationalism.

Works dealing with ethnicity on a cross-national basis began to appear in abundance, among them books by Milton J. Esman, Charles R. Foster, and Jaroslav Krejci and Vitezslav Velimsky.[13] There were investigations into ethnic conflict in the Western world, ethnic minorities in Western Europe, and ethnic pluralism. There even appeared a new scholarly journal called *Ethnicity*, which published scholarly studies on ethnic groups and ethnic pluralism.[14]

Unfortunately, there was a lack of consensus on the definition of ethnicity. An attempt was made by Wsevolod W. Isajiw, in "Definition of Ethnicity," in the journal *Ethnicity*. Isajiw examined scores of references to the term in scholarly studies and only in relatively few cases was he able to find any attempt at definition. In other words, scholars are using the term without making clear exactly what they mean—a dubious means of clarification. When the distinguished sociologist Talcott Parsons sought to elicit the meaning of ethnicity, he found it to be "extraordinarily elusive."[15] Most of those who write about ethnicity undoubtedly consider it to be concerned with distinctive cultural or subcultural characteristics that distinguish one group from others. Here again it must be said that there is not valid justification for appropriating a term concerned with inherited biological traits and giving it a foggy cultural base.

The next step went from ethnicity to "ethnocentrism." Again a new term was applied to the study of nationalism. Anthony D. Smith sought to link "ethnic consciousness" with nationalism.[16] According to Smith, it is important to make a distinction between modern nationalism and the earlier xenopobia, which he calls "ethnocentrism." Like many others, Smith sees "ethnic" as a "fairly large group of people who share a common culture, even though they are no longer related by kinship ties." What he has done here, as have many others, is to mix race with culture. He sees ethnocentrism as the heightened sense of the centrality of one's *ethnie* (synonym for ethnicity). Where the old nationalism was ethnocentric, the new or modern nationalism, in Smith's view, is polycentric. He sees the base of ethnocentrism as an unbreakable faith in the superiority of the nation. The question might well be asked: is this not also the characteristic of modern nationalism?

* * * * *

Recent literature on the relationship of ethnicity and nationalism is examined in an excellent study by Konstantin Symmons-Symonolewicz, Emeritus Professor of Sociology at Allegheny College, in the *Canadian Review of Studies in Nationalism*.[17] With a critical eye and some skepticism Symmons-Symonolewicz examines the steadily expanding recent literature on ethnicity and nationalism and comments brilliantly on its theoretical implications. He, too, is concerned by the lack of consensus on the meaning of the concept. He sees early definitions as linking the cultural distinctiveness of ethnic groups with race,[18] while later ones link it with consciousness of group identity.[19] Most definitions of ethnicity, he writes, emphasize its two basic characteristics. He quotes Talcott Parsons: "It seems to be generally agreed that what we call ethnicity is a primary focus of group identity, that is, the organization of plural persons into distinctive groups, and second, of solidarity and the loyalties of individual members of such groups."[20]

Other observers, such as E. K. Francis, define "ethnicity" as "the social definition of peoples on the basis of common descent, thereby bringing it squarely into the racial mold.[21] Still others, notably George de Vos[22] and Cynthia H. Enloe,[23] both of whom use the term "ethnic" in the titles of their studies, prefer to speak of "ethnic groups" and "ethnic identities" instead of ethnicity.

The fact that a good portion of Symmons-Symonolewicz's bibliographical article is concerned with the confusing nature of the concept of ethnicity, especially among sociologists, indicates the seriousness of the problem of meaning. Thus, E. K. Francis limits the concept to a people who are socially defined as belonging together because of their belief in being descended from a common ancestry (the racial argument).[24] On the other hand, Wendell Bell and Walter E. Freeman present as a minimum definition of ethnicity the characteristic distinctive cultural or subcultural traits that set one group off from others (the cultural argument).[25] These are entirely different approaches to meaning. They reveal the extent of the semantic jumble.

* * * * *

In summary, Béla Király's respect for clarity in his scholarly work plus the Socratic admonition on clear-cut definitions bring to mind a semantic problem in the study of nationalism. The terms "ethnic" and its corollaries "ethnic groups," "ethnocentrism," "ethnonationalism," and the new "ethnicity" have become popular and are being used in such a way as to add confusion to a subject already burdened by severe difficulties in the problem of meaning.

The original definition of "ethnic" refers specifically to physical and mental traits in races or groups of races. As such it becomes close to a synonym for the term "racial" and hence subject to all the difficulties already associated with race. The problem was compounded somewhere along the line when "ethnic" began to be used to describe cultural as well as racial characteristics. Unfortunately, this philological variation received much support among scholars who began to use it repeatedly. What it did, however, was to open a can of linguistic worms, especially when used in conjunction with national groups and nationalism.

The rebuttal holds that language is constantly in change and that persistent use of a different form leads to new, valid definitions. This argument is flawed. Millions of Americans use the term "ain't" in their daily conversation, but this practice has not convinced grammarians to adopt it as an acceptable addition to the American language. Sociologists and anthropologists have taken "ethnic" from its original meaning and applied it to culture, a practice that does not necessarily make it semantically legitimate.

To maintain the purity of language as a means of communication, it would seem best for scholars in most disciplines to leave terms associated with race to the biologists, who already have enough problems in dealing with evanescent myths and fallacies. It is not helpful to give a cultural meaning to a genetic term unless it refers specifically to a major racial group such as the black or white race. To apply it to "ethnic Chicanos," "ethnic Zoroastrians," or "ethnic Welshmen," or to label Jews and Chinese as "ethnics," results merely in confusion.

There is no expectation that the argument presented here will have the slightest effect on continued use of "ethnic" and its corollary terms. We may expect a rising flood of articles and books devoted to the new "ethnicity." But what is attempted here is to seek an explanation for the accumulated and annoying muddle of meaning that has surrounded these faulty terms, a development that makes investigation of nationalism extremely difficult for dedicated scholars.

NOTES

1. In 1954 the present author attempted to clarify the meaning of nationalism and ended up with a definition extending to 208 pages: Louis L. Snyder, *The Meaning of Nationalism*, foreword by Hans Kohn (New Brunswick, NJ, 1954; first Greenwood reprinting 1968; second Greenwood reprinting, 1972).
2. Lenin (Vladimir Ilich Ulyanov), *Collected Works* (New York, 1923), XVII, pp. 142-145, 321-323.
3. *The New York Times*, December 26, 1981. Western diplomats judged that Bolshakov's article was less remarkable for the substance of its claims than for what it revealed about the Kremlin's insecurity and suspicion.
4. Stephen A. Silverman, in the New York *Post*, March 9, 1982.
5. John Lee, in *Time*, March 15, 1982.
6. So overwhelming was the use of "ethnic" in a cultural sense that the editors of *Webster's Third International Dictionary*, in its edition of 1971, added two secondary meanings as follows: 1. ethnic: having originated from racial, linguistic, and cultural ties with a specific group, Negroes, Irish, Italians, Germans, Poles, and other groups; 2. ethnic: originating in an exotic primitive culture (music). Note that in the first of these secondary meanings the word "and" is used in "racial, linguistic, *and* cultural ties," and not the conjunctive "or." Thus, in this important distinction, the racial connotation of the basic definition of "ethnic" is retained. By no means can the Irish, Italians, Germans, and Poles be classified as "races." Even the editors of *Webster's Unabridged* have contributed to the confusion.
7. For extended treatments of race, see Louis L. Snyder, *Race* (New York, 1939); *The Idea of Racialism* (Princeton, NJ, 1962); and *Rassen, Wirkelijkheid: Oorsaken, Achtergronden, Theorien* (Hilversum, The Netherlands, 1966).
8. Karl Pearson, "The Problems of Anthropology," *Scientific Monthly* (November, 1920), p. 455.
9. During World War I Howard Chandler Christy on one of his posters depicted a girl of "pure Nordic type" appealing for Liberty Loans and pointing with pride to a list of names: "Americans All: Dubois, Smith, O'Brian, Knutson, Cejko, Haucke, Kowalski, Chriczanevicz." This was too

much for the racialist Madison Grant, who complained: "The only native American is hidden under the sobriquet Smith."
10. Walter Connor, "The Politics of Ethnonationalism," *Journal of Educational Affairs,* XXVII, 1 (1973).
11. Ibid.
12. Nathan Glazer and Daniel P. Moynihan, eds., *Ethnicity: Theory and Experience* (Cambridge, MA, 1979), introduction.
13. Among such works are Milton J. Esman, ed., *Ethnic Conflict in the Western World* (Ithaca, NY, 1977); Charles R. Foster, ed., *Nations Without State: Ethnic Minorities in Western Europe* (New York, 1980); and Jaroslav Krejci and Vitezslav Velimsky, *Ethnic and Political Nations in Europe* (London, 1981).
14. See for example, Pierre L. Van den Bergh, "Ethnic Pluralism in Industrial Societies: A Special Case," *Ethnicity,* III (3 (1975).
15. Talcott Parsons, "Some Theoretical Considerations in the Nature and Trends of Ethnicity," in Glazer and Moynihan, *Ethnicity,* op. cit., pp. 53-83.
16. Anthony D. Smith, "Ethnocentrism, Nationalism and Social Change," *International Journal of Comparative Sociology,* XIII (1972), pp. 1-20.
17. Konstantin Symmons-Symonolewicz, "Ethnicity and Nationalism: Recent Literature and Its Theoretical Considerations," *Canadian Review of Studies in Nationalism,* VI, 1 (Spring, 1979), pp. 98-102.
18. As, for example, definitions in the *Encyclopedia of the Social Sciences* and the *Dictionary of Anthropology.*
19. Ibid.
20. Talcott Parsons, "Some Theoretical Considerations," op. cit.
21. E. K. Francis, *Interethnic Relations: An Essay in Sociological Theory* (New York, 1976).
22. George de Vos, "Ethnic Pluralism, Conflict and Accommodation," in G. de Vos and Lola Romanucci-Ross, eds., *Ethnic Identity: Cultural Continuities and Change* (Palo Alto, CA, 1972).
23. Cynthia H. Enloe, *Ethnic Conflict and Political Development* (Boston, MA, 1973).
24. Francis, *Interethnic Relations,* op. cit.
25. Wendell Bell and Walter E. Freeman, *Ethnicity and Nation Building: Comparative International and Historical Perspectives* (Beverly Hills, CA, 1964).

Mario D. Fenyő

HARASZTHY: A HUNGARIAN PIONEER IN THE AMERICAN WEST

An explorer, entrepreneur, inventor, lawman, land speculator, politician, Ágoston Haraszthy deserves to be considered a pioneer among pioneers on the American frontier. He is known today as the founder of the California wine industry. But he also founded a city in Wisconsin; ran a steamboat on the Mississippi; led a wagon train across the continent, served as the first sheriff of San Diego; was involved in the Gold Rush as an assayer and refiner; and finally moved on to a new frontier in Nicaragua, where he became master of a sugar plantation and died at the age of fifty-six, apparently the victim of alligators in a jungle stream.

This extraordinary and very American character was in fact a Hungarian nobleman who first set foot in the United States in 1840, when he was twenty-seven. He had come with his cousin Charles Halász to see "this romantic new land" for himself—an imperative felt about the same time by so many young Europeans, aristocrats or commoners, from Alexis de Tocqueville to Charles Dickens. Like so many others, Haraszthy traveled extensively through what he called the "Free States of North America" and wrote a book to describe his adventures and explain the bewildering phenomenon of America to his countrymen. That book, *Travel in North America* [*Utazás Éjszak-Amerikában*] was published in Hungary in 1844 in two volumes.

Ágoston Haraszthy was born on August 30, 1812, at Futak, an estate in what was then southern Hungary. His family belonged to the middle nobility, the title of count having been bestowed upon him by his generous American acquaintances. In his youth Haraszthy served briefly in the Royal Hungarian Guard. Soon thereafter he made the acquaintance of two radicals—Miklós Wesselényi and Lajos Kossuth—who were to play major roles in preparing the Revolution of 1848. In 1834 Haraszthy married Eleonora Dedinsky, a Polish noblewoman. The family chronicle indicates that in 1835 he became a private secretary to Archduke Joseph, the Palatinate of Hungary. We know little about his early life.

Nor do we know for sure what brought him to America in the first place. Charles Halász claimed that the two of them had left Hungary "for no reason, except to wander." After a year and a half of wanderings, highlighted by his founding of *Széptáj* ("Beautiful Region"—now Sauk City, Wisconsin), Haraszthy returned to Hungary and arranged for the publication of his *Travel*. The work became quite popular and may have spurred the emigration of thousands of East Europeans. Even before it was published, in the fall of 1842, he gathered his family and returned to America to settle.

* * * * *

To the immigrant crossing the Atlantic around 1840 the United States was not merely a land of promise. It was also a land of fulfillment, provided he was of an adventurous bent, and was not content to remain in New York City or wherever he happened to disembark, but took the initiative to move westward. Some fifty percent of the recently arrived immigrants did just that.

What, specifically, prompted the immigrants to undertake the still perilous crossing? How did they find out about this land of opportunities?

It was not, in the earlier part of the nineteenth century, a matter of relatives sponsoring relatives, of letters of invitation, or word of mouth: "relatives" could have been but few, immigration—particularly from southern and eastern Europe—was still inconsiderable, the United States was far from having the variegated ethnic composition which distinguishes it at present. Its inhabitants were less heterogeneous; there were Blacks,

Native Americans, Germans, Dutch, and French, but political power and wealth were largely the prerogatives of the Anglo-Saxon element. In the decade ending in 1829 only 128,502 immigrants were recorded, even though the immigration procedures were considerably simpler, so it is not likely that many "aliens" found it necessary to circumvent the laws in order to enter and remain in the country. In the following decade, however, immigrants were arriving at the rate of sixty thousand a year (not quite 100,000 to 200,000, as Haraszthy claimed). Immigration was to reach a first peak in 1854.

Many, perhaps most of these early immigrants were influenced by some book, pamphlet, or handbill. Such handbills were pasted all over Ireland, the most bountiful supplier of American manpower in this period. The Irish came to settle for the most part in the cities along the eastern seaboard, lured by promises of high wages and easy work, long before the potato famine left them with hardly any alternative. But the Irish were not the only ones. Ole Rynning's "True Account of America for the Information and Help of Peasant and Commoner," originally printed in Oslo in 1838, greatly accelerated the arrival of immigrants from Scandinavia.[1] In a minor way, Ágoston Haraszthy's *Travel* had a similar effect upon Hungarians in the days before their revolution, and immediately thereafter. The book sold some 2,000 copies, a considerable number in a small and largely illiterate land. It is clear that Haraszthy's book was yet another example of this genre of "beckoning book," although it was a great deal more besides.

"No human hand or power could create such an earthly paradise though it possess all the treasures of Peru," wrote Haraszthy, "and yet this immensely rich and fertile land is uninhabited and unused even though it costs only $1.25 an acre. Truly a rough diamond! Oh, people of Europe, if you only knew, not for a minute would you hesitate to pack up and settle in this paradise!"[2] Somewhat further on, however, Haraszthy warns his readers that the paradise does not extend over all of North America, nor was it meant for everyone. Florida, for one place, had been overrated. Instead of settling in the South, the immigrant should go west, "to Wisconsin, for example. . . ."[3] It so happened that it was precisely in Wisconsin territory that Haraszthy himself had purchased large tracts of land. Yet he insisted that his original intention in coming to America was not the purchase of real estate, nor any sort of land speculation. And he was wary of the charge of misleading ingenuous immigrants: "In my opinion, those writers who indiscriminately advocate emigration, a dubious undertaking at best, are doing a disservice.... Although I am convinced any sober-minded person could establish his future happiness and even affluence in the United States without too great an effort..., I would not recommend the attempt to anyone who is without determination and a stout heart."[4]

There was nothing underhanded or devious in Haraszthy's endeavor to encourage some (but not all) to emigrate from Hungary and other parts of Europe. His project seems to have jelled already during his first trip to America: "If I wanted to found a city I would have to buy at least 10,000 acres, and immediately build a large inn, a school, several houses, and a grist mill, as well as a sawmill to provide the anticipated poor immigrants from Europe with lumber and other building materials."[5] And no sooner did the thought occur to Haraszthy, than he set about to realize it: "We hired a surveyor to lay out the streets and subdivide the lots; we advertised in the Madison papers for all kinds of craftsmen and for prospective settlers among the immigrants...."[6] Hence his intentions were explicit. And his gross error as regards the statistics on immigration—probably intentional, judging from the fact that the plethora of statistical data elsewhere in his book is mostly accurate—can be dismissed as but a minor instance of manipulation perpetrated for the sake of encouraging readers to follow the author to the United States.

* * * * *

It is surprising that no more than a few thousand Hungarians listened to Haraszthy's summons and took the decision to leave their homeland; for however drastic a solution emigration may be to misery, it should be borne in mind that the people of Haraszthy's native land were victims of stifling internal and external oppression. External, for Hungary was ruled by a foreign dynasty, the Habsburgs, in the interest of a foreign country, Austria; and the Habsburg Monarchy tended to view Hungary not as the see of the dynasty, but as a more or less valuable acquisition, as yet another imperial possession. Hungary was a market for Austrian goods which had but limited access to markets beyond the borders of the Monarchy, whereas capitalist enterprises inside Hungary amounted to only about ten percent of the total number of enterprises within the Empire.[7] Furthermore the rulers of the Monarchy, particularly at this time, in the "Age of Metternich," were fearful of all nationalist or revolutionary symptoms, such as those manifested by elements of the nobility, or by the Hungarian peasants in the aftermath of the devastating cholera epidemic of 1831. The three great conservative powers, Austria, Prussia, and Russia, met at Münchengrätz and in Berlin, in 1833, to revive the Holy Alliance and resolve once again to wage ruthless war on progressive movements within the boundaries of their empires and beyond. It is not surprising, then, that the offer to establish an American consulate in Pest in 1838 (just before Haraszthy was to undertake his journey) was politely but firmly rejected by Metternich: he considered American diplomats "propagandists of the democratic disease."[8] And Metternich was to turn down Count Széchenyi's application for a passport to travel to North America for the same reason.[9] As for Haraszthy, while his name was not unknown to the establishment in Vienna, he was probably too insignificant to be refused a passport.

The deeper evil which determined the fate of most Hungarians, however, was not so much Habsburg domination, but the internal oppression deriving from the feudal conditions which still prevailed. While feudalism had gone out of fashion in Western Europe well before the outbreak of the French Revolution, the Hungarian nobility, and especially the aristocracy, managed to hang on to, and even increase, their inherited privileges. Landowners and the landless gentry, some of the latter hardly distinguishable from the peasant in their mode of life, constituted less than five percent of the population. Even if we were to add the relatively enfranchised population of the "free royal towns," at least ninety percent of the people in Hungary remain unaccounted for. This ninety percent was simply without political existence—they were not part of the "Hungarian nation."[10] As Kölcsey, the poet who wrote the lines of the national anthem, summarized the situation in his diary for 1832: "The constitution must make room for the people, so that ten million of them will regard it as their own and not merely the affair of seven hundred privileged individuals."[11]

Democratic principles, as well as the condition of the serfs are reflected in the writings and activities of the "Reform Generation"—a more or less cohesive group of noblemen and aristocrats who understood the sorry predicament of the souls of Hungary and found inspiration in the conditions that prevailed in Western Europe and the United States. Most prominent among them were Lajos Kossuth, István Széchenyi, Ferenc Deák, Miklós Wesselényi, Lajos Batthyány, Ferenc Kölcsey, and József Eötvös—the Mirabeaux, the Lafayettes, the André Chéniers of the coming Hungarian revolution. Curiously enough, the plans for the bourgeois transformation of society were laid out by progressive nobles and aristocrats acting against their own narrow class interests. Many of them had travelled to France or other "Western" lands and became imbued with the spirit of Western parliamentary democracy (in its still fledgling form) and impressed with Western technology.

The Hungarian lands formed a distinct kingdom with their own national Diet. In 1825 the Diet was convened for the first time in a decade; its members proceeded to challenge Austrian control and agitated for reforms—especially after 1832. Haraszthy, it is said, was a close friend of Kossuth and Wesselényi (and also of Batthyány), two of the more radical agitators. Wesselényi was imprisoned for political reasons shortly before Haraszthy's departure: could there have been a cause and effect relationship? In February 1839 Kossuth himself was sentenced to four years in jail; although, in all fairness, it should be recorded that with the advent of a more liberal turn in Vienna shortly thereafter most political prisoners were released. With the exception of Széchenyi, all the above-mentioned leaders were to take an active part in the Revolution of 1848-1849. Kossuth was to become the leader of the shortlived independent republic and was referred to, in the American press, as "the General Washington of Hungary." In 1851 a vessel was specially dispatched to bring him to this country at public expense, and he was the first foreigner after Lafayette to address the Congress of the United States.[12]

There is no trace of radicalism, however, in the travel book of Haraszthy. Mark Schorer, a critic and novelist who in his novel *A House too Old* portrays the life of generations of German settlers in Wisconsin, devotes the first chapter to the life of a barely disguised likeness of Haraszthy. This hero, upon arrival in Wisconsin, "remembered with pity his friends, the revolutionary leaders, imprisoned by the Viennese court, their cause defeated, less fortunate than himself, who had had money and influence enough to escape with his family and flee to the new land."[13] In many ways Haraszthy's attitude resembled that of Széchenyi, the most conservative member of the Reform Generation, the one who was to remain on the sidelines during the revolution. Although a patriot eventually recognized as "the greatest among the Hungarians," Széchenyi ridiculed the notion that Hungary was the "Garden of Eden on this earth," and that "life was not worth living" outside it. On the very first page of his *Travel* Haraszthy deplores those excessively proud Hungarians who entertain all kinds of delusions and believe their country to be perfect and life beyond its boundaries intolerable; in fact, Haraszthy set out to prove them wrong.

Széchenyi had diagnosed the illness of Hungary as the feudal system. He warned that noble privileges were not identical with real liberties, and that the nobility fell far short of being free and independent (not to mention the peasants who had no political existence whatever), because "only intellectual standing gives real supremacy in this world..."[14] Széchenyi regarded modernization, particularly economic and technological modernization, as the most important concomitant of the struggle against feudalism. His pet projects included the construction of a chain bridge to join the cities of Pest and Buda facing each other across the Danube (the bridge still graces the view of the river beneath the former royal palace), and to render the course of the river navigable all the way from Vienna to the Black Sea. The steamboat, argued Széchenyi, is not for barbarians, but for civilized people. It presupposes a degree of education and the development of a well-to-do middle class. It is incompatible with feudalism under any form.[15] Haraszthy's numerous undertakings in the United States were to include steamship navigation on the Wisconsin River, as we shall see further on.

Little is known of Haraszthy's political activities, if any, in the "old country." There is no evidence that his relationship with Kossuth was close, nor is there any mention of Haraszthy in Kossuth's correspondence, either before the latter's emigration or thereafter. If Haraszthy did mention Kossuth (although not a single Hungarian statesman is named in the travel book), it may simply have been a natural inclination to drop names. Yet, if Haraszthy was hardly "radical" in the contemporary American sense of the term, he certainly was progressive, at least by the standards of the Habsburg Monarchy in the first half of the nineteenth century. His democratic sympathies become evident both in his references to conditions in the United States—a country he insists on calling the Free States of North

America—and in his few, but emotional allusions to conditions in "poor Hungary." Haraszthy seems to have viewed "the masses" and their political ascent far more favorably than the aristocrat from France, de Tocqueville, who had visited these shores exactly ten years earlier. "The whole society seems to have turned into one middle class," noted de Tocqueville perceptively enough, but with a certain lack of enthusiasm,[16] and his pessimistic forebodings regarding the future of American civilization often outweighed his positive impressions. Haraszthy, on the other hand, found little of value in the aristocratic principle of class privilege, at least in the way that principle weighed down on ordinary Hungarians. Whereas he had few if any misgivings about the egalitarianism which seemed to prevail in this country. "In Hungary," wrote Haraszthy, "many of those who wield great power have no more knowledge of economics than they need to count the numbers of their sheep and cattle. . . . They vociferously oppose any progressive idea, their motto being: 'What was good enough for our fathers is good enough for us.' Oh, my unfortunate country! How long will these monsters prevent the flowering of a land so richly endowed by nature!"[17]

In fact, the days of those "monsters" were numbered. In 1848 the revolution broke out in Hungary, as it had in other spots around Europe. The Hungarian Revolution became a war for independence, or of national liberation, and came close to achieving its end. Only in September 1849, long after the revolutionary movements in other parts of Europe had been squashed, were the Hungarian national armies finally brought to their knees by the overwhelming military might of the Russian Empire, to whom the Habsburgs, whose own armies proved unable to cope with the situation, had turned for assistance in order to regain their domains. Ágoston Haraszthy and his family had been exhilarated by the news of the revolution. A Wisconsin historian records that during a celebration at his residence Haraszthy became "so impassioned and enthusiastic" in discussing the revolution "that he lost control of his adopted tongue, and had to talk in his native Hungarian."[18]

* * * * *

Haraszthy claims that, like so many others, he was intrigued by the travelogues about America, and their conflicting interpretations. He came to the conclusion that he "must personally visit this highly praised land, which had been described by countless German, French, and English travelers, and even a Hungarian—Sándor Bölöni Farkas—in so many different ways."[19]

Indeed, the work by Farkas had considerable influence on members of the reform generation. It won the grand prize of the recently established Hungarian Academy of Science, and Farkas himself was elected to membership in that scholarly body.[20] He had visited the United States in 1831-1832, ten years before Haraszthy, at the same time as de Tocqueville. But whereas de Tocqueville came from a land where the bourgeois revolution had already carried the day, hence must have been familiar with the advances of democracy and capitalism, and the concomitant problems, Farkas saw the New World with the eyes of a man living in a feudal state; for him freedom and oppression both seemed timeless principles.[21] Hence the account by Farkas is an uninterrupted paean of praise for this land of freedom and democracy to which he also referred as the "Free States of North America." Indeed, one suspects that Farkas deliberately suspended his critical judgment for the sake of the propaganda effect his book might have on fellow Hungarians back home. The influence of this book on Haraszthy could be demonstrated even if the latter had not given explicit credit to his precursor. It is obvious that Haraszthy follows the itinerary outlined by Farkas up the Hudson River valley and through much of the western part of the state of New York; and Farkas's anecdotes regarding the Niagara Falls are reiterated almost verbatim in Haraszthy's *Travel*.[22]

Even at this late date Hungarian aristocrats tended to look down upon money, upon commercial enterprise, upon business in general, as well as upon manual labor; to Haraszthy, as to Count Széchenyi, none of these activities were demeaning in the least. Haraszthy identifies capitalism with progress and predicts the "greatness and future potential" of North America on such a basis. Back home, in Hungary, the landlords knew next to nothing about economics; or else they would certainly have to know that "the keener the competition, the better it is for the people."[23] In the United States, "to the immense benefit of the public, when a corporation becomes too greedy, competition instantly forces the moderation of the price level..."[24] Clearly, Haraszthy met with American capitalism in its early stage before the monopolies and national or international trusts had changed its configuration.

In fact, Haraszthy was the entrepreneur par excellence, and what freer place to exercise his faculties for enterprise than this land of boundless opportunities, the land where promises come true—the United States of America in the middle of the nineteenth century? "Everybody was a trader" in the United States and "I had no objection to this at all," confessed Haraszthy in Wisconsin.[25] And this is understandable in light of the fact that he sold certain wares he had purchased on the east coast at a 300% profit. At times Haraszthy resembles the free-wheeling heroes of Jack London's stories on the Yukon. At any rate, de Tocqueville's description of the typical American fits Haraszthy fairly well: "Restlessness of character seems to be one of the distinctive traits of this people. The American is devoured by the longing to make his fortune...."[26] If, in the long run, Haraszthy was not quite as successful in business as he might have been, and as some of his fellow immigrants undoubtedly were, it is perhaps because he was burdened by certain qualities not often encountered among typical capitalists of the early nineteenth-century: a proud demeanor, an aristocracy of the spirit.

It was perfectly true that the United States was a land of boundless opportunities for those with the initiative (not the "rugged individualism" of popular parlance) to take advantage of it. Travelers and observant immigrants tended to ascribe the favorable conditions to democracy, to the classless society, to the political power of the common man, to the simplicity of manners. Haraszthy, too, recognized the superiority of democracy, of the levelling process, even though he had not disvested himself completely of aristocratic airs: his acquaintances in Wisconsin seemed to agree that he appeared and behaved just like they imagined a count would and should. But Haraszthy, unlike de Tocqueville, did not deplore "excessive" egalitarianism. On the contrary, he was disappointed by the South where production and industry were lagging because its social elite was not imbued with the same concern for equality.

Yet de Tocqueville, Farkas, Haraszthy, and so many others had largely missed the point: democracy and equality, even if we goodnaturedly assume that these principles did indeed characterize the United States in the first half of the nineteenth century, were not in and of themselves convincing explanations of the peace and prosperity which prevailed over much of the land. Frederick Jackson Turner—it may not be irrelevant to point out—born in 1861 in the very state where Haraszthy had settled when it was still but a "territory" (Wisconsin), offered a more rational, a more satisfactory explanation. Turner wrapped his "frontier thesis" into a certain mysticism about human nature, into a belated Romanticism, exposing himself to facile rebuttals, to attacks from various sides. But shorn of its Romanticism, his argument was simply that the economic and social conditions peculiar to the United States can only be fully understood if we take the West, the American frontier, into consideration: "The men of capital and enterprise come. The settler is ready to sell out and take advantage of the rise in property, push further into the interior and become, himself, a man of capital and enterprise in turn.... Thus wave after wave is rolling westward; the real Eldorado is still further on...."[27] In what way did the frontier impress American culture and history with a distinctive stamp? It was "an area of free land... on the western border of the settled area of the United States. Whenever social conditions tended to crystallize in the East, whenever capital tended to press upon labor or political restraints impede the freedom of the mass, there was this gate of escape to the free conditions of the frontier."[28]

The frontier was not simply the limit of the westward expansion of the United States; it was the western boundary of Europe as well: the western boundary of "Western Civilization," particularly as travel across the ocean was becoming cheaper and easier as a result of the introduction of steam vessels. And though there was an "eastern borderland" of Europe on the other side, and that eastern frontier likewise kept advancing over a period of centuries into Siberia and beyond, it must be conceded that West Europeans and East Central Europeans alike seldom migrated eastward, at least not of their own free will. East Central Europeans, Haraszthy among them, opted for the longer road to the West.

The American frontier explains why industry on the East coast was suffering from a shortage of labor at a time when there was an influx of immigrants. In 1820 the population of the United States was about nine and a half million, that is—if I may be forgiven the incongruity of the comparison—roughly the same as that of the Kingdom of Hungary within the Habsburg Monarchy. But while 350,000 Americans were engaged in manufacture, only about 80,000 Hungarians were employed in workshops and factories. By 1850 the population of the United States had more than doubled, to over 23 million, whereas that of Hungary increased by little over two million. Immigration does not fully account for the soaring rise in the population of the United States, nor does emigration from Hungary account for the relative stagnancy of the population figures there. Life expectancy was also higher in the United States, in more or less direct relationship to the standard of living. Because of the shortage of labor, the real wages in the United States were considerably higher than in other industrialized countries (not to speak of underdeveloped lands such as Hungary). Hence there is a connection, however indirect, between the rise in population and the open frontier.

As illustration of the standard of living in the United States around 1840: the price of wheat was $1.50 per bushel, and a pound of beef cost about 6 cents. According to Haraszthy and others the average per diem pay was 80 cents to a dollar. From this and other data it would appear that eight to twelve cents a day could purchase food for one adult, whereas a day's labor would be sufficient to provide food for three days to a family of six.[29] The gross national product was rising by an estimated 1.5% annually, a rate that was sufficient to keep abreast of the rise in population, and was unequalled elsewhere in the first half of the nineteenth century.[30] The rise in the standard of living and in the GNP was a by-product of the tremendous increase in mechanization and the commensurate rise in productivity.

Progress in technology was constantly spurred by the urge of the industrialist to save on the relatively high cost of labor and remain competitive on the international market. While scientific education and achievement were not yet impressive, Americans were doing imaginative work in the technology of mining and metal processing, in navigation, agriculture, and in the generation and transmission of power. The United States was on the verge of becoming the most technologically advanced nation.[31] Workers in America saw no reason to smash machines, and offered little resistance to technological innovation.

Haraszthy never seems to fail to take note of the technological wonders he encounters, particularly as pertaining to transportation. He is fascinated by railroads, and does not tire of describing them. They were a novelty even in the United States, since the first railroad, the Baltimore and Ohio, went into operation only in 1830, and in 1840 there were still but 2,800 miles of tracks laid in the entire country. On the other hand, in Hungary the construction of the first railroad line was delayed until 1846, partially because of all sorts of objections raised in the Diet, including the argument that trains are dangerous not so much to their passengers, but to the unwary onlooker whose eyesight might become impaired because of exposure to the sight of dazzling speed! Even in the United States accidents were not uncommon: Haraszthy himself tells of being derailed on the Niagara-Buffalo line, because the ties had rotted away, only a few years later the completion of the line.[32]

Haraszthy is equally fascinated by water transportation, whether it be canals, sail or steam vessels (curiously enough, despite his interest in machines, he crossed Atlantic in a packet.) The decade of the forties was the beginning of the age of steam-power. According to a report of the Secretary of Treasury there were, in 1838, 800 steamboats in operation.[33] Haraszthy, whose statistics, as we have seen, are not invariably accurate (but whose very exaggerations are no doubt revealing of his state of mind, of his technological bias, and of the tremendous respect for the machine—a respect he shared with so many of his positivist contemporaries) claims that there were "16,720 steamboats plying the rivers and seas of the Free States," and, most importantly, earning dividends of between fifty and a hundred percent a year![34] Eventually, perhaps under the influence of Széchenyi, jointly with an English friend, Haraszthy purchased a steamer built to navigate the Mississippi and Wisconsin Rivers, for the not inconsiderable sum of $16,000, "to promote" the city he had founded on the banks of the Wisconsin.[35] Haraszthy's steamer, the *Rock River,* carried passengers and freight between Fort Winnebago and Galena, Illinois, the lead mining center, and eventually as far as St. Paul, Minnesota. At least part of the sum invested had come from his successful speculation in real estate. The rental of buildings in the town he had founded yielded 30% annual profit, whereas the lots were selling at about double the sum invested a year earlier, and Haraszthy expected the price to rise tenfold within another year or two.[36] Real estate, Haraszthy discovered, was "surely the safest method of capital investment."[37]

Upon his departure from New York, Haraszthy travelled up the Hudson Valley and the Erie Canal to the Great Lakes. He grew ecstatic over the natural wonder of the Niagara, but he did not tarry. When Farkas and de Tocqueville had visited America, Detroit was an outpost of "civilization," the end of the road. If de Tocqueville decided to penetrate further into Indian country, he must have been prompted by a craving for adventure—not surprising in a young man of twenty-five. By 1840, however, the frontier had advanced far beyond Detroit, into Wisconsin territory. In the census reports the frontier is defined as the margin of that area which has a population density of two or more inhabitants per square mile. The United States west of the Mississippi was considered practically uninhabited; the census takers did not bother to count Native Americans. But the southern fringes of Wisconsin up to the river of the same name already had a population density of more than two (white) persons per square mile.

Haraszthy's *Travel* is filled with figures on population. He provides the readers with statistics on each town of importance he had visited, and is not content with presenting the latest figures, but traces the growth of the town several decades back, decade by decade. Presumably the figures came from the census reports of the United States federal government, but there are occasional discrepancies; thus the population of Philadelphia in 1840 is given as 228,691 whereas the actual figure in the *Census* is but 220,423. It is possible, however, that the 1840 *Census* was not yet in print when Haraszthy was collecting data.

Haraszthy does not explain what led him to Wisconsin, any more than he explains why he came to the United States. Nor are we given an indication of when he actually made up his mind to establish a community. His *Travel* simply avers that the landscape he found there was irresistibly enchanting, a near paradise. When they had reached a certain hill facing Prairie du Sac, Haraszthy and his companions "exclaimed in unison 'Oh, how magnificent!' In truth, the sight was more beautiful than anything I have seen in all my extensive travels in Europe and America."[38] Mark Schorer begins his novel, already quoted, with the arrival of his hero, Count Augustin Karanszcy; the Hungarian Count, wrote Schorer, had already decided to head for Wisconsin before leaving for the United States, on the basis of favorable reports.

Haraszthy founded Sauk City right next to Prairie du Sac, and but a score of miles from the future state capital, Madison. Between 1825 and 1840 there had been a lull in the founding of new communities in the United States; hence it is fair to argue that once again Haraszthy was among the first, a pioneer in more sense than one. He named the town *Széptáj*, but it was soon renamed Haraszthyville. It was to this community that he decided to return, in the summer of 1843, accompanied by his entire family, including parents and children.[39] Eventually "the name of the village was changed [once more], for the older settlers felt that [Haraszthyville] was no proper name...,[and that] it smacked too much of something foreign." Thus they called it Sauk City, after the Sauk (or Sac) Indians who had inhabited the area earlier.[40] When Haraszthy undertook his journey into Indian country, it was partly to befriend the Sac and Fox Indians who had been compelled to retreat from the land he now owned.

Haraszthy's account of his adventures in Indian territory constitute the most exciting chapter of his *Travel*. Yet, it may prove more valuable as a mirror of European attitudes towards the noble savage, than as an anthropological document.

* * * * *

It is a pity Haraszthy did not write an autobiography, or that some powerful poet did not undertake to write his biography, factual or fictionalized, the way Blaise Cendrars had done in his superb epic of John Sutter, the Swiss settler of California, among the very first to cultivate grapes. (To his misfortune, gold was discovered on his land.)[41] For Haraszthy was really the epitome of the pioneer, whose life may be a parable of the westward march. And this march was a long one that stretched from the eastern borderlands of Europe, the easternmost "bastion" of Western Civilization—as Hungarians are wont to call their land—to as far West as one could go, the country around San Francisco. "Migration has become almost a habit in the West" wrote Frederick Jackson Turner. Hundreds of men can be found there, "not over fifty years of age, who have settled for the fourth, fifth, or sixth time on a new spot."[42] Having spent almost eight years in Wisconsin, Haraszthy and his family packed their movable belongings around Christmas of 1848, as the revolutionary regime suffered its first military setback in Hungary. The Haraszthys led the Wisconsin train of "forty-niners" heading toward California, where the goldrush prompted by the discovery on Sutter's land had barely gotten under way. At first, however, Haraszthy did not dig for gold, but settled in the San Diego area long enough to be elected sheriff. Eventually he moved to San Francisco and busied himself with gold, but only as an assayer and director of the United States Mint where he was employed from the very beginning of the Mint's operation in April 1854.[43] He was tried in 1857-58 on charges of embezzlement, and resigned his position even though he was acquitted and exonerated. By that time, however, he had become involved in viticulture, the enterprise on which his fame ultimately rests.

It would not be fair to claim that there was absolutely no wine-making in the United States in the first half of the nineteenth century. Even Farkas, back in 1831, had tasted some local wines in the East, the bouquet of which did not particularly impress him.[44] Haraszthy also gives a hint of his interest in viticulture in his *Travel:* the wine in Ohio, he wrote, is fair "and I do not doubt that wine comparable to our famous Hungarian wines could be made here, if cuttings were imported from Hungary and our methods of cultivation applied. But here they do not understand either the stock or the vine culture. The vines are not pruned and are permitted to spead and grow tall. Cultivation is unheard of and in general viticulture is as unknown here as tea culture would be in Hungary."[45] Although born and raised on the plains of southern Hungary (the Voivodina of present-day Yugoslavia), Haraszthy had often visited his family's estate at Mokcsa in northeastern Hungary, which happens to be near the country's wine producing Tokaj [Tokay] region. It is the same region which produced the "king of wine, and the wine of kings," i.e., the most prestigious and prized wines in eighteenth-century Europe. Hence we may assume that Haraszthy came to the United States with some knowledge in the matter.

As we have seen, Haraszthy was not quite the first to introduce wine to California. In addition to Sutter, the Franciscan fathers at their mission near San Diego had been producing wine for decades, albeit of rather mediocre quality. Jean Louis Vigues, a Frenchman from the Bordeaux region, was successful in transplanting French vinestock to California and produced his first vintage in 1837. Even in the area of the Sonoma Valley, where Haraszthy finally settled with his family, the retired Mexican general, Mariano Guadelupe Vallejo, had preceded him in that endeavor. Nevertheless, Haraszthy deserves major credit for converting

California into a wine-country, and for the fact that California wines can compete with the Bordeaux, the Bourgognes, and other fine wines of Europe.

There, in Sonoma, Harszthy had a "ranch" built, with columns and porticoes, long verandas, and a view equalled by few owners of palaces. "The Prince may boast of a view from his palace," he wrote referring to the Rhenish castle of Prince Metternich, for whom he had no love, "as I can from my ranch in Sonoma; or, rather, I may boast of having scenery equal to that of Prince Metternich. It is true that I have no Rhine River, but in its place there lies the San Pablo Bay."[46]

Yet Haraszthy remained at his "ranch" for hardly a decade. Having cultivated wine with considerable success, but only a modicum of profit, embroiled in litigations, and perhaps tired of leading a sedentary existence, he once again took off in search of new adventures and new frontiers. Not much earlier, in 1856, an adventurer from Tennessee, William Walker, appointed himself president of Nicaragua and was able to remain in power for a year. Haraszthy must have sensed new adventures and new opportunities in Walker's wake. It proved his last adventure. He died not long after his arrival, in 1869. It seems he was attempting to cross a stream by hanging onto the limbs of a tree growing along it bank. But the limb snapped, and he fell into the stream underneath that was infested with alligators. He died the way he lived: adventurously.

Haraszthy was a colorful individual, to be sure. Yet, what makes his life and his travels particularly interesting and valuable is not so much their uniqueness, but rather the extent to which they characterize nineteenth-century America and the American way of life. As Peter Ustinov once quipped: "Americans are always attempting to run away from conformity, but unfortunately they always start running in the same direction."[47] Haraszthy was also running in the same direction, although a bit ahead of most others. In spite of his blue blood, the nobility of his character, his eccentricities, his bravery, his humanity, and his occasional lack of it, he was very much a child of his century as seen from the vantage point of expanding America.

NOTES

1. Edward Channing, *A History of the United States* (5 vols., New York: Macmillan, 1921), V, p. 469.

2. *Utazás Éjszak-Amerikában* [Travels in North America] (2 vols., Pest, 1844), I. p. 98. The quotations are from Theodore Shoenman's translations, soon to be published.
3. Ibid., p. 115.
4. Ibid., p. 116.
5. Ibid., p. 66.
6. Ibid., p. 67.
7. Ervin Pamlényi, ed., *A History of Hungary* (London: Collet, 1975; Budapest: Corvina, 1973), p. 236.
8. George Barany, *Stephen Széchenyi and the Awakening of Hungarian Nationalism, 1791-1841* (Princeton: Princeton University Press, 1968), p. 425.
9. Béla K. Király and George Barany, eds., *East Central European Perception of Early America* (Lisse, The Netherlands: Peter de Ridder Press, 1977), p. 112.
10. Barany, *Széchenyi*, p. 185.
11. Quoted in Pamlényi, *History*, p. 229.
12. Istvan Deak, *The Lawful Revolution: Louis Kossuth and the Hungarians, 1848-1849* (New York: Columbia University Press, 1979).
13. New York: Reynal & Hitchcock, 1935, p. 4.
14. Barany, *Széchenyi*, p. 219.
15. Ibid., p. 269.
16. *Journey to America* (London: Faber and Faber, 1959), p. 274.
17. Haraszthy, *Utazás*, p. 46.
18. Verne Seth Pease, "Ágoston Haraszthy," *Proceedings of the State Historical Society of Wisconsin*, 4th Annual Meeting (Madison, Wisconsin, 1970), p. 242. For other studies on Haraszthy see Paul Fredericksen, "The Authentic Haraszthy Story," reprinted from *Wines and Vines* (1947), 11 pp.; Zoltán Sztáray, *Haraszthy Ágoston a kaliforniai szőlőkultúra atyja* [Ágoston Haraszthy, the Father of California Grape Culture] (San Bernandino, Cal., 1964); and Péter Szente, "Egy elfelejtett amerikás magyar—Haraszthy Ágoston" [A Forgotten Hungarian American—Ágoston Haraszthy], *Századok* [Centuries], CXII (1978), pp. 110-124.
19. Haraszthy, *Utazás*, pp. 8-9.
20. George Barany, "The Appeal and the Echo," in *East Central European Perception of Early America*, p. 124.
21. Alfred A. Reisch, "Sándor Bölöni Farkas's Reflections on American Political and Social Institutions," in ibid., p. 71.

22. Sándor Bölöni Farkas, *Utazás Észak-Amerikában* [Journey in North America] (Kolozsvár: Tilsch János, 1934), p. 193.
23. Haraszthy, *Utazás*, p. 2.
24. Ibid., p. 7.
25. Ibid., p. 65.
26. A. de Tocqueville, *Journey*, p. 182.
27. Frederick Jackson Turner, "The Significance of the Frontier in American History," in *The Turner Thesis*, ed. by George Rogers Taylor (Lexington: D.C. Heath, 1972), p. 16.
28. Ibid., p. 41.
29. Channing, *History*, V, p. 97.
30. Russell Blaine Nye, *Society and Culture in America, 1830-1860* (New York: Harper & Row), p. 272.
31. Ibid., p. 259.
32. Haraszthy, *Utazás*, p. 38.
33. Nye, *Society and Culture*, p. 272.
34. Haraszthy, *Utazás*, p. 3.
35. Ibid., p. 68.
36. Ibid.
37. Ibid., p. 53.
38. Ibid., p. 65.
39. Pease, "Ágoston Haraszthy," p. 232.
40. Schorer, *A House Too Old*, p. 18.
41. The title of Blaise Cendrars's epic is *L'Or*.
42. Turner, "Frontier," p. 16.
43. Documents pertaining to Haraszthy's activities can be found among the General Records of the Department of Treasury, Record Group 56; Records of the Bureau of Mint, Record Group 104; Division of Special Agents, Records of the United States Customs Service, Record Group 36; and the Records of the Bureau of Accounts, Record Group 39; all in the National Archives, Washington, D.C.
44. Farkas, *Utazás*, p. 239.
45. Haraszthy, *Utazás*, p. 48.
46. Theodore Shoenman, ed., *Father of California Wine: Ágoston Haraszthy. Including Grape Culture, Wines and Wine-Making* (Santa Barbara, Ca.: CAPRA, 1979), p. 40.
47. Billington, "Frontier Democracy, Social Aspects," in *The Turner Thesis*, p. 162.

S. B. Vardy

THE GREAT ECONOMIC IMMIGRATION FROM HUNGARY: 1880-1920

Up to the Civil War and for a while even beyond, most of the Hungarians who came to America were either travellers and adventurers, or—as in the case of Kossuth and his followers—political immigrants. True, there were a few exceptions to this rule, for even in the late eighteenth and early nineteenth century we find those who came simply because of the unique economic opportunities offered by the young American Republic. But the number of these were few and far between. Thus, as late as the 1870s, the Hungarian-American community scattered throughout this land consisted almost exclusively of the political emigrants of the Revolution of 1848-49 and of their native-born descendants. Few would have thought even then that within less than a decade a new wave of Hungarians would hit the American shores and inundante this land in such great numbers that their predecessors, who numbered four to five thousand, would simply lose themselves in this sea of compatriots.[1]

This new wave of Hungarian immigrants, however, was made up of totally different kinds of people than those who came between 1849 and the Civil War. The new immigrants came not because of political, but almost exclusively because of economic reasons. The majority of them were young men of the peasant stock, who took to the sea simply to escape from the economic hardships of their native land. They hoped to return to Hungary with sufficient money to be able to buy land and to resume their lives as peasants and farmers. Some of them did return to their mother country, but most of them—for various economic, political and social reasons—remained in the United States. And in this way, although unintentionally, they became the founders of the sizable Hungarian American community, which even today numbers close to 700,000 members.

The great Hungarian emigration during the three and a half decades between 1880 and 1914 was a phenomenon that was not unique to Hungary. It was part of the general intra- and intercontinental migrations that characterized Europe and much of the Western World during that phase of the industrial revolution and the rising free economic system or capitalism. Moreover, within its European context, the Hungarian migration was only of a medium intensity.[2] Of course there had been mass migrations before. But during the previous three or four centuries these migrations were usually the results of religious persecutions and of the search for new frontiers. Nor were they on such a huge scale as the migrations of the nineteenth and the early twentieth century, when the growth of industrialization and the spread of the free economic system produced increasing disparities between the industrially advanced states and the traditional agricultural countries. After a period of painful readjustment, the former were able to increase wages much more rapidly than the latter and thus improved significantly the quality of life for their workers. Consequently, they began to serve as magnets for the underpaid and often underutilized workers of the less-industrialized states.

During the nineteenth century, this phenomenon of mass migration was basically limited to the Europeans, whose primary destination was the United States, which appeared increasingly as the most viable and the most promising among the new non-European countries. Thus, between 1820 and 1914 the United States received over thirty million immigrants, nearly 93 percent of whom were Europeans. During the first and middle part of the nineteenth century these immigrants came largely from western and northern Europe, but by the last third of that century the southern and east Europeans began to outnumber them, and in the first decade of the twentieth century the latter came to constitute 70.8% of the European immigrants to this country. The majority of these "new immigrants" were peasants and farmers who, upon leaving their countries, also left their traditional way of life. Once arriving in the United States they usually settled in the urban centers and in the industrial-mining regions of the country, and thus joined America's growing industrial labor force.

This basic trend also holds true for the majority of the Hungarian immigrants, nearly 90% of whom were of the peasant stock, and almost all of whom became low-paid industrial workers or miners in the United States. This basic pattern remained unchanged right into the interwar period, when the social composition of the much reduced number of immigrants from Hungary underwent a drastic and visible change.

The Three Stages of Economic Immigration

The primary reason for the great Hungarian immigration around the turn of the century was basically the nascent Hungarian industry's inability to use effectively all of those peasants who had been displaced from the countryside and were now streaming into the cities and lesser industrial centers. As noted above, the first major wave of this migration had reached the American shores around 1880, even though the roots of this movement reach back to the early 1850s. Thus, although Hungarian historians generally view the decades following the Hungarian Revolution of 1848-49 largely as a period of political emigration, the same period also saw the beginnings of an almost imperceptible economic emigration from the country. This economic emigration was directed mostly to the neighboring countries, but then increasingly also toward the United States. In light of the above, in the period up to World War I we can distinguish three separate stages in the Hungarian economic immigration to this country: The first between 1849 and 1880, the second between 1880 and 1900, and the third between 1900 and 1914.[3]

During the first of these stages, emigration for economic reasons was still rather sporadic, and perhaps partially for this reason statistical data on this early wave of emigrants are few and mostly unreliable. We know of its existence only from a few contemporary governmental documents and newspaper reports relating particularly to some of Hungary's northern counties. According to these sources, many thousands were apparently leaving the country already in the 1850s and 1860s for economic reasons, although only a fraction of these emigrants ended up in the United States. Contemporary US statistics, for example, which were at that time very unreliable, record only 488 Hungarian immigrants for the decade of the 1860s. In the following decade the pace of this emigration picked up visibly, and this is also reflected in US statistics, according to which, in the period between 1871 and 1880, 13,375 Hungarian citizens settled in the United States. This emigration, however, was still limited to Hungary's northern regions, more specifically to the largely German-speaking burghers of the counties of Sáros and Zemplén, and to a lesser degree to those of the counties of Abaúj-Torna, Ung and Szepes.

It was during this period, in consequence of this early economic emigration, for example, that the earliest Hungarian economic immigrants settled in Cleveland, Ohio, which subsequently developed into the second largest, but the most compact Hungarian-American community in North America.[4] The first of these immigrants were probably the members of the Black family (who originally were probably called "Schwartz"), who arrived in 1851, to be followed a few years later by the Deutsch brothers, by Soma Schweiger, and by many others of lesser significance. In their wake came Tivadar Kundtz in 1873, whose original small machine shop on Cleveland's East Side soon grew into one of the major machine factories of that industrial city. Ultimately, Kundtz's factory employed many thousands of Hungarian immigrants and became one of the focal points of Hungarian community life in Cleveland during the turn of the century.[5]

The second phase of this economic emigration from Hungary during the last two decades of the nineteenth century saw a radical rise in the number of immigrants from a few hundred to tens of thousands per year. During this period, the emigration fever in Hungary gradually spread from the country's northern regions to such Transdanubian counties of Western Hungary as Moson, Veszprém, Győr and Vas, as well as the Transylvania in the east. According to contemporary American statistics—which probably reflect only about two-thirds of the actual number of immigrants—in 1880 over eight thousand (8,135) Hungarians entered the United States, and by 1900 their number exceeded forty thousand (40,963) per year. These last two decades of the century also served as the period when the foundations of a lasting Hungarian-American community and communal life were laid down. Thus, this period witnessed the establishment of the first significant Hungarian social and cultural organizations, the foundation of the first lasting newspapers, churches, theater groups and glee clubs, and most importantly, the creation of the first Hungarian fraternal associations and aid societies.[6] To quote another historian—these decades constituted "the Hungarian Middle Ages in America," when the foundations of this ethnic group's separate little world were firmly established in the New World.[7]

It has been estimated that during the half a century that encompasses the first and the second phases of Hungarian economic emigration about half a million persons have left Hungary, of whom by far the greatest number ended up in the United States. If we accept the figure of 86%—which is the known American share of this emigration during the subsequent period[8]—then the number of Hungarian immigrants to the United States in the second half of the nineteenth century must have been around 430,000.

The third phase of this Hungarian economic emigration lasted from 1900 to 1914, and it was abruptly terminated by the outbreak of World War I. It lasted for less than a decade and a half, yet it saw the coming of more Hungarian immigrants to the United States than all of the other years put together, from the sixteenth century to our own days. According to recent calculations—based both on American and Hungarian statistics, as well as on the data from the major European points of embarkation—between 1899 and July 1914 nearly one and a half million (1,463,592) persons have left Hungary, of whom 86% (1,260,000) ended up in the United States.[9] This amounted to about 75,000 US-bound emigrants per year, which was more than the entire population of some of Hungary's northern counties of that period. In the year 1907 alone—which was the peak of this population flood to the New World—as many as 185,000 Hungarian citizens, (86% of the 209,169 who have left Hungary) or close to 1% of the country's total population, may have landed on America's shores.[10] Migration on such a mass scale was a phenomenon that was bound to affect the position and attitude of the Hungarians both here and in the mother country. Fortunately or unfortunately, the outbreak of World War I ended this human flood abruptly, and the postwar years created a totally new situation, which prevented the repetition of the events of the pre-war decades.

The Problem of Repatriation

Although they came in unprecedented numbers, most of the economic immigrants did not come with the intention of settling permanently. For this reason, until the calamities of the war, repatriation was also a common phenomenon among the Hungarian immigrants. As a matter of fact, a number of them emigrated and repatriated several times and thereby made even more chaotic the already unreliable emigration-immigration statistics both in Hungary and in the United States.[11] Even so—on the basis of Hungarian statistics for the years 1899-1913—we can safely assume that about 25% of the immigrants returned to the mother country. The peak of this repatriation from the New World was reached in 1908, which was a bi-product of the slump in iron ore mining and steel production in the United States. In that year, the number of repatriates almost equalled the number of the immigrants (i.e., 96.3% returned), while in the northern county of Sáros the former outnumbered the latter by nearly 50% (i.e., 148% returned).[12] According to recent calculations, of the roughly two million emigrants who left Hungary between 1849 and 1914 (most of whom ended up in the United States), between 450,000 to 500,000 returned to their native country. At the same time, however, about one-fifth of these repatriates (i.e., 100,000 persons) re-migrated once more to the United States. This means that of the many hundreds of thousands who left Hungary up to 1914 with the intention of returning home, about 80% ultimately settled (or returned to settle) in the United States. Moreover, even those who intended to return after World War I were ultimately prevented from doing so by the new and unexpected political and economic realities in their homeland—be those in truncated post-Trianon Hungary, or in one of the newly created "Succession States."

The National Composition of the Hungarian Immigrants

As pointed out above, the total number of Hungarian immigrants to the United States prior to July 1914 was in the vicinity of 1.7 million (i.e., 430,000 up to 1899 and an additional 1,260 up to 1914), while another 300,000 settled in various other European and overseas countries. But these figures are misleading, for they do not reflect the actual number

The Great Economic Immigration

of real Hungarians (i.e., those who spoke Magyar as their native tongue) who came and settled in this country.

Through much of its history, but especially in the post-Turkish period since the late seventeenth century, the Kingdom of Hungary was a multinational state. Many of its fringe areas were inhabited by non-Magyar speaking nationalities, who, under the influence of modern nationalism, began to consider themselves increasingly as non-Hungarians, i.e., as Slovaks, Rusyns (Ruthenians), Romanians, Serbs, Slovenes, etc. Hungary also had a sizable German minority, who were either urban dwellers who had settled in Hungary during the late Middle Ages, or well-to-do farmers, such as the "Swabians" who migrated into the country during the eighteenth century. Moreover, Hungary's associated state of Croatia, which had become part of Hungary as early as the late eleventh century, was populated largely by Croats (62.5%), along with a number of other nationalities (e.g., Italians, Serbians, as well as Magyars). Thus, in the period under consideration, the Magyar-speaking Hungarians made up only about half of the country's population (including Croatia), although, according to the census of 1910, their share in the population of Hungary proper (without Croatia) was about 54.5%. At the same time the share of the other nationalities was as follows: 16.1% Romanians, 10.7% Slovaks, 10.4% Germans, 2.5% Ruthenians, 2.5% Serbians, 1.1% Croats, and the remaining 2.2% divided among all of the other smaller nationalities. In the case of "Greater Hungary" (including Croatia), this ratio among the various nationalities was altered only slightly, with the Magyars making up 50%, and all the other nationalities put together the other 50% of the population (i.e., 14% Romanians, 9.4% Slovaks, 9% Germans, 8.6% Croats, 5% Serbians, 2% Ruthenians, and 2% for the remaining nationalities).[13]

Naturally, Hungary's multinational character was also reflected in the ethnic-linguistic composition of its citizens who emigrated to the United States—although not necessarily in direct ratio to their relative size in the mother country. Contrary to earlier views expressed by Hungarian historians, we now believe that the share of the Magyars in this emigration was considerably less than their share in the country's population. The specific percentage is unknown, although recent calculations have pushed it down to as far as 31.8%[14] and even 28.9%.[15] The latter figure, however, appears to be far too low, for it is considerably below contemporary US statistics on the country's foreign born population. The US census of

1910, for example, clearly shows that in that year the immigrant Magyars made up 46% of the nationalities stemming from Hungary.[16] At the same time, the next two largest nationalities—the Slovaks and the Germans—constituted only 21.8% and 14.8%, respectively. This seems to indicate that the Hungarian statistics concerning the period between 1899 and 1913—on which the above low figures are based—are incomplete and unreliable. This is all the more likely as immigration statistics do not really reflect the actual number of immigrants. As a matter of fact, we now believe that one-fourth to one-third of the Hungarian immigrants left the country illegally, and that within their ranks there were many more Magyars than non-Magyars. The reason for the latter claim is that Hungarian authorities were generally much more reluctant to grant exit permits to Magyars than to non-Magyars, for the latter's emigration was often viewed as a desirable phenomenon from the point of view of Hungary's national unity and territorial integrity.[17]

If we accept the figure of 1.7 million as the number of those Hungarian citizens who immigrated and eventually settled in the United States prior to 1914, then, on the basis of the above-mentioned percentages, the number of the Magyars among them must have been somewhere between 500,000 and 780,000. For the sake of compromise, and because it is really impossible to arrive at completely reliable figures, we will accept a number between these two extremes. Thus, we shall presume that the number of Magyars who immigrated to this country during the six and a half decades between 1849 and 1914 was around 650,000. This seems to be a rather conservative and acceptable estimate—all the more so as it is still significantly below many of the earlier estimates. If we add to this the approximately 200,000 Hungarians who came to the United States between 1914 and 1982, then we have a total Magyar immigration of around 850,000.

It should also be pointed out here that—contrary to many earlier claims—recent research indicates that the fundamental causes of emigration were basically identical with all of the nationalities of old Hungary. These included such "push" and "pull" factors as the social and economic conditions in the mother country and the economic opportunities offered by the United States. Thus, while there may have been some changes in the comparative ratio among the various immigrating nationalities, the peak of this immigration in every instance was reached between 1905 and 1907. This also applies to the process of repatriation, which peaked for every nationality in 1908, and was the direct result of the economic woes in this country. It should also be noted here that while the centers of the emigration fever in Hungary have moved from region to region, this fever was the direct result of the economic conditions in the affected areas of the country. It may have been the result of agricultural failures, of the lack of sufficient industrialization, of the cessation of public works that were initiated after the Compromise of 1867, or of the combination of any or all of these factors, which had a negative impact on the economic well-being of the population. To these must be added the increasing awareness of the economic opportunities in the "promised land" beyond the sea. In modern terms, the situation may be compared to the recent streaming of the Mexican "wetbacks" into this country, or to the similar influx of the Italian, Yugoslav and Turkish "Gastarbeiter" into West Germany during the 1960s and early 1970s. The various economic "pull" and "push" factors that were bearing upon them and influencing their decisions to leave their native lands, at least temporarily, were identical in both instances.

The Social Composition of the Immigrants

Contrary to the political emigrations that preceded and followed the great economic emigration of the late nineteenth and early twentieth century, the latter was primarily a peasant migration. In other words, the great majority of the Hungarian immigrants of whatever mother tongue who came to this country between 1870 and 1914 were largely of the peasant stock; perhaps even more so than revealed by official statistics. They were the people who had been displaced from their traditional agricultural pursuits by the dislocations that accompanied the economic changes following the Compromise of 1867. Having been made superfluous in their native village, and finding no meaningful employment opportunties in the country's industrial centers, they were forced to seek their fortunes abroad, particularly in the United States.[18]

Although neither American, nor Hungarian statistics are fully reliable, we nonetheless have sufficient data to come up with an acceptable consensus on the percentage of those immigrants who were basically of the peasant class. According to Hungarian statistics concerning the peak years of 1905-1907, for example, we know that 17% of the immigrants from Greater Hungary (including Croatia) were smallholders and 51.6% were landless agricultural workers, making a total of 68.6%. To this must be added such other categories as "day laborers" (9.5%) and "household servants" (5.2%), who are known to have been in contemporary Hungary almost exclusively of peasant background. And this also applies to a sizeable portion (perhaps half) of the category of "unskilled industrial workers and day laborers" (11.3%), many of whom were only recent immigrants from the villages.[19] All this adds up to about 89% (i.e. 68.9 + 9.5 + 5.2 + 5.7) of all of the immigrants. For Hungary proper (without Croatia) this same ratio is 88.3%, while for Croatia alone it is 92.3%.[20]

To a number of researchers these figures may appear to be too high. (István Rácz, for example, believes that only 75-80% of the immigrants were of the peasant stock.)[21] But this disagreement is more apparent than real. It is simply a question of what made one into a "peasant" versus an "industrial worker" in contemporary Hungary. In this connection one should note that, because of Hungary's relatively late industrialization drive, a great majority of the cuntry's industrial day laborers, and even many of its industrial workers, were really ex-peasants, who were only a few years removed from their peasant past. As such, their way of life and mentality was hardly different from that of a typical Hungarian peasant, all the more so as a good number of them were only seasonal industrial day laborers. Thus, even if they appear in contemporary statistical tables in columns other than those reserved for the peasantry, in reality we should still deal with them as with peasant immigrants, i.e., ex-villagers who were totally alien to America's large urban centers, and who thus displayed all the fears and all the basic attitudes of the simple and unsophisticated peasants of contemporary East Central Europe. That this was so, i.e., that nearly 90% of the contemporary Hungarian immigrants had peasant or near-peasant backgrounds, is also substantiated by numerous contemporary observers on both sides of the Atlantic. They spoke of this migration almost exclusively as the movement of the peasants.[22] This was particularly true for the impoverished northeastern counties of contemporary Hungary (e.g. Máramaros), from where nearly 90% of the immigrants (i.e. 88.7% in 1900 and 80% in 1907) were in the category of landless agricultural proletariat.[23]

The Causes of Peasant Emigration

Although the percentage of the peasants among the immigrants was overwhelming, and the landless agrarian proletariat constituted over half of their numbers, they still contained a sizable percentage of independent landed peasants. Thus in the period between 1905 and 1907 they constituted 17% of the immigrants from Hungary including Croatia, and 10.6% without Croatia. The reason behind the emigration of these landed peasants was the fragmentation of the holdings to a point where they were simply unable to support an average peasant family. In looking at the available statistics on some of Hungary's Transdanubian counties (e.g. Vas County in 1914), we find that most of these landed immigrants came from families who held only 4 to 5 *hold*s[24] (c. 6-7 acres) of land. Fewer came from families with 5 to 15 *hold*s (c. 7-21 acres), and very few from those with holdings of 15 or more *hold*s (i.e. 21 or more acres). Those with the smallest holdings tried to supplement their income by hiring themselves out as day laborers to the nearby large estates. Many times, however, this was impossible because of the oversupply of labor. Thus, the only avenue still open to them was to emigrate, with the hope that in a few years' time they would be able to return with sufficient money to buy enough additional lands to support their families.

Insofar as there were emigrations from families with large holdings (i.e. those with 15 or more *hold*s in Transdanubia, and 30 or more *hold*s in the lowlands), this migration was usually limited to the breadwinners of the largest families (i.e. those with six or more children). Their ranks were also swelled by those sons of well-to-do peasant families who were pushed down into the lower ranks through the process of dividing the originally large holdings among several siblings. In such instances some of the brothers gave up their holdings altogether, in return for their siblings' willingness to pay for their transportation costs to America. They did this with the hope that within a few years they would be able to purchase much larger holdings, and thus return into the ranks of the well-to-do peasants.[25]

In addition to being pushed by the lack of sufficient outside work opportunities, these smallholders were also forced to opt for emigration because of their growing indebtedness. Eventually, with several bad agricultural years in sequence, this indebtedness reached the point where many of them were simply deprived of their lands. The only alternative left to them was to seek their fortunes abroad. We know of such examples by the hundreds, particularly from the country's western and northwestern regions.

If economic factors were responsible for forcing a sizable portion of the landed peasants to emigrate, this was even more true for the landless agricultural proletariat, and for the similarly landless and hapless members of the ex-peasant or near-peasant urban day laborers and household servants. Thus, the main factors behind this mass emigration included agricultural overpopulation, the Hungarian industry's inability to employ the displaced peasantry, and the merciless application of the law of supply and demand, which often pushed wages as well as agricultural prices down to an unbearable level.

Like most European countries, in the period between the mid-nineteenth century and 1914, Hungary had also experienced a demographical explosion, even though this explosion was not nearly as steep as in the case of some of the West European states. In the case of Hungary, this growth between 1857 and 1910 was 54.5% (from 12,124,000 to 18,737,000; with Croatia from 13,768,000 to 20,886,000), which averaged out to an annual growth of 0.82% and 0.79% respectively. Although this rate of growth cannot be regarded as extraordinary for those years, because of a major demographic shift that accompanied this growth, the decade of the 1890s and early 1900s witnessed a sudden increase in the young age group whose members were at the peak of their work capacity. Thus, while during the 1880s the 15 to 19 and the 20 to 24 age groups registered a numerical increase of only 1.4% each, in the decade between 1890 and 1900 their natural increase shot up by 26.4% and 11.9% respectively.[26] This sudden increase of manpower in such a short timespan was a phenomenon that the cumbersome Hungarian economy was unable to deal with. It would have caused major dislocations even in much more advanced and much more flexible economies than that of late nineteenth century Hungary. Thus, the only available safety value for many members of this young generation was mass emigration to the United States.

This demographic explosion at the turn of the century was a most important catalyst of Hungarian immigration to this country. Yet, it was not the only one. A factor of almost equal importance was the agricultural workers' inability to shift into native industries, which contemporary

Hungarian society and economy was unable to supply. This is best demonstrated by comparing the growth of industrial workers during those years with the number of immigrants. In the period betwen 1880 and 1910 the number of industrial workers increased by 88,00 in the first decade, by 230,000 in the second decade, and by 260,000 in the third decade, i.e. by a total of 578,000, which is only one-third of the number of immigrants in the same period. If we apply this formula to the most critical first decade of the twentieth century alone, then the ratio between the increase in industrial workers (260,000) and the number of peasant and near-peasant immigrants (1.1 million) is about 4:1.[27] This seems to indicate—particularly in light of the still relatively low Hungarian population density—that this emigration was due perhaps less to real overpopulation, than to the lack of sufficient economic opportunities for the displaced peasantry. To this must be added, of course, their increased awareness about the significantly greater opportunities in the United States.

And herein comes the so-called "pull factor" as a significant cause of this mass emigration from Hungary, i.e. the growing awareness that in the United States one can earn much more in a comparatively brief period of time. This awareness originated from a wide variety of sources. These included letters by earlier immigrants who spoke of hitherto unheard of opportunities;[28] professional emigration agents hired by the large shipping companies (e.g. Hamburg-Amerikanische Paketfahrt Actien-Gesellschaft, Norddeutscher Lloyd, Cunard Lines, etc.) who made it easy even for the simple villagers to emigrate; reports in various local and national papers concerning the economic advantages of going to America; as well as the stories of repatriates, many of whom went home well-healed, self-assured and full of marvelous experiences in the land of opportunities beyond the sea.[29]

Although these stories about America were often inflated and colored beyond recognition, unique economic opportunities did in fact exist in the new American Republic. As a matter of fact, wages in the United States were about five or six times higher than in Hungary;[30] and this holds true even for the early twentieth century when—contrary to popular assumptions—there were also some real and noticeable economic improvements in Hungary.[31] In fact, one of the interesting aspects of this mass exodus was that "the highest level of emigration from Hungary coincided almost completely with economic improvements . . . . However, by this time the idea of emigration had penetrated so deeply into the people's minds . . . that the slight improvement in Hungarian economic conditions failed to produce results which might have been expected. . . . The period of immense prosperity in the USA [simply] proved to be a [too] formidable adversary . . . , frustrating every domestic effort to halt emigration."[32] This pull factor may in fact have been even more significant than the lack of sufficient economic opportunities in Hungary. The difference in the opportunities offered by the two countries was simply too great to have been overcome by the prospective emigrants' basic attachments to the land of their birth. And this holds true notwithstanding the fact that, once reaching the American shores, the newcomers were neatly pushed into the next-to-last layer of the urban working class, just one notch above the still not fully emancipated Blacks.

Although the various economic considerations were the primary and almost exclusive causes of emigration from Hungary, a few other factors may also have played a role.[33] One that is generally mentioned is the so-called "nationality question," even though we are now well aware that this factor had very little to do with the mass migration at the turn of the century. Yet, the relative higher percentage of the non-Magyars among the immigrants still compels us to look at this so-called "nationality factor" even though the ups and downs in the size of this emigration were basically identical for all of the nationalities. In other words, the levels of their exodus from Hungary all peaked and all had their low points at about the same time.[34] Simultaneously, however, a much larger percentage of the Slovaks (20.2%), Ruthenians (11.6%), Germans (11.5%) and Romanians (6.8%) emigrated than Magyars (3.8%),[35] which—notwithstanding the tendency to do so—should not be attributed to their alleged economic and political plight as compared to the latter. The best proof of this is the comparison between the Germans and the Ruthenians, both of whom emigrated in the same percentage, even though there was a great deal of disparity in their social and economic positions. As a matter of fact the Germans were the wealthiest and best-healed of Hungary's nationalities (considerably above the Magyars), while the Ruthenians were on the lowest social and economic rung in the country. In light of the above, therefore, the answer to this puzzle must be sought not so much in the "nationality problem" (which was almost exclusively the "problem" of the intelligentsia and not of the peasantry), but rather in what one of the recent researchers called the "differences in [the] attitudes of the individual nationalities toward emigration."[36] In other words, because of their different historical traditions, ways of life and economy, compounded by the impact of geographical-topographical factors, some nationalities were used to the idea of periodic and seasonal migrations. Thus, while the Germans and the Romanians have long histories of periodic migrations throughout the late medieval and early modern periods, and whereas a sizable portion of the Slovaks and the Ruthenains became migrant workers in the eighteenth and the nineteenth centuries, the Magyars generally refused to be dislodged from their birthplaces. Nor did they become migrant workers in any great numbers as their neighbors in the northern highlands of Hungary. As such, while the coming of the Slovaks, Ruthenians, Germans and Romanians to America was simply another step in their accepted way of life, to the Magyars the idea of leaving their homeland for a new and strange world was much less acceptable.

Nor should we forget the role and significance of the family ties and other close relationships in this mass migration to the New World. A few early emigrants from a specific locality often served as powerful magnets to others from the same family, village or geographical region. And because most of the early economic immigrants of the 1870s and 1880s were non-Magyars, it was the Slovaks, Ruthenians, Germans and Romanians who established the trend for migration in an area and also set the standards of the local intensity of this migration. The Magyars began their migration later, and their exodus was blunted to some degree by the Hungarian Government's efforts to put an end to it. Subsequently their emigration was halted by the outbreak of the First World War, and then almost terminated by the United States quota system introduced during the early 1920s.

The Emigration of the Urbanites and the Intellectuals

While close to 90% of the Hungarian immigrants were peasants or near-peasant urban day laborers and household servants, at least 10% or more were of the non-peasant category. As a matter of fact, the same Hungarian statistics for the years 1905-1907 on which the above calculations are based categorize 15% of the emigrants under various non-peasant headings. These categories included miners (1.2%), independent craftsmen (2.2%), independent merchants (0.3%), and unskilled industrial workers and day laborers (11.3%). But if we deduce half of the latter category as being essentially peasants or near-peasants (5.7%), the above "industrial-merchant-worker" category is reduced to a mere 9.3%. The remaining 1.7% (if we accept the "peasant" category as being 89%) was made up of intelligentsia (0.5%) and of various other persons of unknown occupations (1.2%), some of whom were doubtlessly also of peasant background.[37] On the basis of the above figures we can safely assume that of the nearly 1.7 million Hungarian citizens who emigrated to and settled in the United States prior to 1914, about 90% were basically in the "peasant" and 10% in the "non-peasant" categories.

The question that still remains to be discussed in this connection is the basic social composition of those in the non-peasant category. US statistics concerning the years 1900-1913 identify forty-nine different occupational skills among the Magyar-speaking immigrants. These can be categorized into several occupational areas, such as the leather industry (shoremakers, bootmakers, tanners, furriers, etc.), the textile industry (spinners, weavers, textile makers, taylors, etc.), the wood industry (carvers, decorators, furniture makers, etc.), the paper industry, the iron and steel industry, the glass industry, the milling and food industry (millers, sugar makers, chocolate makers, etc.), the mining industry, as well as such diverse craftsmen as watchmakers, bakers, barbers, carpenters, upholsterers, tinners, butchers, innkeepers, hoteliers, pastry makers, locksmiths, taylors, printers, blacksmiths, silversmiths, goldsmiths, rope makers, lathe operators, wheelwrights, carriage and wagon makers, coopers, barrel makers, etc.[38] The emigration of independent craftsmen and industrial workers affected the whole of Hungary. Yet, proportionately many more craftsmen emigrated from Transylvania and from sections of Northern Hungary than from the country's other regions. We believe this to be the result of the fact that Hungary's nascent industry was more able to absorb the underutilized representatives of the traditional crafts in the country's central and western regions, than in its eastern and northern reaches, where industrialization was proceeding at a slower pace.

While the great majority of the non-peasant immigrants from Hungary were in the craftsmen-industrial workers category, both American and Hungarian statistics also speak of a small category of "intellectuals." This was a very small group, whose numbers in the course of the half century

The Great Economic Immigration

preceding 1914 was no more than six to seven thousand, i.e. less than 0.5% of the total number of immigrants. According to US Census of 1910, for example, in that year there were only 1,739 persons in the category of Hungarian-born intellectuals. That was less than 0.4% of those 495,609 persons who were born in Hungary, although nearly 0.8% of the Magyar-speaking among these foreign born Hungarian immigrants.[39]

In assessing the meaning of the low percentage of the so-called "intellectuals" among the Hungarian immigrants, one should keep in mind that in those days the United States and American society in general had very little drawing power for the educated Europeans. Thus, unless forced by circumstances—such as political or personal reasons—they would seldom opt to come to this land of the hardy self-made men, where a person's stature and position in society depended not so much on his diplomas or titles, as on what he could make of himself through his own abilities. Even so, during the latter part of the period under consideration, i.e., during the 1890s and early 1900s, we find an increasing number of educated people among the Hungarian immigrants. And contrary to Kossuth and his followers, these came not for political reasons, but either to serve their people (e.g., priests, preachers, teachers, journalists, etc.) or to try their fortunes in this land of great opportunities (e.g. engineers, architects, artists, musicians, lawyers, physicians, artists, publishers, businessmen, as well as a few bureaucrats and administrators). Some of the latter may also have come for such personal reasons as the desire to escape from the burdens of economic bankruptcies, unhappy love affairs, overpowering indebtedness, threatening legal entanglements, unexpected demotions, psychological depressions, etc.—conditions from which the only escape appears to have been to wipe out the past completely and to start anew on the other side of the world. Of the many people who came for such reasons, only a few succeeded in adapting themselves to the new conditions. Most of them were torn by the deep longing for the land they had left behind to which it was almost impossible for them ever to return. An example of this is the case of the noted sculptor Sándor Finta (1881-1958),[40] who left Hungary to escape the after-effects of the charge of attempted manslaughter. Although this was the result of his effort to defend the honor of his elder sister, this charge haunted him until he left his country permanently.

The situation was different for those who came to the United States to serve their fellow countrymen. Most of these were preachers or priests, who were driven by their dedication to the cause. As such, notwithstanding the many difficulties they had to face, their lives were filled with sufficient self-satisfaction that they were generally able to escape most of the spiritual self-torments suffered by those whose lives remained unfulfilled and whose past continued to haunt them at least in the form of pangs of conscience.

The Gender and the Age of the Economic Immigrants

When we examine the male-female ratio of the immigrants in the years between 1899 and 1913 as reflected in the Hungarian statistics, we find that men made up over two-thirds (68.2%) and women less than one-third (31.8%) of their numbers.[41] These figures reassert our earlier conclusion that this migration was basically of a temporary nature, motivated by economic considerations. More specifically, it was a search for work by men, who intended to return to their country and to their families as soon as economically feasible.

While men undoubtedly dominated this economic migration, during the final few years the ratio of women began to increase. Thus, in 1908 they passed the 30% mark, and by 1913 they outnumbered men 52.1% to 47.9%.[42] This seems to indicate to us a gradual change in the attitude of the immigrants toward returning to their mother country. For whatever reasons, their resolve to return was weakened in the period before World War I, and this was accompanied by the growing desire to marry and to establish families in their new country; or if already married, to have their wives and children brought over to them. It was this change in attitude that forced the ratio of women up to a point where by 1913 they exceeded the number of male immigrants.

In addition to this change in the attitude of the immigrants, however, there was also an additional "pull" factor that worked upon the young single women in the mother country. During the latter part of the pre-World War I period it became a common practice for professional "white-slavers" (girl merchants) to recruit young peasant girls for immigration with the promise of a quick and worthy marriage to one of their immigrant countrymen in the United States. This obviously implied paying for the expenses and for the expected profits of these merchants of flesh. This was done either by the girls themselves in the form of underpaid obligatory labor or prostitution, or by the prospective husbands who had to pay inflated prices for a wife.[43]

Once married and settled with an established family, the immigrants seldom returned to Hungary. This was also true for those who opted to emigrate with their wives and children. Such immigrants generally resolved to remain permanently in the United States. These factors also explain why so many more men than women repatriated (i.e. 30% versus 13.1%).[44] While most men emigrated with the intention of seeking work and then returning to Hungary with their accumulated wealth, women generally came either to join their husbands or to find suitable husbands, and then to establish families in the new country.

Although the relevant statistics for the period before 1899 are missing, in light of our knowledge of the nature of early economic immigration we can safely assume that in those decades the ratio of men was even higher. Thus, in the course of the whole period of economic emigration from the mid-nineteenth century to 1914, the ratio of males among the immigrants must have been somewhere between 70% and 80%. In fact, in the case of Croatia alone, this ratio was even higher, i.e. in the period between 1899 and 1907 always above 80% and between 1908 and 1913 about 71.6%.[45] This again shows a declining tendency during the final years of the period.

By 1914 the situation changed drastically as the outbreak of World War I immediately reduced the number of immigrants. Moreover, by the end of the war, even those who intended to return were compelled to reassess their positions and to accept the idea of staying permanently. This decision to stay on such a mass scale, and the relative lack of intermarriage between Hungarians and non-Hungarians in those days, increased further the need for the immigration of women. This in turn led to an even greater increase of the proportion of women among the immediate post-war immigrants.

Closely connected with the originally temporary nature of Hungarian immigration to the United States was the age bracket of the immigrants. Those who came in search of temporary employment were largely men (and to a lesser degree women) of the young working age category. Thus, for the peak years of 1905-1907 73.3% of the immigrants were in the 20-49 years old category, 24.1% in the below 20 years of age category, and only 2.6% in the 50 years and older category. But even in the first of these categories the heaviest representation came from the ranks of the 20-29 year olds who made up over one-third (35.4%) of the immigrants. All in all at least 90% of the immigrants of the late nineteenth and early twentieth centuries were in the working age category, with at the most only 10% being composed of non-working dependents.[46]

Literacy Among the Immigrants

Although perhaps nearly 90% of the immigrants came from the ranks of the peasantry or near-peasantry, they did not represent the least able nor the least educated segment of Hungary's population. As a matter of fact, the literacy rate among the immigrants was higher than the literacy rate within Hungary's total population. Thus, whereas the country's literacy rate in 1910 (for those over six years of age) was 68.7% this rate among the immigrants varied between 89% for the Magyars and 70% for the Ruthenians.[47] These figures, however, represent some improvement over those reflected in US statistics for the years 1899-1910, when the literacy rate among the various nationalities from Austria-Hungary above 14 years of age was as follows: 98.3% for the Czechs, 94.8% for the Germans, 88.6% for the Magyars, 76% for the Slovaks, 74% for the Jews, 65% for the Romanians, 64.6% for the Poles, 63.9% for the Croats, 59% for the Dalmatians and Bosnians, 58.9% for the Bulgarians and Serbians, and 46.6% for the Ruthenians.[48] In light of the above, there is much to be said for the view that, while driven primarily by poverty and economic need, the immigrants of the pre-1914 period did not necessarily represent the most forsaken, nor the most underprivileged segment of Hungary's lower classes. Their very decision to face the perils of emigration singled them out as perhaps the hardiest and most determined group among the population, who had more will power and more daring than most of the others of their own socio-economic class. And much of this daring was undoubtedly connected with the fact that they were also the most literate and therefore the most informed among their own kind.

In light of what has been said above, we can safely reassert our earlier contention that those who decided to emigrate to America—whether temporarily or permanently—did so almost without exception with the intention to work so as to improve their economic positions. And they did work, giving their sweat and blood—although as yet little of their brain power—to the land of their choice. The age of the "Hungarian brain power" was still in the future. It came only during the later part of the interwar and during the post-World War II periods, when "the mystery of the Hungarian talent"—to quote Laura Fermi[49]—both enriched and puzzled the American mind.

Hungarian Settlements in the United States

Although—as we have seen—by far the greatest number of the Hungarian immigrants of the pre-World War II period were peasants or near-peasants, very few of them chose to continue agricultural labor in this country. Rather, they settled mainly in the industrial centers of the Northeast. According to a contemporary calculation by József Szász, in 1920 there were about 450,000 Hungarians in the United States, of whom a mere 1,000 were engaged in farm labor.[50] While these figures were perhaps too low both with respect to the number of Hungarians, as well as with regards to the number of farmers and farm workers among them, the unusually low percentage of those engaged in agricultural work (0.2%) does tell us something. Most importantly, it reinforces our basic assertion that the original cause of this mass migration was simply the immigrants' desire to make money and then to return to Hungary with enough capital to be able to buy farms themselves. They could hope to fulfill this goal, however, only if they chose to work in industry, which paid much more than farm labor. As such, virtually all of the Hungarian immigrants gravitated toward America's major industrial regions, more specifically to the large cities and mining areas of the Northeast.

According to the US Census of 1910, there were 710,904 persons in the United States who were born or whose parents were born in Hungary. By 1920 their number had increased to 935,801. These same census figures also reveal that of the "Hungarians" 320,895 (i.e. 45.1%) and 495,845 (i.e. 52.9%) were Magyar speaking, that is real Hungarians.[51] Augmented by the calculations of the above-mentioned József Szász, these statistics also tell us that in 1920 the Magyar-Hungarians were settled primarily in about a dozen northeastern states. Thus, in that year 78,000 lived in New York State (with 64,393 in New York City), 73,000 in Ohio (with 29,724 in Cleveland), 71,000 in Pennsylvania (with 11,519 in Philadelphia and about 26,000 in and around Pittsburgh), 40,000 in

New Jersey (mostly in Perth Amboy, Newark, Passaic, New Brunswick and Trenton), 34,000 in Illinois (with 26,106 in Chicago), 22,000 in Michigan (with 13,564 in Detroit), 20,000 to 25,000 in Connecticut (mostly in Bridgeport, Hartford and South Norwalk), 12,000 in Indiana (mostly in South Bend, Gary and East Chicago), 10,000 in Wisconsin (with 4,803 in Milwaukee), close to 10,000 in Missouri (with 6,637 in St. Louis), 6,200 in West Virginia (with 4,000 in Pocahontas), 5,200 in California (with 1706 in Los Angeles and 1390 in San Francisco), and the rest of them scattered throughout another dozen or so states.[52]

In the course of the next few decades the number of Hungarians in the United States fluctuated, but their geographic distribution remained basically unchanged right up to the 1960s and 1970s. Only in the 1960s was there a gradual shift away from the heavy concentration in the Northeast, largely in the direction of Florida and California. Those moving to Florida were mostly retirees, whose numbers were and are being replenished continuously by newer and newer waves of the elderly population. The majority of those settling in California, however, were young working age people, who were drawn to the Pacific coast by the tremendous economic opportunities presented by that "Golden States." The story of their lives and achievements, however, belongs in a later chapter of Hungarian-American history.

NOTES

1. For the background of Hungarian immigration to the United States see such standard works as: Eugene Piványi, *Hungarian-American Historical Connections from Pre-Columbian Times to the End of the American Civil War* (Budapest: Royal Hungarian University Press, 1927); Géza Kende, *Magyarok Amerikában: Az amerikai magyarság története* [Hungarians in America: The History of Hungarian Americans] (2 vols.; Cleveland: Szabadság Kiadása, 1927); Emil Lengyel, *Americans from Hungary* (Philadelphia and New York: J. B. Lippincott Company, 1948); Leslie Könnyű, *Hungarians in the U.S.A.: An Immigration Study* (St. Louis: The American Hungarian Review, 1967); Joseph Szépalki, *The Hungarians in America, 1583-1974: A Chronology and Fact Book* (Dobbs Ferry, NY: Oceana Publications, Inc., 1975); and Paula Benkart's recent summary, "Hungarians," in the *Harvard Encyclopedia of American Ethnic*

Groups, ed. Stephen Thernstrom, et al. (Cambridge, MA: Harvard University Press, 1980), pp. 462-471; henceforth *HEAEG.*

2. On this whole question of intra- and intercontinental migrations see Hansen Marcus L., *The Atlantic Migration, 1607-1860* (Cambridge, MA: Harvard University Press, 1940); Thomas Brinley, ed., *Economics of International Immigration* (London, 1958); and three revelant studies by Richard A. Easterlin, William S. Bernard and David Ward in *HEAEG,* pp. 476-508. On its Hungarian aspects see J. Puskás, *Emigration from Hungary to the United States before 1914* (Budapest: Akadémiai Kiadó, 1975).

3. Puskás, *Emigration,* p. 5; and István Rácz, *A paraszti migráció és politikai megítélése Magyarországon, 1849-1914* [Peasant Migration and its Political Assessment in Hungary, 1849-1914] (Budapest: Akadémiai Kiadó, 1980), pp. 75-77.

4. The largest, but far less compact Hungarian-American community than that of Cleveland is the community of Greater New York.

5. On the origins and development of the Cleveland Hungarian-American community see Kende, *Magyarok Amerikában,* II, pp. 27-28; Imre Sári-Gál, *Az amerikai Debrecen. Képek a clevelandi magyarság életéből* [American Debrecen. Pictures from the Life of the Cleveland Hungarians] (Toronto: Patria Publishing Co., Ltd., 1966), pp. 17-18; and Susan M. Papp, *Hungarian Americans and their Communities of Cleveland* (Cleveland: The Cleveland State University, 1981), pp. 155-156.

6. Concerning Hungarian-American society and institutions in the late nineteenth and early twentieth centuries I have relied on my soon-to-be published study: "Hungarian-American Society and Organizations, 1880-1940." See also Julianna Puskás, "Magyar szervezetek Amerikában az 1880-as évektől az 1960-as évekig" [Hungarian Organizations in America from the 1880s to the 1960s], *Történelmi Szemle* [Historical Review], XIII, 4 (1970), pp. 528-568; Louis Kalassay, *The Educational and Religious History of the Hungarian Reformed Church in the United States* (Ph.D. Dissertation, University of Pittsburgh, 1939), Otto Árpád Táborszky *The Hungarian Press in America* (MSLS Thesis, The Catholic University of America, 1955); Paula Kaye Benkart, *Religion, Family, and Community among Hungarians Migrating to American Cities, 1880-1930* (Ph.D. Dissertation, The Johns Hopkins University, 1975); István Török, *Katolikus magyarok Észak-Amerikában* [Catholic Hungarians in North America] (Youngstown, OH: A Katolikus Magyarok Vasárnapja, 1978); and Thomas

Szendrey, "The Hungarian Ethnic Theater," in *The Ethnic Theater in the United States*, ed. Maxine S. Seller (Westport, CT: Greenwood Publishing Co., 1982), in press.

7. Kende, *Magyarok Amerikában*, II, p. 47.
8. Rácz, *Migráció*, p. 127.
9. Ibid., pp. 81, 127.
10. U.S. Immigration Commission, *Emigration Conditions in Europe* (Washington, D.C.: Government Printing Office, 1911), p. 353; hereafter cited as *Emigration Conditions*. See also Rácz, *Migráció*, p. 128; and Puskás, *Emigration*, p. 19.
11. The basic contemporary works on Hungarian emigration and repatriation of that period include: *A magyar szent korona országainak kivándorlása és visszavándorlása, 1899-1913* [Emigration from and Repatriation to the Lands of the Hungarian Holy Crown, 1899-1913] (Budapest: Magyar Statisztikai Központi Hivatal, 1918), hereafter *MSKOKV;* and Andor Löherer, *Az amerikai kivándorlás és visszavándorlás* [Emigration to and Repatriation from America] (Budapest: Patria, 1908). For a recent European-wide treatment of this issue see J. D. Gould, "European Inter-Continental Emigration. The Road Home. Return Emigration from the U.S.A.," *Journal of European Economic History*, IX, 1 (1980), pp. 41-112. For a brief summary on Hungarian repatriation see Rácz, *Migráció*, pp. 82-84. Some authorities use a much higher figure for the repatriates (e.g. Leonard Dinnerstein, et al., *Natives and Strangers. Ethnic Groups and the Building of America*. New York: Oxford University Press, 1979, p. 135, which claims that 64% of the Hungarians repatriated), but that is based on incomplete statistics from only a few years before World War I. J. Puskás also gives a higher figure (40%) in her forthcoming book *Kivándorló magyarok az Egyesült Államokban, 1880-1940* [Immigrant Hungarians in the United States, 1880-1940]. I have only glimpsed briefly at a segment of her manuscript.
12. Puskás, *Emigration*, p. 26; Rácz, *Migráció*, p. 84.
13. Concerning Hungary's multinational composition and the relative ratio of the various nationalities see Pál Balogh, *A népfajok Magyarországon* [Ethnic Groups in Hungary] (Budapest: M. Kir. Vallás- és Közoktatási Minisztérium, 1902); *Magyarország története* [History of Hungary], editor-in-chief Zsigmond Pál Pach (Projected 10 vols., Budapest: Akadémiai Kiadó, 1976-), VII, pp. 413-421. For the nationality statistics on the basis

of the official census of 1910 see *Révai Nagy Lexikona* [Révai's Great Lexicon] (21 vols., Budapest: Révai Testvérek, 1910-1935), X, p. 295 and XIII, p. 200.

14. Puskás, *Emigration*, p. 31.
15. Rácz, *Migráció*, p. 107.
16. Concerning these nationality statistics see U.S. Bureau of Census, *Historical Statistics of the United States: Colonial Times to 1970* (Washington, D.C.: U.S.Government Printing Office, 1975). See also Joshua A. Fishman, *Hungarian Language Maintenance in the United States* (Bloomington, IN: Indiana University Publications, 1966), pp. 4-5; and Puskás, *Emigration*, p. 30. Specifically on the Slovak emigration from Hungary see Imre Polányi, "Az északi megyék és a szlovák anyanyelvűek kivándorlása" [Emigration from the Northern Countries and by Those of the Slovak Mother Tongue], in *Szegedi Tanárképző Főiskola Tudományos Közleményei* [Scholar Proceedings of the Teachers' College of Szeged], I (1964), pp. 245-270; M. Mark Stolarik, *Immigration and Urbanization: The Slovak Experience, 1870-1918* (Ph.D. Dissertation, University of Minnesota, 1974), and idem, *HEAEG*, pp. 928-934.
17. On this question see István Rácz, "Attempts to Curb Hungarian Emigration to the United States before 1914," in *Hungarian Studies in English* (Debrecen), VII (1973), pp. 5-33; and its more extensive Hungarian version: "Kisérletek az Egyesült Államokba irányuló magyarországi kivándorlás korlátozására," *Egyetemes Történeti Tanulmányok* [Studies in World History] (Debrecen), V (1971), pp. 53-92. See also István Rácz, "A kivándorlás és a magyar uralkodó osztály, 1849-1914" [Emigration and the Hungarian Ruling Class, 1849-1914], in *A Debreceni Kossuth Lajos Tudományegyetem Történeti Intézetének Évkönyve* [Yearbook of the Historical Institute of the Kossuth Lajos University of Debrecen], I (1962), pp. 85-107.
18. On the nature of this peasant migration see István Rácz, "Parasztok elvándorlása a faluból" [The Migration of the Peasants from the Villages], in *A parasztság Magyarországon a kapitalizmus korában, 1848-1914* [The Peasantry in Hungary in the Age of Capitalism, 1848-1914], ed. István Szabó (2 vols., Budapest: Akadémiai Kiadó, 1965), II, pp. 433-483; and idem, *Migráció*, pp. 19-140.
19. *Magyar Statisztikai Közlemények* [Hungarian Statistical Review], LXVII (1918), p. 35; Rácz, *Migráció*, p. 85.

20. *MSKOKV*, as quoted in Puskás, *Emigration*, p. 26.
21. Rácz, *Migráció*, p. 88. In her soon-to-be-published work J. Puskás pushed this figure even lower. Our disagreement stems largely from the fact that I regard the "artisan" or "industrial laborers" just out of the village as basically still "peasants" in terms of their culture and outlook upon the world.
22. Rácz, *Migráció*, p. 86.
23. Ibid., p. 87. In the case of Szabolcs County the peasants made up between 90.5% (1891-1903) and 92.5% (1905-1907) of the emigrants. Cf. Ferenc Szász, *Az Amerikába irányuló kivándorlás Szabolcs megyéből* [Emigration to America from Szabolcs County] (Nyíregyháza, 1972), pp. 66-67; and idem, "A kivándorlás hatása a Szabolcs megyei parasztságra, 1866-1914" [The Impact of Emigration upon the Peasantry of Szabolcs County, 1866-1914], *Magyar Történeti Tanulmányok* [Studies in Hungarian History] (Debrecen), III (1970), pp. 109-119.
24. One *hold* is equivalent to 1.42 acres or 0.57 hectares.
25. Rácz, "Parasztok elvándorlasa," pp. 460-462; idem, *Migráció*, pp. 89-90; and *Emigration Conditions*, p. 361.
26. Puskás, *Emigration*, pp. 9-10.
27. Ibid., p. 14.
28. For some of these letters and for a discussion of their significance see A. S. Glenn, *Amerikai Levelek* [American Letters] (Budapest: Lamppert Róbert, 1913); and Linda Dégh, "Two Letters from Home," *Journal of American Folklore*, XCI, 361 (1978), pp. 808-822.
29. On the role of the shipping companies see Rácz, *Migráció*, pp. 212-229; Löherer, *Az amerikai kivándorlás*, pp. 189-209; and George J. Pripć, *The Croatian Immigration in America* (New York: Philosophical Library, 1971), pp. 147-149. For one of the small propaganda pamphlets concerning the "Cunard Hungarian-American Line" see Zoltán Fejős, "Kivándorlás Amerikába a Zemplén középső vidékéről" [Emigration to America from the Central Region of Zemplén], in *Herman Ottó Múzeum Évkönyve* [Yearbook of the Herman Ottó Museum] (Miskolc), XIX (1980), p. 303.
30. *Emigration Conditions*, pp. 361-365; Puskás, *Emigration*, p. 16.
31. On these economic improvements see *Magyarország története*, VII, pp. 263-401; and Iván T. Berend and György Ránki, *Hungary: A Century of Economic Development* (New York: Newton Abbot, 1974), chs. I-IV.

32. This assessment by a contemporary Hungarian economist is quoted by Puskás, *Emigration*, pp. 15-16.

33. Some of the other causes for emigration generally mentioned included draft dodging, flight from criminal persecution, and nationality harrassment. But as noted in a contemporary report by the United States Immigration Commission, "in comparison with the main motive, which is economic, other causes of emigration are of little significance and have been greatly overrated." Cf. *Emigration Conditions*, p. 369. For official American and Hungarian views concerning some of the causes of emigration see also Zoltán Kramár, *From the Danube to the Hudson: U.S. Ministerial and Consular Dispatches on Immigration from the Habsburg Monarchy, 1850-1900* (Atlanta: Hungarian Cultural Foundation, 1978).

34. For a comparative graphic portrayal of these peaks and low points see Puskás, *Emigration*, p. 37.

35. Rácz, *Migráció*, p. 107.

36. Puskás, *Emigration*, p. 18.

37. These statistics apply to Greater Hungary, including Croatia. Cf. Rácz, *Migráció*, p. 85. The comparable figures for Hungary without Croatia are: Miners 1.4%, independent craftsmen, 2.2%, independent merchants, 0.3%, unskilled industrial workers and day laborers, 11.8%. Cf. Puskás, *Emigration*, p. 26.

38. *Emigration Conditions*, pp. 367-369; Rácz, *Migráció*, pp. 92-100.

39. Rácz, *Migráció*, p. 101.

40. Concerning Sándor Finta see Miklós Kovalovszky, "Észak- és Dél-Amerika magyar szobrásza" [Hungarian Sculptor of North and South America], *Magyar Hírek* [Hungarian News] XXXIV, 17-18 (August 22, 1981), p. 45.

41. *Magyar Statisztikai Közlemények*, LXVII (1918), p. 70. In US Statistics this ratio is 72.2% men and only 27.8% women, which may be the result of illegal immigration. Cf. *Emigration Conditions*, p. 376.

42. *Magyar Statisztikai Közlemények*, LXVII (1918), p. 9.

43. Rácz, *Migráció*, p. 102. For graphic descriptions of this importation of wives see Thomas Bell, *Out of this Furnace* (Pittsburgh: University of Pittsburg Press, 1976); as well as some of the short stories of the Hungarian-American poet and writer György Szécskay (1880-1958), including his "Szeredás Pista szerelme" [Pista Szeredás's Love] and "Jókus Barnabás házassága" [The Marriage of Barnabás Jókus], in his *Őszi tarlózás*

ötven éves mezőn [Autumn Gleanings on the Field of a Half a Century] (Pittsburgh: Szécskay György Jubileumi Bizottság, 1947), pp. 33-54.

44. *Magyar Statisztikai Közlemények*, LXVII (1918), p. 39.
45. Ibid., pp. 8-9.
46. Rácz, *Migráció*, pp. 105-106.
47. *Révai Nagy Lexikona*, X, p. 219.
48. *Emigration Conditions*, p. 380.
49. Laura Fermi, *Illustrious Immigrants. The Intellectual Migration from Europe, 1930-41* (Chicago and London: The University of Chicago Press, 1968), pp. 53-59.
50. József Szász, "A magyarság Amerikában" [Hungarians in America], *Gazdaság-Politikai Szemle* [Economic-Political Review] (June 1922), pp. 225-288, esp. p. 227.
51. Quoted in Fishman, *Hungarian Language Maintenance*, pp. 4-5.
52. Szász, "A magyarság Amerikában," pp. 227, 275-288. See also Könnyű, *Hungarians in the U.S.A.*, pp. 27-53, which also contains maps on the geogrpahical distribution of Hungarians in the United States.

Stephen Fischer-Galati

THE SIGNIFICANCE AND POSSIBILITIES FOR EXISTENCE OF A NATIONAL MINORITY: THE ROMANIAN SUBCULTURE IN THE USA—HISTORY AND PERSPECTIVES

From an historic point of view the Romanian emigration to the United States is among the least significant of all European population movements to the Western Hemisphere during the last one hundred years. Whatever significance it holds is a function of recent American and Romanian concerns for identifying national and cultural values among persons of Romanian origin living in the United States. The redefinition, if not outright abandonment, of the "melting pot" doctrine combined with the reclaiming of prodigal sons by Ceauşescu's Romania has given rise to a body of literature, produced on both sides of the Atlantic, specifically devoted to the Romanian-American community in the United States, to its contributions—cultural, economic, political, and social—to American and, respectively, Romanian civilization.[1]

We need not dwell at length on the more absurd claims made on behalf of Romanian-Americans and of their contributions. The Romanian-Americans are neither "socialists by instinct or capitalists by nature;" nor are they great Romanian patriots living in the United States or great American patriots concerned with explaining the American way of life to their friends and relatives in the Socialist Republic of Romania. In fact, it would be difficult to discuss Romanian-Americans as a cultural, social, and ethnic unit since the character of the emigration has changed significantly during the last few decades primarily as a result of the assimilation of the second and third generations of early Romanian immigrants and because of the emigration from Romania of individuals of a "new type" since World War II. For these reasons it seems desirable to avoid blanket generalizations and to concentrate on various component parts of what may be regarded as the community of Americans of Romanian descent in the United States. For our part, the discussion will focus almost exclusively on the ethnic Romanian emigration, that is of Romanians of the Orthodox or the Uniate faith.

In the search for a "Romanian grandmother" writers on the Romanian emigration to the United States have been able to locate a "Romanian grandfather" in Colonial America in the person of an Orthodox priest from Transylvania, Samuel Damian.[2] Damian was apparently acquainted with Benjamin Franklin as well as with principles of physics and electricity. He is known to have been in Philadelphia in 1748 but, since he disappeared without a trace in Mexico a short time later, it is doubtful whether he left any direct descendants on the North American continent. Mexico, also, seems to have been at least the ultimate destination of some 120 Romanians who left Constanța in 1856 for California during the days of the "Gold Rush" but whose vessel went under in Ensenada.[3] A Romanian *"hajduk"* is also reported in the oral tradition to have settled somewhere on the Mississippi River around 1800.[4] Be this as it may, the contributions to American civilization made by the aforementioned early Romanians in or en route to the United States are unrecorded.

Also, generally unrecorded are specific contributions by bona fide early immigrants to the United States whose actual number is unclear because of their non-identification by nationality in early American censuses. By means of extrapolations conducted by statistically-oriented social historians it seems fair to say that some 700 persons of Romanian origin lived in the United States by 1870. By 1895, however, emigration of Romanians gained momentum. The census of 1910, for instance, records 87,724 persons of Romanian origin of whom 65,923 were born in pre-World War I Romania.[5] (These figures, however, do not differentiate between ethnic Romanians and persons born in Romania, primarily Jews.)

The majority of these people were Romanians from Transylvania who came to the United States in search of work, and hopefully wealth, with a view of eventually returning to their native villages as *"ţărani înstăriţi."*[6] Various characteristics have been assigned to these individuals, by historians, ranging from anti-Magyar unionist tendencies to a firm commitment to assimilation into the great American democratic society. In truth, the history and contributions to American and Romanian civilization of these early immigrants have been commensurate with their educational, cultural, and professional backgrounds and functions in American society. The immigrants were generally illiterate and unskilled laborers. Unable to communicate in English orally and in any language in writing, unable to engage in agricultural pursuits—except as unskilled farm workers—the immigrants (mostly men from 18 to 45 years of age) worked as a rule as unskilled "day laborers" in the Atlantic and Mid-Western regions of the United States. They managed to lead a meager existence accumulating just enough money to gradually bring spouses from their homeland and to settle in the United States on essentially a permanent basis by the eve of World War I. A few returned to their villages shortly after their arrival in America, a few married non-Romanian women, and a few others merely continued to exist in boarding houses and bars.

This is not a heroic picture but it is a realistic one for immigrants from underdeveloped Eastern Europe. It is thus not surprising to learn that the Romanian immigrants' contributions to American civilization were typical of illiterate ghetto dwellers congregating in "fraternal and cultural societies" and in churches and church organizations.

"Cultural societies" is a misnomer since their only cultural activities were related to maintenance of folk-culture identified with the Romanian village.[7] Rather, they were insurance companies which provided accident and life protection to immigrant Romanian workers. In fact, one of the two principal societies was known as the *"Liga de Ajutor"* (League of Assistance) while the other, the *"Liga Societăţilor Române de Ajutor şi Cultură,"* merely added culture to its official title. Their significance can probably best be measured statistically: at the time of the fusion of the two into the *"Uniunea şi Liga"* in 1928, the combined membership amounted only to 6,000 (or approximately 3% of all Romanians in America).[8] The rest of the Romanian immigrants—including their children born in the United States—were affiliated only with church organizations.

This information is important for understanding the general isolation of the Romanian-Americans or Romanians in America from the mainstream of American social, economic, political, and cultural life. Such contributions as were made to that life were made only by a few professional people, mostly connected with labor problems and trade union activities, or by clerics, Uniate or Romanian Orthodox. Thus, claims originating primarily from contemporary Romania regarding the contributions made by Romanians in America to American awareness of the historic rights of the Romanians and the corollary establishment of Romania, on the eve and during World War I, are indeed far fetched. The evidence would rather show that the two major Romanian language newspapers in the United States *"America"* and *"Românul"* were generally ineffectual in their attempts to awaken their few readers' interest in Romanian affairs and almost totally insignificant in influencing either American public opinion or the U.S. government in favor of Romanian claims and aspirations. It is also doubtful whether some 3,500 U.S. soldiers of Romanian origin who fought in World War I were motivated by pro-unionist sentiments during their military action in the American armed forces. The only incontrovertible evidence is related to efforts by the Romanian government in Bucharest to use the Romanian immigrants in the U.S.A. for political goals by encouraging patriotic manifestations and collections of moneys for the Romanian military effort and by enlisting Romanian leaders, primarily churchmen, in efforts to persuade the U.S. government of the rightness of the Romanian national cause. The evidence is also clear with respect to the insignificance of all efforts—whether initiated by Romanian-Americans, by Romanians in America, or by Romanians in Romania—in affecting American attitudes and policies toward Romania.[9]

The question then arises as to whether Romanians in America or Romanian-Americans had any impact on American life and culture after World War I when an increasingly larger number of second-generation Romanians graduated from American schools, married non-Romanians, worked in American factories and business enterprises, and generally became part of the native, English-speaking, American society.

The answer, unequivocally, is that the impact was very modest indeed. And there were good reasons for that. First, the size of the Romanian community in the United States failed to increase significantly between the two world wars. This was partly due to the returning of some 34,000 immigrants to Romania in the first few years after World War I and the imposition of a rigid quota on Romanian emigration to the U.S.A. in

1924. These factors, when taken in conjunction with a relatively low birthrate, account for the fact that by 1930 only 293,453 persons, or 0.24% of the American population, were of Romanian origin.[10] Of that number, one half represents people actually born in Romania and the other half individuals born in the United States. However, only some 40% of these persons were ethnic Romanians, either Orthodox or Uniate. No relevant changes were recorded in the less complete U.S. census for 1940.

More significant than the numbers themselves, perhaps, is the fact that the majority of these persons continued to live, during the interwar years, in ghettos located mostly in urban centers along the Atlantic coast or in the Midwest and that, as a rule, they were either blue-collar workers or engaged in petit-business activities. Their educational level was strikingly low. In 1930, for instance, only some 800 young people of ethnic Romanian origin were attending high school and the number of those enrolled in colleges or universities was less than one hundred.[11] Moreover, intermarriages with members of more developed ethnic groups were proportionally very small, amounting to only one-sixth of the total number of marriages recorded by 1930.[12]

Under the circumstances, the Romanian-American community—whether first or second generation—was held in low esteem by the American establishment and, for that matter, by Americans of other than East- or Southern European origin. Nor did that community have much value for the Romanian state itself since the Bucharest establishment was fully aware of the political and social insignificance of working-class Romanian-Americans in the United States. Nevertheless, the process of assimilation and development of certain basic characteristics of the Romanian-American communities in the United States in the interwar years are not devoid of importance in the history of the United States or of Romania.

The Romanian-American communities reflected the working class mentality of interwar America with focal concerns on trade unionism and cultural life connected with church organizations. As union members Romanian-Americans were almost uniformly supportive of policies set down by union leaders who, invariably, were of non-Romanian origin. A few industrial workers of Romanian origin were supportive of radical, Marxist, groups but therein too their role was that of followers rather than leaders.[13] It is fair to say that Romanian-Americans were generally disinterested in national and regional politics and that Romanian cultural societies were also generally apolitical. Political attitudes were normally moulded by editors of the Romanian-American press and above all by the clergy. Two separate, and often conflicting, currents were apparent during the interwar years. The prevalent favored political action by trade unions for the advancement of workers' rights within the framework of American democratic practices and institutions; the other favored authoritarian approaches. It is true that Marxist solutions were generally unacceptable to Romanian-Americans; however, populist solutions enjoyed a modicum of support among Romanian-Americans. In fact, the Christian populism— with its strongly anti-Semitic, anti-Magyar, and anti-communist overtones—practiced in Romania by Codreanu's Iron Guard struck a meaningful chord for at least a few members of the Orthodox clergy and their parishioners in America.[14] Still, such national consciousness as Romanian-Americans possessed on the eve of World War II was overwhelmingly American. Their knowledge of and interest in Romanian politics was even more limited than their insignificant participation in and impact on American politics. In truth, on the eve of World War II there were no striking or unique Romanian-American components in the American melting pot which could, for instance, differentiate them from other East European ones. Romanian-Americans were becoming more and more assimilated as the second generation was rapidly losing its sense of ethnicity through loss of knowledge of the Romanian language, ignorance of Romanian culture and civilization, and general indifference toward the ancestral land. And what was true of the second generation was even more true of the third. Also, since the concerns and understanding of the first generation for matters Romanian was at best limited by its own educational and professional levels it seems fair to conclude that the Romanian-American community shared the attitudes and values of other underdeveloped ethnic communities in the U.S.A. and that Romanian-Americans were generally regarded as "second class citizens" by the social and political elites in the United States. But this was to change after World War II.

The changes, often drastic, in the status of Romanian-Americans and of Romanians in America which occurred after World War II must be related to a variety of factors ultimately connected with new American domestic and foreign policies which evolved after the war and which were, in one way or another, related to the war itself and to postwar problems. The most immediate cause for change was the establishment of communist rule in Romania and the adoption by the United States of measures designed to contain Soviet expansionism. At least as significant, however, were American domestic policies which provided new opportunities to World War II veterans for educational, professional, and social advancement. The foreign and domestic policies of the United States were, in a sense, contradictory as far as Romanian-Americans and Romanians in America were concerned and these contradictions continue to affect Romanian-American communities in the 1980s.

The Cold War resulted in a virtual interruption of relations between the United States and Romania. It also required, on the American side, denunciation of Romanian communist practices and policies and, by 1948, support of Romanian political leaders in exile whose participation was sought in the "Crusade for Freedom," whose announced goal was the eventual "liberation" of Romania from communism. The establishment of the Romanian National Committee in the United States and the creation of the National Committee for a Free Europe, with its various anti-communist activities related in one way or another to Radio Free Europe, modified the configuration of the Romanian-American community. The leaders of the Romanian National Committee were, as a rule, middle-aged or elderly political figures whose educational and social backgrounds differed markedly from those of the prewar leaders of the Romanian-Americans. As the Cold War intensified, more and more anti-communist Romanians with similar educational and social backgrounds were admitted to the United States many of whom worked for the National Committee for a Free Europe, Radio Free Europe, the Voice of America, and other governmental or semi-governmental organizations concerned with Romanian affairs. Even the "technocrats" among these "guests" of the United States government were divorced from the Romanian-American community since, at least in theory, they were concerned expressly with the liberation of Romania and with their return to a "Free Romania" as emissaries and/or exponents of American-style democracy. However, as liberation became more and more illusory and anti-communism more and more strident, particularly during the so-called "McCarthy era" of the early 1950s, an increasingly larger number of Romanians—many located in refugee camps in Europe—were admitted to the United States to participate in the anti-communist crusade.[15] This second wave of Romanians proved to be far more significant in the long run because it consisted mostly of individuals unidentified with either democratic politics or with the social and educational standards and values of the early postwar newcomers. In fact, many of the Romanian immigrants who arrived in the fifties had been either identified with the Iron Guard or at least shared its views on matters social, ethnic, and politic. This second emigration assumed even larger proportions in the early sixties as immigration laws were further relaxed. Moreover, these newcomers settled in traditional Romanian-American communities and sought to influence the political thinking, at least as far as Romanian affairs were concerned, of the less educated members of those communities.

Most important, in this respect, was their participation in religious and cultural affairs. The classic case is that of Viorel Trifa, a former leader of the Romanian legionary movement, who became the editor of the Romanian Orthodox Episcopate, *"Solia,"* in 1951 and who was elected Bishop of the Episcopate later in the same year.[16] Whereas Bishop Trifa's was the most dramatic case there were other Romanians with similar backgrounds and views who, slowly but surely, secured positions as clergymen, journalists, instructors and professors within and outside Romanian-American communities in the United States.

The influence exerted by these men on Romanian-Americans is unclear and remains a matter of dispute. It is clear, however, that Bishop Trifa and his associates did instill a sense of Romanianism into many members of his congregation, who were either second or third generation Romanian-Americans, and rekindled or kept alive the Romanianism of first generation Romanian-Americans or of newcomers from Romania. And that Romanianism was heavily nationalistic and generally representative of the ideological and political positions of the Romanian populist right. It is, however, unlikely that—at least during the fifties and sixties—Trifa swayed a majority of the Romanian-American community toward Romanianism or toward acceptance of his political views, most likely because of greater professional and social integration of Romanian-Americans into American society as a whole and corollary Americanization of the younger generation.

The educational opportunities provided by the so-called "G.I. Bill of Rights" to veterans of World War II were exploited, albeit to a limited extent, by Romanian-Americans after the war. There are no meaningful statistics on the number of Romanian-American veterans who graduated from colleges and universities in the forties and fifties but it is known that most Americans, regardless of ethnic origin, graduated from high school during those years and that by the sixties most high school graduates attended at least temporarily one or another institution of higher education. It is also known that second and third generation Romanian-Americans entered the professions after World War II and that the urban ethnic ghetto began to disintegrate rapidly in the fifties and sixties. These changes also led to more intermarriages with other ethnic groups and further Americanization which, in the case of Romanian-Americans, further weakened the already tenuous links with their—and at that time inaccessible—ancestral land. It is important to note that the younger generation seldom possessed any knowledge of the Romanian language and that the number of Romanian-Americans engaged in occupations or professions related to Romania, or of those concentrating on Romanian or East European studies, in the United States was insignificant. It is possible, of course, that even members of the new generation might have been influenced by Bishop Trifa's charismatic personality and messages, but there is no evidence of their having adopted either political or historic views identified specifically with Romania. In fact, ethnicity became a potentially valuable asset to nationalities other than the so-called "Anglos" only during the late sixties and early seventies when, as part of the programs for greater social and cultural integration of races and nationalities in the United States, hyphenated Americanism was to be, at least temporarily, fashionable. Whereas this development as such had relatively little relevance for Romanian-Americans, in combination with another major and mostly independent development, ethnic consciousness became an important factor in the evolution of Romanian-American communities in the seventies.

In the late sixties, largely because of the political and economic needs of Romania, President Nicolae Ceauşescu sought support against Soviet threats to the security of his regime through expansion of relations with the United States.[17] In his quest for obtaining "most favored nation" status, Ceauşescu also sought closer identification of Romanian-Americans with the mother country or ancestral homeland on the assumption that Romanian-Americans could exert political influence in Washington on behalf of Romania's goals.[18] As part of this Romanian ecumenism visits by Romanian-Americans to Romania and by Romanians to their relatives in the United States were facilitated, scholarships were offered to Romanian-Americans for study in Romania, cultural exchanges were intensified, nationalist manifestations were encouraged, and the common bond of Orthodoxy was stressed.

These actions had varying impacts on the Romanian-American community which reacted with varying degrees of enthusiasm and skepticism. The attraction of inexpensive visits to Romania and of relatives visiting families in the United States were largely offset by anti-communist preachings emanating from the pulpits of the Romanian Orthodox Episcopate. Attempts by the Patriarchate in Bucharest to secure control over the Episcopate in the United States were rebuffed by Bishop Trifa and brought on a bitter confrontation between "communist" and "fascist" forces. Two separate Romanian Orthodox episcopates were in fact established: one headed by Archbishop Trifa and the other by the Patriarchate's vicar, Archbishop Victorin. The conflict assumed great virulence during the seventies as several Jewish organizations, with tacit encouragement from Bucharest, launched an all-out campaign against Trifa whom they identified with the Holocaust and whose expulsion from the United States they demanded.[19]

The conflict polarized the Romanian-American community as it became ever more involved in Romanian affairs. Whereas many Romanian-Americans had been indifferent toward matters Romanian in the past, by the beginning of the 1980s the level of involvement, direct or indirect, has reached an all-time high. However, despite intensified cultural and political manifestations, Romanianism, for the majority, is limited to recognition of Romania's problems particularly with respect to Soviet pressures. A substantial minority, however, has become more deeply involved in Romanian matters and has developed political attitudes based on a right-wing nationalist interpretation of Romanian history. That view, partly preached by Trifa and his followers, partly by extremists to the right of Trifa who came to the United States in the fifties and sixties, and partly by recent defectors or legitimate emigrés from Romania, denies the legitimacy of communist rule and advocates the eventual liberation of Romania through political action by the "true" exponents of the Romanian historic tradition, the Christian populists. Jewish participation in the anti-Trifa campaign has also revived or encouraged anti-

Semitism among many a Romanian-American but, more important in the long-run, there appears to be an increase in fascist and neo-fascist tendencies and activities.[20]

This is not to say that by-and-large Romanian-Americans are fascists or, for that matter, have fascist proclivities. It is to say, however, that the lessons of Romanian history have been taught to more and more members of the second and succeeding generations of Romanian-Americans during the last decade or so and that these lessons, combined with the first hand experiences of some 30,000 emigrés who came to the United States since World War II and by other first-generation Romanians who emigrated before the war, are affecting the political, social, and cultural attitudes of individuals of Romanian origin in the United States. Furthermore, those lessons are becoming more and more applicable and relevant to contemporary conditions in the United States at a time when matters related to the rights of racial and ethnic minorities have become of paramount importance and are affecting political and social attitudes both inside and outside the confines of the Romanian-American community.

One thing is certain: the Romanian-American communities which originally comprised primarily unskilled and illiterate workers and which were closely identified, at least until World War II, with the Democratic Party have undergone major changes during the last forty years. The lives and livelihoods of Romanian-Americans have been affected by the recent historic experiences of both the United States and Romania. And, whereas convergence of the two histories is not in the offing, as far as the Romanian-Americans are concerned, limited convergence is taking place at an accelerated pace. The lessons of Romanian history, in matters social and national, are unlikely to have a significant impact on the majority of Romanian-Americans as long as social mobility and professional opportunities will be afforded to them. Many, in fact, are active Republicans and most are staunchly conservative. Whether the lessons of Romanian history will reinforce that conservatism, whether right-wing Republicanism is compatible with that historic experience, whether in fact fascism or neo-fascism are compatible with the views and goals of the American right, are probably irrelevant questions as long as traditional American values and the "American way of life" prevail. However, the process of homogenization of American society does take into account the existence of specific values of component ethnic groups of the American melting pot. The values of the Romanian-Americans must thus be considered and those values are changing under the dual pressure of total assimilation by the educated and professionally successful younger generations and the retention of "Romanian" values and identities usually by the less successful, the more conventional, the less educated, the more biased and gullible members of the community.

NOTES

1. The two most important works are by Gerald J. Bobango, *The Romanian Orthodox Episcopate of America: The First Half Century, 1929-1979* (Jackson, Michigan: Romanian-American Heritage Center, 1979) and the unpublished study by P.R. Toma, *Românii în cele două Americi: O experienţă etnică şi istorică, 1750-1980*, both with ample bibliographic references.

2. Demetrius Dvoichenko-Markov, "A Rumanian Priest in Colonial America," *The American Slavic and East European Review*, XIV:2, 1955, pp. 383-389; L.A. Popovici, "Samuel Damian, primul român în America," *Calendarul Ziarului "America,"* 1971, pp. 158-160.

3. Charles E. George, "Roumanian Colony in Mexico," *Roumania*, October 1, 1917, p. 69.

4. Toma, op. cit., p. 52.

5. Demographic data is to be found in Toma, op. cit., pp. 49 ff. and in Bobango, op. cit., p. 7 ff.

6. Among the most important works on this and related subjects see Christine A. Galitzi, *A Study of Assimilation Among the Roumanians of the United States* (New York: Columbia University Press, 1929) and Joseph J. Barton, *Peasants and Strangers: Italians, Rumanians, and Slovaks in an American City, 1890-1950* (Cambridge: Harvard University Press, 1975).

7. An excellent statement is by Gerald J. Bobango, "The Union and League of Romanian Societies in America," *East European Quarterly*, XII:1, 1978, pp. 29-35.

8. Bobango, *Romanian Orthodox Episcopate*, p. 14.

9. Toma, op. cit., pp. 80 ff. states the basic official Romanian views on the Romanian-Americans' role during World War I. Galitzi, op. cit., and Bobango, *Romanian Orthodox Episcopate*, assume a realistic stance on these issues.

10. Toma, op. cit., p. 167.

11. Bobango, *Romanian Orthodox Episcopate*, p. 53.

12. Toma, op. cit., especially pp. 172 ff. which contain valuable demographic data.

13. Consult the newspaper *"Deșteptarea"* (later known as *"Românul American")* which was the unofficial publication of the Comintern in Romanian in the United States in those years.

14. See Bobango, *Romanian Orthodox Episcopate*, especially pp. 90 ff.

15. Ibid., pp. 198 ff.

16. An important contribution is Gerald J. Bobango, *Religion and Politics: Bishop Valerian Trifa and His Times* (Boulder, Colorado: East European Monographs, 1981).

17. On the entire political background see Stephen Fischer-Galati, *Twentieth Century Rumania* (New York: Columbia University Press, 1970). See also Trond Gilberg, "The Communist Party of Romania," in Stephen Fischer-Galati, Editor, *The Communist Parties of Eastern Europe* (New York: Columbia University Press, 1979), pp. 281-325.

18. Consult any of the issues of *"Tribuna României"* published by the "Asociația România" in Bucharest the purpose of which is to establish and maintain close contacts with the Romanian-American and other hyphenated Romanian communities in the diaspora.

19. Bobango, *Romanian Orthodox Episcopate*, pp. 307 ff.

20. See especially Toma, op. cit., pp. 453 ff.

Ivan Sanders

AMERICA THROUGH HUNGARIAN EYES: IMAGES AND IMPRESSIONS OF AMERICAN CIVILIZATION AS REFLECTED IN RECENT HUNGARIAN WRITINGS ON THE UNITED STATES*

The travelogue or travel journal is a highly popular genre in Hungary, one with a long and distinguished past; and some of the best-known travelogues were written about America. For example, Sándor Bölöni-Farkas's *Journey in North America [Utazás Éjszak-Amerikában]*, first published in 1834, was one of the most widely read Hungarian books of the nineteenth century, much admired by both the political leaders and the literary lights of the time. And during a thirty-year period following the publication of Bölöni-Farkas's famous work no less than eight books appeared in Hungary about the United States.[1] They may not always be aware of it, but the writers of contemporary accounts of American civilization are continuing a tradition begun by these nineteenth-century travelers; for while today's surveyors of American life may be more knowledgeable, more dispassionate about the United States than their nineteenth-century predecessors, they share with them the tendency to compare and contrast conditions in the two countries and thereby present, indirectly, a picture of their own society as well.

Almost without exception the early- and mid-nineteenth-century travelers give a glowing account of life in the United States, and Sándor Bölöni-Farkas's report is nothing less than a paean to America. What they describe is a young, dynamic, enterprising society whose democratic instincts are matched by its institutions. Although many of the voyagers were of noble birth, they applauded America's republican form of government, the absence of noble and ecclesiastic privilege, the notion of grass-roots politics, volunteer armies and the like. Of course Bölöni-Farkas's and his compatriots' enthusiasm for the New World reflected their extreme dissatisfaction with conditions back home. The more they praised the rapidly growing cities, the newly built canals, the thriving farms and factories, the impressive public buildings, the justly proud, civic-minded citizens, the more they were reminded of the economic and cultural backwardness of their native country. It should be noted that the acclaim greeting these travelogues—"Praise be to the Almighty that this book has come out; its usefulness to our citizens is incalculable," Count István Széchenyi wrote to Bölöni-Farkas upon the publication of his *Journey*[2] — was further evidence of a general interest in the Anglo-Saxon world on the part of educated Hungarians. It is well known that for much of the century a veritable Anglomania raged in the highest circles of the liberal Hungarian aristocracy, manifesting itself in everything from admiration for British statecraft to a taste for English gardens and English-style country homes.[3]

The nineteenth-century Hungarian travelers' descriptions of American life and institutions may not be as penetrating—or prophetic—as those found in Tocqueville's classic study of American society, the first volume of which, incidentally, was published a year after Sándor Bölöni-Farkas's book; still, because the accounts were vivid, full of new information, and in the case of Bölöni-Farkas's work, excellently written, the overwhelmingly positive impressions they conveyed contributed significantly to the way America was perceived in the nineteenth century. By the turn of the century the United States became a more familiar and a more real place for much of Europe. The immigrant experience and of course the more readily available information about the New World altered Hungarian perceptions of America considerably. The image of a vigorous, young, idealistic democracy was supplanted by that of a pragmatic industrial giant, a country where fortunes could be made and lost overnight, where freedom could easily turn into lawlessness, where ingenuity, and not probity, was the human quality most in demand. Interestingly enough, even the image of Benjamin Franklin, one of the most popular Americans in Europe, underwent a change. Anna Katona points out in her study of Franklin's reputation in Hungary that by the end of the nineteenth century Franklin the Founding Father and thinker was overshadowed by Franklin the clever and successful businessman.[4]

America didn't cease to fascinate Hungarians during the early nineteen-hundreds; if anything it seemed even more exciting than before—but also more volatile. For many Europeans it was (and to some extent still is) difficult to reconcile America's grand traditions, rooted in Enlightenment ideals, with what was seen as its unruliness, its proneness to violence. It was around the turn of the century that America became known as the land of unlimited opportunities, but also as a place where only paupers, ex-convicts, adventurers, ne'er-do-wells went. Admiration was always tinged with condescension; and what most people admired were the technical achievements, the clever and frivolous innovations, the contributions to populai culture. László Országh demonstrates in his illuminating treatise, *English Elements in the Hungarian Vocabulary [Angol eredetű elemek a magyar szókészletben, 1977]*, that while the most important English words to have entered the Hungarian language during the nineteenth century had to do with statecraft and politics (e.g., cabinet, coalition, petition, reformer, conservative, etc.), among the words added to the Hungarian word-stock at the beginning of the twentieth century, we find many associated with sports, entertainment, fashion, highlife (e.g., breeches, cocktail, bridge, polo, handicap, crack, etc.).[5]

And yet the literature of the period was full of highly favorable, idealized images of America; its people were still seen as forthright, unpretentious, untouched by old-world cynicism. For example, in Kálmán Mikszáth's novel *The Noszty Boy's Affair with Mari Tóth [A Noszty fiú esete Tóth Marival,* 1908], the man who exposes the shenanigans of the corrupt provincial establishment is Mihály Tóth, a landowner who spent his youth in America and who is therefore free of the snobbishness and greed of the local gentry. And in a poem written in 1906 Mihály Babits could still exclaim:

> Ah, to America! There, across the sea is the good life.
> Ah, why won't I go to America with you?
> There is life there, and money, and joy, and room for adventure, room to struggle;
> What's the good of lingering here, and complaining dully about our dear daily bread?[6]

For many years America remained a magnet whose pull proved irresistible for countless Hungarians. During the particularly difficult post-World War I period, even people who would ordinarily be the last to want to leave their native land—successful writers and poets, for instance—thought of emigrating. In a letter that came to light just recently—its addressee is the Hungarian-American critic, Joseph Reményi—we learn that in 1920 Dezső Kosztolányi thought seriously of moving to the States—"until things straighten out."[7] Actually, a number of important Hungarian writers, among them, Áron Tamási, Sándor Hunyady and Zsigmond Remenyik, did cross the Atlantic during the years between the two wars, and wrote about their experiences and impressions. For example, Tamási's three-year stay in the twenties inspired him to write *Abel in America* [*Ábel Amerikában*, 1934] a masterpiece of Hungarian prose fiction and Remenyik's *American Ballad* [*Amerikai ballada*, 1942] remains one of the most incisive surveys of the American scene ever published in Hungarian. These works no doubt deepened some Hungarians' knowledge of the United States, though their perceptions, like those of other Europeans at this time, were influenced far more decisively by American movies, music and popular literature. With the advent of the Second World War the American "presence" in Hungary began to fade, and save for a brief revival of interest after the war, became almost non-existent for about a decade. During the early fifties even English-sounding hotel names, indeed the English language itself, became suspect. Reports about America, its people and culture, published at this time were heavily distorted: most of them strike us, in retrospect, as grotesque caricatures. The following are passages from a journalist's American diary, published in Budapest in 1950:

> There are so many superfluous things in New York, things aimed only at creating a sensation, that they are not so much enthralling as bewildering. . . . This is a city built by formalists, people who knew only one thing about what's beautiful: its size . . . . America is only a halfway house for music. Music is an immigrant here, it's imported; they don't have their own distinctive music, or rather they do, but this is characterless musical hodgepodge. . . . I had the good fortune of espying, in a magazine, a photograph of Truman in swimming trunks. . . . But then again, what should one expect of a man with primitive artistic taste when E. Hemmingway [sic], the head of the American literary snobs, has himself photographed half naked, during the morning feeding of his five or six cats. Unwittingly,

we feel embarrassed for the writer who should show more respect, if not for his own person, than at least for his profession.[8]

* * * * * *

It was only in the more relaxed atmosphere of the sixties that Hungarian curiosity about the United States could once again be satisfied. A host of new books about America was published during the decade. Significantly enough, even American travelogues and diaries written by foreign writers became great successes. For instance the first work by Simone de Beauvoir to appear in Hungarian was her famous travel journal, *L'Amérique au jour le jour,* and over the years chronicles of American life by the Swiss Jürgen Federspiel, the German Edith Anderson were also translated into Hungarian.[9] Many of these travelogues perpetuated old myths and commonplaces about the New World, and in most cases offered a highly critical view of American society, but at the same time provided readers with much sought-after information about daily life in that society. Because the grim dogmatic fifties were still a recent memory, the first travelogues to appear in the sixties—e.g., László Helon's *I Discovered America* [*Felfedeztem Amerikát,* 1966], Zsuzsanna Gál's *I Was a Wife in New York* [*Feleség voltam New Yorkban,* 1967]—took a predictably dim view of the "affluent society." But because Hungary's isolation from the West was not yet a thing of the past either, the authors of these books also got rather excited about the many technological novelties, creature comforts and labor-saving devices they encountered on their visit to the United States. The interest in consumer goods, in gadgets of all kinds is understandable, even the pride in discovering that their own country was "catching up." For example, the journalist Zsuzsanna Gál, who was "only" a wife in New York, writes in the beginning of her book that after she and her husband had returned to Hungary, they discovered America—at home:

> We came across a whole array of little things which we first saw out there and which, by the time we got home, turned up here too. They painted strips on the roads to help traffic. Ambulances, firetrucks, police cars were now equipped with revolving lights on top —just like in New York. In parking places we too had to pay now.

> In a sporting goods store I discovered the same shoe-holder with a zipper lock that I bought in New York—here it was called "camping shelf." We bought someone a car-window washer, but our friend returned it with a smile; he bought the exact replica of ours in an automotive store.[10]

It's instructive to compare this passage with another, in a book by Miklós Almási published seven years later. It's true that Almási's book, *Frequencies—Conversations about Today's America* [*Rezgésszámok—Beszélgetések a mai Amerikáról,* 1974] is not a travelogue in the usual sense but an intellectual's attempt to make sense of the social changes of the sixties; yet the comment does reflect an awareness of the limits of technology—limits which the earlier travelogue writers, impressed even dazzled as they were by American technical know-how, were not yet aware of. Almási tells us that upon returning to Europe and seeing at the Frankfurt Airport familiar cars, ads, neckties, packaged orange juice,

> the realization hit me: it was as though I'd found myself in a smaller, shabbier America. . . . Is there another alternative for Western Europe? And when it comes to such things as technology and plant organization and industrial psychology and technical-scientific development, have we given enough thought to just what we can emulate without finding ourselves at odds with our own objectives?[11]

The early travelogues, aimed at large readership, were for the most part informative, chatty and, inevitably, superficial, though not quite as superficial as eyewitness accounts by reporters stationed in the United States whose stories reflected the even more simplified views of American reality one often encounters in the Hungarian mass media. For instance Pál Ipper's book *Reporting from the Other Side* [*A túlsó partról jelentem,* 1970], a collection of his brief broadcasts from the United States between 1963 and 1969, offers very few insights into political and cultural events; indeed, his comments on American institutions, though always adroit and flippant, at times create confusion. When he remarks in one of his pieces that a group of reporters on a television interview program "threw in" a toothpaste commercial when they felt "cornered" by the visiting French foreign minister, Ipper reveals that he has a rather naive notion about the relationship between broadcaster and sponsor on American television.[12] Of the frustrating and often amusing misconceptions, slips and errors one encounters in some of these travelogues, let me cite just one more example. In surveying New York City's landmarks, Klára Fehér and László Nemes in their otherwise very readable travelogue, *Iroquois and Skyscrapers* [*Irokézek és felhőkarcolók,* 1968] make mention of "dreaded" Ellis Island in New York harbor, where the "fate of immigrants was at one time decided."[13] New Yorkers would be puzzled by this description. Rather than being dreaded, the famous island is adored nowadays by misty-eyed nostalgia buffs who visit the island's dilapidated buildings, searching for scraps of their heritage.

The authors of the more recent travel journals, many of them recipients of American fellowships and grants, try hard to put all preconceived notions about America behind them. In his book, *New York Minute by Minute* [*New York percről percre,* 1971], Iván Boldizsár readily admits that just as many Americans harbor misconceptions about Eastern Europe, there are plenty of Hungarians whose images of America are distorted by outdated information, misinformation, or simply lack of information. He makes the point several times in his travel diary that Hungarians can't be too shocked when Americans do not recognize the names of their great national heroes—he found that at times he was just as ignorant about the names and achievements of American historical personages. What makes *New York Minute by Minute* enjoyable reading is that its author is an energetic and tirelessly inquisitive traveler with an eye for the significant. It is doubtful whether Iván Boldizsár, during his four-month stay, changed his basic attitudes about America, but he did enjoy making new discoveries, and did respond eagerly—and positively—to new stimuli. He liked the idea of using credit cards, for instance ("Why should we allow this system of 'instant goodies' to be enjoyed only by capitalist societies?"[14] he writes), marveled at the power of American unions (in his earlier travel journal, *Doing England with a Giraffe* [*Zsiráffal Angliában,* 1965], he tells us how shocked he was to learn that many English workers actually played the stock market), admired some of the more resourceful American gimmicks, realized that American poverty had to be measured by American, and not European, standards. While reading *New York Minute by Minute,* one can't help feeling that Iván Boldizsár, though no starry-eyed traveler, was nevertheless constantly provoked, challenged, galvanized by what he saw in America. One reason for this may be the fact that he, like many other travelers before him, was fascinated and shocked by the "otherness" of America—by the realization that in the New World everything is radically different. "What I am experiencing now," Boldizsár writes in his book, "is something I couldn't even imagine until now."[15]

In some of the Hungarian literature on America, this fascination is replaced by a sense of dislocation and loss. To some writers America is so frightfully different from Europe that all it evokes in them is an intense longing for home. István Sőtér's account of his journey through the United States, *Dinner in Carmel* [*Vacsora Carmelban*, 1968], is a European intellectual's fastidious, somewhat condescending look at a strange new world. And Sőtér is one traveler who doesn't have much use for the Americans' naive nostalgia for European culture, their reverence for history. On the West Coast especially he is discouraged by "European stage sets"—the potpourri of architectural styles, cultural moods, fake antiques, etc. At one point he comments wrily: "Here on the West Coast we represent, willy-nilly, the whole of European civilization. And we must bear the fame of the Roman Forum and the Champs Elysées, as well as the odium of European tipping customs."[16]

István Sőtér made his trip to the United States in 1965; his book was published in 1968. Interestingly, some of the more recent writings on America reveal a significant change in attitude. Hungarian visitors have become more conscious of the kinds of Americana that are enduring and real. They are amazed to learn that certain cultural, fraternal, religious institutions and organizations, which remind them of their grandfathers' world, have survived intact in America. They discover that many cities have retained their late nineteenth century, Victorian look, and that there are isolated, provincial neighborhoods in almost any large American city, the likes of which can no longer be found in European metropolises. Even Sőtér, who, as we said, was perturbed by the crazy quilt patterns of the American cultural landscape, remarks in his book that a city like New York is made cozy by its fire-escapes and roof-top water tanks. "Its charm," he writes, "lies in the fact that it can still be more provincial than any other big city. New York has not forgotten the small town it once was."[17]

This awareness of what is old in the New World becomes even more pronounced in works published in the mid-to-late seventies. For example, in a book of travel notes and essayistic reflections entitled *I Came from*

America [*Amerikából jöttem,* 1977], the Transylvanian Hungarian writer János Szász invariably associates European encounters with American locales. In New York Szász tracks down the widow of Robert Klopstock, the physician who treated Kafka and acquainted him with the works of Ady and Karinthy. It's also in that city that Szász can finally write about his last meeting with Paul Celan. (In the opening pages of Magda Szabó's novel, *Old-Fashioned Story* [*Régimódi történet,* 1977] we learn that it was in America, in a Milwaukee motel room, to be more precise, that she decided to begin writing her family chronicle.) For János Szász, Magda Szabó and others America is full of reminders; they nostalgically seek out European connections on American soil, and learn in the process that the past in the New World is not obliterated, only submerged.

* * * * *

A survey of the rather large and still growing body of literature on the United States published in the last fifteen years shows that after a spate of travelogues which, as we said, were mostly impressionistic narratives that contained much-needed first-hand information about the country and its people, a number of works tried more systematically, and with greater intellectual discipline, to examine the various facets of American life. Miklós Almási's *Frequencies,* for instance, is an attempt to understand American society in the light of the reigning sociological schools of thought. And though virtually every Hungarian who writes about the United States is interested in the lives and fortunes of Hungarians living here, as well as in Hungary's image in America, the more recent publications also dwell longer on some perennial questions: What does it mean to be a Hungarian abroad? Are things Hungarian (even the celebrated wines and cuisine) really as good as they are cracked up to be? Why isn't Hungarian literature better known in the West? The list is extensive. Imre Szász, in his book *Dry Martini* [*Száraz martini koktél,* 1973], devotes as much space to these questions as he does to his impressions of contemporary American reality.

These same issues became even more urgent in the third group of works about America—the belletristic treatments. It should be noted that from the early nineteen-seventies on, the University of Iowa's International Writing Program has had a Hungarian participant every year. Thus, quite a number of Hungarian poets, novelists and translators have had the opportunity to spend up to a year writing and traveling in the United States. Naturally, many of these writers, upon returning home, published not only travel notes and essays but also poems and stories inspired by their American experiences. The "Iowa connection" has become quite well known. Some parts of Iowa City are probably more familiar to Hungarian readers than they are to Iowa residents; and probably more has been written about the Mayflower Apartments (the building in which the participants are housed) than about all other American landmarks combined. Many of these literary works, though set in America, are really about Hungarian lives, Hungarian problems. For example, Ágnes Gergely's *The Chicago Variant [A chicagói változat,* 1976] is the story of a woman whose ambition was to become a professor of Latin, but who winds up as an actress playing bit parts in her hometown, and then touring the Midwestern United States in the company of amateurs from Nigeria and Uganda. The novel is interesting in that it places dilemmas and conflicts long familiar to East-Central European nationals in an international context, suggesting at once the complexity and universality of certain human predicaments. During the course of the novel the heroine herself has to reexamine her native culture and see her own Hungarianness in a new light.

There are few writers in Hungary who have written as much about their American experiences as has Ferenc Karinthy. His first story with an American setting, "Blue-Green Florida" ["Kék-zöld Florida," 1962], appeared years before he set foot in the New World. Karinthy, too, likes to introduce non-Americans in an American milieu. In one of his best-known American stories, "Long Weekend" ["Hosszú weekend," 1973], we meet an eccentric Brazilian poetess, an outrageous Greek, a taciturn Scotchman, an enigmatic Hungarian divorcée, a worldly-wise Viennese professor—there is hardly a native American in the group that gathers at a New York historian's summer home in the Hudson Valley. Although Karinthy has an unerring feeling for local color and is painstakingly accurate in his details, his American novellas and sketches are Hungarian through and through. Some American novelists—Hemingway, for instance—always have their non-American characters speak in a deliberately strange-sounding, unidiomatic English. Karinthy doesn't care for this advice. All his foreign characters sound as though they were sophisticated denizens of Budapest, which makes translating him more difficult than one might think. Because he is also a quintessentially urban writer, Karinthy is attracted to the large metropolitan areas, most of all to New York. "After New York," he writes in one of his sketches, "all other cities seem dull, provincial, intolerable. I miss it from the moment my plane takes off; it is tugging at me, hurting me, pulling me back."[18]

There are a number of Hungarian writers, poets mainly, who in their depictions of America try to get away from the urban, New York-centered view of the country. Of course, the mere fact that the International Writing Program is located in Iowa City and not New York City has done a lot to shift the focus, to change certain images. In his poems about America, Ottó Orbán, a "graduate" of the Iowa Program, reacts against the still popular European notion that America is simply a magnified, jazzed-up version of the Old World. The poet is exhilarated and perplexed by a different tradition, a different landscape—one that is tough, unsubtle, endearing, and in a strange way closer to the primeval past and open-ended future that's always on his mind than is the East European city with a crazy history which doubles as his home. Having spent months in Iowa, Orbán responds to the Midwestern plains, the Indian heritage, the unabashed provincialism of Smalltown, USA. It is in Iowa that poets like Orbán and Imre Oravecz and József Tornai have found answers to questions that have puzzled foreign travelers from the very beginning: Why is America so self-centered? Why are Americans so much more interested in local news than in national or international happenings? These poets attempt to understand self-sufficient, insular, "un-European" America on its own terms; they are eager to learn more about local history, local characters—about the topography and mythology of the hinterlands. In a Whitmanesque poem entitled "America" Orbán exclaims:

> America your verse is more than poetry
> it's a planet-sized risk
> I saw your face at a truck stop, the face of a Southern kid
> wolfing down his meat, shoving it in, and talking with his mouth
>   full the whole time
> SO YOU'RE ONE O' THEM WRITER FELLAHS, EH? AND
>   WHADAYA WRITE?
> For a moment we were brothers in a beginning-and endless black
>   orphanage.[19]

Perhaps in an attempt to get a better sense of the Midwest and the Far West, the poet Imre Oravecz has even tried his hand at writing a few poems in English. His *haikus* convey his reaction to the stark landscape:

> travelling day and night
> seeking the *western way* lost
> both inside, outside
>
> coyote's body
> run over on 80 West,
> the view undamaged
>
> sagebrush, sand and sign,
> buckaroo's trail continues
> in deserted minds[20]

Although more and more visitors may realize that America in many ways is still a country of small towns and sprawling suburbs, there are many travelers who continue to look for, and write about, the great cities. And New York remains on top of their list, even after they have dutifully repeated the cliché that New York is not really America. One of the most curious recent literary works that has been inspired by an encounter with an American is János Pilinszky's *Conversations with Sheryl Sutton* [Beszélgetések Sheryl Suttonnal, 1977]. In this "novel of a dialogue" we find yet another, highly personal, lyrical evocation of New York. To Pilinszky New York is a dramatic, elusive city, a city without history, a Biblical city—"its radiating effect is the same wherever I stand," he writes. It is "a candle burning by itself."[21]

* * * * *

Many of the books and articles about the U.S. published in Hungary in the last fifteen years or so have been about one period in particular— the sixties. Even the works that came out in the early seventies (e.g., Boldizsár's and Almási's book, or the important collection of essays about American society entitled *Assembly Line and Culture* [*Futószalag és kultúra*, 1972] focus their attention on the major cultural and social upheavals of that decade. An apocalyptic novel like Tibor Déry's *Imaginary*

Report about an American Rock Festival [*Képzelt riport egy amerikai popfesztiválról,* 1971] can also be said to have been inspired by the American sixties. The mere fact that during this period books on America appeared not only in Hungary proper but also in Hungarian communities in the neighboring countries indicates the unusual interest in the subject. We have already mentioned János Szász's *I Came from America.* A few years earlier, in 1971, another book appeared in Cluj [Kolozsvár], Romania, by Mária Tamás, entitled *What Are You Like, America? [Milyen vagy, Amerika?].* In the same year a Hungarian writer in Yugoslavia, Tibor Várady, published his impressions of the United States. His book, bearing the interesting title: *Or Isn't Life Itself the Best Pastime? [Vagy nem maga az élet a legjobb időtöltés?],* contains, among other things, a thoughtful examination of the campus unrest of the last sixties. The Hungarian-speaking world's interest in America is also reflected in the numerous travel notes written during the same general period by writers living in the West, among them, Gyula Borbándi, György Gömöri, Gyula Gombos, and Gyula Schöpflin.[22] The interest in the sixties is not surprising—after all, Vietnam, the Civil Rights movement, Women's Lib, the rise of the counter-culture, etc. made the decade one of the most turbulent and exciting in recent American history. Indeed, some of these Hungarian works may be viewed as contributions to contemporary American social history. In all fairness we should also note that much information about America of the sixties arrived in Hungary somewhat late. Many of the works, by the time they were published,had become dated. A recent case in point is Mihály Sükösd's little volume, *Hippie World [Hippivilág,* 1979], a kind of sourcebook on the hippie phenomenon. As reportage the book is passé, as historical, sociological analysis it is inadequate.

It is difficult to say just how much these newer publications have changed the traditional images of America in Hungary. Some of these older myths and clichés (land of unlimited opportunities, technological paradise, capitalist hell, etc.) no doubt survive on some level, among some people. However, it is safe to assume that this body of literature helped make these images less simplistic, more refined and differentiated. Naturally, we must mention at least some of the other factors influencing Hungarian perceptions of America—American literature, film, popular music, the two-way tourist traffic, etc. For instance, in examining bibliographies of recent American literary works published in Hungary, one becomes convinced that anyone interested can read all the major and sometimes not so major recent American novels and plays in translation.[23] We tend to assume that literature always reveals a great deal about an entire society. However, this is not as true of post-war American literature as it is of the influential works of the twenties and thirties. As we know, recent American literature tends to be much more personal and introspective. "American literature," concludes István Sőtér in his travel journal, "is not a good guide book to America."[24] A word should be said, however, about American *literary* influence. Not enough has been written so far about the impact some of the outstanding figures of modern American literature have had on Hungarian writers, though we do know that someone like Hemingway—after all his works became available in Hungary in the late fifties—had an effect even on some of the older Hungarian prose writers. And it's also common knowledge that the beat poets and someone like J.D. Salinger influenced a whole generation of Hungarian poets and novelists.

The question inevitably arises: How do these writings about America strike the reader who examines them not in Hungary but in the United States? I must confess that the experience is both intriguing and frustrating. The traveling Hungarian writer is not easy to please. He is no doubt correct in observing that, say, culture for many Americans is not within easy reach; but should he also talk about one of the widely accessible cultural institutions, he will invariably point to its snob appeal, the tax dollars saved by its patrons, etc. As an American I feel the Hungarian traveler condescends to me with his constant praise of American efficiency, professionalism, organizational skills, etc. Only rarely (as for example in Miklós Vajda's essays about the American theater[25]) is it acknowledged that this great technical excellence and professionalism can also produce *qualitatively* superior achievements. It's understandable that the visitor is astounded, offended by the "average" American's ignorance about contemporary Hungarian or Eastern European reality. What he doesn't realize (though some of his fellow travelers may have already reminded him) is that while Americans may be gauche, clumsily honest about their ignorance, Europeans can usually conceal their ignorance about America with more finesse.

In general I sense a conflict in the Hungarian visitor, a tug of war between his sense of cultural superiority and his awareness of his own country's technological and organizational inferiority. His ambivalence towards radical American social and cultural experiments is often also the result of a conflict: properly progressive political consciousness may be at odds with more conservative instincts. These conflicts and uncertainties may cause the visitor to be, at times, unreasonable, defensive. Eastern European visitors in America have indeed been portrayed as incurable skeptics, devil's advocates, mischief-makers. In the "Iowa stories" we meet quite a few of them. One of the most memorable is Yurek, the irrepressible Pole in Mihály Sükösd's "The Prince of Babylon" ["Babilon hercege," 1979]. Even Ferenc Karinthy's permanently disheveled Brazilian poet, Dolores Simonovic (in "Long Weekend"), is of vaguely Slavic ancestry. Significantly enough, it is often through these erratic, exasperating characters that their creators suggest something about a society that remains restless, searching, challenging.

Needless to say, there is no shortage of genuine praise for America in the works we have considered. Ironically, there are travelers who are appreciative of the very things many Americans have disdain for—the seemingly empty social rituals, the artificial smile, the penchant for self-celebration. Someone like Ágnes Gergely finds these helpful, comforting. "There is so little joy," she says; "Americans squeeze out of life as much as they can."[26] Other writers do not tire of pointing out just how crucial American innovations, perceptions—in such areas as ecology, urban planning consumer protection, etc.—are to Hungary, to Europe. Imre Szász puts it this way: "Regardless of social systems, America is an example and a warning to any country that has reached a certain stage of industrial development. We must learn from America's mistakes . . . [and] solutions."[27] But above all it's the realization that the United States has lost none of its energy and drive and brashness—the fact that it is still, in Ferenc Karinthy's words, a "Balzacian society"[28]—that creates interest in the country. The very unpredictability of America makes for excitement—and anxiety. According to novelist György Konrád, America as a nation "knows too little about helplessness and humiliations. She hasn't recovered from her defeats because she hasn't yet had real defeats. She doesn't know what it is like not to act, so we cannot be sure when she does act."[29]

We might conclude by saying that it's always easier to write about another country's problems than about our own. Gyula Illyés mentions in *People of the Puszta [Puszták népe]* that in mid-nineteenth-century Hungary ladies' literary magazines published heart-rending stories about the fate of the American Negro slaves, while the plight of millions of landless Hungarian peasants went all but unnoticed. A perfect historical parallel to this is the enthusiastic reception the American people gave to Lajos Kossuth. He was hailed as a champion of freedom at a time when slavery was still an entrenched institution in the South. The fact is that a number of abolitionists, including Frederick Douglass, were disappointed that Kossuth made no mention of the slavery issue in any of his public speeches, evidently for fear of antagonizing would-be supporters for his cause. "We feel for Hungary," declared Douglass in one of his speeches, "but how can we as a nation exert an influence favorable to freedom in the old world while we are oppressors at home?"[30]

Among the works on America published in Hungary in the last decade and a half, the truly valuable and memorable ones are those that are just as fair-minded—and compassionate—about the New World as they are about things closer to home.

NOTES

*The author would like to thank the International Research and Exchanges Board (IREX) of New York for financial support during the preparation of this study.

1. See Anna Katona, "Hungarian Travelogues on Pre-Civil War America," *Hungarian Studies in English* (Debrecen), V (1971), pp. 51-94.
2. See István Gál, "Széchenyi and the U.S.A." *Hungarian Studies in English,* V (1971), p. 105. See also Sándor Bölöni-Farkas, *Utazás Észak-Amerikában* [Journey in North America] (Kolozsvár-Napoca: Dácia Kiadó, 1975), p. 326.
3. See László Országh, "'Anglomania' in Hungary, 1780-1900," *The New Hungarian Quarterly,* no. 82 (1981), pp. 168-179. Muted echoes of this "English connection" can be found even in postwar Hungarian literature. For example, in Gyula Illyés's masterly prose work, *Ebéd a kastélyban* [Luncheon at the Manor] frequent references are made to the relatives of a déclassé Hungarian count, who after the war helped out their poor relations in Hungary with modest food parcels. And the hero

of Mihály Sükösd's novel, *Vizsgálati fogság* [Awaiting Trial], a wartime Hungarian prime minister accused of collaborating with the Nazis, is, in his taste and deportment at least, decidedly un-Eastern European and quite English.

4. See Anna Katona, "The Hungarian Image of Benjamin Franklin," *The Canadian American Review of Hungarian Studies*, IV (Spring 1977), pp. 43-57.

5. See my review of Országh's *Angol eredetű elemek a magyar szókészletben* [English Elements in the Hungarian Vocabulary], in *The New Hungarian Quarterly*, no. 69 (1978), pp. 156-157.

6. Mihály Babits, *Összegyűjtött versei* [Collected Poems] (Budapest: Szépirodalmi Könyvkiadó, 1977), p. 46.

7. Endre Szirmai, "A Reményi-hagyaték: Levelek Reményi Józsefnek Amerikában" [The Reményi Papers: Letters to József Reményi in America], *Új Látóhatár* [New Horizon], XXIX (July, 1978), p. 132.

8. *Bolsevik szemmel a világ körül* [Around the World with Bolshevik Eyes] (Budapest: Szikra, 1950), pp. 297-300.

9. See Jürg Federspiel, *A gyűlölet múzeuma* [The Museum of Hate] (Budapest: Európa Könyvkiadó, 1974); and Edith Anderson, *A megfigyelő nem lát semmit* [The Observer Sees Nothing] (Budapest: Magvető Könyvkiadó, 1976).

10. Zsuzsanna Gál, *Feleség voltam New Yorkban* [I Was a Wife in New York] (Budapest: Táncsics Könyvkiadó, 1967), p. 5.

11. Miklós Almási, *Rezgésszámok: Beszélgetések a mai Amerikáról* [Frequencies: Conversations about Today's America] (Budapest: Magvető Könyvkiadó, 1974), pp. 15-16.

12. Pál Ipper, *A túlsó partról jelentem* [Reporting from the Other Shore] (Budapest: Gondolat Könyvkiadó, 1970), p. 110.

13. Klára Fehér and László Nemes, *Irokézek és felhőkarcolók* [Iroquois and Sky Scrapers] (Budapest: Táncsics Könyvkiadó, 1968), p. 201.

14. Iván Boldizsár, *New York percről percre* [New York Minute by Minute] (Budapest: Magvető Könyvkiadó, 1971), p. 134

15. Ibid., p. 175.

16. István Sőtér, *Vacsora Carmelban* [Dinner in Carmel] (Budapest: Gondolat Könyvkiadó, 1968), p. 213.

17. Ibid., pp. 46-47.

18. Ferenc Karinthy, *Leányfalu és vidéke* [Leányfalu and Vicinity] (Budapest: Szépirodalmi Könyvkiadó, 1973), p. 520.

19. Ottó Orbán, *A visszacsavart láng* [The Turned-Down Flame] (Budapest: Magvető Könyvkiadó, 1979), p. 73.

20. Imre Oravecz, *Egy földterület növénytakarójának változása* [Changes in the Vegetation of a Region] (Budapest: Magvető Könyvkiadó, 1979), p. 66.

21. János Pilinszky, *Beszélgetések Sheryl Suttonnal* [Conversations with Sheryl Sutton] (Budapest: Szépirodalmi Könyvkiadó, 1977), pp. 26, 86.

22. See Gyula Gombos, "Amerikai jegyzetek" [Notes about America], *Új Látóhatár*, XVI (1965), pp. 481-494; Gyula Schöpflin, "Kaliforniai útinapló" [California Travelogue], *Új Látóhatár*, XVII (1969), pp. 55-69; György Gömöri, "Amerikai notesz" [American Notes], *Híd* [Bridge], XXIX (1966), pp. 230-238; idem, "Amerika, 1971," *Híd*, XXXIV (1971), pp. 739-747; and Gyula Borbándi, "Magyar Amerikában" [In Hungarian America], *Új Látóhatár*, XXVIII (1977), pp. 109-142.

23. See "Az amerikai irodalom Magyarországon: Válogatott bibliográfia" [American Literature in Hungary: A Selected Bibliography], in László Országh, *Az amerikai irodalom története* [A History of American Literature] (Budapest: Gondolat Könyvkiadó, 1967), pp. 414-424. See also "Hungarian Essays on American Literature (1945-1977)," *Acta Litteraria*, XX (1978), pp. 179-186; and my review of Gábor Mihályi's *Index of the English Column in "Nagyvilág"*, in *East European Quarterly*, VIII (1974), pp. 387-389. The American scholar Kent Bales is not quite fair in claiming that Hungarian publishers and periodicals have been neglecting the more recent, "post-modernist" American fiction. Cf. his "Factors Determining the Translation of American Belles-Letteres into Hungarian, 1945-1973," *Slavonic and East European Review*, LIV (1976), pp. 171-191. As Gábor Mihályi points out in his response to Bales's article, the fact that fewer works are published in Hungary by avant-garde American novelists is not the result of a political, ideological decision, but of an editorial one, which in turn is based on anticipated reader interest. Cf. Mihályi's "Az amerikai irodalom Magyarországon—amerikai szemmel" [American Literature in Hungary—Through American Eyes], *Nagyvilág* [Wide World], XXII (July, 1977), pp. 1096-1098.

24. *István Sőtér, Vacsora Carmelben*, p. 17.

25. See Miklós Vajda, "Broadway és vidéke" [Broadway and its Vicinity], in István Bart and Miklós Hernádi, eds., *Futószalag és kultúra*

[Assembly Line and Culture] (Budapest: Gondolat Könyvkiadó, 1972), pp. 165-171.

26. Interview with the author, November, 1979.
27. Imre Szász, *Száraz martini koktél* [Dry Martini] (Budapest: Szépirodalmi Könyvkiadó, 1973), p. 311.
28. Interview with the author, November, 1979.
29. György Konrád, "Mit gondolok Amerikáról? " [What Do I Think About America], unpublished essay.
30. Philip S. Foner, ed., *The Life and Writings of Frederick Douglass* (5 vols., New York: International Publishers, 1950-1975), V, p. 228.

Hans L. Trefousse

ABRAHAM LINCOLN VERSUS ANDREW JOHNSON: TWO APPROACHES TO RECONSTRUCTION

Recent scholarship has once again raised crucial questions about the consequences of John Wilkes Booth's crime. If, as has been repeatedly shown, earlier interpretations of the similarity of Abraham Lincoln's and Andrew Johnson's plans of Reconstruction are incorrect, what was the difference between the two? How significant were these discrepancies and what were the reasons for them?

Aside from the obvious fact that Lincoln's policies were designed for a nation at war and Johnson's for one at peace, the first difference lay in the pragmatic nature of Lincoln's approach as compared with the doctrinaire character of his successor's. Devised to undermine the Confederacy in wartime, Lincoln's proposals tended to vary with changing conditions. Phrasing his first references to eventual Reconstruction with care, he repeatedly assured the Southern states that he intended no modification of his purpose of maintaining the Union and the rights of the states inviolate. In his message to Congress of July 4, 1861, he merely qualified this promise by inserting the word, "probably."[1] It was to prove an important modification.

Lincoln was neither able, nor even anxious to maintain his original position. Early in 1862 it became apparent that something other than mere restoration was called for. Tennessee had been partially reconquered, and parts of Louisiana, Arkansas, and North Carolina were under Federal control as well. Carefully weighing all possibilities, the President appointed Andrew Johnson Military Governor of Tennessee. General George F. Shepley took over similar functions in Louisiana, John Phelps Smith in Arkansas, and Edward Stanly, a conservative Unionist, became Military Governor of North Carolina. The last appointment caused trouble because Stanly closed the black schools, but in choosing him, Lincoln doubtless was thinking of winning away from the Confederacy as many wavering Carolinians as possible. It was clear, however, that the time was not yet ripe for the announcement of an overall plan for Reconstruction.[2]

Aware of this, Lincoln refrained from promulgating a general policy. He sanctioned partial solutions, such as the election of congressmen from Louisiana. He also lent his support, however reluctantly, to the project of setting up a separate state in West Virginia, while recognizing the "Restored Government of Virginia" under Governor Francis Pierpoint at Alexandria. Then, when he deemed the time appropriate, he announced his own far-reaching project.[3]

The plan in question was his Amnesty Proclamation of December 8, 1863, the "Ten Percent Plan." Having dealt stunning blows to the Confederacy at Gettysburg, Vicksburg, and Chattanooga, Union forces were now in a position to exert further pressure on the insurgents. Reconstruction policies could support the war effort; many Southerners were thought to be weary of the war and might be lured back to their former allegiance. Accordingly, with a few exceptions, Lincoln promised amnesty to all who were willing to take an oath of allegiance, and as soon as ten percent of the 1860 voters in any state had complied, they might form a new government. This arrangement left out black suffrage, but the President insisted on the acceptance of the Emancipation Proclamation, and, as La Wanda Cox has shown, it could be interpreted as "a means to precipitate an antislavery minority government." If he disregarded Congress, his aim was to undermine the Confederacy, and Lincoln at that time deemed it the best way of doing so.[4]

The subsequent controversy between Lincoln and Congress concerning the Wade-Davis Bill did not charge the fact that he was still pursuing a flexible and pragmatic policy in the midst of war. Even when pocketing the congressional measure, he characterized it "as one very proper plan for the loyal people of any state choosing to adopt it." He sought to reconstruct Louisiana as quickly as possible, and though by the beginning of 1865 he was again at loggerheads with Congress, conditions were changing so rapidly that he was quite prepared to alter his course.[5]

It was Lee's surrender at Appomattox that made it possible for Lincoln to pursue a different policy. When on April 2, 1865, after the fall of Richmond, he visited the former enemy capital, he still agreed to permit a meeting of the Confederate Legislature of Virginia for the purpose of taking the state out of the war. But on April 9, the Army of Northern Virginia capitulated. No longer constrained to use Reconstruction policies as a weapon of war, the President—admitting the validity of the objections of his cabinet, to say nothing of those of the radicals—promptly withdrew his invitation.[6] Active hostilities in Virginia had ceased, and a different policy was called for. How different this policy was was soon to become clear.

The problem of Negro suffrage had long been a divisive issue; as long as he was still mainly concerned with the pursuit of the war, Lincoln was loath to come to grips with the franchise question, at least in public. Yet it was becoming increasingly clear that Reconstruction under Republican auspices would be simplified if it were coupled with at least limited black voting, and many radicals made the concept their own. Although Lincoln had long been careful not to become identified too closely with so revolutionary a change, he soon came to see its logic. His Secretary of the Treasury was committed to some form of black enfranchisement by the end of 1863, and he followed suit not long afterward. Of course he said nothing in public; any pronouncement on so delicate an issue would have interfered with his aim of undermining the Confederacy. Nevertheless, he confided his ideas to a few correspondents in private. In the one paragraph of a letter to General James A. Wadsworth, which even those who have doubted the authenticity of the entire document have conceded to be "in keeping with Lincoln's known sentiments," he wrote early in 1864: "I cannot see, if universal amnesty is granted, how, under the circumstances, I can avoid exacting in return universal suffrage, or at least suffrage on the basis of intelligence and military service." Likewise, on March 13, he admonished Governor Michael Hahn of newly reconstructed Louisiana:

> I congratulate you on having fixed your name in history as the first free-state Governor of Louisiana. Now you are about to have a Convention which, among other things, will probably define the

> elective franchise. I barely suggest for your private consideration, whether some of the colored people may not be let in—as, for instance, the very intelligent, and especially those who have fought gallantly in our ranks. They would probably help, in some trying time to come, to keep the jewel of liberty within the family of freedom.[7]

Hahn never acted on Lincoln's proposal, and the Reconstruction policy the President had inaugurated with his Ten Percent Plan proceeded accordingly. Considering his anxiety to undermine the Confederates' will to fight and to safeguard the abolition of slavery, the President did not protest. After Appomattox, however, he was free from previous constraints. He could now publicly avow his commitment to black suffrage, and on April 11, he did so.

The occasion for his announcement was his last public address, delivered at the White House four days before his death. Speaking to a large crowd, he turned to the subject of Reconstruction in Louisiana. "The amount of constituency, so to speak, on which the Louisiana government rests, would be more satisfactory to all if it contained fifty thousand, or even twenty thousand, instead of twelve thousand, as it does," he said. "It is also unsatisfactory to some that the elective franchise is not given to the colored man. I would myself prefer that it were now conferred on the very intelligent, and on those who serve our cause as soldiers." He even endorsed schools for blacks.[8] Evidently, his publicly announced plans for Reconstruction after Appomattox differed materially from those before.

Johnson's attitude toward Reconstruction, on the contrary, never changed. Convinced that secession was illegal and that all that was needed was the submission of the Southern states to federal authority, he promulgated his policies in May 1865 and never swerved from them. Like Lincoln, he offered amnesty to all but a handful of leading ex-confederates; like Lincoln, he authorized them to set up new state governments. The war was over and there was no longer any need for requiring only ten percent of the old voters to take the oath of loyalty. But the conditions under which the states could be restored were extremely easy, and with the exception of the omission of the ten percent requirement, it would have been difficult to learn from the scheme that the nation was now at peace, no longer engaged in civil war. All the President asked of the

Southerners, with a few exceptions, was that they take an oath of allegiance. Then they could rebuild their governments. He hoped that they would nullify the secession ordinances, repudiate the Confederate debt, and ratify the Thirteenth Amendment, but he did not even insist on these conditions. Congress, he thought, would have to go along with him. And when it refused, his only response was to reiterate his position.[9]

A second difference was the two men's style and method of political operations. Lincoln was a supreme judge of men, who knew how to handle and cajole his political collaborators, as well as his opponents. An extremely flexible practitioner of the fine art of human relations, he achieved his success by astute management. Able to endure temporary personal disappointments without murmur, willing to remain in the background whenever necessary, he yet succeeded in regaining the center of the stage when it counted. Consequently, no matter how severely individual radicals may have criticized the President, he knew very well how to work with the ultras. They were furious because of his disallowance of John C. Frémont's emancipation order, only to be somewhat mollified when Lincoln called for compensated emancipation in the border states. The President, who told Charles Sumner he was only six weeks behind the senator, even read beforehand and approved of a radical speech on abolition which the German-American leader, Carl Schurz, was about to deliver to a group of supporters in New York. After signing the bill for freedom in the District of Columbia, he excited the radicals' fury once more because he disapproved of General David Hunter's emancipation project in the Department of the South. But eventually he gave his assent to the second Confiscation Act and wrote the Emancipation Proclamation.[10]

During the two months between his decision to issue the document and its actual publication, he had to withstand enormous pressure without revealing his secret. How well he knew how to cope with this problem he showed in his answer to Horace Greeley's "Prayer of the Twenty Millions" asking him to free all the slaves at once. Stating that he would save the Union the shortest way under the Constitution, and declaring that his paramount object was neither to save nor destroy slavery but to save the Union, he closed with a ringing affirmation of his own thoughts. "I have here stated my purpose according to my official duty," he concluded, "and I intend no modification of my oft-expressed personal wish that all men, everywhere, could be free." Shortly afterward he issued the Preliminary Emancipation Proclamation, and, despite strong pressure from the conservatives, followed it up with the final document on January 1, 1863.[11]

These actions enabled Lincoln to continue working closely with the radicals in Congress. No matter how much they criticized him, they voted for his war measures, provided legislative support for his policies, and tended to strengthen the Republican Party. If new rifts developed between him and the Missouri "Charcoals," he knew how to bridge them. Considering these ultras "absolutely uncorrosive by the virus of secession," he was certain that he would ultimately have to rely on them. "If one side must be crushed out and the other cherished," he said to John Hay, "there could be no doubt which side we would choose as fuller of hope for the future. We would have to side with the radicals." In fact, as he put it, though the radicals were the "unhandiest devils in the world to deal with," nevertheless, their faces were set "Zionward."[12]

Holding these views, he was able to overcome even the furious opposition to his veto of the Wade-Davis Bill. Execrated by Senator Benjamin F. Wade and Representative Henry Winter Davis, in the end he nevertheless succeeded in placating most of his critics. After dismissing Postmaster General Montgomery Blair, he was able to lead the newly consolidated party to victory in November.[13]

Johnson lacked this ability. He rose by sheer force of personal pluck, betraying a stubborn streak and aggressive habits that made him many personal enemies. Unable to yield until the last moment, he obstinately clung to ideas which remained fixed throughout his career. While this tendency kept him faithful to the Union during the Civil War, thus putting him in line for the Vice Presidency, it also contributed materially to his subsequent troubles with Congress and the party. Instead of seeking to conciliate the moderate Republicans, he alienated them by vetoing the Freedmen's Bureau and Civil Rights Bills. Instead of compromising after his defeat in the fall of 1866, he continued to oppose the ratification of the Fourteenth Amendment and sent truculent messages to the Capitol. Instead of seeking some sort of accommodation in the face of probable impeachment, he openly challenged Congress until the impeachment resolution was passed by a strict party vote. Only when threatened

Two Approaches to Reconstruction

with probable ouster did he finally agree to some concessions which procured his acquittal by one vote. And, in spite of all his appeals to the opposition, in 1868 he failed to obtain the Democratic nomination for President.[14]

These differences in outlook and mode of operation may of course be accounted for by dissimilarities in personality and political ability. There is, however, a more fundamental explanation for their obvious effect on Reconstruction. Because Reconstruction was primarily concerned with the position of the blacks in American society, the two Presidents' diametrically opposed attitude on the race question was the evident cause of their differing approaches.

It is clear that both Lincoln and Johnson grew up in a racist environment. Kentucky was a slave state, and though Lincoln's family eventually moved to southern Indiana and Illinois, the lower Middle West retained many of the bigoted assumptions of the South. Yet Lincoln managed to overcome some of his early prejudices, while Johnson retained the majority of the ideas of his youth throughout his life.

The question of Lincoln's views about race has been extensively debated. Don E. Fehrenbacher and George M. Frederickson, in their standard articles on the subject, emphasize the Emancipator's failure to rid himself of all traces of racism. But as Richard N. Current, writing about Lincoln, has put it so well, "the most remarkable thing about him was his tremendous power of growth." This point of view has been developed further in LaWanda Cox's *Lincoln and Black Freedom,* and the evidence for it is substantial. Toward racial as toward other problems, Lincoln's attitude was flexible.[15]

It is not surprising that Lincoln was not free from the usual prejudices of his neighbors. Born in a slave state and raised there as well as in southern Indiana—as pro-Southern an area as could be found in the North— he associated with poor whites like himself who were deeply imbued with ideas of racial supremacy. Even later, when he met more affluent members of the community, he moved in circles that took the idea of white supremacy for granted. Virtually the only blacks he ever saw were either slaves or the downtrodden victims of the Middle West's harsh racial laws.[16]

Yet for his place and time, the Great Emancipator was very broadminded. His reaction to a coffle of slaves being taken downriver in chains on a boat has often been cited. Amazed that a group of human beings in such circumstances could still be cheerful and apparently happy, he mused on the effect of condition on "human happiness." He later professed to remember that the sight had been "a continual torment" to him, but even if his recollection was exaggerated, as George Frederickson has pointed out he proved that he believed blacks responded "to conditions of common humanity, and not as the result of peculiar racial characteristics."[17]

Many of Lincoln's speeches in the 1850s have been quoted to prove his alleged racism. At Peoria in 1854, he said that he was not contending for the "establishment of social equality between whites and blacks;" at Charleston in 1858, he reemphasized the point by declaring, "I am not, nor ever have been in favor of making voters or jurors of negroes, nor of qualifying them to hold office, nor to intermarry with white people." He even went so far as to predict that the physical differences between whites and blacks would forever forbid their living together on terms of social and political equality. And as this meant that, while they remained together, one of the two must be superior to the other, he "as much as any other man" was "in favor of having the superior position assigned to the white race." Often repeating these statements, he again underscored his basic beliefs in 1859 at Columbus, where he stated that he was not contending for the social and political equality of Negroes and whites.[18] Considering the pressure put upon him by conservative friends who were warning him not to appear to be too radical, his disavowals are easy to understand.[19]

When Lincoln became President, he still adhered to these views. Insisting that the war was a struggle for the Union, and not for the abolition of slavery, he disappointed many a radical.

As time went on, however, he gradually shifted toward ever more advanced positions. Signing into law the first and second Confiscation Acts, the bill to free the slaves in the District of Columbia, and the measure abolishing slavery in the territories, he showed that he was not wedded to a rigid approach to the race question. He issued the Emancipation Proclamation and refused absolutely to rescind it. He raised over 170,000 black troops and used all the powers of his office to secure the passage of the Thirteenth Amendment. Finally he came to support Black suffrage, a clear indication of the tremendous growth of the man who had once said Negroes could never be given equal rights. If he still seemed

Two Approaches to Reconstruction 259

to favor colonization for the freedmen, he must soon have realized that it would never work. But the conservatives were acutely unhappy with his antislavery measures, and the colonization scheme was a means of keeping them contented.[20]

How far he had moved from his earlier conviction that blacks would always remain inferior to whites, socially and politically, he showed by his cordial reception of Frederick Douglass at the White House. "In his company I was never reminded of my humble origin or my unpopular color," the black leader recalled. When at the time of the second inauguration police sought to bar him from the White House, he appealed to the President, who immediately let him in. "Here comes my friend Douglass," Lincoln exclaimed in a loud voice. Taking his visitor by the hand, he asked him how he liked the inaugural address. "There is no man in the country whose opinion I value more than yours," the President added, or at least Douglass remembered it that way. Lincoln's actions were in line with his statements. When a few days later he asked for limited black suffrage, he so horrified John Wilkes Booth, who was in the audience, that the actor made his final decision to kill the President.[21]

Johnson's position on the race question was almost the reverse of Lincoln's. Never outgrowing the influences of his childhood, he not only approved of slavery, but, as the owner of several bondsmen, consistently defended the "peculiar institution." Speaking in 1844 against the repeal of the gag rule, he asked whether the abolitionists were willing to "turn over two million negroes loose upon the country to become a terror and a burden to society, producing disaffection between them and their former masters, finally to be fanned into a flame . . . a servile war, resulting in the entire extirpation of that race in the United States, besides shedding much of the white man's blood." Slavery, he asserted, had existed for over 5,000 years, "If one portion of the country were to be masters and the other menials . . . , he had no hesitancy in bringing his mind to a conclusion on the subject, believing, as he did, that the black race of Africa were inferior to the white man in point of intellect—better calculated in physcial structure to undergo drudgery and hardship—standing as they do, many degrees lower in the scale of gradation that expresses the relative relation between God and all that he has created than the white man." If the laws did not distinguish between white and black, they would "place every spay-footed, bandy-shanked, hump-backed, thick-lipped, flat-nosed, woolly headed, ebon-colored negro in the country upon an equality with the poor white man."

Johnson hardly ever deviated from this fundamental view. In 1848, in a colloquy with James G. Palfrey of Massachusetts, who had spoken of the accomplishments of educated blacks, the Tennessee congressman proceeded to challenge his colleague's basic assumptions. Descending to a new low, he queried whether Palfrey would ever allow his daughter to marry even an accomplished Negro. Johnson believed slavery to be so closely connected with the operations of the government that it might be considered "one of the principal ingredients of our political and social system . . . , a part of the warp and woof that cannot be prematurely removed without spoiling the web." In 1850, in the debates about the Omnibus Bill, he attacked the proposed abolition of the slave trade in the District of Columbia. Declaring that slavery had its foundation, and would find its perpetuity, in the Union, he asserted that the Union would find its continuance in non-interference with slavery. As Negroes were nothing but property, what was property worth if a man could not sell it?[22]

In addition, Johnson was convinced that democracy and slavery, far from being opposites, complemented each other. In the North, the oppression of workers resulted in white slavery; in the South, democracy was based on the blacks' servile condition. "Thus we see that our institution, instead of being antagonistical to democracy, is in perfect harmony with it," he explained in 1856 in an address to the state Democratic convention. Holding these beliefs, he disapproved of the presence of free blacks in the state. As governor, he cheerfully executed the law providing for help to Negroes desiring to emigrate to Liberia, and later favored a state proposal to expel all manumitted slaves from Tennessee.

But his insistence on colonization did not mean either that he was critical of slavery or thought the races could ever achieve equality. In a speech at Raleigh, Tennessee, in 1857, he explained that "he regarded the negro here in a state of slavery in a far better condition than the native African at home. His connection with the white man had an elevating tendency, and many of those negroes who had returned to Liberia had relapsed into the barbarous and savage habits of the natives, showing that the negro is an inferior type of man and incapable of advancing in his native country."[23]

His consistency in maintaining these opinions was remarkable. In a debate about the admission of Minnesota in 1858, he objected to provisions in its constitution conferring citizenship on blacks, and aliens—he did not want Negroes to enjoy such rights, he said. In the debates following John Brown's raid on Harpers Ferry, he sought to demolish the contention that the Declaration of Independence and Jefferson's famous assertion of human equality included Blacks. The idea was ridiculous, he asserted: had not Jefferson himself been a slave holder and were not blacks considered property at the time of the Revolution? And how could blacks and whites, ordained by God to be different, enjoy the same rights and privileges? He even held fast to his fear that the only outcome of emancipation would be the complete destruction of the black race. Should such an event occur, the non slave-holder of the South would unite with the slave holder, and the result would be the extirpation of the Negroes.

It might have been assumed that the secession crisis, during which Johnson stood out because of his loyalty to the Union, might have caused him to modify some of these views, but in fact the contrary was the case. In his great speech of December 18-19, 1860, pleading for reconciliation, he reasserted his conviction that slavery and the Union were inevitably tied together. "If I were an abolitionist and wanted to accomplish the abolition and overthrow of slavery," he stated, "the first step that I would take would be to break the bonds of this Union, and dissolve this Government. I believe the continuance of slavery depends upon the preservation of this Union; and I believe a dissolution of this Union will, in the end ...overthrow the institution of slavery."[24] His arguments were not inconsistent with his support of the Presidential ticket of John C. Breckinridge and its espousal of a federal slave code for the territories.

When, in spite of Johnson's efforts, the South broke up the Union, carried Tennessee with it, and formed the Confederacy, he became famous as the only senator from a seceding state to remain in Washington. This fact led Lincoln, who in time of war was anxious to strengthen national unity and undermine the enemey's popular support, to appoint Johnson military governor of Tennessee and eventually make him his running mate. But Johnson's opinions on slavery and racial equality did not undergo any change. One of the co-sponsors of the Johnson-Crittenden resolutions asserting that the war was not being waged for the purpose of interfering "with the rights or established institutions" of the states, he consistently maintained his position.[25] Taking advantage of the

President's known desire to reanimate Unionism, as Military Governor of Tennessee Johnson was instrumental in securing the state's exemption from the provisions of the Emancipation Proclamation.[26] Only when it became evident that in order to save the Union and win the war slavery would have to go, did he choose his loyalty to the United States over his attachment to the "peculiar institution," but even then he did not for a moment alter his opinions about the alleged racial superiority of the whites.

His position was never in doubt. Forced to supervise the enlistment of blacks in the army, he attempted to restrict them to menial tasks; compelled to assent to emancipation, he sought to reassure his fellow citizens. He advocated freedom for the blacks, he said on New Year's Day, 1864, but while doing so, he did not argue "that the Negro race is equal to the Anglo-Saxon." Continuing to believe that "this is a white man's government," he asserted that if whites and blacks could not get along together in freedom, arrangements must be made to colonize the Negroes.[27]

So unusual was it for Johnson to change his mind that he felt compelled to explain his turnabout. Not he, but those who were trying to break up the Union were responsible for it. "In trying to save slavery, you killed it, and lost your own freedom," he told a Nashville audience on July 4, 1864. "Your slavery is dead, but I did not murder it." As for the blacks, he admonished them that liberty did not mean idleness. It meant the freedom to work and to enjoy the fruits of their own labor. In any case, he believed that he was really freeing more whites than blacks in the state.[28]

The closest Johnson ever came to expressing sympathy for the Blacks was in October 1864, when he addressed a large gathering of Negroes in Nashville and proclaimed them all free. Looking at the eager faces in front of him, he exclaimed that he was almost induced to wish that as in the days of old a Moses might arise to lead them safely to their promised land of freedom and happiness. "You are our Moses," they shouted. Continuing to speak of divine providence preparing an instrument for their redemption and revealing a Moses to them, he merely evoked new outbursts of, "We want no Moses but you." The speaker, carried away by the occasion, retorted: "Well, then, humble and unworthy as I am, if no better should be found, I will indeed be your Moses, and lead you through the Red Sea of war and bondage to a fairer future of liberty and peace." He even promised that loyal men, white or black, should alone control the destinies of the state once the war was over. But this momentary lapse had no permanent significance.[29]

Not even Johnson's subsequent election as Vice President on the Union ticket caused him to modify his opinions. In 1865 he was still telling Senator John Conness of California that he had never been opposed to slavery, "that the blacks were happiest in that condition or one near it," and that white men alone must manage the South.[30] In the fall of that year, he explained to Benjamin B. French, the Commissioner of Public Buildings, that every one would and must admit that the white race was superior to the black, "and while we ought to do our best to bring... the blacks up to our present level, that, in doing so, we should, at the same time raise our own intellectual status so that the relative position of the two races would remain the same."[31]

Nevertheless, Johnson's real position was not generally fully understood. His rambling discourse at the time of Lincoln's second inauguration gave little clue to his opinions about race, and when after the crime at Ford's Theater he became President, many of the leading members of Congress were misled about his attitude. His constantly reiterated denunciations of Southerners as traitors and his demands for stern punishment of rebels caused many observers to overlook the fact that his ideas on black suffrage were very different from theirs. Even Sumner thought Johnson agreed with him, although Frederick Douglass was not fooled. Standing in the crowd at the time of the second inauguration, he saw Lincoln touching Johnson and pointing out the black leader to him. "The first expression which came to his face, and which I think was the true index of his heart," Douglass remembered, "was one of bitter contempt and aversion." Turning to one of his friends, he said, "Whatever Johnson may be, he certainly is no friend to our race."[32]

Douglass was right. In spite of his caution during the first few weeks of his administration, Johnson soon inaugurated his Reconstruction policy which based the Southern electorate on the voters of 1860, thus excluding the blacks. To be sure, in August 1865, superficially following in the footsteps of his predecessor, he urged limited black suffrage upon the Governor of Mississippi. "If you could extend the elective franchise to all persons of color who can read the Constitution of the United States in English and write their names, and to all persons of color who own real estate valued at not less than two hundred and fifty dollars and pay taxes thereon," he wrote to Governor William L. Sharkey, "you would completely disarm the adversary and set an example the other States will follow." But as his language showed, he did not make this suggestion because of conviction. "This you can do with perfect safety," he continued, "and thus place the Southern States in reference to free persons of color upon the same basis with the free States. I hope and trust your convention will do this, and as a consequence the Radicals who are wild upon Negro franchise, will be completely foiled in their attempts to keep the Southern States from renewing their relations to the Union by not accepting their Senators and Representatives."[33] For Lincoln to have made such a statement is inconceivable.

How passionately Johnson held on to his prejudices became obvious the following month. Complaining bitterly about the black troops in his home town, he wrote to General George H. Thomas, the commander of the area:

> I have information of the most reliable character that the negro troops stationed at Greeneville, Tenn. and under little or no restraint . . . are committing depredations throughout the country, domineering over, and in fact running the white people out of the neighborhood . . . . The negro soldiery take possession of and occupy property in the town at discretion, and have even gone so far as to have taken my own house and converted it into a rendez-vous for male and female negroes, who have been congregated there, in fact making it a common negro brothel. It was bad enough to be taken by traitors and converted into a hospital but a negro whore house is infinitely worse.

He asked that the troops be removed as the people of East Tennessee "above all others are the last who should be afflicted with the outrages of the negro soldiery."[34]

Although in public the President still seemed to favor at least some form of limited black suffrage, in private he was unrelenting. Interfering with the local elections in Connecticut by making it clear that he opposed black suffrage, he went so far as to countenance the black codes that were beginning to appear on Southern statute books—legislation that virtually remanded the freedmen to slavery.[35]

Two Approaches to Reconstruction

The depth of his feeling and the effect of his prejudices became evident in February of 1867. In an interview with a delegation of black leaders including Douglass, he stunned his visitors with a chilling reply to their plea for universal male suffrage. As one who had perilled all his means for the colored race, he said, he did not like to be arraigned "by some who can get up handsomely rounded periods and deal in rhetoric." Although he was a friend of the "colored man," he did not intend to adopt a policy he believed would result in a contest between the races and if persisted, in the extermination of one or the other. After some further sharp retorts to Douglass, he dismissed the group.[36]

News of the interview greatly encouraged the President's supporters. Benjamin B. French wrote him how much he appreciated the intelligence. It merely confirmed the sentiments Johnson had expressed to him in the fall. Conservatives in general were delighted with "Andy Johnson's stand on the nigger question," and they had every reason to be. His secretary told the newspaper man Philip Ripley "that the President no more expected that darkey delegation yesterday than he did the cholera. He saw their little game & when they tried to withdraw, he told them to 'hold on.'" As Ripley reported the incident to Manton Marble, "When they went out after his speech he turned to the Secretary . . . and uttered the following terse Saxon: "Those d--d sons of b--s thought they had me in a trap. I know that d--d Douglas; he's just like any nigger, & would sooner cut a white man's throat than not."[37]

This interview showed clearly how little the President had changed. He still clung to the same opinions of white supremacy, of the likelihood of the extermination of the blacks, and of the disadvantage of racial equality for the poor whites that he had always held. Evidently, neither war nor election as a Unionist had made any dent on Johnson's deeply rooted convictions. "Mr. Johnson's olden education and prejudices incline him to attach too much weight to the ancient antagonism between the races," observed John Jay. And as late as 1868, the President's close confidant, Colonel W. G. Moore, wrote in his diary:

> The President has at times exhibited morbid distress and feeling against the negroes. Yesterday noon and this morning a dozen stout negroes were hauling a heavy stone roller over grass and walks of the grounds, around the garden house. He at once wanted to know if all the white men had been discharged; and as I could do no more

> than tell him I would make inquiry, he asked his doorkeeper if the white men were not yet employed about the building and grounds .... The evident discrimination made here in behalf of the negroes was sufficient to excite the disgust of all reflecting men.[38]

Holding such opinions, Johnson naturally approached Reconstruction from a different perspective from Lincoln's. He objected to the Civil Rights Bill on the ground that it discriminated against "large numbers of intelligent, worthy, and patriotic foreigners" in favor of the Negro;[39] he consistently opposed the Fourteenth Amendment with its guarantees of black citizenship and civil rights, and in his annual message of December 1867 he summed up the racial views he had held for so long. Asserting that Negroes had shown less capacity for government than any other race of people, he insisted that, whenever they had been left to their own devices, they had shown a constant tendency to relapse into barbarism. Not even the impeachment trial changed his mind. In his last annual message, he once more gave vent to his views of racial inequality.[40] Whatever may have been Johnson's good qualities, the ability to outgrow his prejudices was not among them.

In view of these facts, it is clear that Booth's crime was a disaster for the country. Not only were Lincoln's and Johnson's policies different,[41] but these differences were highlighted by the two Presidents' different attitudes toward race. These were such that with Johnson in the White House the central problem of Reconstruction could no longer be satisfactorily solved.

NOTES

1. Roy P. Basler, ed., *The Collected Works of Abraham Lincoln* (New Brunswick, NJ: Rutgers University Press, 1953-55), IV, 263, 270, 439.

2. Edward McPherson, *The Political History of the United States of America During the Great Rebellion, 1860-1865* (New York: Da Capo, 1972), 436, 179; William B. Hesseltine, *Lincoln's Plan of Reconstruction* (Chicago: Quadrangle Books, 1967), 64-66; Herman Belz, *Reconstructing the Union: Theory and Policy During the Civil War* (Ithaca, NY: Cornell University Press, 1969), 85-87.

3. Basler, *Collected Works,* VI, 26-28, 130; V, 487-88; Reinhard H. Luthin, *The Real Abraham Lincoln* (Englewood Cliffs, NJ: Prentice Hall, 1960), 474-77, 486-87.

4. Basler, *Collected Works,* VII, 53-56; Hesseltine, *Lincoln's Plan of Reconstruction,* 64-65; Carl Schurz, *The Reminiscences of Carl Schurz* (New York: McClure, 1907), III, 221-22; LaWanda Cox, *Lincoln and Black Freedom: A Study in Presidential Leadership* (Columbia, SC: University of South Carolina Press, 1981), 142.

5. Basler, *Collected Works,* 433-34; Peyton McCrary, *Abraham Lincoln and Reconstruction: The Louisiana Experiment* (Princeton: Princeton University Press, 1978), 169 ff., 288 ff.

6. Hans L. Trefousse, *The Radical Republicans: Lincoln's Vanguard for Racial Justice* (New York: Knopf, 1969), 301-04; J. G. Randall and Richard N. Current, *Last Full Measure: Lincoln the President* (New York: Dodd, Mead, 1955), 308-15.

7. Cox, *Lincoln and Black Freedom,* 38; Salmon P. Chase to Horace Greeley, December 29, 1863, Greeley Papers, New York Public Library; Basler, *Collected Works,* VII, 101, 243; Ludwell H. Johnson, "Lincoln and Equal Rights: The Authenticity of the Wadsworth Letter," *Journal of Southern History,* XXXII (1966), 83-88.

8. Basler, *Collected Works,* VIII, 403.

9. Eric L. McKitrick, *Andrew Johnson and Reconstruction* (Chicago: University of Chicago Press, 1960), 90-92; Edward McPherson, *The Political History of the United States of America During the Period of Reconstruction, April 15, 1965-July 15, 1870* (New York: Da Capo, 1972), 9-12; Albert Castel, *The Presidency of Andrew Johnson* (Lawrence KA: The Regents Press of Kansas, 1979), 26, 44, 65 ff.

10. John J. Duff, *A. Lincoln, Prairie Lawyer* (New York: Holt, 1960), 101. On Lincoln as a politician, cf. Harry J. Carman and Reinhard H. Luthin, *Lincoln and the Patronage* (New York: Columbia University Press, 1943), esp. 336; Richard N. Current, *The Lincoln Nobody Knows* (New York, McGraw Hill, 1958), 187-213; Trefousse, *Radical Republicans,* 176-77, 209-24; Schurz, *Reminiscences,* II, 321-23.

11. Basler, *Collected Works,* V, 388-89; John Hope Franklin, *The Emancipation Proclamation* (Garden City, NY: Doubleday, 1963), 26 ff., 31 ff., 58 ff.

12. David Donald, *Lincoln Reconsidered* (New York: Vintage Books,

1956), 109-27; Tyler Dennett, ed., *Lincoln and the Civil War in the Diaries of John Hay* (New York: Dodd, Mead, 1939), 108, 135; Trefousse, *Radical Republicans*, 231 ff.; David Donald, "Devils Facing Zionward," in Grady McWhiney, ed., *Grant, Lee, Lincoln and the Radicals* (Evanston: Northwestern University Press, 1964), 72-91.

13. Stephen B. Oates, *With Malice Toward None: The Life of Abraham Lincoln* (New York: Harper and Row, 1977), 392-93, 398-400.

14. Patrick W. Riddleberger, *1866, The Critical Year Revisited* (Carbondale, IL: Southern Illinois University Press, 1979), 6-7; Hans L. Trefousse, *Impeachment of a President: Andrew Johnson, the Blacks, and Reconstruction* (Knoxville, TN: University of Tennessee Press, 1975), 30 ff., 67 ff., 115 ff., 157 ff., 182; Oliver P. Temple, *Notable Men of Tennessee from 1833 to 1875, Their Times and Their Contemporaries* (New York: Cosmopolitan Press, 1912), 452-59.

15. Don E. Fehrenbacher, "Only His Stepchildren: Lincoln and the Negro," *Civil War History*, XX (1974), 293-310; George M. Frederickson, "A Man but Not a Brother: Abraham Lincoln and Racial Equality," *Journal of Southern History*, XLI (1975), 39-58; Current, *The Lincoln Nobody Knows*, 235; Cox, *Lincoln and Black Freedom*, 20 ff.

16. Benjamin Quarles, *Lincoln and the Negro* (New York: Oxford University Press, 1962), 16-19.

17. Basler, *Collected Works*, I, 260; II, 320; Frederickson, "A Man but Not a Brother," 44.

18. Basler, *Collected Works*, III, 145-46, 401-03.

19. John L. Scripps to Lincoln, June 22, 1858; Henry C. Whitney to Lincoln, July 31, 1858; David Davis to Lincoln, August 2, 3, 1858, Lincoln Papers, Library of Congress.

20. Hans L. Trefousse, *Lincoln's Decision for Emancipation* (Philadelphia: Lippincott, 1975), 3-57.

21. Frederick Douglass, *Life and Times of Frederick Douglass* (New York: Crowell-Collier, 1962), 355-66; Philip Van Doren Stern, *The Man Who Killed Lincoln* (New York: Dell, 1955), 21 ff.

22. LeRoy P. Graf and Ralph W. Haskins, eds., *The Papers of Andrew Johnson* (Knoxville, TN: University of Tennessee Press, 1967-79), I, 133-46, 418-21, 499, 532; II, 301. For Johnson's attitude toward the blacks, cf. LaWanda and John H. Cox, *Politics, Principle, and Prejudice* (New York: The Free Press of Glencoe, 1963), 151 ff., and David Warren Bowen,

Andrew Johnson and the Negro, Ph. D. dissertation, University of Tenessee, 1976.

23. Graf and Haskins, *Papers of Andrew Johnson,* II, 352-57, 380-81, 360, 447, 450-51, 477; III, 379.

24. Ibid., III, 103, 318-20, 495; IV, 33.

25. *Cong. Globe,* 37th Cong., 2d Ses., 645.

26. James G. Blaine, *Twenty Years of Congress* (Norwich, CN: Henry Bill, 1884), I, 446; Robert W. Winston, *Andrew Johnson, Plebeian and Patriot* (New York: Henry Holt, 1928), 244-45.

27. *The War of the Rebellion: . . . Official Records of the Union and Confederate Armies* (Washington: Government Printing Office, 1880-1901), Series III, Part III, 819-20; Winston, *Johnson,* 251-52; Clifton R. Hall, *Andrew Johnson, Military Governor of Tennessee* (Princeton: Princeton University Press, 1916), 117.

28. Frank Moore, ed., *Speeches of Andrew Johnson, President of the United States* (New York: Burt Franklin, 1970), XXX-XXXI.

29. Ibid., XXXV-XXXVII; Lately Thomas, *The First President Johnson: The Three Lives of the Seventeenth President of the United States of America* (New York: William Morrow, 1968), 279-80.

30. Charles Nordhoff to William Cullen Bryant, February 2, 1867, Bryant-Godwin Papers, New York Public Library.

31. B. B. French to Johnson. February 8, 1866, Johnson Papers.

32. Trefousse, *Impeachment of a President,* 7-9; Douglass, *Life and Times,* 364; Thomas, *Johnson,* 295-97.

33. McPherson, *Reconstruction,* 19-20.

34. Johnson to George H. Thomas, September 4, 1865, Johnson Papers.

35. New York *Tribune,* September 8, 1865; Hartford *Times,* September 19, 1865, W. A. Croffut to Gideon Welles, September 20, 1865, Welles Papers, Library of Congress. For the black codes, cf. John Hope Franklin, *Reconstruction After the Civil War* (Chicago: University of Chicago Press, 1961), 48-50.

36. McPherson, *Reconstruction,* 52-56.

37. Benjamin B. French to Johnson, February 8, 1866, Johnson Papers; Thomas Sites to S. S. Cox, February 22, 1866, Cox Papers Brown University; Philip Ripley to Manton Marble, February 8, 1866, Marble Papers, Library of Congress.

38. John Jay to E. D. Morgan, March 13, 1866, Morgan Papers, State Library, Albany, NY; W. G. Moore, *Diary,* April 9, 1868, Johnson Papers.

39. McPherson, *Reconstruction,* 74-78.

40. Cox and Cox, *Politics, Principle, and Prejudice,* 228 ff.; James D. Richardson, ed., *A Compilation of the Messages and Papers of the Presidents, 1789-1897* (Washington: Government Printing Office, 1896-99), VIII, 3762-63; IX, 3870-71.

41. Observing this difference, many years later Carl Schurz wrote:

> Mr. Lincoln had indeed put forth reconstruction plans which contemplated an early restoration of some of the rebel States. But he had done this while the Civil War was still going on, and for the evident purpose of encouraging loyal movements in those States and of weakening the Confederate State Governments there by opposing to them governments organized in the interest of the Union which could serve as rallying points to the Union men. . . . Had he lived, he would have as ardently wished to stop bloodshed and to reunite all the States as he ever did. But is it to be supposed for a moment that, seeing the late master class in the South, still under the influence of their traditional notions and prejudices and at the same time sorely pressed by the distressing necessities of their situation, intent upon subjecting the freedmen again to a system very much akin to slavery, Lincoln would have consented to abandon those freedmen to the mercies of that master class? Can it be imagined that he would have been deaf to the sinister reports coming up from the South as Johnson was? . . . To assert in the face of all this that the Johnson reconstruction policy was only Lincoln's continued, is little less than a perversion of historical truth.

Cf. Schurz, *Reminiscences,* III, 221-23.

IV

CENTRAL EUROPEAN AND BALKAN SOCIAL AND POLITICAL DEVELOPMENTS

Imre Boba

THE SEVEN HUNGARIAN COUNTIES IN MEDIEVAL TRANSYLVANIA

The purpose of this paper is to investigate the place and significance of the so-called "Seven Hungarian Counties" in Transylvania in the governmental structure of Hungary, and to trace and evaluate the role of the nobility of the "Seven Counties" in the specific developments associated with Transylvania, and in particular her relations with the kings of Hungary.

Since past and recent historiography has emphasized the trends toward separatism or regional particularism in Transylvania, my task will be to scrutinize such opinions and supporting arguments. Many conflicting views could be reconciled if there were an agreement on the terminology used in historical studies. For instance, the terms used in the title of this paper require a precise definition. Through the centuries, these terms and their equivalents in Hungarian, Latin, German, Romanian, and the Slavic languages underwent semantic changes which—if not taken into account—give rise to more controversies than this paper may unwittingly create.

The Term "Hungarian"

Today, the term "Hungarian" (Ungarisch, Wegierski, etc.) refers to a group of people speaking a well-defined language, or to persons and things associated with the country known as "Hungary." The terms "Hungary" and "Hungarian" are not used by the Hungarians themselves, who have as modern equivalents the terms *"Magyarország"* and *"Magyar"*. But the two terms *"Magyar"* and "Hungarian" are equivalent only in modern usage. They were derived from the names of two distinct ethnic and political formations—the Finno-Ugric Magyars and the Turkic Onogurs—who were still separate in the ninth century. Not until about the year 900 A.D., after a political-social merger of the two, did the new political entities appear in sources as *"Ungari"* or *"Hungari"* (as seen from outside the region), or as *"Magyarok"* (as seen from inside). Another difference, even more important, between the modern and medieval uses of these terms is that in the Middle Ages only the ruling class—the chief or the king and his retainers, later the *servientes nobiles*—was named *Magyar* or *Hungari*. The *Magyars* were initially only one group of the multinational federation consisting of several tribes. (The term "tribe" is not precise and is used here in the traditional sense.) The conquering prince, Árpád, and his successors based their power on the *Magyar* tribe. Whoever served the ruler, irrespective of national or ethnic origin, became a Magyar-Hungarian. The class of the *servientes nobiles,* the *natio Hungarica* was multinational and multilingual.

This definition of the multinational Magyar-Hungarian *natio* of *Servientes nobiles*—as distinct from their multinational subjects (among them ethnic Magyars and ethnic Onogurs), the *plebs*—is necessary to show the difference between the *nobiles* on the one hand, and the tribal *Siculi* (Székelys) and the *Saxones* on the other, in Transylvania. With their traditional tribal self-government, the *Siculi* were bound to the person of the Hungarian king by a perpetual contract of military service and occasional gifts. The *Saxones* evolved from a variety of German-speaking groups into one *Universitas* of settlers with territorial self-government and fiscal and military obligations under the overall control of their landlord, the king. In short the *nobiles* served the king as individuals entrusted with military and economic-administrative tasks. The renumeration of the nobility was derived primarily from customary dues exacted from the *plebs*. Since the *Siculi* preserved a form of tribal democracy on their territory, and the Saxon rural and urban settlers had self-government free from the interference of the nobility, only the territories controlled by the Hungarian (multinational) service nobility had a subject population that later was to become a class of serfs. In twelfth and thirteenth-century Transylvania, therefore, one has to distinguish between royal lands with *plebs* controlled by the multinational "Hungarian" nobility, and two sets of districts populated by self-governing *Siculi* and *Saxones*.

The Term "Transylvania"

The second term in need of definition is the name of the region: Transylvania—*Transsilvania* or *Terra Ultrasilvana* in Latin, *Erdély* in Hungarian, *Ardeal* or *Transilvania* in Romanian, *Siebenbürgen* in German. All these words have topographical connotations and are not based on national etymons as are Polonia, Walachia, Bavaria, Hungaria, etc., that also reflect political formations. The terms *Erdély, Terra Ultrasilvana,* and *Transylvania* suggest the notion of a "land lying beyond the forested mountains" as visualized from Hungary proper. The name *Siebenbürgen* (i.e. seven burghs) developed independently of the above forms, probably through folk etymology, from *Sieben Bergen* (Seven Mountains), the name of a region in Germany which the settlers transferred to their new homeland.[10]* The names *Erdély* and *Transylvania* eventually spread from the populated region just east of the "Forest" to the whole region flanked by the Carpathian Mountains, while the names *Siebenbürgen* and *Siebenberg* spread from the southeastern corner of the Saxon-settled area toward other Saxon settlements, finally becoming synonymous with the expanded connotation of *Erdély* or *Transylvania*.

Erdély-Siebenbürgen did not become a single political-administrative entity until the sixteenth century, when the Hungarian realm was divided between two equally legal kings of Hungary. One of these two kings, John of Zápolya (1526-1540), controlled Transylvania and some adjacent regions of Hungary proper. After 1570 these two rulers were reconciled; the one in the East was satisfied to retain his share as *Princeps* under the Habsburg king of the entire realm. The share of the *Princeps* was, and is, referred to in historiography as *Erdély-Transylvania,* but in fact it consisted of much more, for it also included parts of the kingdom proper. The name *Erdély-Transylvania* was not official, the proper name for the principality being *Transylvania et partes Regni Hungariae* (Transylvania

---

*These numbers refer to the numbers in the bibliography.

and parts of the Hungarian Kingdom). These changes in the administration of the lands of the Hungarian Crown, now under a king and a Prince of Transylvania, had an impact on the "Seven Counties" inasmuch as not only the Hungarian nobility, but also the *Siculi* and *Saxones* now came under the direct control of the *Princeps*. The three *nationes* furnished the members for the princely council and were also represented equally in the Diets of Transylvania.

It is only at the present time that most of the region east of the Hungarian-Romanian border toward the Carpathians is referred to officially as Transylvania. Therefore, it is anachronistic to include Bihar, Temes, Szatmár, Csanád, etc. counties in the list of medieval counties of Transylvania.[4]

Hungary's first Christian king, St. Stephen (997/1000-1038) conquered only the inhabited regions to the east and southeast of the "Forest," *Sylva, Erdő*, i.e. the Mountains of Bihar. Soon this territory, the future "Seven Counties", came to be referred to in sources as "The Land Beyond the Forest" (*Terra Ultrasilvana* or *Erdőelue*). The less populated regions toward the east and southeast were subsequently settled by the *Siculi* and the *Saxones*—the latter of whom named their region *Siebenberg* or *Siebenbürgen*. The terms *Terra Ultrasilvana, Transylvania* and *Erdőelue* spread eastward to the regions of the *Saxones* and *Siculi*. The term *Siebenbürgen* spread north-northeast to cover the Germanic settlements in *Transylvania/Erdőelue*, and by the end of the sixteenth century the two terms had become synonymous.[10] The Latin, German and Hungarian terms and their equivalents in other languages referred to a geographical region that became part of the Kingdom of Hungary. This region consisted of three distinct administrative units, each one independent of the others and each placed separately and directly under royal officials: the Count of the *Siculi*, the Royal Judge or Count of the *Saxones*, and the *Voevoda* or *Vajda* in control of the counties of the "Hungarian," royal, multinational *servientes nobiles*.

The Term "Seven"

The number "seven" in the history of the Hungarians, and especially in the history of Transylvania, occurs frequently; in some instances as real numerical references, in other instances as mythical-legendary expressions of "many." This is also true in the case of *Siebenbürgen,* as a result of folk etymology. The number seven in connection with the Hungarian counties in Transylvania falls into the category of real numerical references. However, everything in history undergoes change. The number of counties of the nobility in Transylvania was not always seven; nor were there always seven districts in the lands of the *Siculi* and the *Saxones.*

The process by which the seven counties in Transylvania came into existence is not fully documented. It is, however, evident that they were not established simultaneously, but grew in number from one or two in the beginning to seven in the thirteenth and fourteenth centuries. Thereafter this number remained unchanged right into modern times.

The Term "County"

Finally, the term "county" (*vármegye, megye, comitatus*) also has connotations that have changed with the passage of time. In Hungary, a system of counties was introduced by King St. Stephen either from the West, or on the basis of the practices found among the Slavs in the western part of his realm. St. Stephen found the county system useful for the administration of his private landed possessions, as distinct from the lands held by the tribal nobility of the "conquerors" or by other free people who were not made subjects of the Árpád family, nor to the other lords of the realm. Those landed properties with an indigenous subject population which were confiscated or claimed by the Árpáds were placed under the administration of a "castle count" (*comes castri*), later a "county count" (*comes comitatus*) or *ispán*—the latter Hungarian term being derived from the Slavic *župan.* This Slavic term is, in turn, a derivative of the Avar term *Baján* or *Bán*. Until the early thirteenth century, the primary function of the *comes* or *ispán* was economic and peacekeeping. His officials, the *jobbagiones* and *servientes,* exacted dues from the subjects and merchants, controlled the fiscal interests of the ruler, and formed the policing military force which was available to the king under the command of the *ispán*. The *ispán* and his retainers were private employees of the Árpáds as landowners. The *comes* was generally appointed from among the *servientes* at the court of the king, or from among the free nobility residing in the countryside. The *ispán* also performed public functions, e.g. the enforcement of the administrative and judicial decisions of the church. Eventually the system of royal private counties developed into a public administrative system of the whole realm that made Hungary virtually into a federation of self-governing counties of the nobility.

The Counties in Transylvania

The county system—this unique form of economic administration of royal properties—was introduced into Transylvania (*Erdőelue, Terra Ultrasilvana*) by King St. Stephen (c. 1002) after his conquest of the territory ruled by a certain Gyula about whose background little is known. The inhabited parts of Gyula's realm became the demesne property (dominium-lordship) of the Árpád family. Gyula's subjects became St. Stephen's subjects, while his retainers either accepted service in the household of the Árpád family or became tribute-paying subjects on land claimed by the Árpáds.

King Stephen placed Zoltán, one of his relatives, in charge of the lands previously under the economic and political control of Gyula and his ancestors. Zoltán is referred to in sources as *Erdőelui* or *Transilvanus,* i.e. "Transylvanian." A similar territorial definition is used for the next known administrator of the region: *Mercurius Princeps Ultrasilvanus* (c. 1110). Both Zoltán and Mercurius most probably resided in *Alba Transilvana* (the "Lord's residence beyond the forest")—*Alba* being a noun used to mean a royal residence.

The earliest references to counties in *Terra Ultrasilvana* occur in 1164 for the region and burgh of Doboka, and in 1177 for Alba and Kolozs. It has been suggested that the counties of Doboka and Kolozs were created by detaching their respective territories from an initially large county of Alba. Thus, the first known county in *Terra Ultrasilvana* was the county of Alba (Hungarian: *Fehér* or *Fejér*). Since the term *Alba* or *Fehér* denotes the residence and property of a lord-king, and since Gyula's former realm became the sole property of the Árpáds, the conclusion seems appropriate that the economic control of the demesne of the Árpáds was exercised initially from *Alba Transilvana;* hence the terms *Comes Albe Transilvane* and *Comitatus Alba* (*Fejér Megye*). To suit economic and military exigencies, the demesne lands were reapportioned to form administrative units, such as Kolozs, Doboka, Küküllő, Torda, and Hunyad. The county of Fejér or Alba—although partitioned into Upper and Lower Fejér and constantly shrinking in size—continued to retain its preeminence among the otherwise equal administrative parts of *Terra Ultrasilvana*.

The Voevoda and the Counties

In addition to the "private" administration of the demesne lands under appointed "counts," there was still the public official of the king for *Terra Ultrasilvana* in the person of the *voevoda (vajda)*, an office first attested to in Hungary in 1176. The term and title *voevoda* is an exact Slavic translation of the Latin *dux* or Greek *strategos* (voje + voda = "leader of the warriors"). It was first used by Constantine Porphyrogenitus (c. 950) for Levedi and his chieftains. In medieval Poland the Polish version of this term—*vojewoda*—was used for military commanders, administrative supervisors and other deputies of the king or of one of the dukes. In Romanian populated areas this term was used for the heads of associations of extended families. One may surmise that the term for the ducal function in Transylvania, performed at one time by Zoltán and later by Mercurius, was formulated in vernacular Slavic.

The holders of the office of the *voevoda* or *dux* appear to have been successors to such hereditary lords as Zoltán and the *princeps* Mercurius. The *voevoda* was an officer appointed by the Hungarian Royal Government to administer the military affairs of Transylvania, and also to supervise and to coordinate the administrative functions of the counts. He had no administrative duties himself, but as the deputy of the king, the *voevoda* had the right to appoint the counts. The realm of the defeated Gyula—*Terra Ultrasilvana*—thus remained a distinct political unit under the king's deputy, the appointed *voevoda*, and under the local administrators known as the "counts."

The primary function of the *voevoda* was of a military nature. In the administration of the counties of the nobility his function was supervisory only, while in judicial affairs he acted as an appellate judge. All these functions were exercised by him as the personal representative of the king. Since the king's court officials, including the *voevoda*, were not paid salaries out of the royal treasury, most of them received one or more counties as appanages. The office of count itself was associated largely with economic-fiscal duties. The count could retain one-third of the income gathered from his county. Many of the *voevodas* derived their income from counties outside Transylvania proper, although some of them were also counts of one or more of the seven counties.

The Diminishing Role of the Seven Counties in Transylvania

The terms *Terra Ultrasilvana* or *Erdőelue* (i.e. Transylvania) were associated in the eleventh century only with the former possessions of Gyula, i.e. with the "duchy" of Zoltán. Later they became associated with the bulk of the territory that came to constitute the seven counties of the Hungarian nobility of Transylvania. Subsequently this term received an even larger territorial connotation, when the easternmost parts of the Carpathian Basin, which were still only sparsely inhabited, became settled by the *Siculi*, an originally non-Magyar tribe of several clans, and by German immigrants from the West. Although referred to as *Saxones*, the latter consisted of Bavarians, Rhinelanders, Saxons, as well as several other German-speaking elements. The "Saxons" and the *Siculi* or *Székelys* settled on demesne lands belonging to the king and thus known as "Royal Lands" (*Királyföld, Fundus Regius, Königsboden*). They also received the right to use their own traditional laws. As a result, the whole royal demesne in *Terra Ultrasilvana*—henceforth referred to as Transylvania—was divided into three distinct administrative units—each directly subordinated to the king through three officials of the central government: the *Voevoda* for the "Royal" or "Hungarian" counties, a Royal Count for the *Siculi*, and a Count of the *Saxones* for the Germanic settlements. It must be pointed out that the functions of the Count of the *Siculi* and the Count of the *Saxones* differed from the functions of the royal counts of the Hungarian counties, and resembled more the functions of the *voevoda*. These royal counts had only military, appelate-judiciary and supervisory duties, while all the fiscal, administrative and minor judiciary tasks were exercised fully by the *Siculi* and *Saxones* as part of their chartered territorial self-government. By the early thirteenth century the administration of Transylvania was shared equally by the counts of the royal Hungarian counties and the autonomous nations of the *Siculi* and *Saxones*.

Changes in the Structure of the Counties

As a result of the concessions given to the *jobbagiones* or *servientes* in the Golden Bull of 1222, this heterogeneous class of demesne employees of the king became equal to the class of the free nobility and the latent trend toward local legal self-help organizations on the part of the old and new nobility was recognized and formalized. The community of the old and new nobility, the self-governing county (*comitatus*) was still supervised and presided over by the count (*comes*) appointed by the king, but the details and forms of implementing royal laws and decrees were decided locally by the county assembly. From 1290 on, the nobles were free to elect their own judges (*judex nobilium*) for one year of service. These elected judges were assisted by jurors who were also elected from among the local nobility. The county, or rather the assembly of the county's nobility (*universitas nobilium*) would hire a notary (*notarius*) to keep records, certify documents, and carry on correspondence. In the sixteenth century, as the number of the *literati* increased, the position of the notary became elective. With the growth of self-government, the position of the appointed count faded in significance, but it still remained prestigious as it remained the source of traditional income (one-third of the county's revenues). It was when the duties of the count decreased that it became customary to give one or more countships to royal court officials as a source of income.

In light of the above, it should be clear that in the course of the thirteenth and fourteenth centuries the administration of royal properties by the "castle counts" (*comes castri*) with the help of his employees, "king's servants" (*servientes regis*), changed to a direct administration of smaller entities by the former *servientes*, now the nobility. The *comes* merely transmitted royal decrees to the nobility and ensured that the laws of the country were complied with. The Golden Bull and subsequent royal concessions in favor of *servientes* affected all of the royal counties of the Kingdom of Hungary, including those of Transylvania and Slavonia, except the autonomous regions of the *Saxones* and the *Siculi*, which never had any royal *servientes*. These regions had already enjoyed territorial self-government (the *Siculi* since 1222, the *Saxones*, first by communities, and after 1224 as a province), and they were not subject to royal laws.

The counties administered by the royal *servientes,* now nobility (*nobiles*), in the western and northern parts of Transylvania remained grouped together, and their counts were appointed on behalf of the king by the *voevoda*. The county nobility held periodical assemblies and elected their own judges and jurors. In the case of joint assemblies of two or more counties, the presiding officer was the *voevoda,* a function performed in similar cases in the western part of the realm by the *comes palatinus (nádor, nádorispán)* or by the king himself. Except when attending the joint sessions of the county assemblies (*congregatio generalis*), the *voevoda* spent most of his time at the royal court.

Trends Toward Autonomy or Separatism in Transylvania?

The former "royal counties," now "nobles' counties" in Transylvania possessed no rights or duties that would have made them either more or less autonomous than any of the other counties of the whole Kingdom of Hungary. Their representatives participated in national assemblies, and the decisions of the national assemblies and royal decrees were announced and implemented on the local level in all counties. The alleged constitutional uniqueness of Transylvania within the Kingdom of Hungary has been hypothesized on the basis of the fact that the relations between the royal counties in Transylvania and the person of the king were temporarily severed on two occasions in the thirteenth century: when heirs-apparent (Béla, 1226-35, and Stephen, 1257?-70) were given Transylvania as a "duchy" (*ducatus*), in fact as an appanage and a training ground for their future kingship.

The existence of this temporary situation (*ducatus*) has been used by some historians to conclude that Transylvania always had a natural tendency toward a separate existence. But such opinions are based on selective evidence and on the obvious misinterpretation of the facts. Transylvania was only a part of the share of the realm given to the son in each case. Although he was *dux Transylvanus,* ("Duke of Transylvania"), at the same time he was also *iunior rex Ungarorum,* ("junior King of Hungary"), and as such his share of the realm consisted not only of the seven royal counties of Transylvania, but—as in the case of the junior king Stephen—also of the territories west of Transylvania and east of the Danube. In fact, the *iunior rex* controlled an inalienable part of the patrimony that coincided with the territory of the Archdiocese of Kalocsa. It is true that there were tensions and conflicts between the junior kings (*iunior rex Ungarorum et dux Transylvanus*) and his father the King of Hungary (*rex Hungariae*), but it was a conflict between father and son concerning a single patrimony, and not an attempt at, nor a sign of a permanent division of the realm. The document of 1267, issued jointly by King Béla and his two sons Stephen, the *iunior rex Ungarorum et dux Transilvanus,* and Béla, the *iunior dux totius Sclavoniae,* refers to their respective shares and functions in the realm that was considered without a doubt a single unit as follows: "nobiles Regni Ungariae universi qui servientes Regales dicuntur," ". . . ordinavimus quod singulis annis in festo sancti Regis unus ex nobis Albam venire debeat, et de quolibet comitatu duo vel tres nobiles debeant convenire . . . etc."

The father and his two sons were all interested in controlling all of the realm. The respective shares of the junior king and of the junior duke were meant simply to provide an economic base for their holders. True, they became sources of political dissent and family feuds, but not of permanent political division. The junior king did not want to remain simply the Duke of Transylvania for life, nor to separate his holdings (*regnum*) from the Lands of the Crown of St. Stephen. He wanted to be the king of the whole Kingdom of Hungary.

It has also been suggested that some of the *voevodas* of Transylvania pursued a policy of particularism,[14] or even aimed at gaining sovereignty for Transylvania.[4] Among such *voevodas* the name of László Kán is frequently mentioned. His nearly twenty years in office (in contrast to an average of two years before him), however, cannot be construed as an attempt to establish an independent Transylvanian state for the simple reason that during his tenure in office (1295/7?-1315?) the whole country was in a political chaos. No kings were recognized either by the "oligarchs" (local lords), or by the Papacy, which was the ultimate source of royal authority. László Kán could have opposed King Andrew III (1290-1301), who was not recognized by the Pope, but he did not do so. The little we know about László Kán shows that he was a loyal servant of King Andrew III until the latter's death in 1301. Thereafter, during the prolonged *interregnum,* László Kán remained in his position of *voevoda* and functioned as such with little interference in partisan politics. During this period three, and sometimes four candidates fought for succession, but none of them was in a legal position to remove him from office. It was an accident that László Kán became involved in the conflict. Bribed by the Habsburg candidate Albert, he confiscated the Crown of St. Stephen from Otto of Bavaria, who happened to seek his support. László Kán did so when he realized that Otto was not the strongest candidate for the throne. During the all-Hungarian "electoral" controversy, in which he was involved, he played his own political game. He did not represent the seven nobles' counties of Transylvania, and certainly did not represent the *Saxones* or the *Siculi*. László Kán and the so-called oligarchs of his time played power politics only within the Kingdom of Hungary, and then only in order to secure a better position for themselves in the Hungarian central government. László Kán overplayed his hand, wherefore he and his family lost political influence. Clearly, the *Siculi* and the *Saxones* did not support his policy of weakening the king's position.

The notion that John Hunyadi (Johannes de Hunyad) (1407/09-1456) was a champion of Transylvania's independence is equally baseless. John Hunyadi played a dominant role in Hungarian politics. He became governor of the entire Kingdom of Hungary, with most of his activities occurring outside Transylvania. As governor of Hungary he could hardly have been interested in expanding the already existing autonomy of the counties and provinces (including Transylvania), or that of the *Siculi* and the *Saxones*. His son Matthias—known as Matthias Corvinus—became one of the greatest kings of Hungary (1458-1490) and one of the most vigorous exponents of the country's centralization.

In 1437, the Hungarian nobility of the seven counties of Transylvania took part in a direct political action independent of the central royal government. Possibly on their own initiative, and in the absence of the *voevoda,* they created a "Union of Three Nations" with the *Siculi* and *Saxones* (i.e. Magyars, Székelys and Saxons). The sole purpose of this "Union," however, was to suppress rebellious peasants in Transylvania. Other "unions" followed when prompt and joint military action was needed, e.g. against the Turks. The documents of the Unions of 1437 and 1459, however, were issued by a royal official, the deputy *voevoda.* The text of the Union documents express the fidelity of the Three Nations—i.e. the Hungarians, the *Siculi* and the *Saxones*—to the Holy Crown of Hungary and to the king. Joint assemblies of the Three Nations of Transylvania were held at least fifteen times between 1291 and 1526. A meeting in 1427 was presided over by King Sigismund and was concerned with provisioning soldiers recruited against the Turks.[9] The decisions made by the representatives of the Three Nations were approved by the centrally-appointed *voevoda* or his deputy, or by the king himself (e.g. in 1467 by Matthias Corvinus). The assembly of the Three Nations was not different *in structure and purpose* from regional assemblies of the counties in various other parts of Hungary.

Significant for the position of the seven counties in the joint assemblies was the equal treatment of all three nations; none of them had prerogatives or burdens that were not shared by the others. Decisions on joint issues were taken by all three nations, the rule being that whatever any two of the three nations approved, the third had to accept. Naturally, because both the Hungarians and the *Siculi* were Magyar-speaking, against the German-speaking *Saxones*, the former two usually carried the day.

The hereditary obligations of the heterogeneous nobility to the king, the direct service obligations of the *Siculi* to the king, and the contractual relation of the *Saxones* to the king did not permit for any development that would have freed the three nations from their obligations. They could have revolted or proclaimed their independence, but that never happened. One might even say that the seven counties were more royal, and thus more "Hungarian," than, for instance, the counties of Transdanubia. After 1000 A.D. all the territory of Transylvania became royal property (*Königsboden, Fehér megye,* etc.) and the entire province was administered for the king by his officials, or by the settlers under royal charters of immunity granted by the king. In Transdanubia the royal property in a county initially comprised only a portion of the utilized land, the rest being in "allodial" possession of the descendants of the conquerors and of other free people. Since in the seven counties of Transylvania there were no descendants of the tribal nobility of the conquering Hungarians, the local nobility was a service-nobility, and as such multinational in origin, including Magyars, Magyar-speaking *Siculi*, Croats, Cumans, Romanians, Poles and *Saxones*. The highest offices of the land were also held by the members of these nationalities. Their interests and aspirations were balanced and held in check by this complicated interrelationship. And none of them could aim at a separate status—let alone independence—without the knowledge and consent of the King, the Diet and the Church of Hungary.

Loyalty to the Crown and to the unity of the whole Kingdom of Hungary was expressed even after 1526, when the realm was divided between two kings; as well as after 1570, when it was divided between the King of Hungary and the Prince of Transylvania (*Princeps Transylvaniae*). As an example, John Zápolya, (1526-1540), who legally was one of the two co-kings of Hungary, but actually controlled only the eastern half of the country, including Transylvania, used in his title references to Hungary, Croatia, Dalmatia, etc. but not to Transylvania. Another example was the case of George Rákoczi II (1648-60) who while *Princeps* in Transylvania, referred to his jurisdictional territory as *Patriae Pars,* i.e. part of the (Hungarian) Fatherland.

There were two critical situations that might have led to the separation of the seven counties and the lands of the *Siculi* and *Saxones* from the realms of the Hungarian Crown. The first was the impact of the Protestant movement in Transylvania and the possibility of defying the Catholic king by secession under Turkish protection. The second occasion came during the reign of Maria Theresa, when the Empress made herself Grand "Duke" (*Magnus Princeps*) of Transylvania and subordinated the principality directly to her imperial scepter. This move—favored by some of the *Saxones*—had to be rescinded, however, because of the protests by the Hungarian nobility of the seven counties and by the *Siculi.* The rights of the Hungarian Crown were restored.

Conclusion

The seven counties of Transylvania were part of the royal system of administration of the king's private possession (*fundus regius*) ever since that region's conquest by King St. Stephen. But because Transylvania (*Terra Ultrasilvana, Erdély*) before this conquest was a more or less independent realm under a certain *Gyula*, it remained a "duchy" (*principatus*) under the Hungarian Crown. Its administration was placed in the hands of appointed *comites* supervised by a relative or a son of the king, or by an appointed *voevoda*, whose primary function was military. Newly colonized territories in the region were given autonomy and were placed also under the supervision of royal officials: Counts of the *Siculi (Comes Siculorum)* and Counts of the *Saxones (Comes Saxonum).*

Since they derived their privileges and authority from the King of Hungary, the nobility of the seven counties never manifested any interest in seceding from the Crown. The *voevodas,* who represented the king and not the seven counties, never attempted to make themselves independent. When involved in political activities beyond their assigned duties, it was always during an *interregnum* or crisis in the central government—the *voevoda* in question hoping thereby to increase his power within the central government. The nobility governed by means of royal laws, but shared the administration of Transylvania with the *Siculi* and *Saxones,* both of whom had their own laws. The Three Nations exercised and shared political power in Transylvania only after 1526, during the period of Hungary's trisection, when the country's southern and central parts were occupied by the Turks and when Transylvania itself fell under Turkish suzerainty. Some *Saxones,* on occasion were inclined to shift their allegiance from the realm of St. Stephen to the Habsburgs. Some *Siculi* may have contemplated resettlement in Moldavia or Bukovina. But the nobility of the seven counties remained loyal to the Hungarian Crown. Any armed conflict with the Habsburgs—as Kings of Hungary—was always in the form of resistance (authorized by the Golden Bull of 1222) against the person of the king, and not against the Crown. In short, there is no evidence for the assertion that the *voevodas* or the nobility of the seven counties of Transylvania were ever inclined to dismember the Kingdom of Hungary.

NOTES

1. Bakó, Elemér and William Sólyom-Fekete, *Hungarians in Rumania and Transylvania:* A Bibliography.... Washington, D.C., 1969.
2. Csizmadia, Andor, ed., *Magyar állam- és jogtörténet* /Hungarian State and Legal History/. Budapest, 1972.
3. Deér, József, "A középkori Erdély" /Medieval Transylvania/, *Magyar Szemle,* XXII, (1934), pp. 194-205.
4. Daicoviciu, Constantin, *et al., Din istoria Transilvaniei* /About the History of Transylvania/. Vol. I. Bucharest, 1960.
5. Deér József and László Gáldi, eds., *Magyarok és románok* /Hungarians and Romanians/. 2 vols. Budapest, 1943-1944.
6. Endes, Miklós, *Erdély három nemzete és négy vallása autonómiájának története* /The History of the Three Nations and Four Religions of Transylvania/. Budapest, 1935.
7. Ferdinandy, Ladislaus de. "Das Verhältnis des Fürstentums

Siebengürgen zu Ungarns Heilige Krone," *Ferdinandy-Festschrift.* Wiesbaden, 1972. pp. 327-352.

8. Franknói, Vilmos, *Hunyady Mátyás király élete, 1440-1490* /The Life of King Matthias Hunyady, 1440-1490/. Budapest, 1890.

9. Giurescu, Constantine C., *Transylvania in the History of Romania.* London, 1969.

10. Holtzträger, Fritz, "Siebenbürgen. Ein wort- und sprachgeschichtliche Untersuchung," *Südostdeutsche Archiv,* V (1962), pp. 20-42.

11. Iczkovits, Emma, *Az erdélyi fehér megye a középkorban* /The Transylvanian Fehér County in the Middle Ages/. Budapest, 1939.

12. Kispál, László, *Erdély fejedelmi korszaka* /The Princely Age of Transylvania/. Budapest, 1940.

13. Kristó, Gyula, *A feudális széttagolódás Magyarországon* /Feudal Disunity in Hungary/. Budapest, 1979.

14. Kristó, Gyula, "Kán László és Erdély" /László Kán and Transylvania/, *Valóság,* XXI, 11 (1978), pp. 83-96.

15. Kristó, Gyula, "Különkormányzat az Árpád-kori Drávántúlon és Erdélyben" /Autonomous Governments in the Trans-Drava Region and Transylvania in the Age of the Árpáds /, *Történelmi Szemle,* XXX, 1 (1977), pp. 53-72.

16. Lám, Károly, *Az erdélyi országgyűlés szervezete, 1541-1848* /The Structure of the Transylvanian Diet, 1541-1848/. Kolozsvár, 1908.

17. Lupas, I., *Historic Realities in the Principality of Transylvania.* Bucharest, 1938.

18. Makkai, László, *Erdély története* /History of Transylvania/. Budapest, 1944.

19. Makkai, László, "Honfoglaló magyar nemzetségek Erdélyben" /Conquering Hungarian Clans in Transylvania/, *Századok,* LXXVIII, 4-6 (1944), pp. 162-192.

20. Mályusz, Elemér, "A magyar társadalom a Hunyadiak korában" /Hungarian Society in the Age of the Hunyadis/, in *Mátyás Király Emlékkönyv* /King Matthias Memorial Volume/, 2 vols. Budapest, 1940, vol. I, pp. 309-433.

21. Mályusz, Elemér, ed., *Siebenbürgen und seine Völker.* Budapest, 1943.

22. Marczali, Henrik, *Erdély története* /History of Transylvania/. Budapest, 1935.

23. Mikó Imre, *Erdély különválása Magyarországtól* /The Separation of Transylvania from Hungary/ (*Magyar Tudományos Akadémia Évkönyve,* vol. 9, part 5). Buda, 1860.

24. Szabó, Károly, "Báthori István erdélyi vajda ás székely ispán bukása 1493-ban" /The Fall of István Báthori, Voivoda of Transylvania and Count of the Székelys, in 1493/, *Századok*, XXIII (1889), pp. 701-709.

25. Szilágyi, Sándor, *Erdélyország története* /History of Transylvania/. Pest, 1866.

26. Trócsányi, Zsolt, *Az erdélyi fejedelemség korának országgyűlései* /Transylvanian Diets in the Age of the Principality of Transylvania/. Budapest, 1976.

János M. Bak

DELIQUENT LORDS AND FORSAKEN SERFS: THOUGHTS ON WAR AND SOCIETY DURING THE CRISIS OF FEUDALISM

One of the oft-debated issues in the history of late medieval society is closely related to the interests of Bély Király, and hence it fits well into a volume dedicated to him: war—military service or defense in general—and feudal society. This essay wishes to explore some of its aspects in regard to the crisis of feudalism, especially in East Central Europe.

* * * * * *

It is well known that medieval understanding of social differences and hierarchies was based on the idea that the great majority of the people, the direct producers in town and country, were incapable of defending themselves. Therefore they were to render their surplus produce to the clerical and knightly upper classes, who in return would save them from the attacks of demons and devils or foreign and domestic human enemies respectively. The exchange of dues in kind, coin and labour for protection (*Munt*, etc.) was presented as a legitimate arrangement.

The popular movements of the later Middle Ages, from the Jacquerie through the English uprising of 1381 and the Hussite wars to the peasant revolts of the late fifteenth and early sixteenth centuries, in fact challenged the validity of this justification. By turning against their lords secular and spiritual, peasants expressed their doubts about the legitimacy of this "exchange" by means stronger than words.

Almost all of these rebellions incorporated some element of religious dissent, whereby they attempted to break the clergy's monopoly as the sole dispenser of efficacious remedies against natural and supernatural dangers. In a way, the Church itself introduced this process by granting individual indulgences after 1300 A.D., thus handing over to the laity some of the privilege to "bind and loose". A pardon acquired on a pilgrimage or by other good works placed in the hands of a layman an infinitesimal fraction of the Power of the Keys, up to then an exclusive right of Pope and clergy. Heretical or radical reforming teachings about the mission of the poor and downtrodden to liberate the world from evil were also integral parts of these movements, beginning with the preachings of John Ball in 1381 and culminating in the revolutionary theology of Thomas Münzer. All these elements can be summarized under the heading of a crisis in the legitimation of clerical claims to economic privilege and spiritual domination over laymen, especially peasants. Owing to the identification of the feudal society with the hallowed *ordo* of the world, they inevitably also questioned the eternal validity of the entire system.

A crisis of legitimation in the secular-military sphere, accompanying the decline of feudal economy, is less conspicuous. Of course, one may go back as far as the peoples' crusades in the eleventh and twelfth centuries, in which the belief surfaced that not the feudal knights, but the innocent poor would be the ones to deliver the Holy Sepulchre from heathen occupation. However, these were not mass peasant uprisings. They mobilized as a rule the marginal elements of medieval society: the uprooted, the beggars, the shepherds and the children. Or, as in the "crusade" of Jeanne d'Arc, the leader may have been a peasant girl, but the divine message to fight the enemies of "holy France" was to be entrusted to the king and his knights. These and similar examples reveal some doubt about the ability and suitability of the upper classes, endowed with the exclusive right to bear arms, to fulfill their duty as defenders of society. But this ideological aspect remained marginal in all these movements. In contrast, at least two major peasant revolts in East Central Europe, the Styrian-Carinthian *Bund* of 1478-1479 and the peasant war in Hungary in 1514 wrote on their flags the defense of home and country against the heathen—and ended in open social warfare against those whom they perceived as incapable or unwilling to fulfill their Christian duties: the feudal lords.

These two examples will be more revealing if we briefly consider why the general crisis of feudalism, so obvious in the economic, social and ideological realm all over late medieval Europe did not include in the West a similar military perspective. The question about the secular crisis of legitimation is also interesting insofar as the absence of clear examples for it was reflected in the initial debates about feudalism which influenced even modern scholarship. When arguing the obsolescence of *féodalité* and of noble privilege, neither the Scottish economists nor the jurists and publicists of the Third Estate focused on the contradition between the special status accorded to the *noblesse d'epée* and the actual armed service performed by landowning lords and aristocrats. As we shall see, this matter had been resolved so far in the past and without major social upheavals that it did not bear on the discussions of the eighteenth century, although, theoretically, it would have served the anti-feudal polemic excellently.

Even though there is some evidence on occasional peasant complaints about unwarranted and inequitable burdens placed on the shoulders of the unarmed producers in the defense of the realm (even in 1381), the failure of feudal armies to fulfil their rôle as *bellatores* did not become a major issue in Western and West Central Europe. The main reason is clearly that in the more advanced kingdoms of Europe, monarchs acquired such power and income during the fourteenth and fifteenth centuries that they were able to dispense essentially with the feudal levy and place the defense of the country in the professional hands of mercenary armies loyal only to the crown. These armies may have been a scourge on the peasants, pillaging the countryside even while in royal service (and much more so once dismissed), but they were fairly efficient. They could defend the realm from brigands and foreign enemies and thus deliver the protection for which the peasants had to pay their taxes. Also, even if they failed, the odium of their treachery did not fall upon those lords who were the tenants' seigneurs: these had long relinquished the explicit claim to feudal dues and jurisdiction on the basis of military service and now derived their privilege from royal grace, and rightly so. Besides, and this is also significant, Atlantic Europe (and most of the Mediterranean as well) was not seriously confronted by truly external enemies after the end of the Norman, Hungarian and Sarracene incursions of the ninth and tenth centuries. The numerous and bloody wars fought on French, German and Spanish soil—nothing said of Italy—were devastating, but remained local and "limited" (to use a term of contemporary euphemism). A comparison with the Turkish wars on the Balkan frontier may explain what I mean. Even though foreign mercenaries may have kept their horses in French cathedrals, they did not systematically burn down churches and destroy icons and Madonnas. Even though captured knights were held for ransom by their enemies and peasants robbed, their wives and daughters raped by friend and foe alike, they were not carried off in chains to the slave markets of the Levante by the thousands. Or from another vantage point: once the confrontation passed the limit of traditional feudal warfare, the popular reaction in fact did bring forth "la Pucelle."

In summary, the royal mercenary armies and local "police forces" by and large protected the subjects from enemies and brigands in those centuries, when Western European nobility had, just as their Central European counterparts, abandoned its early medieval military functions. The direct producers had to pay the price, of course. The continuous increase of royal taxation above and beyond feudal dues was a continuous cause for complaints and a trigger for several peasant rebellions. The demand for the reduction of "new burdens" appears in all of them, referring to that centralized feudal rent (*taille,* poll-tax, *Türkenpfennig,* etc.) that went to the support of monarchical pomp and hired troops. But in this way the retreat of the knightly class from performing more or less necessary services for the society at large as its defenders (*bellatores*) did not appear an obvious social contradiction in itself. It was rather subsumed in the increased claims on tenants' lands by the crown and the protests against them.

By this, I do not wish to imply that the feudal theory of a harmonious division of social functions had ever been an adequate reflection of social reality. The armed upper class always performed its defensive functions primarily to protect its monopoly of exploitation from challenging fellow knights or outside competitors. Still, without being able to explore this matter more fully here, it can be stated that the claim of the early medieval lord and his armed retinue to be a godsent protector of the unarmed producers was at least tacitly accepted for many centuries, partially

The Crisis of Feudalism

because of the ecclesiastical-spiritual justification that was supplied for it by the clergy.

In East Central Europe, and more particularly along the southeastern frontier of Christendom, the conditions were in many respects different. For reasons too numerous to be discussed in a short essay, the feudal monarchies, even in their heyday, never succeeded in centralizing as much power and income as their counterparts in the West. To begin with, the economic development set narrow limits to exploitable surplus, while mercenary wages seem to have been not much lower than elsewhere. (Soldiers were a very mobile commodity!) In the Habsburg lands the central authority was often far away and embroiled in the uphill battle for imperial prerogative. In Hungary the county nobility, serving as the mass following of powerful magnates, managed to undermine royal power, especially from the mid-fifteenth century onwards, when *interregna* left the country without government for years in a row. Thus, the kings had neither sufficient power to levy taxes which would have financed a mercenary army, nor enough prerogative to reduce the nobility to courtiers and the obsolete feudal levy to mere pageantry. The nobility was able not only to retain, but widen its privileges, above all its freedom from any kind of taxation and limitation of its local seigneurial power in return for its increasingly worthless military service. The nobles of Hungary or Styria tended to become landed gentlemen in the same way as their Western fellows (about which the commanders of royal armies did not tire to complain), but were still the only significant force on which the countries could call.

At the same time, these very countries were confronted with the one major enemy from outside the European family of nations which had threatened the Continent from the late fourteenth century onwards. Actually it was the only extra-European army which intruded into the subcontinent's affairs between the Mongols of the thirteenth century and the American expeditionary corps of the First World War. The Ottoman Turks reached the Balkans in the late 1300s and before the century was over, carried the day against a crusading army of the European kingdoms. Ironically, then, the modernization of defense was least advanced in those areas that were most immediately exposed to the threat of a massive superior force. The mutual relationships of these two trends would be worth a special study.

From the early fourteenth century onwards, Turkish armies, or at least marauding expeditions, challenged the region's defenses virtually every summer, harrassing the villages and towns in Croatia, southern Hungary and the southeastern parts of Austria (Styria, Carniola, Carinthia). The rural population of a considerable area from Transylvania to the borders of Tyrol was exposed to constant danger, much more than any other segment of the nations in the borderlands. The lords could retreat into their castles or flee to the cities further north and the burghers were reasonably safe behind their town walls, but the peasants were at the mercy of an unusually cruel enemy. The Turkish marauders were much more ruthless than any feudal army or *Landsknecht* troop, not only because they were foreign in their behavior and "heathen", but as they did not intend to return to the same area twice, they destroyed and pillaged all they could and carried thousands of men and women into slavery.

Of course, peasants in Central Europe were as accustomed to protect their homes and families from all manner of soldiery as any other rural folk, whether or not the soldiers claimed to be their allies or enemies. But the Turkish raids were too frequent and too ferocious to be averted by self-help. Many villages built defenses or surrounded the churchyard with strong walls, called *Täber,* referring to either the Hungarian word *"tábor"* (camp, encampment campaign), or the Czech-Hussite name of the peasant's stronghold in Bohemia. But the Turkish raids were often so swift that there was no time to take refuge. Also, many of the rather prosperous villages in the area, active in grain, wine, and cattle-trade with Venice and Italy, were ill-prepared to fight for life and property.

Due to all these factors, the Hungarian-Croat-Austrian borderlands offered several examples of conflict between lords and subjects in which the former's inability or unwillingness to fulfill their task as *bellatores,* protecting their *laboratores,* became a significant issue.

As early as the famous popular crusade of 1456, preached and led by Giovanni di Capistrano, the failure of seigneurial troops to participate in the fighting became a sore point. This campaign—called in the aftermath of the shock felt all over Europe after the Fall of Constantinople—mobilized thousands of peasants and burghers from Hungary and the neighboring countries. Already during the march from the southern plains toward the besieged Belgrade, the peasant crusaders expressed that the sanctions against those refusing to join, both peasants and local clergy, were passed: they were to be excommunicated by the *Bund* and the administration of sacraments prohibited to them by the community. While in the preceding chapters Unrest echoed the general outcry about the Turks being allowed to ravage the country unpunished, he now, against all logic but very much in concert with medieval clerical thinking, denounces the peasants' attempts at armed resistance. "They covered their false behavior (namely attempting to achieve Swiss-type liberty) with the appearance of making an alliance solely against the Turks, but their words and deeds betrayed their lies", he writes, and promptly declares that God sent the Turks to punish the insubordinate peasants.

The allied peasants attacked a few castles and manor houses, while the lords fled to the towns and asked the Emperor for help. But soon the lords were rescued, indeed as though they had been in alliance with the Turks. Two consecutive Ottoman raids in 1478 and 1480 defeated the peasant troops and put an end to the attempts at self-help. In one of the decisive battles, according to Unrest, most of the peasants fled the day before the attack and only a few hundred villagers and some miners (*Erzknappen*) stood their ground and fell from Turkish arms. The lands of Styria and Carinthia were again open to Turkish pillage.

A most mature expression of the conflict between unprotected *laboratores* and inactive *bellatores* was the peasant war in Hungary in 1514: it started out as a crusade, just like the one of 1456, but this time it ended in the bloodiest revolt medieval Hungary had witnessed. The call to the cross, announced in March 1514, brought thousands of peasants to the camp near Buda by the time a commander was named to lead them against the Turks. The crusaders were to march against the Ottoman forces that had besieged an important border castle in the northern Balkans, and to support the operations of an army of the Viceroy [Ban] of Croatia in the west and one of the Voivode of Transylvania in the east. Archbishop Tamás Bakócz entrusted the command to György Székely, in some sources called Dózsa, a lesser nobleman who had served on the southern frontier. Hardly had the 5000-6000 crusaders left the environs of the capital when news reached the Archbishop that *seditio* had arisen throughout the country, and he called on the preachers who were still busy recruiting crusaders, to stop the mobilization and calm the rebellion. The cancellation of the campaign may not yet have been known to the main group of the crusaders, by this time (late May) probably some 12,000 men strong, when it encountered resistance from seigneurial troops near Nagylak [Nadlac]. The peasants rooted the knights and executed their leaders: a bishop and a member of the royal council. These first victims of the rustics were followed by many more who were killed in their country houses; for six weeks the Hungarian Plains were aflame with burning manors and castles. Only the troops of the Voivode of Transylvania, called back by the king from the Turkish front to quell the rebellion, managed to disperse the peasant army under the walls of Temesvár.

The leaders were captured and executed in the most gruesome fashion: Dózsa was burnt alive, while his retainers were forced to bite into his scorched flesh; his quartered body and head were displayed on the gates of four cities of Hungary. A few months later the assembled noble and clerical estates passed retaliatory laws, decreeing *eternam rusticitatem* as a punishment for all peasants in the kingdom. This became the legal basis of the gradually developing hereditary serfdom that was to prevail until the nineteenth century.

According to several contemporary reports, the radical turn by the peasant crusaders against the lords was caused by rumours that some seigneurs were hindering their serfs in joining the campaign. Whether they did so because they feared revolt, or simply did not want to release manpower at the beginning of the summer labours cannot be determined from the few sources available. Neither do we know whether the *conventicula* of rustics in which the *seditio* began (as maintained by the Archbishop) raised other grievances as well. The economic and social changes in the late fifteenth and early sixteenth century caused considerable dislocations in the country's rural economy and supplied plenty of cause for rebellion. Still, the ideology that mobilized the peasants and justified their uprising was the idea of a popular crusade against the enemies of the "poor:" the Turks—and then those, who did not fight against them—the feudal lords.

Dózsa's famous manifesto from mid-summer 1514 does not refer to social and economic matters at all. It is a call to fight the "enemies of the crusade." In it, *Georgius summus capitaneus,* "subject to the Pope, the King and the Primate but not to the lords" announces that the *infideles nobiles* have raised violent hands against the *expeditio sancte congreationis.*

In order to punish and restrain them, all able men are enjoined to appear in the market town of Cegléd, whence the *sancta turma* will proceed against the *maledicti nobiles*. The manifesto closes with a penal formula just like the programme of the peasants of Styria, only the sanctions against those who refused are harsher, including capital punishment for the cowards.

This message, the only authentic text from the surroundings of Székely-Dózsa, marks a full circle from the original programme of a crusade against the Turks, although still constructed from verbal and ideological elements contained in the initial papal bull issued for the campaign. Except that the infidels were now not the heathen without, but rather the vicious nobles within. The peasant army, whose members called themselves crusaders to the last minute, became the "blessed host" fighting for the true cause, punishing the traitors of Christendom. Whatever other weighty reasons may have caused the mass uprising, the main mobilizing force was the peasants' perception of a conflict in the reality of their society: that they were expected to support thousands of nobles who claimed their traditional dues, but did not fulfill their traditional duties.

The charges against the feudal lords were by no means unfounded. The history of Hungary's defense system proves that the nobility, though insisting on its liberties, did not tire to find excuses against supplying men to the besieged castles, nor against giving up a fraction of the surplus expropriated from the tenants for the upkeep of the defenses. In the very diets where the liberties of the tenants and peasant-merchants were curtailed, many empty phrases on national greatness had been reiterated only to cover up the nobility's unwillingness to sacrifice anything for the defense of the realm, while important outposts were lost every year. Turkish raids again reached deep into Hungary and Transylvania. The enthusiastic popular response to the call for a crusade was clearly motivated by a desire for self-defense. No evidence suggests that the many thousands of peasants who assembled in the camp, often under the lead of their local priests or the mendicant friars who preached the crusade, had any other intention but to fight against the fiendish enemy of Christendom and the pillagers of their villages and towns. The fact that they were left alone by their betters and even hindered by some, supplied the kind of dissatisfaction which radical leaders and preachers could turn into rebellion.

To be sure, the crisis of "military" legitimation of noble rule, as expressed in the spontaneous uprisings of undefended peasants was by no means the only, or even the primary, factor in the social conflicts of the area. The other elements were, however, rather similar to those which led to the many revolts that we subsume under the heading of German Peasant War, and even to those of earlier revolts in Western and Central Europe. The issue of defense was peculiar to this area, where no professional royal army (or at least not a sufficiently strong one) could take over the relinquished function of feudal knights.

The implications of all this are manifold. A few hints at problems must suffice for now.

Firstly, the vicious circle into which especially the Kingdom of Hungary got caught is to be noted: by not being able to stop Ottoman raids, the fiscal basis of the country diminished continuously, thus further reducing the available tax-base for defense. This led in the long run to the deterioration of the status quo at the frontier and the final defeats of 1521 and 1526.

Secondly, the attempts to replace or at least augment the feudal host by drafting some kind of auxiliary forces from tenants (in the form of the repeated ordinances on the *portalis militia*) essentially failed, as they too depended on the cooperation of the county nobility. The nobles, in turn, were reluctant to share their revenue with the crown and permit the king to build up a force independent of their control, which would have also undermined their ideological claim to tax-exemption and political rights. They too entered a vicious circle: while in fact moving away from warlike occupations and—especially around the turn of the fifteenth and sixteenth centuries—gradually entering the marketplace, they felt compelled to insist on the ideology of noble military monopoly as the basis for taxation and customs privileges, which were to give them the needed advantage over the commodity producing peasants and *cives* of the agrarian towns. Bereft of its own armed force the crown had no power to force the nobles to sacrifices.

Thirdly, these culs-de-sac—some of the early ones in the development of a nation that was to enter many more in the early modern centuries (as István Bibó aptly pointed out)—enhanced the contradictions between national rhetoric and actual cohesion of the kingdom. That warped national consciousness which was so characteristic for modern Hungary may have had its roots in the decades of Scythian demogogy divorced from any constructive action for the strengthening of the polity.

The solution for the impasse was also different from the "Western" patterns and had far-reaching consequences. While it would be wrong to assume that either before or even after 1514 peasants were not recruited into the different armed forces, massive addition to military manpower was not achieved until after the Turkish occupation of two-thirds of the country. Those marginal elements that already earlier had left peaceful village life—such as the cattle-driver *hajdú* and the refugee South Slav peasant-warriors—became now the main reservoir for the foot-soldiery of the Turkish wars. They, together with the lesser nobles who lost their lands in the Great Plains, constituted that peculiar Hungarian social stratum that was neither fully feudal, nor fully mercenary: the "warrior estate" of the seventeenth and early eighteenth centuries. Their fate was a complex one: some, such as the settled *hajdús* of Bocskai, became the basic stock of a well-to-do free peasantry on the Hungarian Plains, a rural society that developed in the eighteenth and nineteenth centuries along the road some Western European peasantries had taken centuries earlier. Some others, especially the impoverished nobles, became the mainstay of national resistance to both Germanisation and modernisation, in a Janus-faced way that rescued the nation from annihilation, but with it the fetters of medieval privilege and localism. But these contradictions do not belong in this essay: they have been explored by the recipient of this volume in his book on eighteenth century Hungary. May he augment the list of his works that opened with that study— *ad multos annos!*

NOTE

For the medieval perceptions of social inequality I relied, among others, on George Duby, *Les trois ordres ou l'imaginaire du féodalisme* (Paris, 1978), and A. Ia. Gurevich, *Kategorii srednevekovoi kultury* [Categories of Medieval Culture] (Moscow, 1972). The recent book of the latter, *Problemy srednevekovoi narodnoi kultury* [Problems of Medieval Popular Culture] (Moscow, 1981), and Fr. Graus "From Resistance to Revolt: The Late Medieval Peasant Wars in the Context of Social Crisis," in J. Bak, ed., *The German Peasant War of 1525* (London,

1976, pp. 1-9) discuss the clerical "crisis of legitimation" referred to above. The significance of the indulgences has been pointed out to me by Lionel Rothkrug, Montreal. The literature on the West European transformations is too vast to be cited; how generally valid it seemed to be to scholars is attested by the notes of F. Engels, this important pioneer of "war and society" studies, in his manuscript "Decay of Feudalism...", Appendix to *The Peasant War in Germany* (Moscow, 1956), pp. 218-20. For the discussion of this aspect in the literature on feudalism, and the absence thereof, I have consulted only the selections in L. Kuchenbuch-B. Michael, *Feudalismus: Materialien zur Theorie und Geschichte* (Frankfurt a.M., 1977). For the Austrian uprisings the main source is *Jakob Unrest: Österreichische Chronik,* ed. by K. Grossmann, (Weimar, 1957; MGH SS. rer. Germ. N.S. 9), esp. pp. 90-101, and F. Mayer, "Kleinere Mittheilungen zur Geschichte der Bauernunruhen in Steiermark," *Beiträge zur Kunde steiermärk. Geschichtsquellen,* 14 (1877), pp. 117-19. Cf. also J. Szücs, "Die Ideologie des Bauernkrieges," in G. Heckenast, ed., *Aus der Geschichte der Ostmitteleuropäischen Bauernbewegungen im 16.-17. Jahrhundert* (Budapest, 1977), pp 157 ff. For the Hungarian development I have utilized the studies ed. by B. Király and myself, *From Hunyadi to Rákóczi: War and Society in Late Medieval and Early Modern Hungary* (Brooklyn, 1982; East European Monographs No. 104). The sources for 1514 are now assembled in A. Fekete Nagy, V. Kenéz, L. Sólymosi, G. Érszegi, eds., *Monumenta rusticorum in Hungaria rebellium anno MDXIV* (Budapest, 1979; Publ. Arch. Nat. Hung. II, Fontes 12); Dózsa's manifesto is on p. 121f. In the chronology and interpretation I follow G. Barta and J. Szűcs, whose results are summarized in the volume quoted above (Heckenast, ed.). The reference to I. Bibó is to his "Eltorzult magyar alkat, zsákutcás magyar fejlődés" [Distorted Hungarian Character, Deadlocked Hungarian Development] (1948), in *Harmadik út* [Third Road], ed. by Z. Szabó, (London, 1960), pp. 189-226.

Dennis P. Hupchick

SEVENTEENTH-CENTURY BULGARIAN *POMAKS:* FORCED OR VOLUNTARY CONVERTS TO ISLAM?

Bulgarian historical scholarship has traditionally maintained that mass conversions of Christain Bulgarians to Islam were the direct result of an overt Turkish policy of coercion which was continuously applied to the Bulgarian population inhabiting the European possessions of the Ottoman Empire closest to the capital at Istanbul. According to this traditional argument, the two major periods of mass conversion—the first commencing with the reign of Sultan Selim I (1512-1520) and spanning the first half of the sixteenth century; the second stretching through and beyond the second quarter of the seventeenth century under Sultan Mehmed IV (1648-1687) and the Köprülü grand vezirs—stemmed from the rise of Muslim fanaticism in high Ottoman ruling circles, as well as from the necessity for the empire to further insure the security of its Balkan heartlands during periods of conflict with the European Christian powers.[1]

Western scholars have generally accepted the traditional Bulgarian argument because of the rather large number of Turkish and Bulgarian sources concerning the sixteenth and seventeenth centuries which have been edited and published by Bulgarian historians.[2] Furthermore, the argument fits neatly into the general picture painted by Western historians of the Ottoman Empire during these periods. Generally, the rising Ottoman state of the fourteenth and fifteenth centuries is portrayed as a predominantly European power. Except for its Anatolian homelands, the territory encompassed by the Empire lay in Southeast Europe. European Christians constituted the majority in the Empire's population and, under Islamic Sacred Law (the *Sheria*), they were afforded protection by the Muslim Ottoman state upon the condition that they acknowledged the domination of Islam and of its temporal representative, the sultan. This arrangement, known as *zimma*, classified the European Christians as inferior subjects (*zimmis*) of the state and liable for the imposition of discriminatory taxation, most notably the poll-tax (*cizye*), and a number of social and legal restrictions not applicable to Muslim subjects.[3]

A unique system of government, one almost totally in the hands of the sultan's personal slaves, was devised in order to administer and control the heterogeneous Ottoman state. This slave administration was staffed by former Christians acquired primarily through the *devshirme*, a periodic child-levy imposed upon the Christian subjects in the Balkans. Technically illegal under the *Sheria*, the *devshirme*, ironically, furnished the opportunity for the Christian majority of the Empire to be represented in the highest governmental circles, to the near exclusion of born Muslims.[4]

Commencing with the reign of the fanatically Muslim Sultan Selim I, the Empire began to undergo such a transformation that by the close of the seventeenth century the Ottoman state was well on the way toward earning the disreputable title of "Sick Man of Europe" bestowed upon it by the Russian Tsar Nicholas I (1825-1855). In essence, Selim reoriented the Empire in the direction of the Muslim Middle East, which initiated a centuries-long struggle with Persia [Iran] for preeminence in that region. His military conquests in Syria, Palestine, Egypt and Persia increased the Muslim population of the Empire to such an extent that the European Christians fell into the minority. Over the course of the sixteenth and seventeenth centuries the new Muslim majority succeeded in undermining the heretofore efficient slave establishment and gained access to the Ottoman ruling class. Their success played a major role in the decline of the Empire's internal stability and resulted in the obsolescence of the *devshirme*, the decay of the government's standing military forces and the rise of Muslim fanaticism among members of the Ottoman ruling class.[5]

Despite the general acceptance of the traditional interpretation, some contemporary Bulgarian scholars have posited an interpretation which stands in dramatic opposition to the traditional one concerning the mass conversions of Orthodox Bulgarians to Islam during the two centuries of Ottoman internal transformation initiated by Selim. This theory holds that most, if not all, conversions occurred voluntarily, without the use of direct force on the part of the Turkish authorities. Moreover, supporting evidence for this theory is said to exist in the form of unpublished Ottoman documents buried in the archives of the Bulgarian National Library in Sofia.[6] Such a theory, of course, runs counter to the highly nationalistic picture of pre-National Revival Ottoman Bulgaria developed by Bulgarian scholars since the liberation of the country from Turkish rule in 1878. In this picture the Orthodox religion is equated to all that is Bulgarian, Islam to all things Turkish, and the entire period between the years 1393 and 1762 is characterized as the struggle of the downtrodden Bulgarian population to maintain its Orthodox (Bulgarian) identity in the face of continuous Islamic (Turkish) oppression.[7] In as much as the theory of voluntary conversions is dependent upon sources either unpublished or otherwise unavailable, it cannot be readily accepted by serious scholars outright. However, the theory does afford an opportunity for specialists to reexamine the question of mass conversions in Bulgaria in terms of the known sources and of the accepted historical models shown above.

Because this problem is broad and mostly unexplored, this study will concern itself only with the mass conversions which occurred during the seventeenth century, and more specifically with those in the Rhodope Mountains region. The converts there, commonly referred to as *Pomaks* ("Helpers", from the Bulgarian, *pomagach*[8]), have received particular attention in a number of scholarly works dealing with the Ottoman period in Bulgarian history.[9] In all of these, the Rhodopes mass conversions are attributed to the employment of coercive tactics by Turkish military authorities.

The principal source utilized in all studies of the Rhodopes conversions is a rather lengthy chronicular note written upon the final page of an Orthodox liturgical manuscript (*Trebnik*) by a Bulgarian priest from the village of Korovo, Methodiĭ Draginov, and approximately dated 1666.[10] In a literary style quite uncommon for notes of this nature and time, Draginov graphically described the events surrounding the forced conversions among Bulgarians who inhabited the Chepino region of the Rhodopes. Two shorter sources—a note in a liturgical work (1670) once housed in the Pazardzhik Monastery of "Sv. Petŭr"[11] and a page from a chronicle written in the village of Golyamo Belovo (1620 [?])[12] —corroborate Draginov's tale. All told, these three sources comprise the most complete story of forced mass conversions in Bulgaria during the Ottoman period.

In May 1666 (-1670) Sultan Mehmed IV dispatched his Grand Vizier, Ahmed Köprülü, at the head of a massive land and sea expedition against the Venetian city of Candia on the island of Crete. Part of the land forces were mustered in Bulgaria near Plovdiv under the command of the Rumeli *beylerbey* (provincial governor), Pehlivan Mehmed Pasha. Mehmed marched his contingents southward through the Rhodopes in order to effect a junction with other forces being assembled in the Morea. During his march south, Mehmed accomplished the forced conversions of the Chepino Bulgarians.

As a pretext for the conversions, Mehmed declared the Chepino Bulgarians rebels against the state. Gavril, the Greek bishop of Plovdiv, had informed him that the Bulgarians in the area refused to pay the required taxes to the Plovdiv Metropolitanate and were, therefore, rebels. Armed with this excuse, Mehmed, upon entering the village of Kostandovo, threw the village notables and priest into chains and would have had them executed had not one of his Muslim *imams* (prayer leaders), Hasan *hoca*, suggested that the Christians pay for their lives by converting to Islam. The prisoners readily accepted this alternative. Mehmed then declared throughout the region that upon his return from the Candia campaign he would slaughter all of the Christians of Chepino, but offered mercy if they would forsake their Christian beliefs for those of Islam. Added incentive was given to conversion by Mehmed's emphasis upon the tax benefits to be gained by such action.[13] Hasan and four other *imams*, supported by janissary troops, then set about converting the inhabitants of the seven Chepino villages and those of other mountain villages in the area while Mehmed marched off in the direction of Thessaloniki.

Between the months of May and August, Hasan and his assistants successfully fulfilled their task. Their work was aided by a famine which was raging in the area at that time. All who accepted the Islamic faith were given grain from government warehouses in Pazardzhik. Those who refused conversion had their homes destroyed and were forced as refugees into the mountains, where they founded new settlements. In order to fan the flames of conversion, the new converts were given the right to pillage the properties of the Orthodox Church in the region and by August over two hundred churches and as many as thirty-three monasteries were destroyed.[14]

The case for the forced conversion of the Chepino Bulgarians would seem indisputable. However, if the Ottoman Government intentionally forced large numbers of Chepino Christians to leave the *zimmi* class, then it was, in effect, severing itself from a source of much needed tax revenue precisely at a time when the prolonged war with Venice over Crete (1645-1670) made readily available war funds imperative. Therefore, a closer examination of the sources utilized in building the case for forced conversion is necessary.

Unfortunately, none of the three primary sources for the Chepino conversions are known by this author to be extant in the original. All were first published by Bulgarians during the final third of the nineteenth century, which was a period of intense nationalistic fervor in Bulgaria. One may conjecturally question the authenticity of the sources themselves. Draginov's note appeared in printed form in a work by Stefan Zahariev (1870) eight years prior to the liberation of the country and in the midst of intense anti-Greek and anti-Turkish national sentiments over the question of the Bulgarian Exarchate. Draginov's note, as published, contains elements of both. The Pazardzhik Note appeared in 1894, while the *Belovo Chronicle* followed in 1898. Both restated, in abbreviated versions, the tale of Draginov and utilized exactly the same names and descriptions as found in the Draginov Note. The *Belovo Chronicle,* published last, followed almost identically the style and presentation of the Pazardzhik Note in all divergencies from Draginov. Because the conditions under which these sources were "discovered" are relatively unknown and because the time at which they were "discovered" was an intensely nationalistic one, by temporarily setting these sources aside and examining other evidence, we can test the veracity of the interpretation and cast light upon the authenticity of the sources.

A number of authenticated Bulgarian primary sources dating to the seventeenth century support the contention that Muslim fanaticism gave rise to acts of violence perpetrated by the Turkish authorities upon the Christian population throughout this period.[15] The most noted of these is an extensive piece of marginalia written in an Orthodox liturgical work

(*Sbornik*) by the priest Petŭr from the village of Mirkovo.[16] In his note, Petŭr described the wars of Mehmed IV in Poland (1672-1677) and in Transylvania (1684-1687). At the same time, he decried the wanton destruction of Christian properties in Bulgaria and the later cruel suppression by the Turks of the Bulgarian Chiprovtsi Uprising (1688). Although Petŭr and the other sources point out the anti-Christian policy of the Ottoman government and depict the rising tide of Muslim fanaticism among the Turkish authorities, nowhere is there explicitly mentioned attempts at forced conversions.

If the mass conversions of the Rhodopes were not the result of direct Turkish coercion applied toward that end, as implied by the voluntary conversion theory, then one must ask: Why did they occur? The most obvious answer, of course, would be that conversion freed the converts from such arbitrary acts of anti-Christian violence as noted by Petŭr of Mirkovo. Furthermore, conversion brought obvious financial benefits in that converts were freed from the poll-tax, Orthodox clerical taxes of many kinds, mandatory unpaid services demanded of the *zimmi* population by the Ottoman state, as well as the other social and legal restrictions placed upon the *zimmi* class in general. In effect, conversion meant joining the dominant element in Ottoman society and, because of the decay of the *devshirme,* provided the only opportunity for significant social advancement. The abject living conditions of most Bulgarian Christians during the seventeenth century, forced upon them by their *zimmi* status, could well have made the act of conversion quite desirable.[17] Hence, it would logically seem that conversion benefitted the converts more than the Ottoman state.

Individual conversions can be attributed to individual needs or perceptions of the rewards to be attained by such an action. Mass conversions, on the other hand, if not forced, must stem from needs and desires shared in common by a large group of people. In fact, the Chepino Bulgarians formed one of the many enclaves of Bulgarians who were granted certain privileges by the Ottoman state in return for specific services rendered to the state.[18] In the case of Chepino, the Orthodox population of the region had been granted full religious autonomy from the Greek Patriarchate in Istanbul by the Turks at the time of the initial Ottoman conquest of the region during the late fourteenth century. In return, all males from Chepino between the ages of twenty and thirty-five were required to serve with the Ottoman military forces in Europe.[19] The autonomous position of Chepino was maintained into the seventeenth century, aided by the fact that Sultan Süleyman (1520-1566) declared the region to be *wakif* property (a religious endowment) of the Süleymaniye Mosque in Istanbul.[20] Due to *wakif* status, the inhabitants of the Chepino region were freed from certain taxes and special services which the authorities could impose upon non-religous lands by law. Whether due to an outside threat to their religious autonomy (e.g., the Plovdiv Greek Orthodox Metropolitanate) or the existence of Ottoman laws applying to *wakif* lands which permitted *wakif* inhabitants to convert *en masse* (which is implied in the voluntary conversion theory[21]), the Chepino Bulgarians may quite possibly have decided that conversion to Islam was the only alternative open to them in order to maintain their privileged status under an increasingly fanatical Muslim regime.

The purpose of this study has not been to provide any conclusive answer to the question of mass forced conversions in Bulgaria during the seventeenth century. It has merely attempted to draw attention to this topic in the hope that future historical research will result in as definitive an historical account of Bulgarian mass conversions to Islam as possible, free of all nationalistic pretensions and preconceptions.

NOTES

1. Iv. Snegarov, *Turskoto vladichestvo prechka za kulturnoto razvitie na bŭlgarskiya narod i drugite balkanski narodi* [Turkish Domination as an Obstacle to the Cultural Development of the Bulgarian People and Other Balkan Peoples] (Sofia, 1958), pp. 74-5; P. Petrov, *Sŭdbonosni vekove za bŭlgarskata narodnost. Kraya na XIV vek-1912 godina* [Fateful Centuries for the Bulgarian Nationality. The End of the 14th Century— 1912] (Sofia, 1975), pp. 62-121; id., ed., *Asimilatorskata politika na turskite zavoevateli. Sbornik ot dokumenti za mohamedanchvaniya i poturchvaniya, XV-XIX v* [The Assimilatory Policy of the Turkish Conquerors. Collection of Documents Concerning Islam and Conversions to Islam, 15th-19th Centuries] (Sofia, 1962), see Introduction.

2. For example: *Dokumenti za bŭlgarskata istoriya, III, Dokumenti iz turskite durzhavni arhivi (1564-1908)*, pt. 1, *1564-1872* [Documents Concerning Bulgarian History, III, Documents in the Turkish State Archives

(1564-1908)], P. Dorev, ed., (Sofia, 1940); Petrov, ibid.; id., *Po sledite na nasilieto. Dokumenti za pomohamedanchvaniya i poturchvaniya* [On the Trail of Coercion. Documents Concerning Conversions to Islam and Turkism] (Sofia, 1972).

3. These included restrictions: upon the rights to construct or renovate religious structures; upon the height of such structures; upon outward expressions of religious belief; upon the type, color and quality of clothing; upon ownership of horses and wagons; upon bearing legal witness against Muslims; upon inheritance rights if contested by a Muslim, etc.

4. Periodically, young male children of the Orthodox population were collected in the villages, carried off to Istanbul or Anatolia, converted into fanatical Muslims and trained to fill posts at all levels of the government or in the ranks of the janissary standing army. Detailed studies of the *zimma* and *devshirme* can be found in: *The Encyclopaedia of Islam*, II, B. Lewis, C. Pellat, J. Schacht, eds., (London, 1965), pp. 210-13, 227-31; H. A. R. Gibb and H. Bowen, *Islamic Society and the West*, I, *Islamic Society in the Eighteenth Century* (London, 1950-57), *passim;* P. F. Sugar, *Southeast Europe under Ottoman Rule, 1354-1804* (Seattle, 1977), *passim;* and S. J. Shaw, *History of the Ottoman Empire and Modern Turkey*, I, *Empire of the Gazis: The Rise and Decline of the Ottoman Empire, 1280-1808* (Cambridge, 1976), *passim*.

5. Shaw, op. cit., pp. 170-1, refutes this traditional Western model and posits instead that the *devshirme* became so powerful, and the sultans so weak, that Muslims, who could not be legally enslaved, were forced to gain entry into the all-powerful slave class. Either way, the entrance of Muslims into the governmental system was the important fact.

6. From a conversation with the Bulgarian scholar, A. Slavov, November 22, 1979, which took place in the home of J. F. Clarke, Dorseyville, Pennsylvania.

7. When this author broached the subject of this theory to Professor Iv. Duichev, one of Bulgaria's most eminent and internationally recognized historians, at his home in Sofia, July 18, 1980, he immediately erupted into a twenty-minute oration upon Orthodoxy and Bulgarian national consciousness during the Ottoman Period.

8. K. Jireček, *Istoriya na bŭlgarite* [History of the Bulgarians] (Sofia, 1978; reprint of the 3rd. ed., 1929), p. 489. See also S. N. Shishkov,

Pomatsite v treti oblasti: Trakiya, Makedoniya, i Miziya [The Pomaks in Three Regions: Thrace, Macedonia, and Moesia], I (Plovdiv, 1914), pp. 19-31, for the use of the term *Pomak* and for other names acquired by Bulgarian Muslims (i.e., *Ahryanin, Torbesh, Apovnik, Mŭrvak, Poganik*) as well.

9. See, for example: Petrov, *Sŭdbonosni vekove*, pp. 179ff, 184-8, 187-95, 198ff; Snegarov, pp. 74-5; H. Gandev, "Faktori na bulgarskoto vŭzrazhdane, 1600-1830," *Problemi na bŭlgarskoto vŭzrazhdane* ["Factors in the Bulgarian Renaissance, 1600-1830," Problems in the Bulgarian Renaissance] (Sofia, 1976), p. 28; M. Macdermott, *A History of Bulgaria, 1393-1885* (New York, 1962), p. 46; Jireček, *Pŭtuvaniya po Bŭlgariya* [Travels Through Bulgaria] (Sofia, 1974; reprint of Plovdiv, 1899 ed.), pp. 465-7, 527; and a scholarly journal, *Rodopski sbornik* [Rhodope Collection] published by the Bulgarian Academy of Sciences, vol. 1 in 1965.

10. First published in the original seventeenth-century Bulgarian in S. Zahariev, *Geografsko-istoriko-statistichesko opisani na Tatar-Pazardzhishkata kaaza* [Geographical-Historical-Statistical Description of the Tatar-Pazardzhik District] (Vienna, 1870; photocopy ed., Pazardzhik, 1970), pp. 67-8. Two modern Bulgarian transcriptions are to be found in: I. Ivanov, *Starobŭlgarski razkazi. Tekstove, novobŭlgarski prevod i belezhki* [Old Bulgarian Stories. Texts, New Bulgarian Translations and Notes] (Sofia, 1935), pp. 80-1; Petrov, *Po sledite*, pp. 256-7, where the approximate date of the note is discussed.

11. Given in the original in G. Dimitrov, *Knyazhestvo Bŭlgariya v istorichesko, geografichesko i etnografichesko otnoshenie* [The Principality of Bulgaria in Historical, Geographical and Ethnographical Treatment], I (Plovdiv, 1894), p. 111; modern transcript in Petrov, op. cit., pp. 257-58.

12. Published in the original in N. Nachov, "List ot hronika, nameren v s. Golyamo Belovo," [A Page from a Chronicle, Located in the Village of Golyamo Belovo], *Bŭlgarski pregled* [Bulgarian Review], V, 2 (1898), pp. 149-51; modern transcription in Petrov, op. cit., pp. 258-9.

13. Not found in Draginov but explicitly mentioned in both of the other sources.

14. Draginov gives the figures at 218 churches, 33 monasteries; the *Pazardzhik Note* and the *Belovo Chronicle* give 218 churches, 32 monasteries, Petrov, *Po sledite*, pp. 257-9.

15. See, for example, B. Tsonev, *Slavyanski rŭkopisi i staropechatni knigi na Narodnata biblioteka v Plovdiv* [Slavonic Manuscripts and Old Printed Books in the National Library in Plovdiv] (Sofia, 1920), Nos. 18, 66, 84.

16. Tsonev, *Opis na rŭkopisite i staropechatnite knigi na Narodnata biblioteka v Sofiya* [Inventory of the Manuscripts and Old Printed Books in the National Library in Sofia], I (Sofia, 1910), No. 433. This note was also published in its entirely in M. Drinov, "Bŭlgarski letopisen razkaz ot kraya na XVII vek," [Bulgarian Chronicular Tale from the End of the 17th Century], *Izbrani sŭchineniya* [Collected Works], II (Sofia, 1971 reprint of 1882 article), pp. 344-48.

17. Most seventeenth-century foreign travel accounts testify to the abject conditions of existence enjoyed by the Orthodox Bulgarians, relative to those enjoyed by the Muslim population. See: P. Rycaut, *The Present State of the Ottoman Empire* (London, 1687), p. 39; J. Burbury, in M. Leo, *La Bulgarie et son peuple sous la domination ottomane. Tels que ont vus les voyageurs anglo-saxons 1568-1878. Decouverte d'une nationalite* (Sofia, 1949), p. 113; H. Blount, *A Voyage into the Levant* (London, 1636), p. 17; F. Babinger, "Robert Bargrave in Bulgarien (1652)," *Izvestie na istorichesko druzhestvo* [Bulletin of the Historical Society], XIV-XV (1937), pp. 147-8; *Chuzhdi pŭtepisi za Balkanite*, I, *Frenski pŭtepisi za Balkanite, XV-XVIII v* [Foreign Travel Accounts Concerning the Balkans, I, French Travel Accounts Concerning the Balkans, 15th-18th Centuries], B. Tsvetkova, ed., (Sofia, 1975), pp. 252, 254; Snegarov, p. 108.

18. Privileged Bulgarians, often times consisting of entire village populations, served as horse-breeders (*voynuks*), livestock-breeders (*celeps*), falconers (*sokolars*), mountain pass guards (*dervencis*) and militia (*martalosi*) for use against local bandits (*haiduks*). See Jireček, *Istoriya*, pp. 483-8.

19. Ibid., p. 370; Petrov, *Sŭdbonosni vekove*, pp. 187-88.

20. V. Mutafchieva, "Kŭm vŭprosa za statuta na bŭlgarskoto naselenie v Chepinsko pod osmanska vlast" [On the Problem of the Status of the Bulgarian Population in the Chepino Region under Ottoman Rule], *Rodopski sbornik*, I (1965), pp. 118-20.

21. Conversation with Slavov, November 22, 1979. In his remarks from the audience following the presentation of this work at the Fourteenth Annual Duquesne University History Forum on October 27, 1980, Slavov publically denied ever mentioning such documents in our November conservation.

Istvan Deak

BUDAPEST: A DOMINANT CAPITAL IN A DOMINATED COUNTRY?

Budapest is, and has been for the last hundred-odd years, the only great city in Hungary. It is and has been the center of every conceivable type of Hungarian activity, from poetry to parliamentary politics, from prostitution to radical socialism and heavy industry. All this has given rise to a fierce and thus far unsettled debate over the question of, 1) whether the city's numerical superiority and feverish activity have also implied political domination over the rest of the country, and 2) whether the existence of this outsized metropolis has promoted or hampered development and prosperity in the rest of Hungary. The answer to those questions has usually been more ideological than factual. Democrats, Westernizers and other urban intellectuals tend to see the city as an agency for civilization and progress in a rather, crude, primitive and slow-moving country, and to deny that Budapest has ever been politically dominant. Traditionalists, conservatives, agrarian socialists and populists on the other hand, tend to argue that Budapest has corrupted and exploited the countryside, and has often decisively influenced national politics.[1] It is my contention here that the "urbanists" are essentially right: Budapest, despite its splendor and greatness, has never been able to dictate national politics. Also, rather than stunting general growth, the city has always fostered the economic, social and cultural development of the whole country.

Budapest as a metropolis and a capital is of relatively recent date. Less than 150 years ago, it was not yet the capital of the country, and until 1873 there was not even a Budapest as such, only three geographically connected but politically, legally and socially separate townships. The fact that these three municipalities—Buda, Ó-Buda and Pest—were so different from one another, makes the rise of Budapest as a unified metropolis all the more remarkable. Paris, Vienna, London, Rome and other great European cities, radiated out from a historic center, gradually absorbing their suburbs; Budapest, however, came into being as the result of the fusion of several cities, none of which could absorb the others. Unified Budapest inherited the diverse traditions of its three ancestors, which helps to explain why the inhabitants of the capital have not developed any political cohesion or common political goals. This, in turn, might explain why Budapest has never been able to dominate Hungary.

Buda, a hilly, pleasant, and rather sleepy town, with 35,000 inhabitants —mostly German—in 1848, was the traditional seat of the Hungarian kings, and more recently, the seat of the vice-regal administration. But it was not the seat of the cardinal-archbishop, or of the university, or of the Diet. As the administrative but not the cultural, religious, or political center of Hungary, Buda would bequeath to the unified Budapest its bureaucratic tradition, its civil servants, its craftsmen, and its petty bourgeoisie.

Ó-Buda or Old Buda, once the site of an important Roman garrison and, in the early nineteenth century, a small market-town, did not enjoy the historic legal privileges of the "free royal cities" of Buda and Pest. On the other hand, pre-1848 Ó-Buda had a large Jewish community and a bustling shipyard, both heralding two of unified Budapest's characteristic traits: its role as a port in the middle of the Great Hungarian Plain and, much more importantly, as one of the very great European centers of Jewry.[2]

Ó-Buda was subject to the authority of Pest county, which had, however, no authority over either Buda or Pest. This, incidentally, was to become one of Budapest's many anomalies: in the unified capital sat the administration of Pest county, the most powerful territorial unit in Hungary, without this administration having any say over the fate of the very city in which it resided.

Finally, there was Pest, the hub of Budapest's greatness as a metropolis. A small, old walled town, Pest was situated on the eastern side of the historic Danube crossing, with Buda on the opposite bank. If Buda was hilly and pleasant, Pest was flat and dusty or muddy. It served as the starting point for all the main roads leading out onto the Great Hungarian Plain and beyond. Early in the nineteenth century, Pest began a phenomenal growth which was to lead to the creation of modern Budapest and, through it, to the creation of modern Hungary. Development was spurred on by the inauguration of steamship and railroad lines, the investment of Austrian capital in local industry, and a massive influx of people from the countryside in search of jobs and the amenities of urban life.

By 1848, Pest, with its 100,000 inhabitants, harbored enough professionals, students and intellectuals to act as the spark of a national and liberal revolution in Hungary. But as the Hungarian nationalist movement was headed by land-owning noblemen, and as the representatives of these noblemen sat in the Diet at Pressburg [Pozsony, Bratislava] and not at Pest, it soon became clear that the radical lawyers and intellectuals of Pest would be able to play only a very limited role in the upcoming events. They were permitted, nay encouraged, to help the noble elite in its struggle against Habsburg-Austrian centralism and the rebellious non-Magyar nationalists, but the Pest radicals were not allowed to dominate Hungary. When Louis Kossuth, the undisputed leader of the liberal nationalist movement, received a delegation of young radicals from Pest on March 19, 1848, he made amply clear what he and his fellow-noblemen thought of Pest and its radical politics:

> I recognize the inhabitants of Buda-Pest as inexpressibly important in this fatherland; I recognize Buda-Pest as the heart of the country, but I shall never recognize it as [this country's] master.... Just as the word 'nation' cannot be arrogated by one caste, so it cannot be arrogated by any one city.... This nation is so strong in the awareness of its rights, its vocation and its mission, that it can crush anyone who entertains the notion of indispensability to the nation.[3]

A few weeks later the first constitutional cabinet of Hungary, with Kossuth as a member, set up permanent residence at Budapest. This fact, together with Kossuth's speech to the radicals, perfectly illustrated the ruling elite's ambivalent attitude toward the new capital. The Hungarian middle nobility, that social class which had politically triumphed in 1848, was dynamic, progressive, and educated enough to yearn for a splendid capital in a dynamic and progressive country. But the same nobility was not prepared to cede political power to the commoner poets and journalists, German winegrowers and craftsmen, Greek, Serb and Jewish merchants, and Czech and German factory workers of the capital. Budapest, with its trade and industry, with its slums and palaces, with its university, theater, and trade unions, both attracted and alarmed the landed nobility. Never would these nobles be able to make up their minds about the city. Indeed, their relationship with it can best be characterized as a love-hate one. The Hungarian government and parliament would reside in Budapest; the nobility would profit from the cultural and economic creativity of the city, but precisely because this creativity was less their own than that of the city's Jewish, German, and other commoner inhabitants, the nobility would always remain suspicious of Budapest. And when capitalism would revolutionize the economy, toward the end of the century, causing one cultural shock after the other, the suspicion of the landed nobility toward Budapest would be shared by millions of others, including many inhabitants of the city. Finally, when in 1918-19, Budapest would try to dictate politics to the rest of the country, the ruling elite and much of the peasantry were to swear revenge and visit severe punishment on that alien, "sinful city."

A Prosperous Capital in a Growing Country:
Budapest Before the Great War

Following the revolutions of 1848-49, the development of Budapest or, rather, of the three cities, continued rapidly. Geographically and economically it had always been a natural center, and now it quite naturally attracted every modern institution and enterprise, from the railroad to the academy of sciences, from banking to industry. Even though the Vienna-centered, supra-national, absolutistic Austrian regime of Alexander Bach labored to prevent the formation of powerful national capitals, Budapest developed irresistibly.

In 1784, at the time of the first reliable census, Pest, Buda and Ó-Buda together numbered some 50,000 inhabitants which represented only one-half of one percent of Hungary's population. Other places such as Debrecen, Pressburg, and Szeged were not far behind. By 1850, however, Pest,

Buda and Ó-Buda had more than 150,000 inhabitants, constituting two percent of the country's total population; by 1890 the numbers had risen to half a million, and by 1910, to 900,000, or close to five percent of the total population. This meant a six-fold increase between 1850 and 1910; in the same period, the few dozen other self-governing cities of Hungary did not even double their populations. No other European metropolis, except Berlin, matched this rate of increase, and it is no wonder that Budapest, which as late as 1870 ranked only 17th among Europe's cities, had risen to 8th by 1890.[4]

Hand in hand with numerical growth went the Magyarization of the city, a process which had begun well before the Hungarians became undisputed masters of their own country. In 1850, fifty-six percent of the inhabitants of Budapest were Germans; by 1910, almost ninety percent declared themselves to be Hungarian.[5] Even if the assimilation was often only superficial, the overall trend was unmistakable. Because of the pressure of public opinion, the attractiveness of Hungarian culture, the snob-appeal exercised by the Hungarian gentry, and increasingly, too, because of administrative fiat, the German, Jewish, and Slavic inhabitants of the city had become Hungarians.

The Magyarization of Budapest meant much more than just the assimilation of its old-time inhabitants; it also meant the assimilation of its immigrants. Like all big cities, Budapest attracted a mass of immigrants; in 1867 only 367 out of every 1,000 inhabitants were native to the city; 482 had come from the rest of Hungary, 129 from the non-Hungarian provinces of the Habsburg Monarchy, especially Lower-Austria, Moravia and Bohemia, and 22 were from outside the Monarchy.[6] The big cities' role as a melting pot and the virtually unchangeable ethnic boundaries of the countryside are fundamental facts of East Central European history. Big cities in the late nineteenth and early twentieth centuries invariably imposed uniformity of language and culture on their inhabitants, and this language and culture were always those of the countryside surrounding the big city. Thus German-speaking Prague and Brno (Brünn) became Czech, and German, Yiddish, and Slavic-speaking Budapest became a Hungarian city.

There are three crucial dates in the history of Budapest: 1867, when the Compromise of that year made Hungary an equal partner with Austria; 1872/73, when Pest, Buda and Ó-Buda were united; and 1918/19, when Budapest tried, but failed, to impose its politics on the country.

Following the Austro-Hungarian Compromise of 1867, which made Budapest one of the two capitals of the Monarchy, the Hungarian government understandably lavished attention on the city. As Budapest was expected to catch up with Vienna one day, money was poured into construction and industry. Before the official unification of the three cities on January 1, 1873, Europe's largest steam-driven flour mills had been established here, as well as an exemplary waterworks. In the same period, gas lighting and horse-drawn trams were introduced. Following unification, the progress became even more phenomenal, and by 1900, railway lines from eleven directions converged on the capital, the first subway line had been built, and five new bridges spanned the Danube.[7] New public buildings ranged from a gigantomaniac Parliament house to scores of museums, hundreds of schools, and some lovely street-car shelters designed in eclectic style.

And, yet, this development was not artificial, we must insist, because even without politics, Budapest would have been the hub of the tremendous Hungarian railroad network—surpassing that of France in density— and it would have housed the overwhelming majority of the country's credit institutions, printing presses, publishing houses and chemical factories.

Municipal consolidation in 1872/73 brought with it special constitutional privileges for the city, exceeding those of the counties and the other self-governing cities. Still, by creating the position of a Lord-Mayor or *Oberbürgermeister* [*Főpolgármester*], who was a government appointee, and by other means, the government made certain that it would always be able to control the city. A rather unique franchise gave local power to the richest and to the best-educated inhabitants, the two groups not being identical. But as these so-called "virilists" came from the most diverse backgrounds: the old aristocracy, the new Jewish bourgeoisie, the old German and Greek merchant oligarchy, and the new intellectual and professional class, the city's ruling elite was not united in anything, except perhaps in its opposition to the political aspirations of the disenfranchised classes. In fact, the membership of Budapest's city council was to include representatives from every conceivable political trend, from ultra-conservativism to radical socialism.

The Dual Monarchy's economic growth was nothing short of a revolution. The speed of Hungary's progress surpassed that of Austria, and

Budapest's progress surpassed that of the rest of Hungary. Whether the capital's extraordinary growth was detrimental or beneficial to the countryside is very difficult to assess. No doubt, Budapest siphoned off the best talent in Hungary; no doubt, too, professional people and civil servants were reluctant to bury themselves in the countryside, but there is no proof whatsoever that business and capital behaved in a similar way. In fact, there is ample proof to show that capital went wherever it was worth going, and great industrial centers developed in the most remote provinces, when that was warranted by the availability of skilled manpower and raw material.[8] The development of Budapest and the countryside was part of the same capitalist process: they reinforced one another with manpower, innovation and credit.

A Giant Capital in a Small and Poor Country: Budapest During and After World War I

An interruption of this generally healthy process came during the war, when the lingering hostility between city and country flared up over the shortage of food, rolling stock, and industrial goods, leading to mutual accusations that the other side was not pulling its weight. This difficult situation was fatally aggravated in 1918/19, when the star-struck idealist Count Michael Károlyi and the extremist fanatic Béla Kun attempted to impose their political goals on an unready and unwilling country. As these regimes operated with the support of the urban intelligentsia and the Budapest workers, the enmity of the social elite and of large segments of the peasantry toward the city increased tremendously. The urban bourgeoisie, the industrial workers and, in particular, the Jews—all of whom had in fact suffered more from the democratic and socialist experiments than they had drawn profit—were made responsible for the lost war, the revolution, the hunger and the suffering. And, as if that were not enough, the Treaty of Trianon in 1920 deprived Hungary of two-thirds of its territory and over one-half of its inhabitants. As a result, Budapest (as well as Vienna) had become an anomaly, an overgrown head on a puny body. A city of one million in a nation of eight million, a highly developed industry in a country with scarce raw materials and with hostile neighbors: here was truly a source of frustration and conflict. Initially, the Horthy regime exploited this situation, whipping up public sentiment against the big city. But, in reality, popular hostility abated quite early, and the government's enmity proved neither consistent nor lasting. After all, not everybody in Budapest had supported the democratic and soviet republics; nor had everybody in the countryside opposed Károlyi and Kun. On the contrary, much of the Christian middle class and lower middle class in the capital had acted as a most vociferously anti-Semitic and counter-revolutionary force. Furthermore, the government and the political elite continued to profit from the amenities of the capital and from their association with the city's mostly Jewish bankers and industrialists. As a result, interwar governments continued to support Budapest, but without giving it any say in national politics. In fact, the city became politically weak, with a deep chasm separating its liberal-democratic and authoritarian, anti-Semitic political camps.[9]

In the 1930s, the liberal-democratic forces (by which we mean chiefly the Jewish bourgeoisie and the organized workers) were dramatically weakened in Budapest, and local power passed gradually into the hands of the anti-Semitic Right. In the 1939 secret-ballot parliamentary elections, the bourgeois liberals obtained 16.4% of the vote in Budapest, and the Social Democrats 12.7%. This was enormously in excess of their nationwide tally, which was 2% and 4%, respectively. But lest we think that the capital remained firmly progressive in an increasingly rightist country, we should note that the Arrow Cross and other National Socialist parties obtained 29.9% of the vote in Budapest, more than their nationwide proportion of 25%. What was lacking in Budapest in 1939 was a political center: the essentially conservative Government Party received only one-third of the vote in Budapest as opposed to one-half of the vote in the country as a whole.[10]

The radicalism of Budapest was temporary and it did not change the city's dichotomous position of political impotence combined with cultural and intellectual hegemony. Even the peasant-populist poets, the so-called "village explorers," and such heralds of an agrarian-oriented "Third Road" (i.e., neither capitalist nor communist) society as the philosopher-writer László Németh, tended to live in the capital as did, incidentally, most of their readers and followers. It is one of the great anomalies of Hungarian history that the peasant-populist cultural movement, whose output ranged from Béla Bartók's magnificent variations on folk music to the "blood and soil" romanticism of right-wing novelists, was backed and appreciated chiefly by Budapest Jewish bourgeois and intellectuals.[11]

Much of what was said and written in the interwar period about the enmity between city and country and the need for the nation to choose between an immoral, corrupt and alien Budapest and a pure and healthy countryside was nothing but words, an intellectual game between urbanists and populists. Real power was wielded by the bureaucracy that prided itself on its gentry-landowning origins and ideals but was, in reality, composed of mixed elements, partly urban, partly provincial, partly noble, partly common. The dividing line in the nation ran not between Budapest and the countryside, but between rich and poor, between pro-Nazi and anti-Nazi. And even in those difficult interwar years when Budapest, this huge city, barely managed to survive in a poor and small country, the city and the countryside complemented, rather than obstructed, one another.

The end of the war brought terrible hardships to Budapest in the form of a siege that lasted three months. The liberated capital, in ruins, for once depended completely on the good will of the peasants, who alone could, and in fact, did, save the city from starvation. Following liberation, Budapest was even less able to dictate policy to the countryside. Rather, its political development closely paralleled that of the rest of the country.

The Meeting of the City and Country In Post-World War II Hungary

Unlike 1939, when Budapest voted the right-wing or left-wing radical ticket (in 1939, even bourgeois democracy counted as radical), in 1945 the capital closely reflected the political yearnings of the country as a whole, yearnings for social justice and a multi-party democracy. Totally miscalculating the mood of the capital and dogmatically expecting a "Red" vote in a proletarian city, the Communists forced municipal elections in Budapest on October 7, 1945. What happened was precisely the opposite: the most moderate party within the governing anti-fascist coalition, the Smallholders, obtained an absolute majority. Nothing illustrates better the lack of a specifically Budapest-oriented political culture at this time than the fact that the Smallholders, a farmers' party, obtained 285,000 votes at the Budapest municipal elections, whereas the electoral alliance of Socialists and Communists obtained only 250,000 votes, and the two Budapest-based non-Marxist parties, the Bourgeois Democrats and the Radicals together obtained less than 28,000. The national elections, held a few weeks later, confirmed the Budapest political trend by giving 57% to the Smallholders and only 17% to the Communists.[12]

Soon after the elections the autonomy of Budapest, so precariously maintained over the centuries, came to an abrupt end. The Smallholders insisted on continued autonomy, but as police power rested solidly in the hands of the Communists, the Smallholders' absolute majority was worthless. In any case, because of an agreement among the members of the governing coalition, the Smallholders held only a minority of the seats in the Municipal Council.

Between 1945 and 1948, the democratic parties were gradually cheated or driven out of politics, and with the establishment of the Stalinist dictatorship, Budapest ceased to play a special role. Enlarged in 1949/1950 from 206 square kilometers to 525, and from 1,057,000 inhabitants to 1,640,000[13] (and today, over 2 million), Greater Budapest became an even bigger head of the puny body of a country of barely ten millions, but in political terms, the city counted for nothing. The principle of "democratic centralism" concentrated all power at the very top of an enormous party and state apparatus, of which the Budapest apparatus was an organic part. Only in 1956 did the capital initiate developments, when its population set off the Great Revolt. But the spontaneous action of the Budapest workers, students and soldiers was soon imitated by the spontaneous action of such provincial revolutionary centers as Győr, Miskolc and Pécs. During the 13 days of the Revolution the Imre Nagy government in Budapest had to share power or vie for power with several militant national committees that had sprung up in other cities, as well as in the capital. Only the village population remained relatively calm.

Since 1956, power has again been exercised by a centralized bureaucracy that has no intention of yielding any autonomy to the capital and has actively fostered the development of new provincial centers. Budapest is still the hub of most cultural and intellectual activity, as well as of much of the economy, and it is still the goal of those in the provinces who dream of an active and exciting life. But now that Hungary is an industrialized country, the vast differences between capital and province are disappearing rapidly. Maybe Budapest will continue to show the way in the future, but, certainly, it will never dominate.

NOTES

1. For an interesting, although not completely unprejudiced discussion in English of the city-versus-country controversy, see Paul Ignotus, *Hungary* (New York-Washington: Praeger Publishers, 1972), especially pp. 174-184. Paul Ignotus, a "Westernizer," was the son of an even more famous "Westernizer," Ignotus.

2. On the pre-1848 Ó-Buda, see, for example, Elek Fényes, *Magyarország leírása* [A Description of Hungary] (2 vols., Pest: Beimel, 1847), II, 216-217.

3. Kossuth in the Lower House of the Diet on March 19, 1848 (Cited in István Barta, ed. *Kossuth Lajos az utolsó rendi országgyűlésen, 1847=48* [Lajos Kossuth at the Last Estates' Parliament, 1847/48], (Budapest: Magyar Történelmi Társulat, 1951), 675. Translation mine.

4. See Péter Hanák, "Magyarország társadalma a századforduló idején" [Hungarian Society at the Turn of the Century], in P. H., ed. *Magyarország története, 1890-1918* [History of Hungary, 1890-1918] (2 vols., Budapest: Akadémiai Kiadó, 1978), I, 417ff.; László Katus, "A népesedés és a társadalmi szerkezet változásai" [Changes in Demography and in the Structure of Society], in Endre Kovács, ed., *Magyarország története, 1848-1890* [History of Hungary, 1848-1890] (2 vols., Budapest: Akadémiai Kiadó, 1979), II, 1119ff.; and Mária H. Kohut, ed., *Források Budapest történetéhez, 1873-1919* [Sources for the History of Hungary, 1873-1919], (Budapest Főváros Levéltárának kiadványa, 1971), 97.

5. Hanák, I, 417.

6. Károly Vörös, *Egy világváros születése* [The Birth of a Metropolis], (Budapest: Kossuth, 1973), 65.

7. Károly Vörös, "From City to Metropolis (1849-1919)," in Ágnes Ságvári, ed. *Budapest: The History of a Capital* (Budapest: Corvina Press, 1973), 37-43.

8. On the national or regional "blindness" of capital in Hungary, see, for instance, László Katus, "Über die wirtschaftlichen und gesellschaftlichen Grundlagen der Nationalitätenfrage in Ungarn vor dem ersten Weltkrieg," in Péter Hanák, ed., *Die nationale Frage in der Österreichisch-Ungarischen Monarchie, 1900-1918* (Budapest: Akadémiai Kiadó, 1966), 149-216.

9. See Zsuzsa L. Nagy, *A budapesti liberális ellenzék, 1919-1944*

[The Liberal Opposition in Budapest, 1919-1944], (Budapest: Akadémiai Kiadó, 1972).

10. There is a fine analysis of the 1939 elections in Miklós Lackó, *Nyilasok, nemzetiszocialisták, 1935-1944* [Arrow Cross Men, National Socialists, 1935-1944], (Budapest: Kossuth, 1966), 166-176.

11. The best analysis of populism in a Western language is by Gyula Borbándi, *Der ungarische Populismus* (Mainz: v. Hase and Koehler Verlag, 1976).

12. See the 1945 election results in Bennett Kovrig, *Communism in Hungary. From Kun to Kádár* (Stanford, CA: Hoover Institution Press, 1979), 179-181. Also, Imre Kovács, ed., *Facts about Hungary*, revised edition (New York: Hungarian Committee, 1959), 59-60.

13. See Ferenc Gáspár, "From the Liberation to Greater Budapest (1945-1950)," in Ságvári, ed., *Budapest*, 66.

Tamás Aczél

GOD'S VINEYARD: EXCERPTS FROM A POLITICAL AUTOBIOGRAPHY

> *The consummation of time, the extermination of all evils have arrived. . . . All lords, nobles and knights shall be cut down and exterminated in the forests. . . . Accursed be the man who withholds his sword from shedding the blood of the enemies of Christ. . . . The believers shall live together as brothers, none shall be subject to another. . . . The Lord shall reign and the Kingdom shall be handed over to the people of the earth.*
> Articuli et errores Taboritarum, 1422

When I was born, the first World War in mankind's history had barely ended and when I said good-bye to the sooty enclave of my ancient *gymnasium*, (without, incidentally, any noticeable regret), the second was about to begin. During that long, hot summer of 1939, while waiting for the Deluge to burst upon us with its irresistible downpour of steel, explosives and mutilated bodies, my father and I would often discuss our historical and political situation. My father was a life-long social-democrat, a man with a reliable knowledge of socialist theory, a fine sense of social justice and an audaciously anti-social walrus-mustache which made him a close lookalike of a fashionable writer of elegant, if sometimes salty stories about the affairs of impecunious aristocrats, lustful gentries, rich capitalists and ambitious women. He didn't mind the resemblance, though; he rather enjoyed it, tongue-in-cheek. He was a man of simple vanities and a touch of wry humor.

The minor executive of a major bank, he was also a poet *manqué,* and would, accordingly, generously sprinkle his political analyses with poetic images. In between the forbidding mountains of war, he would say in the course of our long walks in the lush, verdant woods of Buda, there lay the desolate valley of a society, *our* society—*what a society!* It was, he continued, prostrated by an unjust peace, torn by revolutions, counter-revolutions, oppression, exploitation, chauvinism, class and racial discrimination, and a general sense of frustration and hopelessness. Small wonder, in his opinion. What else would one expect of a system that left its working people crawling in the mud of history's poverty, and its most thoughtful reformers permanently defeated? That drove its best poets and writers to despair and suicide, its best intellectuals to self-imposed exile in the West, and jailed or often even hanged its radical political opponents?

He was, I knew, referring to a small, sectarian group of underground revolutionaries that called themselves the *Communist Party of Hungary:* though he utterly disagreed with their ideology and disavowed their methods, he was always ready to defend their human and civil rights. One of them, a shy, polite, modest little man, whom nobody could ever have suspected of being a clandestine revolutionary, let alone the leader of a revolutionary party, was once his colleague in the bank; they have shared an office and became quite friendly. When the man was unexpectedly arrested and summarily executed, my father had a nervous breakdown. Though it happened many years ago, he could never forget the day. The shockwaves of that terrible, empty dawn in the cobblestoned yard of Central Prison, were still reverberating in the woods and in his mind; his cheeks, pale and well-shaven, lit-up with the consuming fires of hypertension.

But of course, my father went on, what virtually anywhere in the world would have passed as a bad joke, was reality here: a country without a sea ruled by an admiral without a navy. A former aide-de-camp to the Emperor Franz-Joseph, dressed habitually in the spotless uniform of yesteryear's glory, Admiral Nicholas Horthy, in my father's opinion, was not an evil man, only a weak one. Surrounded by an aristocracy, his kith and kin, that jealously guarded their traditional privileges as well as their enormous estates; supported by an increasingly powerful, yet still thin stratum of capitalists, predominantly Jewish, whom he regarded as upstarts, but nevertheless accepted, (with the customary cynical shrug of the born anti-Semite) both their money and their admiration; and applauded by a timid middle class whose spine had been broken long before it could have evolved into a strong national force, he was, my father pointed out, the best available symbol of his own arch-conservative regime. During his long tenure as Regent of Hungary, the gulf between ruler and ruled, rich and poor grew wider every day, and law and order meant simply the defense and perpetuation of the status quo.

The squalor of the worker's tenements and the menacing omnipresence of the gendarmerie in the villages had gone, however, conveniently unnoticed by those who benefitted from it, and remained carefully hidden from the eyes of visiting Western dignitaries, observers, tourists, curiosity-seekers who came to live well on their hard currency. For indeed, on the thin but sparkling ice of the surface, my father said, life in this beautiful, gifted little country of ours, with its sentimental gypsy music, elegant women, lively theaters, saucy nightclubs, excellent cuisine and intoxicative wines, might well have been a scene straight out of a merry Lehár operetta. Budapest, the "Paris of Eastern Europe," or "Queen of the Danube," as it was both fondly and boastingly called, glittered in the warm summer nights of the prewar interregnum, its impoverished lower classes, political prisoners, obligatory monuments to freedom, and secessionist *fin de siècle* architecture notwithstanding. As hypocrisy's ultimate offence against honesty, decency and justice, the beneficiaries, foreign and indigenous, of those volatile years lived high—but they lived on borrowed time. And, my father would invariably conclude, their time was nearly up.

Nearly, but not yet. And when? This was a question my father could not answer, and was, for me, the big, gaping hole in the thoughtfully woven net of his comments, to which I'd been listening ever since I had, in my mid-teens shown the first discernible signs of moral consciousness and practical interest in political theory and organized labor movement. But now, the time had arrived when I felt compelled to take a more inquisitive look at that *desolate valley of a society,* and words, however compassionate and articulate, no longer satisfied by growing moral indignation. I was still inclined to agree with my father's diagnosis of the *malaise,* but was becoming increasingly reluctant to accept his proposed *panacea.*

True, he was a man of integrity, full of good intention. Granted, he knew a great deal more about socialist theory than I did, and it was from him I first heard the names of Bebel, Kautsky, Bernstein, Luxemburg, Adler and Marx. Yes, he had always worked conscientiously in his trade union—the *Trade Union of Private Employees*—had analyzed the political situation dependably, and campaigned hard for his candidates at municipal or general elections. But what had he really achieved throughout these long, tense years of educating, lecturing, electioneering? With his pleasant smile, correct conjugation, gentlemanly objectivity and unfailing efforts to understand and make himself understood? And, what seemed to me even more disappointing, what had this party achieved with the strikes, dispersed quickly by the mounted police; with the lectures, infiltrated by the secret police; with the newspapers, often suppressed, banned, seized; and with all those vague "reformist" ideas of their small bunch of parliamentary representatives whose voices were invariably drowned in the loud *brouhaha* and sniping witticisms of the government benches? They had achieved nothing and worse: whether they liked it or not, intended or not, they had, instead of bringing it closer, delayed the hour of reckoning and with it, the dawn of socialism. And this was unforgiveable.

There existed, however, a radical alternative to what I felt was the timidity and verbosity of social-democracy. It was the theory and practice of revolutionary communism. Printed abroad, smuggled into the country, circulated through clandestine channels, the works of Lenin and Stalin had found their way into my hands and heart, and those of my generation. Vitriolic in style and content, they lashed out against the injustices and inequalities of the world, revealing the true essence of bourgeois dictatorship behind the smooth facade of pseudo-democracies. Irresistible logic and irrefutable reason took us on a sobering excursion into past, present and future, and life became more meaningful and infinitely more rewarding than ever before.

The leaders of our society, obscured for so long by the galactic distances of status, wealth, myth, came sharply and suddenly into focus. Admiral Horthy was no longer the benevolent, if weak, captain of my father's tales, trying to keep his ship on even keel between the treacherous gusts of brown and red hurricanes. He now emerged as the sinister symbol of a semi-feudal, semi-fascist dictatorship whose sole aim was to destroy the forces of human progress with the tacit support of his secret allies, the social-democrats, and my father—horrifyingly!—was one of them. Yet, however horrifying it all appeared, this was no time for sentimental bourgeois moralizing; it was time to act. High time, indeed.

For the new saints of our new *credo* not only *talked* about the advent of a better world (somewhere in the distant future), as did our social-democratic leaders (ever so calmly, objectively, interminably); they *offered* us the key to the New Jerusalem, the Soviet Union. That was no longer the heavenly city of ancient mystics, fossilized philosophers, antediluvian poets or such latter-day dreamers as my father: the USSR was the shining, earthly fortress of the present becoming the future, and of the future becoming the present. Apart from the clarity, simplicity and universality of Soviet theoretical—or theological?—underpinnings, it was precisely this state of perpetual becoming—the moral imperative of modern revolutionaries—that had attracted us to gather around its walls of utopian messianism. For a bunch of young middle-class intellectuals with no practical experience or skills in politics and hardly any knowledge of the world outside their native land, but who thought of themselves as being morally superior, intellectually more sophisticated and philosophically more penetrating than their elders, (those insufferable old escapists, cowards, traitors!) this must have been—as it was—the supreme religious experience. Into the future we rode with the four horsemen of the Apocalypse.

There seemed to be no other way out of this horrible mess. Neville Chamberlain's umbrella couldn't prevent him from getting soaked on the rainy tarmac of Munich airport, let alone save the peace. Every day, Hitler's grip on the country strengthened. His Hungarian admirers and imitators, the *Arrow Cross* stormtroopers of a hopeless *Lumpenproletariat,* were making threatening noises. Admiral Horthy gave in. Not because he, or his fellow-aristocrats liked Hitler—in fact, they despised him as a *parvenu*—but because their fear of revolutionary social change (probably any change at all) was greater than their distate for a housepainter, still exuding the pungent smell of physical labor. The Jews, then, were relegated into second-class citizenry, despite the vigorous protest of leading intellectuals (poets, writers, scientists, university professors) and some half-hearted remonstrations of the Catholic Church. The last remaining civil rights of the workers had already been taken away under the pretext of an impending war, and inside the stinking huts of landless peasants the gendarmerie—their sickle-feathers fluttering dashingly on their shakos—were searching every nook and cranny for *subversive literature.*

In the Fall, the Poles—brave but defenseless—were already flying their Sunday-gliders against the Nazi *Stukas* in a desperate attempt to resist the advancing *Panzer* columns of the invaders. That scarcely a year before, Stalin had signed a pact with Hitler (that arch-enemy of mankind!) didn't really bother me or, for that matter, my fellow-sympathizers. I was convinced—*weren't we all?*—that Stalin was serving the best interests of the Fatherland of the Revolution—and serving it well. That now, following the collapse of Poland, the advancing Russian bear was more than eager to embrace half of its territory, did not, at the time, strike me as the first, if clumsy steps of a re-awakening imperialist giant, but as the paradigm of Stalin's wisdom and foresight. It was, anyway, as good a time as any to make an important decision, even though I still needed the approval and encouragement of my peers, at least as much as the disapproval and fury of my parents; both came easy.

After some animated discussion over a glass of bubbling-cold *Badacsonyi kéknyelü* in our favorite café-tavern at the Pest side of the Margit Bridge with my friends (promising young poets, writers, journalists, literary historians, teachers, philosophers all) I resolved to help whicheverway I could the underground work of the outlawed Communist Youth League, invisible arm of an equally invisible body, yet the embodiment of a visible future. Some of those present, loyal social-democrats, raised intelligent objections; others, already involved in doing odd jobs for the *Movement*, as pasting red-lettered posters and stickers on the crumbling walls of tenements or distributing illegal newspapers, leaflets, books, supported me vigorously: I knew—I *just* knew—they were right, and I couldn't let them down. The question was thus settled and our attention focused immediately upon the latest and longest poem of one of our poet-friends, published in the first (and, alas, also the last) issue of an obscure, yet exclusive, if somewhat cliquish, literary magazine. For us, innocent sons of Dionysos, literature was still far more important than life, its colorless by-product. So, when my decision—cheek? compulsion? obsession? stupidity?—became known, as it soon did, my mother turned pale and hysterical, my father red, indignant and worried, my larger family disgusted. Predictably so. That I had chosen, while still in *gymnasium,* the insecure and highly dubious career of a writer (like one of my uncles before me) was bad enough; but this was much worse. Yet, surprisingly, the fight I anticipated was, in fact, itching for, never materialized.

I came from a large, sprawling family whose mixture of blood reflected the bloody mixture of Hungarian history: Christians, Jews, believers, agnostics, atheists, freethinkers, freemasons, even an occasional black sheep anarchist or communist (like one of my uncles working for the Comintern in Paris) mingled in its womb with astonishing variety. But despite its voluminous size and teeming diversity, it had preserved, miraculously intact all throughout these years of external danger and internal decay, a distinctive hard core of authoritarian rule, traditional order and inflexible hierarchy which guarded its vulnerable nucleus against the excesses of the individual members. Whether it was the prehistoric instinct of the group collectively to face the unnameable horrors of the antediluvian forest, the only way to secure the survival of the unit, or simply the dead weight of the past, I didn't know, for I was born into it, had grown up under its widespread, protective wings and was not ready to fight it. All I knew was that, whenever I entered the room where my eiders were sitting in their plush, comfortable Victorian armchairs, with fragile and graceful *Meissen* cups in their manicured hands, aglow, as it were, in the reflected lights of crystal chandeliers and argillaceous *Bokharas,* I felt tremors in my stomach and weakness in my legs.

For it was a royal court. Here they were, all those important, powerful and successful men, lawyers, doctors, engineers, high court judges, industrial executives, with their elegant, demanding wives, talking with infuriating competence, about politics, business, literature, music or vacations abroad; arbitrating quarrels; trading *piquant* jokes; rewarding good behavior; giving advice or money to their less successful kinfolk. Symbols of order and permanence, they ruled our lives, sometimes peremptorily, sometimes with a friendly, understanding wink in their bespectacled eyes, enforcing the unwritten laws of the family, its strict code of ethics, its secret communication system, even its collective memory, with the unruffled ease of people accustomed to power. It made my blood-pressure rise—and my heart sink. For now, that I was sitting among them (in one of those plush Victorian *fauteuils,* yet on the outer edge of the inner sanctum's invisible curtain), summoned to account for my decision to become a rebel, an outlaw, I couldn't help feeling simultaneously proud and wretched.

I felt proud because I was capable of turning against them—against their riches, power, success, complacencies and composure—in the name of a higher morality and a greater good. And I felt wretched, because I sensed that I was still attached to them, even loved them, and the lofty motives of my rebellion against Admiral Horthy's fascist regime was inextricably mixed with the uglier personal motives of envy, jealousy and incontinence, my appetite for power and success, both of which were, at least for the moment, lamentably beyond my reach. If they understood my dilemma, (which was likely), they didn't condemn me for it; if they didn't (which was unlikely) they kept silent about their failure. Wise and experienced, they counted on the healing flow of time and listened to my somewhat garbled argument attentively, expressed their disagreement coherently, warned me of the consequences and then—because they still retained a confidence in reason, decency and humaneness—dismissed me with an amicable but condescending pat on my shoulder. For a while, I stood in the well-trimmed garden of my eldest uncle's elegant villa, shivering in the balmy breeze of the Buda hills, left to my own devices, burning with shame, furious.

But this time, sensitive judges of character and circumstances as they were, they misjudged both the situation and my state of mind. For soon afterwards, the world exploded and, even though our personal antagonisms sank beneath the stormy oceans of war and persecution, my youthful sympathies for the left developed into an unshakeable determination and firm commitment: the radical sweep of the fascist right could only be countered—and it must be countered!—by the radical sweep of the communist left. With the endless, frozen plains of the Ukraine, littered with the corpses of soldiers and Jewish youngsters of the forced labor camps, behind me; the giant American *Liberators* transecting cerulean skies above me; and the unspeakable horrors of the systematic genocide of the Jews (that had claimed the lives of many in my family) before my eyes, —where else could I turn for meaning, consolation or purpose?

And so, frightened to death by the swarming, fully-armed ruffians of the Arrow Cross who would often shoot first and ask questions later, I attempted to get close to whatever flimsy resistance movement I could find amidst the ruins of the city, but I got caught and was transported (or, rather, was forced to walk) to *Konzentrazionslager Mauthausen* on Danube, in Upper Austria. In the meantime, however, the big T34 tanks of the Red Army were rolling irresistibly toward the eastern borders of Hungary, and on the bayonets of their infantry there fluttered, I was more than ever convinced, the pennants of freedom, justice, equality and a fighting but better life. Accordingly, after having been liberated by the 7th American Army whose insignia was the buffalo, I returned to what I hoped was going to be a liberated country with the insignia of the red star. The sweet smell of success lingered in the air, and I floated on the soft currents of victory, joyfully blinded by the dazzling flashes of history's vertiginous adventure. The consummation of time had arrived; but the years of innocence had come to an end.

Commitments

> *But of what use is your freedom if you do not commit yourself?*
> J. P. Sartre, *The Age of Reason.*

1949 was a fateful year in Hungary, one of those catastrophic years that are destined to become symbols of defeat and hopelessness in the historical memory of a nation. By then, the groundwork of an eventual and total communist takeover had been laid: the democratic parties of the postwar coalition were destroyed, the last legally and democratically elected Prime Minister Ferenc Nagy, was blackmailed into exile, Cardinal Mindszenty was imprisoned for life, the economy was nationalized—from steel-workers to haberdasheries—and forced collectivization proceeded at an ever-accelerating pace. In the spring, referring of course to Stalin's famous *dictum,* Mátyás Rákosi, Secretary General of the Hungarian Communist Party, proclaimed the arrival of the people's democracy which was, he said, in all essentials, the dictatorship of the proletariat but in the Soviet form. The gates of the newest of all New Jerusalems flew wide open.

They were on the march again: the medieval *prophetae* of the *pauperes* with the chiliastic fantasies of an imminet *Parousia;* the descendants of the spiritualists, enthusiasts, Albigensiens; the progenies of the *perfecti* of the Waldensian *Church of the Pure;* the successors of the Brethren of the Free Spirit of the Low Countries, the Taborites of Prague, the Anabaptists of Münster, the Jacobins of Paris, the nihilists of Moscow, the bolsheviks of St. Petersburg, *homines intelligentiae,* knights of the Apocalypse, the élite guard of history. Unique representatives and sole interpreters of the Divine Will, the General Will, the Will of the People, the Law of Historical Inevitability, armed up to the teeth with the weapons of looted arsenals and their messianic sense of mission, they led the great, subterranean armies of despairing peasants, oppressed artisans, dispossessed burghers, exploited proletarians against the demonic hosts of *Avaritia* and *Luxuria* century after bloody century. In the end, they were always defeated. Yet they rose, time and again, from under the smoldering ruins of a Heavenly City, a Republic of Virtue, a communist state of equality, justice and purity, ready for the next battle, the beguiling mixture of their fanaticism and idealism, innocence and guilt-complex, cynicism and gullibility, moral superiority and amoral destructiveness unchanged and, perhaps, unchangeable.

And now, again, they stood at the threshold of yet another ultimate victory. They were fortified by memories of defeats and self-sacrifice; by the skills, experience and insights they had gained during those interminable years in exile, in prison, in underground skirmishes with a ruthless class enemy. As their forerunners, they were convinced that they had attained a perfection so absolute that it made them immune to sin and error. And last but not least, they were now backed by the Red Army of another Utopia, triumphant in its hour of trial, determined to defend its conquests, and eager to extend the boundaries of its power. Thus, with their customary *élan* and limitless self-confidence, they committed themselves to the realization of their age-old plan of immediate and total world-transformation, never for a moment doubting the enthusiastic support of their perennial protégés. But this time, strangely, there came only a faint echo from the depth of society, an almost inaudible response to the bugle-call of revolution from under the rubble of centuries of suffering, betrayal, hope, cowardice, disgust, despair and fear, neither approval nor denial, neither hatred nor love, just the mute, indifferent rumblings of the deep. That may have, for a moment, surprised them. But they knew well what they had to do.

Soon, the infant democracy, born amidst Nazi terror, American air-raids, and Russian artillery fire, was killed and the stage was set for celebrations with banquets for the victors and with gallows for the vanquished. On the 1st of May, at a lavish reception in the Hotel Gellért, commemorating the people's devotion to the struggle of the international proletariat, László Rajk, Minister of Foreign Affairs and member of the Politburo, was sipping champagne and clinking glasses with General György Pálffy, Inspector General of the Army, relaxed, satisfied and apparently unsuspecting. Two weeks later, he was arrested and, together with General Pálffy and some other high-ranking members of the party hierarchy, charged with Titoist-imperialist conspiracy, tried and, after having confessed to every treachery imaginable, sentenced to death and executed. Ritual celebrations became inextricably lined with ritual murder, the transparency of triumph with the finality of death.

A Political Autobiography

"You see," an old Moscow hand had told me later, in the summer of 1956, when it was not only possible but fashionable to talk about the taboos of past decades, "when after 25 years exile in the Soviet Union we returned to Hungary, we had hoped—hoped against hope—that perhaps this time it was all going to be different. That the madness of those years was not going to be repeated. After all, watching Mátyás Rákosi beaming happily next to Harry Truman on the stairs of the White House, was no ordinary spectacle, believe me!"

"But when Rajk was arrested, we realized that we were deluding ourselves: it *was* going to happen all over again. And we also knew that the only course left open to us was to follow the advice of our old drill-sergeants in the Army of the Austro-Hungarian Monarchy, *maul halten und weiter dienen.* Shut up and obey!"

"So you *knew* Rajk was innocent," I said, terrified.

He looked at me with an unforgettable blend of sympathy, understanding, condescension and contempt, "Didn't you?" No, I didn't. Or, perhaps, I didn't want to.

At once frightened and exhilarated by the storm that enveloped the country, yet which I saw as an ultimately healing force, I was blind but my blindness, that tragicomic lack of knowledge and experience of a significant part of my generation, appeared to me the only way of seeing. Blindness, of course, has always symbolized man's tragic sense of vision, that sublime, luminous, if fleeting insight into his condition, his spasmodic perceptions of the paradoxes and ambiguities of past, present and future, of good and evil, of his bond with the cosmos. Ours, however, was a different kind of blindness—an intellectual and spiritual blackout on whose dark screen the simplifications and petrified dogmas of an obsolete theory sparkled as so many revelations. So, we came to view the past as a series of historically predetermined episodes leading straight up to the present; life as a continuous battle of the fulfillment of future's cloudless Utopia; and the struggle for the happiness of mankind as the only purpose and sole meaning of our existence. It was, no doubt, childishly naive, insanely idealistic, incredibly stupid and intolerably arrogant. Yet somehow, in some curious way, by some singularly illogical interplay between the nobility of the heart and the servility of the mind, it was also understandable.

When for the first time after the war, our old circle of young revolutionary saviors gathered together in our favorite café to take account of the past and celebrate the future, we found the Margit bridge blown into the Danube, our own ranks tragically decimated, the city ravaged but, we thought, the ruins full of promise. At last, Apocalypse was at hand! Yet, to our amazement and dismay, we soon realized that the beginnings were to be anything but apocalyptic. Under the leadership of a coalition government which consisted of the old, prewar opposition parties now joined by the newly legalized Communist Party, which threw its full weight (or so it seemed to us) behind the efforts to stabilize the country's erratic heartbeat, work and more work was the order of the day. Sooner or later we had to understand that our emotional commitment to, and sentimental longing for, a violent and immediate reorganization of social structures and moral precepts was one thing, and party discipline another. But it didn't take too long for us, (or, for that matter, for millions of war-weary, yet assiduously attentive Hungarians) to figure out that beneath that new image of respectability and openness, plans for an attack against the representatives of a "reactionary bourgeois democracy" were already being made and put into operation. We were relieved: so the acceptance of bourgeois slogans, the compliance with bourgeois directives was all tactics, diversionary moves not to be taken seriously. Red-faced, we were also ashamed for doubting the Party's ability to navigate between the Scyllas and Charybdises of the treacherous bourgeois ocean. When the hour of reckoning and redemption finally arrived in the curious guise of forged election results, the coalition collapsed and the Party seized power. And we were happy.

But our happiness was destined to be short-lived. Soon, its clear surface was ruffled by the heavy stones of unexpected announcements about a conspiracy whose magnitude and arrogance seemed to have surpassed everything we had seen before. For we *had* seen this before and there was nothing unusual in it: since the war, plots have been uncovered, conspiracies foiled, imperialist agents—like Cardinal Mindszenty and his spy-ring of fiendish black-clerics—jailed or even hanged and, we thought, quite deservedly. Those were all textbook cases, practical illustrations of well-known theoretical maxims according to which the bourgeoisie was wont to put up a desperate fight for their crumbling power and would become, as their situation deteriorated, less and less fastidious about their methods of subversion.

A Political Autobiography

The arrest of László Rajk and his fellow-conspirators, however, was something entirely new, different, monstrous and despicable. These were not common, run-of-the-mill agents of the CIA or MI5; they were high-ranking functionaries of the Party, all communists with a long, fighting past and apparently impeccable records whose treason now emerged as a turning point both in our lives and in the tactics of the forces of reaction. Until this staggering moment, our task, as we perceived it, was simple. We had to build socialism and, simultaneously, expose and destroy the enemy, "those pygmies, those insects, those contemptible lackeys of the fascists," as Stalin had characterized them with his usual aplomb and theoretical precision.

Exposing the enemy who attacked us, however furiously, *from without,* did not constitute any particular problem. Life was straightforward: there stood the enemy and here the friend; there the forces of imperialist reaction, here those of proletarian progress. I even wrote a long, joyful poem celebrating the symbolic river of our new life *devoid* of its ancient, enigmatic, shadowy undercurrents, twists and turns. But now it was all changed: The enemy was attacking *from within!* The mind boggled: Who was the enemy and who the friend? In a sudden upsurge of shameful uncertainty, we realized that it was increasingly difficult to tell them apart, not only for us, lowly and inexperienced footsoldiers of that mighty proletarian army, but even for so omniscient a general as Mátyás Rákosi who had been—he told us in a speech charged with the high-voltage electricity of righteous indignation after Rajk's arrest—compelled to spend *sleepless nights* in order to disentangle the tangled web of Titoist intrigue and CIA conspiracy. This was a remarkable admission which, apart from revealing the unimaginable complexities of the class war, created in our minds the image of a stern yet loving father guarding vigilantly—day and night—the safety and well-being of his beloved children. But what could we do? Hard work and daily professions of unending faith and loyalty to Stalin and his best Hungarian disciple did not seem to offer a meaningful answer, for the enemy, (clever pygmy and insect that he was in his devious efforts to allay suspicion and worm himself deeper and deeper into the heart and brain of the revolutionary vanguard) worked even harder and professed his faith and loyalty in even more glowing phrases and images. We were, we now understood, trodding a dangerous, slippery path. Our undiminishing enthusiasm, laudable as it may have been, proved only to be the manifestation of our purely *emotional commitment* to the cause and this, in troubled times and without the reinforced concrete foundation of a *scientific ideology* was more source of weakness than of strength, a liability not an asset. We were young, enthusiastic, honest, yes, but also unversed in the intricate subtleties of Marxist-Leninist theory. We needed help badly. In fact, we needed help more than we were able to realize.

Consequently, high in the upper reaches of the party hierarchy, in that rarified atmosphere of power and wisdom where decisions of life and death were common, everyday affairs, a resolution was made. It had been resolved that a one-year *Party Academy* be established—the first in the land—which should offer the firm guidance of theory to the deserving and promising so that, in time, from the chrysalis of the amateur rebel the professional revolutionary could emerge. The decision of the Politburo, as all its decisions, was final and to be implemented without delay. It required setting up a boarding school system, a veritable monastery of learning, a mighty fortress of discipline, puritanically simple in appearance, yet conducive to a total immersion in the proposed studies, directed and supervised by the best instructors available. Charged with the immediate execution of the decision, the Organizational and Cadre Departments of the Central *Apparatus* went to work in haste. In close collaboration with the State Office of Security (fondly known as AVH) the former took care of the physical details, the latter of the selection of both faculty and students. The machine, thus set in motion, soon started to churn out its remarkable products. It was to be, as the Politburo emphasized in the preamble of its decision (but as anybody could tell anyhow) one of the greatest intellectual and spiritual adventures ever offered to young people interested in the scientific redemption of mankind.

Yet, when in the middle of June I received in a crumpled bluish-gray envelope the mimeographed notification, bearing the stamp of the Politburo, which informed me that I was to report on the 16th of October at 8:00 A.M. sharp, at 49 Karolina Avenue in order to attend the one-year *Party Academy,* my heart leaped, but not (I had to admit reluctantly at least to myself) with unbearable joy. To be sure, I felt flattered by this unexpected high honor, reserved, I knew, only for the best, most faithful and most reliable young members of the Party. However, I was touched too, by some uneasiness which, despite its vagueness, was real enough to make me feel queasy about the coming of October.

First, I happened to be working on a novel which I considered quite important, and the time to complete it between then and the opening of the school, seemed to me frustratingly short. Second, I had heard rumors of some strange practices in certain party schools—rumors of denunciations, disclosures, sessions of criticism and self-criticism lasting well into the small hours of the morning—which, though unverifiable, sounded genuine and frightening. Third, the idea of being cooped up for a whole year within the walls of a school (so soon again after my graduate studies) even if it meant honor for me and service for the Party, did not particularly appeal to me, a free and young man of letters, full of exciting plans for the immediate future. Last and most important, however, I felt, in a sudden and unforgivable attack of hubris (for which, as one would expect, I was to pay dearly in the coming months) that my understanding of Marxism-Leninism was extensive and substantial enough, and if it needed some brushing up, I was, I thought, quite capable of doing it myself, without the crutches of any school.

Of course, there was nothing I could do about that flattering draft, except resign myself to the inevitable not with a shrug, as would have been fitting, but with a broad, dignified and self-conscious smile, with a show of humility *and* pride, because I knew that even the smallest hint at certain lingering doubts as to the necessity of my official education would have been tantamount of treason and could have had disastrous consequences. Besides, it was a tumultuous summer, the summer of the *Second World Festival of Youth* (the Party's answer to Boy Scouts jamborees) and it kept me busy for weeks. Large, colorful delegations arrived from the Soviet Union, from the brotherly people's democracies, and smaller groups from the West, including one from England and even from the United States, to bear witness to the happy, joyful life of Hungarian youth, and to participate in what was officially described as the greatest demonstration ever for peace and friendship among the peoples of the world. Whether it was consciously and cleverly timed to coincide with what was going on in the background in order to draw a colorful veil over the prison cells and torture chambers (getting rapidly overcrowded), I didn't know, because I didn't know *what* was going on in the background. The softly-whispered rumors about sudden disappearances and fast-multiplying arrests were drowned by the loud, exotic music of folk ensembles and dancing groups, by the cheers of athletic competitions and by the artificially over-heated arguments of debating teams whose main subject of discussion was, of course, the freedom of socialist society and individual self-fulfillment under the watchful, benevolent eye of the Party, as opposed to the slavery and alienation of Western imperialist societies under the malevolent rule of capitalist oppressors.

I was temporarily appointed as correspondent of the Party's daily, *Szabad Nép* [Free People], and also attached, as interpreter, to the small, but thoroughly enchanted group of English boys and girls. The work kept my mind occupied and the sights lulled my senses into complacency, so much so that sometimes, even if for a few hours, I was inclined to forget the end of the summer and the beginning of my woes. But not entirely. Whatever I did and wherever I went, the shadowy image of the school remained always in the back of my mind—a reminder under bright skies of cloudier days to come. So, I did my job conscientiously, enthusiastically, while waving that little mimeographed note to friend and foe alike, as a symbol of honor and trust, trying desperately to convince myself that I *was* wrong and the Party *was* right—how could it be otherwise?—and I really *did* need to be educated, *didn't I?* Yet, with every passing day, I felt more and more guilty of hypocrisy and duplicity: for the first time in my life in the Party, I was being pushed into a corner from which I was unable to extricate myself. The sacrificial lamb was ready for the slaughter.

God's Vineyard

> *Drive Christ's enemies out from amongst the League of the Elect, for you are the instrument for that purpose. . . . Don't let them live any longer, the evil-doers who turn us away from God! The sword is necessary to exterminate them. . . . If they resist, let them be slaughtered without mercy. . . . At harvest-time one must pluck the weeds out of God's vineyard. . . . For the ungodly have no right to live, save what the Elect chose to allow them.*
> From a sermon by *Thomas Müntzer*, 1524.

By the end of September, I had somehow managed to bring the novel to what I knew was an unsuccessful conclusion, but considering the prevailing atmosphere in the country and my own state of mind, it seemed almost a miracle that I finished it at all. On the 19th of June, the government released the terse, official communiqué of the Minister of Internal Affairs, (headed, incidently, by János Kádár) which informed a stunned populace of the arrest of László Rajk, former political commissar of the Rákosi Brigade in the Spanish Civil War, favorite son of the Party, lionized hero of communist youth, and his accomplices on charges of espionage and conspiracy. The rest was silence; apparently, the case wasn't ready yet for a public trial. Confessions still had to be extracted from the prisoners, sifted, classified, collated until the complex story of their unthinkable treachery emerged in a narrative understandable even to children. Apart from all those secret machinations, the streets, theaters, lecture halls of the capital were still teeming with the starry-eyed participants of the Youth Festival and, obviously, the master-tacticians of the Party must have deemed their presence undesirable for the next attraction. In mid-August, the Festival had ended, and from that moment on the raging tidal wave of a relentless hate-campaign swept through the country, with a force at once irresistible and obscene, reaching its hysterical crescendo on the 19th of September, the day the trial opened.

In cables to the press, letters to the editors, speeches on the radio, at meetings in the factories, party or trade union cells, farm cooperatives, university lecture halls, hospitals, military barracks—workers and peasants, professors and students, doctors and nurses, secretaries and janitors, grave diggers and chimney sweeps, fathers, mothers and children yet to be born but already politically conscious, expressed their "passionate hatred" toward "these vermin" whose inconceivable treachery, they demanded, must be punished forthwith and without mercy. Designed to appear as the spontaneous manifestation of the wrath of a people betrayed, it was, actually, a carefully organized, coldly calculated, and superbly orchestrated orgiastic ritual, offering the *pharmakos*—the scapegoat—on the altar of the class war's avenging god, thus purging the holy body of the Party from the sinful and evil influences of the bourgeois *daimon*. Eventually—and inevitably—the vermin were hanged on the 15th of October, and the news of their well-deserved fate carried next morning by every newspaper in the land. With some distant, yet strangely disturbing apprehension, I read that laconic, official communiqué on the bus that was taking me toward my destination, and, perhaps, my destiny, on Karolina Avenue, amidst gently swaying, sleepy and totally unconcerned faces.

My comrades, the candidates of future power and omniscience, were already gathering in front of the school when I arrived, waiting for the doors to be thrown open, and they did not display any particular animation either: whether or not they had experienced, as I did, that disconcerting mixture of bourgeois pity and communist hatred, I could not tell. If they did (which was possible), they were successfully hiding it behind flashing smiles which, old friends and new acquaintances alike, greeted me and each other. If they didn't (which was equally possible) it was all the better for them and, undoubtedly, for the Party. To all appearances, however, the ominous symbolic coincidence of casual slaughters and great expectations seemed to have left them unruffled—and, perhaps, rightly so. It was a bright, pleasant morning for the festive opening of what promised to be a cheerful *autumnalia* in God's vineyard. In the distance, beyond the lindens and horse chestnuts that lined the long, broad, silent avenue, the misty hills of Buda shone, still green and friendly. Exposed suddenly to the glittering sunshine, the houses of this once clean, quiet, middle class residential area, attempted again—and again in vain—to hide the ugly scars left on them by bombings, street fighting, neglect and decay, behind slowly withering lilacs and forsythias, as if ashamed of their historic misfortunes. Time and again, a man or women would pass by our group, but without even looking at us. Curiosity, they had learned long ago, could be dangerous in this world full of curiosity. We didn't pay much attention to them, however, alien people from another planet. We chatted among ourselves, exchanged thoughts about the coming months that were bound to have a tremendous impact on our lives. At precisely 8:00 A.M. the doors were flung open and we filed in, silently. Instructed to wait in the courtyard, we waited.

Buildings can be used both by reactionary and revolutionary regimes for furthering their respective goals: bricks and plaster, corridors and rooms remain irreverently neutral. Ours, for instance, selected by higher authorities to serve the interests of the proletarian revolution, had earlier served as an Academy for air cadets in Admiral Horthy's tiny and sadly ineffectual Air Force. But the historical ironies of changing fortunes, of war and peace, of progress and reaction, were not reflected by the dust-gray walls of the buildings that were supposed to become our real homes for the year. On our right, we saw a longish edifice which, as we soon learned, housed our future living quarters, study rooms and the library. On our left, there stood the main building for assemblies, lectures and administrative offices. Facing us, on the opposite side of a large courtyard full of potholes, puddles from last week's rain, dirty grass, wildly spreading weeds and a ground for volleyball were situated the dining commons together with the quarters and facilities of a *Six Months School,* already in session.

In the upper right corner of the yard, we also saw the skeleton of the new, giant auditorium, capable of accommodating the students and faculties of both schools and, if occasion warranted, large numbers of invited guests. In a few weeks, the time to celebrate the completion of the new auditorium would arrive. It would be consecrated with ceremonial pomp and with Mátyás Rákosi, as the first speaker ever to set foot on its shining *cathedra,* introducing his admiring audience to the complexities of the 1919 Hungarian Soviet Republic with a simplicty, clarity and humor that was, we thought, at once awe-inspiring and deeply human. He must have known all about it; he was one of its participants! By this time, however, the then insignificant Deputy Commissar of Commerce would have been transformed, as if by a miracle, into one of the greatest and most important—if not *the* greatest and most important—leaders of that unfortunate upheaval, whose personal contribution to its victories and self-effacing heroism in its defeat had already assumed mythological proportions.

But if the past had changed beyond all recognition, the present was changing at an even more dizzying pace. The next guest-exorcist in our functional cathedral of pious orthodoxy was János Kádár, member of the Politburo and Minister of Internal Affairs who delivered a surprisingly dull and uninspiring sermon on "The Problems and Methods of the Infiltration of the Enemy into the Party." Less than five months later, the Inquisitor turned out to be the Devil himself: he was arrested, as an agent of American imperialism and its Titoist lackeys, and disappeared, without trace, under what was then fashionably termed history's rotting rubbish heap.

All that, however, still lay in the cold womb of tomorrow and was none of our concern, not yet anyway. We were assigned now to our rooms, Spartan rooms with sturdy campbeds, rickety chests, straddle-legged tables and highly capricious wooden benches, simple, even slightly forbidding rooms, yet whose freshly painted walls glimmered, white and amicable, in the morning's bright sunshine. Outside, along the gray, narrow corridors of the first floor, we found a long row of dripping faucets for washing and shaving, and heard the hum of endlessly running toilets. There were rooms for two, four and six occupants and, much to my disappointment, a disappointment that remained, of course, unaired, I was assigned one with five others in it who were already unpacking and making themselves comfortable. How could I know that it was all planned in advance and, naturally, for my greatest benefit? That as a writer and what was even worse, a middle class intellectual, I was singled out from the very beginning for a transformation of mythical dimensions? How could I suspect that I was to be engulfed, indeed annihilated first, then triumphantly regenerated by my new mother, the Community, represented here by five jittery young men? That phenomenal idea of my sublime metamorphosis through death and rebirth existed, as yet, only in the minds of my teachers, and neither I nor my roommates had any inkling of their educational methods or quasi-sexual perversions. So, we went about getting acquainted with each other as if our happy encounter—on this moring in that room—were just another accident of life, unplanned, natural and of no particular

A Political Autobiography

consequence. Little did we know that in this small, happy world of ours, accident was only the manifestation of an overpowering inevitability, a tiny, insignificant, almost negligible (if somewhat irritating) pimple on the face of a perfect, historically predetermined universe.

My roommates were nice fellows, a bit tense, perhaps, which was understandable, but apparently gay and carefree, which was also understandable. After all, they knew, they were the *crème de la crème,* who despite being only minor functionaries of a great Party, already held the rewards of future glory in the palms of their hands. They came from all walks of Party-life; from the Cadre Department of the *Apparatus;* the National Center of the Trade Unions; the Communist Youth League or from the *Agitprop* Department of the Party Central Committee. One of them, a well-built, black mustachioed peasant lad, only in his mid-twenties, yet already the Party Secretary of a County Committee somewhere on the eastern plains, seemed to be a very important person indeed. With a polite but hardly apologetic "if-you-don't-mind!" he immediately occupied the bed next to the window because, he said in his husky voice, he liked fresh air—*don't you, comrades?* No, we didn't mind, and yes, we too liked fresh air. Then, we just sat on the edge of our beds somewhat sheepishly, made modestly funny jokes, stood by the window overlooking silent Karolina Avenue, and talked suggestively about the people who lived in those run-down houses, and who, judging by the general reputation of the area, must all be incorrigible, old reactionaries, cunning and bitter enemies of the nation's future and, consequently, our own enemies. Suddenly, the bell rang. We were asked to walk over to the big lecture hall and to wait there until called individually for our first interviews with our teachers.

Michael Sozan

PEASANTS IN TWO POLITICAL SYSTEMS: AN AUSTRIAN AND A HUNGARIAN VILLAGE COMPARED*

The comparison of politics in two villages with disparate ideologies warrants a clarification of theoretical postulates and methodology employed. The nature of the topic and the ramifications of its research themselves invited criticism in Eastern Europe. Some reservations have been voiced about it by my Hungarian colleagues during the fieldwork. Their general consensus was that communities of different political systems could not be meaningfully compared. My response to their scepticism was an assertion of their comparability and my firm intention of doing just that. This is not to say that I did not recognize the pitfalls of the cross-cultural survey in general, or the possible difficulties of comparing the two villages in general, or the possible difficulties of comparing the two villages in specific. What I was actually saying was that I firmly believed in the feasibility of the project, and the validity of the cross-cultural method.

Political scientists and anthropologists disagree considerably as to what a political system constitutes.[1] As a working definition I chose that of

---

* Financial support for this research was given by the International Research and Exchanges Board, the National Academy of Sciences, and the Hungarian Academy of Sciences.

Easton, which states that a political system constitutes "the authoritative allocation of values."[2] The key concepts in this definition are: values, authority, and allocation. Since all three are expressed in human behavior, they may be readily observed.

Both societies under consideration have forms of human behavior which fit the above concepts; both have "values," "authority," and a system of "allocation." Therefore, the two societies are indeed comparable on the theoretical and on the empirical levels.

In addition to defining what one means by "political systems," one should decide—however arbitrarily—what kind of criteria and phenomena are the most profitable for comparison. These criteria (or systemic variables) called "factorial matrix" by Frey[3] are a highly crucial set of research topics—the actual core of the inquiry and they should have cross-cultural validity. A given variable, such as the multi-party system, or hereditary leadership may have great significance in one society and relatively little in another. I have decided to choose the following factorial matrix: a) form of government; b) style of election; and c) manner of articulating the political principles with formal and informal leadership.

The reason for selecting the above three is that I found them to be general enough for comparative purposes and appropriate in the ideal cultures of the two societies under consideration. The data generated through this framework could also be reduced to the level of the lowest common denominator, such as council leadership, voting behavior, informal leadership, etc.

Anthropological fieldwork was carried out in an Eastern Austrian village, Alsóőr [Unterwart] and a Western Hungarian village, Táp, between 1973 and 1979. Although located in Austria, the Hungarian-inhabited Alsóőr and its vicinity had been part of Hungary from the late ninth to the early twentieth century. The two villages, therefore, are similar in their geographic, demographic, ethnic-linguistic composition. Thus the reader is looking at two Hungarian villages on either side of the "Iron Curtain."

The technique of data gathering was restricted almost totally to conversations during participant observation. Opinion surveys or polls, based on questionnaires or interviewing were abandoned because of repeated failures in Hungary. At the risk of suggesting conclusions to the reader, I will give two reasons for this failure. The first is that respondants in

Hungary were not convinced that their anonymity could be insured. One person opined: "I know you won't hand it over to the government, but what if they search you and find notes and tapes?" The second reason—closely related to the first—is that, even those who volunteered information felt they could not answer certain questions honestly or truthfully—either in written or in spoken form—because they were not sure whether the topic of politics was a concern of "common folk." Encouraging them was of no use and was an unacceptable anthropological technique. Others reacted with the opposite attitude. One person, for example, said: "There is freedom of speech in Hungary today, and the government expects its people to be politically active and aware of issues." Yet, when I wanted to cash in on this person's offer to record our conversation, he declined.

The most homogeneous group of politically aware people was the generation over forty, who constituted 44% of Táp's population. They reflected a high degree of disaffection from official ideology and political behavior in general. The overwhelming percentage of their answers was negative. They based most of their opinions on their memories of the 1950s and 1960s, and they were unwilling to recognize recent shifts toward a more human political ideology. Because of their distrust in the entire political process, they also rejected my use of questionnaires and the tape recorder.

There was little else left than to discuss politics with my target families under very informal circumstances, usually during work or a leisure activity, and always in private. Of the several hundred occasions of political discussions, to which altogether thirty-five respondents contributed more than ten constituted what I recognized as essential. These included a series of nine conversations with the council president, four informal discussions with two councillors, two lengthy discussions (four hours each) with an ex-cooperative farm president, and three equally lengthy talks with an active and highly politically conscious worker of the cooperative farm. In addition, I visited the tavern two-to-three times a week where politics are still discussed.

My interaction with people in Alsóőr was much more intense than with those of Táp. I could use the tape recorder as well as questionnaires quite freely. Therefore my knowledge of politics in Alsóőr is greater than that of Táp. A very important factor in this regard was that in Alsóőr I was able to extend my investigations well beyond our target families. In this village virtually anyone could offer information, and did so willingly.

The above differences in the response of the communities can be felt in my present essay.

I. The Austrian Political Model: Present day Austrian ideology rests on the notions of parlimentary democracy shared by most western nations. After gaining independence from the Allied Powers and internationally guaranteed neutrality in 1955, there was no danger of radical shift from this pattern, nor of civil war, social revolution, and other forms of political extremism.[4] In addition to their political choice, the Austrians agreed on the form of economic system that was to be maintained. The choice fell on capitalism, but with vast reforms in the pattern of ownership of natural resources and means of production. In recent years Austria moved very close to socialism with a multi-party system. Political, economic, judiciary and religious institutions are independent of one another, and there is no interference in municipal or village politics by the outside. Personal and property security in Austria is scrupulously maintained and guaranteed. Austria fits all the criteria of the "democratic system" as defined by Inkeles.[5] Both the politician and the electorate perceive the system not merely as the best (people in totalitarian systems may also claim this), but one that affords them the greatest possible freedom of action. But unlike in England and the United States, "freedom" in Austria is not allowed to interfere with ordered political behavior. If there is a choice between freedom and order, Austrians prefer the latter.

A. The Village within the State: The highest level of Austrian political structure is the state, followed by the province, district and the village. A Hungarian speaking village, Alsóőr belongs to the Province of Burgenland and the District of Oberwart [Felsőőr]. The appropriate authorities on these levels are the Austrian Parliament, the Provincial Government (*Landesregierung*) in the city of Eisenstadt [Kismárton] and the District Government (*Politische Bezierke Regierung*) in Oberwart. The laws of the land, political, social and economic legislature pass through this chain of political and administrative bodies. The Parliament in Vienna regulates taxes, social services and the military, whereas the Province's jurisdiction falls on internal security, primary education, housing, health and conservation.[6]

The nine Provinces are subdivided into 98 Districts, which in turn encompass 2,327 *Gemeinde*, or local communities. The District of Oberwart contains 28 *Gemeinde*.

B. Village Politics: The *Gemeinde* are self-governing entities, having a popularly elected village council (*Gemeinderat*), which is established by proportional representation on the basis of political strength.[7] The duration of service for the elected officers is five years. The head of the council is the mayor, or *Bürgermeister* (*bíró* in Hungarian), who is elected by the council from the victorious party. The structure of the village council is illustrated in the following diagram.

        MAYOR (from the winning party)

        DEPUTY (from the opposition party)
        MAYOR

NOTARIES   COUNCIL (8 from winning, 5 from
                          MEMBERS opposition party)

TOWN CRIER

The village council supervises and carries out local laws and ordinances. Although its sphere of influence has been reduced since the last century, it still includes a wide array of matters with substantial effects upon the community. Among these are: land tenure, general safety of buildings and lands, traffic, police, minor disputes ("not worthy of courts"), public utilities, cultural institutions (theaters, museums, libraries, etc.), public housing and health, funeral parlors, communal forests, the village inn, and apartments owned by the village. The state, county or district have no power over these matters. The village government also maintains records of financial transactions and minutes of the meetings that are held during the year. Although according to the law there must be at least four meetings held annually, there are approximately eight meetings annually at the insistence of the village leaders. Daily official business at the townhall is handled by the two notaries. Permanently appointed to this prestigeous position both notaries in Alsóőr are by necessity Hungarian. The head notary commutes from Oberwart, while his deputy is a local man. Their role is one of a middle man: they interpret decisions by the *Gemeinderat* toward the people, and transmit to the *Gemeinderat* information from the public. Their tasks include taking the minutes of the council meetings, registering births, deaths and marriages, officiating civil weddings, authenticating all legal documents, taking the census every year, collecting taxes, and announcing policies through the town crier.

C. Party membership and politics: Since the liberation of serfs (1848) and the subsequent abolition of titles of nobility (1945), Hungarian as well as the subsequent Austrian governments maintained that all political factions within the community must use a single body of political action, the village council. All social classes and class interests must use this body politic to remain legitimate. As it turned out in the past few decades, party affiliation has had a high degree of correspondence with occupational or prestige groups and classes. Almost all peasants favor the Catholic-inspired *Österreichische Volks Partei* (ÖVP), while workers and most of the white collar sympathize with the left-leaning *Sozialistische Partei Österreich* (SPÖ). The primary reason for such a high degree of correlation between party and social class is the difference between the philosophies of the two parties (other parties such as the Freedom Party or the Communist Party have very slight appeal among the rural people of Austria). The ÖVP considers itself to be a "progressive party of the center," and a "party of progress and no experiments." In essence, the "Blacks", as they are popularly referred to, are conservative who believe in a balanced budget, few if any social programs, and a powerful central government. They strongly favor private enterprise, and—this proves important in Austrian politics—in holding a hard line against communism. Although the ÖVP has "softened" in recent years, it has retained its central *Weltanschaung.* In addition to peasants, it gains its strength from businessmen, some white collars, civil servants and unionized workers. Since Alsóőr's political leadership is dominated by the Blacks, it is easy to see which class engineers village politics: the peasants. All the mayors of Alsóőr have run on the ÖVP ticket, and all attempts to break this line of continuity has failed miserably.

The "party of opposition," the SPÖ comes close to a "true socialist party" for which they were branded as "Reds." In recent years the SPÖ eliminated its extreme elements. Today the Reds pursue the policy of equitable distribution of wealth through social legislature. They favor high taxes for the rich, high wages for the working class, federal provincial spending on social welfare, pensions, medicine, unemployment insurance, arts and sciences and education. The SPÖ aims at elevating the working class by guaranteeing better material life, and opportunities for higher education. The Reds are not against private enterprise per se, but neither are they its outspoken champions. Nor are they enthusiastic about the peasants. For example, throughout its years in power the SPÖ has consistently fought raising the prices of agricultural commodities, and when this effort began to fail, it initiated a program of subsidies for the stabilization of retail prices on such food items as dairies, sugar and bread. The displeasure of the peasants with SPÖ policy is understandable. But the modern Austrian village contains many non-peasants and Alsóőr is no exception. There are now more workers in the village than peasants. With an ever-increasing number of workers and other people in sympathy with socialist objectives, the strength of the SPÖ is increasing. This is reflected by the changing ratio of farmers and workers on the town council. The number of workers has grown from a small fraction of the *Gemeinderat* in the 1950s to one third of the council in 1971.

While the Blacks follow the policy of *laissez faire,* the Reds support a policy of economic support of their people.[8] Blacks do not maintain a system of mutual aid through the procurement of loans and jobs, whereas the Reds do. Black party members have switched party because Reds offer loans for building a house and for other expenses.

The broadest support for the SPÖ comes from industrial workers, masons, construction workers and mechanics. In Alsóőr such workers commute to the city. The SPÖ is primarily a city-based party, the party of urbanization and modernization. It is little wonder that Alsóőr's commuters, especially the weekly commuting masons take a strong liking to this party.

The parties tend to have a similar self-image. Both consider themselves to be united and homogeneous, while viewing the other as being fragmented and an ineffective political force. To the non-party affiliate the Blacks appear to be more cohesive because of their vigor in putting forth their beliefs and attitudes. They feel superior to the Reds because the workers do not have "basic property" (i.e., the minimum of 10 hectares of land and 5 full grown cattle), they "live from hand-to-mouth," they are "bare assed" and "drifters". Because Blacks take politics "too seriously," they are quick to snap at the Reds: "What do you know after all? You are away from the village all day. We stay behind to mind the store."

Black party members and their families differ from their counterparts as farmers differ from workers: in sartorial habits, culinary practices, utilization of leisurely time, exterior and interior of their houses, mannerisms, and religious behavior. The most visible sign of party segregation is seen at public performances, such as at village dances organized by the parties. Reds readily attend dances organized by Blacks, but Blacks do not exhibit equal reciprocity. Blacks like to be more distant and isolated from other groups—and from the national culture as well.

Although party policies are finalized at regular monthly meetings, much of the preliminary discussion takes place at informal meetings. The least formal and the most ad hoc gatherings are the "street-bench-talks" typical of the Austro-Hungarian rural scene. Following the evening meal men walk to their gate and "take a look at who might be out there." There are three "main benches" in the upper end of Alsóőr (no longer are there benches in the lower end, and there are only two in the midsection). All three are in front of rich peasants' houses. Conversations are quiet and low key. The number of participants at "bench-talks" is less than five, which allows for lengthy individual expressions and dialogues. For this reason these gatherings are the most intimate and frank interpersonal exchanges in the political as well as social process. Another place of political activity is the tavern.

Let us ask now, what attributes are necessary for political leadership? For the Blacks the most significant personality attributes are the following: 1) To be a good leader. "People must listen to him...they must accept his advice..." Further inquiries into the kind of advice one might ask for, resulted in an unequivocal and unanimous answer: "in matters of farming." Thus a leader was considered to be an authority on such problems as crop usage, crop rotation, fertilizer, machines, the use of farmhands, marketing, and many others.

2) To be a respected person in the community. He must exhibit high moral (and religious) standards. He should be a good family man, and he should not be a drunkard (*részeges*).

3) To be *eszes,* or smart, brainy, almost shrewd. However, a cunning person (*ravasz*) is mistrusted. People feel that he may take advantage of the community if he is too shrewd.

4) To be a good adjudicator of disputes. Partiality in controversial matters and in deciding which party is "right" is disliked in a leader.

People in Alsóőr find this quality to be the most lacking in village leaders. People freely admit that the community always had its share of corruption and nepotism.

The most prominent leaders in Alsóőr come from the ranks of wealthy farmers. The proverb has it that "dogs bark but money speaks." Poor peasants are poor—people claim—because they are not smart enough to be rich. "Dogs do not make good bacon." Therefore, poor people cannot give good advice.

The sphere of decision-making during the past century has shifted from issues of great importance (military defense of the village, communal agriculture, criminal justice, policies regarding newcomers, etc.) to matters of lesser consequences for the community. During this time village politicians had to adjust to dealing with "small stakes". Thus, the parties may engage in prolonged arguments over the repertoire of the Glee Club, the frequency of drills conducted by the Volunteer Fire Association, and the like. The council deliberated for hours on whether the town library ought to be open between 2 and 5 PM or between 1 and 5 PM. "Indeed, it is a miracle that anything is resolved at all," observed an important official. There are more political forums than issues. The Volunteer Fire Association, the Glee Club, the Church Council, the Water Association, party meetings, and the village council. All are fertile grounds upon which political maneuvering can be conducted, statuses can be improved or ruined.

Democracy, or the multi-party system has been a mixed blessing for the once peasant-village now undergoing the most rapid rate of sociocultural transformation it has ever seen. Since Austria's political organization brought to the village two operating and relevant instruments (political parties) for the natives, the political participants of the village began to adjust to these alternatives. Some made their decisions immediately, while others have still not come to grips with the new power alignment. But the overall effectiveness of the village's political process was proven by the local politicians' willingness to "go along with the system" without much reservations. This, of course, meant that the social unification of the village through class unity had to be sacrificed. Peasants became Blacks and workers joined the Reds. The parties have not been able to cut across class interests. If the Reds were to attract more farmers, and Blacks more workers, partisan opposition would be significantly reduced. As things stand, social distance between the classes remain. A knowledgeable councilman reflected thus: "We are just a bit better off than when we were hundred years ago when the noblemen and the commoners had separate political organizations."

Yet, the two-party system—by virtue of allowing legitimate opposition to the establishment, and facilitating an even process of internal adjustment to external (national as well as international) forces—guarantees a smooth and organic form of acculturation. It establishes certain configurations of political decision-making which can eventually dampen the pains of social restratification. By having an unceasing pressure to change its world view, the "village establishment" ("people with basic property") is "given the opportunity" to resign some of its power in favor of village harmony.

It is clear that closed corporate peasant communities in East Central Europe cannot be sustained. Were the Blacks to manage village politics by themselves, it is quite likely that there would be a wholesale abandonment of the local community by the next generation of villagers. The two-party system therefore seems to be the appropriate mechanism that Alsóőr and similar political communities need for the maintenance of sociocultural process.

II. The Hungarian Political Model is neither unique in the history of socialist experimentation, nor is it a perfect replica of the Soviet model from which it was copied. It is an amalgam of East European systems introduced by the October Revolution of 1917 in Russia and the "proletarian dictatorship" established by Hungarian communists in 1919. Its ideology rests on the Marxist-Leninist principles of the collective ownership of natural resources and means of production. "The fundamental law in the Hungarian People's Republic is the Constitution, which safeguards our achievements and guarantees our advancement on the road to socialism."[9] The concept of socialism is not clearly circumscribed in the Constitution, nor by the Hungarian political leadership. The term is used frequently in political communication, both written and verbal, yet few people in Hungary can conceptualize and express its meaning. In the village of Táp, verbal responses to the question: "what is socialism?" ranged from the highly misconstrued to the absurd. Many respondants had no answer, while others dealt with the shortcomings of the system, such as imbalances of power, status, income and treatment of workers. The most common response may be summed up in the following answer: "Socialism is having someone make decisions for you." This misconception of the myth of socialism is certainly not due to a lack of ideological education, but rather, to the discrepancies between ideology and practice. Even those respondents who described socialism as a system based on equality and the sharing of national wealth, felt that the post-World War II governments have not delivered their promises. "Since decisions are made for us, the people do not have political power. Hungarian workers and peasants did not have power in the past and they do not have it today"—opined an informant.

If not the people, then who holds power in Hungary? Political actors have changed dramatically in the past thirty years. "Orthodox communists" turned into revolutionaries during the 1956 uprising, and "reactionary elements" became "good communists"; therefore, it is very difficult to generalize about Hungarian political leadership. However, since the system is designed to contain and restrict political power to the party and to the highly centralized government, the leaders share a common characteristic, which is to act without popular support or even information derived from public opinion. A good leader in Hungary is one who faithfully carries out the party's orders.

Since the Hungarian political system is based on totalitarian principles, there is the obvious need to attract individuals who approve of the principles of totalitarianism. Leaders are selected and trained in this ideology. It is expected of them to share what Inkeles calls the "totalitarian mystique." "The totalitarian," he writes, "is convinced that he has *directly* perceived some immanent law of social development which is dictating necessary action on his part and is guaranteeing the 'correctness' of that action...I believe that only a certain psychological type is likely to have such conceptions.... In other words, the totalitarian mystique is represented not as a quality of the totalitarian society but a quality of the totalitarian *leader* who imposes his conception on society in which he comes to power."[10]

Totalitarian leadership in Hungary may be divided into two types: inspired and dispassionate. The inspired leader is convinced that the "quality of the totalitarian society" is superior to other forms. "Socialism will triumph over capitalism; the dictatorship of the proletariat is stronger than bourgeois democracy"—claims the idealist socialist leader.

This mystique of socialism was characteristic of communists during the interwar period and prior to the ascendance of Mátyás Rákosi, First Secretary of the Hungarian Workers Party in 1949. At this time most idealists were purged or removed from power. Although inspiration was a prerequisite for political leadership during the 1950s, many leaders lacked it and were mere opportunists.

Unlike the inspired leader, dispassionate functionaries do not necessarily believe in the superiority of the socialist model. On the other hand, they stand firm on the issue of totalitarianism based on the leadership of the party. Leaders since the 1956 Revolution may or may not be imbued with the spirit of communism or socialism, and the party does not require of local leaders to be blind followers of Marxist-Leninist ideology. The regime has come to the realization that the maintenance of the mystique of socialism is superfluous and even counter-productive on certain levels of leadership.

The new village leadership may best be characterized as good bureaucrats (in both the positive as well as negative sense), and fair technocrats. The depth of their personal character and ideological conviction seems to be inversely proportional to their willingness to comply with party directives, ultimately designed in Budapest. Some are specialists in economics or agriculture, but most are party-trained *apparachniks* without specialization.

Following the "great changes of 1956" emphasis shifted away from the ideological base to that of "technical competence in solving problems." Local leaders today price themselves of being problem-solvers. Their primary role is to synchronize local needs with the needs of the party. In this dialectic the party is always the winner, and the local leader seldom sides with the loser. For this reason the Party Secretary or the Council President cannot achieve popularity in his own village. "We are not participants in a popularity contest, and we oppose the old-fashioned idea of campaigning for popularity"—observed Táp's Council President.

In order to understand the context within which local leadership operates, it is necessary to look at the broader structure of the Hungarian political system:

1) Fundamental political power in Hungary rests in the Hungarian Socialist Workers Party which rules without opposition. The Party is intricately linked to Soviet leadership through a sophisticated and massive

apparatus of communication which includes Russian "observers", "advisors" and an undisclosed number of Soviet army personnel who have occupied Hungary without interruption since 1945.

2) The Party comprises the basis of all three branches of the government: executive, legislative and judicial. The Parliament and other political organizations (i.e. The People's Patriotic Front) have no decision making or veto power. Since the Party's Committee of Controls consists of party members, the party regulates itself.

3) The decisions of the party are carried out by all levels of the government from the national to the county and local government without significant deviation.

The Hungarian People's Democracy is divided into 19 Counties (Budapest comprises an independent unit, the Capital District). The village Táp belongs to Győr County (*Győr megye*) and one of its four Districts, Győr District (*Győri Járás*). In Győr County there are five cities and 164 villages with a total population of 410,751. Of the 164 villages 74 have their own village administration called *tanács,* or council. The remaining 90 villages share their council with other villages.[11]

The officers of all four levels of the political administration—national, county, district and village—are elected by the Socialist Workers Party. Elections are organized by the Patriotic People's Front (PPF) by whom candidates must be approved. The PPF is a non-party organization which aids the legitimization of political power. However, the fact that the most important members of the PPF are also party members, disqualifies it as a genuine "people's front". On the village level both PPF members and non-members are at a loss of the true role of the PPF. "Who knows what the PPF is for?"—laments a PPF member, active in the village council.

The village government, or council consists of the council president (*tanácselnök*), the Executive Committee (*Végrehajtó Bizottság*) and the council members (*tanácstagok*). The law stipulates that approximately every fifty people be represented by a council member. The council president and the members of the Executive Council must be party members. Council laws circumscribing the authority of the president, the council, the executive council are listed in the *Tanácstörvény* (council laws).[12] These comprehend almost all spheres of community life: public facilities, safety, standards of hygiene, schools and recreation facilities, sanitation, the electorel process, housing and land tenure. Roughly, they correspond to the Austrian *Gemeinderecht* with the exception of matters of adjudication of disputes, which the Hungarian laws leave up to the civil courts. Like the local laws of Austria, the Hungarian laws are also elastic, therefore subject to interpretation. But in the Hungarian case—unlike in Austria—this elasticity works against the community: it gives the county council an opportunity to interpret the law according to "higher interest." One case in point is the "cultural development budget," which in the case of Táp was utilized for purposes that were not in harmony with local interest and sentiment. Under the pressure of the county government the village contributed half a million forints ($25,000) to the reconstruction of the old "cotter's row." This included the purchasing of six thatched-roof, delapidated mud houses, and their renovation for the re-creation of a "historical site." The project was financed by the National Museum Committee, the county as well as the village. While the county felt that the site would have education and "cultural" value, most people felt that this money could have been put to better use, such as to the building of a larger recreational hall, or a public bath. Furthermore, since this part of the village was held in the lowest esteem, villagers saw the project as not only superfluous but degrading. "Why don't they renovate wealthier peasant houses? Why do we have to show our worst side to the world? These houses should be bulldozed. "Why doesn't the village first replace burned-out village lights?"—commented a near-by resident.

Much of village politics hinges on the personal character of the council president. As a salaried public servant, elected for a five-year term, the president has ample opportunities to accumulate political power. More often than not he is an autocrat.[13] In villages such as Táp, where he is a "foreigner," the council president is seldom popular. "This is not a popularity contest," Táp's council president assured me. My informant families agreed with him: "He is better than some of the earlier ones, but we would not say we are in love with him." Another public response is to fuse the president with the entire village council. The reason for this is that many people do not come into personal contact with the president. They leave their request or petition with a secretary, which is eventually returned to them with a stamp of the council and the signature of the president. It is difficult for the petitioner to determine who exactly is responsible for *ügyintézés* (taking care of an official matter). The general consensus in Táp is that ügyintézés is too slow because of either laziness or ill will. Many requests are unheeded for months, sometimes years. Building permits, social allowances and plumbing for village-owned housing are held up wihtout explanation by the council. It is indeed a frustrating politico-administrative scene where the real losers are the people. "Whom can I turn to"—asked the wife of a cooperative farmer—"in my request to reassess the taxes after our garden was subdivided among four heirs two years ago? After the council turned my request down, I sent it to the county, which told me the village council had the last say. But the village council notified me that it was out of their hands."

The thirty-seven councillors of the three-village government are little more than decorations in the political structure. They are so thoroughly disaffected from the political process that one wonders that anyone volunteers for the position. A British anthropologist, C. M. Hann, came to the same conclusion in Tázlár in eastern Hungary. "Many members of the council are apparently resigned to a ceremonial role . . . ."[13]

Of the sixteen councillors of Táp, only four hold annual meetings for their constituents, but even these sometimes skip this opportunity to talk to the people. According to my investigations, less than one-third of the electorate knew who their councillor was, and 85% of the people either had no idea of the role of the councillor, or "did not care." To be sure, this is a very bleak situation since such a degree of apathy restricts the flow of information in the political process. The councillor is an upaid civil servant—similar to his Austrian counterpart. However, all similarities between the two stop here. While the Austrian councillor goes to the monthly meetings with important information from his constituency, "all fired up" to engage in formulating village policy, the Hungarian councillor attends meetings, held every three months, "to hear what the president has to say." The president admitted to me openly that he seldom took into account the councillors' suggestions. All that remains is the reading of his report on past records and future plans to the seemingly bored audience. Voting is always unanimous, since the councillors are carefully chosen by the party and the PPF. Hann noted that "they are . . . chosen very carefully . . . outspoken critics could not expect nomination."[14]

A very large portion of the elderly, who remember the days when the *esküdtek* (sworn representatives) "represented the voice of the villagers," brush the council aside as "contemptible rascals under the leadership of a hyena." Many elderly refuse to enter the townhall (they send a member of the family) and do not receive the greeting of key functionaries. To them politics is "dirty business" one must avoid.

An important political power base within Hungarian villages has been the agricultural cooperative farm since 1960, when private farming was eliminated. This enterprise is the primary employer in the village, and as such, it has formidable economic leverage. The cooperative farm has a separate village-developmental fund which reaches hundreds of thousands of forints (1 dollar = 35 forints). The disbursement of this money is decided by the leadership of the cooperative in consultation with the county and the village council. The fund may be withheld from the village if an agreement has not been reached among the concerned. Much bargaining and politicking ensues as the cooperative generally wants some concessions from the council on such matters as the use of certain roads for farm machines; rezoning land; standards of noise and air pollution, beautification, water purity, etc. Both the village and the cooperative have gained from this relationship.

A political power source of decreasing importance is the office of the local communist party secretary. Local tradition has it "the less we see of him, the better off we are." Although the party secretary still has the power to interfere in the decisions of the council, gone are the years of the 1950s when his power was all-pervasive in all matters of village life. His primary function today is to interpret the party's general policies for the council, and to report to the party's appropriate county cell on the "development of the village," the mood of the people, and the like. The last two party secretaries have been mild-mannered, friendly individuals people recognized on the street but "would not have a drink with them in the *kocsma* [tavern]." They remained outside of daily social interaction. The present secretary is a newcomer to the village. Many people did not even know he was appointed until several weeks after he assumed his role.

Last, but not least, villages in Hungary retain a vestige of the 1950s in the person of an informant to the County Security Office, which is part of the Police Department. He works independently of the single-man police force in the village. Informants come from among school teachers, principals, post office employees, or other government officials who spend their entire time in the village. In Táp it is the school principal. Behind his back some people call him *besugó* (informant). His duties include observation of suspicious behavior, or forms of "anti-socialist agitation." He is to send periodical reports to the county on individuals, who during my stay included an American anthropologist. Shortly after my arrival I was warned to "watch what I was saying in his presence." A month after my first meeting with him the principal invited me to his wine cellar to taste his own wine. He talked about his professional career and how he happend to come to Táp. He commented on mine: "It must be interesting to observe people." Our ensuing relationship was amiable right up to my departure.

CONCLUSIONS

In trying to assess the similarities and differences between the political processes of the two villages, it must be concluded that both Alsóőr and Táp are at the bottom rung of the political structure of the nations of which they are a part. National and county administrations view them as insignificant political entities within the national political scene. Both villages must fight for outside funds over which they attempt to gain control, and both administrations desire less outside interference in their lives. This struggle for local independence should be more intense in the case of Táp because of less abundant local economic resources and because of greater extent of outside interference. Yet, because of the specific nature of the Hungarian political structure and process, the political forces of Táp cannot be easily mobilized. While the body politic of Alsóőr is a dynamic force, representing the often divergent interests of two opposing forces (workers and peasants), the council of Táp is a static, largely ceremonial organization, where whatever power is available, is concentrated in the hands of one person, the council president. He rules without opposition, albeit not without higher control, and his success depends not on his popularity, but on how well he can carry out policies designed by his superiors. Unlike Alsóőr's mayor who gains information from the public through his councillors and the villagers themselves, Táp's council president is isolated by the system from his colleagues and the public. He is seen as a mere administrator, whereas the mayor in Austria is an important village leader to whom people listen, go for advice, and show deference.

Another fundamental difference between the two political processes is in the election of public representatives. It is strictly forbidden in

Hungary for any person to openly and freely campaign for a political office unless he is approved of by the PPF. It is not the individual who volunteers for a political career but the party and the PPF that approach the would-be actor. While the Austrian model requires local politicians to be members of a political party (which, incidentally is not a prerequisite in Hungary, save the job of the council president), a strong sense of voluntarism and a considerable amount of prestige accompanies such status. In Hungary the level of "participatory anxiety" was observable only in the party secretary, while in Austria it seemed to be an integral part of the political process. It is certain that formal political leadership in Hungary is not based on a process of democratic selection and popular representation. When compared with the political process of pre-World War II, when the interests and values of most Hungarian villagers were represented in the body politic and by informal leadership (which is altogether missing today), the contemporary village government in today's Hungary seems like a setback. It is my conclusion that all three accounts mentioned above (i.e. form of government, style of election, and manner of articulating political principles with leadership) the Austrian system serves the people better than the Soviet or Hungarian model. This observation is not based on my personal values, but is heavily underscored by the vast majority of village informants in Austria as well as Hungary.

NOTES

1. See for example, David Apter, "Political Systems and Developmental Change," in Robert T. Holt and John E. Turner, eds., *The Methodology of Comparative Research* (London, 1970), pp. 151-71; Lucy Mair, *Primitive Government* (New York, 1962); Morton Fried, "Anthropology and the Study of Politics," in Sol Tax, ed., *Horizons of Anthropology* (Chicago, 1964); E. Adamson Hoebel, *The Law of Primitive Man* (Cambridge, 1954); Meyer Fortes and E.E. Evas-Pritchard, eds., *African Political Systems* (London, 1940); I. Schapera, *Government and Politics in Tribal Societies* (London, 1956).

2. David Easton, *The Theory of Political Condition,* quoted by Robert T. Holt and John M. Richardson Jr., "Competing Paradigms in Comparative Politics," in Holt and Turner, *The Methodology,* p. 52.

3. Frederick W. Frey, "Cross-Cultural Survey Research in Political Science," in Holt and Turner, *The Methodology*, p. 200.

4. Alex Inkeles, *Social Change in Soviet Russia* (New York, 1968), pp. 401-2.

5. These normative statements came from urban as well as rural people interviewed during 1973-1974.

6. Eugene K. Kefe, *et al., Area Handbook of Austria* (Washington, D.C., 1976), p. 151.

7. Ibid.

8. The same opposition was observed in Oberwart, Alsóőr's neighbor by the linguist Susan Gál in her work *Language Shift* (New York, 1978), p. 58.

9. *A Magyar Népköztársaság Alkotmánya* [The Constitution of the Hungarian People's Republic] (Budapest, 1979), p. 6.

10. Inkeles, *Social Change in Soviet Russia*, p. 66.

11. László Rétvári, *Győr-Sopron megye népesedése* [The demography of Győr-Sopron County] (Budapest, 1977), p. 122.

12. Gyula Fenyő, ed., *Tanácstörvény* [Council Laws], (Budapest, 1971).

13. C.M. Hann, *Tázlár: A Village in Hungary* (London, 1980), p. 109. See also, Antal Végh, *Erdőháton, Nyíren* [In Erdőhát and Nyír] (Budapest, 1972), p. 41.

14. Hann, *Tázlár*, p. 109.

V

CENTRAL EUROPEAN AND BALKAN CULTURAL DEVELOPMENTS

The University of Pécs, 1367

The Universities of Cracow, Vienna and Pécs were all founded during the pontificate of Pope Urban V (1362-1370) and they also share another common feature, namely they all lacked the faculty of theology, which was explicitly prohibited by the pontiff. All available evidence leads us to the conclusion that Urban V viewed the task of University foundations with great seriousness; each foundation being preceded by an elaborate series of steps worked out by him and by the Curia. (Adam Vetulani of the University of Cracow had identified at least fifteen distinct steps in this process.)[3] These actions were designed to insure that the institutions would be indeed viable. Based on the example of Cracow and Vienna—where more ample documentation has survived—we know that the process included lengthy negotiations between the rulers and the Papal Curia, and also involved the opinion of local ecclesiastical and even municipal authorities. In the case of the University of Pécs the surviving documents are meager and it is impossible to determine how thoroughly the ground was prepared for the new foundation. Unfortunately we do not possess the Foundation Charter of Louis the Great, nor the charters issued, respectively, by the Bishop of Pécs and by the representatives of the municipality—if these documents ever existed at all. The Bull of Foundation issued by Urban V at Viterbo on Sept. 1, 1367 has, however, survived and does shed some light on the reasons for the creation of the new university and the major features of its organization.[4] The Pope states that the university foundation was requested by King Louis "not only for the good and prosperity of the public weal and the inhabitants of his kingdom of Hungary, but laudibly keeping in mind the good of the surrounding territory." The Papal Bull continues by saying that the king "desires earnestly that in the city of Pécs, ... being the most eminent city and most suitable and adaptable for this purpose, there be created and established by the Apostolic See, a university provided with every permitted faculty, so that the faith may be spread, the simple instructed, justice preserved, judgment and understanding augmented.... We have decided and also ordain that there be a university in the aforesaid city of Pécs, that it should forever excel in the faculty of civil and canon law, and in any other permitted faculty except theology."[5] The document also states that the doctors, teachers and students should enjoy all the usual privileges, liberties and immunities. Although not explicitly stated, the bishop of Pécs was to be the chancellor of the University. All examinations were to be taken in his presence or in the presence of his vicar. The bishop was to grant the license to candidates and bestow the degrees of Doctor or Magister. Any person who has been granted a degree from the *studium* of Pécs could lecture and teach at any other university. In other words a degree from this institution carried with it the *ius ubique docendi*. Pope Urban expressed anxiety about the financial future of the Hungarian University when he explicitly stated in the foundation document that "We wish furthermore that the masters or doctors who teach in this university be given a just income by the reigning king of Hungary. Otherwise this letter will have no value or weight."[6] To reemphasize this point, the Pope addressed a separate letter to King Louis, dated September 2, 1367, in which he repeated his warning that if the king or his successors failed to provide money for the payment of the professors' salaries, then the Foundation Bull would become void.[7] The Pope's anxiety was not misplaced and the lack of a secure financial basis of the University of Pécs was in all probability one of the major reasons for its early demise.

In order to assist the masters and scholars of the new university, the Pope issued instructions (September, 1367) to the effect that, even without residing at the place of their benefices, the masters and scholars could enjoy the revenues from this source.[8] In 1376 Pope Gregory XI (1370-1378) renewed this same dispensation from residence.[9] It appears that the papacy did its best in promoting the welfare of the *studium*. The question remains, however, whether the newly founded institution received any support from the Hungarian monarch and from the chancellor, who was the Bishop of Pécs. There is no indication that Louis the Great followed the injunction of the papal Foundation Bull to provide for the financial security of the University and its professors. He soon became deeply involved in foreign dynastic schemes designed to secure his election as king of Poland in 1370. His subsequent influence on Pécs is impossible to ascertain. The fact that King Casimir's University of Cracow also became extinct during Louis' reign as king of Poland, does not speak well of the Hungarian monarch as a promoter of higher education on either side of the Carpathian Mountains. We must, therefore, look to the Bishop of Pécs, William Bergzabern, as the person who in all probability was the individual most responsible for the university's organization and operation.[10] Bishop William was well suited for this task, for he was also one of the most trusted servants of the king. He held the office of Chancellor of the Realm and was often dispatched by the king on important diplomatic missions.

The *studium* which William of Bergzabern and his successor as bishop of Pécs, Valentinian Alsáni, were able to bring into, and keep in existence was a modest institution with an Arts and Law Faculty.[11] There are no indications that a Faculty of Medicine ever came into existence at Pécs, nor of a Faculty of Theology that was explicitly forbidden by the Papal Bull.

The most famous professor of the University was the Italian jurist Galvano di Bologna, who taught briefly at Pécs in the early years of the institution's existence. Chancellor William showed his generosity to Galvano by rewarding him with the most enviable salary of 300 silver marks or 600 gold florins, along with a residence in Pécs, as well as with revenues from a nearby village.[12] He was obviously the "star attraction" and the salary was intended to keep him at the university. This attempt did not work for long, as Galvano di Bologna left Pécs and returned to Italy as early as 1372.[13] His brief presence at the Hungarian university did not become a catalyst for the growth of a vigorous Law Faculty. There is the possibility that a certain Hermannus Lurcz, who was mentioned in the *Liber Decanorum* of Prague in 1379, was also a former professor at Pécs. (He is called "de studio Quinclesiensis")[14] Another possible professor was Paul, Provost of Szeben, who received permission from Pope Urban V in April of 1369 to receive the degree of Doctor in Canon Law "observing the privileges, statutes and customs of the University of Pécs."[15]

Most of the other information concerning the University is fragmentary. A few names of possible students, the granting of benefices to members of the faculty, etc., are insufficient evidence to give a clear picture about the life of the institution. It is also difficult to ascertain the exact connection, if there is indeed any, between the University and a collection of sermons entitled *Sermones compilate in studio generali Quinqueecclesiensi in regno Ungarie,* which is at the Bayerische Staatsbibliothek in Munich.[16] It is clear that the sermons were composed by Dominicans and that a number of them are the work of a Hungarian scholar. Yet we do not know if the sermons are the work of one person or several or whether the sermons were ever delivered at Pécs. Although a great deal of discussion has been generated among Hungarian scholars by this collection, the sermons do not tell us much about the university or its intellectual orientation.[17]

Valiant efforts have been made to show that the University of Pécs existed beyond 1390 and that it was a flourishing institution even in the fifteenth and sixteenth centuries, but there is no hard evidence to support this. What has confused a number of scholars is the presence of a vigorous cathedral school in the city, which functioned at least until the disaster of Mohács in 1526.[18] Had the University of Pécs survived much beyond 1390, it would be hard to imagine that permission would have been sought and given in the fifteenth century for the establishment of new institutions of learning within the boundaries of the Hungarian Kingdom.

The Sigismundean Universities of Óbuda, 1395-1410

The second Hungarian university owes its existence to King Sigismund of the Luxemburg dynasty. What prompted him to found a new university is difficult to determine, but it may have been connected with the demise of the University of Pécs and of the consequent lack of an institution of higher learning in Hungary. It is also interesting to note that Sigismund was the brother-in-law of Queen Jadwiga (Hedwig), who played such an important role in the refounding of the University of Cracow. The city where the new Hungarian *studium generale* was to be erected was Óbuda (Alt Ofen), a charming town a few miles north of the capital.[19]

The date of foundation of the University of Óbuda was a much debated problem and has only been satisfactorily resolved in recent years. The original foundation documents, together with all other charters of privileges, statutes and matriculation lists, have been lost or destroyed. For over three centuries the year 1389 has been regarded as the date for the founding of the University. Recent research in the Vatican Archives, however, has resulted in the discovery of a seventeenth-century volume which contains the summary of the Bulls issued by Pope Boniface IX (1389-1404), and provides us finally with the correct foundation date of this second Hungarian university.[20] The summary of the Bull of Boniface, dated October 6, 1395, states that at the request of King Sigismund

University Foundations in the Middle Ages

permission is granted for the establishment of a *studium generale* with all permissible faculties, to be established at Óbuda in the diocese of Veszprém, with all the customary privileges and liberties. The document further states that the Chancellor of the University was to be the Provost of the Church of St. Peter in Óbuda, and that the *capitulum* of St. Peter was to provide for the maintenance of the professors.[21] Unfortunately this summary does not elaborate on the structure of the proposed university. Since there are no indications that any faculty was to be explicitly excluded, we can presume that all four faculties were envisioned by the founder. The naming of the provost of a chapter of canons as the chancellor of a university is not uncommon. Similar development can be found at Vienna, Cologne, Mainz and Tübingen. The same holds true for the stipulation that the payment of professors should be undertaken by the Chapter of St. Peter. Prague, Vienna, Cologne, Erfurt and Leipzig had similar provisions. Although there is nothing unusual about the method used to provide for the financial support of the new university, it is interesting that King Sigismund assumed no responsibility at all for the welfare of the new *studium*. It should have been evident from the start that the revenues from one chapter of canons is not sufficient to build a lasting institution of higher learning.

The first Chancellor of the University of Óbuda was Lucas Demetrius, Provost of the Church of St. Peter. At the time when Pope Boniface IX issued the Bull of Foundation for the new *studium*, the Provost was in Rome and probably played an active role in the preparations which preceded the issuing of the foundation document. On the same day when the Pope issued the Foundation Chapter of the University, i.e. October 6, 1395, Lucas Demetrius was given permission to hold the office of Chancellor of the new University, even though he was not a doctor in any faculty. He was also given assurances that he would remain Chancellor and Provost of St. Peter even if eventually he would receive a bishopric—which in fact did occur later.[22]

The only shred of evidence about the existence of the University of Óbuda in the years immediately following its foundation comes from the Acts of the Faculty of Arts of the University of Vienna. On July 2, 1396 a certain Magister Johannes Horow petitioned the congregation of the Arts Faculty for permission to leave Vienna and to go to the University of Buda (*in universitate Budensi*).[23] Whether Master Horow ever left

Vienna, and if he did, what position he held at the Hungarian *studium* remains a mystery. Nor do we know how long the University of Óbuda functioned. Internal and external problems made Sigismund's reign most stormy during this period. There was active warfare around the Hungarian capital, and the military actions might have disrupted the infant institution.[24]

Not until the first decade of the fifteenth century do we hear again about the University of Óbuda. On August 1, 1410 Pope John XXIII (1410-1415) issued a new Foundation Bull.[25] The copy of this Bull is the only major surviving document of the University. According to this document, the restructured or refounded University of Óbuda was to have all four faculties, and was to enjoy all the privileges, exemptions and immunities which the Universities of Paris, Bologna, Oxford and Cologne enjoyed. Those who completed their studies at Óbuda could enter the higher faculties of any other university, or having received their license to teach, could lecture any place. The Bull of Pope John restated that the Provost of the Church of St. Peter was to hold the office of Chancellor and that examinations were to be held in his presence. Curiously, however, this document does not mention that this is a refoundation of a previous *studium.* Some instruction must have followed this second foundation, for subsequently two ex-students of the University of Óbuda were admitted into the rank of bachelors at Vienna in 1412 and 1415, respectively.[26]

Our last source for the history of the Óbuda *studium generale* is the appearance of a sizable delegation of professors from the University at the Council of Constance. According to the *Concilium Book* of Ulrich von Richental, the Hungarian university delegation consisted of seven members. This is an unusually large number in comparison with some of the most famous and established institutions. Of the delegations mentioned by Richental only Paris, Vienna, Heidelberg and Orleans had more members than Óbuda.[27] It would be erroneous to assume that all seven individuals mentioned by Richental were actually professors. It is hard to imagine that a university which four years previously was in such state of decay, or more probably non-existent and had to be refounded, could all of a sudden gather such a large delegation of masters to send to the Ecumenical Council. Some of the members probably just attached themselves to the official delegation of the University, and travelled in a group with them. At the head of the delegation was Lambertus, the Provost of Óbuda and thus Chancellor of the university. He was a canon lawyer. Other members included a master of medicine, two doctors of theology, two doctors of civil and canon law, and the *lector* of the Chapter in Óbuda.[28]

Following the Council of Constance darkness descends again upon the Hungarian universities. This second attempt to found an institution of higher learning on Hungarian soil, therefore, shared the same fate as the University of Pécs.

The Academia Istropolitana, Pozsony, 1465

Hungary was not destined to have another university until the reign of Matthias Corvinus (1458-1490). It is not surprising that this monarch would show an inclination in the establishment of a *studium generale* in his kingdom. Matthias Hunyadi was greatly interested in the promotion of culture, was an avid builder and bibliophile, as well as a renowned and most generous patron of scholars and artists. This love of learning and scholarship was encouraged in Matthias by his trusted friend, Archbishop Vitéz of Esztergom (1408?-1472), who was also the Chancellor of the Realm, and himself a great admirer of Renaissance culture.[29]

In 1465 Matthias Corvinus sent the Italian educated Hungarian Humanist Janus Pannonius (1434-1472) on a diplomatic mission to Pope Paul II (1464-1471). The primary objective of the Hungarian king was to get financial aid from the Pope for a major campaign against the Turks. A secondary objective of Janus Pannonius's mission was to deliver to Pope Paul a request from King Matthias for the establishment of a university on Hungarian soil. The king pointed out to the Pope that, although a large and fertile country, Hungary had no university. ("In regno Ungarie, licet amplo et fertili, non viget aliquod studium generale.") This clearly indicates that in the meanwhile the Universities of Pécs and Óbuda had ceased to exist. King Matthias's petition was recorded in the Supplication Registers on May 19, 1465, and a Bull of Foundation was issued on the same day.[30]

The Papal Bull is unusual in several aspects. First of all, Pope Paul II addressed himself both to Archbishop Vitéz and to Janus Pannonius in the opening of the letter, but referred only to Vitéz in the body of the text. The Pope explained that, at the request of King Matthias, he gave them permission to establish a university in any city of Hungary designated by the King. The new institution was to be a *studium generale* with all four faculties.[31] The office of Chancellor of the new University was to be filled by Archbishop Vitéz. The Pope furthermore instructed Vitéz to draw up statutes and ordinances for the government of the University, following the pattern of those of the University of Bologna. Once this was done and papal approval was granted for the statutes, the new institution would be empowered to grant degrees with all the privileges and insignia that went with a university.

Since the Bull of Paul II indicated that the university could be established in any Hungarian city found suitable by King Matthias, the choice fell on Pozsony, a beautiful and well-developed city on the Danube. It was only a few miles from the frontiers of the Archduchy of Austria and about forty miles east of Vienna. In establishing the new University at Pozsony, the King and Vitéz were motivated by two main considerations. First, after Buda Pozsony was probably the most important urban center in Hungary. An even more important reason for selecting Pozsony was its proximity to the Holy Roman Empire and to the flourishing University of Vienna. The founders apparently felt that the Austrian institution would have a beneficial influence on both the teachers and the student body of the new university.[32]

The building which was to house the new institution was provided by the King. A noble citizen of considerable wealth, Stephanus Gmaintl, had recently died without a male heir and his house became Crown property. It was this building that became the seat of the University, with the professors and students living in one of its wings, and instruction being given in the other.[33]

Although the building and the grounds were large, it is most probable that some of the students and masters did not live there, but, following the medieval custom, established themselves in private houses around the town.[34]

While the building for the university was provided by King Matthias, Vitéz took upon himself to find professors to staff the new institution. This was no easy task, and it probably accounts for the two-year lapse between the issuing of the Papal Bull in 1465, and the inauguration of the university in 1467.

Vitéz was certainly not idle during this period. His personal influence enabled him to attract some professors of such note that any university would have been proud to have them. The most notable of these were Johannes Regiomontanus (1436-1476), the great German astronomer and Martinus Bylica of Ilkusz (1433-1494?), famous alumnus of the University of Cracow. These noted scholars arrived at Esztergom, Hungary's ecclesiastical center, sometime in spring or early summer of 1467, where they were welcomed by the Archbishop and by King Matthias Corvinus. While at Esztergom Regiomontanus and his Polish friend undertook the task of preparing a horoscope for the new University. Dated June 20, 1467 the horoscope was designed to ensure an auspicious beginning and a long life for the Pozsony *studium*.[35] Based upon subsequent events it seems, however, that Regiomontanus and Martinus Bylica were rather inept prognosticators. From Esztergom the assembled professors made their way to their new home. In a letter dated July 18, 1467, Vitéz informed the City of Pozsony about the arrival of several professors and indicated that he had sent for others who would shortly arrive from Italy and France.[36]

In organizing the new university, Vitéz assumed the important function of Chancellor and kept this position until his death in 1472. He became entirely identified with the University. In fact, the records of the Theological Faculty of Vienna talk of the University of Pozsony as "his [i.e. Vitéz's] university."[37] One of the members of the Theology Faculty, an Austrian Dominican by the name of Leonhard Huntpichler, exchanged extensive correspondence with Archbishop Vitéz in 1467 encouraging him in his efforts to create a viable institution.[38] Huntpichler believed that the selection of Pozsony as the site of the new university was wise, since it could be reached without difficulty from all points of the Kingdom of Hungary, as well as from other parts of Europe. He furthermore urged Vitéz to be guided by the example of Heidelberg, where both the *via antiqua* and the *via moderna* were taught, and also cautioned against the example of the University of Basel, which was undergoing a great deal of difficulty because of differences between the adherents of these two systems. Another item of Huntpichler's advice was the need for a capable vice-chancellor for the university: he recommended for this position the Provost of Pozsony, Gregorius Schönberg. Finally, the friar assured the Archbishop that he could be certain of the support of the University of

Vienna and recommended a certain Nicolaus Schrickher of Hittendorf, former dean of the Arts faculty, as an excellent prospective professor. In another letter, Huntpichler informed the Archbishop that one of his confreres, Johannes Gatti, delivered a commemorative oration in Vienna at the time of the inauguration of the University of Pozsony.[39]

This correspondence is important because it illustrates the close contact between the University of Vienna and the newly established Hungarian University. Huntpichler probably hoped that several members of his Order would be invited to become professors at Pozsony. How many, if any, Viennese Dominicans taught at Pozsony cannot be determined on the basis of these letters. But it is interesting that about at this time (January 31, 1469) King Matthias petitioned Pope Paul II to grant him permission to settle Hungarian Dominicans at Pozsony in order to strengthen the *studium* in that city.[40] Apparently this request was never granted, for the Dominican friars did not have a convent at Pozsony in the fifteenth century. Whether this would have prolonged the existence of the university is something we can only speculate about.

There is more information concerning the University of Pozsony than about any of the other institutions founded in Medieval Hungary. We have the names of several professors who taught there, and also know that a number of students who received their bachelor's degree at that institution, were subsequently admitted to the University of Vienna.[41] Yet when all the pieces of information are fitted together, the end result is still meager. The Pozsony *studium* started auspiciously, but in less than a half decade it had already burned itself out. The death of Archbishop Vitéz in 1472 was undoubtedly a great blow to the institution. The University did not cease to exist with the death of its Chancellor, but it was clearly ailing. All the famous professors left. Although we know that the Faculty of Arts continued to exist for some time, the final curtain came down during the hostilities between the Emperor Maximilian and Hungary, following the death of Matthias Corvinus in 1490.

The Dominican Studium at Buda

The University of Pozsony was still in existence, when Matthias Corvinus made a half-hearted attempt to somehow raise the *studium* of the Dominican friars in Buda to a full university. This *studium*, established perhaps as early as 1304, was located in the convent of St. Nicholas on Castle Hill in Buda. The Dominican *studium generale* was specifically designed for the purpose of teaching members of the Order, and its emphasis was on philosophy and theology.[42] All indications are that King Matthias was unable to make it into a regular university with four faculties, and that the Buda *studium* remained through most of its existence simply a typical *Ordenstudium*[43]

In the sixteenth century the scholarly printer Gáspár Heltai (1490/ 1510-1574) claimed that King Matthias planned a university on the banks of the Danube for 40,000 students, and that he had actually seen the plans for this great enterprise.[44] Not only did Matthias Corvinus fail to found such an incredibly huge institution, but he did not even attempt to rescue the University of Pozsony from decay.

Conclusions

If we look at the repeated failures of Hungarian university foundations in the course of the fourteenth and fifteenth centuries, we inevitably have to raise the question: Why this series of failures? Was Hungary incapable of supporting a university during those centuries? Was there no genuine interest in scholarship and learning? Was the country that backward? The answers to these questions must generally be negative. Hungary of those centuries certainly had both the need and the wealth necessary for the maintenance of an institution of higher learning. Its social development was not inferior to those of the neighboring countries, with the exception of Italy and the Germanic lands. There was a hunger for knowledge, and Hungarian students flocked in large numbers to foreign universities such as those of Paris, Bologna, Padua, Ferrara and later also to Prague, Cracow and Vienna. By the fifteenth century many of the officials of the Royal Chancery, as well as the leading churchmen of the realm were graduates of universities. The interest in higher education was certainly evident. But if this was true—as it certainly was—what went wrong with the university foundations? I think that the answer is twofold. First and most importantly, there was no secure financial basis for the new foundations. Second, there was a lack of consistency in the support for these institutions. The surviving documents lead us to conclude that King Louis the Great, Sigismund and Matthias Corvinus all failed to take the necessary steps to ensure that their newly founded universities would have economically sound bases. The anxiety expressed by Pope Urban V in the Foundation Charter of the University of Pécs proved to be prophetic. There does not appear to have been any long-range planning for an adequate and constant source of income to supply the institutions with needed revenues. We get the impression that the three monarchs were willing to petition the Holy See for the foundation charters, but when it came to matters of finances, they seem to have lost interest.

Another regrettable sign of failure is the lack of permanent residential colleges in connection with the universities. Among the country's wealthy lay and ecclesiastical lords, not one offered an endowment to any of the universities. The presence of even a few well-financed colleges could have prevented the extinction of these universities. Somebody in Hungary should have read Jean Gerson of the University of Paris, who gave clear warnings about the prospective failure of colleges and universities unless well endowed.[45]

Almost as serious as the absence of proper funding was the lack of consistency. Four different places were chosen by the Hungarian monarchs as locations for universities. Instead of moving from city to city, however, it would have been wiser to concentrate on a single location, and if the original foundation did not succeed, then to try again and again in the same place. None of the Hungarian towns selected for the universities had much of the necessary intellectual and scholarly milieu. Moreover, because this milieu never really developed until much later, Hungary remained without a university until 1635, and impoverished in matters of scholarly heritage for even longer. This impoverishment is evident both in the absence of physical reminders of the academic world, as well as in the lack of sufficient number of noted professors, theologians and legal scholars. The ephemeral nature of their medieval universities has also prevented the Hungarians from producing university graduates who could have risen in the administrative structure of the Church and State. Nor do we hear much of stimulating debates and intellectual wranglings, or of other similar excitements generated by a functioning university. The situation is equally sad when it comes to the paucity of material objects connected with a *stadium generale*. No university or college buildings, no major libraries, no charters of scholarly privileges, no matriculation lists, no deliberations by the nations or faculties of universities, no maces and scepters have survived, perhaps because few of these have ever existed in Hungary.

In light of these realities, the influence of the four or five medieval Hungarian universities upon Hungarian intellectual, spiritual and artistic life must also have been rather limited. This influence was certainly much less than could have been, had one or more of these universities managed to survive.

NOTES

1. H. Denifle, *Die Entstehung der Universitäten des Mittelalters bis 1400* (Graz: Akademische Druck u. Verlagsanstalt, 1956; repr. of 1885 edit.). On Prague: pp. 582-603; Vienna, pp. 604-625; Cracow, 625-629; Pécs, 413-418. Also: Hastings Rashdall, *The Universities of Europe in the Middle Ages,* eds. F.M. Powicke—A.B. Emden (3 vols.; Oxford University Press, 1958), II, Prague: pp. 211-234; Vienna, pp. 234-245; Cracow, pp. 289-294; Pécs, pp. 294-295.

2. The standard treatment of medieval university foundations in Hungary is the work of Jenő Ábel, *Egyetemeink a középkorban* [Our Universities in the Middle Ages], (Budapest: Akadémiai Könyvkiadó, 1881). Also see: H. Schönebaum, "Die Ungarischen Universitäten in Mittelalter," *Archiv für Kulturgeschichte,* XVI (1925), pp. 41-59; L.S. Domonkos "The State of Education in Hungary on the Eve of the Battle of Mohács (1526)," *Canadian-American Review of Hungarian Studies,* II (1975), pp. 4-8.

3. A. Vetulani, "A pécsi egyetem, valamint a krakkói és bécsi testvéregyetemek alapításának körülményeiről" [The University of Pécs, as well as the Cricumstances of Foundation of the Sister Institutions of Cracow and Vienna], in *Jubileumi tanulmányok a pécsi egyetem történetéből* [Jubilee Studies Concerning the History of the University of Pécs], (Pécs: Tudományegyetem, 1967), I, pp. 39-40; and the excellent study of T. Klaniczay, "Megoldott és megoldatlan kérdések az első magyar egyetem körül" [Solved and Unsolved Questions Concerning the First Hungarian University], *Irodalomtörténeti Közlemények,* LXXVIII (1974), p. 163.

4. Vatican Archives, Reg. Vat. no. 256, fol. 68v.-69r. For the text of the Foundation Bull see: R. Békefi, *A pécsi egyetem* [The University

of Pécs] (Budapest: Magyar Tudományos Akadémia, 1909), pp. 13-21; also in J. Koller, *Historia episcopatus Quinqueecclesiarum* (Pozsony: Wagner, 1784), III, pp. 96-99.

5. English translation of the Bull in: A.L. Gabriel, *The Mediaeval Universities of Pécs and Pozsony,* (Frankfurt a. M.; Joseph Knecht, 1969), pp. 18-21.

6. Ibid., p. 21; Békefi, *A pécsi egyetem,* p. 19, col. 2 and p. 21 col. 2.

7. Letter in Vatican Archives, Reg. Vat. no. 258, fol. 68v. Gabriel, op. cit., Plate no. 1; also: Bekéfi, op.cit., pp. 22-25.

8. Letter in Vatican Archives, Reg. Avenion. no. 164, fol. 502 r. Gabriel, op. cit., Plate no. 2; also: Békefi, op. cit., pp. 124-125.

9. Koller, *Hist. Episc. Quinqueecl.* III, pp. 178-180; Békefi, op. cit., p. 129.

10. Gabriel, *Medieval Universities of Pécs and Pozsony,* pp. 22-23; Békefi, *A pécsi egyetem,* pp. 28-30.

11. Concerning Alsáni see: E. Fűgedi "Alsáni Bálint, a pécsi egyetem második kancellárja" [Bálint Alsáni, the Second Chancellor of the University of Pécs], in *Jubileumi tanulmányok,* pp. 97-107; also: A. Aldásy, *Alsáni Bálint Bibornok* [Cardinal Bálint Alsáni], (Budapest: A Magyar Történelmi Társulat, 1903), pp. 54-56.

12. Koller, *Hist. Episc. Quinqueecl.,* III, pp. 130-131.

13. A. Csizmadia, "Galvano di Bologna pécsi működése és a középkori magyar jogi oktatás egyes kérdései" [The Activities of G. di Bologna at Pécs and the Problems of Legal Education in Medieval Hungary], in *Jubileumi tanulmányok,* pp. 111-128.

14. See: *Liber decanorum facultatis philsophicae Universitatis Pragenis* [Monumenta Historica Universitatis Carolo-Ferdinandeae Pragenis], (Prague: 1830), I, p. 186. Also: František Kavak, "A prágai Károly egyetem, a pécsi egyetem és Dél-Magyarország a XIV. sz. és a XV. sz. elején [The Charles University of Prague, the University of Pécs and Southern Hungary in the 14th and early 15th century], in *Jubileumi tanulmányok,* pp. 87-88; E. Petrovich, "A középkori pécsi egyetem ismeretlen tanárai" [The Unknown Professors of the Medieval University of Pécs], *Irodalomtörténeti Közlemények,* LXVII (1967), pp. 290-296.

15. Vatican Archives, Reg. Avenion., no. 170, fol. 541 r.; Gabriel, *Mediaeval Universities of Pécs and Pozsony,* p. 27, Plate no. 4.

16. Munich, Bayerische Staatsbibliothek, Cod. Lat. Mon. 22, 363^b Part II, pp. 1-156.

17. See the excellent study of Pál Timkovich, "A 'Pécsi egyetemi beszédek' szellemi háttere" [The Spiritual Background of the University of Pécs Sermons], in *Irodalomtörténeti Közlemények*, LXXXIII (1979), pp. 1-14.

18. E. Petrovich, "A középkori pécsi egyetem megszünése" [The Disappearance of the Medieval University of Pécs], in *A Janus Pannonius Múzeum Évkönyve: 1966*, (Pécs: 1967), pp. 166-167.

19. Ábel, *Egyetemeink a középkorban*, pp. 17-27; 57-64; K. Heilig, "Zur Geschichte der ältesten ungarischen Universitäten und des Magisters Benedikt von Makra," *Jahrbuch des Wiener ungarischen Historischen Instituts*, I (1931), pp. 42-64; Gy. Székely, "A pécsi és óbudai egyetem alapítása a középeurópai egyetemlétesítések összefüggéseiben" [The Foundation of the Universities of Pécs and Óbuda in Relation to the Establishment of Universities in Central Europe], in *A Janus Pannonius Múzeum Évkönyve, 1967* (Pécs: 1968), pp. 155-174.

20. H. Diener, "Zur Geschichte der Universität Gründungen in Alt-Ofen (1395) und Nantes (1423)," *Quellen und Forschungen aus italienische Archiven und Bibliotheken*, XLII (1963), p. 265.

21. Vatican Library, Cod. Lat. 6952, fol. 164 v; Diener, op. cit., 270; L.S. Domonkos, "The History of the Sigismundean Foundation of the University of Óbuda (Hungary)," in *Studium Generale, Studies Offered to Astrik L. Gabriel* [Texts and Studies in the History of Mediaeval Education, XI], (Notre Dame, Ind.: Mediaeval Institute, 1967), pp. 5-6.

22. V. Fraknói, ed., *Monumenta Vaticana Historiam Regni Hungariae illustrantia* (Budapest: Magyar Tudományos Akadémia, 1888), Ser. I, III, p. 301; E. Mályusz, *Zsigmondkori* okmánytár, *1387-1399* [Chartulary from the Age of Sigismund] (Budapest: Akadémiai Kiadó, 1951), I, p. 450, no. 4102.

23. Vienna, Universität Archiv: *Acta Fac. Artium*, Lib. I, fol. 76v.

24. Master Benedict of Makra might have been a professor at Óbuda during these troubled periods. See: Heilig, op. cit., pp. 46-47; Domonkos, "Sigismundean Foundation," *Studium Generale*, pp. 15-16.

25. Text of the Bull of Foundation: V. Fraknói, "Oklevelek a pápai levéltárakból" [Charters from Papal Archives], *Történelmi Tár*, XV (1892), pp. 398-401; also: Domonkos, "Sigismundean Foundation," *Studium Generale*, pp. 30-33, Appendix III. Concerning the events surrounding the refounding of the university see: T. Foffano, "Ripporti

tra Italie e Ungheria in occasione delle legazioni del Card. Branda Castiglioni," in *Venezia e Ungheria nel rinascimento,* ed. V. Branca [Civilta Venezia Studi, 28], (Florence: Leo Olschki, 1973), pp. 70-72.

26. *Acta Fac. Artium,* Lib. I, fol. 143 r.; fol. 179r.

27. Ulrich von Richental, *Das Concilium so zu Constanz gehalten ist worden...*, (Augsburg: 1536; Facsimile edition, Leipzig: 1936), pp. 121v-124r.

28. Domonkos, "Sigismundean Foundation," *Studium Generale,* pp. 26-28.

29. Concerning Vitéz see my study: "János Vitéz: The Father of Hungarian Humanism, 1408-1472," *The New Hungarian Quarterly,* XX (1979), pp. 142-150.

30. Text of the Petition of King Matthias in Vatican Archives, Reg. Supplic. 810, fol. 56; also: Békefi, *A pécsi egyetem,* p. 131.

Text of Papal Bull of Foundation in: Koller, *Historia Episc. Quinqueecl.,* IV, pp. 146-148.

31. M. Császár, *Academia Istropolitana. Mátyás király pozsonyi egyeteme* [The Academia Istropolitana, King Matthias's University at Pozsony], (Pozsony: Eder István nyomda, 1914), pp. 11-14; Ábel, *Egyetemeink a középkorban,* pp. 27-37, 64-83; Gabriel, *The Mediaeval Universities of Pécs and Pozsony,* pp. 39-40. There is the possibility that a law faculty did not develop at the University of Pozsony. See: Karol Rebro, "Istropolitana a Bologna" [Istropolitana and Bologna], in *Humanizmus a renesancia na Slovensku v 15.-16. storoci* [Humanism and Renaissance in Slovakia during the 15th and 16th Centuries], (Bratislava: 1967), pp. 17-23.

32. L.S. Domonkos, "The Origins of the University of Pozsony," *The New Review: A Journal of East European History,* IX, (1969), pp. 270, 275.

33. There is evidence that a *bursa* for students existed at the University in 1470. See: Gy. Bónis, "Einflüsse des römischen Rechts in Ungarn," in *Ius Romanum medii aevi,* Pars V, (Milan: Typis Guiffre, 1964), p. 45 and note 173, 174.

34. Concerning the buildings of the university see: V. Janković, "O budovach Academie Istropolitany" [Concerning the Buildings of the A.I.], in *Humanizmus a renesancia na Slovensku,* pp. 94-99.

35. Vienna, Österreichische Nationalbibliothek, Cod. Lat. 24, fol. 212r.

36. Ábel, *Egyetemeink a középkorban,* pp. 68-69; Császar, *Academia Istropolitana,* pp. 106-107; Gabriel, *Mediaeval Universities of Pécs and Pozsony,* p. 60, n. 89.

37. *Acta Fac. Theol.,* Lib. II, fol. 25 verso.

38. The correspondence of Huntpichler is found in: Vatican Library, Cod. Ottobon. Lat. 689, fol. 131r.-142r. See: I.W. Frank, "Leonhard Huntpichler O.P. Theologie-professor und Ordensreformer in Wien," *Archivum Fratrum Praedicatorum,* XXIV (1966), pp. 338-340.

39. Frank, op. cit. 340 calls him Watt. This must be a misreading for Gatti, a Dominican who probably taught at the University for a few years. This information was conveyed to me by Prof. Tibor Klaniczay of the Institute for Literary History, Budapest. I hereby acknowledge his excellent suggestions.

40. V. Franknói, *Magyarország egyházi és politikai összeköttetései a római szent-székkel* [Ecclesiastical and Political Relations of Hungary with the Holy See], (Budapest: Szent István Társulat, 1902) II, p. 240 and p. 453 note 741.

41. Gabriel, *Mediaeval Universities of Pécs and Pozsony,* pp. 46-47; Domonkos, "Origins of the University of Pozsony," pp. 281-282.

42. A. Harsányi, *A Domonkosrend Magyarországon a reformáció elött* [The Dominican Order in Hungary Before the Reformation], (Debrecen; Nagy Károly nyomda, 1938), pp. 146-148.

43. The General Chapter of the Dominican Order made several attempts to expand the Buda *Studium* and even ordered the transfer of eight teachers from Paris to strengthen the school of Buda. See: *Monumenta Ordinis Fratrum Praedicatorum Historica,* Vol. IX, *Acta Capitolorum Generalium,* (Rome: 1899), IV, pp. 68-69. It is improbable that any of the assigned teachers ever left Paris.

44. G. Heltai, *Chronica az magyaroknak dolgairól* [Chronicle Concerning the Deeds of the Hungarians], (Kolozsvár: Heltai Gáspár, 1575; facsimile edition Budapest: Akadémiai Kiadó 1973), pp. 177-178. Also see: P. Kulcsár "Az óbudai egyetem Heltai Gáspár krónikájában" [The University of Óbuda in the Chronicle of H.G.], *Acta Historiae Litterarum*

Hungaricarum, X-XI (1971), pp. 5-7. Concerning the building plans see: R. Feuerné-Tóth, "A budai 'Schola' Mátyás király és Chimenti Camicia reneszánsz ideál városnegyed terve" [The "Schola" of Buda: The Plans of King Matthias and Chimenti Camicia for an Ideal Renaissance City], *Épités-Épitészettudomány,* V (1973), pp. 373-385.

45. J. Gerson, "Considerationes pro volentibus condere testamentum," *Opera Omnia,* Ellies du Pin, ed. (Antwerpen: 1706), III, p. 759. See: A.L. Gabriel, "The College System in the Fourteenth-Century Universities," *The Forward Movement of the Fourteenth Century,* ed. F.L. Utley, (Columbus: Ohio State University Press, 1961; also reprint: Baltimore, 1962), p. 8., n. 85.

Thomas Szendrey

HUNGARIAN HISTORIOGRAPHY AND EUROPEAN CURRENTS OF THOUGHT FROM LATE BAROQUE TO EARLY ROMANTICISM 1700-1830

During the late seventeenth and eighteenth centuries one can point to the appearance of a relatively great number of Hungarian memoirists and scholars, who by their pioneering efforts in introducing the new historical methods and attitudes of Western Europe, mainly reflecting the influence of the Bollandist School and the memoir literature in evidence throughout Baroque Europe, did much to put down the foundations of subsequent historical scholarship in Hungary. Their efforts were significant for the gathering of a large amount of historical material and for their early critical efforts, subsequently making possible some of the remarkable achievements of nineteenth-century historians. However, they paid but little attention to the fostering of the Hungarian language and related national issues and thus most of their studies and historical collections were preserved and published in Latin.[1] Gábor Hevenesi, Mátyás Bél, and most other historians of that period were certainly not directly instrumental in the promotion of linguistic and nationally-inspired cultural reform movements; indeed the scholars were mostly isolated from the rapidly growing national movement in Hungary in the second half of the eighteenth century.[2] This isolation nonetheless had a positive dimension; scholars such as Bél, Péter Bod, and numerous others were able to carry on their work without interference from the basically literary oriented national movement. This isolation, however, did not remove them from the censorship effort of the ruling Habsburg dynasty, since the imperial censors often found assertions in their works or in the collected documents which they deemed not in accord with the interests of the dynasty and the ruling classes of that era.

Any discussion of the major features and tendencies of eighteenth-century Hungarian historiography must take into account not only Baroque spirituality and inwardness, but also the role of the Enlightenment and the movement for a national language with implications which extended beyond the realm of linguistic concerns.[3] The conflict between Baroque ideals and Enlightenment ideas generally characterized the history of Hungary during the course of the eighteenth century. While the royal absolutism of the time did its best to keep the new ideas out of the Hungarian lands, it was not usually successful. However, when an enlightened absolutist such as Joseph II attempted to introduce uniform systems of administration and decreed the German language compulsory in official dealings, such changes were deeply resented by the politically conscious elements of the Hungarian population. This resentment against Joseph II's policies took numerous forms, manifesting itself especially in a renewed and extensive emphasis on linguistic modernization and rationalization together with the promotion of national values in literary expression.[4] Scholarly activity and publications remained somewhat isolated from this movement, as attested to by the fact that virtually all such works, especially in history, were generally written and published outside the sphere of influence and inspiration of this nascent national movement.[5]

The impact of the Enlightenment on Hungarian public institutions and intellectual and cultural life generally did not reach the same crescendo as it did in Western Europe. During the reign of Maria Theresa these enlightened ideas found expression mostly in a reduced intensity in the religious struggles and a turning away from a pronounced theological orientation. For example, the two best known Protestant scholars, Bod and Bél, were concerned in their writings more with literature and history respectively.[6] The best known among the Catholic "enlightenment philosophes", mostly Jesuit priests, were instrumental in establishing history as an autonomous academic discipline.[7] There was also emerging an interest in various philosophical movements, especially the thought of Immanuel Kant; among other such writings, one should take note of a critique of Kant's philosophy written by József Rozgony (1756-1823), entitled *Dubia de initiis transcendentalis idealismi Kantiani*.[8] The intellectual life of Hungary was thus becoming by degrees more cognizant of affairs outside the Habsburg realms and this was further augmented by the impact of other enlightened ideas and indeed the events of the French Revolution as well.[9] This series of seminal events caused a two-fold reaction in Hungary. Some enthusiastic democrats welcomed it, such as the poet János Bacsányi; his poem, "About the Changes in France", ["A franciaországi változásokra"], written in 1789, reflected this attitude:

> Nations, countries, who are now in an ugly snare
> And groan under the painful knout of slavery,
> And could not, until now, remove these iron
> Implements which condemned them to the grave.
>
> You also, whose blood is desired by nature,
> Ordained executioners of your loyal serfs,
> Come, so that you may see your fate in
> Advance, turn your watchful eyes upon Paris.[10]

Other politically conscious elements were outraged by the more extreme and radical aspects of the French Revolution and sometimes this feeling was coupled with indignation for the centralizing and Germanizing tendencies of Joseph II. The situation which arose out of this was described in these terms by one writer:

> This is how there developed at the end of the eighteenth century that Hungarian attitude, which, in its contacts with Vienna and the power of the king, was as enlightened as any revolutionary, but in defense of the constitution and especially the aristocratic privileges, more Baroque than the Baroque itself.[11]

Even though the influence of the Enlightenment and the French Revolution was experienced in numerous ways, the social and political condition of Hungary could neither extensively nor deeply assimilate such movements and ideas. For example, the Martinovics conspiracy (1794-1795) only led to further confusion in political and intellectual life and it was only a fortunate turn of events that the ideas and attitudes associated with an enlightened romantic nationalism soon broke this intellectual, cultural, and political stalemate in Hungary. Thus, this was the flow of events in which the historically-minded scholar functioned and searched for the meaning of his historical and political experiences.

The search for the understanding of the often rapid altercation of events and ideas found expression in the extensive memoir literature of the seventeenth and early eighteenth centuries, specifically in the writings of such individuals as Mihály Cserei, Péter Apor, Pál Ráday, Ferencz Szakál, Sándor Károlyi and numerous others.[12] Being, however, the classical period of the collection of sources, many of the documents, which were later synthesized into large-scale historical presentations, were discovered, identified, and organized by these scholars, who so often worked tirelessly under trying political conditions, mostly without reward and due recognition. Their activities may be divided into three successive phases, although the lines of demarcation are not always exact or evident. There was, however, a certain development from one phase to the next: namely the collection of documents, their systematic organization, and finally their being subjected to historical criticism and then ultimate use as a historical source.[13]

The collection of historical documents in Hungary was intimately bound up with the activities of Protestant ministers and Jesuit priests. They were assisted and supported by numerous members of the aristocracy, not only as memoirists and correspondents, but also as collectors and preservers of family records.[14]

The pioneer in the collection of historical sources in this period was Gábor Hevenesi (1656-1717), a Jesuit and one-time director of the *Pázmaneum* in Vienna. Having been influenced by the work of the Bollandists, he left behind a collection of approximately 140 volumes of historical sources, dealing mostly with the ecclesiastical history of Hungary in the sixteenth and seventeenth centuries.[15] There can be little doubt that the religious controversies of the age failed to exercise an impact on either the selection or the tone of the critical work performed by him.

Among the early Protestant collectors of historical documents, the name of Pál Ember Debreczeni (1660-1710), was probably the most significant. As in the case of Hevenesi and so many others, the Dutch Bollandists also influenced his work; indeed, Debreczeni had studied in

Holland for two years and after his return he became a minister and continued his activity as a historian and collector of documents. His major work, also reflective of the religious controversies of the age, *Historia ecclesiae reformatae in Hungaria et Transylvania,* was published only posthumously in 1728.[16] These religious polemics tended to foster historical scholarship and the commitment to the collection of sources insofar as the arguments were conducted mostly in terms of the religious history of the Hungarian people.

In spite of this significant religious cast to these historical efforts, cultural history was by no means neglected; this can be seen especially in the collecting and editorial work of Dávid Czvittinger (1676-1743), the first to collect documents concerning the lives and activities of Hungarian literary figures. The results of his work were published at Frankfurt and Leipzig in 1711 under the title *Specimen Hungariae Literatae.*[17]

Significant as a distinct undertaking was the historical work dealing with Transylvania specifically. Active in this field was János Kénösi-Tőzsér (1708-1772), who compiled and organized many of the sources for the history of Transylvania, and near the end of his life began to write a minutely detailed work, in reality a collection of documents with connecting passages, on this topic.[18] The work was left unfinished and was continued by others in the latter decades of the eighteenth century.[19]

The Jesuit tradition reaching back to Hevenesi was continued by Sámuel Timon (1675-1736), who collected and subjected to expert criticism the sources of Hungarian history to 1662; his work was updated and published after his death by his fellow Jesuit Ferenc Kazy under the title *Historia regni Hungariae.*[20] Timon was undoubtedly a better handler of sources than most of his contemporaries, and although he could not fully overcome his Catholic orientation, he was by all means more concerned with the search for truth than the fostering of historical polemics. Furthermore, his works reveal an interest in questions of chronology. More significant than that, however, especially in terms of subsequent Hungarian historiography, was his attempt to deal with the history of the numerous nationalities living in Hungary.

Ferenc Kazy (1695-1759), who as Timon's successor finished his work, was especially active at the Jesuit-established University of Nagyszombat [Tyrnavia] and provided the historian of intellectual and cultural life with one of the most comprehensive accounts of this institution of higher learning. Kazy was also one of the first among the documentary historians who turned his attention to the rather misty proto-history of the Hungarian people; his work on this topic, entitled *Hunnias sive Hunnorum et Scythia Asiatica egressus* was published at Nagyszombat in 1731.[21] Interest in this topic, ranging from poorly informed speculation through romantic theorizing to acceptable scholarship, has become an indispensable dimension of virtually all subsequent Hungarian historiography.

The work of another Jesuit collector of sources must be mentioned, namely István Kaprinai (1714-1785), who collected approximately 102 volumes of historical records; however, only a small amount of it has been published, but is nonetheless preserved in manuscript. Much of it is of great value, specifically the materials dealing with the diplomacy of King Matthias.[22]

The Protestant tradition of documentary historiography reaching back to Debreczeni found a worthy successor in Péter Bod (1712-1769), a cultural and ecclesiastical historian. In his *Magyar Athenas* (Nagyszeben, 1766) he gathered together the biographies of 500 Hungarian men of letters and in the introduction expressed in his intent to use the Hungarian language as the vehicle of his scholarship. In this respect he foreshadowed the eventual dominance of the Hungarian language in scholarly life as well.[23]

The individuals mentioned up to this point were primarily collectors of sources and documents, even though some of them engaged in some initial efforts to organize what had been discovered and collected. Another group of scholars, their activities made possible by these collectors, were more instrumental in the task of organizing this vast amount of information into coherent and useful patterns and structures. Especially significant in this respect was the scholarly work and organizational activity of Mátyás Bél (1684-1749), one of the most prodigious scholars of the early decades of the eighteenth century. He was a Lutheran minister, an historian, indeed, the leading polyhistor of his time. His dedication to scholarship, coupled with his knowledge of the major currents of European thought, resulted in his major work, *Notitia Hungariae novae historico-geographica*, published between 1735 and 1742, in which he attempted to give a comprehensive picture of the Hungary of his day. However, only the part dealing with the northwestern counties was completed. This comprehensive picture of the old and new Hungary was put together mainly by the use of a method properly classed historical, included a study of political and physical geography, history, linguistics, folklore, economics, and even public health questions.[24] However, Bél's first concern was with using all the necessary sources to arrive at his more comprehensive account.[25] Not only his methods and example, but his skills as a scholarly organizer made it possible for him to establish a school of followers, who then were quite influential in Hungarian scholarly life in the second half of the eighteenth century.

Another representative figure of the same school of thought as Bél was Márton Schmeizel (1679-1747), who taught Hungarian bibliography, history, and statistics at the University of Jena. His influence extended to a whole generation of Transylvanian-Saxon scholars, who then gathered together and organized the sources of their own history.[26] The Jesuit school of documentary history also turned more toward the organization of source materials, even though the collecting activity always remained a part of their work. The Jesuit school's major historical scholar in the first half of the eighteenth century was Miklós Schmitth (1707-1767), who not only collected sources for all periods of Hungarian history, but also wrote about the life and activities of numerous palatines. However, his major contribution was his role as the teacher of the yet to be discussed two best-known representatives of the Jesuit school, György Pray and István Katona.

Accompanying this resurgence in the gathering and organization of documents, a revival of interest in the more remote periods of the Hungarian past became evident and widespread, which revival went hand in hand with the growing national movement. This became especially obvious in the works and activities of András Dugonics (1740-1818), a priest of the Piarist order, whose scholarly activity centered around the collection of sources for the earliest periods of Hungarian history. His collections and the works based upon them are generally characterized by an obvious sense of aristocratic nationalism. This may well be due to the fact that Dugonics was also a literary figure of some note and was influenced by the national movement that was still largely limited to the upper classes.[27]

Others involved in this extensive interest in Hungarian proto-history were Incze József Desericzky (1702-1763), and Ferenc Ottrocski-Fóris (1648-1718). Desericzky arrived in Rome in 1742 as a member of the council of the Piarist order and during the four years spent there also collected historical documents, an activity he continued later at Vienna and Nagyszombat. He was especially interested in the relations among the early Hungarians and those peoples he believed were related to them, specifically the Scythians, Huns, Avars, and Cumans. The results of his labors were gathered together in a large five-volume work entitled *De initiis ac majoribus Hungarorum commentaria*.[28] Although his method of presenting these documents disregarded some of the canons of editorial and critical work, he thus made available many documents for the study of early Hungarian history, and as such performed a valuable historical task. The other collector of documents concerning the early history of the Magyars, Ferenc Ottrocski-Fóris, published one of the first collections on the pre-history of the Magyars. His *Origines Hungaricae* appeared in 1693, and anticipated some of the subsequent activities in this field, including some of the works mentioned in this brief survey.

In the field of cultural history the name of Pál Wallaszky (1742-1824), the author of the first systematic history of Hungarian literature must be mentioned. Although he wrote his major works in Latin, they are nevertheless permeated by a powerful Hungarian spirit, which is especially true of his major work, *Conspectus Reipublicae litterariae in Hungaria ab initiis Regni ad nostra usque tempora delineatus*.[29] He dealt with literature in the broadest sense and his work comprised not only the history of literary expression, but also the history of art and the history of the various academic disciplines.

In addition to Wallaszky, some other individuals deserve mention. Strongly influenced by the Jesuit tradition was Ádám Ferenc Kollár (1718-1783), who for a time was a member of that order, but later left it and became the director of the library at the Vienna court. He was thus acquainted not only with the rich collections of the Jesuits, but extended his horizon to other significant collections, especially those in the capital of the Empire. He carried out extensive collecting and copying work, and made available in his collections many hitherto unpublished documents.[30] One of his colleagues at Vienna, Boldizsár Ádám Kercselich (1715-1778), engaged in extensive research work as well, and is especially remembered for gathering together documents concerning the history of Croatia, Dalmatia, and Slavonia.[31]

* * * * * *

If the eighteenth century broadly conceived was the classic age of documentary collections and the organization and critique of historical documents in Hungary, then the early years of the nineteenth century (indeed even the waning years of the eighteenth) were characterized by attempts to write meaningful historical narratives.[31] This, however, was made possible by the labors of both the known and unknown collectors and organizers of the eighteenth century. After all, these were the individuals who sought out, gathered together, and classified many of the documents which were then used as the building blocks of the historical narratives and supported the evidence for historical understanding. The critical spirit developed and was formalized in the late eighteenth century and early nineteenth centuries and the individuals who developed these principles of criticism and also wrote historical narratives occupy the central ground between the document-gathering generation and the Romantic historiographers of the next generation. One must thus discuss the activities, ideas, and influences of this middle generation of critically-minded scholars and writers, because these individuals served as the connecting link between the Baroque and semi-Enlightened world on the one hand, and the earliest exponents of Romanticism and consciously expressed national sentiment in historical writing on the other.[32]

In terms of obvious influence, the work of the Jesuit historian István Katona (1732-1811) provided many of the early nineteenth-century historians with a collection of well-edited and admirably organized documentary volumes that not only made their work possible, but also made it easier as well. The organizational and critical apparatus that Katona imposed upon the vast amount of material he had so assiduously collected and evaluated remains of inestimable value to the historian of Hungary even in our own day.[33]

In his most significant work, *Historica critica regum Hungariae*,[34] published in 42 volumes between 1779 and 1817, he presented an account of the development of Hungarian history from the earliest times through the eighteenth century. He gathered together a prodigious amount of information, source quotations, scholarly opinions, and whatever else might prove useful or pertinent, and then used all of the published and many of the unpublished and hiterto scarcely known sources of Hungarian history to put together the largest and most comprehensive compendium of the historical development of his country and its peoples. While it is generally agreed that he did not possess the same high degree of critical acumen as his contemporary György Pray,[35] he made up for this apparent shortcoming by a correspondingly greater emphasis upon scholarly apparatus and an almost superhuman effort in collecting source material and presenting it in a coherent and well-organized manner.[36] This extensive work was not only a learned chronological account of the events of Hungarian history, but a careful compendium of scholarly opinions on numerous controversial points, all of which were then fully discussed and illuminated by careful and precise documentary references.[37]

In addition to this major work, Katona wrote and published extensively. Some of the more significant of his smaller works were general outline accounts of Hungarian history for use by his students, such as *Synopsis chronologica historiarum ad sublevadam memoriam historiophilorum concinnata*[38] and *Historia critica primorum hungariae ducum.*[39] He also wrote about the history of the Roman Empire, as well as about the significance of the Crown of St. Stephen.[40] While the aforementioned works were all in Latin, he did compose one brief book in Hungarian, a discussion of the significance and greatness of St. Stephen. One might also note that this work was more didatic in tone than his other writings.[41]

The events of Katona's life are not particularly significant, nor do they possess any intrinsic biographical information worthy of special note; nonetheless, these details may help in understanding some of his attitudes, especially his perseverance in the study of history, in spite of the numerous obstacles placed in his path by the political conditions of his time. The one essential fact about his life was his membership in the Jesuit order and indeed his early interest in history was largely conditioned by this influence on his life. He was always very concerned with teaching, but due to the limitations placed upon Hungarian educational policies, he retired from active teaching already in 1784. Later in his life, however, he returned to this profession, and a few years before his death he became the rector of a seminary.[42] He was always very devoted both to his Catholic faith and to his nation, and the influence he had upon his students attests to these attitudes and commitments. In addition to this marked devotion to faith and nation, he was especially deeply attached to his order; its dissolution left a deep wound on his sensitive spirit.[43] In spite of these difficulties in conjunction with the dissolution of the Jesuits, Katona continued his scholarly activity, still within the service of the Church. While it would be anachronistic to attribute undue significance to the forces of modern nationalism in this part of Europe in Katona's age, the stirrings of national sentiment were becoming audible and did not fail to exercise an impact upon scholarship, although to a lesser extent than on literature. It was in this setting that one must assess the extent of the impact of national sentiment upon the scholarly activities of Katona and many other scholars of this generation in Hungary. It would be reasonable to argue, based upon the corpus of his lifetime involvement in historical studies and the judgments made by others since, that Katona was indeed concerned with the fate and destiny of his nation, but he understood the concept of nation more in terms of categories derived from Enlightened rather than Romantic thought. Indeed, he may not have been fully aware of the transitional character of his concept of nation.

In a memorial tribute written on the 200th anniversary of Katona's death, the historian György Balanyi (1886-1963) made the following observation about his national feelings: "In the defense of the truth of his nation he did not admit of forebearance. At times like these he even placed himself beyond the otherwise fostered solidarity of his order."[44] Katona certainly had a passionate devotion to historical truth and this can be seen not only in his professional commitments, but also in his human ones. Thus, he was a historian dedicated to truth not only by external circumstances, but also on account of a commitment to research and a passionate interest in the past.

In this works he was primarily interested in the solution of historical problems, rather than in connected and graceful narrative. As a consequence of this attitude he presented the results of his researches in a strictly chronological order. Indeed, Katona was and remains renowned for his solution to many chronological disputes in Hungarian history. Another of his great contributions was the fact that he established the validity of many of the documents which previous Jesuit historians had gathered together. One might also add that his emphasis upon chronological accuracy made his work especially useful to he great synthesizers of subsequent generations of scholars.[45]

Katona encountered many obstacles in the course of his scholarly career, not the least of which was gaining access to archives. It was a difficult enough task to locate all of the extant sources and then find that some of these were zealously guarded by individuals with political influence sufficient to deny access. Nonetheless, the perseverance of Katona made it possible for him to overcome some of these difficulties and assemble vast amounts of source material. The completion of this task to the best of his ability was only the smaller of the tasks faced by him as a historian. The organization and criticism of what was discovered consumed most of his efforts. He, as well as the other scholars of that era, also faced difficulties with the censorship. Literary figures, who were in the forefront of the Hungarian national movement, could be found there precisely because of the artistic and invariably allegorical character of literary work. But a historian with a passionate dedication to the search for truth was certain to have difficulties, as Katona certainly had. Owing to good fortune, he managed to obtain the assistance of the Palatine Joseph (1776-1847), the founder of the Hungarian branch of the Habsburgs, and thus was spared at least some of the difficulties with the censorship. In spite of these difficulties and opportunities, he perservered in his chosen profession and in the preface to the last volume of his great work to appear in his lifetime, he wrote as follows about his attitudes and his dedication to the work of the historian:

> For all of this work, undertaken so laboriously and by the sweat of my brow, it is only to God that praise is due. This is because it was He who gave me the inspiration to begin this great task and it was He who with His blessed goodness gave me enough energy to be able to continue and finish this seemingly endless task. God be with you, benevolent reader, pray for me, who am rapidly approaching the grave.[46]

The significance of Katona's work for the subsequent evolution of Hungarian historiography can hardly be denied; not only in terms of the work he left behind, but also in terms of his human qualities. The value of his work is obvious. His commitment to a life of scholarship, especially as manifested by his devotion to truth, could serve as a model. Alexander Flegler (1803-1892), among the earliest chroniclers of the story of Hungarian historical scholarship, made the following observation concerning Katona:

> Katona was a critical individual, who moved with certainty among the given facts, but was not a creative spirit. It is certain that the

exact, not spurious, examination of documents and other historical facts is the first requirement of historical scholarship, without which neither historical research nor effective historical writing is imaginable. But once the dry work has occurred, the facts are further tied together with an invisible spiritual fastener, which has to be discovered in history and put in its proper place, just as the life of man is moved by ideas, feelings, passions and good and bad instincts.[47]

This observation certainly emphasized the dedication to accuracy which permeated the historical works of Katona, but it judged the value of Katona's writings from a different perspective than Katona himself would have judged them. Katona was not concerned with the spiritual connections in and among historical events; rather, his concern was with factual accuracy.

Judged from that perspective, István Katona certainly made a basic contribution to subsequent work in Hungarian history.

The other great figure in the critical and documentary tradition of eighteenth-century historiography was György Pray (1723-1801), who became better known than Katona, probably because he was more intimately involved with other scholars through a wide-ranging correspondence and was also appointed the official historian of Hungary by Maria Theresa in 1773. As in the case of Katona, the events of Pray's life are not especially significant. Born in Érsekujvár [Neuhäusel, Novezamki] in northwestern Hungary, he entered the Jesuit order in 1740, became a librarian at the university of Buda in 1777, canon of Nagyvárad in 1790, a member of the Hungarian Diet in the same year, and then died as an abbot eleven years later.[48]

Pray was the best critical historian among the early historiographers. Indeed, one can state that by his historical work he established the critical spirit as one of the building blocks of Hungarian historiography. Virtually all of his major works exhibit his critical spirit, including also the practice of judicious selection from among diverse sources on related themes.[49] He was concerned, as indeed Katona also was, with chronological accuracy, which was especially evident in his work entitled *Historia regum Hungariae*.[50]

He was influenced not only by his Jesuit predecessors, and especially Miklós Schmitth, but also came into contact with Erasmus Frőlich, an eminent Jesuit historian in Vienna, who encouraged him to collect and study the sources for Hungarian history available there. Pray's attitude toward history and his conception of the nature of historical scholarship was generally typical of his age. He espoused a basically Roman Catholic view of the world, and his ideal can be summed up in terms of these Catholic teachings coupled with a certain measure of patriotism, integrated with a sense of loyalty to the Habsburgs. In spite of these commitments, however, he was rather scrupulous in his dedication to the canons of scholarship. Bálint Hóman (1885-1951), in his brief study of the origins of Hungarian historiography, summed up quite aptly the attitudes and values of Pray: "He was a good Catholic, active member of his order, a loyal subject of the king and a good patriot, but he was not a sectarian and not a politician."[51] An attentive and critical reading of his works permits one to make certain observations concerning both the content and attitudes of his writings. First of all, the main focus of his attention was invariably upon political history, but then this was a general characteristic of that age. Because of this basic political orientation, he was especially concerned with the development of the state and the external history of the institution of kingship. Secondly, it is worthy of note that Pray hardly concerned himself with questions of religion and culture in his writings, in spite of the fact that some of his predecessors and contemporaries in the scholarly world were carrying on extensive documentary research and polemically motivated writing in these areas. Pray was also the best Latin prose stylist of these historians; his style and presentation seemed to be more coherent and his transitions of thought and expression smoother and more meaningful.

It was certainly a positive feature of his life's work that he attempted, and not without success, to foster cooperation among the scholars of his time and he was able to accomplish this because of his position as the official historiographer of Hungary after 1773. Being in almost constant correspondence with most of the historians of his day, Pray became the center of scholarly life. Upon his death there appeared a memorial volume which provided telling testimony of the extent of his influence:

> Elderly Pray is gone. Sunken into a sad sorrow, the banks of both Tisza and Danube bemoan his name. PRAY! Who, with an everlasting pen, could take note of the heroic acts of the whole nation, is dead. No! He will live until the sound of the shepherd's flute can be heard from the Mátra mountains, while Badacsony looks down upon

Balaton, until there will be a Hungarian nation; and that will remain forever, certainly until the Scythian blood of our ancestors flows in our veins.[52]

This panegyric to Pray illustrated not only the esteem in which he was held by his contemporaries, but it undoubtedly manifested an emerging Magyar nationalism, albeit still within the confines of an absolute monarchy and with the necessary and due respect rendered to the existing order. One could argue that the nationalism manifest in this panegyric represented the attitude of those who, while loyal to their own nation and heritage, were loyal to the dynasty as well. This was probably the attitude of Pray and many other scholars of the time, although this was beginning to change under the impact and inspiration of the activities and writings of the circle centered on György Bessenyei (1747-1811) and Ferenc Kazinczy (1759-1831), and more evidently in the activities and writings of the romantic synthesizers and writers looming on the intellectual and cultural landscape.

The Lutheran tradition of historical scholarship was represented in this era by Dániel Cornides (1732-1787), who after Katona and Pray, was the greatest critical historian of the late eighteenth century. He followed in the footsteps of Mátyás Bél and his well-organized personal library collection of historical documents attested to his critical skills.[53] Another representative figure of the Lutheran tradition was János Ribiny (1722-1788), who did extensive work in church history. Among the Calvinists one must mention the scholarly work of Miklós Sinay (1730-1808), who was also involved in the work of gathering and organizing the documents of church history.[54] Members of the proscribed Jesuit order continued their activities, but members of other religious orders also engaged in scholarly activities. Especially significant was the work of the Piarist priest Elek Horányi (1736-1809), who, in his lexical collections dealing with literature and related fields, supplemented the work of the more political history-oriented Pray School by an emphasis upon broadly conceived intellectual history.[55] One cannot conclude even a brief account of eighteenth century Hungarian historical scholarship without at least mentioning Márton György Kovachich (1744-1821) and his son József Miklós Kovachich (1798-1878). They were concerned mostly with the collection and publication of the legal sources of Hungarian history.[56]

The critical tradition in Hungarian historiography found a nineteenth century successor in the person of György Fejér (1766-1851), a student of István Katona, who attempted to perpetuate the ideals which he had learned from that master of historical criticism. Although Fejér's critical acumen was by no means on the same level as that of his teacher, he did edit some significant collections of historical documents, specifically those dealing with diplomatic history.[57] However, Fejér's significance extended beyond historical scholarship proper; many of his publications dealt with theological and philosophical issues. In one of these philosophical writings, *The Development and Shaping of the Human Person* [*Az ember kiformáltatása*], he reflected on his works and aspirations and his affirmation can be construed as a scholar's credo:

> To search for the truth with open eyes and to defend it with valor, to refute the false, to direct the doubtful, to point out the certain, to speak in an understandable manner, to remedy one of the missing dimensions of our national literature—this was my goal.[58]

This statement was certainly more reflective of nationalist sentiment influenced by a Romantic sensibility than some of the previously cited ones. Fejér carried on extensive and far-ranging intellectual activities, and when he died in 1851 he left behind a corpus of work amazing mostly for its quantity and scope of interest. He had continued the methods of the eighteenth century historians with less than consummate skill and coupled it with a still imperfectly and incompletely assimilated romantic sensibility. His work is transitional in character, as ineed the Reform Era (1825-1848) in Hungarian history served as the transition between an imperfectly assimilated Enlightenment heritage and a fully developed National Romanticism. One must also add that the work of some other historians, such as János Keresztély Engel (1770-1814) and Ignác Fessler (1756-1839) was also transitional, but reflected more the synthesis of the skillful use of critical methods and represented a more consciously romantic attitude toward the past.

The activities of these scholars found a valuable supportive dimension in the collections of the various noble families who, influenced by a patriotic fervor, continued to collect not only their family records, but played an active role in the support of scholarship. This work found an institutional dimension in their contributions to newly established national libraries and scholarly associations, and together with the work of writers, poets, and scholars, contributed immeasurably to the fostering of cultural life in the service of national goals immediately before and during the Reform Era. However, the history of this National Romantic orientation in scholarship falls beyond the scope of this brief survey.

NOTES

1. On this point see especially Gyula Dudás, "Történetírásunk a XVIII. században" [Our Historical Writing in the 18th Century], *Hazánk* [Homeland], III (1885), pp. 330-333. Concerning eighteenth and early nineteenth century Hungarian historiography in general, see my doctoral dissertation, *The Ideological and Methodological Foundations of Hungarian Historiography* (New York: St. John's University, 1972), pp. 10-104; and Steven Bela Vardy, *Modern Hungarian Historiography* (Boulder: East European Quarterly, Distributed by Columbia University Press, 1976), pp. 19-37.

2. Márta Mezei, *Történetszemlélet a magyar felvilágosodáas irodalmában* [Attitudes toward History in the Literature of the Hungarian Enlightenment] (Budapest: Akadémiai Kiadó, 1958), p. 11. Especially instructive is the following passage: "Until the serious historical research does not begin in the 1770's, and until the prodigious material gathered together by Katona—Pray—Mátyás Bél, does not make inroads among a broader circle at the beginning of the nineteenth century, it is the literary works which guard over and foster the glory, grief, and lessons of the Hungarian past."

3. See esp. Gyula Szekfű, ed., *Iratok a magyar államnyelv kérdésének történetéhez* [Documents Relative to the Question of the Historical Development of the Language of the Hungarian State] (Budapest: Magyar Történelmi Társulat, 1926), and Gyula Kornis, *A magyar művelődés eszményei* [The Ideals of Hungarian Cultural Development] (Budapest: Királyi Magyar Egyetemi Nyomda, 1927), I, pp. 141-176.

4. There is an extensive literature on Joseph II and Hungary. On the issue of linguistic reform, Henrik Marczali, *Az 1790-1-diki országgyülés*, [The Diet of 1790-1] (Budapest: Magyar Tudományos Akadémia, 1907), I, pp. 341-393.

5. There were hardly any meaningful interpretative works produced on the history of Hungary during the eighteenth century, with the exception of some textbooks and works in Latin. The discussion concerning the

role of the scholar in the rebirth of Hungarian culture is evident only after 1790. Kornis, op. cit., vol. I, pp. 387-391.

6. László Ravasz, "A világnézet," [The World View], in Sándor Domanovszky, ed., *Magyar művelődéstörténet* [History of Hungarian Culture] (Budapest: Magyar Történelmi Társulat, 1942), vol. 5, pp. 316-317.

7. The activities of the Jesuits is discussed in more detail in my doctoral dissertation, *The Ideological and Methodological Foundations of Hungarian Historiography*, chaps. I-II.

8. Published at Pest by Mathias Trattner in 1792.

9. Peter F. Sugar, "The Influence of the Enlightenment and the French Revolution in Eighteenth Century Hungary," *Journal of Central European Affairs*, XVII (January 1958), pp. 331-355.

10. The text of the poem is given in János Horváth, ed., *Magyar versek könyve* [Book of Hungarian Poems] (Budapest: Magyar Szemle Társaság, 1942), p. 216.

11. Ravasz, op. cit., p. 317.

12. Jószef Szinnyei, "A magyar történetirodalom" [Hungarian Historial Literature], *Századok* [Centuries], V (1871), pp. 396-404.

13. This tripartite division was pointed out by Bálint Hóman, *A forráskutatás és forráskritika története Magyarországon* [The History of Source Collection and Source Criticism in Hungary], reprinted in Bálint Hóman, *Történetirás és forráskritika* [Historical Writing and Source Criticism] (Budapest: Magyar Történelmi Társulat, 1938), p. 416.

14. Ibid., p. 415 and Dudás, op. cit., p. 333.

15. Concerning Hevenesi, Hóman, op. cit., pp. 337-351.

16. Concerning Debreczeni, see Gyula Ferenczy, *Debreczeni Pál életrajza* [The Biography of Pál Debreczeni] (Debrecen, 1882).

17. Czvittinger was also considered one of the pioneers of the writing of literary history. See esp., Károly Máté, "Irodalomtörténetirásunk kialakulása" [The Development of the Writing of Literary History], *Minerva*, VII (1928), pp. 83, 131-133.

18. Published in 1753; Hóman, op. cit., p. 398.

19. The work was eventually finished by István Fosztó, Mihály Kozma, and János Kozma.

20. Published in three volumes at Nagyszombat, 1737-1749.

21. Concerning Kazy, Hóman, op. cit., p. 399. His work in educational history, *Historia Universitatis Tyrnaviensis*, 1737.

22. *Hungaria diplomatica temporibus Mathias de Hunyad* (2 vols., Vienna, 1767-1771).

23. On Bőd see esp. Imre Révész, *Bőd Péter mint történetiró* [Péter Bód as a Historian] (Kolozsvár, 1916).

24. On Bél, a good summary is Imre Wellman, "Bél Mátyás," *Történelmi Szemle* [Historical Review], XXII (1979), pp. 381-391.

25. Bél wrote as follows about this: "And I was always truly convinced that what the Bible is for the theologian, the written law for the legal scholar, common sense for the philosopher, the document is for the historian. If only the grudging archives would finally open before us." Introduction to *Adparatus ad historiam Hungariae,* quoted by Alexander Flegler, *A magyar történetirás története* [The History of Hungarian Historical Writing] (Pest: Franklin Társulat, 1877), pp. 147-148.

26. M. Schmeizel was instrumental in the training of a whole generation of Transylvanian Saxon historians, among them József Teutsch, György Haner, and Márton Felmer. Most of their works remained in manuscript. Mihály Rotarides was also one of the disciples of Schmeizel. He was actively involved in the collection and criticism of sources concerning the history of Hungarian science.

27. Concerning Dugonics consult Pál Pándi, ed., *A magyar irodalom története 1772-től 1849-ig* [The History of Hungarian Literature from 1772 to 1849] (Budapest: Akadémiai Kiadó, 1965), pp. 114-118.

28. Buda, 1748-1760.

29. Pozsony, 1785. See the biography by Mihály Szilinszky, *Wallaszky Pál élete* [The Life of Pál Wallaszky] (Budapest, 1910), and Máté, op. cit., p. 133.

30. *Analecta monumentorum omnis aevi vindobonensia* (2 vols., Vienna, 1761-1762). He also published the writings of Ursinus Velius and Miklós Oláh. See L. Gyurkovits, "Kollár Ádámnak élete, tudós munkáji s kéziratok gyüjteménye" [The Life, Scholarly Work and Collected Documents of Ádám Kollár], *Tudományos Gyüjtemény* [Scientific Collection], X (1823), pp. 3-26.

31. Concerning these early attempts at historical writing, Louis Lékai, "Historiography in Hungary, 1790-1848," *Journal of Central European Affairs,* XIV (1954), pp. 3-18. A more extensive account is the same writer's *A magyar történetirás, 1790-1830* [Hungarian Historical Writing, 1790-1830] (Budapest: Stephaneum, 1942).

32. The best known among these were Benedek Virág and István Horvát.

33. For bibliographical information, József Szinnyei, *Magyar irók élete és munkái* [The Life and Works of Hungarian Writers] (Budapest: Hornyánszky Viktor, 1891-1914), VI, pp. 1201-1202.

34. István Katona, *Historia critica regum Hungariae* (42 vols., Pest, Pozsony, Kassa, Buda, Kolozsvár, Vác, and Kalocsa, 1779-1817). The last volume was published after Katona's death.

35. Hóman, op. cit., p. 410.

36. Jenő Pintér, *A magyar irodalom története* [The History of Hungarian Literature] (Budapest, Bibliotheca, 1942), I, pp. 553-554; and Dudás, op. cit., pp. 327-328.

37. Szinnyei, op. cit., VI, p. 1199.

38. Tyrnaviae, 1771-1775.

39. Pest, 1775-1778.

40. These works are entitled as follows: *Synopsis Historiae Romanorum* (Buda, 1782), and *Dissertatio critica in Commentarium Alexii Horányi . . . de Sacra Hungariae Corona* (Buda, 1790).

41. *Szent István magyarok első királya dicsérete* [The Praise of St. Stephen, the First King of the Hungarians] (Vienna, 1738). It was originally delivered as a sermon.

42. Szinnyei, op. cit., VI, pp. 1197-1202.

43. György Balanyi, "Katona István emlékezete" [The Remembrance of István Katona], *Magyar kultúra* [Hungarian Culture], XXXIX, (1932), p. 499.

44. Ibid., p. 500.

45. Hóman, op. cit., p. 410. Hóman's observation is worth quoting: "The great synthesizers of the nineteenth century—Fessler, Szalay, and Horváth—were able to write their comprehensive accounts first of all by relying on the material published by Katona."

46. Preface to vol. 41 of *Historia critica regum Hungariae*, cited in Balanyi, op. cit., p. 502.

47. Flegler, op. cit., pp. 159-160.

48. Szinnyei, op. cit., II, pp. 111-118.

49. See esp. the following: *Annales veteres Hunnorum, Avarum, et Hungarorum, ab anno ante natum Christum 210 ad annum Christi 997 deducti* (Vienna, 1761); *Dissertatio historico-critica de Sancto Ladislao*

Hungariae rege (Poszony, 1774); and *Annales regum Hungariae* (5 vols., Vienna, 1763-1770).

50. Buda, 1801; Flegler, op. cit., pp. 152-154 makes reference to the chronological accuracy considered so important by Pray.

51. Hóman, op. cit., p. 379.

52. Anonymous, *Fő Tisztelendő Pray György Magyar Ország történetírójának emlékezete* [In Rememberance of the Very Reverend György Pray, the Historian of Hungary] (Pest: Trattner Mátyás betüivel, 1801), p. 1.

53. Hóman, op. cit., p. 410.

54. Ibid., pp. 411-412.

55. Pintér, op. cit., I, pp. 559-560.

56. Flegler, op. cit., pp. 211-213.

57. His most important work in the collection of diplomatic documents was the *Codex diplomaticus Hungariae ecclesiasticus ac civiles* (43 vols., Budae, 1829-1844). Lékai, in his study of Hungarian historiography, makes only passing references to Fejér, and passes judgment on him in the following terms: "The development was a downward path there too, and the lowpoint is marked by Fejér's *Codex diplomaticus,* in which it is difficult to praise anything except the dedication of the editor." Lékai, op. cit., p. 170.

58. The book, *Az ember kiformáltatása* [The Development and Shaping of the Human Person], was published at Buda in 1835. The quoted passage is from Szinnyei, op. cit., III, pp. 254-255.

James F. Clarke

Venelin and Bulgarian Origins*

For the founding fathers of Slavistics at the beginning of the nineteenth century, a central preoccupation was the "Bulgarian Problem" that was expressed in the following questions: Who were Cyril and Methodius (since 1981 "Apostles to Europe")? What kind of Slavic language did they use? Where was the homeland of this language and where was it first employed? What came first, Cyrillic or Glagolitic? And finally: who and what were the Bulgarians? The last question was obviously at the heart of this whole problem. One may rightly say that Bulgaristics (as it is now called) was the core of Slavic Studies.[1] There were heated arguments, even quarrels, among J. Dobrovský, B. Kopitar, P. J. Šafařik and others, each of whom had his pet theory. All were interested in the interrelationship of the Slavic peoples and their languages.[2] Counting and comparing Slavic languages continues to be a favored occupation. At first there was a tendency to classify Modern

---

* This essay is an elaboration of a paper given at a conference on Southeast European Studies at Ohio State University, Columbus, in 1981, in connection with the 1300th anniversary of the Bulgarian state. I wish to acknowledge the assistance of a former graduate student, Luba Bilyj; as well as of a paper on Venelin by Mons. Basil Shereghy at a special session on the 1300th anniversary at the Duquesne University History Forum organized by Professor Steven B. Vardy in 1981.

Bulgarian as a sub-species of "Orthodox Serbian."[3] None of the pioneer Slavists got to Bulgaria. Although Šafařik for years lived in Novi Sad (Neusatz, Újvidék) and would have given his eyeteeth for the chance, he never made it to Bulgaria. Vuk Karadžić, author of the first analytical description of Bulgaria, depended on Bulgarian informants from Macedonia. His Russian counterpart, Peter Koeppen, did get to see some Bulgarians in Transylvania.[4]

The Bulgarian problem was complicated by what might be called a "layered" people and history, with an earlier Slavic substructure and a non-Slav Bulgar or "Proto-Bulgarian," overlay, a situation common to Russia and other European countries. It was hard to distinguish the two kinds of Bulgarians. Regarding the Proto-Bulgars there were two main schools: the Finno-Ugric and the more common Turko-Tatar. Whereas considerable information was available on the medieval, basically Byzantine period, very little was known about contemporary Bulgaria.

Into this equivocal situation, there stepped an unknown young Carpatho-Ruthenian, Iuri Venelin, in 1829, with a 230-page book on *The Ancient and Present-Day Bulgarians in their Political, Ethnographic, Historical and Religious Relationship to the Russians. Historical-Critical Researches,* demolishing existing theories of Bulgarian origins.[5]

Iuri Venelin was born Iuri Hutsa (Hucza) in 1802) in Nagy Tibava, Bereg County in Carpathian Northeast Hungary. His father, a Uniate priest, died when he was ten. At his uncle's insistence he studied theology at Ungvár (Uzhgorod) and Szatmár (Satu Mare), but escaped it and his relatives by changing his name and enrolling in his hobby, history, at the University of Lemberg (Lvov, Lviv). With his cousin, I. I. Molnár, he took off over the mountains in 1823 for the "promised land" of Russia. On his way he stopped off at Kishinev, a center of the large Bulgarian emigration in Bessarabia, where he was well received by the Governor-General, Imzov, a Bulgarophile, and given a job as mathematics teacher at the local seminary. His two years in Kishinev, where he got to know many Bulgarians, were decisive for the rest of his life. He arrived in Moscow in 1825 with six rubles. There, after 1829, he got acquainted with a number of prominent Slavophiles.

For practical reasons Venelin was persuaded to enroll in medicine in Moscow University, but he continued with history, his passion since Lvov. He was encouraged by Mihail P. Pogodin, the influential editor of *Moskovskie Vedomosti* (Moscow Gazette) and a blatant Russian nationalist, who shared Venelin's Slavophile views. Pogodin, in whose house Venelin lived for some time, encouraged him in his writing and helped him financially in publishing his first major historical work in 1829. In the same year he successfully finished medicine.[6] Venelin's historical study caused quite a furor and gained him immediate notoriety. It also brought him, with Pogodin's recommendation, 6000 rubles for a travelling fellowship in 1830 from the Russian Academy. His goal was to spend two years in Bulgaria, Thrace, part of Macedonia, Athos, Wallachia and Moldavia to study modern Bulgarian and bring back historical, philosophical and archeological material. Venelin even hoped to go on to Venice and Rome in search of Slavs.

Venelin's study trip was over-ambitious and unfortunate in its timing. Acually he was preceded by at least one other Russian, V. G. Teplyakov, who had been assigned to archeological and historical research in Bulgaria by General M. S. Vorontsov, commander of the Russian Army occupying Varna. Teplyakov spent three months there in 1829 and later wrote his *Letters from Bulgaria*.[7]

In 1830 Bulgaria had not yet settled down after the latest Russo-Turkish War (1828-1829).[8] After a long delay in Odessa, Venelin, with Russian military protection, spent three weeks in Varna and vicinity, found those natives who had not fled ignorant and suspicious; heard and scolded Bulgarians speaking Turkish (perhaps Gagauzi who still live near Varna); but avoided the cholera epidemic. Venelin moved on to Kavarna (Dobrudja) and Silistria on the Danube and then spent some time in Bucharest. In the Metropolitan Library he found an unfriendly reception, but also books he had not seen in Russia and a number of charters. He returned to Moscow at the end of 1831 with 66 Slavonic charters from the fifteenth to the seventeenth century, mostly from the Principalities and Bessarabia, 20 facsimiles, and about 50 Bulgarian folksongs, 40 of which he got from refugees in Odessa, plus a knowledge of Modern Bulgarian. He presented a more than 300-page "Grammar of the Present-Day Bulgarian Dialect" to the Academy. The reviewer of his manuscript, the leading Russian Slavist, A. H. Vostokov, concluded in his report of 1835 that, although he disagreed with a number of points, he thought its publication would be useful. However, two years later Venelin was informed that it did not merit publication by the Academy. It never has been published, probably because it reflected Venelin's view of the Bulgarian language, which he felt was (or should be) a Russian dialect. The Academy did publish Venelin's charters after his death.[9]

One of Venelin's great interests was the study of folk songs, which he felt had great importance for a nation's history and characteristics. He collected some Bulgarian songs on his trip. Others came from a collection by Vuk Karadžić. In 1835 Venelin himself published a small book, *On the Character of the Folk Songs of Transdanubian Slavs,* which had considerable influence.[10]

At the Sofia Congress of Bulgaristics in 1918, an authority on Venelin, Elka Dorosieva, began her paper on Venelin by saying he was so well known no biographical introduction was needed.[11] On the other hand, a Russian chairman of a Slavic Department of a prominent Southern university confessed he had never heard of Venelin. Even so I cannot afford the luxury of recounting in detail Venelin's multifaceted life and achievements, although his public life lasted scarcely a dozen years. Living in the heyday of Romantic Panslavism and nascent Slavistics, Venelin was an ultra Slavophile, one might even say a dedicated Slavomaniac. His romantic Slavophilism embraced all the Slavs, but over and above that he was an admirer of Russia, his spiritual fatherland. Among the other Slavs his predilection was for the South Slavs, but because of the Bulgarian impact of his 1829 book, he became a lifelong Bulgarophile. He adopted the Bulgarians and they him.

Venelin obtained a doctorate in medicine instead of history, but he never practiced his profession. Instead, he supported himself by tutoring. In 1834 he turned down the offer (via Pogodin) of a three-year job tutoring (for 4000 rubles) the children of the Russian ambassador in Constantinople, A. P. Butenev. He did this because of the vain hope of getting the Moscow University chair of Slavic studies. Eventually he did get a minor post as inspector of the Institutes of the Order of St. Catherine and Alexander (orphanages?). He died and was buried in Moscow in 1839, after a short and unhappy life of only thirty-seven years.

All his life Venelin had been a voracious and indiscriminate reader and note-taker. He was fluent in Greek and Latin, knew German, French, Italian, Spanish, Magyar and some English, and of course all the Slavic languages and some Turkish.[12] In Kishinev he even started to learn Albanian. He was almost as much, and as bad a philologist (at heart) as a historian. This may have been part of his undoing, as he was obsessed with pseudo-etimology and the seeming similarity of words and names in different languages, as evidence. He was very conversant with Byzantine sources.

In 1835 Venelin was asked by Moscow University to prepare a prospectus or syllabus for the University for the teaching of Slavic languages and literatures, a sort of area studies program. By doing this, along with his Bulgarian grammar, he hoped to be appointed to the Slavic chair at Moscow University. But he was frustrated in this goal. After J. P. Šafařik and other Czech and Slovak Slavists had turned down the offers of Slavic chairs at Russian universities, four young Russians were given extended traveling fellowships to study in Slavic countries, prior to their university appointments. One of these was O. M. Bodyanski, a disciple and supporter of Venelin, who was eventually appointed to the Moscow chair. The others were P. I. Preis (St. Petersburg), I. I. Sreznevski (Harkov), and Victor Grigorovich (Kazan). All were instructed to visit Bulgaria, but the only one to get there was Grigorovich (1844-1845) who brought back "rich loot," to quote the envious Šafařik.[13] Preis was warned by the prince-bishop (*vladika*) of Montenegro not to go to Bulgaria unless he had two heads.

Venelin left unpublished in the hands of Molnár as much or more than he had published. Some of his publications were published posthumously, thanks to Bodyanski.[14] Venelin was a Slavic Don Quixote, tilting in all directions. His bibliography, almost as much a mess as his biography, consists of about forty-one published items.[15] His unpublished work, much of it unfinished, and on all kinds of unrelated subjects, including a piece on the Etruscan language, has forty-four items.[16] In addition, he left many boxes full of notes.[17] Although there were some who wanted everything Venelin wrote published, fortunately this has not materialized.

Venelin had intended putting out major works on each of the Slavic peoples, but the only such work he managed to publish in his lifetime was his already mentioned study, *Ancient and Present-Day Bulgarians*, published in 1829.[18] In spite of entreaties from Bulgarians, Venelin laid aside the continuation of his first work. He reported that one reason for so long delaying a reply to Vasili Aprilov's first letter was that he had decided to give up his Bulgarian research and did not want to upset his Bulgarian friend on that account. Yet in his letter to Aprilov dated April 9, 1837, he referred to a second volume of his Bulgarian work, which would not be a history, but a critical discussion of many side issues of no interest to the ordinary Bulgarian reader.[19]

However, a second book on Bulgaria by Venelin did appear in 1849, edited by his cousin Molnár, with a long introduction by Piotr Bezsonov, who had known Venelin. It was published with the aid of a rich Bulgarian merchant, I. N. Denkoglu, under the title: *Critical Researches on the History of the Bulgarians, by I. I. Venelin. From the Arrival of the Bulgarians on the Thracian Peninsula to 968, or the Subjection of Bulgaria by the Russian Grand Prince Svyatoslav.*[20] The censor, Feodor Golubinski, professor of history in the Moscow Theological Seminary, removed about 50 pages of repetitions and errors, some of which he corrected in footnotes. An example is Venelin's assertion that Cyril and Methodius labored only in Bulgaria. However, for the Bulgarian version of 1853, most of the excisions were restored by Bodyanski in the thought that the Bulgarian national ego would be flattered.[21]

Venelin gives a spirited defense of the Bulgarian character of Cyril and Methodius.[22] He also has a discussion of their language, in a typical Venelin rebuttal:

> And now we are left with 'Bulgaro-Macedonian.' But does this last word designate some new language or dialect? No: Macedonia is the name of a country, but its inhabitants are Bulgarians, who can be called Macedonians because they live in Macedonia. Therefore, Macedonian means Bulgarian. And as for the question, what to call the form of the general Slavic language? It is enough to call it simply Bulgarian. And for the further and more exact translation of the Scriptures, the word Macedonian can be added, since it is known that the Bulgarian language is subdivided into its dialects.[23]

Venelin's 1849 sequel is largely a historical narrative from the conclusion of his 1829 book. It carries the history of the Bulgarians up to 968, based largely on Byzantine sources. The most useful part of the 1849 volume is the long introduction by Piotr Bezsonov.[24] Obviously Venelin's second book on Bulgaria, even though translated, could have no current impact on Venelin's Bulgarian connection.

Meanwhile, Venelin's only other work on the Slavs was published by Molnár in 1846 under the title: *The Ancient and Present-Day Slovenes, in their Political, Ethnographic, Historical and Religious Relations with the Russians. Historical-Critical Researches.*[25] According to Molnár, Bulgarians insisted on having the fifteen sheets on the Slovenes, which Venelin had started printing in 1834, published in 1841.[26] For the sake of completeness Molnár decided to add "relevant" items from Venelin's papers, changing the title page. The title page reads "1841," the censor's OK is dated 1841, Molnár's Preface is dated June 1846, and his biographical sketch of Venelin, April 1846.

The Slovenes is an extraordinary hodge-podge of related and irrelevant material on Slovenes, Slovaks and Slavs, whom Venelin (or Molnár) appears to have equated. It begins Slovene history in 9 A.D. There is a long chapter (XI) on Slovene letters (123 pages), which includes Etruscan and Albanian. Obviously, much of the "credit" for this compilation must go to Molnár. An extraordinary feature is that it received 319 advance subscriptions from Bulgarians, mostly from Odessa and from the Left Bank Bulgarians. It must have been a shock when they opened their copies. The best part and prime source is a long introductory biographical sketch of Venelin's private and scholarly life by Molnár.[27]

In 1856 Molnár put out a second edition of the pioneer 1829 work, unfortunately without Venelin's introduction, but with a useful introduction by Bezsonov and with minor footnote corrections and additions.[28] As an appendix it includes (as does the first edition) excerpts from Chaplain R. Walsh's interesting journey from Constantinople to Bucharest, which Venelin added to make up for his paucity of knowledge of contemporary Bulgaria.[29]

Venelin's basic iconoclastic thesis of the Slavic character of the Proto-Bulgars and their history had few takers in the learned Slavic world, but it did stir up a bitter controversy from which Venelin's patron Pogodin did not escape. In his classic *Slavic Antiquities,* the dean of European Slavists, P. J. Šafařik, wrote:

> Recently a number of scholars have wanted to declare the Bulgarians as originally Slavs, but wrongly, since all Byzantine historians declare the Bulgarians who came from the Don and Volga as ethnic relatives of the Huns and Kuturgurs. Even Nestor, who followed popular tradition, did not include the Bulgarians among the Slavic peoples, but along with the Avars, Hungarians and Khazars.

To this Safarik added a footnote, asserting that Venelin, who in his *Ancient and Present-Day Bulgarians* (1829)—in contrast to the well-known historian Engel and others—"considers the Bulgarians Slavs, must soon likewise designate the Huns, Khazars, Magyars as Slavs, which will please no one."[30] Indeed, by insisting on the Slavic character of the Proto-Bulgars, Venelin had painted himself into a corner. In a letter to Bartolomej Kopitar, Šafařik wrote: "Nothing is more repulsive for me than exaggerated Slavomania . . . ."[31]

Given the state of literacy and political upheaval among Bulgarians in 1829, the impact of Venelin's first Bulgarian work on them was gradual and indirect, but decisive, even though there never was a Bulgarian translation. The Bulgarians were suffering from an inferiority complex and shame at their alleged Turkic origins. With a stroke of the pen (in 230 pages!) Venelin rescued them from the Turks (and Greeks) and gave them a Slavic identity, as well as a splendid history and a membership in the community of Slavic nations, headed by the Russians.

Venelin's 1829 book had scarcely 20 pages on the contemporary Bulgarians. The bulk of the book is a polemic refutation of the conclusions of such German historians as Schlözer, Thuneman and Engel and of the Serbian Rajić. Venelin based his arguments largely on a play on words, more specifically on the seeming similarity of names, largely derived from Byzantine sources. He was obsessed with names as historical evidence. "Rudolph," for example, is not German, but the Slavic *Radulo;* "Baudoine" is the Serbian *Baldovich,* and so forth.[32]

Aside from his obsession with Slavs, Venelin had many other interests derived from his omnivorous and eclectic reading, most of which were reflected in his published and unpublished works. Among the forty-four unpublished subjects, his literary executor Molnár lists studies on Julius Caesar, the Etruscans, the names of all of Attila's relatives, Russian sea trade in the eleventh century, comments on Hungarian orthography, negotiations of Sir Thomas Roe at the Porte, etc. A list of his forty-one published works, from 1828 to 1896, is given by his biographer, Tamara Baitsura.[33]

A subject which came naturally to Venelin and which endeared him to Russian nationalists was the Normanist controversy. As might be expected, Venelin was a staunch anti-Normanist. He was the author of *Skandinavomania,* which ties in with his thesis of the southern origin of Russians, Ukrainians and Bulgars.[34]

Why did Venelin adopt the Bulgarians and vice versa? Aside from his Bulgarian contacts in Kishinev, at the beginning of his 1829 book he gives the following reasons: The Russian wars with Turkey drew attention to Bulgaria; there was the mystery about Church Slavonic language origins; even the notable Dobrovský put Macedonia under the Serbs and referred to "Serbo-Bulgaro-Macedonia"; Karamzin (the first modern Russian historian) did not even mention the Bulgarians; most ethnographers in enumerating the Slavs omit them as though they did not exist, like the Pomeranian Slavs. As he wrote, "It is unforgivable to forget the Bulgarians from whose hands we received our baptism, who taught us to write and to read, in whose native language is held the church liturgy, [and] in whose language for the most part everything was written until Lomonosov... *quod erat demonstrandum.*"[35]

In Chapter II of his work entitled: "Evaluation of the Evidence of the Tatar Origin of the Bulgars" (pages 23-60), Venelin undertakes to demolish Engel's "dogma" based on evidence concerning the Tatar origin of the Bulgarians and their alleged transformation into Slavs. In his view, to deduce the Tatar origin of the Bulgars from the title of their rulers (hagan/khagan, han/khan) is like Latinizing the Russians for using "imperator," or Slavicizing the Magyars for "király."[36] Venelin had it in for Engel. After 37 pages Venelin concluded his "refutation" of Engel as follows: "Having analyzed and reviewed briefly the so-called evidence to the Tatarism of the ancient Bulgars, it is necessary to revert to the true historical situation, [namely] that the ancient Bulgars were not of a Tatar, nor of a Turkish, but of a still existing Slavic race."[37] Likewise Venelin disposes of Engel's second thesis concerning the Bulgars' linguistic transformation. How could the Tatar Bulgars, asks Venelin, be metamorphosed into Slavs between 680 and 863 (their conversion to Christianity), when the Greeks have survived as Greeks for 2000 years in spite of all comers! To Engel's arguments for the Slavicizing of Tatar Bulgars through trade, literature, religion, etc., Venelin replies, "Ba, ba!"[38] In conclusion he repeats: "The Bulgars were a Slavic race, not just in the 9th century, but also in the 8th, 7th, 6th, 5th, 4th, 3rd, 2nd and 1st, right back to the ancient past."[39]

Venelin's Chapter V is on "The Bulgars on the Volga and their Migration under the Name of Huns (Avars, Khazars) to the Danube," (pages 95-104). In this case "Volga" does not mean Volga, but the area between the Volga and the Don (p. 105). Similarly, the Russian chronicler Nestor's reference to the Bulgars coming from "Khazaria" really means Bulgaria, a place rather than an ethnic name (p. 138), like Bulgarians from Macedonia.

Although the title of the 1829 book includes the Bulgars' relations with the Russians, there is very little specifically on that topic. In his view, the Volga Bulgars were one of three (and the leading) related Slavic elements in Russia, along with the Russians and the Little Russians (Ukrainians). The Bulgarian-Russian empire in the fourth century and later extended from the Volga to perhaps beyond the Caucasus and the Danube in the south, and the Baltic in the north. Venelin's evidence for the alleged relationship between the Bulgars and the Russians is that they had similar plural gods and similar customs, as seen in Priscus. "Ergo the Bulgars are part of the Russian people."[40]

Venelin equates "Bulgar" and "Hun." The Hun-Avar-Khazar state actually was the kingdom of the Russians, of which the Bulgars were the largest part.[41] Venelin includes, in Russian translation, Priscus's embassy from Byzantium to Attila (pages 111-42) as evidence for the Huns' alleged Slavicism.

In his last chapter entitled "The Military-Political Role Played by Russia in Europe under the Rule of Attila and its Dominion Over Other States" (pages 199-224), Venelin follows Attila—the "Russian (Bulgarian) Tsar" all around Europe. The book ends with the grandiose funeral of Attila, the "Slavic patriot." He compares this funeral with contemporary funeral customs in Carpatho-Ruthenia, and then concludes with a panagyric to Attila.[42]

There is no need to say much more about Venelin's Bulgarian sequel published by Molnár in 1849. It continues Slavic Bulgarian history from the death of Attila to the defeat of Bulgaria by the Russian Grand Prince Svyatoslav in 968. It is based largely on Byzantine sources and on Lebeau's *Le Bas Empire*. After Venelin gets past 681, his narrative becomes more Orthodox. It had the advantage, however, of having been translated into Bulgarian soon after it was published (1849-1853). By then the Bulgarian national revival was well under way, even though triggered by a phony start in 1829. One can imagine how flattered Bulgarians were by Venelin's "discoveries."

Although Venelin had studied some history and philology at Lvov and Szeged, he was basically an autodidact and amateur scholar. While he often refers to "historical criticism," he was carried away by his own preconceived theories. He was also inclined to be conceited, snobbish and intolerant. But he had enormous motivation, energy, and enthusiasm, in spite of his poor health.

It is unlikely that anyone has read any of Venelin's books lately. They are virtually unreadable, although in their day they were "best sellers."[43] Most writers, especially Bulgarians, tend to ignore or avoid, or at best treat with kid gloves Venelin's crackpot theories of Slavic, including Bulgarian and Russian origins and early history. They dwell rather on his unquestioned positive impact on the Bulgarian national revival.[44]

If it can be said that any one person helped revitalize a whole people, in this case the Bulgarians, that man was Venelin. Venelin unwittingly upstaged his eighteenth-century predecessor, Paisii of Hilendar, and temporarily even, overshadowed him. Yet, who knows what might have become of Paisii's legacy, if Venelin had not come along to keep the spark alive. Paisii may be likened to John the Baptist, heralding the "pre-renaissance," while Venelin was the "savior" of Bulgarian national consciousness. Paisii remained unpublished until fifteen years after Venelin's history was printed and could therefore circulate only anonymously until 1844. Yet Venelin knew about and valued Paisii. Paisii was rediscovered and rehabilitated in 1871 by Bulgaria's first professionally trained historian, Marin Drinov, professor of history at Harkov University.[45] Naturally, Drinov was critical of Venelin's Slav origins theories.

Venelin's role in the Bulgarian national revival is an oft-told story. It was in the nature of a delayed chain reaction. It began with a classic "Saul to Paul" episode: Vasili Aprilov, a wealthy Bulgarian vodka merchant in Odessa, and an active Hellenophile, accidentally came across Venelin's book in 1831 and became an instant Bulgarian nationalist—a "born-again" Bulgarian, to use his phrase. After a long delay, because he could not locate Venelin, Aprilov finally wrote to him in 1836. Venelin's reply was written in 1836. Then he lost Aprilov's address (or so he claimed), rewrote the letter in March 1837, and then, after getting another letter from Aprilov in June, finally dispatched it on September 27th of that year.[46] This first letter became a blueprint for collaboration and for the collection of all kinds of Bulgarian folklore, and was circularized by Aprilov via Neofit Rilski to the small Bulgarian intelligentsia. In spite of this lame start, a fruitful collaboration resulted. Aprilov became a clearing house between Venelin and Bulgaria. He and his Odessa colleagues, the Palauzov brothers, established the first "modern" Bulgarian Lancastrian-type school in their home town Gabrovo and installed the Bucharest-trained Rila monk Neofit Rilski as teacher. Neofit became a focal point of the Venelin transmission belt in Bulgaria. He was the author of the first systematic Bulgarian grammar and many other textbooks. He also translated the New Testament, and is generally regarded as the "patriarch" of the first stages of the national revival.[47] His pupils disseminated the Venelin-Aprilov initiatives all over Bulgaria, and even within the Bulgarian colony of Bucharest. One of these disciples, Anastas Kipilovski, boasted he had read Venelin's book six times,[48] while another, G. Th. Peshakov, wrote an ode to Venelin. But Venelin is reported to have said that he would have preferred a Bulgarian folk song.[49]

Venelin became the first, somewhat caustic, chronicler of nascent Bulgarian literature, stimulated in part by himself. In 1838, he published a book *On the Birth of New Bulgarian Literature,* with selections from his correspondence with Aprilov. Aprilov in 1841 published his *Dawn of New Bulgarian Education.* These two works are important sources for the Bulgarian Renaissance.[50]

Because Venelin was elevated overnight to the position of oracle and arbiter of all things Bulgarian, and because he was a devotee of Old Bulgarian and of the Russian language, he decreed against the Bulgarian post-positive article ("ta-ta-ta"), which was missing from all other Slavic languages, including Russian. With this he worsened the already chaotic state of the infant Bulgarian literary language and ruined the career of at least one Bulgarian writer. He castigated Vuk Karadžić, creator of the modern Serbian language for reducing literary Serbian to the spoken (vulgar) "swine-herd" level and for eliminating several Russian letters.[51] Venelin was appalled by Bulgarian orthography, as was Neofit, who also opposed the literary use of the vernacular. Neofit exclaimed in his 1835 *Grammar,* "Oh you language, degenerate and uncontrolled!" Another pro-Venelin writer, referring to linguistic "modernisms," compared them to unnatural "filth," like a monkey giving birth to a human (or vice versa).[52] Nevertheless, Venelin's insistence on a single literary language was a positive contribution.[53]

One might say Venelin came to look on himself as the "guru" of the Bulgarian national revival, for so he was hailed by his admirers. In the language question he failed: Bulgarian has retained the "ta-ta-ta," but it has borrowed freely from Russian vocabulary—over 2000 words up to World War II. But we may credit Venelin with stimulating the beginnings of Bulgarian historiography. Aprilov himself became the first amateur Bulgarian historian (not counting Paisii) with his *Bulgarian Charters.*[54]

Venelin was impressed with the importance of folk songs as historical and ethnographic sources. His instructions to Aprilov for undiscriminatingly collecting Bulgarian folklore inaugurated this aspect of Bulgarian literary activity.[55] Nevertheless, there were Greek-educated Bulgarians at home, including Neofit Rilski, who were jealous of the patronizing emigré Bulgarians and of Venelin's pontifications. In a letter to his fellow Hellenist, Raina Popovich, Neofit complained of Odessa trying to lead Bulgarians around like monkeys or blind men.[56] Inside Bulgarians were cautious about Russian connections and suspicious of creeping Russomania. Venelin obviously gets much credit for saving the Bulgarians from the Turks and diverting them from the Greeks, but Aprilov should get some of this credit. Venelin took his Bulgarian rebuffs too personally.

Finally, one of Venelin's most important and lasting contributions was to draw Russian attention to the contemporary Bulgarians and vice versa at a time when the Bulgarian intelligentsia were going to school in Athens and the Austro-Slavs were eyeing the Bulgarians. As Elka Dorosieva has pointed out, Venelin may not have been chronologically the first, but what he started was destined to grow at the hands of Pogodin, the Aksakovs, Bodyanski and many more Bulgarophiles until it climaxed in Russia's liberation of Bulgaria in 1878. Venelin's 1830-1831 tour and that of Bodyanski, Preis, Sreznevski, Grigorivich and others had got the wind up in Vienna and Prague; Venelin helped undercut the Austro-Slavism of Šafařik, Kopitar and the Vienna authorities regarding Bulgarians.

Venelin was legally a Hungarian, ethnically a Carpatho-Ruthenian, but at heart a Russian, even a Great Russian. But he was also a Slavophile and a Bulgarophile. He had a special interest in Ukrainians and fondly remembered his Carpatho-Ruthenian-Russian birthplace. No doubt, he would have been pleased to see it back in the Russian-Ukrainian fold. Venelin was also a Romantic. At one time he wanted to write a novel about fourteenth-century Bulgaria. He may be credited with starting the Romantic movement in Bulgarian literature, perhaps less by what he wrote, than by how he wrote it; less by his erudition, than through the effect of his personal enthusiasm on others. All who knew him speak of this.[57]

Venelin died prematurely in 1839, poor, sick and lonely. The promise of his early years had petered out. But he has remained a prophet honored in his adopted country, canonized as a saint of the Bulgarian national revival. Bulgarians were grief-stricken at the news of his early demise. On his marble tombstone in the Danilov Monastery cemetery in Moscow the following epitaph is inscribed: "He reminded the world of the downtrodden, but once famous and powerful Bulgarian race and passionately desired to see its rebirth. Almighty God fulfill the prayer of Thy servant." On the reverse side is: "To Iurii Ivanovich Venelin. The Odessa Bulgarians, 1841."[58] A touching tribute came from the Macedonian Bulgarian, Jordan Dzhinot, ten years later: "He rests with the heavenly angels and archangels, he rescued our Bulgarians from dark obscurity.... All we Bulgarians are bound to weave wreaths for him for ever and ever."[59] His adopted countrymen are still placing wreaths in his memory.

But the neatest verdict comes from P.R. Slaveikov, leading literary personality of the Bulgarian revival: "He died after having reawakened us to life." In discussing Venelin, Bulgarians still get emotional. Understandably, they hesitate to call a spade a spade. For example, here is a conclusion by the eminent historian of Slavistics, Emil Georgiev:

> Venelin (1802-1839) occupies an enviable place among the creators of Russian Slavistics. His scholarly activity was directed exclusively towards the Bulgarians, their history, language and culture. Venelin uncovered the Slavic connection of the Bulgarian people and assigned it a leading place in the history of the Slav peoples and of Slavic culture.[60]

According to the authoritative *Bulgarian Encyclopedia:*

> On occasion [Venelin] yielded to his romantic enthusiasm, thus going against scientific truth.... Venelin's activity in the areas of Bulgarian language, folklore, ethnography and history, his role in the formation of Bulgarian national consciousness, confirm him as one of the most prominent actors in the Bulgarian renaissance.[61]

The *Great Soviet Encyclopedia* disposes of Venelin more tersely: His 1829 book refuted the accepted Turco-Tatar origin of the Bulgars, placing them with the Slavo-Russians; his Vlacho-Bulgarian charters have scholarly value; his other works long ago lost their scholarly significance.

The harshest but perhaps most objective verdict is reserved for the foremost Slavist in his day, Vatroslav Jagić, in the *Encyclopedia of Slavic*

Philology. It irked Jagić that no Bulgarian had written anything but praise, including the centennial tribute of Bulgaria's foremost historian, Vasil Zlatarski.[62] According to Jagić, the source of Venelin's shortcomings lay in his lack of proper education and in his personal character. A zealous researcher, he read and copied everything that came his way, most of which remained undigested. "Venelin may be called the product and even the victim of romantic enthusiasm." It would have been better for Venelin if his 1829 work had received its deserved criticism, but did not because of Pogodin's prestige. Venelin was more at home in his studies of Russian (Ukrainian) and Serbian folksongs, but here too he suffered from his unfettered imagination. His best work was his review of current Bulgarian literature. Of his historical work Jagić wrote: "As for [his] scholarship, it has proved to be almost entirely unnecessary and has lapsed without trace." Of his book on the Slovenes, Jagić commented: "In one word, this work is a horrible example of enormous reading with complete absence of criticism." It should be noted here that Jagić appears to overlook Molnár's share of the responsibility.[63]

But we need no longer worry about Venelin's scholarship or lack of it. To borrow a phrase from the "father" of Russian "Westernizers," Peter Chaadayev, Venelin wrote on the blank pages of Bulgarian history. Had he been more critical, his effect on Bulgarians would have been less. The modern historian of Bulgaria, Alois Hajek, concluded that for his moral contributions to the Bulgarian renaissance, Venelin fully deserved the accolades he received.[64]

Suffice it to say that he will always justly remain one of the first in the hearts of his adopted countrymen, the Bulgarians.

NOTES

1. Emil Georgiev, "Bŭlgaristika-osnovna distsiplina na slavistikata" [Bulgaristics—the Basic Discipline of Slavistics], *Osnovi na slavistikata i bulgaristikata* [The Foundations of Slavistics and Bulgaristics] (Sofia, 1979), pp. 78-93.

2. L. Miletich, "Dr. Frants Mikloshich i slavyanskata filologiya" [Dr. Franz Mikloshich and Slavic Philology], *Sbornik za Narodni Umotvoreniya, Nauka i Knizhnina* [Collection of Popular Folklore, Science and Literature], V (1891), pp. 355-499, 400.

3. For example, P.J. Šafařik, *Geschichte der slavischen Sprache und*

Literatur nach allen Mundarten (Ofen, 1826). In this, as in almost everything else, he was followed by Talvj, "the first American Slavist." J. F. Clarke, "Therese Albertine Louise von Jakob (Talvj) and P.J. Šafařik," *Culture and History of the Bulgarian People*, ed. by W. Kolar (Pittsburgh, 1982), pp. 13-30.

4. J.F. Clarke, "The Russian Bible Society and the Bulgarians," *Harvard Slavic Studies*, III (1957), pp. 67-103, 69.

5. *Drevnije i nynieshnie bolgare v politicheskom, narodopisnom, istoricheskom i religioznom ih otnoshenii k rossiyanam. Istoriko-kriticheskiya izyskaniya* (Moscow, 1829). The first edition does not seem to exist in this country. I have used the 2nd, 1856 ed., with minor changes. Hereafter cited as "1829" (1856).

6. One of the best sources for Venelin's biography is N. Barsukov, *Zhizn i trudy M. P. Pogodina* [The Life and Works of M.P. Pogodin], (St. Petersburg, 1889 ff.) in 22 vols., esp. vols. 3-4.

7. V.A. Popruzhenko, "Odesa i bŭlgarskoto vŭzrazhdane" [Odessa and the Bulgarian Renaissance] in *Kliment Tŭrnovski* [Clement of Tŭrnovo], ed. by M. Arnaudov (Sofia, ? ?), pp. 87-100, 90. Popruzhenko, authority on Russo-Bulgarian relations during the Bulgarian national revival and the last Old Regime librarian of the Odessa Public Library, wrote one of the best short accounts of Venelin: *I.I. Venelin i negovoto znachenie v istoriyata na bŭlgarskoto vŭzrazhdane* [I. I. Venelin and his Significance for the History of the Bulgarian Renaissance] (Sofia, 1903], 24 pp. An emigré in Bulgaria, Popruzhenko told me that after the Revolution he bought in European antiquarian bookstores books from Venelin's personal library in Odessa.

8. V.D. Konobeev, "Natsionalosvoboditelnoto dvizhenie v Bŭlgariya, 1829-1830" [The National Liberation Movement in Bulgaria, 1829-1830], pp. 180-271 of his *Bulgarskoto natsionalosvoboditelnoto Dzizhenie* [The Bulgarian National Liberation Movement] (Sofia, 1972). The author, a Russian, used Soviet archives.

9. *Vlaho-bolgarskiya ili dako-slavyanskiya gramoty* [Vlacho-Bulgarian or Daco-Slavic Charters] (St. Petersburg, 1840), 350 pp.

10. *O haraktere narodnyh pesen u slavyan zadunaiskih* (Moscow, 1835). Excerpts from Venelin's *Travel Notes*, published in 1857, are in Popruzhenko's *Venelin*.

11. Elka Dorosieva, "Za mestoto na Iurii Ivanovich Venelin v ruskata

bŭlgaristika" [The Place of Iuri Ivanovich Venelin in Russian Bulgaristics], in press. See also her *Stanovlenie russkoi bolgaristika (do serediny XIX n.)* [State of Russian Bulgaristics—to the Middle of the 19th c.] (Leningrad, 1980), which is a summary of her dissertation.

12. "Necrology," *Moskovskie Vedomosti,* May, 1839, in "The Private and Scholarly Life of Iuri Ivanovich Venelin" by his cousin, I.I. Molnár. See note 27.

13. Clarke, "Russian Bible Society," 102; and L. Minkova, *Osip Maksimovich Bodyanski i bŭlgarskoto vŭzrazhdane* [O.M. Bodyanski and the Bulgarian Renaissance] (Sofia, 1978), p. 20. Grigorovich published his valuable *Ocherki Puteshestviya po evropeiskoi Turksii* [Sketches of Travels in European Turkey] in Kazan in 1848. In 1877 it was also published in book form.

14. A dozen of posthumous articles appeared in the proceedings (*Chteniya*) of the Moscow University Society for Russian History and Antiquities, edited by Bodyanski, of which society Venelin was elected member in 1833.

15. A complete list of Venelin's publications is in T. Baitsura, *Iurii Ivanovich Venelin* (Bratislava-Prešov, 1968), pp. 295-298, including posthumous items.

16. Listed by Molnár at the end of his introduction to Venelin's second work, *The Slovenes* (1846).

17. I.D. Shishmanov, *Venelinovite knizha v Moskva* [Venelin's Papers in Moscow], *Bŭlgarski Pregled* [Bulgarian Review] (Sofia, 1897). Venelin's papers were in the library of the Society for Russian History and Antiquities.

18. Molnár, Preface to the *Slovenes,* i-iii.

19. Venelin, Moscow, Oct. 9, 1837, to Vasil Aprilov, Odessa, in "Dve pisma ot Iurii Ivanovich Venelin do Vasilya Aprilov" [Two letters from Iurii Ivanovich Aprilov to Vasili Aprilov], *Sbornik za Narodni Umotvoreniya, Nauka i Knizhnina,* I (Sofia, 1889), pp. 176-190, p. 189.

20. *Kriticheskiya izsledovaniya ob istorii bolgar. I.I. Venelina. S prihoda bolgar na thrakiiskii poluostrov do 968 goda, ili pokoreniya bolgarii velikom knyazom russkim Svyatoslavom* (Moscow, 1849), 342 pp. A Bulgarian translation by Botiu Petkov (father of Bulgaria's favorite poet and revolutionary, Hristo Botev) (Zemun, 1853), 2 parts, 380 pp., with portrait of Venelin and a record 881 advance subscriptions, 94 from the small town of Kalofer.

21. Minkova, *Bodyanski*, pp. 100-102.

22. Cf. K. Mechev, "Iurii Ivanovich Venelin i vopros o natsionalnoi prinadlezhnosti Kirilla i Metodiya," [Iurii Ivanovich Venelin and the Question of the National Affiliation of Cyril and Methodius), *Bulgarian Historical Review* (1978), No. 2, pp. 72-83. Mechev is currently the leading Bulgarian authority on the Brothers.

23. *The Bulgarians* (1846), pp. 65 ff. Among Venelin's many digressions is a discussion of Magyar (Tatar) origins.

24. Bezsonov (1828-1898) was a prominent Slavophile, philologist and folklorist, to whom Molnár gave carte blanche regarding Venelin's papers. Bezsonov is the author of "Iurii Ivanovich Venelin," *Zhurnal Ministerstva Narodnago Prosveshchenie* [Journal of the Ministry of Public Education] (June, 1882), pp. 159-206.

25. *Drevnie i nyneshnie Slovene, v politicheskom, narodopisnom, istoricheskom i religioznom ih otnoshenii k Rossiyanam. Historical-Critical Researches,* II (Moscow, 1841 [1846]). According to Molnár's preface, Venelin began printing vol. II of his *Researches,* i.e. the *Slovenes* (vol. I of *Historical-Critical Researches* being his 1829 book) in 1834, but stopped at p. 48. There does seem to be a difference in type after p. 71. But according to Bodyanski, Molnár took back the 1849 Bulgarian Ms. after printing, including the title page, had started. Cf. Minkova, *Bodyanski,* pp. 184-185. Molnár also states that some copies of *The Slovenes* had "Bulgarians" on the title page, later changed. The 1849 Bulgarian work was to be vol. III of the *Historical-Critical Researches,* but only the second vol. of Venelin's Bulgarian work. Needless to say there is bibliographical confusion. For example, *Bulgarian Encyclopedia* gives 3 vols. for his Bulgarian works. Hristo Gandev has Venelin's 2nd vol. on Bulgaria published in 1846 (*Problemi,* 485).

26. I can find no record of such a publication, but this might explain the 1841 date and "Bulgaria" on some of the title pages. This information is from Molnár's preface to *The Slovenes* and in his "Venelin," p. xxviii. See also Bezsonov's introduction to the 2nd. ed. of the 1829 work, xxx ff., but with reference to the 1849 book.

27. "Cherti iz chastnoi i uchenoi zhivot Iuriya Ivanovicha Venelina," vii-lxxix. A similar item is N.H. Palauzov, tr., *Zhiznepoisanie Iuriya Ivanovicha Venelina* [Biography of . . .] (Odessa, 1851), 32 pp.

28. Same title as in 1829 with "Second Edition" added, 230 pp.

29. R. Walsh, *Narrative of a Journey from Constantinople to England*. (Philadelphia, 1828).

30. *Slavische Alterthümer* (Leipzig, 1844-1845), vol. II, 165-66. Šafařik devotes ch. 3 (pp. 152-236) to the "Bulgarian" Slavs conquered by the Bulgars. The original, *Slovanske Starožitnosti*, was published in Prague in 1837 in 2 vols.

31. Novi Sad, Sept. 3, 1827, in Vaclav Burian, *Šafařikovy dopisy slovinci Jer. Kopitarovi v letech 1826 a 1827* [Safarik's Slavic Correspondence with J. Kopitar in the Period between 1826 and 1827] (Prague, 1931), p. 33.

32. "1829" (1856), p. 44.

33. *Venelin*, pp. 295-298.

34. *Skandinavomaniya ili poklonniki ili stoletnie izyskaniya o varyagah* [Scandinavomania and its Devotees, or a Century of Research on the Varangians] (Moscow, 1842), first as articles in 1836. 114 p. In this he "demolished" A.L. von Schlőzer, *Probe russische Annalen* (1768), and *Allgemeine nordische Geschichte* (1771).

35. "1829" (1856), 9-10. N.M. Karamzin, *Istoriya Gosudarstva Rossiiskago* [History of the Russian State]. Karamzin refers to Bulgarian as "the coarsest of all Slavic tongues." 3rd ed., pp. 121-122. Venelin intemperately attacked Karamzin in his "1829" (1856), pp. 196-197.

36. "1829" (1856), p. 41.

37. Ibid., p. 50.

38. Ibid., p. 57.

39. Ibid., p. 60.

40. Ibid., p. 187.

41. Ibid., p. 195.

42. Marin Pundeff describes the 1829 book as "the first major investigation of medieval influences of Balkan Slavs (especially Bulgarians) on Russia" (which it was not) "by Venelin born in Austria" (which he was not). "Bulgarian Nationalism," *Nationalism in Eastern Europe*, ed. by Peter Sugar and I.J. Lederer (Seattle and London, 1969), p. 106.

43. An exception may be L. Minkova, "Istoriyata na edna istoriya. Knigata na Iurii Venelin, *Kriticheski issledovaniya ob istorii bolgar*, i neiniyat prevod na bŭlgarski napraven ot Botiu Petkov" [The History of a History. The Book of Iurii Venelin, *Critical Researches on Bulgarian History*, and its Translation into Bulgarian by Botiu Petkov], *Litera-*

turna Misl, XVI (1972), no. 6, pp. 82-96. This is Venelin's more readable 1849 work.

44. Dorosieva is critical but stresses positive elements. On Venelin there is nothing in English to speak of. More surprising, there is no Bulgarian biography, the longest account probably being B. Penev's chapter on Venelin, in *Istoriya na novata bŭlgarska literatura* [History of the New Bulgarian Literature], ed. by B. Iotsov, vol. III (Sofia, 1933), pp. 583-640. Much Venelin material is in Arnaudov's biography of *Aprilov* and in Barsukov's *Pogodin.* One of the best short accounts is Popruzhenko's *Venelin.* There is only one biography, by T. Baitsura (Baicura), *Iurii Ivanovich Venelin,* 304 pp., with an extensive bibliography.

45. "Otets Paisii. Negovoto vreme, negovata istoriya i uchenitsite mu" [Father Paisii. His Times, his History and his Pupils], *Periodichesko Spisanie* [Periodical Review], I, 4 (1871). Chronologically, M.B. Petrovich is correct in noting that "next to Paisii (1722-98), the Ruthenian Iurii Venelin (1802-39), was the greatest awakener of the Bulgarian People, thanks to his historical research and collection of Bulgarian folklore." Cf. *The Origins of Russian Panslavism* (New York, 1956), p. 18. On Paisii see J.F. Clarke, "Father Paisii and Bulgarian History," *Teachers of History,* ed. by H.S. Hughes (Ithaca, 1954), p. 258-283.

46. According to Bezsonov, Venelin said that he delayed replying to Aprilov's first letter (1836, written in Greek) because he did not want to tell him he had given up his concern for Bulgarian history. Cf. his "Venelin," p. 201. Aprilov continued to use Greek until 1841. For Venelin-Aprilov, see M. Arnaudov, *Aprilov. Zhivot, deinost, sŭvremennitsi 1789-1947* [Aprilov. Life, Activity, Contemporaries] (Sofia, 1935); also *G.S. Rakovski, Zhivot, proizvedeniya, idei* [G.S. Rakovski. Life, Works, Ideas] (Sofia, 1922).

47. R. Radkova, *Neofit Rilski i novo-bŭlgarskata kultura* [Neofit Rilski and the New Bulgarian Culture] (Sofia, 1975).

48. Popruzhenko, *Venelin,* p. 19. Kipilovski wrote Venelin's publisher for his address "so that we could address him a message of gratitude which the whole Bulgarian people owes this immortal restorer of Bulgaria's existence."

49. Both Peshakov's Ode and his Elegy (1839) are in Molnár's "Venelin," pp. l-li and lxxvi-lxix.

50. *Dennitsa novobŭlgarskago obrazovanie* (Odessa, 1841), and

Supplement (St. Petersburg, 1842). Venelin was twice translated into Bulgarian, by M. Kefalov (Bucharest, 1842) and N. Daskalov (Constantinople, 1860). Venelin's and Aprilov's booklets are highly important sources and influences on the Bulgarian national revival.

51. Venelin on Vuk, *The Slovenes,* p. 270. According to Bezsonov, Venelin would have liked to make Bulgarian a Russian dialect.

52. Hristaki Pavlovich, 2nd ed. of his revised *Slaveno-Bulgarian Grammar* (1836).

53. G.K. Venediktov, "Nekotorie voprosi formirovaniya bolgarskago literaturnogo yazika v epohu vozrozhdeniya" [Some Questions Concerning the Formation of the Bulgarian Literary Language in the Period of the Renaissance), *Natsionalnoe vozrozhdenie i formirovanie slavyanskih literaturnyh yazykov* [National Renaissance and the Formation of Slavic Literary Languages], pp. 207-268 and 246 ff. Cf. S. Mladenov, *Istoriya na bŭlgarskiya ezik* [History of the Bulgarian language] (Sofia, 1979), tr. from the German ed. of 1929.

54. *Bolgarskiya grammoty* (Odessa, 1845). For other pan-Russianists see L. Leger, *Le Monde Slav* (Paris, 1897), 305-344.

55. Venelin and his followers contributed his collection (some of it via Aprilov) to the first significant collection of Bulgarian folksongs by Piotr Bezsonov, *Bolgarskie pesni iz sbornikov I.I. Venelina, N.D. Katranova i drugih bolgar* [Bulgarian Songs from the Collections of I.I. Venelin, N.D. Katranov and Other Bulgarians], (2 vols., Moscow, 1855), 790 pp. This included copious comments on Venelin and the Bulgarian language.

56. Arnaudov, *Aprilov,* pp. 179 ff.

57. E. Georgiev, in *Istoriya na bŭlgarskata literatura* [History of Bulgarian Literature], vol. II, *Literatura na vuzrazhdaneto* [The Literature of the Renaissance] (Sofia, 1960), pp. 90-92. However, Dimitry Cizevsky denies there is any such thing as Bulgarian Romanticism. Cf. *Outline of Comparative Slavic Literature* (Boston, 1952).

58. Molnár, "Venelin," pp. lxxi. One is reminded of present-day Bulgarian pilgrims to the grave in New Lexington, Ohio, of J.A. MacGahan, on whose tombstone is inscribed, "Liberator of Bulgaria," referring to his reporting of the 1876 massacres, which led to the Russo-Turkish War and liberation in 1878.

59. Published in *Tsarigradski Vestnik* [Constantinople News], 1851, no. 63. Cf. Arnaudov, *Aprilov,* p. 52.

60. *Osnovi na slavistikata i bŭlgaristikata,* pp. 55-56, 85. He lists the date of Venelin's first Bulgarian book as 1829-1841.
61. *Entsiklopediya Bŭlgariya,* I, A-V (Sofia, 1978).
62. V. Zlatarski, "Iurii Ivanovich Venelin i znachenieto mu za bulgarite" [Iurii Ivanovich Venelin and his significance for the Bulgarians], *Letopis na bŭlgarskoto knizhovno druzhestvo v Sofia,* No. 3, 1901-1902 (Sofia, 1903).
63. *Istoriya slavyanskoi filologii,* (Vol. I of *Entsiklopediya slavyanskoi filologii)* (St. Petersburg, 1910), pp. 449-456.
64. *Bulgarien unter der Türkenherrschaft* (Stuttgart, 1925), pp. 131-137. Hajek was the son-in-law of Konstantin Jireček, who published the first scholarly history of Bulgaria in 1876, and who was the grandson of Šafařik.

Peter F. Sugar

THE EVALUATION OF LEOPOLD II
IN HUNGARIAN HISTORIOGRAPHY

Most historians accept as at least partially valid the often heard statement that "each generation writes its own history." Even if history is limited to works of authors who honestly tried to tell their readers "wie es eigentlich gewesen ist" by conscientiously avoiding omissions or comissions that could introduce biases into their narratives, it is impossible to point to two works which describe, let alone evaluate, the same events or personalities in exactly the same manner. This is true even of volumes of roughly equal length which were written in the same country at about the same time with the help of the same primary and secondary sources. The personalities of the authors, their value judgments, and their interpretations of meticulously and correctly described events will account for these differences. These variations will be even greater when studies are involved whose lengths are very uneven and whose origins go back to periods in history in which the views of those who wrote them were colored, even if unconsciously, by the realities of the day. This holds true even if the authors lived in the same country.

Studying histories written in the same country at different times permits various analyses, e.g., what source materials were known, which events or developments received the most attention, what "interpretation" was the most "fashionable" at any given time, and many others. What this short essay will try to do is to establish, by concentrating not on the description of events but on evaluative statements, what if any biases the selected authors displayed and to what extent these can be explained by the political circumstances that prevailed in Hungary when they wrote their works.

Leopold II's reign (1790-1792) was selected as the test case because—while short and managable—it was very important and open to various interpretations. Of the six Hungarian histories selected, five were written by well-known and respected historians whose works were—or are—"the histories" of their own days (i.e. Henrik Marczali, 1856-1940; Ignác Acsády, 1845-1906; Gyula Szekfű, 1883-1955; János Varga, 1927- ; and Kálmán Benda, 1913-).[1] The sixth work, also authored by a respected historian (Vilmos Franknói, 1843-1921), represents on these pages mainly the efforts of the first post-*Ausgleich* generation of scholars.[2]

The six studies are of various lengths and, consequently, the number of pages devoted to the reign of Leopold II differs considerably.[3] The following major aspects of Leopold's reign are mentioned by all authors:

> Leopold II's foreign policy,
> The 1790-1792 Session of the Hungarian Diet
> The 1790-1791 Session of the Transylvanian Diet
> Leopold II's "propaganda" campaign
> The Serb Congress of 1791 at Temesvár [Timişoara]

Furthermore, in connection with the second and fourth of these aspects, every author said something about the ruler's approach to the various social classes. None of them, not even Franknói who is limited to the fewest number of pages, can be accused of errors of omission although the thoroughness with which details are handled varies greatly. Nor can these scholars be accused of errors of commission, if under these we understand the inclusion of hearsay, the undocumented attribution of statements, or similar practices. The differences in their handling of Leopold II become clear when their interpretations of the king's motives and their evaluations of his rule are compared.

All authors agree that Leopold II was a talented man and able ruler. Franknói, who in general refrains from expressing judgments, described him as a "wise ruler," while Marczali praised "his wisdom, moderation and energy."[4] Acsády noted his "even character" which "saved him from hasty action, rashness and from using undue force."[5] Szekfű, who did not like Leopold II, refrained from evaluating his abilities, although he held very strong views concerning his activities. The same approach characterizes the short pages of Varga. While representing different time periods and working under different political regimes, Szekfű and Varga are highly critical of Leopold II, as will be demonstrated below, and maybe they did not even want to give him credit for wisdom and moderation. Benda's introductory remarks to his treatment of Leopold II's rule contain the strongest and most positive evaluation of his ability. He writes about him as "an outstanding ruling personality, a determined, highly educated person, who inherited not only the practical way of thinking of his father, but also the humane tactfulness of his mother."[6]

While only one other author makes reference to the Emperor Francis I (1745-1765), comparisons between Leopold II and his brother, Joseph II (1780-1790) are much more numerous. Once again, it is interesting how close Szekfű and Varga are even in this respect. According to the former, Leopold II "possessed the extraordinary political talents of his older brother," while the latter mentions the younger man's "political abilities that resembled those of his older brother."[7] That all authors stress that Leopold II was more tactful and patient than his predecessor goes without saying; this fact was too obvious either to miss or to omit. Yet, differences of opinion appear when the relationship between the imperial brothers is assessed.

Three different interpretations emerge from the study of these volumes. According to Acsády, Leopold II disapproved of his brother's actions while Joseph II still ruled, although he loved his brother dearly. The fact that this brotherly love existed, at least originally, is implied in Benda's remark about the gradual cooling of the relationship between the two, while Szekfű assures his readers that the relationship between them was bad for many years.[8] Each author tied the personal feelings of the brothers, irrespective of the picture they paint, to political considerations.

For example, Acsády underlines that in spite of the good personal relation between brothers, Leopold II "did approve neither his [Joseph II's] domestic, nor his foreign policy... He urged him to go slower in introducing his domestic reforms and to take, if possible, the legal way."[9] Szekfű was even sharper when he wrote that everybody knew that the new ruler condemned and was determined to discontinue his older brother's "autocratic people-fooling ways."[10] Benda stated that "Leopold disapproved Joseph II's methods of government from the very beginning, and, as long as their relationship was good, even voiced his misgivings."[11] One wonders: are personal feelings among brothers determined solely by political considerations especially, as will become clear soon, if the differences were in fact not very great?

Naturally, Leopold II's approach to politics illustrated by his long rule in Tuscany (1766-1790) was used by the historians to explain the differences that separated the ruling brothers. "He [Leopold II] was familiar with the ideas of his time and his 24 years long rule in Tuscany was based on Montesquieu's *Spirit of the Laws*.... He preferred people who were involved in... [reforming] activities or those who worked for legal progress."[12] What Acsády, who wrote these lines, did not mention was that Joseph II was at least as familiar with and guided by the principles of the enlightenment as was the Tuscan ruler and certainly did not tolerate in his presence people who did not work for his reform. The other historians make similar statements about Leopold II, but stress only in passing the similarities between the aims of Maria Theresa's two sons. On the other hand, they stress that the major difference in their approach to rule was merely tactical. Joseph II was the proverbial bull in the china shop, Leopold II the diplomat. In short, they were not divided by political, but simply by tactical considerations.

Apart from minor disagreements, the picture that emerges from what the six authors had to say about these rulers is not very different. Their disagreements become evident when they analyze and evaluate more closely the methods of rule and the aims of Leopold II. According to Marczali, Leopold II's "reign, although it lasted for only two years, belongs among the most distinguished in our history.... The reestablishment of constitutional life based on historical precedents... is tied to his name." Marczali's evaluation echoes that of Fraknói, who spoke of 1790-1792 as the years "which destroyed the new institutions and with great enthusiasm reestablished those which were inherited from the forefathers."[13] Both of these men believed that one of Leopold II's greatest achievements was that he was able to use the old, well-established Hungarian institutions, especially the Diet, to introduce and have them sanction reforms to which practically everybody in the country objected vehemently during the last years of Joseph II's rule. Benda agreed with

The Evaluation of Leopold II

them when he wrote that Leopold II "while he recognized the right of the Diet to legislate, and reserved for himself only the executive power . . . , always found the way to lead to victory his own concepts behind the cloak of constitutional action."[14] Even this evaluation, when read in context, is positive and appreciative of the king's work.

The unexpected pair, Szekfű and Varga, not only saw things differently, but expressed itself, once again, in practically identical terms. Szekfű concluded that Leopold II's behavior is explained by the fact that he used "the Machiavellian methods and [followed] the Italian models, which he learned during his years in Tuscany." According to Varga, "Leopold used all the tools of diplomatic trickery and of the Machiavellian system of government which he learned while he ruled in Tuscany."[15] In the evaluations of these two historians the clever, flexible diplomat is replaced by the basest schemer ready to use the faulest methods to achieve his aims.

These assessments are contradictory and result from the authors' evaluation of Leopold II's methods and goals. The methods, discussed by all, although at different length, include the measures taken by the new ruler to counter the domination of Diet and local assemblies by the gentry, which not only tried to eradicate the last vestiges of Josephinism—"the new institutions" to which Fraknói referred—but also attempted to become the dominant political force in the country. Leopold II mobilized all forces opposed to the gentry's aspirations, from the even more reactionary aristocracy and Catholic episcopacy to those ranking lower on the social scale, whom he intended to use as allies in his struggle to "lead to victory his own concepts," mainly the urban middle class, but also the peasantry. To counter Magyar nationalism, he permitted the Serbs (who subsequently got nothing from Vienna) to gather at Temesvár to show the Hungarians that he was capable of finding allies even in their own country. To popularize his "own concepts" Leopold II commissioned various political pamphlets and tracts and had petitions drafted in which people asked him to do what he wanted to do in the first place and, then, graciously granted them what they requested. Was this way of acting the result of clever politics or of Machiavellianism?

Benda is the only one who not only gives a clear answer, but also a plausible explanation. "The obvious thing to do for Leopold would have been to make his views known through the various organs and institutions of government, but these were unsuitable." All those, with very few exceptions, who served in the various offices "stood firmly behind the concept of Hungary's estates-based constitution, even if they rejected the extremist concepts of the gentry."[16] A ruler who had to calm his realm (not only Hungary) on the verge of revolution in response to Joseph II's rule, who could not use the people who served in his administration, and who, at the same time, was determined to end the "old regime" and reform his domain in accordance with the principles contained in *Spirit of the Laws* had to find means to make his views known. The publication of tracts was a well-established practice as was the submitting of petitions to the ruler. These methods of "communications" were, therefore, the least "suspect" and their use had to be obvious to any clever politician even if, on occasion, the form in which they were presented had something Machiavellian about it. Leopold selected authors, told them what to write, and, in general, tried to use the means of the contemporary "communications system" to propagate his views.

A completely different evaluation emerges from Szekfű's pages. He does not see in the men Leopold engaged as his publicists either the ruler's collaborators or, at worst, opportunists, but base, anti-Magyar individuals, "informers and spies... who, in their secret reports, maligned Magyardom, while simultaneously trying to cause trouble by purposefully disseminating rumors."[17] That the selection of this kind of men reflected dishonor on the king is assumed as evident. The implication is clear: Leopold's agents were enemies of the Magyars, they were liars and fabricators, they acted under the ruler's direction, and their activities reflected the attitude of Leopold II toward Hungary.

Both interpretations pose the following unanswered question: Was Leopold clever or maligned? If one agrees with the aims pursued by Leopold II which—thanks to his methods and actions—he did achieve, the judgment will be: Leopold was extremely clever. If the king's aims or motives are not shared by his judges, the answer to the question will be: he was a malign Machiavellian who achieved his goals by foul means.

Fraknói is short and positive in his evaluation of the "wise-ruler who saved the throne and the country under very difficult circumstances." Marczali rated as a major achievement that Leopold II "regained for the royal dignity not only its brilliance and prestige, but also the nation's confidence. Only the consolidation of the monarchical, constitutional and national principles made it possible that the dynasty and Hungary were able to triumph over attacks that were mightier than anything else had been in the past." This is high praise, indeed, with which Acsády agrees in a few words when he states that Leopold was "the kind of ruler whom Hungary and the hereditary provinces badly needed." According to Szekfű, Leopold II's aim was narrow and purely dynastic designed to secure the future supremacy of the Habsburg family in Hungary.[18] For Szekfű, a staunch monarchist, when he wrote those lines, this was a positive goal. While not *Kaisertreu* and, therefore, not satisfied with Leopold II's motivation, Varga agrees with Szekfű in assessing that the aim of Leopold II was only "to maintain his dynasty's rule in Hungary."[19] Benda devotes several pages to the evaluation of Leopold's activities under the revealing heading: "The Contradictions in the Policy of Leopold II."[20] Towards the end of his evaluation he points out that Leopold II's "reforming of the constitution had practical political aims and was not the result of any ideological concept."[21] Gone is the man who acted in conformity "with the ideas of his age" following the principles he found in *Spirit of the Laws*. His place is taken by an experienced, pragmatic, goal-oriented politician. According to Benda, to use only some of his arguments and evaluations, Leopold II "did not break with absolute rule . . . . Office holding was predicated on loyalty to the dynasty . . . . Reforms were based on the ruler's understanding that revolution could only be avoided by making available safety valves through which discontent could be released."[22] Benda summarized his evaluation as follows:

> Leopold did not break with absolutism or with dynastic policy. His absolutism was, nevertheless, enlightened, and once he felt that his throne and power were secure . . . he worked to improve the lot of the non-nobles and to mitigate the feudal system . . . while maintaining not only constitutional forms, but even strengthening constitutions. . . . The essence of reform was the same in all his lands: to bring the non-nobles into the various legislatures. The admission of the urban classes and the peasantry within the walls of feudal constitutions signified both the breaking of the political power which the nobility and clergy exercised exclusively for centuries, and the strengthening of the absolute power of the monarch.[23]

In these lines most of the favorable and unfavorable, idealistic and pragmatic, reactionary and progressive evaluations of Leopold II are explained in a few words. He lived at a time, after the enlightenment and before his lands got involved in the wars of the French Revolution, when an intelligent monarch was able to reconcile the dynastic and popular principles, and he took advantage of the opportunities which the local and international situations presented to him. These allowed him to regain the "nation's confidence" and to bring into harmony "the monarchical, constitutional and national principles."

Benda's judgment covers Leopold II's achievements in all his lands. When his actions are reviewed by Hungarian historians, the reader will look for their assessment of his rule as it affected specifically Hungary: was his short reign good or bad for this country? The six authors expressed differing views when they attempted to answer this question, and these, in turn, clearly reflect the ages in which they wrote. They represent distinct "generations," each of which "wrote its own history."

Fraknói, who Magyarized his name from Frankl two years after he published the volume utilized for this survey, and who subsequently wrote several works of lasting value, was a young man of twenty-nine when he wrote his *The History of the Hungarian Nation*.[24] I do not know when he began working on it, but its publication date, 1872, makes it one of the earliest histories of Hungary published after the *Ausgleich* of 1867, when pro-Hungarian sentiments could again be openly expressed without the intervention of the censors. While his relatively slender volume has all the hallmarks of being the work of an inexperienced, cautious historian who avoids expressing opinions, it gives clear indications of two approaches to Hungarian history that have the stamp of the period. The first of these is the delight of the Hungarians at regaining their independence and constitutional rule reflected by Fraknói's pleasure with the reestablishment of "inherited institutions." The second characteristic, based on the achievement of the *Ausgleich* and the "good feeling" prevailing between ruler and nations, is the equating of "throne and country" as practically identical entities.

While the Hungarians had several objections to the dualist system, by the time they celebrated the millennium of the founding of their state, the festive mood of this occasion and the prestige which Francis Joseph enjoyed made it quite natural that in the millenary history Marczali expressed fairly similar sentiments. As has been indicated already, Marczali too underlined the importance of the "reestablishment of constitutional life based on historical precedents" and the consolidation "of the monarchical, constitutional and national principles" when he evaluated Leopold II's achievements.

Acsády's work represents a more interesting case, especially because his volume was published only a few years after Marczali's. He refrained from including in his study a section, even a short one, devoted entirely and exclusively to the evaluation of Leopold II's life work. This Magyar nationalist, whose work is devoted according to its title to the history of the "Hungarian Empire" expressed preferences and criticisms in a subtle but clear manner. While he did not pass judgment on Leopold II as Emperor-King, he detailed his previous achievements in Tuscany and underlined the "progressive" nature of his rule in that country. He, furthermore, wrote about Leopold II as "an atypical Habsburg" and listed the monarch's basic beliefs as follows:

— Rulers can only legislate in partnership with the people's representatives.
— Only legislatures can approve taxes.
— Rulers must account for their actions, especially for the manner in which tax revenues are expended.[25]

Was, in Acsády's opinion, Francis Joseph a typical Habsburg who had to be reminded of these principles? Did Acsády simply attempt to describe Leopold II's principles and personality, or did he try to criticize the Vienna of his days? I do not know the answer to these questions, but raising them when Acsády did, assuming that he raised them, would perfectly illustrate the dissatisfaction with the *Ausgleich* already openly expressed by the Independence Party which came to power only one year after Acsády's history was published. The same mood that produced this critical evaluation of the *Ausgleich* and the growing difficulties in the relationship between Magyars and the other inhabitants of Hungary, could, if the author did it on purpose, even explain the "imperial" title of his history.

Szekfű who—with his coauthor of the volumes dealing with earlier periods, Bálint Hóman (1885-1951)—was the dominant figure of Hungarian historiography in the interwar period, represents a very interesting case. As it is well known to those familiar with Hungarian historical writing, this very talented historian had two distinct careers representing two approaches to history and reflecting the two equally distinct historical periods in which he worked separated by the second World War. In the first of the periods, when he wrote about Leopold II, Szekfű was one of the spokesmen of the Magyar nationalist-revisionist thinkers, who saw in the Peace Treaty of Trianon one of the greatest injustices ever committed. At the same time, Szekfű was a conservative who believed in the monarchical principle in almost the same manner in which the upholders of the *ancien régime* defended it prior, during and right after the French Revolution. He not only preferred the centralized absolutist state to the nation state, but also saw advantages in a social order based on estates. Furthermore, he was a believer in the historic importance and role of the Catholic Church as the upholder of the moral principles on which a state had to be based. He was, therefore, opposed to the principles proclaimed by the enlightenment, to the equality of the people professing various religions, and to legislative bodies elected by universal suffrage. He was, in his writings, highly critical of Maria Theresa,[26] Joseph II and especially Leopold II. In his view the latter succeeded in perverting the Hungarian Estates and forced them to "legitimate" the Enlightenment-based measures of his two predecessors. In the Leopoldine reforms he saw the roots of development that culminated in the tragedy of Trianon.

That Varga was not a monarchical conservative is obvious, if for no other reason that the publication date of the volume (1964) in which his evaluation of Leopold appeared.[27] This is an important work because it is the first major synthesis of Hungarian history to be written by Hungarian historians since the Stalinist/Rákosi period. That a Marxist historian would object to a policy which, in his eyes, aimed at nothing more but the "maintenance of dynastic rule in Hungary"[28] is understandable. What is surprising is his agreement with Szekfű in his evaluation of Leopold II's methods. If our stereotyped image of "the Marxist historian" is correct, Varga should have been delighted with Leopold II's attempts to break the power of the nobility and the clergy securing a larger role in the life of the country for the members of the third estate and he should have been sympathetic to a ruler who was willing to listen to all his subjects irrespective of their nationality. Varga did not approve these actions of Leopold II. While Szekfű was clearly a partisan of the *ancien régime,* Varga's heroes belong to a significant class within the old order, the gentry, which was the largest single segment of the First Estate. This group, Leopold II's most dangerous foe, represents to Varga the most "radical national" element against which the king mobilized everybody, including "the bourgeoisie that was not Magyar in speech and was indifferent to national slogans."[29] Similarly, according to Varga, Leopold II permitted the calling of the Serb Congress in order to sharpen the Magyar-Serb controversy and to gain "a new tool for the suppression of the resistance of the Hungarian nobility."[30]

It is perfectly true that the Hungarian gentry was the most nationally-minded segment of the Magyar population of Hungary in 1790-1792, but was it, from a Marxist point-of-view, the most progressive? If the gentry would have been revolutionary, anti-monarchist, and on occasions even republican, they could be regarded as those who moved the dialectical process of history in the correct direction. But what the gentry really wanted was the reestablishment of the constitutional order in its pre-Josephinian form so as to ensure its dominance in the central and local legislative bodies, and thus its dominance over middle class and peasantry. This is not what a Marxist would call a "progressive" program. Yet Varga was not going against the prevailing ideology of his country when he wrote what he did. On the contrary, he is a perfect representative of the time in which he wrote, a period in which national-communism made its appearance. One of the changes which the end of the Rákosi regime brought to Hungary was the possibility for the historians to write, once again, national history free from many of the obligatory distortions that Stalinism had imposed on them. Varga's lines simply mirror the pleasure he and his colleagues felt when they were, once again, allowed to write as Hungarians.

Those who follow the development of the writing of history in Hungary have watched with great interest their colleagues' work during those years that separate Varga's evaluation of Leopold II from Benda's. During this period Hungarian historians have gained a deserved reputation for thoroughness, impartiality (even when writing about their own country), and the absence of dogmatism in their work. Among the Hungarians who earned this reputation, Benda occupies a leading position. Yet, his work too mirrors the mood and the self-image of the country and its inhabitants. Moderation, caution, freedom from illusions, dedication to country and profession, disinclination to judge too rapidly or harshly, a curiosity in discovering what the present is, how and why it follows from the past, cautious optimism when looking to the future, and a Hungarian version of undogmatic Marxism are among the characteristics of present-day Hungarian historians. Not all of these features are evident from the few lines of Benda's writings that could be included in these pages. But hopefully enough has been quoted to show that he too is the son of the Hungary of his days. His Leopold II is a very capable ruler, a good diplomat, a clever, although often cunning politician, and first and foremost a Habsburg. He is judged by Benda not according to the criteria applied to him by the various segments of the society in which he lived and by those that motivated subsequent generations (including the other historians quoted in these pages), but according to the aims Leopold II himself tried to achieve, which are the only true measures of his accomplishments. While I agree with Benda's image of Leopold II, I cannot forget that both he and I are children of our time, and am certain that future generations will again rewrite the history of Leopold II in accordance with the demands of their own age.

NOTES

1. In order of publication: Sándor Szilágyi, editor-in-chief, *A Magyar Nemzet Története* [The History of the Hungarian Nation] (10 vols., Budapest: Athenaeum, 1895-8). This was the work that was published to celebrate the millenium of the establishment of the Hungarian state. The eighth volume (published in 1896), which deals with Leopold II, was written by Henrik Marczali and has the title, *Magyarország Története III. Károlytól a bécsi congressusig (1711-1815)* [The History of Hungary from Charles III to the Congress of Vienna (1711-1815)]. Subsequent citations will refer to Marczali. The name of authors will be used for citations in the cases of all other works listed below: Ignácz Acsády, *A Magyar Birodalom Története. A kútfők alapján. A művelt közönség számára* [The History of the Hungarian Empire. Based on the Sources. For the Educated Public] (2 vols., Budapest: Athenaeum, 1904). Bálint Hóman and Gyula Szekfű, *Magyar Történet* [Hungarian History] (5 vols., Budapest: Magyar Királyi Egyetemi Nyomda, 1st ed., 1928-34). The relevant fifth volume was written by Gyula Szekfű. Erik Molnár, ed., *Magyarország Története* [The History of Hungary] (2 vols., Budapest: Gondolat, 1964). Chapter 3 of Part IV in Volume I deals with Leopold and was written by János Varga. Zsigmond Pál Pach, editor-in-chief, *Magyarország Története tiz kötetben* [The History of Hungary in Ten Volumes] (Budapest: Akadémiai Kiadó, 1976-). The reign of Leopold, written by Kálmán Benda, is covered in Part I of Volume V, edited by Gyula Mérei and Károly Vörös, *Magyarország Története, 1790-1848* [The History of Hungary, 1790-1848]. It appeared in 1980.

2. Vilmos Frankl [Fraknói], *A Magyar Nemzet Története* [The History of the Hungarian Nation] (Pest: Szent-István Társulat, 1872).
3. Fraknói, pp. 353-66; Marczali, pp. 467-544; Acsády, pp. 577-90; Szekfű, pp. 53-97; Varga, pp. 408-11; Benda, pp. 29-115.
4. Fraknói, p. 359; Marczali, p. 544.
5. Acsády, p. 571.
6. Benda, p. 53.
7. Szekfű, p. 69; Varga, p. 397.
8. Acsády, p. 571; Benda, p. 54; Szekfű, p. 53.
9. Acsády, p. 571.
10. Szekfű, p. 53.
11. Benda, p. 54.
12. Acsády, p. 571.
13. Marczali, p. 544; Fraknói, p. 353.
14. Benda, p. 54.
15. Szekfű, p. 69; Varga, p. 397.
16. Benda, p. 61.
17. Szekfű, p. 66.
18. Fraknói, p. 359; Marczali, p. 544; Acsády, p. 571; Szekfű, p. 69.
19. Varga, p. 397.
20. Benda, pp. 108-15.
21. Benda, p. 112.
22. Benda, pp. 108, 110, 111.
23. Benda, pp. 110, 111.
24. Concerning young Fraknói see Ferenc Rottler, "Fraknói Vilmos történetírói pályakezdése, 1861-1871" [Vilmos Fraknói as a Young Historian, 1861-1871], *Századok* [Centuries], CIII, 5-6 (1969), pp. 1046-76.
25. Acsády, pp. 570-1.
26. Concerning Szefkű's views on Maria Theresa see Kálmán Benda, "Mária Terézia királynő a magyar történetírásban" [Queen Maria Theresa in Hungarian Historiography], *Történelmi Szemle* [Historical Review] XXVI, 3 (1981), pp. 485-92.
27. Work on this volume started in 1957.
28. Varga, p. 397.
29. Varga, pp. 397-8.
30. Varga, p. 399.

Agnes Huszar Vardy

THE TURKS AND THE OTTOMAN CIVILIZATION IN JÓKAI'S "HISTORICAL NOVELS" AND SHORT STORIES

Jókai as a Novelist

Mór Jókai, (1825-1904)[1] the nineteenth century Romantic novelist, is still Hungary's most popular and most widely read author.[2] His works, which comprise well over one hundred volumes, have been published year after year in hundreds of thousands of copies and are eagerly received by the reading public, both young and old. He is also the best-known Hungarian writer abroad: his works have been translated into over thirty languages.[3]

Jókai's readers as well as his critics are impressed by his mastery of fiction, vividness of plot, quality of suspense, picturesque descriptions and his sense of humor that serve as vehicles of escape from the dullness of everyday existence. Jókai was a storyteller *par excellence* whose magic wand with one stroke could recreate exotic lands and characters far beyond the experience of ordinary mortals. As one of his eulogizers said at Jókai's funeral,

> If all the persons whom he had called to life in his novels were to appear—Hungarian peasants, knights of the Middle Ages, great magnates, 'honvéds,' /soldiers/ beggars, Roman senators, Greek sailors,

> Indian maharajahs, Turkish janissaries, nomadic Arabs, English lords, Assyrian kings, Christian martyrs, modern stockholders, Negroes, Russians, Armenians and Gypsies—the multitude would line the streets for more than a mile.[4]

It was precisely Jókai's inexhaustible imaginative power and talent as a fabulist that brought these greatly varied characters to life, and shaped the image of the past of Hungary and that of other nations in the minds of his readers.[5] Although Jókai was less concerned with accuracy than with telling a good story, many of his readers took the historical reliability of his stories for granted. Consequently, the views found in his writings play an unusually significant role in the formulation of popular attitudes even though the "historicity" or historical accuracy of these writings is highly debatable.[6] In most instances they are a strange mixture of fact and fiction which Jókai accomplished in such a fashion that the facts and the historical personalities assume new identities, and thus throw history completely out of perspective. This tendency in itself should not necessarily be considered a sign of his shortcomings, for as a novelist, Jókai had poetic license to shape the past whichever way he pleased. Yet, a problem develops when his mostly youthful and less-than-sophisticated readers—to whom he has the widest appeal—accept the "historicity" of his "historical" novels at face value. And because most of them do, they gain a false and distorted view of the past; a view that is perpetuated generation after generation, and which is so difficult to alter.

Historical inaccuracies and the idealization of the past in creative literature do not necessarily produce negative results. In fact, some idealization is useful and beneficial: man needs ideals and heroes to serve as models for the present. The situation is different, however, when totally negative stereotypes are continued, and in particular, when these stereotypes are applied to a nation or an entire civilization. And this is undoubtedly the case with the Turks and with the Ottoman Civilization as a whole, as portrayed in the "historical novels" and short stories of Jókai.

Jókai's Dilemma in Dealing with the Turks

Jókai's writings that deal with the Turks and with Turkish-Hungarian topics occupy a special place among his works. The most relevant of these include five novels and over a dozen short stories that were written during the 1850s.[7] But references to the Turks are scattered in dozens of his other writings as well.

The personal and cultural portraits presented in these works are almost always negative. Moreover, the total image also displays the same irreconcilable dichotomy or dualism that characterized much of the Hungarian mind on this matter in the second half of the nineteenth century. On the one hand, it reflects the standard anti-Turkish attitude rooted in the fundamental anti-Moslem bias of Christianity and in the anti-Ottoman prejudice of the awakening and growingly nationalistic Southeast European nations; on the other hand, it displays the gradually rising pro-Turkish sentiment that began among Hungarians in the middle of the nineteenth century. This sentiment was fueled partially by the growing sense of loneliness of the Magyars among the nations of Europe, and by the accompanying search for relatives, and partially by their increasing antipathy against the Habsburgs that was further enhanced by the brotherly hand extended by the Turks to the defeated and fleeing Hungarian revolutionaries after 1849.[8]

These contradictory views and emotions placed most Magyar intellectuals—including Jókai—into a difficult position. While convinced of the "inferior" and "destructive" nature of the Ottoman past and civilization in general, they began to view the Turks as their long-lost brothers, and felt obliged to say something positive about them. In doing so, they often had to forget their knowledge of history (or presumed history) and had to act against their own inner convictions. Moreover, they felt the need to dress up the past by portraying at least some Turks in a more favorable light.

Jókai also took this path in his Turkish-related writings. Thus, he combined his extremely unfavorable portrayal of Ottoman history with the creation of a few extremely idealized Turkish heroes. He did this either by changing the personality and identity of known historical figures, or simply creating such figures where none existed. This did not necessarily produce a likeable past for the Turks, but it made that past more readable and more consumable for contemporary Hungarians who were becoming increasingly sympathetic toward the Turks.

Jókai's Initial Turkish Short Stories

Jókai's turning to Turkish topics was motivated not only by his growing interest in the Turkish-Hungarian past, but also by the Habsburg censor's unwillingness to permit his continued treatment of the events of 1848-1849 and those that preceded it.[9] His early attempts were all short stories, including "The Stones of Nicodemia" (1850) and "Süleyman's Dream" (1851). Both of these are fairy tale-like writings displaying more of Jókai's imagination than his knowledge of Turkish history. In the first of these stories, an ambitious young man who participated in the Revolution of 1848-1849, has to flee to Turkey. Before leaving Hungary, however, he visits the keeper of the Turkish mosque of Buda, the 150 year old Abud Shirzad Eddin. The old sheik advises him to go to Nicodemia (Iznik) where he will be allowed to glimpse at those "precious stones" that persons of great fame and fortune receive as their rewards. Upon arriving in the city, he is led to a secret altar made of these "precious stones," which turns out to be tombstones of Hannibal, Scipio Asiaticus, Imre Thököly and his wife Ilona Zrínyi. There the young man also learns that Kossuth and his followers are likewise destined to receive such stones in exile. Upon having learned the price of fame and greatness, he relinquishes his dreams, returns home, and becomes a humble tiller of the soil in one of the provincial regions of Hungary.[10]

"The Stones of Nicodemia" is only partially Turkish in its subject matter. It was soon followed by Jókai's first fully Turkish story, "Süleyman's Dream," which narrates Sultan Süleyman Kanuni's role in the death of his son-in-law, the grand vizier Ibrahim. Although based on specific facts of history, as presented by Jókai, the whole story is the product of his own imagination.[11] The world he depicts in this story has very little to do with the world of Süleyman the Magnificent. It is rather the re-creation of the presumed world of Khalif Harun al-Rashid and of Sheherazade. This applies equally to the setting as well as to the major characters of the story, including the Sultan himself. Süleyman appears in Jókai's world not as the pragmatic statesman and conqueror that he really was, but as the fairy-tale khalif of Aladdin and his wonder lamp, and of the other stories of the *Thousand and One Nights*.

Jókai's Hungarian-Turkish Novels

While interesting as well as enchanting, these early stories had very little to do with the Turks or with the Turkish world of the seventeenth or of the nineteenth century. From our point of view they are important only as Jókai's halting steps in the direction of the Turkish past. But these short stories were soon followed in quick succession by several major novels. Three of these treat the Hungarian-Turkish encounter in Transylvania and in Hungary proper, and two of them discuss the fate of the janissaries in the Ottoman Empire from the early eighteenth century until their destruction in 1826.

The three Turkish-related novels include the mis-named *The Golden Age of Transylvania* (1852), its sequence, *The Turkish World in Hungary* (1853), and finally the somewhat side-tracked and mostly ahistorical *The Man with the Two Horns* (1853).[12]

The first two of these are basically historical novels that encompass three decades of Transylvanian-Hungarian history between 1660-1690. Both novels pay particular attention to Transylvanian-Turkish relations at the time when the Magyars were caught in the renewed violent confrontation between the Habsburg and the Ottoman Empires. The third work, however, is closer to a phantasy-novel than to historical prose. And this holds true, even though many of the characters of this novel are historical figures, who have also appeared on the pages of the *Golden Age* and of the *Turkish World*.

The title of the *Golden Age* is derived from Jókai's mistaken belief that the Battle of St. Gotthard and the Treaty of Vasvár in 1664 were followed by a period of real peace that also permitted a relatively unhindered evolution of Transylvania. This assessment, of course, is too optimistic, and is belied by Jókai's own summary of the events of the 1860s and the 1870s. The so-called "golden age" under the leadership of the weak and vacillating Prince Mihály Apafi was really a period of internal and external turmoil. It was characterized both by unceasing multi-sided external pressures upon the principality, and also by the inability of Transylvania's Magyar political leaders to agree on a desirable foreign policy for their country. There were those who wished to continue the policy of relying upon the Ottoman Empire; others who wanted to steer the rudder of the state toward a pro-Habsburg course; and still others, who simply wanted to survive and to save Transylvania's so-called "independence." The latter, who came to be known as "Transylvanianists" wished to keep their state out of any and all involvements in the Turkish-Habsburg conflict, even if this meant abandoning their Magyar brethren in Hungary proper.[13]

The primary source of Jókai's Turkish-Hungarian historical novels was Mihály Cserei's *Historia,* which was written in the spirit of "Transylvanism."[14] Jókai followed Cserei's narrative very closely, and his characters often recite the chronicler's words almost verbatim. With the exception of a few secondary personalities (e.g. the shrewd and amoral odalisque Azraele), these heroes can all be found in Cserei's *Historia,* and they include even the idealized Küchük Pasha, and his "valiant young son" Feriz Bey, although their personalities are fully the creation of Jókai's imagination. In addition to Cserei's *Historia,* however, Jókai also used Count Miklós Bethlen's apocryphal *Memoires* (really authored by the French abbé Dominique Reverend), János Bethlen's *Historia Rerum Transylvanicarum,* György Pray's *Specimen Hierarchiae Hungaricae,* Sámuel Decsy's *Osmanographia,* as well as a few other works. These sources all display, to a lesser or greater degree an anti-Turkish bias, which, in light of the conditions and general consensus of those days was quite understandable. But none of the latter works were as influential in shaping Jókai's views and historical knowledge as Cserei's *Historia.*[15]

Jókai's Image of the Turks

Because his sources were almost unilaterally negative about the Turks, Jókai's views were also negative, and thus conformed to the stereotyped image that was being popularized by nineteenth-century historians. According to these views the Moslem Turks always represented the "evil," and the Christian Westerners always the "good" in the unceasing struggle between good and evil. Turkish rule was always depicted as a corrupt, aggressive and vicious system, whose primary goal was to conquer, to enslave, and to massacre the Christians, and to live off their sweat and blood, and most importantly, to exploit their women for pleasure and for the propagation of the Turkish race. These alleged features of the conquering Turkish Civilization were deeply ingrained in Jókai's and his informants' minds, making that civilization one of the most barbaric cultures known to man.

The Christians, of course, were not alone in viewing their own civilization as being far superior to that of their rivals and adversaries. The

Turks had a similarly low opinion about Christian Civilization.[16] These mutually degrading views were actually cultural biases, and stemmed from the inability of both sides to recognize that this alleged "inferiority" was simply "differentness." And consequently these two notions were equated in the minds of both the Turks and the Christians. While a power balance existed between the two, the negative impact of this state of affairs was felt equally by both sides. But once this power balance was destroyed at the expense of the Turks, it was primarily the latter who had to suffer the consequences of their "differentness." They were obliged to face, and eventually even to accept the notion of their alleged lower cultural and social status.

The image that emerged in Hungary about the Turks was no different. They were thought of primarily as "powerful barbarians" who exploited Hungary's internal weakness to impose their rule over a much more highly cultured land. It was this view that came down into the nineteenth century, and was popularized by Hungary's historians and novelists, including the most widely read and most highly regarded of them all, Mór Jókai.

The deeds, speeches and behavioral patterns of most of Jókai's main Turkish characters display the above features. Whether he happened to be Ali, the Pasha of Nagyvárad, who attempted to dictate a "typically" offensive Turkish letter to the newly elevated Prince Apafi of Transylvania;[17] or the notorious Korsar Bey of northern Hungary, who lived off the land like a medieval robber baron;[18] or Haji Baba, the "most notorious slave merchant in Istanbul;"[19] or Hassan Pasha, the lecherous, old and incompetent Beylerbey of Buda;[20] or Olay Bey, the smiling killer, whose special role in life was to offer the notorious "silk rope" to those Ottoman leaders who have fallen out of the Padishah's graces;[21] or Azraele, the beautiful but demon-like and totally amoral odalisque who always bound her fate to the man on the way up;[22] or Baruch Tawaif the cruel Seraskier who possessed all the right features of an opportunist renegade[23] — these "heroes" were all typical "Turkish" figures, as imagined, shaped and molded by the Christian mind, and as amended by Jókai's fertile imagination. Jókai's imaginative power was particularly evident in the shaping of such fictional characters as Korsar Bey, Azraele and of Tawaif. Regardless whether they were fictional heroes, or fictionalized historical personalities, Jókai's characterization always conformed to the generally accepted view about the Turks as depicted and popularized by contemporary historians.

Manifestations of "Oriental Despotism"

One of the most important features that characterized Jókai's Turkish heroes is what we might call manifestations of "oriental despotism." These manifestations include a total disregard for the rights, desires and aspirations of subordinates, inability to view social inferiors and those under their control as full-fledged human beings, and utter contempt for and total exploitation of the conquered population. This attitude is always evident in communications with subjects or inferiors, be they in a written or in an oral form. Thus, when Ali Pasha of Nagyvárad instructed Prince Apafi to convene with the Hungarian and the Transylvanian nobility, he saw nothing wrong in addressing them as "wretched slaves."[24] To him this was just as natural as calling the Prince of Transylvania the Sultan's "serf"—as it was done by Grand Vizier Kara Mustapha in Jókai's *Turkish World*.[25]

These signs of "cultural barbarism" are accompanied in Jókai's novels by numerous examples of "physical barbarism," paralleled by an apparent lack of recognition of the cruelty and viciousness of these deeds. Thus, Prince George Strudza's murder in Istanbul by a "wandering sheik," simply for having touched the sheik's gown, is taken for granted and without the slightest hint of moral indignation.[26]

This lack of moral indignation also holds true concerning the widespread bribery that plagued the Ottoman Empire. Not even the highest leadership was immune to it, and apparently the Grand Vizier could be bribed right in the Divan. Thus—according to Jókai's portrayal—Grand Vizier Ahmed Köprülü saw nothing wrong with accepting bribes from Prince Apafi's emissaries, while calling them "pagan dogs," and then openly soliciting higher bribes from Apafi's opponents: "If you wish your justice to triumph," the interpreter tells Pál Béldy and his friends in Köprülü's presence, "then offer him seventy more pouches/of gold coins/than did the envoys of the Prince. I promise to you that then they /Apafi's envoys/ will all be sewn into leather sacks and thrown into the Bosphorus, while you will be able to return as lords to your country."[27]

Coarseness and brutality are manifested even by Jókai's most likeable positive heroes, including the idealized Küchük Pasha. Thus, when the renegade Seraskier Baruch Tawaif is just about to drown Ádám Boór (the man he had deformed by having two goat horns affixed to his forehead) in a large bowl of wine, Küchük Pasha saves Boór by drowning the evil Seraskier in his own wine: "You will be the one to die for your treachery," says Küchük to Baruch Tawaif. And then the hapless Seraskier is cast into the bowl. "He bobs up to the surface of the wine again and again with protruding eyes. His desperate screams resound frightfully through the whole room. Then he goes under again, with only a few air bubbles coming to the surface, containing in them the tiny soul of the /Seraskier's/immense body."[28] Justice was undoubtedly done, but in what a cruel and crude fashion. Apparently, not even Jókai's positive heroes could refrain from acting the way Turks had to act according to the Christian view of things. Not even they managed to alter the presumed basic barbarism of the Turks and of the Turkish Civilization in general.

The Good Turks (Positive Heroes) in Jókai's Novels

Although not really successful at this, under the pressure of his evolving Turkophilism during the 1850s, Jókai did create a number of fictional heroes, whom he endowed with all the positive features he could without destroying their basic Turkish identity. The two most notable of these are the already-mentioned Küchük Pasha and his son Feriz Bey, both of whom conform to the requirements of Jókai's over-idealized and therefore "unreal" positive heroes.

Insofar as we know there did live a certain Küchük Mehmet, the Bey of Jenő and subsequently the Pasha of Nagyvárad, and he may even have been of Hungarian birth. But the scanty historical sources that are available show him to have been an unscrupulous tyrant, who had periodically sacked and denuded sections of Transylvania between 1661 and 1663.[29] The chronicler Cserei also mentions that Küchük had a "young and valiant son," but without mentioing his name.[30] It was this nameless son who became Feriz Bey in Jókai's novels. An unsubstantiated family tradition also holds that Küchük Pasha courted and then married a certain Katalin from the noted Kállay family, whom "he kept according to Christian laws as his one and only wife."[31] Supposedly, it was this Hungarian girl who became Feriz Bey's mother.

Küchük Pasha appears on the pages of Jókai's *Golden Age* as a "middle-sized, sunburnt man, with eyes as bold and bellicose as an eagle's."[32]

Although coming as the Sultan's envoy whose task was to put Apafi on Transylvania's throne, he displays unusual fairness and justice in dealing with the local population. This is apparent immediately when he commands Ferhad Aga and twelve of his men to go to the nearby village and "to respectfully ask the magistrate" to supply them with "forty hundredweights of bread, the same amount of meat, and twice as much of hay and oats at four aspers per pound in general, neither less, nor more."[33] This is an uncommon mode of behavior on the part of a Turkish pasha, who—according to the standard accounts—should not have gone through such niceties. He simply would have robbed the villagers of most of their belongings. Then, turning to his Vlach subordinates (*kurtány*), who apparently constituted a group of freebooters, Küchük warns them: "You dogs! Don't think that we have come here to plunder. Don't even dare to move from your places, for if I learn that so much as a goose has been stolen from the village, I will hang your leaders and then decimate the rest of you."[34] This again is a very un-Turkish-like protection of the natives against plunderings. Yet, at the same time it also displays those elements of "oriental despotism" to which we have already alluded as allegedly typical of the Turks.

In his effort to further improve the image of his positive Turkish heroes, Jókai also draws a parallel between the idealized Küchük Pasha and the unduly maligned Prince János Kemény of Transylvania.[35] Whereas he portrays Küchük as the virtual reincarnation of a medieval knight, with all the bravery and chivalry associated with knighthood, Jókai depicts Kemény as a boastful and incompetent drunkard, who is ultimately given the *coup d'grace* by Küchük's twelve year-old son, Feriz Bey.[36] The encounter between Kemény and young Feriz is so unrealistic that no one but Jókai could have written it with the hope of getting away with it.

And thus the noble figure of Küchük Pasha reappears again and again in Jókai's above-mentioned novels, represented as the epitome of fairness, justice and chivalry. Jókai transferred these characteristics also to Küchük's son, Feriz Bey, who lived and fought only for honor and for the love of his chosen one, Aranka, the daughter of the "Transylvanianist" Pál Béldy. Feriz Bey's manly beauty and chivalry eventually captured even Azraele's love. And the hitherto completely amoral odalisque sacrificed herself so as to gain at least Feriz Bey's respect, if she was unable to gain his love.[37]

After the death of his beloved Aranka, the valiant and chivalrous Feriz Bey becomes deranged. However, later in the novel he re-appears like a seventeenth century Jean d'Arc. And like the Virgin of Orleans two and a half centuries earlier, he too manages to infuse new vitality into his dejected people, saving thereby at least the Balkans for the declining Ottoman Empire. Feriz eventually dies a hero's death, but only after revenging the death of his beloved by killing the treacherous Count Mihály Teleki in the Battle of Zernyest in 1690.[38]

The Turkish Image in Jókai's Wholly Turkish Novels

Having completed his novels on seventeenth-century Hungarian-Turkish relations, Jókai decided to turn his attention to a fully Turkish topic, namely to the role of the janissaries in the declining Ottoman Empire of the eighteenth and early nineteenth centuries. In addition to a number of short stories, he devoted two novels to this question. In one of them (*The White Rose*, 1853) he dealt with the 1730 revolt of Patrona Halil which resulted in Sultan Ahmed III's deposition, and in the second one (*The Last Days of the Janissaries*, 1854) he treated the revolt of Ali Pasha of Janina and the extermination of the janissaries in 1826.[39]

The stories of Patrona Halil and Ali of Janina are too well known to need repetition here. We are more interested in Jókai's portrayal of these historical figures, and even more in the way the image of the Turks emerges from these novels.

Although Jókai dealt with historical personalities in his *White Rose* and *Last Days*, both novels are more the products of his imagination than of historical research. Thus, in Jókai's interpretation Patrona Halil emerges both as a progressive reformer, as well as one of his over-idealized positive heroes, who is virtually devoid of any shortcomings.

This does not hold true for Ali of Janina, but on many occasions even he comes forth as a pleasant old gentleman. Not even his wanton and vicious deeds (e.g. the murdering of his own mother, sons and grandson) appear that horrible in Jókai's portrayal. One often has the feeling of walking in a fairy-tale land where real crime is impossible, and yet, where everything is possible.

Some of these fairy tale-like features may have been introduced by Jókai to smooth over the rough edges of the unilaterally negative view about the entire Ottoman world. But, if this was his wish, he did not really succeed, for ultimately he still reproduced the same stereotype view that had been universally accepted in his own age. As an example, let us cite a brief passage from his discussion of the foundation of the Janissary Corps by Haji Bektash in the fourteenth century:[40]

> When accompanying Turkish armies, who upon entering Christian villages, began to murder their inhabitants, the dervish /Bektash/ would force his way through the bloodthirsty warriors. Then, if he saw Bashkir or Kurdish fighters who were about to bash against the wall a weeping child crying for his mother, he would grab their hands, remove the child, cover him with his mantle, caress him and take him home. And thus he would continue...[41]

Although this was simply an effort to summarize a basically generous and humane deed on the part of the holy man Bektash, it still turned into a negative description of Turkish customs. For the main idea that a reader retains from Jókai's words is that the primary occupation of the Turkish janissaries was to go around, cutting down inhabitants of conquered villages and smashing the heads of orphaned children against the wall. In all probability Jókai truly believed all this, and despite his growing Turkophilism, he never considered the possibility that these alleged deeds may not be more than pure fabrications; or that, insofar as they did occur, they were not much different from similar deeds of various Christian armies. Thus, when wishing to improve the general image of the Turks, he did not question the reliability of his sources, but fabricated totally unrealistic positive heroes out of nowhere. This is the method he employed in his earlier works, and he followed a similar course in the novels *The White Rose* and *The Last Days*. In these works the role of the positive heroes was played by a completely re-made Patrona Halil (who had nothing in common with his historical counterpart), and his son Behram, who lived for nearly a century to carry his father's dreams to completion.

Like Küchük Pasha and Feriz Bey, Halil and Behram are endowed with characteristics that make them unreal. Thus, instead of appearing as a typical, self-seeking janissary spokesman of the early eighteenth century, Halil emerges as a virtuous, chivalrous and almost totally selfless knight, who sacrifices himself for the well-being of his nation, and dies with the following last words on his lips: "I shall die, but my son will live."[42]

And so Behram does live. He grows up to be a dervish, who dedicates his life to the realization of his father's goal: the purging of the Empire from the plague of the janissaries, who have become a cancerous growth on the body of the Turkish nation. According to Jókai, Behram achieves his goal by guiding the hands of Sultan Mahmud, who eventually sends 20,000 janissaries to the Bridge of Alshirat, where Patrona Halil has been waiting for them for nearly a century.[43]

Last Short Stories on Turkish Topics

By the time Jókai completed his Turkish-related novels, the situation in Hungary changed sufficiently that he was again allowed to deal with more recent Hungarian topics. The results of this new orientation were some of his best-loved and most highly regarded novels, including *A Hungarian Nábob* (1853) *Zoltán Kárpáthy* (1854) *The New Landlord* (1863) and several others. Simultaneously, however, he also retained his interest in, as well as his affection for the Turks.

Jókai's sympathy for the Turks, and his corresponding antipathy for the Russians is amply evident from his so-called *Book of Blood* (1855), a collection of short stories, many of which deal with the Russo-Turkish struggles of the nineteenth century. In these stories, he generally portrays the Turks with greater sympathy, while at the same time condemning Russian aggression and imperialistic designs.[44]

Although obviously rooting for the Turks in their struggle with the "Colossus of the North" (Russia), Jókai was still unable to free himself from the stereotyped negative view of the Turkish past. This is evident, among others, from the short stories incorporated into the collection that he published under the title *From the Chronicle of Debrecen* (1857). Here he again depicts the Turkish conquerors of the seventeenth century as the products of a corrupt, amoral and in a sense "barbaric" system. In his short story "The Heavenly Sling Stones" he even goes as far as to alter the character of his Turkish hero, Küchük Pasha, presenting him as a "merciless plunderer" instead of the chivalrous knight he had made him out to be a few years earlier.[45]

Jókai's inability to alter his negative views about Turkish history is particularly evident from his lengthy short story, "The Last Pasha of Buda" (1859).[46] The title of this story is misleading, for its real hero is not Abdurrahman (Abdi) Pasha, the last Beylerbey of Buda, but the ex-*kuruc* colonel Dávid Petneházy. Although this is one of Jókai's most interesting short stories, his portrayal of the Turks is most unfair. And this is all the more reprehensible, since the incriminating parts are all the products of his imagination, including the unusually contradictory personality and alleged deeds of Abdi Pasha.[47] Thus, the man who fought bravely and died honorably under the most adverse circumstances, while defending this westernmost outpost of the once mighty Ottoman Empire, is also portrayed as the man who was planning the murder of his prospective son-in-law Petneházy. Furthermore, Abdi Pasha is depicted as standing there unmoved while his beloved daughter (Telli) is becoming a harlot, willing to prostitute herself during one and the same night with an African (Osman Bey), with a filthy, seventy year-old ex-Jewish merchant (Seyton), as well as with her future husband Petneházy, who is already under the death sentence. And then, to top it all off, this same heroic Pasha is portrayed by Jókai as having his wife (Telli's mother) sewn into a leather sack, in company of snakes and rats, and then having her cast into the Danube.

Moreover, while all this is happening, and this alleged "amoral murderer" Abdi Pasha is preparing to defend Buda even at the expense of his life, all the Sultan does is to continue his customary hunting expeditions. But how? If we are willing to believe Jókai, then with 60,000 horsemen and 10,000 infantry, of whom 12,000 froze to death in a single night.[48]

And so Jókai goes on and on, feeding his readers with the most incredible stories, which they seem to believe nonetheless. As a matter of fact, most of them are inclined to take Jókai's words for granted even when he gives a totally ridiculous description of the Sultan's procession after the fall of Buda. According to Jókai, this procession included "thirty highranking viziers" who were obliged to cover their heads with "rags soaked in the blood of Jews and donkeys." In this same procession, Christian and Jewish slaves were cut to pieces at intervals of every mile, and then they were left there to die in their own blood.[49]

Jókai's description is colorful indeed. But again, it reveals more of his fertile imagination, than of his knowledge of history. And it certainly does not display any effort on his part to create any kind of sympathy for the Turks. Apparently, he reserved his sympathy only for the Turks of his own age, but made no attempt to question standard views and assumptions of the past. This is also evident from his brief assessment of the Turkish rule in Hungary: "They /the Turks/ were rich and powerful. They did whatever they wanted to do. They could build, or they could destroy. They could kill or enslave anyone who opposed them. The country was theirs! But what remained of them? Nothing, but bad memories!" Then, going along the same lines, and simultaneously professing his faith in the durability of his nation, Jókai continued: "They brought fire upon us. But did we melt? They created a sea out of our blood. But did we drown in it?" His answer was an obvious "no," which also applied to the future: "The Magyars live, and will continue to live on and on, sprouting forth like wheat growing from a grain that has been planted in the mouth of a mummy for a thousand years."[50]

And thus, while condemning the Turkish role in Hungarian history, Jókai also professed his faith in the future of his nation, as well as his willingness to extend a brotherly hand to the Turks. In other words, while unable to forget the past, or what he thought to be the past, he was willing to forge a common future with these re-discovered brethren of the Magyars.

Summary

In recent decades, historians of Southeastern Europe have done a great deal to try to give justice to the Turks and to the Ottoman Empire.[51] Their work, however, is very slow and painful in gaining recognition. Popular histories, novels and other writings are still filled with the traditional negative image that had been formed in the eighteenth and nineteenth centuries, and had been continued right into our own period.

In Hungary, Jókai had much to do with the perpetuation of this image of the Turks. As the most popular of Hungary's novelists, whose writings are still eagerly read today, the image that he has created is still being ingrained into the minds of the young generations of Hungarians. This is most unfortunate. Were Jókai alive today, in all probability he would not approve of it.

What is the answer to this dilemma? Certainly not the prohibiting, nor the censoring of his novels. That would be an overt act against one of Hungary's greatest novelists. It is not Jókai, but the study of history that should be changed. Perhaps historians should write more popular histories that reflect a revised view of the past to counterbalance the views of Jókai and others of similar bent. Jókai's works should therefore be viewed as fiction, as products of his boundless imagination, and not as "historical" novels and short stories that present a reliable portrait of the past.

NOTES

1. Some of the important biographies on Jókai are as follows: (Place of publication is Budapest unless otherwise indicated.) László Szabó, *Jókai élete és művei* [Jókai's Life and Works] (1904); Kálmán Mikszáth, *Jókai Mór élete és kora* [Mór Jókai's Life and Times] 2 vols. (1907, 1960); Ferenc Zsigmond, *Jókai* (1924); János Gál, *Jókai élete és irói jelleme* [Jókai's Life and Literary Character] (Berlin, 1925); István Sőtér, *Jókai* (1941); Miklós Nagy, *Jókai* [His Career until 1868] (1968); Dénes Lengyel, *Jókai Mór* (1968); Gyula Dávid, *Jókai* [Jókai and Transylvania] (Cluj-Kolozsvár, 1971); Miklós Nagy, *Jókai Mór* (1975). For specific aspects of his work see Jenő Péterfy, "Jókai Mór," *Péterfy Jenő összegyüjtött munkai* [Jenő Péterfy's Collected Works], ed. Dávid Angyal, 3 vols. (1901-1903), I, 59-105; Pál Gyulai, "Újabb magyar regények" [Recent Hungarian Novels] in Gyulai, *Birálatok 1861-1903* [Critiques, 1861-1903] (1911), 73-99; idem., "Jókai mint hirlapiró" [Jókai as a Journalist], ibid., 133-152; Ferenc Szinnyei, *Novella és regényirodalmunk a Bach-korszakban* [Our Short Stories and Novels during the Bach Regime], 4 vols., (1939), I, 163-455; János Barta, "Jókai és a müvészi igazság" [Jókai and Artistic Truth], *Irodalomtörténet* [Literary History], XLII (1954), 401-417; Miklós Nagy, "Két százéves Jókai regény" [Two One-Hundred Years Old Jókai Novels], *A Magyar Tudományos Akadémia Nyelv és Irodalomtudományi Osztályának Közleményei* [Proceedings of the Sections on Language and Literature of the Hungarian Academy of Sciences], VII, (1955), 65-89; István Sőtér, "Két Jókai tanulmány" [Two Jókai Studies], *Romantika és Realizmus* [Romanticism and Realism] (1956), 363-549; Miklós Nagy, "A kőszívű ember fiai" [The Sons of the Man with a Stone Heart], *Irodalomtörténet*, LXII (1958), 231-246; Zsigmond Vita, *Jókai Erdélyben* [Jókai in Transylvania] (Bukarest, 1975); Imre Bori, "A magyar 'fin de siècle' irója—Jókai Mór" [The Author of the Hungarian 'Fin de Siècle'—Mór Jókai], *Híd* [Bridge] (Novi Sad-Újvidék), XXIX (November-December 1975), 1215-1243, 1404-1426, and XXX (January 1976), 1-17.

For English language studies see: H. W. V. Temperley, "Maurus Jokai and the Historical Novel," in *Hungarian Quarterly* Vol. V, No. 4 (Winter 1939-1940), 722-731; Frederick Riedl, *A History of Hungarian Literature* (New York, 1906), 183-189; Joseph Reményi, *Hungarian Writers and Literature,* ed. with an introduction by August J. Molnár (New Brunswick, 1964), 165-177; T. Klaniczay, J. Szauder, M. Szabolcsi, *History of Hungarian Literature* (1914), 155-159.

2. A survey taken among both Slovak and Hungarian readers in Czechoslovakia in the summer of 1974 demonstrates Jókai's immense popularity even outside of Hungary. Cf. László Végh, "Könyvek és Olvasók" [Books and Readers] in *Irodalmi Szemle* [Literary Gazette] (Bratislava-Pozsony) (February 1979), 173-178.

3. For Jókai's popularity and reception in England cf.: Lóránt Czigány, *A magyar irodalom fogadtatása a viktoriánus Angliában 1830-1914* [The Reception of Hungarian Literature in Victorian England 1830-1914] (Budapest, 1976), 201-272.

4. Riedl, 184.

5. For the treatment of Germans, Romanians, Poles, and other nationalities in Jókai's novels and short stories see: Magdolna Bernfeld, *A németség Jókai Mór megvilágitásában* [Germandom in Jókai's View], (1927); László Rajka, *Jókai román tárgyú novellái* [Jókai's Short Stories with Romanian Themes], (Cluj-Kolozsvár, 1935); József Nacsády, "Jókai müveinek lengyel alakjai" [Polish Characters in Jókai's Works], *In memoriam Gedeon Mészöly* (Szeged, 1961), 97-114; István Csukás, *Jókai és a nemzetiségek* [Jókai and the Nationalities], in *Acta Historiae Litterarum Hungaricarum* (Szeged, 1973).

6. For a discussion of Jókai's historical novels and dramas in general see: Lajos Dézsi, *Magyar történeti tárgyú szépirodalom* [Hungarian Creative Writings with Historical Themes] (1927), 118-128.

7. The five novels are: *Erdély aranykora* [The Golden Age of Transylvania] (1851), *Törökvilág Magyarországon* [Turkish World in Hungary] (1852), *A kétszarvú ember* [The Man with the Two Horns] (1852), *A fehér rózsa* [The White Rose] (1854), and *A janicsárok végnapjai* [The Last Days of the Janissaries] (1854). For a cursory discussion of Jókai's novels and short stories with Turkish themes see Szinnyei, 220-235, 291-307; and Géza Hegedüs's epilogue to a 1959 popular edition of *A janicsárok végnapjai,* 338-345. Of the above novels, the following appeared in

English translations: *Erdély aranykora* [Midst the Wild Carpathians], tr. by R. Nisbet Bain. London, 1894; *The Golden Age of Transylvania*, tr. by S. L. and A. V. Wite, New York, 1898; *Török világ Magyarországon* [The Slaves of the Padishah], London, 1902, 1918; *A fehér rózsa* [Halil the Pedlar], tr. by R. Nisbet Bain. London, 1892; *A janicsárok végnapjai* [The Lion of Janina, or the Last of the Janissaries], tr. by R. Nisbet Bain. London, 1897.

8. On the problems of this dichotomy, on Turkish-Hungarian relations, and on the rising Turkophilism starting with the mid-nineteenth century see: Lajos Fekete, *Magyarság, törökség: két világnézet bajvívói* [Hungarians and the Turks: Champions of Two Ideologies] (1847); Ladislaus Rásonyi, "Ungarn und die Türken," *Ungarn und die Nachbarvölker*, ed. Stefan Gál (1943), 224-242; József Somogyi, "Magyarok és törökök," [Hungarians and Turks], *Magyarság és Keleteurópa* [Hungary and Eastern Europe], ed. István Gál (1947), 241-266; and István Hajnal, *A Kossuthemigráció Törökországban* [The Kossuth-Emigration in Turkey] (1927).

9. This whole question is treated by Sándor Orr, *Jókai első történeti regényei* [Jókai's Initial Historical Novels] (Ph.D. Dissertation, University of Budapest, 1923.) Cf. Ambrus Oltványi's notes to the critical edition of Jókai's *Erdély aranykora* (1962), 307-310.

10. Szinnyei, I, 221-222.

11. Jókai, *Elbeszélések* [Short Stories], III (1973), 114-127, 356-363; and Szinnyei, I, 222-223.

12. See note 7. All subsequent references to and quotations from Jókai, unless otherwise noted, are from the critical edition of Jókai's works now in the process of publication. *Jókai Mór Összes művei* [The Complete Works of Mór Jókai], ed. Miklós Nagy and Dénes Lengyel (1962-).

13. On the historical background of Jókai's novels under discussion see Bálint Hóman and Gyula Szekfű, *Magyar történet* [Magyar History], 7th ed., 5 vols. (1941-1943), IV, 51-91, 145-232; L. Makkai, *Histoire de Transylvania* (Paris, 1946), 238-257; Denis Sinor, *History of Hungary* (London, 1959), 198-208; Katalin Péter, *A magyar romlásnak századában* [In the Century of Hungarian Decline] (1975); and *A History of Hungary*, ed. Ervin Pamlényi (London, 1975), 160-170.

14. *Miklósvárszéki Nagyajtai Cserei Mihály históriája 1661-1711* [The History of Mihály Cserei of Miklósvárszék and Nagyajta], ed. Gábor Kazinczy (Pest, 1852).

15. For a discussion of Jókai's historical sources, see Miklós Czunya, *Jókai töröktárgyú regényeinek forrásairól* [On the sources of Jókai's Novels with Turkish Themes] (1934); István Jánosi, "Az Erdély aranykora forrásainak problémáihoz" [On the Problems of the Sources of The Golden Age of Transylvania], *Irodalomtörténet* (1956), 336-345; and Dénes Lengyel, "Jókai Mór: Törökvilág Magyarországon [Mór Jókai: Turkish World in Hungary], *Irodalomtörténet* (1956), 106-109. See also the relevant sections of the notes in the critical editions of the novels under discussion: *Erdély aranykora*, 310-339; *A kétszarvú ember*, 152-175; *A fehér rózsa*, 388-399; and *A janicsárok végnapjai*, 434-441. I was unable to secure a copy of the critical edition of *Török világ Magyarországon*.

16. This is evident from the generally demeaning and even offensive tone of the letters of the Turkish administrators to their Christian subjects, as well as from the general tone of the contemporary Ottoman chroniclers and travelers, when discussing the culture and way of life of the non-Muslims. For examples of such demeaning and offensive Turkish letters see, Hóman-Szekfű, *Magyar történet*, III, 422-423. For additional related documents see *Okmánytár a hódoltság történetéhez Magyarországon* [Documents on the History of Conquest of Hungary], 2 vols., ed. Áron Szilády and Sándor Szilágyi (Pest, 1863). Even the learned Evliya Chelebi displayed such a demeaning tone. Cf. *Evlia Cselebi világutazó magyarországi utazásai 1660-1664* [The World Traveler Evliya Chelebi's Travels in Hungary 1660-1664], tr. and ed. Imre Karácson (1904); and *Evlia Cselebi magyarországi utazásainak folytatólagos leírása az 1664-1666 közti években* [The Continuing Description of Evliya Chelebi's Travels in Hungary between 1664 and 1666] (1908).

17. *Erdély aranykora*, 41.
18. Ibid., 102-103, 113-121.
19. *Török világ Magyarországon*, 117-125.
20. Ibid., 132-139, 210-231, 249-251, 256-263, 270-272, 286.
21. Ibid., 186-195, 224-230, 254-255, 286.
22. *Erdély aranykora*, 108-121, 172-175, 278-284; *Török világ Magyarországon*, 126-150, 256-262, 270-285.
23. *A kétszarvú ember*, 27-28, 31-38, 79-84.
24. *Török világ Magyarországon*, 41.
25. Ibid., 376.

26. Ibid., 25.
27. Ibid., 306-307.
28. *A kétszarvú ember*, 83-84.
29. See the critical notes in *Erdély aranykora*, 411; and *A kétszarvú ember*, 227.
30. *Cserei históriája*, 7; and Gyula Németh, "Feriz Bég," *A Magyar Tudományos Akadémia Nyelv és Irodalomtudományi Osztályának Közleményei*, XIII (1958), 89-94.
31. Critical notes to *Erdély aranykora*, 414.
32. Ibid., 55.
33. Ibid., 56.
34. Ibid.
35. Ibid., 71-81.
36. Ibid., 80.
37. *Török világ Magyarországon*, 280-285, 386-392, 407.
38. Ibid., 407.
39. On the historical background of these events see Bernard Lewis, *The Emergence of Modern Turkey*, (London, 1961), 77-79.
40. On recent scholarly views concerning the origin of the janissaries see: J. A. B. Palmer, "The Origins of the Janissaries," *Bulletin of the John Rylands Library*, XXXV, 2 (1953), 448-481.
41. *A janicsárok végnapjai*, 301-302.
42. *A fehér rózsa*, 155.
43. *A janicsárok végnapjai*, 379.
44. Szinnyei, 228-234.
45. Ibid., 311-312; Ferenc Zsigmond, *Jókai és Debreczen* [Jókai and Debrecen] (Debrecen, 1925); and Jókai, *Válogatott elbeszélések* [Selected Short Stories], 3 vols, (1955), II, 189-217.
46. *Válogatott elbeszélések*, II, 410-411.
47. On the noble and heroic figure of the historical Abdurraham (Abdi) Pasha see Árpád Károlyi, *Buda és Pest visszavívása 1868-ban* [The Re-Conquest of Buda and Pest in 1868] (1886; rev. ed. 1936). His final stand is described on pp. 374-375.
48. *Válogatott elbeszélések*, II, 410-411.
49. Ibid., 436-437.
50. Ibid., 418.
51. This change is evident in virtually all of the more recent publications on Ottoman history in the West. On the Hungarian aspect of this

question see: S. B. Vardy, "The Ottoman Empire in European Historiography: A Re-evaluation by Sándor Takáts," *Turkish Review* (Pittsburgh), 2/9 (1972), 1-16, also reprinted in *Duquesne University Studies in History* (Pittsburgh, 1977); and idem, "The Changing Image of the Turks in Twentieth-Century Hungarian Historiography," Paper presented at the Fourth International Congress of Southeast European Studies, Ankara, Turkey, August 13-18, 1979.

Louis J. Elteto

THE HUNGARIAN POET'S TASK:
THE HISTORIC AND HISTORICAL MISSION
OF HUNGARIAN POETRY THROUGH FIVE CENTURIES

In 1847, young Sándor Petőfi, destined to become Hungary's best-known poet, summed up his view of his art as follows:

> Let no-one start to strike the strings
> Irresponsibly.
> He who takes the lyre now
> Assumes a great task.
> If all you can do is to sing
> Of your own pain and joy,
> The world has then no need of you—
> Lay down the holy lyre therefore.[1]

These thoughts are a formulation of an old Hungarian poetic tradition. At the same time, they are nothing less than a literary program, which Hungary's better poets have followed ever since.

That the poet is not merely molded by his milieu but also shapes it in turn, that he has a moral responsibility in forming history by affecting the thinking of others, is not a widely-held view in the traditions of the West. In Hungary, it has always been otherwise. For the Hungarian poet, life means, more often than not, a state of crisis, in which his nation, his culture, even his language is threatened. He may—and does—sing his own pain and joy, of love, life, death and the human condition, but to be a good artist in a hostile world, he must do more: nurture the language, keep faith alive, give hope, and lead the way to action when that is needed. Petőfi, who was to fall on the battlefield two years later, makes the task clear:

> We wander in the desert,
> As Moses did with his people,
> Following a column of fire
> Sent by God to guide them.
> In recent times God has ordered
> Poets to be such fire-columns,
> That they should lead
> The people into Canaan.[2]

The language is revolutionary and, at the same time, religious: the poet's charge to lead his people into the future is really a divine imperative.

Hungary's national literature first blossomed during the sixteenth century, at the time of the Reformation. Split into a Catholic West, a Protestant East and a Turkish South, the country became, for nearly two hundred years, a theater of military operations of theretofore unheard-of size, interrupted by long periods of skirmishing and guerrilla war. The poetry that sprouted over the battlefields and graveyards is a powerful, soldierly lyric, written by and for men who fought, loved and prayed hard.

Bálint Balassi (1554-1594) is the best representative of this era's early part. A polished gentleman well versed also in Latin, Italian, German, Polish, Turkish and Romanian, his "flower songs" [*virágénekek*]—as the baroque love poems are known in Hungary—are a joy to read and recite even today, and his religious verses are a fine example of the biblically inspired poetry of the age, revealing genuine repentance and the struggle of a true sinner with God. But it is his war poems that really distinguish Balassi, for they are unmatched in any other European literature of the period. He wrote from experience, spending most of his life in the saddle, until he fell at Esztergom in 1594. Here is how he describes the Turkish frontier that he knew so well:

> Under bloody banners
> The soldiers bear lances,
> Standards flutter in the breeze;

The Hungarian Poet's Task

Mighty armies spying,
Across the fields flying,
They ride swiftly, as the wind;
Panther-skin capes trailing,
Shiny helmets glaring,
They're handsome in everything.

Good Saracen chargers
Prance under their masters
When a distant bugle calls;
Some of them mount the guard
While the rest, who dismount,
Greet the morning, at daybreak,
Where in the dark of night
After the wearying fight
They had laid themselves to rest.

The breadth of the meadows,
The woods with their shadows,
Are like palaces to them;
Ambushes on byways,
Skirmishes on highways,
The only schooling they get;
Starvation, thirst and heat
Out on the battlefield
And wear are their amusement.

In their sharp sabres bright
They take a just delight,
For they're collectors of heads;
Over the battlegrounds
In bloody, mangled mounds,
Unburied comrades lie, dead;
Bellies of beasts and birds
Often become the urns
Of a good soldier's ashes.

Oh, army glorious
Of brave young warriors
Serving on the wide frontier!
The whole world respects you;
May God still protect you

> And increase your name and fame:
> As He gives trees apples,
> May He in your battles
> Grant you victory in the field![3]

Balassi is *engagé* in the modern sense; his poetry has a moral quality that the works of studio-poets lack. Even his romanticism is honest and realistic—the blood, the wounds, the severed heads, the heat, thirst, and the pain of battle: this was his life, and he did not write his songs for his desk drawer. He read them, sang them to the troops, and inspired younger companions, such as Rimay, to write in turn. How much Balassi and his pupils added to the consciousness, the pride and spirit without which Hungary could not have survived, we cannot tell, but the question is not merely academic as far as Hungary's history is concerned.

Petőfi's generation knew Balassi's work, as they did that of Miklós Zrínyi (1620-1664), the most important master of the next, the seventeenth century. A superbly educated aristocrat, Zrínyi was tutored by Cardinal Pázmány (1570-1637), the most famous proponent of the Hungarian Counter-Reformation. He attended the universities of Graz, Vienna and Nagyszombat [Tyrnau, Trnava] and sojourned in Italy. He knew and wrote Latin, Italian, Croatian and German besides Hungarian. A man of the world on a grander scale than Balassi, Zrínyi was a general at 26 and Viceroy of Croatia at 27. He lived out his life leading armies, building fortifications, writing on military and political matters, and feuding with Vienna for support—but his real love was poetry, which he pursued to the end, in 1664, when he was killed, allegedly by a wounded boar. The rumor still persists that he was in fact assassinated on imperial orders—for Zrínyi saw in German expansion no less a danger than in the might of the Turk. His greatest literary achievement is a long epic, *The Peril of Sziget [Szigeti veszedelem]*,[4] in which he describes the campaign culminating in the fall of Szigetvár (Fort Sziget) a century before. Szigetvár's defender, Zrínyi's great-grandfather, perished with his entire garrison of 2000 men in that battle, but broke the Turkish onslaught for several years.

The Peril of Sziget is still exciting reading. Most fascinating about the work is its attention to detail and its historic accuracy, which is rarely sacrificed for literary effect. We are introduced to dozens of characters intimately, know their feelings, hopes and fears, and never doubt that these were real men, not heroes of fiction. In telling their story, Zrínyi combines the novelist's sweeping vision with the dramatist's skill in building tension. To cite an example: It is a dark night and Mehmet Pasha, a young dandy from Istanbul, is encamped with his regiment under the walls of Siklós. In vain does the commander of the local garrison beseech him to quarter himself within the walls; Mehmet would like nothing better than the prestige of fighting Zrínyi. "Besides," he remarks, "it's raining and Zrínyi will not attack now." The local officer knows better, as does the reader; for while the two are sipping coffee, Zrínyi is quietly moving down the valley. A Turkish youth with a lute steps into Mehmet's tent and sings of fortune, love, peace and happiness, while wolves lurk out in the night. The camp is massacred and Mehmet killed—a historical fact, as it was this engagement that diverted Süleyman from his drive to the north, against the stronghold of Eger.

Zrínyi wrote his magnificent work, as he tells us, in a few winter weeks, between campaigns. In his closing "Peroration" he calls it "my great work, which neither jealous time nor fire can undo, nor the wrath of heaven, nor iron destroy, nor the enemy harm," but adds:

> Yet I seek fame not only with the word,
> But also with my terrible battle-sword;
> Until I die, I'll fight the Turkish horde
> And strew, with glee, its ashes over the world.

Otherwise—what matter? A true soldier, he wrote in a later verse:

> The blue will shroud me if I have no coffin.
> If I find honor in my final hour,
> Let wolves devour me, let ravens digest me—
> The sky will be above, the earth below.[5]

Zrínyi was right. By 1700, the Turkish moon had waned, and in its stead the Germans ruled the land. One yoke had replaced another. The result was the *Kuruc* wars, between pro and anti-Habsburg forces, whose height was reached in Ferenc Rákóczi's fight for independence (1703-1711). In many ways, this was Hungary's—and Europe's—first "democratic" war, and its populism is seen in the best poetry of the period. Most of the extensive collection of lyrics from this time is of anonymous authorship. They are songs made by and for the troops, recording tales of battles, having both positive and negative propaganda value:

> Crane-legged, magpie-nosed
> Miserable Germans!
> Run before us, fearful of us,
> Despicable nation.
>
> Up and at them, chase them, cut them,
> They are our enemies;
> Let us show our Magyar people
> What good soldiering is!
>
> The good *Kuruc* horseman
> Wears a tailored dolman,
> Jangling spurs upon his boots, and
> Rides on a swift stallion.
>
> The Germans had better get out
> Of our noble country,
> Before we make, before we cut
> Their hides into belting![6]

But after eight tiring years, when French support was withdrawn, the end had to come. Outnumbered, outgunned, with more and more of the nobility deserting the cause, the *Kuruc* armies lay down their arms at Nagymajtény. The sadness and the disappointment that followed gave birth to the so-called *bujdosó*-songs, fugitive-songs that turned to God for consolation:

> The dew of the green woods,
> The track of my red boots
> Winter covers up with snow.
>
> Friends that I had, and loved,
> Comrades with whom I fought—
> Oh, they have betrayed me.
>
> I'll go far, far away,
> Find a new place to stay:
> God will guide my wandering.[7]

The Hungarian Poet's Task

A battleground for 185 years, Hungary seemed ruined, its population reduced to less than what it had been two centuries before. Recovery, now tied to Viennese directives, was painfully slow. The nobility, who had managed to come out ahead in 1711, now had to pay the piper by fighting the Dynasty's wars abroad. Tax and tariff policies made Hungary an Austrian colony in fact if not in name. Foreign homesteaders were imported to replace the lost Magyar peasantry, changing the land's ethnography. Such a climate did not encourage literary pursuits and, indeed, the first half of the eighteenth century is the low-point in Hungarian letters.

The very existence of the Magyar tongue was threatened. The leading families were becoming cosmopolitan, and the centralist tendencies encouraged the introduction of German as the official language. Joseph II even decreed the teaching of Hungarian to be illegal. The decree was never enforced, but that it could be issued at all shows the weakness of Hungarian society at the time.

Yet by the end of the century there were no fewer than two dozen outstanding poets writing in Hungarian, starting literary societies, founding journals, and involving themselves in the political life of the country. Their efforts led to the rebirth of the nation, the beginning of modern Hungarian letters, culture and language. Without them, there might not be a Hungary today.

The magnificent, explosive phenomenon of the Hungarian Enlightenment is too complex to sketch. To state its essence: young Hungarians discovered Western Europe and, at the same time, their own heritage. In previous ages, education meant a knowledge of Latin, Italian, perhaps of ancient Greek; now it meant knowing French, English and German, though Latin remained important. Instead of schooling themselves on Vergil and Petrarch, the new generation devoured Voltaire, Rousseau, Shakespeare and Locke, Gottsched and Kant. Nor did they shy away from political activism, and many suffered for their views. Ferenc Kazinczy (1759-1831) spent seven years behind bars, Ferenc Verseghy (1757-1822) nine. János Batsányi (1763-1845), perhaps the most talented among them, was imprisoned twice, and never returned to Hungary from his Austrian exile.

The slogan of the new literary movement was that the Hungarian writer must be

> Like a burning torch that blazes in the darkness
> And, itself consuming, casts a light for others. . . .[8]

Accordingly, one of the major concerns of the poets of the time was to instruct the next generation and to induce it to take up the pen, too. Count Stephen Széchenyi's (1791-1860) famous adage that "the nation lives in its language"[9] was formulated much earlier in a poem by Dávid Baróti Szabó (1739-1819), a Jesuit, from whom the concluding line is startling:

> Awaken, Hungarian youth! Behold, your national language,
> The mark of a handsome race, rushes unto its death.
> Take the pen; start writing; strike up an acquaintance
> With lyric Apollo in the native tongue of your land.
> There's no better means, nor will there ever be, ever: so do
> All witty Britons, Frenchmen, Italians and Dutch.
> And what beautiful verses fill their books and their journals!
> How they bear them to you! How eager you are to receive them!
> How your land is filled with the dazzling treasures of others!
> How Árpád's language[10] and race hasten to disappear!
> Awake from your slumber, take pity at last on the language
> Of your land—which, if it die, know, you're eternally dead![11]

The younger generation listened, and after the greatest genius of the era, Mihály Csokonai Vitéz (1773-1805) had shown the way, albeit with tragic results,[12] many were ready to write for a career, dedicating their lives to letters, though of course not to poetry alone. Professional publishing and journalism were rapidly becoming a source of income and a means for influencing the thinking no longer only of the intellectual elite, but of the entire nation. And if earlier poets had built a Hungarian tradition of engagement, those of the nineteenth century became fully aware and conscious of their role. Of the dozens of outstanding names, we need to mention but three to show this: Mihály Vörösmarty, Sándor Petőfi and János Arany.

Born in 1800, Vörösmarty left a career at law to become a writer in 1826. His epic, *The Rout of Zalán* [*Zalán futása*] (1825) had brought him instant fame; in it he told a fanciful story of the Magyar conquest of the Carpathian Basin in the ninth century. He wrote for various journals, became an editor and a member of the Hungarian Academy of Sciences. Today he is best remembered for his lyric poetry, especially for those works in which he tried to instill pride in the nation, to remind it of its past, which had to be made glorious even when it was not quite so. Yet Vörösmarty's intent was always of the highest morality possible:

> What is our role in life? It is to struggle
> As best we can for that which is most noble.
> Before us lies an entire nation's fate.
> When we have fought it from its deep morass,
> And in the light of intellecual battle
> Have raised it to the greatest possible height,
> Then we may say, returning unto dust:
> Thank you, oh Life, for having blest us so—
> It was good pleasure, a work fit for men![13]

Active in the War of 1848-1849 on the political front, Vörösmarty was crushed by the defeat dealt Hungary by Austria and Russia. He took to drink and died in 1855.

Petőfi was born the son of a saloon-keeper and butcher, in 1823. We have already noted his view of the poet's role, and know that he lived in accord with it. Yet, for all that, his greatest achievement was not political, but purely cultural. It was he who first became a *popular* poet—read and loved by the entire nation. While his martyrdom in 1849 had a lot to do with his becoming a hero, a better explanation for his popularity is to be found in his style—for Petőfi transformed the everyday language of everyday people into an artistic medium. Because he de-intellectualized poetry and made it accessible to all, he had a greater impact on Hungary's rank and file than any other poet, even to this day.

His friend János Arany (1817-1882) is a possible exception. Born five years before Petőfi, Arany was destined to become Hungary's narrative poet *par excellence,* one who won every honor that could be bestowed upon a writer. Active in developing a cultural policy for the defeated nation, he became the entire country's teacher in literature and criticism. Like that of Petőfi, his poetry was realistic and built on folk tradition. He also founded a school of translation unique to Hungary. It is sometimes claimed that Hungarian translations are improvements on the originals— and while that is certainly an overstatement, it is true that translating literature has been entrusted to the best talents in Hungary every since Arany. The pliability of the Hungarian language enabled these masters to do outstanding work in this regard.

Arany's personal task, as he saw it, was to define the essence of being a Hungarian poet. He sums up his role thus:

> I'm not ashamed, nor do I care
> That, since I had to write,
> My writing is Hungarian
> And isn't read abroad.
> It's not the wonder of two worlds,
> Of mine I am but *one*. . . .
>
> Let the might aggrandize
> Their tongue, their land, their god!
> A tide that washes all away,
> They ruin and fructify.
> In a *small* land, whose role it is
> To bar destruction's way,
> The poet's place is with his own—
> To want more is to die.[14]

The end of the nineteenth century is much underrated by current Hungarian literary criticism. The reason is political: Marxist scholarship is hard put to find its own justification in the poetry of this period, which was largely bourgeois in outlook. But while no one of Arany's stature dominated these years, many outstanding poets were writing, for an ever widening public: Pál Gyulai (1826-1909), Károly Szász (1829-1905), János Vajda (1827-1897), Gyula Reviczky (1855-1889), Jenő Komjáthy (1858-1895), Emil Ábrányi (1851-1920), Andor Kozma (1861-1933), Jenő Heltai (1871-1957), to mention but a few, are names with which every Hungarian school child is (or ought to be) familiar. Since this was a time of construction, expansion and optimism, we see none of Petőfi's fire-columns. Many people thought, indeed, that the Promised Land had already arrived, but that was not so: by the beginning of our own century, a general malaise had overcome Europe, and Hungary was no exception. An agrarian and urban proletariat had evolved, minority questions were plaguing the country, and abroad; war was in the air. Over a million Hungarian nationals left the country before World War I to seek their fortunes in other climes. Internally, the political response to the problems was rigidity, even corrupt impotence.

During this time Hungarian poets again felt the need to become involved. Endre Ady is the most important by far. Born in 1877, he was a

The Hungarian Poet's Task

professional journalist before he dedicated himself wholly to poetry. He became an opponent of the Hungarian establishment, political, clerical and literary, and challenged it, almost single-handed. As controversial a figure as ever one can find in the Hungarian tradition, he was a man full of paradoxes: deeply Christian, yet pagan; modern, yet conservative; decadent, but a worshiper of life; thoroughly moral, but a debauched fornicator; revolutionary, yet contemptuous of the rabble; humble, yet not above comparing himself with Jesus. There is no poetry more Hungarian than his, but no Hungarian poetry more European in outlook. Because he is so deceptively western, he is translated more often than other Hungarian poets, yet his is the least understandable poetry in even the better foreign renditions, so Hungarian are his language, his imagery, symbolism, emotional and spiritual world. And Ady loved Hungary more than any other poet, yet hated her intensely. Though he died in 1919, pupils in secondary schools were forbidden to read him until the 1930s, and then only in strictly censored editions; only the boldest critics dared defend him; and, until the end of the Second World War, even his name was almost unmentionable in many so-called better homes. Marxist critics try to claim him, but do not know quite what to make of him. Ady is more popular than ever, as apropos as ever, as dangerous to the establishment as ever. He is read by the younger generation like an Old-Testament prophet, whom he, for all his modernism, perhaps best resembles:

> Our Lord of Hosts scatters his people, too:
> Such is the custom of the stricter gods,
> As a sad Transylvanian preacher
> Of long ago once wrote,
> Seeking our kinship with the Jews.
>
> With wrong morals we came to the wrong place,
> Highwaymen once, then merely in the way,
> And while our lords devoured each other and the people,
> Our lazy dreams were beaten down by hail,
> And we haven't even built the Temple.
>
> We were unable *then* to stand our ground,
> And wound up *here*—that's our initial curse.
> Our blood, adulterous, is no longer ours,
> Anything can come and take our place:
> We've killed ourselves, we've sinned ourselves to death.

> And we, in our dispersal, shall not be
> Forsaken, yet victorious a race:
> Not hardened in the raging fire of ages,
> The furnace of the world will melt us down,
> And we'll be gone, because we've lost ourselves.[15]

A literary program incarnate, Ady must be read in entirety to be understood—a poem or two cannot give a true picture of his poetic views. He is the most eminent example of the engaged Hungarian poet, whether we take a religious, a patriotic, a socialist, a humanist, or just about any other approach to his work, so wide is his scope, so broad his vision.

Before turning to contemporary Hungary, we must make an all-too-brief mention of three other men who had an impact on Hungarian poetry almost as great as Ady, and the "almost" is admittedly a matter of opinion: Mihály Babits (1883-1941), Dezső Kosztolányi (1885-1936), and Attila József (1905-1937). The former two were Ady's contemporaries, but outlived him by about two decades. Both were intellectual poets, master craftsmen whose verse has been equaled rarely, if ever, by others. Both were "involved" in our sense of the word, though Kosztolányi far less so than Babits. Here is an example from each, showing their conceptions of the poet's duty. Commenting on the dehumanized horror of materiel-war in 1916, Babits continues:

> still, I do not sing of machines,
> this March, now, when
> in the air, the strength of the wind,
> you can taste the wet
> of our blood-juices, the drink of
> dear Hungarian blood:
> my lips, when I drank this salty air,
> became chapped and the words
> now hurt in my mouth:
> but even if my lips crack, even then,
> a Hungarian song, in this March season,
> a bloody song will break the wind!
> I do not sing the victor,
> not the nation-machine, the blind hero,
> whose every stop is death,
> whose glance stifles words,
> whose handshake is slavery,
> but him I sing, whoever, anyone,

The Hungarian Poet's Task

> who will first utter the word,
> who first dares to say,
> to shout, the brave one, brave one,
> the magic word, awaited by the
> hundred-thousands, the breath-giving, holy,
> man-redeeming, man-restoring,
> nation-saving, gate-opening,
> liberating, precious word:
> enough! enough! it's been enough!
> and: peace! peace! peace! peace!
> peace! peace now!
> Let it end now!
> Let the sleeping sleep,
> the living live,
> the poor hero rest,
> the poor people hope.
> Let the bells ring,
> let's alleluyah sing,
> by the time that March returns,
> let's blossom anew![16]

And Kosztolányi's poem, "Flag":

> Just a stick and canvas,
> but it's not a stick and canvas,
> it's a flag.
>
> Always talking.
> Always waving.
> Always feverish.
> Always in a frenzy
> above the street,
> fluttering on high
> up in the sky,
> proclaiming something
> madly.
> Even when they're used to it and pay it no attention,
> even when they're asleep,
> night and day,
> till it gets all worn thin,
> and still it stands, like a skinny, apostolic preacher
> on the rooftop
> above,

> wrestling the stillness and the wind,
> useless, yet ever more majestic,
> fluttering, talking.
> My soul, you too, you too—
> not a stick and canvas—
> be a flag.[17]

József is different from Babits and Kosztolányi: younger than they, he was born in 1905, the son of a cobbler who deserted his family. He grew up in miserable circumstances, and committed suicide in 1937. Because he became an avowed communist, he was an outcast in the Hungary of his lifetime. Not until after 1945 did he become famous—unfortunately, for political reasons, though his genius with words is enough justification for his fame. József's life was committed to political struggle, but he fought with the pen, and with the mores of a saint:

> The glass-makers build large fires
> and with their blood and their sweat
> they mix the mold
> that cooks transparent in their kettles.
> They then pour it into panes,
> and with the waning strength of their powerful arms
> they roll them smooth.
> And when day breaks,
> they bear light with them
> into cities and farm shacks.
>
> Sometimes you call them workers,
> sometimes they are called poets,
> though neither is more than the other.
> Slowly the blood of both ebbs away,
> they themselves become transparent,
> sparkling, huge crystal-windows
> on the future being built of you.[18]

Trained as a teacher of Hungarian and French, József was denied certification because of the alleged immorality of his poems. Recalling the incident bitterly shortly before his death, he swore: "I shall teach my whole people, and not on the high-school level!"—a promise he has kept, from the grave.

A man who did literally that was Miklós Radnóti (1909-1944), who represents a transition to post-war Hungary. Radnóti would have remained strictly second-rate if we did not possess the beautiful, deeply humanistic poetry he wrote in the concentration camps he served in before he was shot to death in November, 1944. His moving odes, written in a traditional, classical meter, are morally incomparable: in spite of his fate, they contain not one word of hatred, nor of reproach, for the Hungary he still loved, or against the German guards who were to shoot him. Here are the last lines he wrote, about a week before his death, discovered on his body after it was exhumed from a mass grave:

> I fell beside him. His body turned over
> and tautened like a string before it breaks.
> Shot in the head. "So that's how *you* will end it,"
> I whispered to myself, "just lie real still."
> Flowers of death blossom on patience now.
> *"Der springt noch auf!"*—I heard a shout above.
> Dry blood is on my earlobe, caked with mud.[19]

More than any other poet, Radnóti has taught Hungary to become reconciled with its past of 1944-1945. But the horror was not yet over, and the better Hungarian poets, involved as always, did their best to fight it.

The events of 1956 and the role played in them by poets and writers is too well known to neeed retelling here. The debates of the Petőfi Circle, the publications during the brief period of freedom in October, the writers' strike that lasted until amnesty was granted to the last imprisoned colleague, is still current events for us. So is the recent activity of Hungarian men of letters in support of human rights. The chapter is by no means closed.

Today's Hungary has no lack of outstanding poets, but we are too close to them to attempt an evaluation of their moral effect. Gyula Illyés (1902-), the *eminence gris* of Hungarian literature, no doubt enjoys the highest respect. He, László Benjámin (1915-), Imre Csanádi (1920-), Ferenc Juhász (1928-), Sándor Weöres (1913-), Ágnes Nemes-Nagy (1922-), János Pilinszky (1921-1981), and others, living or deceased, will surely find their way into the nation's poetic hall of fame—and if the country's traditions are a guide, those will be the first who were best able to sing of more than just their own pain and joy, or—we must add today—of the joys of scientific socialism. Style and language change, but the poet's task remains:

> Why cry for that which was?
> And why for what will not be?
> Every day we are born,
> our every new work and word is our last.

> By now every child of this earth,
> if he has not lived with closed eyes and heart,
> has seen and suffered the agony of the begetting Era,
> dying with it by the minute; and while here
> veins burst and vertebrae cracked,
> there, a new generation, a new Laocoön-group
> girded itself, unsuspecting, for victory.

> I do not fear the Law. Will day break
> tomorrow, too?—My only care is
> that I do the task allotted for today,
> that I utter that word yet:
> then let the snake come.[20]

NOTES

1. Sándor Petőfi, "A XIX század költői" [Poets of the 19th Century]. Excerpt. The Hungarian text of the poems cited in this essay are so well-known that they may be found in most good anthologies. *Hét évszázad magyar versei* [Hungarian Poems of Seven Centuries], eds. István Király, Tibor Klaniczay, Pál Pándi and Miklós Szabolcsi (3 vols., Budapest: Szépirodalmi Kiadó, 1972), is one such—and an excellent—collection. All translations are mine.
2. Ibid.
3. Bálint Balassi, "Egy katonaének" [A Soldier Song]. Excerpt.
4. Count Miklós Zrínyi, "Szigeti veszedelem" [Peril of Sziget]. Excerpt.
5. Zrínyi, "Az idő és hírnév" [Time and Fame].
6. "Csínom Palkó" [a nickname for *kuruc* soldiers]. Anonymous. Excerpt.
7. "Zöld erdő harmatát" [The Dew of the Green Woods]. Anonymous. Excerpt.

8. János Batsányi, "Magyar író" [The Hungarian Writer]. Excerpt.
9. Count István (Stephen) Széchenyi, a prominent Hungarian statesman and philosopher.
10. "Árpád's language"–Magyar, or Hungarian. From Árpád, who led the Magyar conquest of the Carpathian Basin in 896.
11. Dávid Baróti-Szabó, "A magyar ifjúsághoz" [To Hungarian Youth]
12. Mihály Csokonai-Vitéz, tried to earn his living exclusively as a writer, but without success; his poverty contributed to his illness and early death.
13. Mihály Vörösmarty, "Gondolatok a könyvtárban" [Reflections in the Library]. Excerpt.
14. János Arany, "Kozmopolita költészet" [Cosmopolitan Poetry]. Excerpt.
15. Endre Ady, "A szétszóródás előtt" [Before Diaspora].
16. Mihály Babits, "Húsvét előtt" [Before Easter]. Excerpt.
17. Dezső Kosztolányi, "Zászló" [Flag].
18. Attila József, "Tanítások" [Teachings]. Excerpt.
19. Miklós Radnóti, "Razglednicák" [Croatian for "picture postcard", with Hungarian plural]. Excerpt.
20. László Benjámin. Untitled.

Paula Sutter Fichtner

"DIE FRAU OHNE SCHATTEN:"
OPERA AS CONSERVATIVE ALLEGORY

Nationalist revolutionaries in nineteenth-century Europe were quick to see that the opera could be politically useful. Music, combined with words and stage action could stir up the mass enthusiasm on which the success of their programs depended. Supporters of Italian unification went perhaps farther than any, turning even the name of Verdi into an acronym which stood for their final goal—*Vittorio Emmanuele Re d'Italia*.[1]

But liberals have not had a monopoly on opera as an ideological weapon. Conservatives have turned the music drama to their ends as well, though examples are more difficult to find. Commenting on the relationship between opera and politics, James H. Billington seems to think that the absence of revolutionary themes in the works of the Russian Modeste Moussorgsky and the German Richard Wagner qualifies them for the label conservative.[2] Far more explicit examples of his point would have been some of the libretti which the Austrian poet, dramatist, and essayist, Hugo von Hofmannsthal, developed for the composer Richard Strauss in their collaboration of twenty years. Uncannily attuned to the symbolic meaning of human relationships, Hofmannsthal came to see these more in political than aesthetic terms as he lived through the last chaotic days of the Habsburg Monarchy and the equally troubled beginning of the first Austrian republic. The destructiveness of political nationalism had been amply proven as far as he was concerned; Bolshevism, though it marched under international banners, was no better. He therefore became a spokesman for yet another vision of a regenerated Europe—one in which social and political harmony would come about not through the violent re-ordering of boundaries, class distinctions, and economies, but through changes in human beings themselves.[3]

Few ideas sound more radical than that of re-shaping the very nature of man. However, the notion has venerable conservative antecedents. No less a figure than Edmund Burke had voiced such sentiments in his *Reflections on the Revolution in France*. For him it was a way of stressing the futility of tampering with traditional social and political arrangements. The very real evil in the world, according to him, came from human passions, not the structures which disciplined them. If such evil were to be eradicated, it was the hearts of men that must be altered, not the forms of their government.[4] Faced with what they regarded as institutional collapse all around them after World War I, Central European conservatives such as Hofmannsthal felt that such a philosophy offered the only alternative to national and class warfare. By the Austrian poet's own admission, his most successful artistic effort to promote these ideas came in "Die Frau ohne Schatten." Indeed, he was so engaged by the material that he did two versions of it—the opera libretto was followed by a far more elaborate prose narrative. Due to the limitations of the war economy on theatrical production in Central Europe, both were first presented to the public in 1919. The texts differ—whole episodes in the prose version are missing from the opera. The social content of the stage work is more overt. However, the thematic texture of both pieces is nearly identical, so that one can reasonably assume that Hofmannsthal had the same moral purpose in mind when he wrote each of them.[5]

Drawn from German re-workings of Persian and Arabic sources, the opera tells of an Emperor of "the Southeastern Islands" who, on one of his frequent hunts, brings down a gazelle with the aid of a favorite falcon. About to kill his prey, the Emperor sees that it is not a beast at all, but the temporarily transformed daughter of Keikobad, the ruler of the spirit world. Instead of slaying the young woman, he is passionately attracted to her and takes her as his Empress. However, despite their physical infatuation with one another, they can have no children. The Empress, still part of her father's incorporeal realm, casts no shadow. Unless she acquires one, and with it the capacity to bear mortal progeny, the vengeful Keikobad will turn her husband to stone.[6]

Opera as Conservative Allegory

Resolved to find such a shadow, she and her mysterious nurse-companion enter the world of common men and women. Disguised as servants, the two women take up residence in the house of a good-natured, but naive and unperceptive dyer, Barak, and his wife.[7] Procreative troubles afflict this pair too. The dyer longs to have children; his petulant and dissatisfied bride, though possessed of a shadow, does not want them. Taking advantage of her discontent, the Empress and her nurse persuade the woman to give up her shadow in return for promises of finery and a handsome lover. But overcome by guilt for what she is doing to Barak, the Empress cannot accept the shadow she has schemed away from his wife. Nor can the latter cast off her husband when she sees his outrage at her impending unfaithfulness. The Empress's sacrifice transforms them all. She receives a shadow of her own, the Emperor retains his fleshy estate, and Barak and his wife, once again with her shadow, are reunited. The opera closes with a chorus of unborn children, some of whom will presumably receive the gift of life from one or the other couple, and a celebration of human brotherhood on all sides. The prose version ends somewhat less jubilantly, but in the same vein, with a remark about "...the eternal mystery of the interconnectedness of all earthly things."[8]

Ideological messages are usually cast out of materials far more transparent than these. Indeed, Hofmannsthal himself thought that "Die Frau ohne Schatten" was somewhat unaccessible. It is perhaps for this reason that the opera has not become a repertory staple, even though its score is one of Strauss's lushest and most inventive. Yet, Hofmannsthal called "Die Frau ohne Schatten" an "...allegory of the social...," and at least some of his contemporaries, especially those with conservative leanings, apparently knew what he meant.[9] Though at one point he thought that the libretto might need an introduction, he did not plan to do it himself. Rather, he felt that he could entrust the job to the Austrian writer Max Mell, a close sympathizer.[10] Describing the opera after its premier in Vienna, a reviewer in the *Österreichische Rundschau* called it "...the first opera libretto since Wagner which is not merely to listen to and to view, but also to think about, [and] which contains a moral idea."[11] Some years later, discussing the prose version in the Catholic and conservative *Schweizerische Rundschau,* Olga Brand said that the story directly addressed problems of modern life. The Austrian journal thought the central idea of the opera to be that of a younger generation coming into being through the purification of its elders. Brand went into greater detail. In her view, such a cleansing took place when the adults of the tale rejected hedonism and isolation, thereby allowing the unborn to enter the world of the living. Love, in the process, becomes the agent of a higher purpose rather than an expression of pure egoism. In the Empress, the character whom Hofmannsthal claimed was central to the dramatic development of the entire plot, motherhood embodies "...self-sacrificing, redemptive love."[12] Even Hofmannsthal's critics, such as his erstwhile friend and correspondent, Count Harry Kessler, found a social and moral message in the opera.[13]

Many of the basic themes of "Die Frau ohne Schatten" were commonplace in German and Austrian literature. The comedies of the early nineteenth-century Viennese playwright Ferdinand Raimund are peopled with characters of a higher social station who are saved from dire straits by contact with more humble folk. German romantic writing often treated love as a bridge linking the isolated ego to the universal, thereby completing the personal development of the individual.[14] Nor was Hofmannsthal using these and other ideas prominent in the opera for the first time in his own work. As early as 1907, he had spoken of the need to integrate all classes of society to counteract the *anomie* of his contemporary industrial environment.[15] The shadow as a symbol of the links between one human and another figures in his famous poem "Manche freilich . . . ," written around 1895:

> Doch ein Schatten fällt von jenen Leben
> In die anderen Leben hinüber,
> Und die leichten sind an die schweren
> Wie an Luft und Erde gebunden.[16]

But it was World War I that made Hofmannsthal's preoccupation with the spiritual bonds of society politically compelling. His growing activism led him to put forth these thoughts in lecture tours he undertook on Austria's behalf and in the propaganda which he enthusiastically edited and wrote. Analyzing Grillparzer in a volume which he put together for such purposes, he praised the nineteenth-century dramatist for what he called his "...responsibility for the totality."[17] As the war ground on, Hofmannsthal came to believe that Europe was undergoing a general purgation, after which, for its own deliverance, it would have to examine the roots of Austrian history very closely. From it, he felt the entire continent could learn the ideas of supra-nationality which were, to him, the lone avenue of its survival.[18]

First-hand contact with the national hatred unleashed by the war deepened his convictions. Two weeks in Prague in the middle of 1917, during which the once friendly local press took no notice of him, were crucial in his development. Shocked by the intensity of Czech opposition to "us," as he put it, he argued that internationalism was the only way to counteract such feelings. He advanced the old Holy Roman Empire as a kind of organizational model, since, in his view, it owed its authority not to "... power and continuity and self-assertion..." but to "... something higher...."[19] He did not specify what this higher principle was beyond emphasizing the "holy" in the title. At the very least, however, he seems to have felt as European conservatives traditionally have, that human institutions required some spiritual underpinning in order for them to be effective. Even as the dramatist was finishing the libretto of "Die Frau ohne Schatten" in 1916, the future Christian Socialist chancellor of post-war Austria, Ignaz Seipel, was saying much the same thing in his newly-published *Nation und Staat*. The priest-statesman argued that the corrosive toll which chauvinism took of practical government could be lessened only through a merger of political internationalism and cultural nationalism. Like Hofmannsthal, he believed that the state had an obligation to care for all its people. Again like the poet, Seipel thought that secular institutions must have a morally transcendent element in them to arbitrate human affairs successfully.[20]

But Hofmannsthal was neither a politician nor a professional propagandist. He was an artist, and "Die Frau ohne Schatten" was the best way for him to present these views and the experiences which had shaped them. The libretto was difficult for him to finish; it was only under the stimulation of the trip to Prague in 1917 that his creative powers rose to a level where he could work "feverishly" on the manuscript.[21] Additional inspiration came to him from reading Houston Stewart Chamberlain's *Goethe,* where he learned that the great German dramatist had also considered doing a text for the music drama. Interestingly, the theme of irreconcilability emerges in this work as well, for Chamberlain argues that Goethe dropped it as a subject for tragedy.[22]

"Die Frau ohne Schatten" is, above all, a tale of reconciliation and harmonization brought about by the inward transformation of all its characters.

In Hofmannsthal's own words, the opera was to be made up of eleven scenes in which "...two worlds, two pairs of human beings, two conflicts alternately succeed one another, mirror one another, heighten one another, and finally resolve one another."[23] From the moment he began his first sketches for the libretto, the theme of overcoming the self was central to his conception of the story.[24] Only after the Empress concerns herself with the fates of both her husband and Barak are the problems of all participants in the drama solved. Through her caring for others, willingness to sacrifice her membership in the spirit world not only for the Emperor but for the plebeian dyer—that is, for the larger community—the difficulties troubling both couples vanish.[25] One human transformation brings both levels of society closer together. This situation exemplified what Hofmannsthal called the "allomatic," a Greek derivative meaning transformation through the influence of another. This he contrasted with the "automatic," or change of the self through the self, in his view the normal state of affairs of men in a fragmented society. Indeed, for Hofmannsthal "Die Frau ohne Schatten" embodied the "triumph of the allomatic."[26]

Closely interwoven with the theme of shared humanity is a second one —the need to appreciate people for what they are rather than for what they can be used. Hofmannsthal saw the problems of male-female relations as the most telling way to make this point. In the opening scene of the opera, the Emperor describes his wife as "quarry;" in the prose narrative, a group of children whom he had met accuse him of surrounding her with walls.[27] The resentment of the dyer's wife toward Barak and her situation stems from her feeling that her husband takes no interest in her for what she is—an attractive if short-tempered woman. Wholly absorbed in his trade and his desire for progeny, he confesses in the prose tale that it was the hope of riches, children, and a long life that had led him to marry in the first place.[28] It is only when Barak threatens to kill the unhappy woman because of her supposed infidelity that she begins to realize, as does he, that she is of some intrinsic value to him.

Again, Hofmannsthal was not the only Austrian conservative to see mutual appreciation of male and female as a way to a more harmonious society. The idea also appears in the work of Othmar Spann, the economist and social philosopher who was one of the developers of the idea of the corporate state. In his *Gesellschaftslehre,* a ponderous compendium of his theories and those of others, he argued that men and women, though different, should realize that they complement one another. In a world increasingly preoccupied by meaningless externals and endangered by the dissolution of the family through female employment, husbands and wives were losing their deepest ties to one another. Women were growing "masculinized" and men were sacrificing themselves to "empty activity." Both sexes needed to re-establish their true natures—for the male to be the ruler and leader of the family, the female to give him emotional depth and direction.[29]

"Die Frau ohne Schatten" speaks to this last point as well. The reknitting of intra-family hierarchy with the emotionally receptive male at its head is the way that Barak and his wife resolve their difficulties. "Stern judge, noble husband," and, for the first time, "my beloved," she calls him as she sees that he is genuinely angered by her supposed betrayal.[30] In his very assertion of his masculine role, he shows that he is vulnerable to her, and the process of reconciliation between them begins.

But the community to which these two people are tied is not confined to themselves and their contemporaries. They bear some measure of responsibility for the future of humanity as well. This is the thought that lies behind the motif of the unborn children present at crucial points in the opera and in its prose counterpart. Once more, the notion of crossgenerational unity was a common one in conservative thought, used to underscore a variety of arguments. For Burke, the linkage of one generation to another through biology and inherited property was a reason not to destroy casually the social and political institutions which tradition had also passed down. Juan Donoso-Cortés, the nineteenth-century Spanish Catholic polemicist with whose work Hofmannsthal had some acquaintance, liked to speak of the love of God uniting generations as a way of arguing that the divine creation could be simultaneously one and diverse.[31] For Hofmannsthal, the act of begetting children was his way of joining the self with all of being.[32]

Done in the state of wedlock, procreation raised man's moral stature as well. In the acts of marriage and parenthood, Hofmannsthal saw love moving men and women beyond the level of the selfish and sensual. Here too, the poet was again at home with the classical strain of European conservative thought which consistently rejected sexual libertinism as an expression of radical privatism and egoism. The ultimate form of such egoism was the sin of separation from God himself, a condition which Donoso-Cortés, for one, thought that prurience encouraged. The Vicomte de Bonald, the early nineteenth-century French conservative whom Hofmannsthal had also read, argued the point in more explicitly social terms. Marriage, to him, was a union of male and female expressly designed to foster society. Libertinage, on the other hand, was an equally conscious way of avoiding larger social responsibilities.[33]

The need to transform the sensual into the moral is a familiar theme in Hofmannsthal's later work; nowhere is it more clearly underscored than in "Die Frau ohne Schatten."[34] The change in the relationship of the Emperor and Empress is especially significant. At the outset of both the opera and prose narrative, the author makes it clear that the two have a deep carnal attachment. Beyond this, they give little thought to the meaning of their relationship. "He is a hunter and a lover, otherwise nothing," says the nurse of the Emperor.[35] The dyer's wife too, is overly engrossed in her bodily charms and how to enhance them.

Hofmannsthal, however, clearly believes that the sexual relationship has far greater significance for society as a while. His ideal emerges in the watchmen's chorus at the end of the first act, which is the musical high point of the opera as well.

> Ihr Gatten in den Häusern dieser Stadt,
> liebet einander mehr als euer Leben,
> und wisset: nicht um eueres Lebens willen
> ist euch die Saat des Lebens anvertraut, . . .
>   *   *   *
> Ihr Gatten die ihr liebend euch in Armen liegt,
> ihr seid die Brücke, überm Abgrund ausgespannt,
> auf der die Toten wiederum ins Leben gehn!
> Geheiligt sei eurer Liebe Werk![36]

The appearance of the Emperor's shadow at the end of the opera and the rejoining of the dyer's wife to hers betokens the approach of motherhood for both women as well as a relationship to humanity as a whole reaching far beyond their immediate surroundings. All of this, it should be noted, takes place without any external changes in the socio-political order itself.[37] Emperor and Empress remain rulers, Barak and his wife, simple proletarians. All, however, are fully sensitized to the humanity of others, and society, both present and future, is much the happier for it.

Through such means did Hofmannsthal impress his vision of eternal human varieties upon his audiences. Persuaded by the war that human institutions could do very little to promote human welfare, he turned to the human heart instead for a way to improve the earthly lot of mankind. The message, issued through "Die Frau ohne Schatten" and other works, was familiar to conservatives of his own time and would not have been altogether foreign to earlier ones. But the ability to incorporate this into the music drama was uniquely his.

NOTES

1. James H. Billington, *Fire in the Minds: Origins of Revolutionary Faith* (New York: Basic Books, 1980), pp. 152, 156.
2. Ibid., p. 359. To be sure Billington does find traces of "conservative nationalism" in Wagner's *Die Meistersinger von Nürnberg* (p. 361), but he does not define the term.
3. For a detailed analysis of these themes from a literary-philosophical point of view see Peter Christoph Kern, *Zur Gedankenwelt des späten Hofmannsthal. Die Idee einer schöpferischen Restauration* (Heidelberg: Carl Winter, 1972). A useful early treatment is Jean-Jacques Anstett, "Les idées sociales de Hugo von Hofmannsthal," *Revue Germanique,* 22 (1931): 23-24. On the general question of Hofmannsthal's political transformation during the war, see Brian Coghlan, "The Cultural-Political Development of Hugo von Hofmannsthal during the First World War," *Publications of the English Goethe Society,* 27 (1958): 1-32 and my "Schorske's Garden Transformed Again: Aesthetics, War Propaganda, and the Conservative Revolution," forthcoming in Peter Pastor and Samuel B. Williamson, Jr., eds., *World War I and East Central Europe* (New York: Brooklyn College Press, 1982).
4. *Reflections on the Revolution in France,* ed. Thomas H. D. Mahoney (Indianapolis, IN: Bobbs-Merrill, 1955), pp. 162-163.
5. Walter Brecht, "Hugo von Hofmannsthal's *Ad me ipsum* und seine Bedeutung," *Jahrbuch des freien deutschen Hochstifts* (1930): 328; Belma Çakmur, *Hofmannsthals Erzählung Die Frau ohne Schatten. Studien zu Werk und Innenwelt des Dichters.* Veröffentlichungen der philosophischen Fakultät der Universität Ankara, 85 (1952), pp. 13-39, 249-250.
6. On the literary sources of the libretto see William Mann, *Richard Strauss: A Critical Study of the Operas* (London: Cassell, 1964), p. 174.

7. For the character of Barak, whose good nature is stressed far more than his stupidity in synopses of the opera, see Gloria Ascher, *Die Zauberflöte und die Frau ohne Schatten. Ein Vergleich zwischen zwei Operndichtungen der Humanität* (Bern-Munich: Francke, 1972), p. 11.

8. *Die Frau ohne Schatten* (n. p.: Boosey and Hawkes, 1964), pp. 48-49; "Die Frau ohne Schatten," in Hugo von Hofmannsthal, *Gesammelte Werke*, ed. Herbert Steiner (15 vols., Frankfurt a.M.: Fischer, 1946-1959), *Erzählungen*, p. 375.

9. Gerhard Pfaff, "Hugo von Hofmannsthals Märchendichtung 'Die Frau ohne Schatten.' Die Bedeutung der Hauptgestalten" (Dissertation, University of Frankfurt, 1957), p. 37; Brecht, *"Ad me ipsum,"* p. 328; Joseph Gregor, *Kulturgeschichte der Oper,* 2nd. ed. (Vienna-Zürich: Gallen-Scientia, 1950), p. 459.

10. Hugo von Hofmannsthal to Richard Strauss, April, 1915, in *Briefwechsel,* ed. Franz and Alice Strauss, revised by Willi Schuh (Zürich: Atlantis, 1954), p. 256.

11. D. [J.] B[ach], "Die Frau ohne Schatten," *Österreichische Rundschau,* 61 (October 1919), p. 92.

12. "Die Frau ohne Schatten," *Schweizerische Rundschau,* 33 (1933/34): 822; B[ach], p. 92; Jakob Knaus, *Hofmannsthals Weg zur Oper Die Frau ohne Schatten.* Quellen und Forschungen zur Sprach- und Kulturgeschichte der germanischen Völker, 38 (1977), p. 91.

13. Jürgen Haupt, *Konstellationen Hugo von Hofmannsthals. Harry Graf Kessler. Ernst Stadler. Bertolt Brecht* (Salzburg: Residenz, 1979), p. 54.

14. Roger Bauer, "Hugo von Hofmannstahl et la théâtre populaire viennoise: Die Frau ohne Schatten," in *Un dialogue des nations. Albert Fuchs zum 70. Geburtstag* (Munich-Paris: Herder-Klincksieck, 1967), p. 185; Çakmur, *Frau ohne Schatten,* pp. 229-230.

15. C. E. Williams, *The Broken Eagle. The Politics of Austrian Literature from Empire to Anschluss* (New York: Barnes and Noble, 1974), pp. 8-9.

16. *Gesammelte Werke. Gedichte und lyrische Dramen,* p. 19.

17. Ibid., *Prosa,* part 3, p. 506. For a thorough discussion of Hofmannsthal's political work during the war see Heinz Lunzer, *Hofmannsthals politische Tätigkeit in den Jahren 1914 bis 1917* (Frankfurt a.M.-Bern: Fritz Lang, 1981).

18. Peter Pawlowsky, "Die Idee Österreichs bei Hugo von Hofmannsthal," *Österreich in Geschichte und Literatur,* 7 (1963): 178, 184.

19. Hugo von Hofmannsthal to Eberhard von Bodenhausen, July 10, 1917, in *Briefe der Freundschaft* (Düsseldorf: Diedrichs, 1953), pp. 235-236; Alois Hofmann, "Hugo von Hofmannsthal und die Tschechen," *Hofmannsthal Forschungen,* 6 (1981): 236.

20. Klemens von Klemperer, *Ignaz Seipel: Christian Statesman in a Time of Crisis* (Princeton: Princeton University, 1972), pp. 54-65; William T. Bluhm, *Building an Austrian Nation: the Political Integration of a Western State* (New Haven: Yale University, 1973), pp. 17-20; Coghlan, "Hugo von Hofmannsthal," pp. 17-20.

21. Hugo von Hofmannsthal to Alfred von Nostitz-Wallwitz, August 5, 1917, in Hugo von Hofmannsthal-Helene von Nostitz, *Briefwechsel* (Frankfurt a.M.: Fischer, 1965), p. 140.

22. Hugo von Hofmannsthal to Richard Strauss, January 20, 1913, *Briefwechsel,* pp. 181-182; Houston Stewart Chamberlain, *Goethe* (Munich: Bruckmann, 1912), p. 554ff.

23. Hugo von Hofmannsthal to Richard Strauss, January 20, 1913, *Briefwechsel,* p. 182.

24. "Aus Hugo von Hofmannsthals Tagebüchern," *Corona,* 6 (1936): 68.

25. Mann, *Strauss,* p. 174; Ascher, *Humanität,* pp. 28-29.

26. Norman Del Mar, *Richard Strauss: a Critical Commentary on his Life and Work* (3 vols., New York: Free Press, 1962), 2: 158; Brecht, *"Ad me ipsum,"* p. 328.

27. *Die Frau ohne Schatten* (libretto), p. 3; *Erzählungen,* pp. 319-320.

28. *Die Frau ohne Schatten* (libretto), pp. 14, 27; *Erzählungen,* p. 334. See also Ascher, *Humanität,* pp. 34-35.

29. Othmar Spann, *Gesellschaftslehre* in Gesamtausgabe, vol. 4 (Graz: Akademische Druck und Verlagsanstalt, 1969), p. 525.

30. Ibid., pp. 136-137; *Die Frau ohne Schatten* (libretto), p. 35.

31. Burke, *Reflections,* p. 38; Juan Donoso Cortés, "Essai sur le catholicisme, le libéralisme et le socialisme," in *Oeuvres* (3 vols., Paris: Vaton, 1858-1859), 3: 74. For Hofmannsthal's mention of his acquaintance with the works of Donoso Cortés and the Vicomte de Bonald see Hugo von Hofmannsthal-Joseph Redlich, *Briefwechsel,* ed. Helga Fußgänger (Frankfurt a.M.: Fischer, 1971), p. 77.

32. Brecht, *"Ad me ipsum,"* pp. 320-321.
33. Ascher, *Humanität,* p. 25; Edward Shorter, "Illegitimacy, Sexual Revolution, and Social Change in Modern Europe," in *Marriage and Fertility: Studies in Interdisciplinary History,* ed. Robert I. Rotberg and Theodore K. Rabb (Princeton: Princeton University, 1980), p. 96; Donoso Cortés, "Essai," pp. 216-217; Louis Gabriel, vicomte de Bonald, *Du divorce, considéré au XIXe siècle relativement à l'état domestique et à l'état public de société* (Paris: d'Adrien le Clere, 1847), p. 176.
34. Horst Althaus, *Zwischen Monarchie und Republik. Schnitzler, Kafka, Hofmannsthal, Musil* (Munich: Fink, 1976), p. 127.
35. *Die Frau ohne Schatten* (libretto), p. 2; Mann, *Richard Strauss,* p. 175.
36. *Die Frau ohne Schatten* (libretto), p. 16; Ascher, *Humanität,* p. 26. Cf. Geneviève Bianquis, "Le testament moral de Hofmannsthal," in *Mélanges Henri Lichtenberger* (Paris: Stock, 1934), pp. 355-356.
37. Haupt, *Konstellationen,* p. 70.

Frank J. Coppa

VILFREDO PARETO'S LOVE/HATE RELATIONSHIP TO ITALY AND HIS TRANSITION FROM ECONOMICS TO SOCIOLOGY

Vilfredo Pareto, the Italian economist, political theorist, and sociologist, born in Paris during the revolutionary upheaval of 1848, grew up in an age dominated by faith in man's rationality and perfectibility. He imbibed the prevailing ideas of the period and favored freedom of trade, removal of restraints from the press, primary education for all, and universal suffrage. In 1868, when twenty, Pareto was both a liberal and a humanitarian.[1] He believed that militarism and religion were the major scourages of mankind, and humanity's future could be best assured by the triumph of democracy.[2] A missionary of the classical school of economics, he regarded liberty as the universal panacea.[3] Although Pareto moved in aristocratic circles, he ardently championed democracy and disarmament. He adhered to the sovereignty of the people as an axiom and in his first political writing favored proportional representation.[4] Indeed this self-confessed agnostic embraced liberalism as a surrogate religion.[5]

As the nineteenth century drew to a close, the consensus in favor of reason, the market economy, and the perfectibility of man began to disintegrate. Just as parliamentarianism triumphed in Europe, parliamentary government was subject to a blistering critique and the viability of representative institutions questioned. So far reaching was the challenge to earlier assumptions, that some have called it an intellectual revolution.[6]

Pareto, too, experienced a radical conversion. He explained that until the end of the century his ideas had been shaped by the optimism of the earlier age. With the passage of time, he concluded that the premises of the nineteenth century had been erroneous and reached other conclusions.[7] He warned that strict adherence to the dogmas of humanitarianism would lead to the destruction of society.[8] In fact the Marquis played an important role in the fin de siècle movement against positivism, becoming a bitter opponent of parliamentary government and a critic of nineteenth-century rationalism.

Pareto's conversion occurred within a broader European disenchantment with nineteenth-century thought. Certainly he was not alone in appreciating the intrusion of the subjective into what had been considered the realm of the objective, and was not unique in his interest in the irrational. Durkheim, Sorel, and Freud were equally interested in probing the nonlogical and inexplicable.[9] Likewise his preoccupation with the nature of knowledge, and his reexamination of political institutions, was typical of much of the intellectual ferment at the turn of the century. Thus Pareto's pessimism can be seen as part of the growing skepticism that troubled the European world at the end of a century of peace, prosperity, and progress.

Pareto's polemic against humanitarianism and parliamentary government suggest a personal involvement transcending the wider revolt against reason. This is corroborated by the fact that paralleling his philosophical change there was a noticeable chilling of temperament that would eventually lead him to prefer the company of cats to people.[10] What led this apostle of rationalism to abandon his principles and conclude that man cannot be governed by reason, insisting instead that force is the foundation of all social organization?[11] It is upon this question that the essay focuses as well as the impact of this conversion upon Pareto's transition from economics to sociology.

According to one biographer of Pareto, Franz Borkenau, conflict between father and son influenced the latter in turning against democracy, for in reality Vilfredo was turning against Mazzini's doctrine and his father who cherished them.[12] This analysis flows from the fact that the Marquis Raffaele Pareto was forced to abandon his native Genoa in 1835 or 1836 for his republican and revolutionary ideas.[13] Unfortunately, the younger Pareto's childhood is shrouded in darkness, so one can only speculate that tension between father and son influenced Vilfredo's intellectual development. The fact that he followed in his father's steps in studying engineering, and assumed many of his father's beliefs, would seem to negate such conjecture. Furthermore, until the 1890's Vilfredo remained well disposed toward the followers of Mazzini.[14]

There are indications that Pareto's alienation from his country and its political institutions affected his development and studies. Having a French mother and influenced by Gallic culture during the first decade of his life, Pareto loved France, and was grateful to the Swiss for the hospitality they offered him, but Italy always had a special place in his heart, and he refused to abandon his Italian citizenship despite the problems this created for him.[15] Although most of his scholarly works were written abroad, they were inspired by his Italian years. It was in the peninsula that he fell under the spell of Auguste Comte's philosophy of positivism, began to despise metaphysics, and sought to solve the problems of scientific sociology. Indeed many of his subsequent positions on scientific methodology found their origins in this Italian period of his life.[16]

His father, the Marquis Raffaele Pareto, critical of Italian patriots for their inability to expel the foreigner, gave his son two German names, Fritz Wilfrid. These were the names his son used in his early correspondence, but after 1870 almost always preferred the Italian Vilfredo.[17] Although he chose to emphasize his Italian name and background, there was much in Italy that did not please him. Tommaso Giacalone-Monaco has stressed the interrelationship between his personal humiliations and the skepticism of his scholarship.[18] To understand Pareto, writes Paola Maria Arcari, one must appreciate that he was exiled or alienated from his country, social class, profession, and official science.[19] Rejection in his country was the most traumatic blow of all, and his love/hate relationship with Italy not only colored his perspective but influenced his scholarship.

The intellectual evolution of Pareto has a geography of its own, which included Paris, Turin, Rome, Florence, and Lausanne. After graduation in 1870, he went from Turin to Rome, where he served as a managerial engineer with the Roman Railway Company and was scandalized by the client relationships he encountered.[20] In Florence, where he transferred to assume the directorship of the Ironworks of the Valdarno, he found fault with his colleagues, the bureaucrats, and the politicians. He complained that though an engineer, he was constrained to play the part of an intrigant.[21] As the manager of an important business enterprise, he was especially critical of the government's intervention in economic affairs.[22] His twenty-year crusade against protectionism in Italy, and caustic criticism of one government after another, contributed to his isolation. He sought solace in his books.[23]

The Marquis opposed the government's assumption of functions he believed best left to individual activity. In Italy, he explained, too many were expert at extracting concessions from the authorities. Thus while parasitical behavior was found in all countries, it was most pronounced in the Peninsula where industry was not developed, and the state was perceived as the fount of favors. He deplored this situation asserting that the Italian Government performed its functions poorly and labeled its administration the worst in Europe, save that of the moribund Ottoman Empire.[24] Following the "parliamentary revolution" of 1876 which saw the fall of the Destra and the accession of the Sinistra to power, Pareto was disturbed by the Transformism of Agostino Depretis, which brought together Left and Right in a coalition government. He was outraged by the fact that once the Left assumed power, citizens no longer grouped themselves on the basis of ideas but only according to interests.[25] At this juncture Pareto already realized that his liberal theories did not correspond to reality and that matters he had earlier considered simple, were complex.[26]

Pareto's disappointment with the coalition governments of the Left in Italy after 1876 colored his view of democracy. Distressed first by the transformism of Depretis and later by the abuses of Crispi, he argued that Cavour had provided a liberal inspiration whose effects continued to be felt some time after his death. Unfortunately this faded with the passage of time and Pareto condemned the tendency towards centralization, the growth in the functions of the state, and the move towards a disguised form of state socialism. In his view Italy had the misfortune of experiencing the worst possible regime, a parliamentary dictatorship in control of the forces of centralization.[27]

Pareto commenced a critique of parliamentary government in Italy that degenerated into a vendetta. Initially he tended to believe that matters could be set straight, and he could play a part in this reformation. Thus as early as 1880 he considered presenting himself as a candidate for the Italian Chamber.[28] After his assessment of the situation in the College of Monevarchi, he decided not to do so.[29] In 1882 he did run for Parliament in the district of Pistoia. The sensitive and irascible Marquis suffered a defeat that contributed to turning his former appreciation of democracy into scorn, as he began to ponder whether the people knew best. He would never again seek elective office.[30]

In 1887 the Italian Government adopted a new, and more protective tariff, which aroused the anger of Pareto and increased his opposition to the parliamentary regime. He claimed that its duties aided and abetted the special interest groups represented in the Chamber to the detriment of the majority. Scandalized, he compared Italian parliamentary groups to the condottieri of a former age, arguing that by means of votes and influence, they succeeded in amassing private fortunes. Protectionism, he deemed, one of the causes for the plight of the Peninsula.[31]

Despite his vocal condemnation of Italian political and economic policies, Pareto still considered himself a democrat and remained convinced that it was one's duty to secure the well-being of the majority.[32] Education was the means to do so, for he believed that society's ills flowed from the ignorance of the public. Above all, he wished to demonstrate that the tenets of economic liberalism could uplift the Italian people.[33] To do so he sought a chair in economics, but found academic Italy enchanted by the theories of the German "socialism of the chair" which favored state intervention to correct inequities in society. Laissez-faire theorists, such as he, were not even invited to the Congress of Italian Economists called by Fedele Lampertico. Thus he found the doors of academic Italy closed to him.

Pareto proved unable to penetrate either the political or the academic world of his country and resented this double rejection. In his mind the two were interrelated for he believed the government, which he had long criticized, interfered in every aspect of Italian life including higher education. The Marquis' constant criticism of the government provoked subsequent reprisals. Not surprisingly he found it difficult to publish his works at home.[34] In 1891 the police prevented Pareto from delivering a series of public talks in Milan, which increased his exasperation and made him all the more disenchanted with Italian political life and parliamentary government in general. Retiring as director of the Valdarno Iron Works in 1890, he assumed a consultantship and used his time to launch a literary crusade against the domestic and foreign policy of the state.[35]

In the years before he left for Lausanne in 1893, he wrote over 160 articles, most of which were critical of the regime. Commenting on the Banca Romana Scandal, which led to the collapse of the first Giolitti Ministry in 1893, Pareto admitted that his first impulse was to blame individuals for the mess, but concluded that it was the Italian political system which was responsible.[36] He argued that the politicians ruined the banks of issue, as they had earlier ruined the railroad, and almost everything else.[37] Statism, he insisted, proved disastrous for Italy.[38]

Despite his despair concerning the prevailing political situation in Italy, and personal disappointment,[39] Pareto continued to believe that political economy could improve the lot of the poor. Biology prevented it from providing universal happiness. Having studied Malthus and Darwin, Pareto claimed that the struggle for existence and natural selection improved humanity by eliminating the weak and infirm.[40] This assumption was reinforced by his studies of Draper, Spencer, and Buckle.[41] Government intervention, this champion of laissez-faire posited, only made the plight of the downtrodden worse. He therefore called upon his countrymen to elect those who would curb government activity.[42] He was unsuccessful in this effort, ignored both by the masses and by academicians.

A frequent contributor to the free trade periodical *Giornale degli Economisti,* Pareto's enthusiasm for economic liberalism made him a bitter opponent of the existing order and a trenchant critic of governmental policies. What most exasperated him was the realization that he was battling for a cause that did not arouse his countrymen.[43] The article that he published in the *Revue des Deux Mondes* the summer of 1891, won him the applause of a coterie of liberals, but was not well received by the Italian press and public. Fearing that the authorities might take action against him, he promised at the beginning of 1893 that, despite persecution, the truth would still be made known. Comparing himself to Mazzini, who wrote abroad when he could not do so at home, Pareto indicated that he, too, was prepared to depart, and like the master would not remain silent.[44] He proved true to his word.

The Marquis was to leave Italy sooner than he had anticipated. In 1893 he accepted a teaching position at the University of Lausanne and with the retirement of Leon Walras, assumed his chair of political economy. This was a significant event in his life and marked a new epoch in his intellectual development.[45] Pareto never reconciled himself to his failure in Italy. Convinced that the fault was not his own, he sought the reasons in his country's institutions and practices. In 1893, the year he left for Switzerland, he explained:

> There is no place in Italy for a citizen who, to preserve his independence, refuses to be a party to political patronage. He finds himself in about the same position as a Hindu who has no caste. He is an outlaw, a man whom everyone can attack. If a lawyer, he has no clients; if an engineer, nobody employs him; if a merchant or tradesman, he is ruined; if a landowner, he is exposed to petty annoyances from prefects and syndics. Every door is closed to him.[46]

Years later, still bristling at the humiliation, he wrote his friend Maffeo Pantaleoni that, while academic Italy rejected him, he repudiated her. He would not forget that no academy, not even a less well-known one, deemed him worthy. Pouting at this rejection, Pareto claimed that had these Italian institutions admitted him, they, not he, would have been honored.[47] He also claimed that it was fortunate that the members of the scientific community in Italy considered him a donkey, for had they treated him well, and had he accepted their flattery, he would have lost the independence indispensable for the study he wished to pursue.[48] Thus Pareto frankly acknowledged the importance of the rejection he experienced in Italy and the impact this had upon his subsequent work.

The Marquis wrote another friend, shortly after his transfer to Switzerland, of his activities in that "free and honest country." "I would be completely happy," he confessed, "were it not for the thought of my country."[49] He recognized his attachment to Italy as a prejudice. It was one he would never overcome as indicated by his constant concern with developments in the Peninsula and his tendency to evaluate parliamentary institutions in light of his Italian experience. Later he attacked English and even American political institutions and interpreted such terms as "general will" and "majority" as abstractions used by the few to exploit the many.[50] He concluded that the abuses which he had earlier witnessed in Italy were not extraordinary events, but manifestations of the weakness of parliamentary life, humanitarianism, and democracy.

Following Pareto's move to Lausanne, his interest in Italian affairs and his commitment to the anti-protectionist campaign continued, and both were reflected in the 53 articles written in the *Giornale degli Economisti* from 1893 to 1897. By this time he had come to the conclusion that the reason for the deplorable government in Italy was not the fault of this or that minister, but of the majority that supported it.[51] Transformism, he explained, was not invented by Depretis, but was practiced from 1860 onwards.[52] Thus it was Italian political forms and parliamentary life in general that were flawed. While he acknowledged that there were thieves everywhere, at home they seemed to concentrate in the government. Despairing of an improvement from the political progress, he observed that only a change in the psychology of his countrymen could lead to meaningful reform.[53]

Pareto's disdain for political solutions was reflected in his refusal to run for the Italian Chamber in 1896.[54] While his enthusiasm for parliamentary government had diminished, he had not yet abandoned the belief that reason could affect the course of social and economic progress. This was made clear in his first important publication, his *Cours d'economie politique* (1896-97) which incorporated the material he had included in his lectures at Lausanne his first years there.[55] In these two volumes, he sought to prove by means of mathematics the superiority of the free trade system over all others.[56]

At the time of the publication of the *Cours,* another Pareto began to emerge; less optimistic and far less willing to accept the underlying assumptions even of economic liberalism. The turning point occurred in 1896 when the Marquis Di Rudini and the party of the Destra returned to power in Italy. Pareto hoped that this Ministry would restore the economic liberalism of Cavour, but he was to be disappointed. His disillusionment was reflected in the newspaper articles of 1896. So long as the country was governed by the Crispi clique, he admitted, he had clung to the illusion that when Destra returned things would improve. He learned otherwise: "What advantages have the people derived from Di Rudini replacing Crispi," asked Pareto. And he answered: "Absolutely none."[57] Outraged that the Italian people had rejected economic liberalism and those like himself who espoused it, he became critical not only of the Italian regime, but of parliamentary democracy in general.

In light of his Italian experience, Pareto also began to question his conviction that man behaved rationally and could be guided by political economy. His crisis occurred with the realization that logical actions, or those in which means were appropriate to ends, on which he had concentrated in his economic studies, only constituted one type of human action. Other actions were motivated by non-logical considerations.[58] When this student of economics understood that his science could not provide the answers he sought, and did not affect the political reality in Italy, he moved toward sociology.[59]

That men were not guided by reason could be deduced from the position Italians assumed toward socialism and protectionism. He was convinced that his country would have had a splendid future if it had remained faithful to the liberal doctrines of Cavour.[60] Political economy, he argued, had demonstrated that protectionism leads to the destruction of wealth, yet there was no popular outcry against it. This led him to conclude that to have certain principles accepted, it was not sufficient to demonstrate their validity.[61] He elaborated upon this in his subsequent works where he argued that the accord of a doctrine with reality is one thing, but its social importance quite another.[62] Pareto learned this lesson in Italy where he had failed to convince the government to return to economic liberalism.[63] All of his reasoned arguments and statistical proofs had been to no avail. Finding economics unable to provide an explanation for this failure, he turned to sociology.[64]

The Marquis was also puzzled by the popularity of Marxism in Italy whose principles he held to be demonstrably false. He only understood its continuing appeal when he realized that the bulk of human activity was not based upon rational judgments but sentiments.[65] It was therefore useless to reveal that *Das Kapital* contained scientific and logical errors, for most who believed in Marx never read this work, and would never be in a position to do so.[66] He concluded it was foolish to suppose that men could be persuaded by logical demonstrations and reasoned discourse.

At this juncture Pareto offered his first course in sociology at the University of Lausanne.[67] That same year, 1897, he published an article entitled "Il compito della sociologia fra le scienze sociali," which serves as a testimony of his transition from economics to sociology.[68] Acknowledging that no one was absolutely logical, he added that the principal task of his sociology was that of separating logical actions from non-logical ones and showing that for the most part, the non-logical were more important.[69] Reason, he wrote in 1897, played little part in determining social phenomena.[70]

In another article published in the *Rivista Italiana di Sociologia,* Pareto observed that the greater part of human actions derived not from reason, but sentiment. Concomitantly, he indicated that except for brief intervals, men were always governed by an "aristocracy," which he thought to consist of those who were strongest, most energetic, and most capable. It was an illusion to believe that there was a struggle between the dominant class and the people, as the socialists liked to pretend. Rather it was one aristocracy pitted against another, and if the old one were to be overturned, only a new one could accomplish the task.[71]

During the half decade from the publication of the *Cours* in 1896 to the appearance of *Les systèmes socialistes* in 1902, Pareto sank into a deeper depression. This was not alleviated by the considerable inheritance left him by his uncle Domenico in 1898, for he used the money to purchase a villa at Céligny to which he withdrew with his Angora cats, shutting out the world.[72] In his despair, Pareto considered the unreasonable opposition to liberalism impossible to overcome. He resigned himself to the fact that the parties in Italy would not implement his free trade program, despite its obvious merits.[73] He now questioned whether his first political battles at home had been worth the effort.[74]

Frustrated in his private and public life, Pareto sought explanations in psychology and sociology. He found solace in Gustave Le Bon's *Psychologie de Socialisme* which maintained that religions founded upon chimera have had an impact upon all civilizations, while philosophical systems based on reason have played an insignificant role. He seconded this author's interpretation of socialism, considering it more a state of mind than a doctrine.[75] Pareto warned Pantaleoni that in seeking to persuade people with reason, he was one of those figures cited by Le Bon, who are amazed to discover that their potent logic has not the least effect upon the crowd. He did not know if mass opinion could be changed by an appeal to sentiments, but he was certain that reason could not change it.[76] The failure of his anti-protectionist campaign in Italy provided proof positive.

In part his approval of Le Bon's work reflected his own change in attitude towards socialism in Italy. By this time he no longer viewed the socialists as opponents of the government, and therefore praiseworthy, but saw bourgeois elements in the movement exploiting humanitarian ideologies primarily to attain their own ends. Consequently the Marquis included them in his overall criticism of the political class. In an article of July, 1900, he warned that while the party was then open to all, when it achieved power it would become a new elite, and like all others it would be rigid and closed.[77]

In 1902 Pareto published his *Les systèmes socialistes,* refining a concept on which he had been brooding for several years, the paramountcy of the non-rational in human conduct:

> The sources of men's illusions about the motives determining their behavior are manifold. A main one lies in the fact that a very large number of human actions are not the outcome of reasoning. They are purely instinctive actions, although the man performing them experiences a feeling of pleasure in giving them, quite arbitrarily, logical causes.[78]

Economists, he observed, were mistaken in stressing reason as the dominant motive determining human actions. They deluded themselves when they believed that by exposing the flaws in the theories of their adversaries, they could reduce them to impotence. This critique represented self-criticism for Pareto. It revealed his frustration in being unable to convince the public in Italy of the evils of protectionism and represented a disavowal of his earlier attitude.[79] With one brush, he exposed the weakness of the liberal position as well as the logical inconsistencies of socialist doctrines.[80]

In his *Systèmes* he also revealed that democracy did not operate as he had earlier assumed. The lower classes, he insisted, were incapable of ruling. Those at the bottom could play an important role insofar as they helped to produce a new elite.[81] On the other hand, he saw within the bourgeoisie the signs of decadence, the intrusion of humanitarian feelings which prevented it from defending its position. This created a dangerous situation which called for strong measures.

By 1902 Pareto determined that without the use of force, law and order in a society could not be assured. "The living creature, which shrinks from giving blow for blow and from shedding its adversary's blood, puts itself at the mercy of its adversary," he wrote in the *Systèmes.*[82] He later observed that in the nineteenth century an attempt had been made to govern by reason, but the experiment had failed. Instead of instituting the government of reason, the liberals had only succeeded in substituting the force of one elite with another.[83]

In his *Manuale di economia politica,* completed between 1903 and 1905, Pareto sought to investigate the social sciences in a manner similar to that employed in the physical sciences he had studied in Turin. His observations led him to conclude that men followed their sentiments and self-interests, but liked to imagine they followed reason. Convinced by his experiences in Italy that faith alone moved men to act, he did not deem it desirable, nor practical for them to deal with social matters scientifically.[84] Those like himself, who praised free trade, restricting themselves to its economic effects, did not construct a faulty theory of international commerce, but rather made an incorrect application of an intrinsically true theory. Their failure stemmed from disregarding political and social consequences which were subject to other considerations. Humanitarianism was flawed not because it lacked scientific foundation, for religions moved society, but because it befitted the weak rather than the strong. In his view the history of human societies was molded by a succession of aristocracies.[85] It his *Manuale* Pareto also continued his polemic against the Italian Government and its practices.[86] Democracy, too, was criticized, as he observed that when the suffrage was given to all men, including madmen and criminals, when it was extended to women, and if you like to children, it would have to stop—unless it was extended to animals! Pareto feared that democracy would lead the masses to seek a redistribution of wealth, and this would prove dangerous, if not disastrous. Pareto's own inheritance, which enabled him to live in self-imposed seclusion, strengthened his conviction that the rights of inheritance and private property provided the essential elements for stability in society.[87] While in Italy he had been convinced that economic liberty was threatened by the political intrigants and their hangers on, but in pondering the situation while abroad, he had come to the realization that the problem was broader. Indeed he was forced to the conclusion that democracy was the worst enemy of liberty and, therefore, had to abandon another illusion.[88]

Pareto's ideas were elaborated in the *Trattato di sociologia generale* (1916), his major sociological work, which he insisted be published in Italy first. He explained therein that every social phenomenon might be considered under two aspects: as it is in reality, and as it presents itself to the mind of this or that individual. The first aspect he termed objective, the second, subjective; adding that the names provided these classes should not lead one astray, because all human knowledge is subjective and these phenomena are not of a different nature, but are characterized by a smaller or greater knowledge of the facts. Furthermore, there were actions that logically link means to ends, and others in which such a trait is missing. Pareto dubbed the first logical and the second non-logical.[89]

In Pareto's framework the non-logical nuclei are "residues" and the secondary pseudo-logical explanations, "derivations."[90] He stressed that individuals were primarily motivated by sentiments or clusters of primordial psychological forces which were non-logical and push men to move in one direction rather than another.[91] Corresponding to certain instincts, he considered them without exact determination and inaccessible to reason. What Freud termed "drives" Pareto dubbed "residues;"[92] he categorized them in six groups.[93] Since most men remained enamoured of logic, they sought to provide rational explanations for their non-logical conduct, hence the "derivations."[94] These "derivations" which comprised logical reasoning, unsound reasoning, and sentiments, were manifestations of humanity's hunger for thinking. Although they appealed to reason, nature, and more recently to science, they all covered indistinct and incoherent sentiments.[95] This had political as well as social implications.

Pareto explained that while all governments assert they are founded on reason, they all rely on force. Whether universal suffrage prevails or not, an oligarchy governs, disguising its actions by invoking the will of the people. As a result, the people send to Parliament men pledged to do one thing, but once in power they often do the opposite. He had witnessed this firsthand in Italy. Consequently he considered popular representation a fiction. Every people was governed by an elite.[96]

The Marquis observed in the *Trattato* that every sect, every party accuses its adversaries of immoral acts, while it fails to see its own.[97] Referring again to the Italian situation, he related that when the Right was governing there, the various sections of the Left raised a hullabaloo over the corruption of their adversaries, but once they attained power they behaved worse than their predecessors. He generalized that whatever the form of government, men holding power have as a rule, the inclination to use power to keep themselves in the saddle and to abuse it to secure personal gain.[98] Thus he was able to explain "scientifically" what he had seen and criticized in Italy years before.[99]

In his major sociological work, Pareto warned that in the practice of the social sciences one must be ever on guard to prevent the intrusion of personal sentiments, citing the danger that flowed from man's inclination to transcend what is, and to attempt to determine what ought to be.[100] He called upon investigators to cast aside their sentiments, preoccupations, and beliefs while engaged in scientific pursuits, resuming them later. Pareto realized that this was easier said than done.[101] Nonetheless, as early as the turn of the century, the Marquis claimed that he was tied to no party, religion, or country, and, therefore, was relatively free of the passions that haunted most social scientists.[102] Despite these frequent protestations of objectivity, he was influenced by his prejudices, and above all by his troubled relationship with his country.

After a visit to Italy in 1907, Pareto reiterated his earlier claim that it was his good fortune that his country had rejected him, and its leading lights had insulted him, for, when at home, he could not remain detached and impartial.[103] In fact, as we have seen, he could not remain objective toward Italy while abroad. Behind his expression of disinterested realism that often degenerated into cynicism, there lurked a profound exasperation with the social and political situation in the Peninsula. His sociology, which made a distinction between logical and non-logical action, and objective and subjective phenomena, was inspired by his need to explain the disappointments he had endured there.[104]

Much of his critique of parliamentary government, as well as his theory of elites was drawn from the Italian example as he depicted Agostino Depretis as "the leader of a syndicate of speculators" and Giovanni Giolitti "a master in the art of using interests and sentiments."[105] He was convinced that in Italy the extension of the suffrage was brought about by calculating politicians. In fact his analysis of the Italian political scene led him to conclude that whatever the form of government, men exercising power have an inclination to abuse it to secure personal gains.[106]

As early as 1893 when forced to leave his homeland, the seeds of contempt for parliamentary democracy were planted in Pareto's mind. These were nourished by his continued obsession with Italian events as he viewed developments there with dismay.[107] Following the World War, the political and social problems of his country continued to haunt Pareto, whose essays and articles during these years mirrored his preoccupation. In his articles in the anti-Giolittian *Rivista di Milano*, he depicted the troubled Italian situation as a manifestation of the transformation, one might say, the degeneration of democracy. He denied the notion that the Italian Parliament represented the nation, indicating that it represented only that element which controlled the others.[108] Distressed by the confusion which burdened his homeland, and sensing the need for a return to authority, he was inclined to look upon Fascism as a healthy reaction to a deteriorating situation.[109] Had he lived to see its direction, it is likely that this champion of individualism would have found it as wanting as the parliamentary regime which so influenced his scholarship.

NOTES

1. Giovanni Busino, *Gli Studi su Vilfredo Pareto oggi* (Rome, 1974), p. 19.
2. Vilfredo Pareto to A. Antonucci, December 7, 1907, *Alcune lettere di Vilfredo Pareto pubblicate e commentate a cura di A. Antonucci* (Rome, 1938), pp. 19-23.
3. Pareto to Luigi Ridolfi, April 11, 1874, in Giovanni Busino, *Vilfredo Pareto e l'industria del ferro nel Valdarno* (Melon, 1977), p. 259.
4. Vilfredo Pareto, "Suffragio universale. Lettera al Machese Trivulzio Pallavicino," in *L'Italiano-Gazzetta del Popolo,* November 12, 1872, and published in V. Pareto, *Scritti politici. Lo sviluppo del Capitalismo* (1872-1895), edited by G. Busino (Turin, 1974), I, pp. 47-51.
5. R. Cirillo, *The Economics of Vilfredo Pareto* (London, 1979), p. 7.
6. H. Stuart Hughes, *Consciousness and Society: The Reconstruction of Social Thought* 1890-1930 (New York, 1958), p. 33.
7. Pareto to Maffeo Pantaleoni, July 15, 1908, in Vilfredo Pareto, *Lettere a Maffeo Pantaleoni,* ed. G. de Rosa (Rome, 1962), III, 108-109.
8. Vilfredo Pareto, *The Mind and Society: A Treatise on General Sociology,* ed. by Arthur Livingston, (New York, 1963), III, 1249.
9. H. Stuart Hughes, *Consciousness and Society,* p. 35.
10. Franco Ferrarotti, ed., *Per Conoscere Pareto* (Rome, 1973), p. 14.
11. Vilfredo Pareto, *Manual of Political Economy,* trans. by Ann S. Schwier, edited by A. Schwier and Alfred N. Page (New York, 1971), p. 94.
12. Franz Borkenau, *Pareto* (London, 1936), pp. 10-11.
13. The Marquis found refuge in Paris where he married the French woman Marie Mettenier who bore him two daughters, and on July 15, 1848, a son, Vilfredo. Cirillo, p. 25; Arthur Livingston, "Introduction,"

V.P., *The Mind and Society: A Treatise on General Sociology*, ed. by A. Livingston (New York, 1963), I, xv.

14. Vilfredo Pareto, "The Parliamentary Regime in Italy," *The Ruling Class in Italy before 1900* (New York, 1974), p. 19.

15. Paola Maria Arcari, "La Formazione psicologica della teoria della circolazione delle aristocrazie," *Cahiers Vilfredo Pareto*, no. 5 (1965), p. 218.

16. Vincent J. Tarascio, *Pareto's Methodological Approach to Economics* (Chapel Hill, NC, 1968), p. 8.

17. See his letters to Domenico Pareto, November 26, 1864, to Prospero Richelmy, December 22, 1869 and to Ubaldino Peruzzi, September 18, 1872 in Busino, *Vilfredo Pareto e l'industria del ferro nel Valdarno*, pp. 250-253.

18. Giovanni Busino, *Introduction a une histoire de la Sociologie de Pareto* (Geneva, 1968), pp. 98-110.

19. Arcari, *Cahiers Vilfredo Pareto*, no. 5 (1965), p. 214.

20. T. Giacolone-Monaco, "L'Ing. Vilfredo Pareto nella Società delle strade ferrate romane (1870-1873)," in *Giornale degli Economisti e Annali di Economia*, July-August 1963, pp. 537-578.

21. Ferrarotti, *Per Conoscere Pareto*, pp. 11-12.

22. T. Giacalone-Monaco, "Preface," *Cronache Italiane* (Brescia, 1965), p. 15.

23. Pareto to Celestino Bianchi, November 24, 1874, Vilfredo Pareto, *Lettere ai Peruzzi, 1872-1900*, ed. by T. Giacalone-Monaco (Rome, 1968), I, pp. 457-459.

24. Pareto's observations before the parliamentary commission examining how the railway system in Italy operated, 1880, in Giovanni Busino, *Vilfredo Pareto e l'industria del ferro nel Valdarno* (Melon, 1977), pp. 418-428.

25. Vilfredo Pareto, *La Liberté Économique et les Événements d'Italie*, (New York, 1968), pp. 33-34.

26. *Alcune Lettere de Vilfredo Pareto. . . a cura di A. Antonucci*, pp. 19-23.

27. Pareto, *La Liberté. . .* , pp. 32-33.

28. Pareto to Ulbadino Peruzzi, May 3, 1880, in Busino, *Vilfredo Pareto e l'industria del ferro nel Valdarno*, p. 436.

29. Pareto to Ulbadino Peruzzi, May 6, 1880, ibid., p. 438.

30. Pareto to Ulbadino Peruzzi, September 22, 1886, Vilfredo Pareto, *Lettere ai Peruzzi,* II, 628.

31. Pareto, *La Liberté...*, pp. 25-29.

32. Pareto to Francesco Papafava, December 2, 1888, in Busino, *Vilfredo Pareto e l'industria del ferro nel Valdarno,* p. 819. Pareto to Francesco Papafava, December 3, 1888, ibid., p. 824.

33. Pareto, *The Ruling Class in Italy before 1900,* p. 46.

34. Borkenau, p. 13; Pareto, *Lettere a Maffeo Pantaleoni,* I, 93-96.

35. Pareto, *La Liberté...*, p. 33.

36. Pareto, *The Ruling Class in Italy before 1900,* pp. 76-77.

37. Cronaca of November 1, 1894, Vilfredo Pareto, *Cronache Italiane,* ed. by Carlo Mongardini, preface by T. Giacalone-Monaco (Brescia, 1965), p. 273.

38. Pareto, *La Liberté...*, p. 97.

39. Pareto's personal life was less than happy and following the death of his father in 1882 and his mother in 1889, both he and his sister, Cristina, to whom he was very attached, suffered from poor health. At the end of 1889 he was less than enthusiastic as he married Alexandra Bakounine. Given his admitted lack of interest in the woman he married, it was largely his fault that the marriage was not a success. Children he could not abide. Small wonder that his wife, tired of Pareto's showering more time and attention on his cats than her, eventually left her all too busy husband. Cf. Busino, *Vilfredo Pareto e l'industria del ferro nel Valdarno,* p. 873; Cirillo, pp. 11 and 25; Werner Stark, "In Search of the True Pareto," in Meisel, ed., *Pareto and Mosca,* p. 49.

40. Vilfredo Pareto to Francesco Papafava, December 2, 1888, Busino, *Vilfredo Pareto e l'industria del ferro nel Valdarno,* pp. 830-831.

41. Vilfredo Pareto to Francesco Papafava, December 3, 1888, ibid., p. 823.

42. Vilfredo Pareto to Francesco Papafava, December 5, 1888, ibid., pp. 829-830, 832.

43. Busino, *Gli Studi su Vilfredo Pareto oggi,* p. 16.

44. Giacalone-Monaco, "Preface," *Cronache Italiane,* p. 21.

45. Busino, *Gli Studi su Vilfredo Pareto oggi,* p. 27.

46. Pareto, *The Ruling Class in Italy before 1900,* p. 57.

47. Vilfredo Pareto to M. Pantaleoni, February 2, 1909. Vilfredo Pareto, *Lettere a Maffeo Pantaleoni,* ed. G. De Rosa (Rome, 1962), III, p. 129.

48. Pareto to M. Pantaleoni, October 26, 1907, ibid., III, pp. 70-71.
49. Carlo Mongardini, "Introduction," in Vilfredo Pareto, *Cronache Italiane*, p. 38.
50. Pareto, *The Mind and Society*, III, p. 73.
51. Cronaca of March 1, 1896, Pareto, *Cronache Italiane*, p. 393.
52. Cronaca of October 1, 1896, ibid., p. 38.
53. Vilfredo Pareto, Cronaca di November 1, 1896 and January 1, 1897, *Cronache Italiane*, pp. 452-467.
54. Tomaso Giacalone-Monaco, "Due Sconfitte elettorali di Vilfredo Pareto," in *Cahiers Vilfredo Pareto*, no. 5 (1965), 39.
55. Vilfredo Pareto, *Cours d'économie Politique* in Sociological Writings, ed. by S. E. Finer (New York, 1966), p. 97.
56. Tarascio, p. 44; Borkenau, p. 16.
57. Vilfredo Pareto, Cronaca of August 1, 1896, *Cronache Italiane*, pp. 428-432.
58. Arcari, *Cahiers Vilfredo Pareto*, no. 5 (1965), 227-228.
59. Mongardini, "Mosca, Pareto e Taine," ibid., 179.
60. Cronaca of May 1, 1897, Pareto, *Cronache Italiane*, p. 502.
61. Carlo Mongardini, *Vilfredo Pareto dall' Economia alla Sociologia*, (Rome, 1973), pp. 118-119.
62. Vilfredo Pareto, *The Mind and Society: A Treatise on General Sociology*, ed. Arthur Livingston (New York, 1963), III, p. 1112.
63. Cronaca of May 1, 1897, *Cronache Italiane*, p. 502.
64. Franco Ferrarotti, "Breve nota intorno all teoria dell'equilibrio in Pareto," *Cahiers Vilfredo Pareto*, no. 5, (1965), p. 226.
65. J. E. Finer, "Introduction," in Vilfredo Pareto's *Sociological Writings* (New York, 1966), p. 11.
66. Arcari, *Cahiers Vilfredo Pareto*, no. 5 (1967), p. 226.
67. In the broadest sense Pareto described sociology as the body of all that which pertains to the organization of life, and development of human society.
68. Mongardini, *Vilfredo Pareto dall'Economia alla Sociologia*, p. 12.
69. Pareto to Pantaleoni, May 17, 1897, Vilfredo Pareto *Lettere da Maffeo Pantaleoni*, III, p. 73.
70. Pareto to Pantaleoni, November 11, 1897, ibid., III, p. 121.
71. Mongardini, *Vilfredo Pareto dall'Economia alla Sociologia*, pp. 122-123.

72. Manon Michels Einaudi, "Pareto as I Knew Him," *The Atlantic Monthly* (LVIC September, 1935), pp. 336-338; Cirillo, p. 11.
73. Borkenau, p. 12.
74. Mongardini, *Vilfredo Pareto dall'Economia alla Sociologia*, p. 27.
75. Ferrarotti, *Per Conoscere Pareto*, pp. 139-140.
76. Pareto to Pantaleoni, October 24, 1902, Vilfredo Pareto, *Lettere a Maffeo Pantaleoni*, III, p. 406.
77. Mongardini, *Vilfredo Pareto dall'Economia alla Sociologia*, pp. 25-26, 59-60, 180-184.
78. Pareto, "Les Systèmes Socialistes," in *Sociological Writings*, p. 124.
79. Mongardini, *Vilfredo Pareto dall'Economia alla Sociologia*, p. 24.
80. Busino, *Introduction a une histoire de la Sociologie de Pareto*, p. 23.
81. Pareto, "Les Systèmes Socialistes," in *Sociological Writings*, p. 135.
82. Ibid., p. 135.
83. Pareto to Pantaleoni, February 22, 1905, *Lettere a Maffeo Pantaleoni*, III, pp. 436-437.
84. Vilfredo Pareto, *Manual of Political Economy*, trans. by Ann S. Schwier, ed. by A. Schwier and Alfred N. Page (New York, 1971), p. 86.
85. Ibid., pp. 14, 312, 364.
86. Ibid., pp. 354-355.
87. Ibid., pp. 91, 100-101, 314.
88. Luigi dal Pane, "Due Lettere di Vilfredo Pareto a Tullio Martello," *Cahiers Vilfredo Pareto*, no. 5 (1965), pp. 58-59.
89. Pareto, *The Mind and Society*, I, pp. 75-78.
90. Ibid., III, p. 1185.
91. Giuseppe Palumba, "Quattro medaglioni in Sociologia. Pareto-Spengler-Toynbee-Jung," *Cahiers Vilfredo Pareto*, no. 5 (1965), p. 189.
92. J. H. Meisel, "A Question of Affinities: Pareto and Marx," *Cahiers Vilfredo Pareto*, no. 5 (1965), p. 166.
93. In his list of residues two main principles of grouping appear, on the one hand the contrast between conservatism and progress, and on the other hand the contrast between individualism and collectivism. Pareto listed the residues of (1) combinations, (2) persistence, (3) manifestation of sentiments by external acts, (4) sociability, (5) integrity of personality and (6) sex residues.

Pierre-Louis Reynand, "Pareto et la Psychologie Économique Moderne," ibid., p. 137.

94. Pareto lists the deviations as follows: (1) affirmations, (2) authority, (3) accord with sentiments or principles, (4) verbal proofs. Borkenau, p. 79.

95. Pareto, *The Mind and Society,* III, pp. 885, 964.
96. Ibid., IV, pp. 69, 1526-1528, 1569-1575.
97. Ibid., III, p. 1269.
98. Ibid., IV, pp. 1608-1609.
99. Pareto, *La Liberté...* , p. 33.
100. Pareto, *The Mind and Society,* IV, p. 1737.
101. Ibid., I, p. 72.
102. Pareto to Pantaleoni, November 21, 1899, Pareto, *Lettere a Maffeo Pantaleoni,* III, p. 281.
103. Pareto to Pantaleoni, October 26, 1907, ibid., III, pp. 70-71.
104. Mongardini, *Vilfredo Pareto dall'Economia alla Sociologia,* pp. 23-26.
105. Pareto, *The Mind and Society,* IV, p. 1579.
106. Ibid., III, p. 974; IV, pp. 1607-1608.
107. Ibid., III, p. 974.
108. Vilfredo Pareto, *Trasformazioni della democrazia* (Rocco San Casciano, 1964), pp. 80, 93.
109. Ibid., pp. 19-20; Borkenau, pp. 17-19.

VI

INTER-NATIONALITY RELATIONS IN THE DANUBE VALLEY

Stephen Borsody

HUNGARY IN THE HABSBURG MONARCHY: FROM INDEPENDENCE STRUGGLE TO HEGEMONY

In two world wars Germany and Hungary were allies. On a different scale, but under similar circumstances, each suffered defeat. Germany was stopped in a reckless bid for supremacy and world power. Hungary failed in her ambition to dominate the mid-Danubian region. Defeat solved neither the German nor the Hungarian problems. The status quo of 1945 keeps Germany divided into two parts in a partitioned Europe. National boundaries in the Danube region keep the Hungarian people divided into five parts. Both situations are abnormal and potential threats to peace. Defeat, however, dissolved the partnership between German and Hungarian imperialism. And this is good for the peace of Central Europe.

The alliance that led to a short-lived German-Hungarian hegemony in Central Europe before the First World War is dead. But short-lived as it was, its impact was far-reaching. The alliance between Hungary (a small nation) and modern Germany (one of the great powers) set the pattern for the policy of imperialism among Central Europe's smaller nations. It served as an unfortunate source of inspiration for the small to seek domination over their equals in association with powers greater than themselves.

This is not to say that Hungarians invented small-nation imperialism. Nobody had to invent that. It was in the air in the age of modern nationlism.

The Hungarians, however, set in motion a chain-reaction of hegemonistic aspirations among the Danube region's small nations which was hard to stop. They also paid a heavy price for the folly of power rivalry among the small nations of the Danube region. Hungary's offended neighbors (mostly Slavs) took vengeance on their oppressors after the First World War. The new postwar order of independent nation-states in Central Europe was emphatically anti-Hungarian and pro-Slav. But the punishment of Hungary did not hurt the Hungarians alone. It further aggravated the postwar political climate of Central Europe, poisoned primarily by the restlessness of the Germans under the punitive peace settlement. New solutions of old problems had thus led only to new tragedies. And the dismal consequences of rival solutions are still with us, frustrating everybody's hope for peace in Central Europe.

That the Hungarians (or Magyars, as the Hungarians call themselves in their own language[1]) should land in the camp of the Germans in the age of modern nationalism is not without irony. For the role of the Hungarians in European history has been anything but friendly to German power. Hungary showed no particular fondness for a German political orientation, and never became a captive of it until the latter part of the nineteenth century.

The position of the Hungarians as allies of the Germans and enemies of the Slavs is of nineteenth-century origin. But, due to the emotionalism of nationalist historiography, this nineteenth-century alignment of national positions has been blown up by Hungary's rivals into a theory of historical interpretation covering centuries. The most influential modern popularizer of that theory, who proclaimed the very presence of the Hungarians in Central Europe as an unmitigated evil for the Slavs, was the nineteenth-century Czech historian František Palacký. Placing recent Hungarian-Slav hostility on the same footing as the age-old Slav-German struggle, he concluded that the arrival of the Magyars (people of Eastern origin who migrated from the Dnieper region to the Danube region in the ninth century) was "the greatest misfortune that has befallen the Slavonic world for thousands of years."[2]

Unhappy with the inferior position of the Slavs in his own time, Palacký blamed the Germans and Hungarians for it. In his interpretation, the crime the "Asiatic Magyars" committed against the European Slavs was twofold: They destroyed, in collusion with the Germans, the Great

Moravian Empire, and they ruined for good the unity of the Slavs by driving an East-West wedge between them. Palacký's angry view mirrors well the bitterness of modern national conflicts, but does not do justice to a thousand years of Danubian history. The fact of the matter is that in the ninth century it did not take much Magyar effort to destroy the Moravian Empire because it was already rent by Slav dissent. And as for the founding of the Hungarian state in predominantly Slavic Eastern Europe, the Hungarians did not seem to have aggravated Slavic discord. If anything, relations among Slavs seem to have been better where Hungarians kept them apart than in places where nobody stood between them.[3]

Palacký's fondness for dating the modern Hungarian-German alliance back to the fall of the Great Moravian Empire rings no more true than the rest of his anti-Hungarian interpretation of Danubian history. Actually, between the ninth and the nineteenth century, the Hungarians more often fought Germans than Slavs. The real place of the Hungarians in European history has been better defined by a twentieth-century historian Denis Sinor who, commenting on one of the eleventh-century collisions between the Magyars and the Germans wrote: "It was the first episode of a struggle which was to last for over nine centuries: the struggle of Hungary to maintain her independence against German ravenousness."[4]

The modern scene of the Hungarian struggle for independence—not unlike that of many Slavs—was the Danubian empire of the Habsburgs. Between the fifteenth and nineteenth centuries, in addition to the Hungarians, a number of Slavic people in central, eastern and southeastern Europe came under the German domination of Habsburg Austria. The Habsburgs, however, were not the first to deprive some of these people of their self-rule. The Ottoman invasion in the late Middle Ages had been the original cause of the eclipse or extinction of independent statehood in the Balkans and the Danube regions of Central Europe. A number of once flourishing medieval states (Bulgaria, Serbia, Hungary) lost their independence to the invading Turks, one by one, in much the same way as smaller nations have succumbed to larger powers in the eastern half of Europe so many times since. Habsburg empire-building in the Danube region began as a defensive move against the Turkish advance on Europe from the Balkans. The Habsburg claim of defending Christian Europe never vanished, although it turned into an aggressive policy of dynastic imperialism. Dynastic ambition, embellished by Christian pretensions, inspired the German branch of the Habsburgs to liberate Central Europe from the Moslem Turks in the seventeenth century. But naked dynastic ambition expanded Habsburg rule in all directions at the same time and continued into the twentieth century.

The liberation of Hungary from the Turks toward the end of the seventeenth century was a momentous event in the formation of the Danubian empire of the Austrian Habsburgs. Another equally important seventeenth-century success, entitling Habsburg Austria to call herself an empire, was the subjugation of the Bohemian kingdom following the defeat of the Czechs in the Battle of the White Mountain in 1620.

The Austrian Empire was the dynastic creation of the Habsburg family. Before being officially named an empire in 1804, Austria had very properly been known in European diplomacy merely as *Maison d'Autriche*, the state that belonged to the House of Habsburg. Apart from family interests, the only sense of loyalty the Habsburgs ever cultivated consistently was their devotion to the Roman Catholic Church.[5] This latter interest expressed itself for a long time in ruthless persecution of Protestants, in particular among Czechs and Hungarians. Counter-Reformation, Germanization, Centralization—these were, in the opinion of most historians, the three principal instruments of Habsburg imperial policy. The Habsburgs introduced some uniformity into the lives of the Danubian people brought under their rule. They expanded elements of Western Civilization eastward. But neither the talents of the Habsburgs, nor the times into which their Danubian empire was born were suitable for molding the various people under their domination into a modern commonwealth of nations.

The lands and peoples under Habsburg rule were a spectrum of Europe's ethnic, linguistic, religious and cultural varieties. With such a cosmopolitan composition the Habsburg Empire might have been a suitable beginning for a European federation of nations. But such a political mission was alien to the minds of the Habsburgs, who leaned toward medieval Christian visions of unity and who were hostile to almost all ideas of the modern world. The Catholic Habsburg vision of a conservative commonwealth went against the grain of modern times, guided by Western secularism, inspired by the ideas of liberalism and nationalism. Under the impact of European modernization, the head-on clash between Habsburgs and their peoples was inevitable.

The Habsburgs tried to stop the clock of history. They opposed modern nationmaking as much as they could. They were highly successful in that time-honored Roman political game known as *divide et impera*. They set one national aspiration against another. But, in the meantime, they also missed all opportunity for taking the initiative in a direction different from the Western nation-state. By the time they thought of taking such an initiative and proposed a program of democratic federalization, as Emperor Charles did in 1918, in the last days of the First World War, it was too late. By then the Habsburgs had neither the power nor the opportunity to act as modern federators of nations.

It is not uncommon in politics to mistake a divide-and-rule policy for true statesmanship. This common mistake was the undoing of the super-aristocratic Habsburgs, and the people who succeeded the Habsburgs in democratized Europe were no better than the Habsburgs. Divide-and-rule tactics in Danubian politics continued long after the demise of the Habsburg dynasty.

The first among the Habsburg people to rise and claim the rights of modern national independence were the Magyars of Hungary. They showed a stronger sense of nationality in the early stages of national awakening then their neighbors. What accounted for the difference was Hungary's different history.

Hungary had never lost her identity and continuity as a state and nation both under the Turks and under the Habsburgs. The Magyars never suffered such a blackout of their national existence as did the Czechs under Habsburg domination. Even the Pragmatic Sanction of 1723, which proclaimed the unity and indivisibility of the Habsburg lands, treated Hungary differently from the rest of the Austrian Empire. Already in the eighteenth century, some form of a "Dual System" had existed in Austro-Hungarian relations, as R.W. Seton-Watson has pointed out, hinting, as others have too, at deeper historic origins of the ill-fated Austro-Hungarian Dualism of the second half of the nineteenth century.[6] Of course, in the eighteenth century, in the wake of an eight-year war fought under Ferenc Rákóczi, and with memories of a much longer struggle against the Habsburg liberators from the Turks, the Hungarians were less than satisfied with their special status. Despite the Pragmatic Sanction, which assured the continued Habsburg succession on the Hungarian throne, Hungary to the Hungarians remained a *"regnum liberum,"* a free kingdom, "which is not subject to any other state or people."[7] If not "free", as contemporary Hungarian nobility fancied it, or party to a "Dual System," as later observers saw it, Hungary certainly was special among the Habsburg lands, although it too suffered a steady erosion of its special status under Habsburg absolutism.[8]

At any rate, Hungary was allowed to have a Council with the Palatine at its head throughout the age of Habsburg absolutism. The Diet, that symbol of Hungary's constitutional continuity since the Middle Ages, was never allowed to die. Most of the Magyar aristocracy were subject only to superficial Germanization and became Magyar again a century later, while the large crowd of lesser nobility (one of Europe's most populous nobilities), remained staunchly Magyar, and in control of that uniquely Hungarian institution of privileged liberty: the county autonomy of the gentry. At a later date, the dead hand of this gentry past became an obnoxious burden, and a fatal obstacle to Hungarian democratization and modernization. But in the early days of national awakening, under the leadership of the powerful nobility—or, rather, thanks to the gifted and educated elite of that highly heterogeneous and mostly undistinguished class that called itself the Hungarian nobility—the Magyars made so much progress toward national independence that the non-Magyar people of multiethnic Hungary were later unable to catch up fast enough with them.

A complex problem of independence struggles within the Magyar independence struggle developed when the non-Magyars of multiethnic Hungary began to demand from the Magyars the kind of national freedoms the Magyars themselves were demanding from Austria. The Magyars were thus caught between two fires. They were fighting against Austria, while Hungary's non-Magyars were fighting against them. And their once privileged position became all the more precarious vis-à-vis their rivals since Hungary's non-Magyars ethnically outnumbered the Magyars.

The unfavorable ethnic ratio of the Magyars in their own historic kingdom of Hungary was the result of both Turkish domination and Habsburg liberation. Before the Ottoman Turks conquered Hungary, in the wake of their victory in the Battle of Mohács in 1526, an estimated 77-87 percent of the medieval Hungarian kingdom's population was Magyar.[9] Due to the enormous ethnic losses suffered under Ottoman conquest and Habsburg liberation, however, the Magyars were reduced to a minority in modern Hungary. A reliable estimate in 1720 put the Magyar ratio in the devastated country at only 45 percent of the total population. Random Slav and Romanian migration, as well as systematic German colonization, further decreased the Magyar ethnic ratio. It hit an all-time low in 1787, at 29 percent. In fact, this ethnic minority status became an emotion-laden point of argument against the right of the Magyars to claim multiethnic Hungary as a nation-state of their own.

However, despite radically reduced numbers and rising hostility against Magyar rule, the Magyars never doubted their right to Hungary as their own state.[10] And, under the impact of modern Western nationalism, they also saw to it that their ethnic ratio should improve. Mostly by natural assimilation of non-Magyars, but increasingly also by forcible Magyarization, the Magyar ratio rose to 44 percent by 1850, and to 54.5 percent by 1910, according to the last Hungarian census taken before the First World War.[11] In the long run, however, this phenomenal success of Hungary's so-called Magyarization turned out to be a mixed blessing for the Magyars. Their enemies in the Danube region multiplied faster than the ethnic stock of the Magyar people. The harmony among the peoples of mixed ethnic origins, which modern Hungarians have always proudly extolled as the foremost legacy of their country's medieval founders, vanished forever.[12]

National conflicts between Hungarians and their Danubian neighbors burst into the open with force for the first time during the European revolutions of 1848-49. The conflict remained unresolved and has plagued the Danube region ever since.

The Revolution of 1848-49 forged the Hungarian people into a nation in the contemporary modern sense—a feat achieved only by a few ethnic groups of the world at that early date in the history of modern nationalism. The Hungarian revolution against Austria was a spectacular manifestation of the spirit of a new age of freedom. When its initial compromise with the old regime collapsed, the revolution deposed the Habsburg king. The country was proclaimed a republic and Lajos (Louis) Kossuth, leader of the revolution and a fiery Magyar nationalist, was named its governor. The victories of the hastily recruited and poorly equipped Hungarian armies made revolutionary history. Only with Tsarist Russian help was Imperial Austria capable of stopping the Magyars from wrecking the Danubian Monarchy. Encircled and outnumbered, the Hungarians surrendered to the invading Russian armies on the battlefield of Világos in the summer of 1849—one in a series of modern national tragedies in that region's history.

Subdued only by the combined forces of two despised tyrannies, those of the Romanovs and of the Habsburgs, the Hungarians became heroes in the eyes of the rising liberal world, both in Europe and overseas. But, unlike their prestige abroad, the Magyar's popularity at home was undermined by the growing hostility of rival nationalities. The Magyar struggle for independence from Habsburg Austria spurred Hungary's non-Magyars to claim their own right to be equal with—and independent from—the Magyars.

Three weeks before the Világos surrender, in the summer of 1849, Bertalan Szemere, last premier of the crumbling republican regime, introduced a liberal nationality law during one of the final sessions of the National Assembly, as it was fleeing before the victorious Habsburg forces. The law pledged equality to Hungary's nationalities in an effort to appease the Romanians, Croats, Serbs, Slovaks, Germans and Ruthenes —all of whom were offended in varying degrees by Magyar nationalism. The Hungarian gesture toward the nationalities had come too late, but the gesture was sincere.[13] Even then, it had its opponents among the conservative nobility of the National Assembly. But Szemere silenced them by denouncing their "aristocratic conception" which denied equal rights to the nationalities. Such an attitude, at variance with the spirit of the new times, he warned, "if the nation is unable at long last to transcend it, will be the ruin of Hungary."[14]

Kossuth himself, during his subsequent exile of almost half a century, became an advocate of Danubian federalism. His concept of federalism, however, was predicated on Hungary's territorial integrity. He opposed Hungary's "internal federalization," advocated at that time by Kossuth's fellow exile, Count László Teleki. Not unlike Szemere's nationality law of 1849, Kossuth, the exile, stood for granting "perfect equality" to all nationalities. But only under the condition of Hungary's "undivided territory" was he willing to federate his country with neighboring states.[15]

At any rate, Kossuth's federalist messages from abroad did not get through, neither to the Hungarians nor to their Danubian neighbors. To his contemporaries, Hungarians and non-Hungarians alike, Kossuth remained a symbol of intransigent Magyar nationalism—and thus no guide toward a Danubian reconciliation. Only much later, among progressive

Hungarians, did Kossuth's conciliatory ideas become a source of inspiration for proposing a Danubian democratic federation. But, when in 1918, Oszkár (Oscar) Jászi proposed Hungary's internal federalization, it came as late as did Emperor Charles's proposal to federalize the defeated Habsburg realm's Austrian half.

As seen from the vantage point of later times, a particularly ominous conflict of the 1848-49 revolutions in Central Europe was the one between Czech and Hungarian policies. This clash was the curtain raiser to a dramatic polarization from which Czechs and Hungarians later emerged as modern protagonists of two rival, aggressively nationalist systems: one resting on German-Hungarian hegemony, the other on Slav supremacy in Central Europe.

In 1848, following a brief revolutionary episode, the Czechs, led by the historian-politician František Palacký, rallied loyally behind Austria. What they feared most at that time was not Habsburg absolutism but German nationalism. The Czech lands of Bohemia and Moravia (ethnically only two-thirds Czech and one-third German) had since the Middle Ages been united with Germany in the Holy Roman Empire. In 1848, the German nationalists, although eager to transform the German Confederation of the former Holy Roman Empire into a modern German nation-state, invited the Czechs to their National Assembly in Frankfurt. Palacký, sensing a German design to submerge the Czechs in a German nation-state, refused to go. Instead, he appealed to Vienna for Habsburg protection of Czech national rights against the Frankfurt Germans.

In one of the most prophetic Danubian documents of modern history, Palacký implored the Habsburgs to act as guardians of smaller nations living between the German and Russian giants. He urged the Habsburgs to transform the Danubian Empire of Austria into a Danubian Federation of free nations. It was Austria's great peace mission, argued Palacký, to federate Central Europe's smaller nations. To prove his point, and flatter the Habsburgs, Palacký coined a few memorable phrases—such as "Europe, indeed mankind and civilization need Austria," and the more familiar "If there weren't an Austria, it would be necessary to invent her."

Palacký had no objection to the Czechs being in close association with the Germans. He did not even oppose the idea of a larger Central European customs union combining federated Austria with a German nation-state. He was in fact lending his support to a plan similar to the German idea which later came to be known as *"Mitteleuropa."* What aroused Palacký's anger was the prospect of a division of the Austrian Empire along national lines into what he derisively called a series of independent "dwarf republics." Small states in that part of Europe, he warned prophetically, could never maintain their independence. They would never be able to defend themselves against the double danger of German and Russian imperialism.

No less angrily, Palacký lashed out against Magyar nationalism which he felt threatened Austria's existence and the peace of Europe. He saw nothing heroic in the Hungarian revolution against the Habsburgs. Rather, he considered it a menace to peace because of Magyar chauvinistic national intolerance. Magyar nationalism, he thundered, was an outrage against equality among nations and among men. To Magyar chauvinists, he said derisively "a man must first be a Magyar before he can be a human being."[16]

The common cause Palacký made with the Habsburg enemies of liberalism during the revolutions of 1848-49 earned for the Czechs the contempt of contemporary liberals, including some angry comments from the vitriolic pen of Karl Marx. That was soon forgotten. Czech-Hungarian rivalry was not.

From the Hungarian point of view, fighting against Austria had always meant fighting Germans. The war of national independence in 1848-49 was the climax of a centuries-old Hungarian struggle against German power spreading along the Danube eastward from Vienna. But in 1848-49, while fighting the German enemy which, to them, was Austria, the Hungarians also found a German ally, namely liberal German nationalism rising against the Habsburgs both from Vienna and Frankfurt.

In Hungarian eyes, the Vienna liberals stood too close to the hated German Habsburgs to become friends overnight. But there was no obstacle to the Hungarians' falling in love with the faraway German liberals of the Frankfurt Parliament. Hungary, unlike the Czech lands, had never been part of the Holy Roman Empire of the medieval Germans, nor of the German Confederation of modern times; therefore, in 1848, the Hungarians received no invitation to come to Frankfurt. Nonetheless, they did send two Magyar deputies to Frankfurt to salute the German National Assembly. Thus was born the first "brotherhood-in-arms" between German and Hungarian nationalism. The Frankfurt Parliament passed unopposed a motion of alliance with the Magyars, while the Hungarian Parliament approved unanimously the German-Magyar alliance.[17]

The 1848 alliance between Hungarian and German nationalists helped drive the Slav nationalists into the arms of Habsburgs. Simultaneously the 1848 Habsburg-Slav alliance helped engender sentiments of Hungarian-German fraternity. The Habsburgs did not reward Slav loyalty. Absolutism, once it had triumphed over the liberal revolutions, stamped out freedom indiscriminately. The German nationalists, for their part, were too weak to support even their own cause, let alone to help the Hungarians. The temporary convergence of German and Hungarian national interests nonetheless did not pass unnoticed: It alerted the Slav nationalists to the threat of a German-Hungarian front against them.

After 1849, the idea of a Hungarian-German alliance fell for awhile into oblivion. In fact, all things German were hated more than ever by the Hungarians, who were suffering under the counter-revolutionary Bach era of Austrian absolutism, under its centralization, clericalism and Germanization. After 1849, the hope of finding allies for Hungarian national resurrection was rerouted for awhile in the direction of faraway France and Italy.

The French emperor Napoleon III has emerged at mid-century as the chief advocate of Europe's nationalist reorganization. He supported, above all, Italian unification. He challenged Austria, the power that presided over Italian disunity. Hungarian exiles, seeking European support against the Habsburgs, were elated at the thought of Austria's impending defeat and partition in a war with the French and Italians. Their hopes, however, of receiving help from the French-Italian quarter were met with disappointment. Italy was liberated and united with French assistance all right, but Austria's fate was not sealed by the Franco-Italian coalition. Habsburg defeat at Solferino, in the Austro-Sardinian War of 1859 did not cause the Habsburg Empire's collapse as the Hungarians had hoped.

Soon after Solferino, Hungarian nationalists resumed once again their German orientation, and Hungarian nationalist policies remained tied to Germany through the age of Bismarck, through two World Wars, all the way to a disastrous ending of the German alliance in 1945.

Interest in a Hungarian alliance with Germany against Austria was rekindled when Bismarck seized the helm of Prussian politics in the

1860's. Once again, Hungarian exiles anticipated Austria's doom, this time as a result of a showdown between Prussia and Austria for German leadership in Central Europe. On the eve of the Austro-Prussian War, in the spring of 1866, a Hungarian legion stood by in Prussia to liberate Hungary. Bismarck was also thinking of stirring up insurrections among the Czechs in Bohemia. Had he done so, he might have forged an alliance between Czechs and Magyars against Habsburg Austria. But, as Bismarck recorded in his memoirs, the necessity of insurrection in Hungary and Bohemia depended on three "ifs"—if Napoleon III intervened in the Austro-Prussian War on Austria's side, if Russia's attitude remained doubtful, and if cholera made further ravages in Prussian ranks.[18] None of the three "ifs" materialized, and Prussian success against Austria was assured without insurrections either in Hungary or in Bohemia.

At Sadowa, in the summer of 1866, Prussia won a lightning victory over Austria without Czech or Hungarian help. Yet, Prussian victory did help usher in a Hungarian triumph: It cleared the way for the Austro-Hungarian Compromise of 1867, which fulfilled the Magyars' demands for self-government within Hungary's historic boundaries, though not their dream of full national independence. Many Hungarians, eager for complete separation from Austria, disagreed with the Hungarian makers of the Compromise with Austria. The exile Kossuth was among them. He foresaw the future better than any Hungarian of his time. The privileged position the Magyars had gained under the Compromise of 1867, he warned, would ultimately make Hungary share Austria's inevitable doom.[19]

It was easier for the Czechs than for the Hungarians to be of one mind about the Austro-Hungarian Compromise. Austria's transformation into Austria-Hungary, most Czechs believed, spelled ruin for the fulfillment of Czech national freedom under the Habsburgs. And, even before the signing of the Compromise of 1867, confronted with the threat of a Dualist solution, Palacký lost his faith altogether in Austria as a power capable of making peace among the Habsburg Monarchy's rival nations. He coined on this occasion another of his famous aphorisms on Austria. He said: "We were here before Austria, and we will be here after her."[20] It took half a century for the Czech Palacký's optimistic prophecy and the Hungarian Kossuth's pessimistic one to come true.

Bismarck's achievement in unifying Germany under the Second German Empire, and its corollary, the dualist transformation of Austria, have served as Central European stepping stones in the march modern nationalism has taken toward global triumph. In carrying mankind toward a global embrace of nationalism, Bismarck's role is comparable only to that of the peacemakers of 1919, acting under the spell of the Wilsonian principle of national self-determination. Of the two heroes in the history of modern nationalism, only the liberal Wilson was a true believer in the European reorganization according to the nationality principle. Bismarck too, was in the position to break up the Austrian Empire into its national components. But, with his conservative flair and concern for the European balance of power, he preferred a Central Europe of empires to one of small nation-states. Yet, with different intentions, both Bismarck and Wilson moved European history, as well as world history, in the same direction— toward national transformation and ethnic division.

The progress modern nationalism made with Prince Bismarck's and President Wilson's intervention gave rise to two opposite peace systems in Central Europe. The Wilsonian system favored as much, if not more, the Slavs than Bismarck's did the Hungarians.[21] However, neither system was favorable to making national equality into a condition of peace in Central Europe. And, ever since, no peacemaking that tackled the intricate nationality problems of that region succeeded in banning the vicious tradition of national inequality.

The period of German-Hungarian hegemony in Central Europe was brief. Its formal beginning may be dated from 1867, from the Austro-Hungarian Compromise. But its functioning was actually assured only by the defeat of the Schäffle-Hohenwart plan of an Austro-Czech compromise in 1871, and by the conclusion of the alliance between Austria-Hungary and Germany in 1878. Both were personal triumphs for Count Gyula Andrássy, Hungarian Premier in 1871, and Austro-Hungarian Foreign Minister in 1879.[22]

Hungarian hegemony ended in the First World War of 1914-1918, with Hungary's defeat and punishment as Germany's ally. From the pinnacle of power in modern times, millennial Hungary fell into the abyss of its deepest humiliation. In 1920, under the aegis of the Western democracies, the punitive Trianon peace settlement inflicted a double catastrophe upon the Hungarians. Not only was the Hungarian state territorially partitioned —a disaster the Hungarians had experienced before, during Turkish and Habsburg times—but the Hungarian people were dismembered as well. The latter aspects of the Hungarian catastrophe was the really painful one. Forced under hostile rule of neighboring nation-states, one-third of the Hungarians were condemned to a loss of their national identity. This was a heavy price indeed the Hungarians were made to pay for the short period of hegemony they shared with the Germans in Central Europe before the First World War.

NOTES

1. As a rule I am calling the Hungarians "Hungarian" because that is their name in the English language. However, I am calling them "Magyar" whenever the emphasis is on the ethnic distinction between Hungary's Hungarians and non-Hungarians.

2. As quoted from Palacký's *Geschichte von Böhmen* (5 vols., Prague, 1844-1867), by R.W. Seton-Watson, *A History of the Czechs and Slovaks* (London: Hutchinson & Co. Ltd., 1943), p. 15.

3. Cf. Hans Kohn, *Pan Slavism: Its History and Ideology* (New York: Vintage Books, 1960), p. XVI: "The affinity of the Slav languages and the belief in very doubtful common ancestry in prehistoric times offered no solid foundations for unity. On the contrary.... Nor did proximity create good neighborly relations."

4. Denis Sinor, *History of Hungary* (London: George Allen and Unwin Ltd.; New York: Frederick A. Praeger, Inc., 1945), p. 37.

5. Loyalty and devotion to the Church survives in the politics of Otto von Habsburg, so-called "heir" to the vanished Habsburg throne. During World War II, he advocated federalist plans for the Danube region, and for the reorganization of Europe in general, in order to "permit Europe to reassume her mission of Christian culture." Otto of Austria (sic), "Danubian Reconstruction," *Foreign Affairs,* XX, 2 (1941-42), p. 252. As a member of the European Parliament from the Federal Republic of Germany, he is currently advocating European unity under Christian auspices.

6. R.W. Seton-Watson, op. cit., p. 141.

7. Act 10/1791 of the Hungarian Diet, as quoted in Dominic G. Kosáry, *A History of Hungary* (Cleveland and New York: The Benjamin Franklin Bibliophile Society, 1941), p. 175.

8. Béla K. Király, *Hungary in the Late Eighteenth Century* (New York: Columbia University Press, 1969), p. 80.

9. Jules (Gyula) Szekfű, *État et nation* (Paris: Les Presses Universitaires de France, 1945), p. 136.

10. The Hungarian language recognizes no distinction between "Magyar," the name of the people, and "Hungary," the name of the country. The same is true, for the same historic reason, of the Czech language which does not know the difference between "Czech" and "Bohemia."

11. Oszkár Jászi, *A nemzeti államok kialakulása és a nemzetiségi kérdés* [The Formation of Nation-States and the Nationality Question] (Budapest: Grill Károly, 1912) pp. 360, and 377. Robert A. Kann, *The Multinational Empire: Nationalism and National Reform in the Habsburg Monarchy, 1848-1918*. New York: Columbia University Press, 1950), II, p. 303.

12. Hungarian scholars, whether of conservative or radical persuasion agree: peace among Hungary's nationalities is one of the distinct features of Hungary's history. Cf. Jászi, op. cit., p. 323. Szekfű, op. cit., p. 137. This point of view, however, is not shared by historians of Hungary's neighbors, and seldom supported since the turn of the century by the Western democracies.

13. Cf. Istvan Deak, *The Lawful Revolution: Louis Kossuth and the Hungarians, 1848-1849* (New York: Columbia University Press, 1979), p. 315.

14. Jászi, op. cit., p. 337.

15. On Kossuth's federalist views and on his conflict with Teleki, see Oscar Jászi, "Kossuth and the Treaty of Trianon," *Foreign Affairs,* XII, 1 (October 1933), pp. 86-97.

16. All the above on Palacky's views quoted from Hans Kohn, op.cit., pp. 65-70 passim.

17. Lewis Namier, 1848: *The Revolution of the Intellectuals* (Garden City, New York: Anchor Books, Doubleday & Company, Inc., 1964), p. 117. (Originally published by Oxford University Press in 1946.)

18. *Bismarck: The Man and the Statesman: Being the Reflections and Reminiscences of Otto Prince von Bismarck. Written and Dictated by Himself After His Retirement from Office* (London: Smith, Elder, & Co., 1898), II, p. 38.

19. The Hungarian role in defeating the plans for an Austro-Czech compromise in 1871 only aggravated Kossuth's pessimism. Cf. István (Stephen) Borsody, *Magyar-szlovák kiegyezés* [Hungarian-Slovak Compromise] (Budapest: Officina, 1945), p. 46.

20. Palacký's famous dictum on the European necessity of Austria's existence is quoted usually on the pattern of Voltaire's well-known saying about the existence of God. (This is how I quoted it; see above, Palacký's public letter to the Frankfurt Assembly in 1848.) On the other hand, there is no standard English version of Palacký's other famous statement on the existence of the Czechs. (I quoted it from the Czech in my own translation.) For less idiomatic but more verbatim English renditions of the two Palacký pronouncements, see, respectively, Hans Kohn, op. cit., p. 77, and Joseph F. Začek, *Palacký: The Historian as Scholar and Nationalist* (The Hague–Paris: Mouton, 1970), p. 27. Kohn: "Certainly, if the Austrian state had not existed for ages, we would be obliged in the interest of Europe and even of mankind to endeavor to create it as fast as possible." Začek: "We existed before Austria, we shall exist when it is gone."

21. The Romanians, the only non-Slav rivals of the Hungarians in the Danube region, had also been favored by the victors, ending as they did both World Wars on the Allied side, although they started on the German side.

22. For a perceptive analysis of the 1870's see A.J.P. Taylor, *The Habsburg Monarchy, 1809-1918: A History of the Austrian Empire and Austria-Hungary* (London: Hamish Hamilton, 1948), pp. 145-155.

N. F. Dreisziger

CENTRAL EUROPEAN FEDERALISM IN THE THOUGHT OF OSCAR JÁSZI* AND HIS SUCCESSORS

> There does not exist for me an isolated Hungarian problem; and though with an unbroken loyalty to my own, I have the same sympathy for all the suffering peoples of the Danube Basin.
>
> (Oscar Jászi quoted by Béla K. Király)

Few regions of the world have seen more and larger-scale political transformations over the past seven decades than East Central Europe. Within this period the peoples of this region have experienced monarchical rule, national independence, German subjugation, and communist domination under Soviet aegis. About the only major political alternative they had not been able to taste has been the so-called "federal solution." The non-existence of the federal experience in the history of this region is at once lamentable and surprising. It is lamentable because none of the solutions that have been tried have really solved the problems of the area, and it is surprising as there has been steady support for the idea in the region ever since the mid-nineteenth century.[1]

A future history of Central European federalism will probably point out that Hungarians had been quite numerous among the advocates of what they usually call the Danubian Confederation. Such history will also no doubt reveal that most prominent among these people have been a handful of Magyar intellectuals in Western emigration. Of course, all students of Central and East European history are familiar with at least some of the concepts of Oscar [Oszkár] Jászi, the undisputed doyen of Hungarian emigré scholars in North America in the interwar years. What is less well known is that Jászi has had numerous followers, some of whom are still active in the promotion of the idea of a federal solution for the problems of Central and East Central Europe.

* * * * *

Jászi embraced the cause of East Central European federalism rather late in life. His book outlining his scheme for a federation of Danubian Europe appeared only in 1918, nearly two decades after he had attained national prominence as an advocate of social reform. Nevertheless it seems evident that the pre-1918 period in his intellectual development had served as the gestation time for the federalist ideas that he would cherish for the rest of his long life. In other words, Jászi's federalist ideas can be traced back to concepts he had developed well before 1918: respect for the dignity of the individual, devotion to the idea of human rights for everyone, regardless of race or creed, and an unshakable belief in social progress.

Jászi's advocacy of reform and democracy inevitably turned him into a critic of contemporary Hungary. As such he scrutinized and criticized most aspects of Hungarian society, none so attentively as the country's nationality problem. His attitudes to this issue deserve analysis as they serve as the key to the understanding of his approach to the issue of East Central European or Danubian federalism.

Jászi's first major pronouncement on the nationality question in Hungary appeared in 1911 under the title *The Nationality Question and Hungary's Future [A nemzetiségi kérdés és Magyarország jövője]*.[2] The work, based upon one of Jászi's public lectures, began with an outline of contemporary Hungarian attitudes to the issue. One of these Jászi described as the *"úrlovas"* [gentlemen-horseman] conception held by those who wanted to ride roughshod through the whole issue and solve it by governmental decrees. Another commonly held approach Jászi labelled the *"jó fiú"* [good boy] view, whose proponents believed that kind-heartedness, in the form of granting equal rights to all citizens, will resolve the problem once and for all. Neither of these approaches held any prospect of success according to Jászi. The use of administrative measures could not solve nationality problems. Citing as examples Russian policies toward the Jews, and pre-reform British policies in Ireland, Jászi warned that repression and forcible assimilation had undesirable consequences for the state, increased tensions among nationalities, and were self-defeating. In his view assimilation could only be a natural process, the result of the attraction of a superior culture on a less advanced one. In reply to those who believed that the granting of equal rights to all citizens would eliminate the nationality issue Jászi answered that more than this was needed. He asserted that the fundamental needs of each nationality had to be guaranteed: good schools, good government and a good judicial system—all of which could only be satisfactory if offered in the minorities' own languages. Besides this, each nationality had its inalienable right to express its culture in its own way.[3]

Jászi's solution to Hungary's nationality problem was natural assimilation. The precondition for this was the country's social and economic transformation through extensive reforms. In a tone of pessimism Jászi predicted that his country would not embark on such reforms as this could be only done in a democracy, and in Hungary the attainment of democracy was not possible because the country's rulers used the "threat" of the nationality issue as a pretext for preventing its introduction. What was needed was a party of reform which, in the interest of peace and intra-national reconciliation, would unite within its ranks all the nationalities. Cooperation among the nationalities would facilitate economic and social progress, which in turn would lead to a permanent solution of the issue.[4]

Jászi's ideas on this question were further refined and elaborated upon in his major work, *The Evolution of Nation States and the Nationality Question [A nemzeti államok kialakulása és a nemzetiségi kérdés]*, which appeared in 1912.[5] In this study Jászi traced the evolution of nation states from earliest times, and examined the situation in contemporary Europe. His reflections on the problem led him to the conclusion that, in most cases, nationality relations within individual states assumed the form of a struggle. In such Western European countries as France and England these struggles had been resolved, but they were intense elsewhere, particularly in Eastern Europe.[6] The roots of these nationality struggles lay in the natural aspiration of peoples for linguistic and cultural self-realization and the decision of ruling circles of the state to oppose these. Where these aspirations were not opposed, as for example in the United States of America, the nationality struggle did not appear. In such states nationalities, except for inassimilable groups such as Chinese and Negroes, readily melted into the national culture. The explanation for this phenomenon lay in the existence of civil rights and democracy in America, and foremost of all, the superiority of American culture.[7] Jászi found the contemporary situation in Europe quite a contrast. There the cultural aspirations of nationalities were opposed. The extreme example was Russia, where the tsarist regime was trying to russify peoples who often had a higher culture than the Russian masses—only to find increased resistance to these policies.[8]

Within the Habsburg realm, the nationality problem became an issue with the awakening of the "lesser" nations. Here, as elsewhere, the situation was complicated by the fact that the aspiration of the minorities for cultural self-realization was reinforced by their desire for social and economic betterment. The result was a more intense form of struggle between the minorities and their masters. The latter perceived the former's aspirations as desire for separation, and reacted to them by implementing policies of forced assimilation. According to Jászi, this phenomenon was characteristic of states with great landed estates, stratified class system, and in general the lack of democratic tradition. This situation could be overcome only in modern, industrialized societies.[9]

Of the many laws Jászi detected in the development of nation states and nationalities, two more deserve to be mentioned. One was his belief in the evolution of larger and larger states, i.e. units of international society. The other was the principle that, in the interaction of two societies within a single state, the culturally superior one would assimilate the less advanced one—even if the latter was politically or militarily more powerful. Other factors, such as geographic, economic, demographic and sociological realities, would only influence the rate and effectiveness of the assimilation process.[10]

Belief in these two "laws" of historical development greatly influenced Jászi's prescription for the solution of contemporary Hungary's nationality problem, as well as his later thoughts on federalism in East Central Europe. First of all, Jászi would not and could not envisage the solution

Central European Federalism

of the nationalities question in the Carpathian Basin in other than a single political unit comprising this area. To dissolve the economic unity of this region would be to hinder commerce and the free flow of ideas, which in turn would make economic and political progress more difficult. It would also contradict the law of the evolution of larger and larger political units. It would be retrogression rather than progress. When in 1918 Jászi was confronted with the prospect of precisely this "territorial solution" that he had so emphatically rejected, he came out with his famous alternate plan for East Central Europe, the concept of the federation of the Danubian nations.

Jászi's work containing his federalist ideas was written early in 1918 but it did not appear in print until the fall of that year. It was entitled *The Future of the Monarchy, the Collapse of Dualism and the Danubian United States* [*A monarchia jövője a dualizmus bukása és a Dunai egyesült Államok*]. What Jászi proposed to establish was the replacement of the dual monarchy of Austria-Hungary by a "Pentarchy," a federation of the kingdoms of five of the major nations in East Central Europe: the Hungarian, the German or Austrian, the Polish, the Czech and the South Slav. The member states would form a customs union, and would have a united defence and foreign policy; there would be a single "supreme court" for the federation. The establishment of such a political unit—and the solution of economic problems and nationality issues within it—was essential according to Jászi for the elimination of the "danger zone" on the continent and the guarantee of lasting peace.[11]

Although Jászi became the Minister of Nationalities in Mihály Károlyi's revolutionary government in October of 1918, it proved impossible for him to implement his plan, or even a more modest version of it: the disintegration of the Habsburg Monarchy, and within it, of the Kingdom of Hungary, had advanced too far toward a "territorial" rather than a federative solution. Accordingly, Jászi resigned his ministerial post in December and left for Vienna. He would never return to his homeland except as a visitor. Although the opportunity to create a "Danubian Confederation" was missed in 1918, Jászi did not give up hope for its realization. In the preface to the German edition of this book, published late that same year, he could still express the belief that the "logic of the idea" would in the end prove "stronger than the logic of people."[12]

* * * * *

In 1923 Jászi came to the United States and two years later he became a member of Oberlin College's faculty. In 1929 he published his best known English language book *The Dissolution of the Habsburg Monarchy*. Throughout this period his writings were characterized by enthusiasm for the newly created democracies in East Central Europe, especially Czechoslovakia, coupled with bitter hostility toward the conservative regime of Hungary. He constantly stressed that the Danube region constituted a "danger zone" in Europe. The peace settlements, he argued, failed to solve effectively and permanently the problems of this area. Although the transformation of 1918-1920 had "de-feudalized" part of it and allowed the local peasantry to enter the mainstream of political life, the peace settlements had disrupted the region's economic unity, embittered race relations, and created new and strong irredentas. Jászi acknowledged the impossibility of drawing clear-cut ethnic boundaries in this part of Europe without injustice to some nationalities, but he insisted that the peace treaties "inflicted unnecessary cruelties which could have been avoided by a wiser spirit of justice and benevolence."[13]

As far as Hungary was concerned, the way out of this situation according to Jászi was the country's de-feudalization, de-militarization, the introduction of democracy and agrarain reform coupled with the attainment of good relations between Hungary and her neighbors. Jászi called for the restoration of the Magyar nation's integrity through "securing free economic and cultural intercourse between the mother country and her detached territories."[14] Believing that the countries of the Little Entente were led by reasonable men, he felt that frontier revision in favor of Hungary would be possible, if only Horthy's regime could be eliminated in Hungary. In this connection this is what Jászi wrote in 1924 in the preface of the English language edition of his *Revolution and Counter-Revolution in Hungary:*

> Only a thorough-going democratization of Hungary, and loyal and intimate relations between this democratized Hungary and the new States can create such an atmosphere in Central Europe as can cure the greatest evils of the present situation and clear the way for a democratic confederation of all the small nations which are not tormented by the rigid dogma of national sovereignty.[15]

"Only a democratic confederation," he continued, "could really solve the question of the minorities in these states...." This confederation, based on free trade and honest national autonomy for all the minorities, would end the rule of the selfish principle of national sovereignty and thereby "cure" Europe's ills.[16]

Early in 1935 Jászi visited Czechoslovakia, Romania and Yugoslavia. His visit made a deep impression on him. Hitherto he seems to have belived that all that was needed for an improvement in the prospects of federalism in Danubian Europe was the reform and de-militarization of Hungary. But his findings during his trip made him much more pessimistic. What he found during his visit, especially in Romania and Yugoslavia, was tensions, hate-mongering, nationalistic mass hysteria, and the "undue influence" of "unbalanced" intellectuals, resulting in a "hidden *bellum omnium contra omnes.*"[17] It became evident to Jászi that the new states were plagued by the same nationality problem and intra-national antagonisms that Austria-Hungary had been plagued with earlier. This state of affairs reinforced Jászi's conviction that the "only possible solution" to the region's problems was not dismemberment but "a federal structure" combined with cultural and administrative autonomy for all the nationalities.[18]

There can be little doubt that the developments of the years following 1935 did little to encourage Jászi's hopes for the realization of his dreams. As the tide of the Second World War began to turn in 1942 and 1943, Jászi could once again anticipate the coming of a chance for what he called the "federal organization of the whole Danube-Vistula region."[19] By 1944, however, a new complication entered into the picture. It became obvious that Soviet Russia would have a say in the reorganization of post-war East Central Europe. Jászi kept hoping though that the threats of Russian territorial aggrandizement, or possible Russian-German collusion at the expense of the East European nations could be averted through an agreement between the Western democracies and the USSR.[20] In fact, the first post-war disappointment which awaited Jászi was not caused by Russian actions but by developments in Danubian Europe itself.

In 1945 the nations of East Central Europe embarked on a policy of expelling undesirable minorities from their territory. This policy was vigorously pursued even by Czechoslovakia, a state which Jászi had admired in the interwar period. These events deeply dissapointed Jászi, and he condemned them with all his heart. To him, these policies destroyed that spirit of cooperation which would have been absolutely essential for a federal reorganization of the region. With much sorrow he concluded that the expulsion of Hungarians from Slovakia, and the Germans from everywhere "utterly demolished" the hopes for a Danubian and Balkan confederation.[21]

The events of the post World War II period caused Jászi to reassess his attitudes toward the nations of East Central Europe. While before the war he tended to have a high opinion of the peoples of the new successor states, especially Czechoslovakia, now his disillusionment prompted him to have a better opinion of his own co-nationals. In an article written at this time he described the Magyars as a "sober, hard-working, extremely intelligent ethnic group, remarkably free from the mysticism and the extreme racial fanaticism of the Slavs and the Romanians.[22]

After a while Jászi recovered to some extent from the shock and pain which the turnabout of Czechoslovakia's nationality policy had caused him. In 1947, in an open letter to the students of the town of Eger in Hungary he reasserted his faith in the future of the Danubian confederation:

> As I approach the end of my life, it is very gratifying for me to know that an independent group of young Hungarians appreciates the truth that, after the enormous catastrophe [of the war], true democracy and true freedom is inconceivable without Kossuth's plan for the Danubian Confederation.... The terrible sufferings of the peoples of the Danube region will not have been in vain if from them could develop a fraternal alliance [*testvéri szövetség*] which would guarantee independence and human rights [*emberi szabadságjogok*].[23]

Following this statement Jászi urged his young correspondents to further the cause of federalism by working for the freedom of commercial intercourse among nations, the enhancement of the masses' culture and morality, the growth of cultural interaction among peoples, and for the securing of human rights in all countries.[24] Although Jászi lived for another decade, lack of finances and growing old age prevented him from further extensive efforts to promote his cherished plan of a federation in the Danube Valley.

* * * * *

During and after the Second World War numerous Hungarian intellectuals arrived in the United States. Many among these were also advocates of a federal reorganization of East Central Europe. And as Jászi and his contemporaries retired from the struggle, these new arrivals took it upon themselves to promote the idea.

For some time during and immediately after the war it seemed that the most influential Hungarian exile in the United States would be Tibor Eckhardt. Eckhardt was a publicist, diplomat and politician who had been sent to America in 1941 by the Hungarian regime with the idea that he should prepare the ground for the establishment of a Hungarian government in exile should circumstances in Central Europe warrant it.[25] While Eckhardt never had to perform this task, he did become a leading figure of the Hungarian community in the New World. This fact is of some consequence from the point of view of our subject as Eckhardt was also a federalist. He seems to have become a convert to this idea during the numerous national and international crises which affected Central Europe in the 1930s. By the end of the decade, and early during the war years, he formulated a scheme for Danubian confederation which he continued to advocate during his American exile. The diagnostic characteristic of Eckhardt's federalist plan was that, unlike Kossuth and Jászi before him and other thinkers later, he wished to leave the South Slavs and the Romanians out of any future Danubian federal state. The "three pillars" of the confederation envisaged by him were the ancient capitals of Vienna, Prague, and Budapest; that is, the peoples living in the Austrian, Bohemian and Carpathian basins.[26]

Eckhardt never managed to rival Jászi's reputation either as a federalist or as an exile intellectual and publicist. He published little in English and, in any case, by the mid-1950s there were other Hungarian intellectuals in the West advocating the cause of the Danubian federation with more vigor and effectiveness than Eckhardt. Some of these people eventually coalesced around a journal maintained purposely for the promotion of this cause, the *Studies for a New Central Europe*. This periodical served as a major forum for Central European federalist ideas in the West for almost a decade. It was maintained through the efforts of a group of Hungarian emigré intellectuals. The most important among them were: Eugene Padányi-Gulyás, an architect who had been a member of Hungary's pre-1945 parliament; Béla Talbot-Kardos, an economist with a keen interest in history, Alexander Gallus, an anthropologist who served as the journal's editor, and Francis S. Wagner, a former diplomat and prolific writer on the problems of the Danube region. The journal evidently also received considerable moral and other support from exiled intellectuals of other Danubian nations.[27]

In the *Studies* there emerged a somewhat more elaborate and to some extent different concept of a Central European federation. Padányi-Gulyás explained this idea this way: "The people living in this area are looking for a *realistic Third Way* in foreign policy, economy and in ideology, different from that of their neighbors." In foreign policy, the region would be neutral on the pattern of Switzerland. In the economy a system would evolve which was neither communist nor capitalist, but would stress "self-management" of vital industries and public services. The political system would be pluralistic, while society as a whole would be a reflection of local national traditions rather than Eastern or Western ideologies.[28]

In the early 1970s the *Studies* group of federalists embarked on a scheme to prepare a "Blueprint" for the creation of a neutral "Mid-European" buffer zone between the Soviet Union and the West. Incorporated into this plan was a proposal for a possible federal organization of the region, as well as a detailed scheme for the solution of nationality problems there. This latter scheme envisaged that in the treatment of minorities the model of Switzerland should be followed by the states of Mid-Europe. The rights of minorities should be internationally guaranteed. The United Nations and its various organizations should be empowered to mediate in disputes, or to investigate complaints. They should even have the power to order plebiscites and enforce their decisions.[29]

* * * * *

While the *Studies* group of Hungarian federalist publicized their ideas and lobbied in Washington, London and elsewhere to have them endorsed by the West's leaders, other emigré Hungarian intellectuals served the cause through their own writings. Among them was Professor Béla K. Király, an avowed Danubian federalist. In a 1965 article in the *Hungarian Quarterly* he reviewed Jászi's approach to the issue of East Central European federalism. He explained Jászi's Danubian Confederation scheme of 1918:

The basis for Jászi's concept... was the half-century-old Kossuth project. Jászi's federalist project was predicated on a progressive social philosophy ... his basic teaching was that the federalist solution of the peaceful organic cooperation of free nations could be realized only with the simultaneous realization of a democratic form of government.[30]

According to Király, Jászi's most important achievement was his vision that his proposed Danubian Confederation would serve as a starting point for a larger constellation of federative states—the Pentarchia would expand into an Octarchia embracing the Balkans as well—leading eventually to a United States of Europe "and larger regional federations, securing peace and happiness of all mankind." In his conclusions, Király compared Jászi and Kossuth and observed about them: "Both... broke out from the framework of national self-indulgence" and through their federalist ideas ascended "onto the proud plateau" where they placed "human progress" as their first political priority. Király closed his study by remarking that after his visit to Danubian Europe in 1948 Jászi reiterated his old conviction that federalism was the "only possible means of reconciling states and nations."[31]

The Hungarian-American academic who devoted the most time and effort to the propagation of Jászi's federalist ideas is without doubt Professor Stephen Borsody. In fact, with his own major work concentrating on the problem of the political organization of East Central Europe, and with his numerous publications concerning the work and ideas of Jászi, Borsody should be regarded as the proper heir to the grand old man's "federalist" mantle.[32] While a detailed review of Borsody's writings on Jászi is beyond the scope of a brief paper such as this one, it might be worthwhile to mention here a few of his observations. The first concerns Jászi's Hungarian intellectual heritage. In this connection Borsody makes the interesting remark that while much of Jászi's 1918 scheme derived from Kossuth's earlier federalist plans, the thinkers he respected most were the Hungarian statesmen István Széchenyi and József Eötvös, in fact, it was these two men whose pictures adorned Jászi's private study in Oberlin.[33]

Another piece of interesting commentary Borsody provides is his comparison of the careers and ideologies of Jászi and Thomas G. Masaryk. Indeed, the comparison is a useful one. It constrasts the political success of the latter with the failure of the former to realize his ideas and to gain public acclaim. Yet the differences separating the two men were few. Both were prominent intellectuals before the fateful year of 1918 when their fortunes parted. Both were advocates of social progress, but they differed in their solution to the problem of the organization of post-World War I East Central Europe. Masaryk opted for the national solution, while Jászi insisted on the federalist idea. Their choices pre-determined their political fortunes. In an age of rampant nationalism, Masaryk's success and Jászi's failure should not surprise us at all. Borsody, however, goes beyond pointing out the contrast between the two men's fortunes: he also offers an explanation of the different approaches the two adopted for the solution of East Central Europe's problems. This explanation lies in the two men's national experience. For a Czech whose nation had been denied the experience of national self-determination, the hope of a better future seemed independence. For Jászi the national experience had been different. After centuries of Habsburg rule, between 1867 and 1918 Hungary had achieved near-total self-determination. But in Jászi's view, this experiment resulted in catastrophic mistakes. This conclusion enabled him, in the words of Borsody, "to reach the vision of the post-nationalist age;" Masaryk wanted to "eradicate" the past, Jászi sought a "synthesis between the past and the future."[34]

* * * * *

All the Hungarian advocates of Danubian federalism who have been mentioned so far had spent most of their lives since leaving Hungary in the United States. This fact does not suggest that the Hungarian advocates of this cause have been predominately or even largely confined to the United States. In fact, one of the more recent developments in the history of Hungarian federalist thinking has emerged from a more distant part of the world, Australia. This has been the publication of a book containing several analyses of the past and present of East Central Europe, and essays on the problems of a federal solution for the area. The volume in question is the *Quest for a New Central Europe,* edited by the Hungarian-Australian expert on international law, Julius Varsányi.[35] Its chapters were written by Hungarian and non-Hungarian scholars from various parts of the world. One of the most distinguished essays is by an Australian, David St. L. Kelly.

Among the papers produced by emigré Hungarians in this volume, Varsányi's is probably the most important. It investigates the principle of "concurrent interstate jurisdiction" as it could be applied to a future East Central European federal state. Varsányi envisages four types of jurisdiction for a Danubian confederation: federal, state, federal-state and "interstate." The first three would provide public order, security, public services and economic guidance; the fourth would deal with matters of culture and would have an ethnic rather than territorial basis. The territorially based federal, state and federal-state types of jurisdiction would co-exist with the ethnically oriented fourth type very much as temporal and religious jurisdiction had co-existed in Europe during the Middle Ages.[36] Varsányi explains further:

> The prescribed... law by a member state A for its ethnically or linguistically related conationals living within the borders of member state B (and vice-versa), should be implemented by means of the same federal agency as the one responsible for the implementation of law for the subject matter of exclusive federal jurisdiction.[37]

* * * * *

Nearly three-quarters of a century had passed between the time of Jászi's first significant writings on the nationality issue in the Carpathian basin and Varsányi's and his colleagues' schemes for the attainment of the harmonious coexistence of the peoples of East Central Europe. Throughout these decades a number of Hungarians living in Western exile persisted in voicing the belief that the most promising solution to the national rivalries of the region was the one that was not tried in the post-World War I or any of the subsequent reorganizations of the Danubian Basin.

While the message of these intellectuals has been very much the same throughout this period, their means of promoting it varied somewhat. Jászi emphasized the need for a "federalist solution" whenever he could, both in his scholarly and his popular writings. The historians among his followers tended to focus attention on the issue by writing on the history of East Central European federalism and especially on the schemes of Kossuth and Jászi. Most of the scholars associated with the cause had also been involved in editorial work aimed at the same purpose. Kardos and Wagner had been involved with the already mentioned *Studies for a New*

Central Europe. Borsody and Király at one time or another did much of the editing of the *Central European Federalist.* A number of volumes of essays have also been edited and published though none quite as ambitious in scope as Varsányi's volume mentioned above. And while the scholars published, an ex-politician such as Padányi-Gulyás lobbied for the endorsment of their schemes by the leaders of the Western World.

Differences also existed among these men as to the precise federation they envisaged. To illustrate this fact it is enough to refer to the issue of the geographic extent of the proposed federation. Jászi thought very much in terms of the territory of the former Habsburg Empire. Here he differed from Kossuth who in his post-1849 writings envisaged a confederation of the nations of the middle and lower Danube Valley, leaving out Austria and Bohemia. With Eckhardt, the territory of the coveted federation shifted very much to the West, abandoning plans for the inclusion of any Balkan nations. And with the Padányi-Gulyás group, the proposed federation "expanded" to the North and Northeast envisaging the incorporation of the nations of Scandinavia and the Baltic.

But these men differed in at least one other respect as well. They seem to have had, to some extent at least, differing reasons for devoting so much of their time and energies to their cause. Jászi's advocacy of a Danubian federation derived mainly from his concepts of the laws of historical development, coupled with the lessons he drew from the experience of pre-1918 Hungary. As has been seen, the laws of history taught Jászi to expect larger and larger state formations (to assure economic and social progress), while the experience of his native country suggested to him that nationality problems were unlikely to be solved in unitary nation states.[38] One can also detect some anti-German elements in Jászi's federalist plans, but these were probably secondary in importance. This type of fear has obviously played a more important role in the thoughts of Jászi's followers. Eckhardt's conversion to the cause has been obviously brought on by his rejection of German imperialism, while there can be no doubt that the devotion of the post-war and post-1956 emigrés to the idea has been motivated largely by the realization that the political independence of East Central Europe from both the West and the East can be achieved only through a federation of the region's nations.

It would be misleading to end an analysis of Jászi and his successors with a discussion of their differences, for there was much more that united these men than what divided them. They undoubtedly shared a common belief in the need for human progress, for the economic, social, cultural and moral advancement of mankind. They also seem to have developed a keen awareness of the common history of the nations of the Danube Valley, an awareness which has been only heightened by sufferings that have been inflicted on these peoples by outside powers in the past four-and-a-half decades. For these Hungarian federalists this awareness of the present and the past has been coupled with an intense concern for the future of the region's nations, a future that, in their view, could only be mastered through close and harmonious cooperation. Jászi and his intellectual heirs then, had transcended their own national particularisms, and while they remained devoted to their Hungarian nation, they worked —and continue to work—for the better future of all the peoples of East Central Europe.

NOTES

* My interest in Oscar Jászi and other Hungarian federalists had been first aroused in a graduate seminar I had taken from Professor Peter Brock of the University of Toronto. I had returned to this subject in a paper prepared for the 1981 Slovak World Congress in Toronto. Various drafts of this paper were commented on by Dr. Francis S. Wagner of Washington, Professor Stanislaw Kirschbaum of Glendon College in Toronto, and Professor Peter Pastor of Montclair State College. Their suggestions were most useful. Professor Stephen Borsody of Pittsburgh has greatly facilitated my research by sending me copies of his publications which I had been unable to obtain in or through libraries in Kingston and Toronto. My research on this paper and other related subjects has been periodically supported by funds from my college's Arts Division Research Fund, and Social Sciences and Humanities Research Council funds.

1. See Stephen Borsody, *The Triumph of Tyranny: The Nazi and Soviet Conquest of Central Europe* (London: Jonathan Cape, 1960), esp. Chapter II. A new edition of this book has been recently released: *The Tragedy of Central Europe* (New Haven, CT: Yale Concilium on International and Area Studies, 1980). For a brief discussion of recent East European attitudes on federalism see Bennet Kovrig, *Communism in Hungary from Kun to Kádár* (Stanford, CA: Hoover Institution Press, 1979), p. 430.

2. Published in Budapest by the Galilei Kör [Galielo Circle], in 1911.
3. Ibid., pp. 5-15.
4. Ibid., pp. 23-30.
5. Published in Budapest by Grill.
6. Ibid., pp. 109-123, passim.
7. Ibid., pp. 113-121.
8. Ibid., pp. 135-168, passim.
9. Ibid., pp. 209-236.
10. Ibid., pp. 228--231.
11. For a detailed analysis of this book see Béla K. Király, "The Danubian Problem in Oscar Jászi's Political Thought," *The Hungarian Quarterly*, Vol. V, nos. 1-2, (1965), pp. 124-130.
12. *Der Zuzammenbruch des Dualismus und die Zukunft der Donaustaten* (Vienna, 1918), see the preface.
13. Oscar Jászi, "Dismembered Hungary and Peace in Central Europe," *Foreign Affairs*, Vol. II, no. 2 (December 1923), pp. 270ff.
14. Ibid., pp. 279ff.
15. Oscar Jászi, *Revolution and Counter-Revolution in Hungary* (London, King, 1924), p. ix.
16. Ibid. Also, "Dismembered Hungary," p. 280.
17. Oscar Jászi, "Neglected Aspects of the Danubian Drama," *Slavonic Review*, Vol. XIV, no. 1 (July 1935), pp. 54-56.
18. Oscar Jászi, "The Future of Danubia," *Journal of Central European Affairs*, Vol. I, no. 2 (July 1941), p. 135.
19. Oscar Jászi, "Central Europe and Russia," *Journal of Central European Affairs*, Vol. V, no. 1 (Spring 1945), p. 2.
20. Ibid., pp. 4-6; also, Oscar Jászi, "Postwar Pacification in Europe," in H. O. Eaton, ed., *Federation: The Coming Structure of World Government* (Norman, OK: The University of Oklahoma Press, 1944), pp. 147-54.
21. Oscar Jászi, "The Choices in Hungary," *Foreign Affairs*, Vol. 24, no. 3 (1946), p. 463. See also Borsody, *Triumph*, p. 153.
22. Jászi, "Choices," p. 456.
23. Oszkár [Oscar] Jászi, "Üzenet az egri diákokhoz a Dunai Konföderációról" [Message to the Students of Eger about the Danubian Confederation], *Huszadik Század* [Twentieth Century], Vol. XXXV, no. 2 (May 1947), pp. 97ff.

24. Ibid., p. 98.

25. János Pelényi, "The Secret Plan for a Hungarian Government in the West at the Outbreak of World War II," *Journal of Modern History*, Vol. XXXVI, no. 2 (June 1964), pp. 171-175. For a much more recent comment on Eckhardt's American mission see Hajdu Tibor, *Károlyi Mihály, politikai életrajz* [Mihály Károlyi: A Political Biography] (Budapest: Kossuth, 1978), pp. 474ff.

26. For some of Eckhardt's English-language writings see his article "The Problem of the Middle Danube Basin," *Hungarian Quarterly*, Vol. VI, no. 1 (1940), especially pp. 3-14, and his memoirs, *Regicide at Marseille: The Recollections of Tibor Eckhardt* (New York: The American Hungarian Library, 1964), especially pp. 74-75.

27. I have reviewed the work of these people in somewhat greater detail in a paper "Free Hungarians and the Future of East Central Europe," given at the 1981 Slovak World Congress in Toronto. The publication of a revised version of this paper is in progress.

28. Eugene Padányi-Gulyás, "Toward a Constructive Ideology and Policy in a New Central Europe," in Francis S. Wagner, ed., *Toward a New Central Europe: A Symposium on the Problems of the Danubian Nations* (Astor Park, FL: Danubian Press, 1970), p. 29. Emphasis in the original.

29. *Blueprint for a New Central Europe*, special issue of the *Studies*, Ser. 3, no. 1 (1971-72), pp. 6-28.

30. Király, "The Danubian Problem," pp. 124f. (See note 11 above).

31. Ibid., p. 133.

32. Borsody, *Triumph*, (see note 1 above), István Borsody, "Az Úttörő" [The Pioneer] in István Borsody, ed., *Jászi Oszkár élete és műve: Írások 80. születésnapjára* [Oscar Jászi's Life and Work: Writings on the Occasion of his 80th Birthday] special issue of *Látóhatár* [Horizon], Vol. 6, no. 2 (1955), pp. 66-77; "Jászi és Masaryk" [Jászi and Masaryk] in the same journal, Vol. 10, no. 1-2 (1959), pp. 56-61; "A magyar helyzet: Jászi Oszkár születése századik évfordulójára" [The Hungarian Situation: On the Occasion of Oscar Jászi's Hundredth Birthday] *Új Látóhatár* [New Horizon] Vol. XXVI, no. 2 (April 1975), pp. 89-101; and "Division and Reunion: Problems of Peace and Federation in Central Europe," in Harold J. Gordon Jr. and Nancy M. Gordon, eds., *The Austrian Empire: Abortive Federation?* (Lexington, MA: D.C. Heath and Company, 1974), pp. 149-154, are some of Borsody's publications on the subject.

33. Borsody, "Az Úttörő," p. 68; see also Borsordy's preface to the re-issue of Jászi's book: *Magyar kálvária—Magyar feltámadás* [Hungarian Calvary—Hungarian Ressurection] (Munich: Aurora, 1969), p. 8.
34. Borsody, "Jászi és Masaryk," pp. 58f.
35. The volume was published by the Australian Carpathian Federation (Adelaide-Sydney) and printed by the Dai Nippon Printing Company of Hong Kong, making it a truly international undertaking. The work appeared in 1979.
36. Julius Varsanyi, "The Legal Aspect: Concurrent Jurisdiction," in the above volume, pp. 247-254.
37. Ibid., p. 255.
38. Despite the considerable volume of writings on Jászi, there is no comprehensive analysis of his ideological development. There is one monograph which examines him as a radical, from a Marxist viewpoint: György Fukász, *A magyarországi polgári radikalizmus történetéhez, 1900-1918: Jászi Oszkár ideológiájának birálata* [On the History of Hungary's Bourgeois Radicalism, 1900-1918: An Evaluation of Oscar Jászi's Ideology] (Budapest: Gondolat, 1960). Two North American scholars, Mary Gluck and Lee Congdon, are studying the intectualls of Hungary's "Second Reform Generation" of which Jászi was a prominent member. Hopefully, they will come up with an authoritative and detailed examination of Jászi's intellectual development.

Andrew Ludanyi

SOCIALIST PATRIOTISM AND NATIONAL MINORITIES: A COMPARISON OF YUGOSLAV AND ROMANIAN THEORY AND PRACTICE

Communist ascendancy in Romania and Yugoslavia resulted in a complete reformulation of the "nationalities question" on the basis of Marxist-Leninist nationalities theory.[1] This changed ideological context provided Romania and Yugoslavia with new guidelines for the treatment of their minorities. Henceforth, the ethnic minorities of both states were guaranteed an existence which was "national in form," but "socialist in content." This paper will examine the ideological and other modes of self-definition which are related to this formula and its application.

The Ideological[2] Position of the National Minorities

The ideological position of the Hungarians and other minorities of Transylvania and the Vojvodina have undergone significant changes since the communists first come to power. These changes have been a consequence of altered power relationships within the communist bloc, as well as certain developments within the communist parties of Romania and Yugoslavia respectively.

Within and outside the bloc the tendency toward "polycentrism" has provided the opportunities for differing policies. Polycentrism designates the numerous centers of ideological authority which emerged following the Tito-Stalin split of 1948. This process of ideological fragmentation followed the expansion of communist rule into East Central Europe and Asia. It was a consequence of political developments within the expanded empire as well as changes within Soviet leadership.[3]

Within the expanded communist orbit the events most responsible were the Tito-Stalin split, the death of Stalin in 1953, the riots in Poland and revolt in Hungary in 1956, the rift between communist China and the USSR, the more recent Romanian opposition to economic integration into COMECON, and the Warsaw Pact invasion of Czechoslovakia in 1968. These events were closely tied to changes in the Party leadership of the USSR. Stalin's death was followed by an acceleration of these tendencies, because his successors initiated policies which allowed more freedom of action to party leaders in the satellite states.

Until Stalin's demise, satellite leaders simply mimicked Soviet nationalities policy as well as constitutional forms.[4] Even in Yugoslavia, the Soviet pattern was assiduously followed until 1949.[5] However, as de-Stalinization unfolded within the bloc, the Soviet pattern was moulded to fit the national peculiarities within each state. This process affected both the ideological and the constitutional context of nationality policies in Romania and Yugoslavia.

Soviet National Policy

Before we examine the application of Soviet nationalities policy in Eastern Europe, a number of its major features will be noted. Flexibility is, perhaps, its most obvious feature. It has been able to adapt itself to all sorts of political situations, among various ethnic groups and nationalities, in drastically different economic and geographic settings.[6] But this adaptability was always guided by the political interests of the Soviet Union. As a result, "proletarian internationalism" meant the subordination of all local and ethnic "nationalisms" to the interests of the Soviet Union as a whole.[7] The theoretical right to "secession" and "self-determination" or the right to local "autonomy" within a federal constitutional context, were always contingent on the intra- and international political needs of the Soviet Union.[8] This was also the case for the East European communist states until Stalin's death.[9]

Since Marx had written very little on the "nationalities question," Soviet policies in this regard were formulated mainly by Lenin and Stalin to meet the needs of power seizure and power consolidation.[10] As such,

Soviet nationalities theory incorporated the lessons learned by the Bolsheviks in the turbulent two decades which followed the 1905 Revolution. These lessons reflected the particular characteristics and problems of the multinational Russian Empire, as seen by revolutionaries who desired to utilize existing contradictions (i.e., national conflicts) to further their own quest for power.[11]

This utilitarian and even opportunistic development of Soviet nationalities policy, allowed for theoretical as well as practical inconsistenceis and contradictions. As a consequence, the same ideological precepts were used to justify such vastly different events as the Soviet acquiescence to Finnish independence and the bloody reincorporation of the Caucasian republics.[12] Although present-day ideologues blame some of these admitted contradictions on the distortions caused by the "Stalinist personality cult," in actuality the inconsistencies were already manifest before Lenin's death in 1924.[13] Stalin only exaggerated these contradictions by enabling Russian nationalism to resurface in the 1930s, after an ineffective war of words against "great Russian chauvinism" and "local bourgeois nationalisms."[14]

Both Romania and Yugoslavia adopted Soviet nationalities theory to solve the problems of their own multinational existence. In the case of Romania this adoption was really Soviet-imposed. But in Yugoslavia the adoption was a matter of international communist solidarity as well as domestic political necessity.[15] In both cases, however, the nationalities policy so adopted, was fashioned after the prevailing theory in Stalin's Soviet domains. While the communist parties of both these countries had paid lip service to this policy in the interwar years, their rise to power following World War II gave them the opportunity to practice that which they had been preaching.[16]

The Vojvodina and Transylvania

For the analysis of Yugoslav and Romanian nationalities policies the present study has focused primarily on the regions of the Vojvodina and Transylvania, respectively. These two areas are the most diverse in nationality make-up and they include minority problems which are potentially volatile. Both areas include large minority groups which are linguistically, religiously and culturally quite distinct from the "official" nationality(ies) of the state. They also contain "border" nationalities which are the source or can become the source, of international tensions.

Recent changes in the ethnic composition of the Vojvodina have had a strong bearing on Yugoslavia's post-World War II nationalities policy there. The changes that concern us relate to the difference between the prewar and postwar ethnic make-up of the area as well as its current composition as reflected in the census of 1971. A comparison of 1931 and 1948 data indicates that Vojvodina's German population was reduced during the war from 317,000 to about 35,000. This drastic change is a consequence of deportations and liquidations that took place during the last year of the war. In general the change has altered the population ratio in the Vojvodina—where most of the Germans lived—from about one-third German, one-third Hungarian, and one-third Serb to about one-fourth Hungarian, over one-half Serb, and nearly one-fourth other South Slavs. (The rise of the Serb, Croat, etc. overall percentage was due to the extensive colonization of the lands left vacant by the deported Germans.)[17]

The Hungarian population has been stagnating, and since 1961 has actually declined drastically. Thus, while between 1961 and 1971 Yugoslavia's population increased from 18.5 million to 20.5 million, and the Albanians within Yugoslavia from 915,000 to 1,309,000, the Hungarian population during the same period dropped from 504,000 to 477,000. From a bio-political perspective, the Hungarians, in comparison to the dynamism of the Albanians, are in definite decline within the overall population. This demographic stagnation may be the result of their more effective "integration," or it may be propelling them toward greater integration. It could also be a sign of their alienation, if the population losses were due to emigration, a low birthrate, or assimilation by other ethnic groups.[18]

In Romania, similar stagnation is evident according to official census results, not only among the Hungarians, but also among the Germans and the Jews. The Romanians have doubled their population between 1910 and 1966. At the same time, the Germans have been reduced from 565,000 in 1910 to 372,000 in 1966, and the Jews from 182,000 in 1910 to 14,000 in 1966. The largest minority, the Hungarians, have gone from 1,664,000 in 1910 to 1,597,000 in 1966.

What have been the reasons for these dramatic demographic changes in Transylvania? As in Yugoslavia, so in Romania, World War II has produced the most drastic consequences, particularly for the Germans and the Jews.[19] These changes were due to the dislocations of the war, including deportations, territorial transfers and exterminations. The net result of these changes has been to leave only the Hungarians as a strong minority (although they too have been weakened),[20] and to accentuate the predominant role of the Romanians.

The Jewish ethnic group suffered greatly during the war years. At this time the Iron Guardists and the Antonescu dictatorship carried to fulfillment the Nazi "solution" of the Jewish problem.[21] Besides outright extermination, the Jews also diminished in proportion to the other minorities as a result of the cession of Bessarabia and Bukovina to the USSR and Dobruja to Bulgaria. More recently their numbers have been further reduced by emigration to Israel.

The Germans suffered mostly during the closing phase of World War II and during the early postwar years.[22] These losses were of various kinds, including the effects of the war among the male population[23] and deportations to Russia.[24] But, perhaps, the greatest reductions came when Hitler transferred Romanian Germans to newly conquered areas in Poland and Czechoslovakia as colonists.[25] Later, these "colonists" suffered immense losses when the Poles and Czechs reasserted their rule following the German collapse.[26]

Other ethnic minorities like the Bulgarians, Ukrainians, Tatars and Turks were also reduced in size and significance. These reductions came with the cessions of Bukovina, Bessarabia and Dobruja. Unlike the Germans and the Jews, however, these other minority reductions did not affect greatly the minority situation in Transylvania. But they did eliminate the problems posed by these lesser minorities. Consequently, it left the Romanian regime more time to concentrate its attention on its greatest minority problem—the Hungarians or Magyars of Transylvania.[27]

In relation to the Hungarians of Transylvania—who did not suffer deportation, extermination or encouraged emigration—the stagnation of population requires some other explanation. Is it due to forced or voluntary assimilation, to low birthrate or to falsification of census results? The aggressive nationalism of most Romanian administrations since 1918-20 would seem to suggest that all of the above have been contributing factors. At least one significant study on the population profile of Transylvania has made the claim that the Hungarians are not reported accurately in the Romanian census. According to Satmarescu's study of 1975,[28] the actual number of Hungarians in Transylvania is definitely over two million, and is perhaps closer to 2.3 million than to 1.6 million indicated in the official statistics. Whatever the case may be, the present study will focus on these minorities to reflect on nationalities policies as they have emerged under the Yugoslav and the Romanian versions of "proletarian internationalism."

The Romanian Ideological Position

In Romania the communists immediately applied the "national form" and "socialist content" of Soviet nationality policy. As in the Soviet Union, so in Romania, the reason for adopting this policy was closely tied to considerations of power seizure and power consolidation. The policy attempted to popularize the Communist Party of Romania among the country's national minorities. It entailed guaranteeing to them the right to use their language in public discourse, in education and in their relations with the government. It also guaranteed for them equality with the Romanians in political, social and economic relations. In fact, in the Sacuesc (Székely) districts it even provided for "autonomy" in line with the Soviet example.[29]

In the Stalinist years, the ideological justification for these enlightened policies were simple and straightforward. "Proletarian internationalism" (i.e., Soviet foreign policy) demanded such enlightenment.[30] In the writings of Romanians dealing with the question of nationalities policy, this was definitely the central concept. The concept of "patriotism" or "socialist patriotism," on the other hand, was treated only as an afterthought. It was viewed merely as an appendage of "proletarian internationalism." Consequently, pro-Soviet attitudes, expressions, and actions were both internationalist and patriotic, while any anti-Soviet manifestation was considered to be *ipso facto* "bourgeois nationalism" and "chauvinism."[31]

For this reason interwar Romania was condemned for its "monstrous antipatriotic, antinational struggle against the Soviet Union."[32] It was also described as a cruel oppressor of nationalities which inflamed "chauvinism and racial hatred" by its "brutal exploitation," wherein:

> Workers belonging to national minorities were deprived of political and civil rights. Their native languages were prohibited in government

institutions. There were no government schools in the native languages. The culture of national minorities was persecuted and suppressed. The bourgeois-landlord government promulgated no fewer than 400 laws and decrees against the national minorities.[33]

For all these inequities, the "bourgeois-landlord" class basis of interwar Romania was held responsible.[34]

In the late 1950s the ideological discussion of the nationalities question began to take on added dimensions. It began first as a change of emphasis, but ended in making Romania a new dissident center within the polycentric communist camp. Besides the policies of de-Stalinization in the CPSU, the Hungarian revolt of 1956 and the withdrawal of Soviet troops from Romania in 1958, provided the opportunity for asserting more ideological independence.[35] It is ironic that more ideological independence for Romanian communists has led to less ideological and political freedom for the country's national minorities.

Recent Romanian formulations of "proletarian internationalism" have stressed its interstate rather than intrastate role. Thus, very little is done about the rights of national minorities.[36] Even when the rights of minorities are mentioned, it is only to show that their treatment has "cemented the unity of the nation," by "strengthening friendship and brotherhood between the Romanian working people and those belonging to the coinhabiting nationalities."[37] In this way, the intrastate considerations of proletarian internationalism are all subsumed under the concept of socialist patriotism. The latter has now moved to the center of the Romanian ideological stage. Nationalism, defined as the selfish prejudice which leads to imperialism and discord, is still decried. But, it is contrasted against the positive force of "patriotism" which is the "intimate union of the ideas of socialism and national consciousness."[38]

In recent ideological formulations "socialist patriotism" is definitely viewed as the constructive national force which animates Romanians who follow the leadership of the CPR.[39] It is the element necessary for achieving an inseparable unity and cohesion within Romania. Such national unity is in turn a prerequisite for unity within the international communist movement, because concrete "socialist construction" goes on within national boundaries.[40] It is a "national creation—because socialist revolution can neither be the object of import or export, a transplanted hybrid ... [but] can only be an outcome of the struggle of each people."[41]

By making unity within the international communist movement dependent on unity within each national communist party, the Romanians have ventured so far as to say "that there is no national communism or international communism—but there is a unitary national...and...international [task] ...of carrying through socialist construction in good conditions."[42] Such conditions are available only if all parties within the international communist movement "resolutely defend [their] ... autonomy."[43] This calls for an "internationalist solidarity" which is based on "the principles of independence, equal rights, noninterference in internal affairs, respect for the right of each party to decide by itself its policy and practical activity."[44] In short, "there cannot be parties 'standing above others' [parties]." On the international plane the principle of democratic centralism is "absolutely inapplicable." It is only meant for "the inner [national] party plane."[45]

For the Hungarians living in Transylvania this means that they have no alternative but to struggle "shoulder to shoulder" together with other "coinhabiting nationals" for the "freedom and prosperity of Romania."[46] They cannot look for assistance from the international communist movement, since their problems of existence are considered ideologically to be strictly an internal Romanian national matter. In fact, they are not supposed to have interests which conflict with "the most sacred national interests" of Romania. Such a conflict is theoretically inconceivable, since the unity, cohesion and solidarity of the entire people is "welded" by "the community of political and economic interests" of the developing socialist system of Romania.[47]

The Yugoslav Ideological Position

The Yugoslav reinterpretation of Soviet nationality policies began much earlier than the Romanian development outlined above, but it has provided the national minorities of the country somewhat more tangible safeguards for their rights. Like the Romanian reinterpretation, it has been developed to provide guidance in both intra- and inter-state relations. However, unlike the Romanian nationality policy, the Yugoslav policy has not become repressive as a consequence of the country's greater ideological independence.

The major point of difference between the ideological stance of these two countries is that the Yugoslavs believe that unity in both intra- and interstate relations is best served by a policy of tolerance for local variations and ethnic differences.[48] The Romanians, on the other hand, only believe in such tolerance on the international front. In intrastate affairs they definitely demand unity through uniformity.[49]

The ideological positions of both these communist states are very similar on the international level.[50] This similarity blurs the fact that in intrastate relations Yugoslavia and Romania have vastly different interpretations of "proletarian internationalism." Because both of them stress that "independent paths to socialism" are possible, they have changed the meaning of internationalism from a solidarity based on the leadership of the Soviet Union, to an ideological solidarity with equality among all socialist states and "progressive movements" in the world.[51] While, both these states describe this relationship with similar formulas (e.g., equal rights, independence, noninterference in internal affairs, etc.), even in the international field there are some important differences. The Yugoslavs stress that their national minorities perform the role of "bridges."[52] They link Yugoslavia with neighboring countries. They promote cooperation rather than discord between the countries of the area.[53] Romanian theorists have also discussed this possibility—but only rarely in recent years.[54]

In Yugoslavia the discussion of nationalities problems is frequent and candid.[55] The same is not true of Romania. In the latter, it is assumed that the nationalities question has been solved.[56] The Yugoslavs, on the other hand, openly admit that there are many problems in this area that require special attention and a great deal of effort and understanding.[57] So they discuss these problems frequently and in detail. There are usually fewer attempts to hide existing conflicts behind a facade of slogans. Instead, it is stressed that words are worthless even if written into the constitution, if they are not backed up with action. An everyday effort must be made to transform ideals into reality.[58]

According to the Yugoslavs this effort must be guided by national unity based on the free development of each and every nationality living in the country. Real unity is unachieveable unless the "individuality" of each nationality within the country is safeguarded. "Yugoslavism" presupposes a diversity of national languages and cultures.[59] In present-day Romania there is little talk on the intrastate level of individual national developments. Instead, emphasis is always placed on common struggles and on a "unitary" Romanian national development.[60] In the latter context there is no room for the type of statement, made by a Hungarian recently in a Yugoslav publication, that the Yugoslav Hungarians support the present regime, because of its humane nationality policy. The *support* of the government, therefore, *is contingent* on its correct treatment of such national groups.[61]

The Yugoslav nationality policy, like its Romanian counterpart, has as its goal greater unity within the country. In both cases, nationalism is viewed as the greatest threat to such unity.[62] However, the two states have adopted different policies to combat this threat. In Yugoslavia the government sees nationalism as basically of two sorts: One is local or minority nationalism, while the other is the nationalism of "bureaucratic centralism and hegemony."[63] Both these forms are considered detrimental to the development of a truly unified Yugoslavia. "Bureaucratic centralism" or "superstate hegemony" harks back to the Serbian-dominated Yugoslavia of interwar days. Local nationalism, on the other hand, represents the disintegrative force which destroyed Yugoslavia on the eve of World War II. These two forms of nationalism feed upon one another. Consequently, the Communist League of Yugoslavia combats both.[64]

In Romania no such distinction is made. Majority and minority nationalisms are not combatted equally, because "nationalism" *per se* is the enemy.[65] Thus, while theoretically nationalism is always decried, the socialist patriotism of the majority is never viewed as nationalism. Any sign of localism or "isolationism" among national minorities, on the other hand, is immediately labelled as chauvinism.[66] Thus, the Romanians lack the theoretical safeguard of the Yugoslavs, which condemns both minority and majority nationalism, rather than just nationalism in the abstract.

Yugoslav and Romanian Self-Images

Theoretical differences between communist states do not indicate the actual nature of their policies. It is, therefore, necessary to consider the "self-image" of the respective communist states to ascertain what is and what is not "nationalistic." These self-images are the products of the national setting, the party developments, and the ideological heritage.

We have already examined the ideological development of both Yugoslav and Romanian nationalities policies. Parallel to this, the "national image" in both of these societies also underwent change.[67] In the immediate postwar years both states drew on the experiences of the war and the process of "liberation" as their source of historical self-interpretation and legitimacy. The Yugoslavs still use this event as their point of reference in defining their historical role.[68] The Romanians, on the other hand, have recently reinterpreted their own role in World War II and have drawn on pre-communist historical events to define their present self-image.[69]

Yugoslavia's self-image is based on what we can describe as the "Partisan Myth."[70] Its purpose is twofold: First, to ensure the leading role of the communists in the country, secondly, to provide the country's numerous nationalities with a sense of common destiny. The "Partisan Myth" pervades their everyday existence. It is the criterion of both leadership and "Yugoslavism."[71]

The myth is based on the national liberation struggles of World War II. This concrete historical experience consecrates the Partisan leaders of the time as the saviors of national independence and honor.[72] It provides, at the same time, a common enemy, a common danger, against which all Yugoslavs must unite. This outside threat is German imperialism. Even in present-day Yugoslavia it is viewed as one of the foremost outside threats to the independence of the country.[73] It is played up in the press and in formal government foreign policy pronouncements. The persistence of anti-German sentiment, is one of the most effective means of uniting the country internally. After the Tito-Stalin split of 1948, the danger of Cominformist intervention was also utilized in a similar way.[74] But, the "German threat" is more effective because it is based on a bloodier historical experience and at the same time is more easily fitted into the ideological prerequisites of Yugoslavia.[75]

The "Partisan Myth" is not just based on antagonism to Germany, but also contains a sense of mission, which gives the myth its supernational appeal. The Partisans in World War II had been fighting not just against Germany, but also against World Reaction and racism.[76] The legacy of fighting both these retrogade tendencies, has given the present-day leaders of the country the reputation of being true internationalists. As leaders of the "progressive forces" of history, they have depended on the unity and solidarity of all nationalities within the country. Partisans were not just Serbs, Croatians, or Macedonians, but primarily Yugoslavs. They wanted to rid the whole country of German occupation and not just certain parts of it.[77]

One has to be in Yugoslavia only a few days to see and feel the everyday role of the Partisan myth. This distinctly communist Yugoslav "political culture" is manifest everywhere. One encounters this supra-ethnic glue not only in the Partisan dominance of the government, but also in the everyday existence of the people. Radio programs devote a great deal of attention to it. For example, programs called "Partisan Songs" are a part of the weekly schedule of most Yugoslav radio stations.[78] Besides radio and television, the myth is propagated in the history books, schools, journals, and periodicals of Yugoslavia.[79]

In Romania, the country's political-cultural self-image is similarly disseminated by the ruling elite. However, the self-image of Romania lacks the supra-national appeal of the "Partisan Myth." It is much more ethnocentric in its emphasis. However, even if it is more narrowly "socialist patriotic," it does *not* possess the coherence of its Yugoslav counterpart. In Romania, we encounter two, rather than just one, self-image myths. For the sake of brevity, we have called them the "August 23rd Myth" and the "Daco-Roman Myth," respectively.

The "August 23rd Myth" is based on the Romanian switch from the Axis to the Allied camp.[80] To the early 1960s this "heroic act" of the Romanian people—led by the Romanian Communist Party—was not used to belittle the role of other national groups in the country. But it always had the potential of becoming the "progressive tradition" only of the Romanians. The reason for this was twofold. First, Romania had been an active, and in some ways the most enthusiastic, supporter of the Nazi onslaught against the USSR. Thus, the Germans were never looked upon as "the enemy." In this way, the overthrow of Antonescu and the desertion of the German cause, became an indication of repentence rather than the unfolding of a great "national liberation struggle" as was the case in Yugoslavia.[81] This made a scapegoat of Romania's past rather than of German imperialism. The "August 23rd Myth" was, therefore, rooted in an intranational purgation, a national "desire" for repentence. This made it a distinctly Romanian experience, since the nationalities in Transylvania did not partake in this "historic" event.[82]

The second reason why the August event was more narrowly Romanian, was its motivation. The realization that Germany was losing the war and that the Red Army was already on the country's eastern borders, made it evident that only a switch would give Romania the opportunity to diminish its territorial losses. The ownership of Transylvania hung in the balance. The switch, therefore, became symbolic of the Romanian campaign to make territorial gains in Transylvania. This campaign was, of course, the exact opposite of what the Hungarians in Northern Transylvania desired.[83]

The only consideration that kept the "August 23rd Myth" from becoming a purely Romanian tradition, was the role of the Red Army. Its advance was the most direct reason for the overthrow of Antonescu and the redeployment of the Romanian army against the Germans and Hungarians in Transylvania. Furthermore, the Red Army carried the brunt of the fighting against both the Germans and the Hungarians. It also kept the Romanians from carrying out atrocities against the nationalities of Transylvania. Thus, the process of "liberation" was not a purely Romanian achievement, but more a consequence of Soviet military might.[84]

More recent Romanian interpretations of this event contradict this assessment. While in the past the assistance of the Red Army was always acknowledged, more recent statements on the significance of this event have de-emphasized the Soviet role, and have even attempted to judge the event as a great national act of emancipation.[85]

Apparently this "myth" has not been enough to provide present-day Romania with an adequate historical foundation. To make up for its deficiencies, it has been supplemented with the "Daco-Roman Myth."[86] The latter had provided the foundations for the pre-communist Romanian self-image. This does not seem to disturb the present leaders of the country. While the readoption of this national myth was gradual, it is at present at least as important as the "August 23rd Myth." Already in the middle of the 1950s there were indications that this myth would be resuscitated, but it was only in the early 1960s that this process was completed.[87] Ever since, it has been incorporated into party statements, university studies, historical education, and every other phase of Romanian life where selfconsciousness is developed and inculcated.[88] This has gone so far that party leaders talking about agricultural development, for example, will refer to the "flourishing agriculture" of "our ancestors, the Dacians."[89]

The growing importance of the "Daco-Roman Myth" is particularly menacing for the non-Romanian inhabitants of Transylvania, because it is based on purely "ethnic" Romanian beliefs and traditions. At least in the case of the "August 23rd Myth," the role of communist solidarity was not completely lost from sight. This, however, is completely missing from the "Daco-Roman Myth." Thus, the non-Romanians become, in effect, "foreigners" in the land.[90]

A Comparative Assessment of Yugoslav and Romanian Self-Images

National self-images in both Romania and Yugoslavia, provide citizens with a simplified and symbolic definition of their origins, their present state of development, and their glorious future. These self-images are less precise than the ideological basis of the two countries. But, at the same time these "myths" orient the everyday behavior of the man in the street. This has far-reaching implications for the national minorities of both countries. In Yugoslavia, the "Partisan Myth" guarantees for the Vojvodinian Hungarians a part of the past, present, and future of the country. In Romania, on the other hand, both the "Daco-Roman" and the "August 23rd myths" deny them a part of the past.[91] This means, in effect, that they will have a present and a future only insofar as they assimilate themselves into the traditions of the "indivisible" and "unitary" Romanian nation-state.

The comparison can be carried one step further by reflecting briefly on Romanian and Yugoslav self-definitions in their respective constitutions. The *legal* self-definition for Romania can be found in Article I of its constitution. The Article states:

> The Socialist Republic of Romania is a *sovereign, independent* and *unitary* state of the working people of the towns and villages. Its territory is *inalienable* and *indivisible*.[92]

In the Yugoslav Constitution, the corresponding Article maintains:

> The Socialist Federal Republic of Yugoslavia is a *federal* state of *voluntarily united* and *equal peoples* and a socialist democratic community based on the powers of the working people and on *self-government*.[93]

True, these self-definitions are to a great degree propaganda. But, not completely so. They are also statements of certain ideals toward which the two states are striving. Considered in this light, the nationalities of the Vojvodina possess greater constitutional defense of their national cultures than the non-Romanians of Transylvania. Although neither Yugoslavia nor Romania give their minority inhabitants "group" or "corporate" recognition and rights, the tendency toward decentralization and self-government in Yugoslavia provides those of the Vojvodina with more opportunities and less restrictions than those of Transylvania.

As in the case of ideology, so in the constitutions of the two countries, it is possible to discern distinctive and different approaches to the nationality question. While both documents are based on the understanding that nationalism is the greatest threat to the cohesion and unity of the country, they have developed in different directions to meet this threat.

In Yugoslavia, the intranational heterogeneity makes no *one* nationality a majority of the population. Consequently, the interests and needs of all nationalities have been balanced against one another. This has been achieved by granting self-government on the local level, without tying it to "national self-government."

In Romania, the exact opposite has happened. While the 1948 and 1953 constitutions had guaranteed many Hungarians self-government as a group in the "Autonomous Magyar Region," the 1965 constitution has taken from them all such self-government. It has placed them directly under the central government of the unitary Romanian state. Thus, the *imbalance* of Romania's ethnic make-up, has led to the subjugation of the minority to the majority. The *balance* of nationalities in Yugoslavia, on the other hand, has tried to keep them from becoming subject to one another—at least in theory.

* * * * *

On the basis of the foregoing comparison of ideological and national self-definitions and their legal reflections we can conclude that each aspect of the Yugoslav and Romanian experience reinforces every other aspect. Thus, it is not surprising that these different levels of self-definition parallel the actual treatment of the minority nationalities in the Vojvodina and Transylvania. In Yugoslavia, even if conditions are not idyllic, they are acceptable as far as government policy is concerned. Discrimination on a non-official level is of course widespread even in the Vojvodina. But in Romania, discrimination is the rule on both the official and the non-official levels. The minorities in Transylvania suffer on practically every level relative to educational, cultural, economic, social and political existence.

What came first, one may ask, the reality or the self-definition? Probably, they have been mutually re-enforcing. At least the Romanian and Yugoslav experiences in theory *and* practice seem to indicate as much.

NOTES

1. The "nationalities theory" and "policy" which has been copied from the Soviet Union, has been variously designated. Recently, the designation "Marxist-Leninist" has become more and more popular. In Yugoslavia this is most commonly used. In Romania, on the other hand, the designation is simply "Leninist." Prior to de-Stalinization, in Romania this policy was also referred to as "Leninist-Stalinist." In Yugoslavia this was also the designation until the Tito-Stalin split in 1948.

2. Under ideological relationships I am thinking mainly of communism. But, nationalism is also an "ideology." It is an ideology according to *A Dictionary of the Social Sciences* (New York: The Free Press, 1964), p. 455, when it seeks "to justify the nation-state as the ideal form of political organization." When it does this, nationalism like communism, becomes a pattern of beliefs and concepts which gives its adherents guidelines for behavior. Of course, communism is a much more complex and intellectualized ideology, but as a consequence, it is also less appealing to the masses. In the present context, I will view both communism and nationalism as nonphysical political "forces" which are at the disposal of ruling elites in Romania and Yugoslavia. Unlike George W. Hoffman and Fred Warner Neal, *Yugoslavia and the New Communism* (New York: Twentieth Century Fund, 1962), p. 5, I do not believe that communism "uses" nationalism or that nationalism "uses" communism. Rather, the members of the new ruling elites in Romania and Yugoslavia are not only communists, but also nationals of their respective countries. They are, therefore, a product of both communist and national traditions, and borrow freely from both to undergird their own positions of power.

3. See Walter Laqueur and Leopold Labedz, eds., *Polycentrism* (New York: Frederick A. Praeger, Inc., 1962).

4. Boris Levitski, "Coexistence within the Bloc," *Survey*, No. 42 (June, 1962), 28-29, 33-34. A good example of such mimickry is I. Nistor, "Example of the Soviet Union is a Guiding Light," under heading "Rumania," *The Current Digest of the Soviet Press*, IV (Feb. 7, 1953), p. 18. The original article appeared in the December 27, 1953 issue of *Izvestia*, p. 3.

5. Hoffman, *Yugoslavia and the New Communism*, pp. 81-85, 91-102; Robert Lee Wolff, *The Balkans in Our Time* (Paperback Edition; New York: W.W. Norton Company, Inc., 1967), pp. 325, 329, 339, 352.

6. The history of this flexibility is traced sympathetically by István Dolmányos, *A nemzetiségi politika története a Szovjetunióban* [The History of Nationality Policy in the Soviet Union] (Budapest: Kossuth Könyvkiadó, 1964). A more objective analysis of early Soviet nationalities policies is Richard Pipes, *The Formation of the Soviet Union: Communism and Nationalism* (Revised Edition; Cambridge, Mass.: Harvard University Press, 1964).

7. For a more precise definition of "proletarian internationalism" and related terms see the Soviet political dictionary *Politicheskii Slovar'* (Russian Series No. 5; Ann Arbor, Michigan: Edwards Brothers, Inc., 1948), "bourgeois nationalists," p. 70; "internationalism," p. 219; "patriotism," p. 410; "proletariat," pp. 451-52; "socialism," pp. 528-29.

8. Alfred D. Low, "Soviet Nationality Policy and the New Program of the Communist Party of the Soviet Union," *The Russian Review*, XXII (Jan., 1963), p. 12.

9. In relation to Eastern Europe, this opportunism is reflected in Stalin's utilization of minority nationalities discontent against Tito. See: "Minorities in Eastern Europe—", *East Europe*, VIII (April, 1959), pp. 9-11; Hugh Seton-Watson, *The East European Revolution* (New York: Frederick A. Praeger, Inc., 1951), pp. 342-45; Wolff, *The Balkans in Our Time*, pp. 459-61.

10. Low, "Soviet Nationality Policy and the New Program of the Communist Party of the Soviet Union," pp. 10-12.

11. Dolmányos, *A nemzetiségi politika története a Szovjetunióban*, pp. 5-36.

12. Ibid., pp. 47-50, 83-104, 118-22; Pipes, *The Formation of the Soviet Union*, pp. 43, 56, 93-108, 193-241.

13. Low, "Soviet Nationality Policy and the New Program of the Communist Party of the Soviet Union," pp. 10-12; Dolmányos, *A nemzetiségi politika története a Szovjetunióban*, pp. 77-122.

14. Continuity, rather than change, has characterized Soviet nationalities policies. Low, "Soviet Nationality Policy and the New Program of the Communist Party of the Soviet Union," p. 10, points out that while de-Stalinization has affected most areas of Soviet life, it has not altered to an appreciable degree the country's nationality policy. For additional observations on this continuity, see Frederick C. Barghoorn, *Soviet Russian Nationalism* (New York: Oxford University Press, 1956), ch. I; *Program of the Communist Party of the Soviet Union: Adopted by the 22nd Congress of the C.P.S.U. October 31, 1961* (New York: Crosscurrents Press, 1961), pp. 114-118; Alex Inkeles, "Soviet Nationality Policy in Perspective," *Problems of Communism*, IX (May-June, 1960), pp. 25-34; Frederick C. Barghoorn, "Nationality Doctrine in Soviet Political Strategy," *The Review of Politics*, XVI (July, 1954), pp. 283-304.

15. The reasons for these national differences have been treated extensively by others. See for example Wolff, *The Balkans in Our Time*, pp. 267-74, 278-92.

16. As Hoffman, *Yugoslavia and the New Communism*, p. 155, points out: "Communists... [Yugoslavs, Romanians, and others] are essentially theoretical beings. No greater mistake could be made than to assume that Communists do not believe their theories. This does not mean that Communist theories have not originated as little more than rationalizations. It does mean, however, that ideology provides a binding orientation for the direction of society, a view of both tactical and strategic goals and a guide to the thinking of at least the leadership."

17. For an excellent overview of population changes in Eastern Europe, see Leszek Antoni Kosinski, "Population Censuses in East-Central Europe in the Twentieth Century," *East European Quarterly*, V (1971), pp. 274-301.

18. For speculations about the Hungarian demographic picture in Yugoslavia, see Károly Mirnics, "Fogyatkozásunk számadatai: Nemzetiségi politikusainknak ajánlva" [Data Concerning Our Population Decline: Dedicated to Our Nationality Politicians], *Új Symposion* (Novi Sad) (February, 1971), p. 112; and Csaba Utasi, "Bizalmatlanság vagy primí-

tivizmus?" [Distrust or Primitivism?], *Új Symposion* (May, 19710, pp. 216-217.

19. Regarding the classification of Jews in the census of 1910, 1930, and 1956, it must be noted that the latter two place them in the nationality category. This was not the case in the census of 1910. According to this early census a Jew could designate—on the basis of preference—what nationality he belonged to; only on religious grounds was he differentiated in statistics. The Romanians have placed the Jews in a separate category in order to weaken the statistics of the Magyars, for in the past the Jews have, on most occasions, opted for that nationality.

20. C.A. Macartney, *October Fifteenth, A History of Modern Hungary 1929-1945* (2d. ed., 2 vols., Edinburgh: Edinburgh Univ. Press, 1961), vol. II, pp. 346-47; Reuben H. Markham, *Rumania Under the Soviet Yoke* (Boston: Meador Publishing Company, 1949), pp. 513-14.

21. For the prewar development of the problem see Oscar I. Janowsky, *People at Bay: The Jewish Problem in East-Central Europe* (London: Oxford University Press, 1938), pp. 68-71. For postwar changes see sources in Randolph L. Braham, *Jews in the Communist World: A Bibliography 1945-1960* (New York: Twayne Publishers, Inc., 1961), pp. 30-32.

22. Theodore Schieder, ed., *The Expulsion of the German Population from Hungary and Rumania*. A Selection and Translation from *Dokumentation Der Vertreibung Der Deutschen Aus Ost-Mitteleuropa* (Bonn: The Federal Ministry for Expellees, Refugees, and War Victims, 1961), III, p. 42.

23. Ibid., pp. 61-62.

24. Ibid., pp. 78-79, 80-82; Markham, *Rumania Under the Soviet Yoke*, p. 410.

25. Macartney, *October Fifteenth*, II, p. 347; Schieder, *The Expulsion of the German Population from Hungary and Rumania*, III, pp. 49-50, 54-55. In this same source also see Annex 6 and 7, pp. 136-47.

26. Ibid., pp. 55, 96.

27. Leszek Kosinski, "Changes in the Ethnic Structure in Countries of East-Central Europe," A Paper Presented at Louisiana State University, Feb. 29, 1968.

28. G.D. Satmarescu, "The Changing Demographic Structure of the

Population of Transylvania," *East European Quarterly,* VIII (Jan., 1975), pp. 432-433.
29. Nistor, "Example of the Soviet Union is a Guiding Light," p. 18, enumerates these rights. Alfred D. Low, *Lenin on the Question of Nationality* (New York: Bookman Associates, 1958), pp. 30-35, points out, however, that for Lenin (and Stalin, we may add) such "rights" were really secondary.
30. Hadak Utján, "A nemzeti kérdes és a kommunizmus," *A Hét,* III (April 7, 1967), p. 1.
31. Nistor, "Example of the Soviet Union is a Guiding Light," p. 18.
32. Ibid.
33. Ibid.
34. For some communist Hungarian reflections on the class basis of such inequalities, see: *Imre Nagy on Communism* (New York: Frederick A. Praeger, Inc., 1957), p. 233; Mátyás Rákosi, *A békéért és a szocializmus épitéséért* (Budapest: Szikra, 1951), p. 279; János Kádár, *Socialist Construction in Hungary: Selected Speeches 1957-1961* (Budapest: Corvina Press, 1962), pp. 107-8.
35. "Magyarok Romániában" [Hungarians in Romania], *Lármafa* [Distress Bell], XI, 4 (1964), p. 9, and Gyula Zathureczky, *Transylvania: Citadel of the West,* trans. and ed. by A. Wass de Czege (Gainesville, Florida: The AHLG Research Center, 1965?), p. 55, indicate that Gheorghiu-Dej's policy statement on February 19, 1959, inaugurated the change in Romanian nationality policy.
36. Some characteristic indicators of this trend include: V. Iliescu, "Ensuring the Unity and Cohesion of the International Communist Movement—Major Imperative of our Day," *Documents, Articles and Information on Romania,* XIX (February 10, 1968), pp. 11-14; Nicolae Corbu and Constantin Mitea, "Development of the Socialist Nation and Proletarian Internationalism," in ibid. (February 1, 1968), pp. 14-17; Miklós Kallós, "A dolgozók szocialista politikai tudatának kialakulása és fejlődése hazánkban" [The Development and Evolution of the Socialist Political Consciousness of the Workers in Our Country], *Igaz Szó* [True Word] (Tirgu Mureş-Marosvásárhely), XII (August, 1964), pp. 266-277; Zoltán Farkas, "Allam, nemzet és szuverénitás a szocializmusban" [The State, the Nation, and Sovereignty in Socialism], *Studia. Universitas Babeş-Bolyai. Series Philosophia* (Cluj-Kolozsvár), XI (1966), pp. 19-27.

Socialist Patriotism and National Minorities 577

37. Corbu, "Development of the Socialist Nation and Proletarian Internationalism," p. 14.
38. Ibid.
39. Kallós, "A dolgozók szocialista politikai tudatának kialakulása és fejlődése hazánkban," pp. 272-76.
40. Farkas, "Állam, nemzet és szuverénitás a szocializmusban," pp. 22-24.
41. Corbu, "Development of the Socialist Nation and Proletarian Internationalism," p. 16.
42. Ibid.
43. Iliescu, "Ensuring the Unity and Cohesion of the International Communist Movement—Major Imperative of Our Day," p. 12.
44. Ibid.
45. Ibid., pp. 12-13.
46. Corbu, "Development of the Socialist Nation and Proletarian Internationalism," p. 15.
47. Ibid., p. 14. This exaggerated stress on unity, indivisibility and sovereignty, is carried one step further by Farkas, "Állam, nemzet és szuverénitás a szocializmusban," p. 23, when he states that: "Szocialista államunk egységes nemzeti állam. Területén, *egyetlen* nemzet el: a roman szocialista nemzet, amely a nemzetiségekkel testvéri egységben fejlődik és épiti a szocialista társadalmat." [Our socialist state is a unitary national state. It is inhabited by only a *single* nation: the Romanian socialist nation, which develops and builds a socialist society in brotherly unity with the coinhabiting nationalities.]
48. Hoffman, *Yugoslavia and the New Communism,* pp. 157-60, 162, 168-70; Josip Broz Tito, "Concerning the National Question and Socialist Patriotism," *Selected Speeches and Articles 1941-1961* (Zagreb: Naprijed, 1963), pp. 97, 102-3.
49. Iliescu, "Ensuring the Unity and Cohesion of the International Communist Movement—Major Imperative of Our Day," pp. 12-13; Corbu, "Development of the Socialist Nation and Proletarian Internationalism," pp. 16-17.
50. "Yugoslav Visit by Romanian Party and State Delegation Led by Nicolae Ceausescu," *Documents, Articles and Information on Romania,* XI (Jun. 15, 1968), pp. 1, 5.
51. Hoffman, *Yugoslavia and the New Communism,* p. 162; Corbu,

"Development of the Socialist Nation and Proletarian Internationalism," pp. 15-17; "Yugoslav Visit by Romanian Party and State Delegation Led by Nicolae Ceausescu," p. 5.

52. Paul Shoup, "Yugoslavia's National Minorities Under Communism," *Slavic Review,* XXII (March 1963), p. 79; Florián Kis, "Új szempontok a nemzetiségi kérdésekben," *Magyar Képes Újság* [Hungarian Illustrated News] (Zagreb), XV (July 1, 1966), p. 3.

53. Ibid.

54. In Romania this ideal was chiefly espoused by Petru Groza. Since his death in 1958, only some writers have paid lip service to it. An example of this is Veronica Porumbacu, "Aranyhíd" [Golden Bridge], *Igaz Szó,* VII (October, 1959), p. 641.

55. Some examples of this include: Kis, "Új szempontok a nemzetiségi kérdésekben," p. 3; Tito, "Concerning the Nationality Question and Socialist Patriotism," pp. 96-105; Tibor Minda, "A nemzeti kisebbségek helyzete Vajdaságban" [The Position of the National Minorities in the Voivodina], *Híd* [Bridge] (Novi Sad-Újvidék), XXVII (January, 1963), pp. 102-107; Dobrica Cošić, "A korszerű korszerűtlen nacionalizmusról" [About the Up-To-Date Outdated Nationalism], *Híd,* XXVI (January, 1962), pp. 21-31; László Varga, "Figyelő: Kétnyelvű oktatás Vajdaságban" [Observer: Bi-Lingual Education in Vojvodina], *Híd,* XXV (February, 1961), pp. 157-165; Olga Pennavin, "A magyar tanszék" [The Hungarian University Chair], *Híd,* XXIV (July-August, 1960), pp. 595-596; János Kóssa, "Az anyanyelv kérdése napjainkban" [The Question of the Mother Tongue in Our Days], XX (January, 1956), pp. 26-35; Edvard Kardelj, "A nemzeti kérdésről" [About the Nationality Question], *Híd,* SVIII (January, 1954), pp. 31-40; Edvard Kardelj-Sperans, *A szlovén nemzeti kérdés fejlődése* [The Development of the Slovenian Nationality Question], trans. by István Bodrits, et al., (Novi Sad: Fórum Könyvkiadó, 1961).

56. Igaz Szó szerkesztősége, "Életünk alaptörvénye" [The Fundamental Law of Our Lives], *Igaz Szó,* XIII (September 1965), pp. 315-317; "Speech by Emil Bodnaras," in *Documents, Articles and Information on Romania,* XVI (August 10, 1965), p. 34; Nicolae Ceausescu, "Exposition on the Improvement of the Administrative Organization of the Territory of the Socialist Republic of Romania: Special Session of the Grand National Assembly, February 15-16, 1968," in *Documents, Articles and Information on Romania,* Supplement no. 2 (February 17, 1968),

pp. 13-15.
57. Kis, "Új szempontok a nemzetiségi kérdésekben," p. 3.
58. Ibid.
59. *Yugoslavia's Way: The Program of the League of Communists of Yugoslavia* trans. Stoyan Pribechevich (New York: All Nations Press, 1958), p. 193.
60. Farkas, "Állam, nemzet és szuverénitás a szocializmusban," p. 23.
61. Kis, "Új szempontok a nemzetiségi kérdésekben," p. 3.
62. *Yugoslavia's Way*, pp. 195-96; Kallós, "A dolgozók szocialista politikai tudatának kialakulása és fejlődése hazánkban," p. 270.
63. *Yugoslavia's Way*, p. 195.
64. Ibid.
65. Kallós, "A dolgozók szocialista politikai tudatának kialakulása és fejlődése hazánkban," p. 270.
66. Stephen Fischer-Galati, "Rumania," *East Central Europe and the World*, ed. Stephen D. Kertesz (Notre Dame, Ind.: University of Notre Dame Press, 1962), pp. 164-165.
67. It is, of course, impossible to say which came first. However, it was the power seizure by the respective communist parties that made such a cultural-ideological transformation possible. For a general consideration of this East European development, see: Francis S. Wagner, *Cultural Revolution in East Europe* (New York: Danubian Research Service, 1955), pp. iii-xii.
68. Danilo Kečić, "Figyelő: A JKP Vajdaságban a felkelés előkészítésének és megindításának napjaiban" [Observer: The Yugoslav Communist Party in the Vojvodina in the Days of the Preparation and Initiation of the Uprising], trans. by József Kollin, *Híd*, XXV (September, 1961), pp. 784-792; *idem*, "Emlékalbum a forradalom 20. évfordulójára: A háború és a jugoszláv népek forradalma 1941-től 1945-ig" [Memorial Volume for the Twentieth Anniversary of the Revolution: The War and the Revolution of the Yugoslav Peoples from 1941 to 1945], trans. by József Kollin, *Híd*, XXV (November 1961), pp. 981-983.
69. Constantin Daicoviciu, et al., *Rumania* (Bucharest: Foreign Languages Publishing House, 1959), p. 92f.; Keith Hitchins, "Book Review: Istoria Rominiei, Vol. I," *Balkan Studies*, IV (1963), pp. 181-83; G. Unc, "Book Review; E.I. Rubinshteyn: The Downfall of the

Austro-Hungarian Monarchy," and T. Lungu, "Book Review: History of Rumania, Vol. 4," *Analele Institutului De Istoria A Partidului De Pe Langa CC AL PMR*, Vol. 10 (1964), trans. in *Rumania Press Survey No. 451* (Radio Free Europe, Sept. 26, 1964), pp. 2-8; "New Books: 'Transylvania in the History of the Romanian People'—C.C. Giurescu," *Documents, Articles and Information on Romania*, XIX (June 30, 1968), pp. 14-15.

70. In the present context "myth" designates a "world picture" held by a particular group. It performs the indispensable role of self-definition by reference to specific formative historical events, developments and traditions. This involves the group's entire value system, including standards of social morality, certain rituals and practical rules of guidance. Myth is less precise and intellectual than an ideology, but as a consequence it is also more pervasive. It is based on traditions, customs, folklore and mores, many of which have a mystical rather than a rational foundation. For a more precise definition see *A Dictionary of the Social Sciences*, p. 450. The definition of myth is very similar to the definition of legend (King, "Legend," Ibid., p. 384). *Funk and Wagnalls New "Standard" Dictionary* differentiates them by stating that: "Myth is the creation of a fact out of an idea," while legend is "the seeing of an idea in a fact." Thus, "myth is purely the work of imagination," while "legend has a nucleus of fact." According to this dichotomy, in the Yugoslavian "Partisan Myth" and in the "August 23 Myth" and "Daco-Roman Myth" of the Romanians, elements of both myth and legend are present. Consequently, in the present context myth will be given a broader meaning, as a belief including elements of both fact and imagination. Myth in this sense is what *Webster's Third New International Dictionary* calls, "a belief given uncritical acceptance by the members of a group especially in support of existing or traditional practices and institutions (e.g., of racial superiority used to justify discrimination)."

71. *Yugoslavia's Way*, pp. 188-89, 192-93; Dennison I. Rusinow, "A note on Yugoslavia," *American University Field Staff Reports Service*, Southeast Europe Series, XI, No. 5 (DIR-5-64), pp. 558-560; Bogdan Smiljević and Dorde Knezević, *A Legújabb kor története* [The History of the Most Recent Period], trans. Kálmán Csehák (Subotica, Yugoslavia: Minerva Könyvkiadó Vállalat, 1965), pp. 221-224.

72. Ibid., Ch. V. particularly pp. 206-216; Kečić, "Figyelő: A JKP

Vajdaságban a felkelés előkészítésének és megindításának napjaiban," pp. 786-792.

73. See particularly Joseip Broz Tito, "What We Need is Peace," *Socialist Thought and Practice*, No. 22 (Apr.-Jun., 1966), p. 51. Also see Punisa Perović, "Twenty-Five years of the Yugoslav Revolution," *Socialist Thought and Practice*, No. 22 (Apr.-Jun., 1966), pp. 3-28; Koca Popović, "Power-Politics—The Greatest Danger," *Socialist Thought and Practice*, no. 18 (April.-Jun., 1965), pp. 32-44.

74. Smiljević, *A legújabb kor története*, pp. 244-48; Hoffman, *Yugoslavia and the New Communism*, pp. 128-151; Wolff, *The Balkans in Our Time*, pp. 352-377.

75. "Proletarian internationalism" as such demands more understanding of Soviet errors than of the errors of "capitalist" West Germany. See *Yugoslavia's Way*, pp. 65-67, 72-74, 76-79.

76. Ibid., pp. xviii-xix, 18-19; Hoffman, *Yugoslavia and the New Communism*, pp. 69-80.

77. Ibid., pp. 71-77.

78. Radio Belgrade has had "Partisan Songs" as a regular program on Saturday mornings at 10:15 A.M. See "Belgrádi Müsor" [The Belgrade Program], *Dolgozók* [Workers], XIX (July 22, 1966), p. 14. Also see the writer's "Titoist Integration of Yugoslavia: The Partisan Myth and the Hungarians of the Vojvodina," *Polity*, XII, no. 2 (Winter, 1979), pp. 225-252.

79. Smiljević, *A legújabb kor története*, pp. 146-224; Kečić, "Figyelő: A JKP Vajdaságban a felkelés előkészítésének és megindításának napjaiban," pp. 784-792.

80. Ibid.

81. An example of this "guilt complex" is Nistor, "Example of the Soviet Union is a Guiding Light," p. 18.

82. While the switch as a whole was primarily a Romanian undertaking, the nationalities were strongly represented in the Romanian Communist Party. The latter, in turn, played a role in engineering Antonescu's overthrow. See Wolff, *The Balkans in Our Time*, pp. 278-92. For an overstatement of this role also consult "Celebration of August 23," *Documents, Articles and Information on Romania*, XVIII (Sept. 5, 1967), p. 1.

83. This fear of Romanian rule led many to welcome the Soviet occupation of the area, as well as to support the communists. See Schieder,

The Expulsion of the German Population from Hungary and Rumania, III, p. 85; Markham, *Rumania Under the Soviet Yoke*, pp. 215-217.

84. Schieder, *The Expulsion of the German Population from Hungary and Rumania*, III, pp. 63-68, 77-78; Wolff, *The Balkans in Our Time*, pp. 239-242.

85. While in 1959, Daicoviciu, et al., *Rumania*, p. 143, praised the role of the "glorious Soviet Armies" in the liberation of the country, by the summer of 1964—on the occasion of the 20th anniversary of Romania's "liberation"—the role of the Red Army was ignored or merely mentioned. See for example, "The Great Anniversary" and "It Happened in August, 1944," *Rumania Today*, 116 (1964), pp. 1-5; David Binder, "Bucharest Plays Down Arrival of Mikoyan for Liberation Fete," *New York Times* (Aug. 21, 1964), p. 2; David Binder, "Rumania Enjoys Being Red Mecca," *New York Times* (Aug. 24, 1964); George Bailey, "Trouble Over Transylvania," *The Reporter*, XXXI (Nov. 19, 1964), p. 27.

86. The "Daco-Roman" presupposition provides the basis for the Romanian claim to prior settlement of Transylvania. Briefly, the Romanians claim that they are the descendents of Romans and Dacians who came into contact with one another in the early second century A.D. At this time Emperor Trajan (98-117 A.D.) had successfully subjugated the Dacians. A hundred-seventy years of Roman rule followed, which according to the Romanians, also entailed intermixture with the Dacians. Consequently, when the Roman legions were withdrawn from the area to defend the Empire against Barbarian invasions, they left behind many of their progeny. The consideration that makes this thesis doubtful—or hypothetical at least— is that there are no historical records of "Romanians" (i.e. Wallachians) living in Transylvania until almost a thousand years later, when they appear in Hungarian documents. For the Rumanian side of this controversy see Walter Hoffmann, *Rumanien Von Heute* (Leipzig: Felix Meiner, 1942), pp. 32-35; and the communist Romanian reassertion of this claim by Constantin Daicoviciu and others, *Rumania* (Bucharest: Foreign Languages Publishing House, 1959), pp. 92ff. For the Hungarian side see Eugene Horvath, *Transylvania and the History of the Roumanians*, pp. 5-16. For more detached opinions consult Macartney, *Hungary and Her Successors*, pp. 256ff; Robert Strauss-Hupe, "Rumanian Nationalism," *The Annals*, no. 232 (March, 1944), pp. 86-87.

87. Daicoviciu, et al., *Rumania*, pp. 92ff., presents one of the earlier reiterations of the Daco-Roman presupposition. Since 1959, the theme has become more and more popular in historical interpretations.

88. As an example see "Culture, Art, Science: Premiere of the Film 'The Dacians,'" *Documents, Articles and Information on Romania,* XVIII (February 20, 1967), pp. 8-9.

89. "Speech by Nicolae Ceausescu, General Secretary of the Central Committee of the Romanian Communist Party," *Documents, Articles and Information on Romania,* XVII (March 15, 1966), p. 2.

90. Officially they are designated as "co-inhabiting nationalities." This designation and the context in which it is frequently used gives the impression that these non-Romanians were late-comers in Transylvania. In actuality both Magyars and Saxons have a longer *recorded* history in the area than the Romanians. This mistake is anadvertantly picked up and perpetuated by some Western reports. See for example Kenneth Ames, "Rumania is Home for 15 Different 'Nationalities,'" *The Washington Post* (November 26, 1967), p. H5.

91. To be fair, the nationalities are given a place in Romania's history. Whenever "class unity" is stressed, the role of the nationalities— "fighting shoulder to shoulder" with their Romanian brothers—is always mentioned in peasant uprisings, as well as in the revolutions of 1848. Along this line see Pál Binder, "Avram Iancu levelezése" [The Correspondence of Avram Iancu], *Korunk* [Our Age] (Cluj-Kolozsvár), XXIII (March 1964), pp. 425-427; Tibor Oláh, "Moldva és Havasalföld egyesülésének centenáriuma" [The Centennial of the Unification of Wallachia and Moldavia], *Igaz Szó,* VII (January 1959), p. 7; "Party and State Leaders' Visit to the Mures Magyar Autonomous Region," *Documents, Articles and Information on Romania,* XVII (September 6, 1966), p. 13.

92. "Rumanian Draft Constitution of 1965," p. 3; emphasis added.

93. "Yugoslav Socialist Constitution of 1963," Art. 1, p. 12; emphasis added.

Károly Nagy

PATTERNS OF MINORITY LIFE: RECENT HUNGARIAN LITERARY REPORTS IN ROMANIA*

In the best traditions of Hungarian literature—which has frequently assumed the role of the herald of the nation's struggle for freedom—a few courageous Hungarian writers in Romania are offering a frank diagnosis of the prevailing negative atmosphere in the country. This atmosphere is the result of the "double yoke" faced by the country's more than two million Hungarians, who constitute the largest single national minority in Europe. In Romania they are subjects to a regime which denies to them their basic rights both as human beings, as well as members of a national minority.[1] Although couched in allegories, some of their difficulties are expressed in the following two poems by two of their noted lyricists:

NOT EASY

It's not easy now that the hard autumn is here
for the sober or the lunatic
not easy, when night gets longer
for the evil or the good
not easy when the wind gets furious
for the believer or the doubter
not easy when the lights get dimmer
for the idle or the busy
not easy when there is no head on the stem
to be awake or to dream

not easy when winter lurks
not easy now even for the easy
not easy now only for the stones
which bear down on our chests
    Imre Horváth 1978
    Nagyvárad [Oradea]

I AM GOING TO DIE

I am going to die
so that even my last sigh
will be held back
and recorded on tape
by somebody
who will rewind it a couple of times
and will muffle it
or erase it
so that it be polite
let that mild smile stay
without the bitterness, of course,
that's what he always had on his lips
that mild smile
without a sigh
somebody will say that
whose choking hand
I felt on my throat
through all my miserable life.
    Sándor Kányádi, 1978
    Kolozsvár [Cluj-Napoca]

It is very difficult under circumstances described in the above two poems for Hungarian writers in Romania to give expression to the vicissitudes faced by their people. Some of them, however, still do so; writing about the painful realities of minority life at considerable risk to themselves. Nowhere are these realities better depicted than in the sociographic prose of some of the best writers, where they let the facts speak for themselves.

What follows is not an attempt to analyze contemporary Hungarian sociographic prose in Romania, but to provide a brief introduction to the topic, offering some excerpts from books published there during the 1970s.

* * * * *

Sociographic literature has had an exceptional place in Hungarian letters, especially during the past fifty years. It could be considered part of one of the most significant intellectual trends in modern Hungarian history: the so-called populist movement. Beginning with the folksong collecting activities of Béla Bartók and Zoltán Kodály in the early decades of this century, writers, social scientists, politicians, and other concerned and influential individuals and groups of the country turned their attention to the peasantry. They were searching for authentic art, for identity, for strength, and for a way to lift the peasant class out of its miserable and exploited condition. This is when sociographic literature—a new *genre*—emerged: a blend of art and science, of engaged emotions and hard hitting data, of interesting reportage and factual documentation. Some of the best writers produced sociographic works in the 1930s, and since the mid-1960s, renaissance of this trend can be witnessed in Hungarian literature, as well as in the literature of Hungarians in Romania, Czechoslovakia and Yugoslavia.

Since the early 1970s, it has been increasingly possible, althought still risky, for Hungarian writers in Romania to write about some societal problems. They write about the recent past, as well as about the contemporary situation. One of the most painful governmental acts which they describe and documents is the abuse of the peasantry in the 1950s, when in accordance with the Soviet scenarii, agriculture was collectivized with full coercive force and some peasants in every village were designated "kulaks." They were labeled exploiters and enemies of the people, who were then ostracized, expelled from their homes, sometimes jailed and beaten, and executed. The Hungarian peasants—who are in the minority in Romania, although they constitute majorities or even the entire population in many villages—were treated worse than any of the other classes or groups during these Stalinist times.

Árpád Farkas (1944-) one of the most significant poets of the younger generation, quoted an old peasant in one of his reports:

> After the Second World War when I returned home and we began to settle in, they soon made me out to be a 'kulák.' I don't know why, because when I went off to war I closed my door, when I came home, I opened it. I don't know how I could have become an exploiter when all my ancestors were servants. When they organized the collectives, I submitted some six acres of land, but what's the

use, I gave up feeling sorry about it, those were difficult times....[2]

Gyula Szabó (1930-) a short story writer, quotes from one of his father's letters written to him in 1958 with tongue in cheek:

> And now, not giving a hoot anymore about family censorship, I will turn to the more realistic side of our present life. The 'still life' continues in our village, that is, they are organizing the collective like a steam roller. They do it, of course, in the spirit of socialist law, with different paragraphs for the ones who signed up and for those who did not. Our family is affected only by the general paragraphs, because our acreage is in such parts which are not too attractive to anybody. But there are many who are not willing to go dozens of miles every day to plough or mow in outlying, distant areas, by giving up their lands near the village. Such people have separate paragraphs coming to them. So, we can't complain that we are the state's foster children, because it has begun to show that it cares....[3]

László Király (1943-) a poet and prose writer, described a truck ride in the moonlit, snowy night of a New Year's Eve in the 1950s. His father, a teacher, was charged with being a "kulák sympathizer" and was ordered to leave his village with his wife, his two children, and as many belongings as would fit into the truck. The family arrived at their new village in the dead of the night, and unloaded into their one-room "new home."

> In the morning—writes Király—a short, stocky man came to visit us with a policeman. 'Good morning,' said the one in civilian clothes, 'I am the Council President and this is the Comrade Sergeant.' My father also introduced himself and offered them chairs. 'Thanks, we won't sit down,' said the president when the sergeant already had. At this, the sergeant stood up again. The president looked around in the room. 'I would like to ask something,' he said. 'Please, do!' 'Could you tell me,' the president swayed back and forth, 'how is it, what is the reason, that you, Comrade Teacher, had to leave your place now, in the very middle of the school year? I mean: why did you come here, to our village?' My father was surprised at this rude question which conveyed suspicion, but he answered calmly. 'They denounced me that I sympathize with 'kuláks'.' The president gave the sergeant an 'I told you so' look. 'Who denounced you?'—'More than one person.' 'Uh-huh. And why? I mean—on what did they base their denunciation of you?'—'They saw me talk with 'kuláks' many a time on the streets.'—'Yes—yes,' nodded the president, like one for

whom this whole case has been clear for a long time. 'So you sympathize with 'kuláks?' 'This was said by those who denounced me' —corrected my father. 'Of course, of course. And did the higher authorities believe it?' 'They believed it.'—'Why did they believe it?' My father shrugged his shoulders: 'I have no way of knowing that.' —'Uh-huh. But why didn't you defend yourself?.—'Nobody asked me.'—'Clear. It's still strange that you had to come away exactly on New Year's Eve. Isn't it?' He addressed this question to the sergeant, who started to nod eagerly at this. 'Strange,' said my father 'and mainly unpleasant. But they issued a truck only for this night. Look, Comrade President. It may not be nice, but I am going to brag a little. They loved me in that village, strange as it may sound. Not my denouncers, of course. Well, and they said if I was going to be expelled, that would come to nothing, because they simply wouldn't let me go. So what's the logical solution? I had to be taken out when everybody was busy with something else. As you can see, the plan worked. We are here. But I see the reception here is somewhat mixed.' The president did not continue the interrogation.[4]

András Sütő (1927-), who is already a "living classic" as a novelist, short story writer and dramatist, has written one of the most significant sociographic books of Hungarian literature about his native village in the 1950s. His work became a best-seller and a milestone in East Central Europe. "I don't know where she got the pen and ink," writes Sütő,

when, in December, 1952, my mother wrote the following letter to me in Bucharest: 'Dear Son, it's been four weeks now that we've been living out in the stable and in the woodshed, and we are very cold. . . . September 9 was a very dark day for us. I saw that a lot of officials were coming across the field. I couldn't image why so many were coming to see us. I was just taking some straw to make fire. I stopped and, of course, said come on in, and what do you want. First came the policemen, then the council president, the other office men trudged along behind them, altogether five of them. I was already trembling because no policeman has ever visited our home before. Then the policeman said that I should move out to Mr. Bucur's and that I should vacate the house. Then I turned to the officials and said isn't that nice. You have made us out to be 'kuláks' and now you are even putting us out of our house. And then I went up to the porch and cried and cried and remembered how much we had struggled with your father and with you, our children, to build this little two room house and, alas, now that we are old, they put us out of it. And then I said that we would vacate the house, but asked them to let us move into the woodshed, and the secretary said that they would. And then I started to cry again, because then it seemed certain that they would put us out of our house, and then I felt that I would like to die.'[5]

Zoltán Tófalvi (1944-), another writer cites a former inhabitant of the village of Alsósófalva [Sus] who remembers that in those years they "placed on the 'kulák'-list some people in this village—one of the poorest villages of this entire region—who hardly had two-three acres of land."

> That was the time when I came home from the city—on foot—to persuade my father to join the collective farm. I didn't have anyone to lecture to, because they had put my father onto the 'kulak'-list and took him down to the town hall and kept him there for days. My mother was whimpering in fear. At times she roused me in the dead of the night and we ran half dressed to some of our neighbors to hide from the harassments.[6]

The working-class author, György Lőrincz (1946-), traces some current problems to these harassments, as a result of which—as he put it—"something was broken in the depths of the people's soul." Some of these problems include the rapid depopulation of entire rural regions: the people are virtually fleeing from the villages, some of which have existed for four to six-hundred years as viable and cohesive Hungarian communities.[7] Another problem is suicide. Lőrincz reports that "in the Udvarhely [Odorheu] region, sixty-two persons—according to official medical records: forty-six men and sixteen women—have committed suicide in 1977 and 1978. Of these sixty-two persons, three were children and eleven were in the twenty to twenty-five age group. The region's over-all population is approximately 100,000. Thus they had an annual suicide rate of 31 per 100,000."[8] (By way of comparison the suicide rate in the United States in 1974 was 12.1 per 100,000. In the following year the rates for Great Britain, Czechoslovakia, Austria, Yugoslavia and Sweden, respectively, were 7.5, 22, 24.1, 13.5 and 19.4 per 100,000.)

* * * * *

Of the many problems that affect Hungarians in today's Romania, the most acute is connected with the difficulties they face in trying to maintain and develop their own language and culture. This problem is observed and recorded by many sociographers, who try to catalogue some of their difficulties and urge improvements. There are two basic institutions in every town and every village that have bearing on this problem: the library and the school. But are these institutions fulfilling their mission in maintaining and transmitting the Hungarian heritage in Romania? This is the one question that is always asked by the writers as they explore the countryside—village by village and town by town.

One of these "exploring" writers, who has emerged during the 1970s as one of the most persistent, prolific and talented sociographers is György Beke (1927-). Books containing his collected reports offer an uncompromisingly truthful inside view of Hungarian life under Romanian rule today. When he visits a Hungarian town, he always goes to the library and to the school; the two institutions that are most reflective of the cultural realities under which his people live. Some of his observations are most telling:

"The Gyimesközéplok [Lunca de Jos] library last year received altogether 376 books and not always those which it had asked for or would have liked," wrote Beke in one of his recent books. "In the village there are 1,100 steady readers who visit the library regularly. From this I can calculate when a popular book gets around to everybody. The neighboring village is Felsőlok [Lunca de Sus]. The library here acquired a total of 51 books last year! True, there are fewer steady readers here; only 400. But Mrs. András Tímár, the librarian, wants to raise that number to 900. What would be needed to accomplish this goal is more books!"[9] And the situation is similar in many other towns:

> The school library of Kraszna [Crasna] has no catalogue. It also doesn't have any copies of Petőfi's *János Vitéz* [John the Hero] in spite of the fact that it is required reading in the fifth grade. István Asztalos's *Jóska* [Joe] can be had in two torn copies. It is needed for a hundred and fifty students at the same time. There are also two copies of Ady's poems; that, too, is required material. The total number of books that the library has is impressive: 10,547 volumes. And there are some works which can be found in multiple copies here. The volumes of art history line the shelves in 130 undisturbed copies. 'The book distribution center of Kolozsvár doesn't send us what we request,' says Edit Seres, the school librarian. Antal Emil, the school principal, says: 'The distribution official is interested only

in fulfilling the plan. He ships us the number of books which fit the annual budget; he doesn't care what those books are.' Benjámin Molnár, a teacher, says: 'We had visitors from the government's education department and they just shook their heads when they saw our library. We gave them a list of the missing books which we absolutely need.' In the town library of Kraszna the shelves are dusty and so are the books. Either the windows are opened too often in windy, dusty weather, or the books get taken off the shelves too seldom. The few volumes, that is, which can be had here at all. I am looking for the poems of Kányádi. If students cannot find more than one copy of this book in the school library, they could come here for it. No use in coming. There is no Kányádi volume here. András Sütő's *Anyám Könnyű álmot igér* [My Mother Promises Light Dreams] can be had in a single copy, and even that only in Romanian translation. The library does not have a copy of it in the original Hungarian. Gyula Szabó's *Gondos Atyafiak* [Caring Relatives] is available also in Romanian translation only. Should I go on? According to Mrs. Jakó, the librarian, Kraszna could have at least 2,500 steady library users. It has only 826. They don't have anything to read.[10]

Many schools, just like many of the libraries of the Hungarian parts of Romania, are struggling with problems which stem from discrimination against the Hungarian population. These are problems which could easily be remedied, if the regime would cease its anti-Hungarian policies.

Barno Marosi (1931 —) has published many sociographic reports. In a 1974 volume of his recent writings, he describes Hungarian life in a region of scattered farmsteads around Pálpataka [Valea Lui Pavel], on one of the mountain plateaus in the Hargita region.

The school has 130 students—on paper. When I visited them, about 30 had come to school, the rest were working with their parents out in the fields. They are absent from the school at harvest time, later because of the heavy rains, the snow, and the ice. In wintertime it gets light only shortly before eight o'clock in the morning. The students arrive at the school in the farmstead center at around nine or ten o'clock. There are many parents who don't let their eight to ten year old children walk two or three miles through forests in drifting snow where there are no houses in sight in most parts. When the children get home, they have to work; some parents don't take into consideration that the students have homework. Some don't want to send their 6th or 7th grade sons to school at all any more. 'His place is with his father, on the fields'—they say.[11]

György Beke often visits the schools during his journeys. In a small town, Alpestes [Peştişul Mare], near Vajdahunyad [Hunedoara], there is only one Hungarian class in the school, although about half of the town's population consists of Hungarians. The one Hungarian class has ten 6 to 10 year old students in the same room, learning the curriculum of the four elementary grades. "When they first step into the classroom," writes Beke,

> they practice their Hungarian mother tongue with words as well as hand signals. It is very difficult to teach them the correct spoken language. And they can get only a taste of spelling during the four years they attend this class, because the teacher has to teach four classes in one room at the same time. István Bíró, the 54 year old teacher, has tired eyes. 'Will there be more students here in the future, Mr. Bíró?'—'Next year we will have five first graders in the Hungarian class. Two students will leave us because they will have completed the fourth grade.'—'Where can they go to school if they want to continue their studies in their native Hungarian?'—'In cities of some distance. Therefore about half of them stay home in this town and attend the Romanian fifth and upper grades.'[12]

In another village, Gyimes [Ghimeş], where the majority of the population is Hungarian, only 6 of the school's 236 students are of Romanian nationality, but Hungarian is taught there only as an elective subject. Writes Beke:

> In the school where András Deáky is the principal, fourteen teachers teach 236 students. 230 of the students are Hungarian by nationality; they speak their native Hungarian at home and in the school yards during recesses. Inside the school, Hungarian language and literature is taught only as an elective subject and the level of instruction there is very low. 'What is your specialty,' I ask the principal. 'Hungarian and Romanian,' he answers, but I could have guessed it from the books covering the walls of the pleasant room: an enviable selection of the newest, most valuable Hungarian literary works. 'Forgive me, I am embarrassed. . . . Surely you are the one who teaches the elective Hungarian subject.' András Deáky smiles bitterly: 'No, sir, it isn't I who teaches it.' 'Who then? Another Hungarian teacher?' 'A colleague, who didn't even finish high school. His name is János Gergely. He can't even spell right.'—'Unbelievable! You are the specialist, and you are the principal!' 'But I have the

district superintendent above me. And he demands this.'—'Why?'—'I am sorry, but I cannot make a statement about my superiors. In this village many things happen the way he wants it and not the way the parents would wish.'[13]

* * * * *

How helpful are these reports? Can they bring about some corrective measures? Can they help solve some problems? What are the future possibilities for the *genre* itself? Will it be allowed to continue? Or will these courageous writings remain "messages in bottles" amidst furious waves of a hopelessly deep ocean?—as described by Kányádi's poem below:

MESSAGE IN A BOTTLE

The last paddle broke, the waves
were towering, the storm didn't subside,
it got bigger and more furious,
it swayed the Moon, like mad,
kept blowing it out and then
threw it out to some distant shore or perhaps
into the hopelessly deep Ocean.
We were bailing water all night.
We stiffened our shoulders and feet
against the cracking ribs of the boat.
Only in the morning, when the waves
were bowing on their knees towards
the rising Sun like a horde
of pious Muslims, only then
did we feel how useless was our fight!
We will have to await our ultimate humiliation
without a swallow of water!
We scrambled up, peered into
the bright and empty horizon
and gathering our last strength
we went under.
          Sándor Kányádi
          Kolozsvár [Cluj-Napoca]

The present legal and social measures of the forced assimilation program of the Romanian state against Hungarians does not promise any improvements. As recent events in Romania show, the campaign against allowing Hungarians to maintain their culture is continuing with full force, and those who speak out are in constant danger.

Messages in bottles are acts of hope, however. The passengers of the boat these days are stiffening their resolve and are still bailing water.

NOTES

* All translations in this article are by Károly Nagy.

1. George Schöpflin, *The Hungarians in Rumania* (London, Minority Rights Group Report No. 37, 1978), p. 17.
2. Árpád Farkas, "Gyalogolni kell," [One Must Go on Foot] in György Beke, et al, *Bővizű patakok mentén* [Along Brooks with Water Plenty] (Bucharest: Kriterion, 1972), p. 57.
3. Gyula Szabó, *Gólya szállt a csűrre* [A Stork Flew on the Shed] (Bucharest: Kriterion, 1974), pp. 169-170.
4. László Király, *Kék farkasok* [Blue Wolfs] (Bucharest: Kriterion, 1972), pp. 77-78.
5. András Sütő, *Anyám könnyű álmot igér* [My Mother Promises Light Dreams] (Bucharest: Kriterion, 1971), pp. 122-124.
6. Zoltán Tófalvi, *Pogány fohászok faluja* [Village of Pagan Prayers] (Bucharest: Kriterion, 1979), p. 43.
7. György Lőrincz, *Amíg csak él az ember* [As Long As One Lives] (Bucharest: Kriterion, 1980), pp. 101-115.
8. Ibid., p. 127.
9. György Beke, *Magunk keresése* [Searching for Ourselves] (Bucharest: Kriterion, 1972), p. 58.
10. György Beke, *Szilágysági hepehupa* [Ups and Downs in the Szilágy Region] (Bucharest: Kriterion, 1976), pp. 38-39.
11. Barna Marosi, *Megbolygatott világ* [Stirred-up World] (Bucharest: Kriterion, 1974), pp. 185-186.
12. György Beke, et al., *Csőposta* [Mail Through the Tube] (Bucharest, 1974), p. 47.
13. György Beke, *Magunk keresése*, op. cit., pp. 62-63.

VII

INTER-STATE RELATIONS IN CENTRAL AND EASTERN EUROPE

János Decsy

ANDRÁSSY'S VIEWS ON AUSTRIA-HUNGARY'S FOREIGN POLICY TOWARD RUSSIA

The Compromise of 1867, particularly the powerful position Hungary attained in the Austro-Hungarian partnership, profoundly affected the foreign policy of the Dual Monarchy. As a result, Count Gyula [Julius] Andrássy (the Elder), the first dualist prime minister of Hungary (1867-1871), who weighed the security of his country and the Dual Monarchy in terms of foreign policy, could successfully impose his views on the common government.[1]

The basic aim of Andrássy's foreign policy was to prevent developments that would be contrary both to Hungary's national interests and to the security of Austria-Hungary. To achieve this goal, he wanted to maintain the *status quo* within, and also preserve the territorial integrity of the Dual Monarchy, that was Hungary's shield against hostile neighbors. Well-informed on the internal and external peculiarities of the multinational Austro-Hungarian Empire, Andrássy professed the view that, since the geopolitical situation of the monarchy left it open to unremitting pressure from without, foreign policy had to have priority over domestic. This, he believed, required a vigilant, active and firm policy.[2] "There scarcely exists a state," Andrássy maintained, "that by virtue of its make-up and geographical location is interested in so many significant European questions as is the Austrian Empire." Therefore, "Austria cannot shirk the need to make its influence felt on certain issues."[3]

Andrássy, who had a diplomatic talent of the first order, and an intimate knowledge of Europe and the various problems of European affairs, analyzed with great perception the basic foreign policy questions of the Monarchy. He devised an effective system of policy to stave off dangers threatening the security of the Empire.

Andrássy's foreign policy was simple in its underlying principles. One of its fundamental axioms was the need to turn the Dual Monarchy's energies toward the east to check aggressive Russian expansionism. Andrássy saw in Russia and the Pan-Slav-inspired national movements the most dangerous enemy. In his view, if they joined forces, they would endanger the territorial integrity of Hungary and the very existence of the Dual Monarchy. From this sprang the second principle of his policy. Andrássy regarded friendship and alliance with Bismarckian Germany as the best guarantee against Russian expansion and against Austria's absorbtion by Germany, that would enable Vienna to undo dualism. It suited Bismarck's aims and this is why he endeavored to strengthen Hungary's voice in the councils of the Dual Monarchy. For similar reasons, the preservation of the Ottoman Empire and the *status quo* in the Balkans also suited Andrássy's policy.

Contrary to Foreign Minister Count Friedrich von Beust's anti-Prussian intentions, Andrássy reflected decidedly anti-Russian, anti-Pan-Slav sentiments, due both to Russia's role in crushing the Hungarian struggle for freedom and independence in 1848-49, and to his awareness of Russia's machinations in Hungary to incite and keep alive Slavic movements.[4] Walter Platzhoff, the noted interwar German historian, observed that the Hungarians felt themselves engulfed in the great Slavic sea of Eastern Europe and by the 1860s saw their only hope in an alliance with Germany.[5] The idea of German-Hungarian cooperation against Russia and the Pan-Slav danger was the legacy of the Hungarian liberals of the Reform Period.[6] The events of 1848-49 only reinforced the need for such cooperation.[7]

It is widely held that Andrássy's "turn to the east" was motivated by "blind hatred of Russia" and that his main principle was "revanche pour Világos."[8] This interpretation does not hold water, however. Andrássy was a realist and a moderate, as recognized by contemporary diplomats[9] and prominent historians of the present;[10] hatred and revenge had little place in his diplomacy. He could always keep his internal fires in check while dealing with state affairs or conducting foreign policy.[11] Andrássy believed that "passion is only an obstacle in politics and reason dictates that it should be disregarded."[12] But it would be incorrect to claim that he had wholly forgotten Russia's part in the suppression of Hungarian freedom in 1849, his personal experiences in that struggle, and the movements among the Slovaks and Ruthenians in his native North Hungary which made Andrássy so keenly aware of the Russian-Slav danger. All this, coupled with the malevolence of the Russian Pan-Slavits[13] and a barrage of unwise and hateful pronouncements by František Palacky,[14] one of the most important leaders of the Old Czech party, developed in Andrássy the conviction that the Monarchy has to discard once and for all its "German impulses." He pointed out to Béla Orczy that "now, when we are threatened from the east, retention of German supremacy is next to impossible."[15] "Instead of this," he confided to Benjamin Kállay, "the Empire's attention must turn completely to the east."[16]

Baron Ludwig von Wächer-Gotter, the Prussian consul in Pest, reported that "facing the east" was regarded by Andrássy "as the prime purpose of his policy... Russia is in his mind day and night."[17] The Italian consul general, Luigi Salvini, had a similar impression of the Hungarian statesman's attitude. It was "fear of Russia" that seemed to move Andrássy the most, he wrote following a meeting with him.[18] Salvini added: "Besides the antipathy for that power [Russia] that has existed here since the war of 1849, Russia is and has always been the obsession, the specter, of Hungary."[19] Kálmán Ghiczy, one of the leaders of the Hungarian Left-Center Party, expressed similar sentiments: "We have only Russia to fear,"[20] he declared. Russophobia was apparently not restricted to the "Hungarian liberals," nor the "Hungarian ruling classes," as suggested by some historians.[21] It was a national phenomenon. But were Andrássy's fears exaggerated? Francis Deák, the prominent Hungarian statesman, did not think so. On one occasion in 1868, he admonished a deputy of his party who called Andrássy's attitude toward the Eastern Question an "absured infatuation." Speaking in his usual quiet manner, Deák observed: "Forgive me, my friend, but with all due respect, I think Gyula [Andrássy] sees further than you do."[22] It is ironic that Kálmán Tisza's pro-Prussian Left-Center Party, in spite of its conceptual differences over Hungary's position within the Monarchy, was more united in its support of Andrássy's Russian policy than his own party, the so-called Deák Party.[23]

The motive behind Andrássy's foreign policy seems to have been fear of Russian aggression. Andrássy believed that, as soon as Russia had completed its railroad network and the reorganization of its armed forces, it would attack the Monarchy.[24] The threat posed by the secret Russian-Pan-Slav support for the Slav national movements within the Monarchy and in the Balkans haunted him with special force. In his view—and this he repeated often—these Pan-Slavic activities endangered not only the territorial integrity of Hungary, but also the very existence of the Monarchy.[25] Salvini, who was a perspicatious observer, came much to the same conclusion: "Russia, leaning on the Slavic population living in Hungary, is disposed to annihilate the Hungarian nationality and walk over its corpse to possess Serbia and...assure itself of the Danube."[26] No doubt, the writings of the Russian Pan-Slavs also contributed considerably to this pessimistic view.[27] The late Robert Kann rightly stresses that "this very factor of irredentism backed by a Great Power spurred Austrian foreign policy from the older Andrássy to Berchtold to a kind of preventive dynamism."[28]

In view of this evidence, it is not surprising at all that the Russian-Pan-Slav problem was the main focus of Andrássy's foreign policy. All other considerations, including the German question, were secondary. "I have always maintained," he told Adolph Thiers, the French statesman, "that we were not a German nation, but a European nation placed on the borders of all nationalities." Therefore, "we must not adopt a policy of rancor, but one of equilibrium,...and intervene only when the interests of Europe absolutely demand it."[29] Here emerges another guiding principle of Andrássy's foreign policy, eminently "European" in that it went beyond the pursuit of specifically Hungarian and imperial interests. It aimed at containing the expansionist tendencies of other powers, above all Imperial Russia, in the wider interest of European balance.[30] In an interesting piece of political journalism that Andrássy published in *The Eclectic Review* (England) in 1850, he had already expressed his belief that "the existence of Austria can be an advantage to the other powers as a balance to the power of Russia."[31] Twenty years later he voiced the same idea that it was Austria's task "to constitute a bulwark against Russia." As long as it did, "its continuance will be a European necessity."[32] Andrássy, however, like Metternich, perceived the peril inherent in being merely a "European necessity;" he felt that it would make the Monarchy "mute among our nearest neighbors"[33] and dependent on the goodwill of others. To avoid this, "a state must have a mission." "Ours lies in the East ... where our most important interests are at stake,"[34] he commented in his personal notes. Andrássy apparently felt that a sense of mission would command the loyalty of the Monarchy's nationalities and guarantee its independence in international affairs.

To avert the Russian-Pan-Slav danger, Andrássy championed the containment of Russia, preferably by diplomatic means. This involved the maintenance of the *status quo* in the Balkans and particularly the preservation of Turkey as long as possible.[35] Andrássy explained his reasons at the Council of Ministers for Common Affairs on January 29, 1875: "Turkey is almost a providential utility to Austria. Its existence is essential to our well-understood interests. It preserves the *status quo* among the small states and hinders their aspirations to our advantage. If it were not for Turkey, then all these heavy obligations would fall on us."[36] Furthermore, Andrássy believed, the Monarchy's foreign policy should aim to prevent the coalition of Russian diplomacy and the Slav national movements, and to disrupt their relations where already established. "It could not but be to the advantage of Turkey," Andrássy told Sir Henry Elliot, the British ambassador at Constantinople, in 1874, "if its people—the Slavonic communities—were taught to turn their eyes to Austria, which was a thoroughly friendly power, and to look to her for sympathy and support in obtaining redress of their grievances, instead of to Russia of whose hostility to Turkey every one was aware."[37] And Andrássy was precisely the statesman "who, by virtue of his Hungarian nationality and European breadth of view, recognized this objective considered to be of vital importance from the Monarchy's point of view,"[38] concedes one of Andrássy's severest critics.

Andrássy seems to have been willing to win over the South Slavs by concessions.[39] He sought honestly to avoid the appearance of conquest, for he believed that "any growth of territory can only be harmful to the Monarchy."[40] He made it quite clear that "we want to make headway in the east by peaceful means, not by war."[41] His attitude was conciliatory toward both the South Slavs (especially the Serbs)[42] and the Romanians.[43] Andrássy hoped to gain their cooperation against Russia or, at least, to neutralize them. He hoped in this fashion to establish a definite sphere of influence in the Balkans. But he never preached the doctrine of national or racial superiority, nor the conquest of lands surrounding the Dual Monarchy.

In any consideration of this policy, two important points needed to be emphasized: first, the already mentioned deep-set Hungarian suspicion, distrust and fear of Russia and Pan-Slavism; secondly, Russia's aggressive expansionist policy in the Balkans, where it could count on the support of the fanatical forces of Pan-Slavism.[44]

The various diplomatic and military plans of action that Andrássy conceived by the eve of the Franco-German War of 1870-71 were to answer the exigencies of a possible eastern war—then or in the not too distant years. Examining them, it is obvious that the Hungarian statesman had an independent and purposeful concept of foreign policy. Andrássy's strategic considerations in dealing with the Russian danger were oriented to defensive purposes. His plans envisaged either a preemptive strike (which he feared Austria-Hungary would be forced into),[45] or a defensive-offensive strategy against Russia. In considering a suitable program of action, Andrássy had to weigh with great care the pros and cons of his plans in order to ensure that no harm came to the vital interests of Hungary and the Monarchy.

The war psychology, created by wanton Russian actions and unyielding, Pan-Slav agitation, seems to have affected Andrássy deeply. The Hungarian consul general at Belgrade recorded in July 1870: "He [Andrássy] does not want war, but it will hardly be avoidable."[46] In one of his dispatches Isacco Artom, Italy's special envoy, reported: "according to him [Andrássy], Russia is making preparations in great haste and Austria could be forced to forestall them."[47] Two weeks later Andrássy told Artom: "The danger exists in their [the Russians'] secret manipulation of the Slav population of the Danube.... There is peril that Austria must avoid at all cost: that is, dying like a scorpion immersed in excess carbolic." Finally, Andrássy stressed: "in the face of that danger, a strong initiative would become inevitable."[48]

Andrássy thus appears to have contemplated a preemptive war, which has certain advantages from a strictly military point of view, as the 1967 Israeli-Arab war so brilliantly attests. He seems to have been considering the advisability of striking first, before Russian preparations were complete.

Another plan can also be discerned, a defensive-offensive strategy. It seems that Andrássy has eschewed preventive war in favor of the latter concept. He confided to Kállay in the summer of 1870 that he "holds a triumphant war necessary for the empire; we cannot wage this war against anyone but Russia, and if we win, we simultaneously break Russian power."[49] Andrássy deemed it necessary "that Russia initiate the war,"[50] Kállay noted. In the first phase, spirited Austrian defense would blunt the main Russian trust. In the second, after the aggressor had exhausted its forces in fruitless assault, the common army of the Monarchy, reinforced by the Hungarian *Honvéd* forces and in close cooperation with the allies, would shatter the Russians with a powerful counteroffensive.[51]

Wächer-Gotter reported to Berlin that Andrássy considered a conflict with Russia inevitable, and believed that preparations should be made and the opportune moment chosen for it. For the sake of security in the east—so the Prussian consul believed—Andrássy desired close cooperation with Germany and was convinced that the latter would not forget its obligation toward the Europeans in the area.[52] This implies that Andrássy was not thinking in terms of an Austro-Russian war. He knew that Austria-Hungary—although a great power on the basis of its area and population—did not have the strength to fight a victorious war alone against Russia—if for no other reason, than because of its multinational composition. But he also saw, along Metternichian-Palmerstonian lines, that Austria was an important element in the European balance of power system. Indeed, the Iron Chancellor valued the Dual Monarchy as a "dam against Pan-Slavism,"[53] France regarded it as a "guarantee of French security,"[54] and Britain considered its cooperation essential against predatory Russian expansionism.[55] Andrássy hoped to gain the cooperation of these powers for mutual aid and security; he wished to check Russia's policy of expansionism by joint European action. It was an ambitious diplomatic scheme, worthy of an imaginative and creative statesman. By an interesting coincidence, Bismarck, like Andrássy, expressed the conviction that the real future enemy of "civilized Europe" would be Russia, which only a European coalition could withstand.[56]

Before condemning Andrássy as an advocate of war,[57] it is well to consider three points. First, his ideas were not connected with any plan of action, nor did he make any serious attempts to translate them into reality. Strategic considerations were oriented to defensive purposes. Speaking to the German ambassador in 1872, Andrássy said: "We have been thrown out of Germany, and that is well; we lost Italy and we became stronger; we do not want to make annexations, but desire peace to defend our vital interests, which are threatened so far as our Slavic population is concerned."[58] Second, in a fluid situation, he felt it unwise to commit himself to a definite course too early,[59] and he held to this all the more because he knew that this was a weakness to which his countrymen were susceptible. "We Hungarians get excited easily," he observed. Therefore, "it must be our leaders' concern to point out the whirlpool toward which we are running." Then, with his usual optimism, he added: "Once we perceive it, we do not have to be restrained by force; we turn back on our own."[60] To the end of his career, Andrássy set himself steadfastly against delusions. The third point is that, aware of the dangers of an all-out conflict, as Austria-Hungary's foreign minister (1871-79), his policy was dedicated to the avoidance of war. In accordance with the political principles of his time, Andrássy too considered war as the *ultima ratio*. His considerable intuition and experiences enabled him to discern factors that would limit his freedom of choice and action.[61] Austria and Russia, Andrássy observed in 1878, "are immediate neighbors and must live with one another, either on terms of peace or war. A conflict between the two empires would not be decided by one single campaign but would be inherited by generations to come . . . ; and its end could hardly be other than the total destruction of one of the two states. Before embarking upon such a contest there had to be reasons . . . that made a death struggle inevitable."[62] Andrássy's desire for peace, in any case, was a worthy desire. The will to preserve it was not lacking.

The defensive prognosis of his policy toward Russia is in sharp contrast to the image of the "warlike Andrássy" projected by his critics. In reality, his policies were always pacific and within constitutional limits. His sometimes aggressive tone suggests fear rather than a desire for confrontation. As has been shown, he was aware that not even a successful war could bring many tangible gains to the Dual Monarchy, and that the dangers involved in resorting to armed conflict were simply too great. Andrássy's policy was thus limited in aim and defensive in nature.

NOTES

1. For details see János Decsy, *Prime Minister Gyula Andrássy's Influence on Habsburg Foreign Policy During the Franco-German War of 1870-1871* (New York, 1979), pp. 11-17.

2. Ibid., p. 22.

3. Quoted in Béla Lederer, ed., *Gróf Andrássy Gyula beszédei* [Speeches of Count Julius Andrássy] (2 vols.; Budapest, 1891), I, 306.

4. Ladenberg to Bismarck, Vienna, Sept. 16, 1967, Deutsches Hauptarchiv des Auswärtige Amts (hereafter cited as DHAA), I.A.A. 1 (Österreich) 54, Acta betr. Schriftwechsel mit der Kgl. Gesandschaft in Wien, sowie mit anderen Kgl. Missionen und fremden Kabinetten über die innere Zustände und Verhältnisse Österreichs, III (hereafter cited as Austria, File 54), No. A 3896.

5. Cf. Walter Platzhoff, "Die Anfänge des Dreikaiserbundes," *Preussische Jahrbücher*, CLXXXVIII (June, 1922), pp. 298-306. See also William Langer, *European Alliances and Alignments, 1871-1890* (2nd ed.; New York, 1950), p. 20.

6. See George Barany, "Hungary: The Upcompromising Compromise," *Austrian History Yearbook*, III, Pt. 1 (1967), pp. 245-247.

7. The Hungarian desire for close cooperation with Germany was personified by Andrássy. For details, see Decsy, *Andrássy*, pp. 28-29.

8. See, for instance, Heinrich Ritter von Srbik, *Aus Österreichs Vergangenheit von Prinz Eugen zu Kaiser Franz Joseph* (Salzburg, 1949), pp. 77, 80, 90. Srbik's contentions seem to represent a delayed revenge of the Austrian conservatives and reactionaries of 1866-1870, who were pushed aside by Andrássy.

9. Contemptuous of abstract speculation, theories and ideologies, he always aimed at the practical in dealing with problems of politics. When asked to autograph a lady's album with "what he sought in art," he wrote: "What I despise most in politics—the ideal." Cited by Ede Wertheimer, *Gróf Andrássy Gyula élete és kora* [Life and Times of Count Julius Andrássy] (3 vols.; Budapest, 1910-1913), III, 431; see also Count Julius Andrássy, Jr., *Bismarck, Andrássy and their Successors* (London, 1927), pp. 43-44.

10. Despite his extreme animosity toward the Magyars, even A.J.P. Taylor agrees with this proposition. See his *The Habsburg Monarchy, 1809-1918* (New York, 1956), p. 126. For a realistic and highly scholarly appraisal consult Arthur J. May, *The Habsburg Monarchy, 1967-1918* (Cambridge, Mass., 1960), pp. 34, 112-113.

11. Cf. Decsy, *Andrássy*, p. 19.

12. Cited by Lederer, *Andrássy*, I, 137.

13. For details, see Michael B. Petrovich, *The Emergence of Russian Panslavism, 1859-1870* (New York, 1956), pp. 273-274.

14. Certain startling and ugly utterances by Palacký are quoted in Joseph F. Začek, *Palacký and the Austro-Hungarian Compromise of 1867.* A Report to the International Conference on the *Ausgleich* of 1867, Bratislava, Aug. 28 to Sept. 2, 1967 (Los Angeles, 1967), pp. 8-10, 24-25, n. 16. For the latest monograph on Palacký, see Začek's *Palacký: The Historian as Scholar and Nationalist* (Paris, 1970).

15. Béla Orczy diary, entry of Oct. 31, 1868, in Wertheimer, *Andrássy*, I, 569. To make his opposition to Beust's anti-Prussian, pro-French policy more effective, Andrássy arranged to have his confidant, Baron Béla Orczy, appointed head of a department in the foreign ministry. The latter served in this capacity between 1868 and 1879. It was Orczy's duty, among others, to uphold Andrássy's views against Beust. Cf. Karl Tschuppik, *The Reign of Emperor Francis Joseph* (London, 1930), p. 205.

16. Béni Kállay, *Belgrádi Napoló*, XXXI-XXXIV, Magyar Országos Levéltár [Béni Kállay, Belgrade Diary, XXXI-XXXIV, Hungarian National Archives] (hereafter cited as Kállay diary, MNA), XXXI, entry of April 4, 1869. Béni Kállay distinguished diplomat, historian and an expert on Balkan affairs, had been a close friend of Andrássy who pressed Foreign Minister Beust to appoint Kállay to the sensitive position of consul general in the Serbian capital, Belgrade (1868-1875). It was Kállay's duty among others to prepare the ground for Serbia's removal from Russian influence, and to learn the real motives behind Beust's Balkan policy. Furthermore, Kállay was charged with keeping a sharp eye on the activities of the military members of the Court party in the frontier region. Evidence of their continuing agitation among the area's inhabitants had been causing considerable anxiety in Budapest. Reactionary circles in Vienna apparently still considered the Military Frontier District Hungary's potential Vendée. For details, see Kállay diary, XXXI, entry of Aug. 19, Oct. 31, and Nov. 11, 1868, MNA.

17. Wächer-Gotter to Bismarck, Pest Nov. 22, 1871, DHAA, Austria, File 58, II, A4730. See also Protokoll vom 22 Aug. 1870, Ministerrath für gemeinsame Angelegenheiten (hereafter cited as Ministerrath), Haus-, Hof-, und Staatsarchiv, Vienna, Politische Archiv (hereafter cited as HHSA, PA), XL, 285.

18. Salvini to Visconti-Venosta, Pest Nov. 3, 1870, No. R. 10, Ministero degli affari esteri, Archivo storico (hereafter cited as M.A.E., AS), Serie politica (1867-1888), Austria-Ungheria, busta 1253: 1867-1870.
19. Salvini to Visconti-Venosta, Pest Nov. 13, 1870, No. R. 11, ibid.
20. The full text of Ghiczy's remarks is printed in Lederer, *Andrássy,* I, 304.
21. See István Diószegi, *Ausztria-Magyarország és a francia porosz háború, 1870-1871* [Austria-Hungary and the Franco-Prussian War, 1870-1871] (Budapest, 1965), pp. 42-43. Diószegi's extreme view is contradicted further by Wächer-Gotter's report of December. "In their enmity toward Russia," wrote the Prussian consul general, "all Hungarian parties are united, ..." Cf. Wäcker-Gotter to Bismarck, Pest, Dec. 21, 1869, DHAA, Austria, File 58, I, No. A 4243. For public opinion, see also the *Pesti Napló* (Pest Journal), July 14, 17, 1870, and *Pester Lloyd,* July 15, 1870.
22. Cited by Florence Foster-Arnold, *Francis Deák Hungarian Statesman: A Memoir* (London, 1880), pp. 301-307.
23. Count István Tisza, "Wertheimer 'Andrássy'-ja" [Wertheimer's Andrássy], Magyar Figyelő [Magyar Observer], I, January-March, 1911, 337. Cf. Victória Kondor, *Az 1875-ös pártfúzió* [The Party Merger of 1875] (Budapest, 1959), pp. 62-66.
24. Ministerrath, Aug. 22, 1870, HHSA, PA, XL, 285.
25. Thus Andrássy expressed himself to the special emissary of the Italian foreign minister, Artom to Visconti-Venosta, Vienna, Aug. 7, 1870, private and unnumbered, M.A.E., AS, Archivi di gabinetto (1861-1887), busta 219: Guerra franco-prussiana e trattative segrete 8 luglio 14-settembre 1870, fascicolo 3.
26. Salvini to Visconti-Venosta, Pest, Nov. 13, 1870, No. R. 11, M.A.E., AS, Austria-Ungheria, busta 1253.
27. For the anti-Magyar orientation of the Pan-Slavists, see Petrovich, *Russian Panslavism,* pp. 273-276.
28. Robert A. Kann, *The Austro-Hungarian Compromise in Retrospect. A Report to the International Conference on the Ausgleich of 1867,* Bratislava, Aug. 28 to Sept. 2, 1967 (Los Angeles, 1967), p. 15.
29. Adolphe Thiers, *Memoirs of M. Thiers, 1870-1873* (London, 1916), p. 29.

30. Decsy, *Andrássy*, p. 33.
31. [Andrássy], "The Present Position and Policy of Austria," *The Eclectic Review*, XXVIII (November, 1850), p. 628. It was written ostensibly as a comment on the works of E. Zsedényi, *Ungarns Gegenwart* (Wien, 1850); and Paul von Somssich, *Das legitime Recht Ungarns und seines Königs* (Wien, 1850), but since the article contains no reference to these works, it may be regarded as an independent study.
32. Ministerrath, Aug. 22, 1870, HHSA, PA, XL, 285.
33. Personal notes of Andrássy, published in Róland Hegedüs, "The Foreign Policy of Julius Andrássy," *The Hungarian Quarterly*, III, No. 4 (Winter, 1937/38), p. 633.
34. Ibid., pp. 632-633. Cf. István Diószegi, "Honvédőrnagy Metternich íroasztalánál: 150 éve születet Andrássy Gyula [A major at Metternich's Desk: Julius Andrássy Was Born One Hundred Fifty Years Ago], *Élet és irodalom* [Life and Literature], XVII, No. 9 (March 5, 1973), p. 7.
35. "The integrity of the Turkish Empire" is a must, Andrássy told Kállay. Kállay diary, XXXI, entry of Aug. 19, 1868, MNA. To the Russian chancellor Andrássy declared emphatically that "we desire the preservation of Turkey as it is." Gorchakov to Alexander II, Berlin Aug. 28-Sept. 9, 1872. The full text is printed in Baron A.F. Mayendorff, "Conversations of Gorchakov, Andrássy and Bismarck in 1872," *Slavonic and East European Review*, VIII, (December, 1929), p. 405.
36. Quoted in M.D. Stoyanovich, *The Great Powers and the Balkans, 1875-1878* (Cambridge, 1939), pp. 30-31.
37. Cited by Sir Spencer Walpole, *History of Twenty-five Years, 1856-1880* (4 vols., London, 1904), p. 71.
38. István Diószegi, *Ausztria-Magyarország és Bulgária a San Stefanói Béke után, 1875-1878* [Austria-Hungary after the Treaty of San Stefano, 1875-1878] (Budapest, 1961), pp. 7-8.
39. Kállay diary, XXXI, entry of Aug. 19, 1868, MNA.
40. As quoted in Hegedüs, "The Foreign Policy of Count Julius Andrássy," p. 630.
41. Anton Freiherr von Mollinary, *Sechsundvierzig Jahre im österreichischen-ungarischen Heere* (2 vols.; Zürich, 1905), II, 257.
42. Kállay's diary reveals that Andrássy made several steps toward winning the cooperation of Turkey and Serbia. Kállay diary, XXXI, entry of July 29, 1870.

43. Karl von Rumänien, König, *Aus dem Leben König Karls von Rumänien* (4 vols.: Stuttgart, 1894), I, 309.
44. Cf. Decsy, *Andrássy*, p. 34.
45. Artom to Visconti-Venosta, Vienna, July 20-21, 1870, private and unnumbered, M.A.E., AS, Archivi di gabinetto, busta 219, fascicolo 3.
46. Kállay diary, XXXII, entry of July 29, 1870, MNA.
47. Artom to Visconti-Venosta, Vienna, July 20, 1870, private and unnumbered, M.A.E., AS, Archivi di gabinetto, busta 219, fascicolo 3.
48. Artom to Visconti-Venosta, Vienna, Aug. 7, 1870, private and unnumbered, ibid.
49. Kállay diary, entry of Aug. 19, 1868, MNA.
50. Ibid.
51. See Decsy, *Andrássy*, p. 100.
52. Wächer-Gotter to Bismarck, Pest, Nov. 22, 1871, DHAA, Austria, File 58, II, No. A 4330.
53. Gerhard Ritter, "Das Bismarckproblem," *Merkur*, IV (1950), p. 663.
54. Moustier to Gramont, Paris, July 3, 1867, France. Ministére des affaires étrangéres. *Les Origines diplomatiques de la querre de 1870-1871* (herefater cited as ODG), (29 vols.; Paris, 1910-1932), XXVII, No. 5263.
55. Cf. May, *The Habsburg Monarchy*, p. 92.
56. See the account of Arthur, Graf Scherr-Thoss, "Erinnerungen aus meinem Leben," *Deutsche Rundschau* (Berlin, 1881), pp. 78-79. Cf. Bismarck to Benstorff, Berlin, Jan. 18, 1869, DHAA, Austria, File 41, XII, No. A 4132.
57. See, for instance, Diószegi, *Ausztria-Magyarország és a franciaporosz háború*, pp. 42-43.
58. Quoted in Hans Lothar von Schweinitz, *Denkwürdigkeiten des Botschafters General von Schweinitz* (2 vols.; Berlin, 1927), I, 297.
59. Béni Kállay testified to this in his memorial speech. See Béni Kállay, "Gróf Andrássy Gyula emlékezete" [Remembrance of Count Julius Andrássy], *Akadémiai Értesítő* [Bulletin of the Academy], II (June 15, 1891), p. 341; see also Andrássy, Jr., *Bismarck, Andrássy and their Successors*, p. 43.
60. Cited by Sándor Okolicsányi, "Adalékok gróf Andrássy Gyula jellemrajzához" [Additional Data on the Character Study of Count Julius Andrássy], *Budapesti Szemle* [Budapest Review], LXII (1890), p. 119.

61. This contention is well demonstrated by Andrássy's speech in the Hungarian Delegation in 1882. See *A magyar delegáció naplója* [The Minutes of the Hungarian Delegation], IV, April 23, 1882.

62. Memorandum of Andrássy to Beust, Vienna, June 22, 1877. The full text is printed in Miksa Falk, *Kor és jellemrajzok* [Time and Character Studies] (Budapest, 1903), pp. 286-289.

Peter Pastor

MIHÁLY KÁROLYI AND HIS VIEWS ON HUNGARIAN-RUSSIAN TIES

Among the statesmen of twentieth-century Hungary, few are considered more controversial than the late Mihály Károlyi (1875-1955). It was only during the short-lived Hungarian Peoples' Republic that he held power. During the early tenure of the second Hungarian Peoples' Republic, thirty years later (from August 1947 to 1949), he was Hungary's Ambassador in Paris. Following his resignation from this position, he chose exile, just as he had earlier, following the collapse of his regime in 1919. His first exile lasted until 1946; his second, in Vence, France, until his death in 1955.

Whether as an active politician in Hungary or the spiritual leader of the liberal-democratic exiles, Károlyi always emphasized foreign affairs as a primary force in internal Hungarian politics. Unlike most of Hungary's leading politicians, Károlyi considered Germany as Hungary's greatest threat to sovereignty. On the other hand, he was almost consistently in favor of some kind of cooperation with Russia.

Before the outbreak of World War I, he saw Russia as the only power capable of counterbalancing the German threat, while at the same time moderating neighboring Slav enmities against Hungary. Following the collapse of the Károlyi regime and the eventual victory and twenty-five-year domination of the autocratic reactionary Horthy regime, Károlyi looked at Russia as a country where some of the reforms he had dreamed of for Hungary had already been established. His constant rejection by the West—be it the abandonment of the democratic People's Republic, or the American refusal to permit Károly to settle in the United States—all contributed to his perception that Hungary had to depend on the East, rather than on the West.

Károlyi's political career began in 1905 in the Hungarian Parliament. As a scion of one of the richest magnate families in Hungary, his election to the Lower House presented no great difficulties.

By the early 1910s Károlyi became one of the leaders of the Independence Party. During these prewar years, he became increasingly interested in foreign affairs. He was among the first of the opposition politicians to recognize that the changes in internal politics favored by his partisans called for a change in Hungary's external policy. Károlyi feared that Germany's predominance in the Triple Alliance threatened the endeavors of the Independence Party to create a truly independent and sovereign Hungary.[1]

The outbreak of the Balkan Wars in 1912 seemed to threaten a clash between the Dual Monarchy and Russia. To avoid such an eventuality, Károlyi went to Paris in November 1912 in search of contacts. His intentions were to find out if the French Prime Minister, Raymond Poincaré, was receptive to the idea of a new political party in Hungary which would favor a pro-Entente and pro-Serbian foreign policy. Although his attempts to see Poincaré were unsuccessful, Károlyi continued to stress a pro-Entente line upon his return.

He stressed that Russian involvement in the Balkans indicated a need for coexistence between the Slavs and the Hungarians. For this view, he was labeled in the pro-government press as a "Slavophile."[2] In the spring of 1914, Károly continued his search for Russian contacts and a rapprochement between Hungary and Tsarist Russia. During the visit of some conservative Russian journalists to Hungary, Károlyi was informed that St. Petersburg would favor starting a dialogue with those politicians who were interested in putting distance between the Dual Monarchy and Germany. The Russian consul in Budapest reinforced this claim of the Russian journalists.

When Károlyi visited Paris in March 1914, he contacted Alexander P. Izvolsky, hoping to gain some meaningful commitment from this former foreign minister. The appointment set up by Izvolsky, however, could not be kept, as Károlyi was in a rush to meet his boat and embark on a visit to the United States. Upon his return from the United States the planned visit to Russia was again put on the back burner, Károlyi having to prepare for another trip to the United States. The Independence Party in its official declaration stated that a St. Petersburg visit by party leaders could not be envisaged before August of that year. The lack of an official Russian invitation contributed to the postponement of the trip. This may have been caused by Ambassador Nikolai S. Shebeko's negative report from Vienna. The Russian envoy opposed Károlyi's visit to St. Petersburg on the grounds that it was inspired by the needs of internal Hungarian politics and it had no chance to alter Austro-Hungarian foreign policies.[3]

The guns of August drew Austria-Hungary into a war against Russia that Károlyi had sought to avoid. Károlyi, upon his return from the United States, thought that it was his patriotic duty to follow his government's policy and went to fight on the Galician front against Russia. By late 1916, however, Károlyi had become the leader of those who called for a negotiated peace. The increasing superiority of Germany and the German *Mitteleuropa* plan seemed to reinforce Károlyi's worst fears about the threat of Germany's domination over Hungary.

For these reasons, Károlyi welcomed the March Revolution in Russia. In his official statement he declared that "we are at war not with the Russian people, but with Tsarism." He hoped that peace would result from changes in Russia. At the same time he also belived that the Russian events would serve as a warning to the Hungarian Government not to stand in the way of electoral reform.[4]

The continuation of the war and military defeat led to revolutions and to the collapse of the Austro-Hungarian Monarchy nineteen months later. In Hungary, the revolution of October 30, 1918 brought Károlyi to power as Prime Minister of a liberal-democratic state. After the armistice of November 3 and the abdication of the King, it became the Peoples' Republic of Hungary. The government was supported by three parties: Károlyi's own Independence Party, the Radical Party of Oszkár Jászi, and the Social Democratic Party. This latter was the only mass party in the coalition.

The Hungarian Revolution and the other revolutions in East Central Europe and in Germany were welcomed by the Bolshevik Government in Russia. The communists, however, were seen by Károlyi as anarchists. Nor could a Bolshevik Russia, then in the throws of civil war, be seen as a potential ally. Rather, Károlyi and his colleagues believed that it would be Wilsonianism which would be instrumental in helping him create a new Hungary, with some Western, but mostly American support.

The Western crusade against Bolshevism in Russia was coupled by the zeal of Hungary's neighbors to justify their incursions into Hungary against the alleged Hungarian Bolshevik threat. These made Károlyi even more careful and he did his best to keep his contacts with Russia at a minimum.

The Soviet Government's propaganda message was kept from the Hungarian people. The Hungarian Government, upon French pressure, arrested the Soviet Red Cross representatives in Budapest (January 1919), and it never appointed an ambassador to Russia—despite the fact that the Russians had indicated that they were sending Christian Rakovsky as their ambassador to Budapest. Consequently, the Hungarian prisoners of war in Russia could only be represented by Hungarian Red Cross delegations.

The famous Vix Ultimatum of the Allies, which on March 20, 1919 called for the further withdrawal of Hungarian troops from Hungarian territories, led to the resignation of President Károlyi and his Prime Minister, Dénes Berinkey and his government. The ministers resigned with the expectation that a purely socialist government would be formed which would take up the struggle with the support of international socialism. Russia's position in this struggle was also taken into consideration by Károlyi. He advised the socialists to come to an understanding with the imprisoned Hungarian communist leaders. That way, the Red Army, which was reported to be operating near Hungary's borders, would not attack Hungary from the back. With this in mind, the communists were liberated from prison.[5]

The communists, however, were invited by the socialists to fuse with them, and the 133-day Béla Kun interlude in Hungary represented the communist ascendence. An alliance on paper was established between Soviet Russia and Soviet Hungary. Disapproving of the Kun regime, Károlyi left Hungary in June, not to return again until twenty-eight years later.

The betrayal of Wilsonian ideals by the West, and its recognition of the autocratic and reactionary Horthy regime in Hungary greatly disappointed and embittered Károlyi. To add insult to injury, the United States Government refused to allow Károlyi to accompany his wife on a speaking tour in 1925. Nor was Károlyi allowed to settle down in the United States, although he believed that it was the only country where he could live and work in comfort. His Marxist-socialist sympathies, which he openly espoused in the fall of 1919 slowly evolved into a pro-Soviet position. In the twenties he came to favor a United Front policy with the Russians. In a letter to György Lukács in 1928, he proudly pointed out that, though not a communist but a left-winger, he never criticized Russia during the ten years of his exile.[6]

In June 1931, Károlyi and his wife arrived in Russia in the company of Lucien Vogel, editor of the pictorial journal, the French *Vu* magazine. He, like so many of the left-wing sympathizers of the communist experiment, was most impressed by what he saw there. He had arrived in the midst of forced collectivization, yet rather than seeing evil in the deeds of Stalin, he saw it as a positive act.

Károlyi, who used to be the president of the *Hangya* (Ant) cooperative movement in Hungary before the war, and who in February 1919 had divided up his lands among the poor Hungarian peasants, considered the *kolhoz* as the way of the future.

No doubt behind his views was a great deal of wishful thinking. He wanted to see Russia recover its strength so that it could act as a counterweight to Germany, the country that Károlyi still considered as the prime threat to Hungary. The party purges of the 1930s disturbed Károlyi a great deal. He did not believe in the fake confessions of the purged. Yet he still refused to make an open break with Stalin. He believed that this would only help capitalism and weaken the chances for survival of the only socialist state in the world. It would also undermine the chances of victory for the loyalists in the civil war in Spain.[7]

The Nazi-German Pact was yet another blow to his trust of Russia. He saw in this act his wished-for end to capitalism, but at the expense of communism and of Europe.[8]

His pessimism was tempered by Nazi Germany's attack on Russia, although he did not seem to be willing to forgive Stalin for the Pact. By 1944, with a Russian-Western victory in sight, Károlyi expected that Hungary, backed by the Russians, would embark on socialist reforms and would embrace the democratic traditions of the West. He thus saw Hungary's postwar role as a bridge between Russia in the East and Britain and France in the West.

For these reasons, he welcomed the land reforms of the Hungarian Provisional Government which was set up in Debrecen by the Russians in December 1944. He was also pleased to see that these reforms were instituted by the politicians and military men of the Old Regime. He hoped that this would preclude the possibility of the creation of a new "stab in the back" legend. He expected that the land reforms in Hungary would lead to the organization of *kolhoz*-type collectives, believing that there was not enough land for all the Hungarian peasants.

Liberation in April 1945, the end of the war in May, and the victory of the British Labour Party in August filled Károlyi with greater hopes. Perceiving the United States as the great enemy of Europe, he hoped that the British and the Russians could form some kind of united socialist front. This was perceived as a further assurance that Hungary could become a sovereign state.[9]

Károlyi expected that the British would protect an Octobrist Hungary because they were guilty for the betrayal of Hungary in 1919. Just like they had felt remorse for the Munich Pact and had subsequently gone to war with the Nazis, he believed that the British would come to Hungary's aid. He therefore saw certain parallels between 1918 and 1945: the land reforms, a break with Germany and a pro-Slav orientation.[10]

While Károlyi was pro-Slav, he did not intend to see Hungary toeing the Russian line and was critical of those who became blind supporters of the Russian position.[11] Karl Polányi justly saw in Károlyi's reluctance to return to Hungary immediately after the war a refusal to be a Hungarian Quisling.[12]

Károlyi was infuriated by Russia's failure to stop the outbreak of resurgent nationalism among the Hungarians and among their neighbors. He was critical of Czechoslovakia's expulsion of the Hungarians, and of Hungary's expulsion of the *Volksdeutsche* population. He began to suspect that Russia was up to the old technique of dividing and conquering. His doubts about Russian motives, however, were dismissed on the basis that the Russians were not foolish and would not support a policy that would lead to a Smallholder Party victory instead of one by a left-wing party.[13] Obviously, Károlyi had forgotten the devious mind of Stalin, who might possibly have preferred to see the victory of the right, rather than a non-Muscovite left.

The fears of a Smallholder victory in Hungary proved correct. In November 1945 the Smallholder Party, supported by Cardinal Mindszenty's pastoral letter, won 57% of the electorate against 17% for the Communist Party and 17.4% for the Socialist Democratic Party.[14] When Károlyi returned to Hungary in May 1946 as a national hero he soon came to look on this victory as the perpetuation of the traditions of the hated interwar establishment. In this belief he was not alone.[15] The destruction of the unrepentant establishment with Russian support was welcome. It is for this reason that in 1947 he supported the "bogus coalition," which was dominated by the communists. During this year he came to be an admirer of László Rajk, who as Minister of the Interior busied himself in eliminating the "old order."

Károlyi offered his services to the government in the field of foreign policy. In 1947 it seemed that he was to be sent to Prague, which to all seemed as a backwater of diplomacy. Károlyi, however, perceived himself as having excellent contacts with Jan Masaryk, Edvard Beneš and Hubert Ripka. He therefore hoped that he could win the Czechoslovak leaders to a less hostile policy toward Hungary. Moreover, he saw Czechoslovakia as a Slav bridge between Hungary and Russia.[16]

Instead, he was sent to Paris. Among his major activities in France in 1948 was the defense of Mindszenty's arrest. He applauded his government's action, perceiving that the Prelate would become a politician standing in the way of changes in Hungary. But Károlyi—as his memorandum to Rajk indicates—objected to the repressive means used by the Hungarian Government and favored instead the expulsion of Mindszenty to Rome.[17]

In Hungary, the purge of the purgers led to the arrest, trial and "confession" of Rajk and many others. Károlyi returned briefly to Hungary and professed Rajk's innocence before the Hungarian Premier and the Communist Party Secretary, Mátyás Rákosi. In August of 1949 Károlyi resigned his Paris post so as to return to Hungary and clear the name of his friend. The mass resignations and defections in the Hungarian diplomatic corps, however, persuaded Károlyi of the futility of his plans. Instead, he chose exile in France.[18]

The death of Stalin in 1953 filled him with hopes of what he called a European *détente*. In an interview granted to a Yugoslav paper he indicated that he expected the Soviet Government to adjust to the new realities and to allow Hungary to choose Yugoslavia's independent way to socialism. His death in 1955 perhaps saved him from yet another disappointment.

Károlyi's consistent inclusion and calculation of Russia in the Hungarian picture indicated a realism that escaped other Hungarian politicians. Where he was proven wrong was in his assumption that Russia's interest, as perceived by its leaders, would overlap with his own. This error, however, has also been made by other statesmen of great repute.

NOTES

1. Ferenc Pölöskei, *Kormányzati politika és kormányzati ellenzék* [Governmental Policy and Governmental Opposition] (Budapest, 1968), p. 32.
2. Tibor Hajdu, *Károlyi Mihály. Politikai Életrajz* [Mihály Károlyi. A Political Biography] (Budapest, 1978), p. 145.
3. Mihály Károlyi, *Az egész világ ellen* [Against the Whole World] (Budapest, 1965), pp. 68-72; István Dolmányos, "Károlyi Mihály és a 'szentpétervári út'. Az orosz-magyar szövetség gondolata 1914-ben" [Mihály Károlyi and the 'Road to St. Petersburg.' The Idea of a Russian-Hungarian Alliance in 1914], *Történelmi Szemle* [Historical Review], VI, 2 (1963), pp. 167-174.
4. *Magyarország,* April 1, 1917.
5. Hungary, Council of Ministers, *Minisztertanácsi jegyzőkönyvek* [Minutes of the Ministerial Council], March 19 and 20, 1919; and Peter Pastor, *Hungary between Wilson and Lenin* (New York, 1976).
6. Hungary, *Károlyi hagyaték* [Károlyi Papers], Mihály Károlyi to György Lukács, Paris, April 4, 1928.
7. Michael Károlyi, *Memoirs of Michael Károlyi. Faith Without Illusions* (London, 1957), pp. 249, 282.
8. Columbia University, *Jászi Papers,* Károlyi to Jászi, October 9, 1939.
9. Hungary, *Károlyi hagyaték,* Károlyi to Jászi, May 22, 1945; Jászi to Garbai, July 27, 1945.
10. Hungary, *Károlyi hagyaték,* Károlyi to Bölöni, September 21, 1945.
11. Hungary, *Hatvani hagyaték* [Hatvani Papers], Mrs. Mihály Károlyi to Lajos Hatvani, July 28, 1945.
12. Hungary, *Károlyi hagyaték,* Károly Polányi to Mihály Károlyi, April 16, 1946.

13. Hungary, *Károlyi hagyaték,* Károlyi to Károly Polányi, April 1, 1946.
14. Bennet Kovrig, *Communism in Hungary* (Stanford, 1979), pp. 179-180.
15. For example, Anna Kéthly, a Social Democratic party leader, bitterly noted that the elections demonstrated the successful destruction of the democratic intelligentsia by the defunct Horthy regime. She believed that only the presence of Soviet troops prevented the outbreak of civil war in Hungary and that it would take the passing of a generation as "with the people of Moses," before the rebirth of democracy and freedom was possible in Hungary. See Hoover Institution on War, Revolution and Peace, *Rusztem Vámbéry Collection,* Kéthly to Vámbéry, April 22, 1946.
16. Hungary, *Károlyi hagyaték,* Károlyi to Hatvani, June 14, 1945: *Memoirs of Michael Károlyi,* pp. 341-342.
17. Hungary, *Károlyi hagyaték,* undated.
18. Hungary, *Károlyi hagyaték,* undated; *Memoirs of Michael Károlyi,* pp. 351-359.

Michael Palumbo

GOERING'S ITALIAN EXILE, 1924-1925

Among Hermann Goering's many titles and unique responsibilities during the Third Reich, one of his favorite roles was as a leading intermediary and advisor for Hitler on relations with Fascist Italy. Goering's expertise in Italian affairs dates from 1924, when he took refuge in Italy after the abortive *putsch* in Munich. There has been very little reliable information on this important early example of Nazi-Fascist relations. It is unfortunate that most later works on Goering base their description of this episode on his earlier biographers' inaccurate accounts, sometimes adding details that can only be described as sheer invention. With recently available material, however, it is now possible to give a clear picture of Goering's Italian exile.

The story begins when Goering, as leader of the SA, participated in Hitler's uprising in Munich of 1923. He received a bad wound in the leg which was complicated by an infection resulting in fever and severe pain. With his wife Carin, Goering eventually escaped into Austria.[1] There he met Kurt Ludecke who had undertaken two missions for Hitler to Italy in 1922 and 1923. Goering spoke to Ludecke about the recent abortive *putsch* in Munich. They probably also discussed Ludecke's trips to Fascist Italy and his meetings with Benito Mussolini. In his memoirs Ludecke gives the impression that his missions to Italy were widely known in Nazi circles, so that Goering was sure to raise this subject. Whether Ludecke influenced Goering to go to Italy is not known, but the discussion probably left him with the impression that Mussolini's regime was accessible to an emissary from the NSDAP.

While in Innsbruck, Goering was operated on in the local hospital. Still suffering from agonizing pain, he acquired a dependence on morphine, which was administered copiously. It is during this period that the future Reich Marshal developed his well-known drug addiction. Goering's wound failed to heal properly, and he experienced a number of relapses. Many of those whom he met in Austria and Italy report that he limped rather badly. He also lost his youthful physique and began to develop the girth that characterized him later on. When his health permitted, Goering took part in various political activities. He established contact with Austrian Nazis and German followers of Hitler who were also in exile. His activities aroused the interest of the authorities—particularly his efforts to raise funds for the National Socialist movement. When one of his associates was arrested in Vienna, Goering was quietly asked to leave the country. The Nazi exile and his wife were fortunate to receive aid from the Wagner family. As Friedeling Wagner relates, his bills in Innsbruck were paid by her father and arrangements were made for the Goerings to go to Venice to live at a hotel which was owned by a Nazi sympathizer.[2]

The couple arrived in Venice in the spring of 1924. They took up residence in the Hotel Britannia. Its owner, Rudolfo Walther, was a German national whose family had lived in Italy for many years. Carin's first reaction to Italy was one of sheer enchantment by the charm and beauty of Venice; she regretted only that her knowledge of the language was so poor. Her husband's command of Italian, however, was substantial, and he decided to utilize his visit to carry on the work of his movement. There is no evidence that he was invited to Italy by Mussolini or any Fascist offical. His choice in going there appears to have been motivated chiefly by the offer from Walther. However, it could not have failed to cross his mind that this trip might provide an opportunity to further the cause of Nazi-Fascist relations; it seems safe to assume that this was at least a secondary consideration. After a short stay in Venice, the couple set out for Rome.

There has been considerable misinformation about Goering's visit to Rome in 1924. Though the exact chronology of his stay is still unclear, it is possible to document much of what he did in the Italian capital. Most important is the question of whether he actually met Mussolini. Carin, Goering's sister, states in her book that Goering met the Italian dictator "often." This contention has been repeated and embellished by many biographers.[3] But a number of letters written by Goering at a later date requesting an interview with Mussolini make it evident that the Nazi exile never met the Duce in 1924-1925. However, Goering did have considerable dealings with the Fascist government while he was in Rome. His contact was Giuseppe Bastianini,[4] the chief of a department responsible for relations with foreign groups of Fascist orientation. According to Bastianini's memoirs, Goering came to Rome with Giuseppe Renzetti, who was Mussolini's personal agent in Germany. Bastianini met Goering several times in Rome; they talked at length in his office, at restaurants and at certain castles in the Rome area. The Italian diplomat records that Goering gave him a letter addressed from Hitler to Mussolini concerning the question of South Tyrol, the German-speaking region occupied by Italy after World War I. According to Renzo de Felice, the leading contemporary historian of the Fascist era, no trace of this document has ever been found.[5] However, Goering himself wrote a letter to Mussolini while he was in Rome, which may well be the document referred to by Bastianini.[6] In this memorandum Goering pledges that if the Nazis came to power there would be no quarrel over the South Tyrol. A National Socialist Germany, he said, would guarantee the reparations awarded to Italy by the Versailles treaty. Goering also promised that the Nazi press would work for good relations between Germany and Italy. In return, the letter requests Italian help for the Hitler movement, which would include favorable press reports, public statements of support, and financial assistance. Mussolini was also asked to adopt an attitude of neutrality in regard to the Treaty of Versailles, including the question of reparations. Goering's memorandum is remarkably similar to the goals established by Hitler for Ludecke's second mission to Italy. Though there is no evidence that Goering received any direct commission from Hitler, there is reason to suspect that he decided to promote Ludecke's objectives after speaking to him in Innsbruck.

Of potentially great importance in this memorandum is Goering's assertion that the NSDAP might come to power by "legal or illegal means." This statement runs counter to the prevailing interpretation that after the failure of the Munich *putsch,* the Nazis gave up all plans to come to power by violent methods. Goering in his letter to Mussolini does not rule out the possibility of another Nazi uprising. It is not clear if this reflects only his attitude or was a widely held viewpoint with the NSDAP at that time. It is possible that the dogma of abandonment of armed revolt was not as fully accepted in the party as is generally believed. In any evident, Goering dropped this hint to Mussolini that the Nazis were considering a new revolt in which they hoped for Italian Fascist support.

Unfortunately for the Nazis, Goering's visit to Rome coincided with the Matteotti affair, which was the greatest initial crisis of Italian Fascism. There are many indications that Mussolini was overwhelmingly absorbed with the crisis and was not in a position to make new commitments. Thus no concrete agreement was reached. Goering returned to Venice, possibly at the request of Bastianini. It was there that he began a long and aggravating correspondence with Dr. Leo Negrelli of the *Corriere d'Italia*. This Italian journalist had been in Germany, where he had interviewed Hitler in October 1923. He was known to be sympathetic to Nazism, and Goering hoped to use him as an intermediary between himself and Mussolini. Negrelli worked as a functionary for the Italian dictator, and the Nazi exile believed he might have some influence on or at least access to Mussolini. His letters are filled with requests which he hoped Negrelli would convey to the Duce.

One of Goering's most persistent requests was his petition on behalf of Rudolfo Walther, his host in Venice. As a result of the Treaty of Versailles, the Hotel Britannia had been sequestered because it was German-owned. Goering argued that Walther would make an ideal Nazi representative in Italy, and that since he had always been pro-Italian, the property of his family should be spared. No fewer than ten letters written in 1924 and 1925 reflect Goering's constant efforts to gain a favorable judgment for Walther. He had raised the question with Bastianini in Rome, but had received no satisfaction and did not trust the youthful Fascist official on this question. Of course a large part of Goering's motivation may simply have been a desire to repay Walther for the hospitality he had shown him and his wife for so long.[7] However, this seemingly trivial incident provides us with some significant information, for Goering's letters on this subject reflect a quite virulent anti-Semitism.

Many biographers of the future Reich Marshal describe him as a "moderate" on the Jewish question.[8] While of course he was certainly not as obsessed with anti-Semitism as Hitler, there is abundant evidence from this period that he had a very deep and personal hatred for the Jews. In a private letter from Austria on February 22, 1924, he indicated his unwillingness to return to Germany so long as it was a "Jew Republic." In Rome, Bastianini was unfavorably impressed by Goering's tirades against the evil influence of world Jewry.[9] In his letters on the Walther affair, Goering argued that there was a Jewish plot against the proposed Nazi representative in Italy. He stated that the Jewish-owned Banca Commerciale wished to gain control of the Hotel Britannia and thus form a monopoly of hotels in Venice. On September 23, Goering wrote to Negrelli: ". . . I have found out that the Jewish Banca Commerciale, behind the scenes and in typical Jewish lowness, wants to seize the hotel."[10] Ironically, the official who had the power to decide in the Walther matter was Guido Jung, the Italian Minister of the Treasury, who was of Jewish origin. Goering in his correspondence displayed a great distrust for Jung because of his Jewish background, and he warned Negrelli against him on that basis. He saw the Jews as enemies of both Fascism and Nazism:

> The Jew above all—out of racial unity—must be against a national movement because he is the final leader of internationalism, so the national groups must form a closed phalanx against him. Most of the national movements today are already anti-Semitic. . . . [He then lists ten such groups in various countries] . . . . At this moment anti-Semitism grows everywhere. Why did the Fascists in a great outcry declare the Banca Commerciale to be their greatest enemy? This already displays an unconscious anti-Semitic tendency!![11]

Such an outpouring of hatred against the Jews could have been written by Hitler himself, and it is typical of Goering's attitude during this period. Like the Fuehrer, Goering believed that the Fascists were really anti-Semitic, and that this unconscious tendency would eventually manifest itself. It should be noted that the Nazi exile received no satisfaction on the Walther issue. It is doubtful that his expressions of anti-Semitism did anything to help his cause. This is also true of his attacks on the Catholic Church.

Goering's antagonism toward the Vatican and the clerical forces in Italy was almost as consistent and as vicious as his attacks on the Jews. On September 23, he wrote to Negrelli: "The Vatican is cunning. . . . Spiritually and basically, the Vatican is an enemy of Fascism."[12] A few weeks later, the Nazi exile continued his attack on the Catholic Church:

The Vatican is very deceptive. While in Italy it is apparently very well disposed toward Mussolini, in other countries... it is entirely against Mussolini.... Mussolini made powerful temporary concessions to the Pope and he may some day regret this... the large Catholic Party in Germany in expressly anti-Italian and anti-Fascist.[13]

Like his anti-Semitism, Goering's attacks on the Church could gain him few friends in Italy. While Mussolini and the Fascists had an anticlercial tendency, any overt opposition to the Church was not good policy in Catholic Italy. On these issues, Goering showed a distinct lack of tact that was typical of the Nazi movement.

Along with his prejudices Goering's letters also exhibit a deep and apparently sincere admiration for Mussolini and the Fascist movement. When he heard of the political assassination of a Fascist Party official by the Socialists, Goering offered to fight to defend Mussolini's regime if the murder proved to be a prelude to a left-wing uprising. He wrote to Negrelli: "I put myself in the place of a simple Fascist and await orders.... I ask that you do all you can so that I may be a co-fighter."[14] The former World War ace volunteered to go as a reporter, but if necessary he would serve as a pilot in the struggle against an anti-Fascist uprising. Such sentiments on the part of the Nazi exile suggest that he saw the NSDAP as a German auxiliary of the Fascist Party. Of course he may have been seeking to impress his Italian hosts, but there is little doubt that Goering believed that the Nazi party should emulate the Duce's movement.

The main purpose, however, of Goering's letters to Negrelli was not to express his opinions, but to get aid for the Nazi movement from Mussolini's government. This of course meant primarily financial assistance. The Nazi exile claimed that a loan was needed to pay for a pro-Fascist propaganda campaign in Germany: "... a *loan* of two million. For this you would have in your press an important speaking trumpet. Besides you will get your two million back in five years at the latest."[15] In an undated memorandum to the Directorate of the Fascist Party, Goering made his most serious bid for a loan. He indicated that it would be kept secret and listed several reasons for it. In addition to the plan of building a pro-Fascist press in Germany, the need to fight Communism was also stressed. According to Goering, the large debt incurred by the movement in electoral campaigns necessitated the loan, especially since Nazi property was under sequestration as a result of the Munich *Putsch*.[16] The evidence available indicates that Goering never received any money while he was in Italy and gradually dropped the request for a loan. However, a Fascist offical in Munich wrote many years later that after the Nazi *putsch* the Italian Consulate provided money to the survivors of Hitler's abortive revolt.[17] But Goering probably did not know about this. It should be noted that at this time the Nazis were involved in a court case against a political opponent who accused them of receiving financial support from the French;[18] actually it was the Italians whom the Nazis were looking to for such aid.

In exchange for the financial support he was requesting, Goering promised a position by the Nazis on the key question of the South Tyrol that would be favorable to Italian interests. This issue, involving Italian rule of a German-speaking area, aroused nearly unanimous opposition in Germany. Almost every political party, right, left, and center was outraged by Mussolini's efforts to Italianize the region which the Fascists called the Alto-Adige. Goering was not far from the truth when he stated that a pro-Italian position on this issue would mean that "all the rest of the press will come down on us [National Socialists]." He added that "therefore we must be prepared and fore-armed—that is [we must] already have the money for the strengthening of our press."[19] The NSDAP was the only party that took a moderate position on this issue, though it should be mentioned that Hitler was not unopposed even within its own movement. Goering stressed the fact "that Hitler had been denied his Austrian citizenship because of his sharp support of the Italian point of view in regard to the South Tyrol question."[20] This was not true since Hitler remained an Austrian until April 7, 1925, when he resigned his citizenship voluntarily. But Goering was more accurate when he stated that the NSDAP position on the South Tyrol question demonstrated the sincerity of the movement's friendship toward Fascism. He wrote: "Mussolini has an assured ally in Germany, and that is us! This is proved by our sacrifice of the South Tyrol."[21] As early as November 1922, in a discussion with an Italian diplomat, Adolfo Tedaldi, the Fuehrer had given up any claim by a future Nazi Germany to the South Tyrol. In September 1923, he authorized Kurt Ludecke to agree to Italian sovereignty over the Alto-Adige in his meeting with the Duce. And in October of the same year, in his interview with Leo Negrelli, Hitler dwelt on the South Tyrol, affirming his acceptance of the Brenner frontier.[22] Thus Goering was following Hitler's policy on this question.

The Nazi exile emphasized the foreign policy implications of the South Tyrol question. An anti-Fascist German Government, Goering wrote, would be forced to ally itself with France and Yugoslavia against Italy because of the South Tyrol issue. Thus it was in Mussolini's interest to have the Nazis in power in Germany, so as to prevent this anti-Italian coalition. Of course Goering believed that this was a major reason for Fascist Italy to support the Nazis. It should be noted that Goering advocated an alliance of Italy, Germany and Britain. Bastianini mentions that Goering spoke in favor of such a grouping in their conversations in Rome.[23] This was a coalition which Hitler continually advocated during this period, and it was also the key aim of his foreign policy in the 1930s. Like his Fuehrer, Goering was to dedicate much of his career to a Rome-Berlin-London alliance.

Goering's greatest desire, while he was in Italy, was to express his views on foreign policy and other matters to Mussolini directly. Since he did not get a chance to visit the Duce, he constantly brought up the subject of an audience with the Italian dictator in his correspondence with Negrelli from Venice. In a letter that was probably written in early 1925, Goering wrote:

> ...I ask that you do all that you can to arrange an audience in the next few days, since I can no longer wait and must soon depart. ...I am to write a little book about him [Mussolini] and Fascism for propaganda in Germany. It would be stupid to do this if I had never seen him.[24]

Goering linked his request for an interview with the Duce with a supposedly impending visit by Hitler to Italy. On October 15, 1924, he wrote: "...Hitler will certainly be released in the next few days and will then perhaps go to Rome with me.... This will happen only if he could be sure of having an audience with Mussolini...."[25] But by January 25, 1925, Goering wrote: "Hitler will soon have a meeting and an audience with Mussolini. I don't know how this was arranged, but it has been done."[26] The Nazi exile went on to claim that because of the Fuehrer's impending visit, it was even more important that he have a prior audience as a press representative. A few weeks later, Goering wrote: "Hitler has commissioned me to speak to an influential member of the Fascist Party who had promised Hitler to take our matter and secure for me an audience with Mussolini."[27]

Goering's letters of this period suggest a number of interesting possibilities. First we see that Goering claims to have corresponded with Hitler while he was in exile. This has been alleged by some biographers, but no proof has ever been produced. We also have the suggestion that Hitler was in contact with Fascist agents in Germany while he was in prison working on *Mein Kampf*. If these revelations are true, it would mean that Hitler was involved politically, while he was in prison, to a much greater degree than previously believed. Most accounts maintain that Hitler tended to avoid involvement in party affairs while he was at Landsberg. Perhaps he made an exception with regard to relations with Fascist Italy. At any rate it would be interesting if we could get an accurate list of visitors to Landsberg prison to see if it included any possible Fascist agents.

The fact that Hitler would try to arrange a meeting with Mussolini is plausible, for during the *Kampfzeit* he made repeated efforts toward this end. As early as 1922, he had indicated his desire to meet with Mussolini. Other requests are known to have been made in the late 1920s and even in 1932, while Hitler was in the middle of an election campaign.[28] The revelations about Hitler in Goering's letters are consistent with the previously available information we have on this attitude toward Mussolini; it fills a gap and suggests that the Fuehrer's efforts to meet the Duce were even more persistent than previously believed.

Although Renzo de Felice denies that there were plans for a Hitler visit to Italy in 1925,[29] there is some evidence to verify Goering's statements that the Fuehrer planned a trip at this time. We know that Hitler was reported to have told the Nazi *Gauleiter* of Würtemberg that in order to meet Mussolini he needed a large retinue of cars so that he could make the appropriate impression. It is interesting to note that a police report (*Lagebericht*) of March 2, 1925, states: "Hitler now possesses a second car which he also uses on his trips outside Germany."[30] It is possible that this second automobile was purchased during a time when the Nazi Party was short of funds, in anticipation of a trip to Rome to see Mussolini. But as with the Fuehrer's other plans to visit Mussolini between 1922 and 1933, his trip in 1925 was probably prevented by the Duce's refusal to see him.[31]

The question we must ask is why Goering did not get a chance to meet Mussolini. One possibility is that Negrelli never passed on to the Duce

Goering's urgent requests. One gets the impression from the letters that Negrelli may not have been as close to Mussolini as he claimed. But it is unlikely that both Bastianini and Negrelli would have dealt with Goering without some indication of this reaching Mussolini. Why should they risk their positions in unauthorized negotiations without the Duce's approval? What is more plausible is that Mussolini knew of the negotiations, but for various reasons did not wish to make any commitments to Goering. What must be emphasized in this connection is the previously mentioned fact that Goering's stay in Italy coincided with the Matteotti crisis, which surely occupied much if not all of the Duce's attention; for the outbreak of public indignation following the murder of the opposition leader posed a direct threat to his regime. The Italian diplomatic documents show that Mussolini was particularly sensitive about foreign reaction during this period—including opinion in Germany.[32] He was certainly in no mood to make any commitments to a revolutionary leader who was exiled after an unsuccessful coup.

There were a number of factors besides the Matteotti crisis which may explain why Mussolini refused to make any firm commitment to Goering. Although Goering and Hitler were known to favor Fascism, the Nazi Party at that time was controlled by groups opposed to Mussolini's Italy. Typical was Adolph Dresler who wrote a biography of Mussolini in 1924 in which he speculated that the Duce was really a Jew who emigrated to Italy from Poland. In 1925, the editor of the party newspaper *Voelkischer Beobachter,* Alfred Rosenberg, wrote "Mussolini has allowed the dictatorship of Jewish finance."[33] Despite Goering's assurances Mussolini surely must have been aware of the true feelings of a great many leading Nazis. It was to take Hitler a considerable time after he returned from prison to suppress the anti-Italian element in Nazism. While Goering was in Italy, such tendencies were definitely dominant in the NSDAP.

This anti-Italian attitude was of course not appreciated in Fascist circles. Also, Nazi anti-Semitism was not popular in Italy. Although not as numerous as claimed by the Nazis, there were many Jews prominent in Italian life, including the government and the Fascist Party. Many Nazis, when dealing with the Fascists in the 1920s, lost considerable support by their imprudent verbal attacks on the Jews. This happened to Hitler in October 1923 when he was interviewed by Negrelli in Munich, and to Kurt Ludecke when he visited Italy in 1922 and 1923 as a Nazi emissary to

Mussolini. The story is often told that when two other Nazi delegates came to Mussolini and asked for joint cooperation on an anti-Semitic basis, he referred them to his Minister of the Interior, Aldo Finzi, who was of Jewish origin. This story may not be literally true, but it gives a good indication of the attitude of Mussolini and many othe Fascists toward the Nazis' anti-Semitism. Also unpopular in Italy were the Nazi attacks on the Catholic Church and its influence in German life. Many Fascists saw Nazism as pagan and un-Christian. Despite a number of superficial similarities, there was a considerable undertow of resentment against Nazism in Fascist Italy.

Another reason why Mussolini was reluctant to collaborate with the Nazis was his support of the more conservative established right-wing groups in Weimar Germany. In 1924, Mussolini sent General Luigi Capello to Germany, where he conferred with Hans von Seeckt and other military leaders.[34] Capello also spoke with various nationalist politicians such as Karl Helfferich, chairman of the DNVP (German National People's Party). These parleys ultimately resulted in the supplying of weapons to the Reichswehr and promises of support for the DNVP. Capello made no attempt to contact the Nazis. It is obvious that during this period, the Duce was hedging his bets on the NSDAP which had made such a poor showing during the Munich uprising. That failure and the apparent eclipse of Hitler's movement politically were perhaps the main reason why Mussolini was unwilling to make any firm commitment to Goering. In his letters, the Nazi exile attempted to answer Negrelli's charge that the NSDAP was a spent force. One gets the impression that he was rather hard put to deny that the movement had sustained a heavy blow. He calls Hitler "the coming man in Germany."[35] In other passages, too, he speaks of the future potential of the movement, but avoids any references to the current situation of the NSDAP. Such was the weak position in which Goering found himself.

Although Mussolini was obviously not overly anxious to grant Goering's requests, his policy was to give the Nazi exile just enough encouragement to prevent a complete break. After all, he could have expelled Goering or refused to allow Bastianini or Negrelli to have any dealings with him. Mussolini may have believed that the Nazis might serve some useful function at a later date. A memorandum on this subject was written by Bastianini to Mussolini in February 1925.[36] Although we cannot be sure that Mussolini received the report, it gives a good indication of the Fascist attitude toward the Nazis in this period. Bastianini indicated that an agreement in substance if not in form had been made by Goering and Negrelli on a pact between the Fascist and the Nazis.[37] But Goering (probably out of frustration) asked Negrelli to drop the question of this agreement. He now requested only two things: a press interview with Mussolini and settlement of the Walther affair. In his memorandum to Mussolini, Bastianini argued against "a dangerous break of contact and relations with the Nazis." Bastianini suggested that Goering should receive some satisfaction before leaving Italy. There is no indication of Mussolini's response to this memorandum, but Goering left Italy without obtaining either an interview or a settlement of the Walther affair. His letters, however, give the impression that he received assurances on at least some of his requests. Mussolini's policy was probably in line with Bastianini's suggestion. Apparently the Duce allowed Negrelli and Bastianini to make statements to Goering that were just encouraging enough to avoid an open break, but without yielding anything of substance that could embarrass the Fascist regime. One gets the impression from Goering's letters that he suspected what was happening, and that he decided to leave Italy when he realized that there was nothing to be gained.

There is a small possibility, however, that Mussolini may finally have given his consent to a meeting. On February 14, 1925, Goering sent a telegram to Negrelli in which he stated "Thanks for Telegram. Everything all right."[38] He could have meant this as a positive response to Negrelli's notification that a meeting had finally been arranged. This interview with Mussolini may have failed to take place because of Mussolini's preoccupation with the Matteoti affair or because of illness. The Duce's ghost-written autobiography indicates that he was ill throughout most of February and March 1925.[39] Though this source is unreliable in political matters, there is no reason to believe that the authors would fabricate an illness on the part of the Duce. In view of his often stated impatience to get to Sweden, it is possible that Goering may have left Italy even though he was promised a meeting with Mussolini. There is no way of knowing if this was the situation, but a telegram by Goering from Sweden makes it clear that the Nazi exile never met the Duce whether a promise of a meeting was given or not.

There is also an unnecessary misunderstanding over Fanny von Williamowitz-Moellendorf's assertion in her book that her sister Carin Goering visited

Germany several times, where she met Hitler while the couple was living in Italy. Many historians have accepted as genuine a photo given by Hitler to Carin. However, the date on the photo is April 15, 1924, not April 15, 1925 as reported by most writers. Carin received this photo from the Fuehrer while he was incarcerated in Landsberg Prison. This is another example of Hitler's involvement in Nazi-Fascist relations while in prison. But the story that he gave Carin money is probably a fabrication.[40] Also untrue is a German police report that Hermann Goering was requested to leave Italy.[41] There is no evidence for this. It is possible that the couple had outstayed their welcome at the Britannia Hotel in Venice, especially since Rudolfo Walther had received no satisfaction on his petition despite Goering's intervention.

The Goerings arrived in Sweden in April 1925. Carin, who had preceded Hermann, had gone by way of Germany, where she sold their house in Munich. On Arpil 22, 1925, Hermann Goering sent a letter indicating that the couple was settled in Stockholm.[42] During Goering's first year in Sweden, his drug problem became severe, and ultimately he was placed in an asylum. After considerable effort, he managed to divest himself of his morphine addiction. In 1926 he was ready to consider his political career once again. At this time, Goering began to play his role as a leading Nazi expert on Fascist Italy. He had promised Negrelli that he would make propaganda favorable to Mussolini while he was in Sweden. But he never admitted that there was need for such propaganda within the Nazi ranks. From Sweden, Goering sent to the *Voelkischer Beobachter,* the party newspaper, a series of articles in which he argued for a close link between the Nazis and Fascist Italy. This was necessary to support Hitler's struggle to suppress the strong anti-Italian sentiment within the movement. On March 3, 1926, the Nazi paper published the first article: "Zum Deutsch-Italienischen Konflikt I." In this piece, Goering blamed the dispute between Italy and Germany over the South Tyrol on the Jews. He was forced to admit that the Germans living under Italian rule were mistreated, but he believed that the Fascists would soon recognize their error. He wrote:

> As much as we condemn and reject this suppression of our Tyrolean brothers, we nevertheless entertain the hope that the Fascist will soon recognize how much they are harming themselves by

these violent measures and how the common enemy—Jewish Freemasonry—is as always helped by them.[43]

In his second article of this series, Goering continued his anti-Semitic outbursts. He also tried to show a close affinity between Fascism and Nazism. He wrote: "Although Fascism is a purely Italian movement, there is much in its basic make-up that is related to our National Socialist *Weltanschauung.*"[44] Goering mentioned the fight against Marxism, parliamentarianism and degenerate capitalism, as well as love of the native land and cultivation of race as basic similarities of the two movements. He called Mussolini's Rome "the model and example for the national movements"[45] all over Europe. In the last article of the series,[46] Goering stressed foreign policy and Italy's quarrel with France and Yugoslavia. He stated that at Locarno the Weimar Government reconciled itself with France, Italy's foe and the true enemy of the German people. This, he said, forced Mussolini into a harsh policy in the South Tyrol. A new Nazi Government would seek eastern expansion by working together with Italy against France. This and the other articles written by the Nazi exile while he was in Sweden are noticeably similar in tone to the letters which Goering wrote while he was in Italy.

The contacts with Fascist officials which Goering made constitute an important chapter in Nazi-Fascist relations. It has long been known that in 1922 and 1923, Kurt Ludecke travelled to Italy and established contact with Mussolini. There is also reason to believe that Mussolini may have been involved in the Munich *Putsch* to the extent of providing financial support.[47] In the late 1920s and early 1930s there are numerous examples of close contact between leading members of both movements. But the period after the *Putsch*, between 1924 and 1925, has long been presumed to have been devoid of any demonstrable Nazi-Fascist relations. Goering's correspondence during his stay in Italy, including his references to Hitler's contact with Fascist agents, go a long way toward filling in this gap in the story of the relationship between the two movements. We also have a somewhat better idea of Mussolini's attitude toward the Nazis during one of their worst moments. The Duce's treatment of Goering is very consistent with the way he dealt with the Nazis throughout the years 1922-1933. Mussolini never really gave wholehearted support to the Nazis. Perhaps he feared that a Nazified Germany was bound to have an aggressive foreign policy that would ultimately be a threat to Italy. But he always felt it was in his interest to keep on good terms with a group that might one day be in power in Berlin.

Goering's stay in Italy probably had a noticeable effect on the Nazis' view of Fascist Italy. André Francois-Poncet, the knowledgeable French ambassador to Rome and Berlin in the 1930s, states that Hitler's admiration for Mussolini was largely based on the refuge offered to Goering after the Munich *Putsch*.[48] This is probably an exaggeration, but Goering's Italian exile was a step on the road that culminated in the Axis Alliance of the 1930s.

NOTES

1. For Goering's exile in Austria, see Kurt G. W. Ludecke, *I Knew Hitler* (New York, 1937), pp. 177-181; the letter sent by Carin from Innsbruck on November 13, 1923, is reproduced in her sister's book, viz. Fanny von Williamowitz-Moellendorf, *Karin Goering* (Berlin, 1934), pp. 68-69; NSDAP Hauptarchiv: reel 52/Folder 1225 Stanford University, California (hereafter cited as HA).

2. Friedelind Wagner, *Heritage of Fire* (New York, 1945), pp. 13-14. This story is confirmed in a personal letter by Frau Winifred Wagner to Ben E. Swearingen. The author would like to thank Mr. Swearingen for his kind permission to use the Goering-Negrelli Correspondence. Facsimiles of this collection of 16 letters and memoranda may be examined at the Library of the Graduate School and University Center of The City University of New York (hereafter cited as GNC).

3. Williamowitz-Moellendorf, p. 106. See biographies Charles Bewley, *Herman Goering and the Third Reich* (New York, 1962), p. 59; Leonard Mosley, *The Reich Marshal* (Garden City, 1974), p. 96; Roger Manvell and Heinrich Fraenkel, *Goering* (New York, 1962), p. 60. At least half a dozen other writers repeat the story that Goering met Mussolini at this time.

4. For additional information on Bastianini see T-586 [Mussolini's personal file] roll 1200 United States National Archives (hereafter cited as NA), Washington, D.C.

5. Giuseppe Bastianini, *Uomini, cose, fatti: Memorie di un ambasciatore* (Milan, 1959), pp. 147, 183; Renzo de Felice, *Hitler e Mussolini: i rapporti segreti 1922-1933* (Florence, 1975), p. 25.

6. GNC: Goering to Mussolini, September 1924.
7. In 1931-32, Walther, who was then a *Stahlhelm* leader in Venice, had serious economic problems. He was accused by the local Fascists of unethical business practices. Walther appealed to Goering for help but there is no evidence that he was ever repaid for allowing the Nazi exile and his wife to live at his hotel for over a year completely rent free. Letter from Stutzpunkt Venedig to Nieland, December 14, 1931, Kapfer to Nieland, March 5, 1932, NA: T-580 [no frame numbers in this series] roll 58; see also GNC: Goering to Negrelli, September 23, 1924.
8. For a typical example, see Mosley, p. 168.
9. Bastianini, p. 185; Williamowitz-Moellendorf, p. 93.
10. GNC: Goering to Negrelli, September 23, 1924.
11. GNC: Goering to Negrelli, October 15, 1924.
12. GNC: Goering to Negrelli, September 23, 1924.
13. GNC: Goering to Negrelli, October 15, 1924.
14. GNC: Goering to Negrelli, September 12, 1924.
15. GNC: Goering to Negrelli, September 19, 1924.
16. GNC: Goering to the Directorate of the Fascist Party, n.d.
17. Giuliano Cora, "Un diplomatico durante l'era Fascista," *Storia e Politica,* V (1966), pp. 90-91.
18. Report of March 1, 1925, HA: reel 85/1738.
19. GNC: Goering to Negrelli, September 19, 1924.
20. GNC: Goering to Negrelli, January 25, 1925, Goering memorandum November 1924, Report of May 25, 1925, HA: reel 85/1738.
21. GNC: Goering to Negrelli, October 15, 1924.
22. *I Documenti Diplomatici Italiani,* Commissione per le publicazioni (Rome, 1953); Series 7, Vol. I, no. 131 (hereafter cited as DDI); Ludecke, p. 135; *Il Corriere Italiano,* October 16, 1923.
23. Bastianini, p. 186.
24. GNC: Goering to Negrelli, n.d.
25. GNC: Goering to Negrelli, October 15, 1924.
26. GNC: Goering to Negrelli, January 25, 1925. Hoepke's assertion that Goering while in Italy helped arrange an invitation for Hitler is unfounded. Klaus-Peter Hoepke, *Die Deutsche Rechte und der Italienische Faschismus* (Düsseldorf, 1968), p. 314.
27. GNC: Goering to Negrelli, February 12, 1925.
28. DDI: Series 7, Vol. I, no. 131; vol. VII, nos. 412, 421. NA: T-586/491/050253, 050262-4.

29. de Felice, p. 127.
30. Munich police report, March 2, 1925, HA: reel 85/1738.
31. At about this time Mussolini told the Chief Rabbi of Rome that the Nazis were angry because he had refused to receive Hitler. Guido Bedarida, *Ebrei d'Italia* (Livorno, 1950), p. 10.
32. DDI Series 7, vol. III, nos. 39, 85.
33. *Voelkischer Beobachter,* July 7, 1925 (hereafter cited as VB); Adolph Dresler, *Mussolini* (Leipzig, 1924), p. 51.
34. DDI Series 7, vol. III, nos. 39, 85.
35. GNC: Goering to Negrelli, October 15, 1924.
36. GNC: Bastianini to Mussolini, February 1925.
37. Though not specified in Bastianini's memorandum, this tentative agreement probably included Fascist loans to the NSDAP, Nazi recognition of the Alto Adige, mutual press support, Italian promises of recognition of a new Hitler regime when it came, Nazi guarantees of reparations to Italy, Fascist neutrality on conflicts over the Treaty of Versailles imposed on Germany. GNC: Goering to Mussolini, September 1924.
38. GNC: Goering to Negrelli, February 14, 1925.
39. Benito Mussolini, *My Autobiography* (London, 1928), p. 236.
40. Mosley, p. 98; Williamowitz-Moellendorf, pp. 108-109. Mr. Swearington is an expert on Hitler's handwriting.
41. See cumulative police file, June 12, 1924. HA: reel 51/1225.
42. GNC: Goering to Negrelli, April 22, 1925.
43. VE: March 3, 1926.
44. VB: March 6, 1926.
45. Ibid.
46. VB: March 9, 1926.
47. See Michael Palumbo, "Mussolini and the Munich *Putsch*," in *Intellect,* January 1978.
48. André Francois-Poncet, *The Fateful Years* (New York, 9172), p. 238.

György Ránki

HITLER AND THE STATESMEN OF EAST CENTRAL EUROPE: 1939-1945*

After Germany's swift and successful campaign against Poland at the start of the Second World War in September 1939, Hitler turned his attention westwards and it appeared that his interest in the region of Southeastern Europe had lessened considerably. That was reflected in formalities too. There was a brief, quite unimportant protocoll meeting on October 21, 1939, with the speaker of the Hungarian Parliament, András Tasnády Nagy, and then for almost nine months, right up until July 10, 1940, Hitler received no other politician or statesman from the region at all. Of course there was a very simple reason for this apparent lack of interest: it was the very region in which he had promised a strong influence and interest to Italy, and he had no desire to disturb in any way an alliance that was still in its formative phase. One should also remember that his success in Poland had allowed Hitler to avert the danger of being involved in a war on two fronts. While he was tied down in the West, he strove, understandably, to avoid any kind of disturbance in his own backyard. Moreover the foodstuffs and strategic raw materials he needed from the region seemed to be arriving as expected, and the economic contracts forced through with the application of strong political pressure in 1939 operated without a hitch.

But in the summer of 1940 the situation changed in several ways. For one thing the Soviet Union made an attempt to use the new situation in order to settle the outstanding border disputes to her own advantage.

For another, Italy took the view that the increase of Germany's power and influence in the west ought to be balanced by an Italian surge towards the Balkans. The subject was broached by Ciano in July 1940 as follows:

> Bisher habe zwar auch Italien auf dem Standpunkt gestanden, dass der Balkan möglichst unberührt gelassen werden solle. Jetzt aber glaube der Duce, dass man in ungefähr einem Monat die jugoslawische Frage liquidieren müsse.
> Italien sei nun einmal am Adriatischen Meer sehr stark interessiert, während Rumänien und das Schwarze Meer mehr zum deutschen Interessengebiet gehören.

Thus the Italian foreign minister tried once again to clear the issue of spheres of interest.

The Führer saw things differently. Of course, he did not communicate to his chief ally that nothing was further from his thoughts than to approve such a division of spheres of interests. Instead he drew Italy's attention to the possible repercussions of an attack on Yugoslavia.

> Wenn Italien Jugoslawien angreife, so würde Ungarn sofort über Rumänien herfallen, da Ungarn ja dann nichts mehr von seinem jugoslawischen Nachbarn zu fürchten hätte. Bei einem Angriff Ungarns auf Rumänien würden aber zweifellos auch die Russen wieder lebendig werden, die Donau überschreiten und die Verbindung mit Bulgarien aufsuchen.
> So würden die Russen sicherlich auf ihr altes historisches Byzanz, die Dardanellen und Konstantinopel vorrücken. Es frage sich nun, wie Italien dazu stehe.

Ciano retreated quite speedily, and Hitler then reaffirmed orally the 1936 division of spheres of interests, which had recognized Italy's historical claims in the Mediterranean and the Adriatic. Given this situation, Italy postponed her attack on Yugoslavia. Hungary's claims against Romania, however, were not so easily removed from the agenda. It was decided therefore that the Hungarian prime minister, Pál Teleki, should be summoned to Berlin for joint discussions. The main aim (which will be cited again in another context) was to talk Hungary's bellicose politicians out of a military intervention and force them back into the diplomatic channel of negotiation.

In the course of his discussions with the Hungarians, Hitler never sketched Germany's interests in the region in any detail. All he did was to express his concern at the risk that armed conflict between Hungary and Romania might provide good grounds for interference in the region's affairs by the Soviet Union or Britain. Nevertheless, a few days later Hitler told the new Romanian prime minister that Germany's interests in the Balkans were not political but economic, and he repeated the arguments which had proved so effective in the 1930s:

> Ohne Deutschland gäbe es keine ausgeglichene kontinentale Wirtschaft. Das Deutsche Reich sei nicht nur ein grosser Lieferant— das seien andere Länder auch—, sonder als Konsument von entscheidender Bedeutung. Es wolle nicht nur exportieren, sondern auch seine eigenen Bedürfnisse befriedigen. Es sei daher der einzige für Rumänien und die Balkanländer wertvolle Wirtschaftsfaktor.

Germany's political interests extended as far as the Northwestern Carpathians (i.e., Slovakia). During the discussions Hitler returned to the point of her political disinterestedness, as opposed to the economic interests, on several occasions: "Wirtschaftlich sei Deutschland an allen Balkanländern interessiert, da diese für den Austausch zwischen Agrarprodukten, zu denen im Falle Rumänien noch das Öl hinzukomme, und Industrieprodukten für Deutschland geradezu ideale Handelspartner darstellten."

Naturally, by claiming that Germany's economic interests demanded the maintenance of the peace in the region, Hitler also had Germany's political interests in mind. Thus, although it was a blatantly political act to do so in return for certain territorial concessions towards Hungary and Bulgaria, Hitler agreed to guarantee Romania's borders.

The following day, Hitler's tone to the Bulgarian foreign minister was the same. He distorted the truth by saying that in the event of a war in the Balkans, Germany would not interfere even if Romanian oil supplies were jeopardized. A clearer picture of the economic aspects of German interests can be had from one of Hitler's table talks:

> Romania would do well to give up, as far as possible, the idea of having her own industry. She would direct the wealth of her soil, and especially her wheat, towards the German market. She would

receive from us, in exchange, the manufactured goods she needs. Bessarabia is a real granary. Thus the Romanian proletariat, which is contaminated by Bolshevism, would disappear, and the country would never lack anything.[1]

In Slovakia's case Hitler made no secret of the fact that a guarantee of Germany's economic interests would not suffice. He also had political concerns there, which were the results of military considerations. While on the subject of the strategic importance of the Carpathians, he mentioned reproachingly that certain countries were discoursing about thousand-year-old borders (i.e., Hungary) and thus threatening Slovakia's independence. He made it known that "der Gedanke einer unabhängigen Slowakei, ... Deutschland am Herzen liege." Hitler also clarified during the discussion what he meant by the guarantee he gave Slovakia. Having stationed German troops in Eastern Slovakia, and having forced the resignation of Interior and Foreign Minister Durčansky—who has been trying to salvage some freedom of monoeuvre in the new state's foreign policy— Hitler managed to have these two posts filled by two of his reliable supporters: by Sanyo Mach, the leader of the fascist Hlinka Guards, and by Prime Minister Adalbert Tuka. Two days earlier in Bratislava the German Ambassador had already made it clear that "Slovakia lies within our *Lebensraum*, which means that only our wishes are decisive."

Hitler was not thinking of an intergovernmental agreement; cooperation, he declared, should be rooted in the two peoples. In his view this meant that newspapers should not be allowed to write anything against Germany, that books criticizing National Socialism should not be published, and that public speeches of that nature should not be made. Germany was following Slovakia's domestic policy attentively, for Hitler was determined to "promote the cooperation of [these two] nations in the best possible way." Politicians who worked on behalf of that cooperation were to be supported, while those who entertained different views concerning Slovakia's relations to Germany were to be suppressed and removed.

After the Second Vienna Award (August 30, 1940) Germany's economic interest in the Balkans took on a far clearer form. At the beginning of September Hitler informed the Hungarian Ambassador Döme Sztójay of his decision to take the defense of the Romanian oilfields into his own hands. In the final months of 1940 Hitler repeatedly announced that Germany's interests in the Balkans were purely economic, even though German troops had been sent to Romania and it was more or less clear to everybody how matters stood. Another sign that Southeastern Europe was coming up on Hitler's agenda was the increasing emphasis in his discussions on the alleged danger from Russia, as is evident from the content of his remarks to Antonescu on November 22, 1940:

> Um diesen Plan in einem neuen Europa durchführen zu können, sei er [der Führer] entschlossen, so lange zu kämpfen, bis England endgültig vom Kontinent ausgeschaltet sei.
> In seinen Besprechungen mit Molotow habe er versucht, eine Neuorientierung der russischen Expansion herbeizuführen. Er habe jedoch Molotow keinen Zweifel darüber gelassen, dass es Deutschland mit seiner Garantie Rumänien gegenüber ernst meine....

Hitler also explained in relative detail how he imagined Germany's links with Romania and with the other countries in his *Grossraum Wirtschaft*. He promised long-term economic agreements under which Germany would accept all surplus agricultural products at fixed prices. The occasion for his talks with Antonescu was provided by Romania's accession to the Three Power Pact (i.e, the Berlin-Rome-Tokyo Axis). Since Hungary and Slovakia had already joined this military alliance, which had been signed by Germany, Italy and Japan on September 29, 1940, the German Chancellor now discarded his earlier stand and made it increasingly clear that he also wished to include Bulgaria and Yugoslavia into the Axis.

To the Bulgarians Hitler stressed the Russian danger, while in his discussions with the Yugoslavs he augmented his usual economic arguments by asserting that Germany had no territorial claims in the Balkans and that he himself was ready to defend Yugoslavia even against Germany's own ally, Italy. Hitler went so far as to promise the Greek city of Salonica to Yugoslavia, if the latter would only take sides with Germany. He made Bulgaria similar promises, asserting that their claims against Greece would be honored.

In February 1941 Hitler provided a further interpretation of German interests during his talks with the Yugoslav Prime Minister, Čvetković. He first laid particular emphasis on economic relations, which had played a major part in winning over the country which in the 1930s was still a member of the French-sponsored Little Entente. Hitler then pointed out that one difference between Britain's and Germany's policies was that it was in Germany's particular interest that "die europäischen Staaten von starken und national gesinnten Regimen getragen würden". And then he added: "Deutschland und Italien die autoritär gerichteten Kräfte der Ordnung unterstützen."

When Hitler finally forced Yugoslavia to join the Three Power Pact, he again asserted that he had no territorial claims on the region. The wording, however, was already different in that Hitler stated that he would not recall the German soldiers from the Balkans until the war had ended and all danger has passed. The danger that actually threatened the Balkans became manifest four days later, when Hitler ordered that Yugoslavia be crushed as a state and as a military force.

Hitler imagined that the new Croatian puppet régime he strove to consolidate would prevent the danger of the re-emergence of Yugoslavia, and that "dadurch...würde der Weg über den Balkan wieder versperrt...." As he explained to Ante Pavelić on September 24, 1942, "die Festigung des jetzigen kroatischen Regimes sei das beste Mittel, um die Notwendigkeit eines neuerlichen Kampfes zur Offenhaltung des Balkanweges zu vermeiden."

After the change in the course of the war, Hitler no longer mentioned his earlier ideas about Southeastern Europe. He focused instead on holding back his hesitant and intimidated allies and thus prevent them from seeking a separate peace with the British. His chief argument was the threat of Bolshevism. Again and again it proved to be his best card, particularly when he stressed that "Deutschland und seine Verbündeten sässen alle in einem Schiff." He liked to speak of Germany's altruism and self-sacrifice, claiming that his country became involved in the war with the Soviet Union largely to save the Balkan countries from the Soviet threat. He repeatedly asserted that the Balkan countries could only choose between Bolshevism and National Socialism.

In 1944 he returned on two occasions to the question of what the Balkan region represented to him. His monologue to Sztójay—according to the protocoll—runs as follows:

> Wenn wir den Krieg verlören, könnten wir uns zur Bekräftigung der deutsch-ungarischen Freundschaft an einem gemeinsamen Strick aufgängen; gewännen wir den Krieg—wovon der Führer fest überzeugt sei—, so hätten wir so viel zu tun, dass wir uns mit anderen Ländern nicht befassen könnten. Wir würden 200 Jahre brauchen, um die Gebiete, die dann an Deutschland fielen, nutzbar zu machen. Wir würden dazu auch die Wirtschaft des Balkans brauchen und müssten daher mit diesem zusammenarbeiten. Es werde eine Zeit kommen, wo kein Soldat und kein SD-Mann am Balkan und in Ungarn stehen würde, aber jeder gerechte Ungar werde dann sagen, dass die Befreiung und das Aufblühen Ungarns damals, als wir ins Land gekommen seien, begonnen habe.

A few weeks later Hitler defined his position to General Béla Miklós even more clearly:

> Wenn Ungarn ein Staat wäre, der an der Peripherie läge und an dem Deutschland daher kein Interesse habe, die Zustände, die in diesem Lande herrschten, völlig gleichgültig sein würden. Er mische sich ja auch nicht in die Verhältnisse in Irak und Afghanistan ein. Bezüglich Ungarns aber lägen die Verhältnisse anders. Träte dort eine Katastrophe ein, so bedeute dies gleichzeiti eine Katastrophe für den ganzen Balkan. Deutschland würde dann von Rumänien und dessen Ölfeldern sowie von weiteren Balkanländern abgeschnürt werden, die ihm wichtige Rohstoffe wie Mangan, Kupfer und dergleichen lieferten.... Als Steuermann des Schiffes "Europa" werde er [der Führer], solange ihn die Vorsehung am Leben erhalte, in jeder Hinsicht stets so handeln, wie er es vor seinem Gewissen für nötig befinde.... Daher sei er [der Führer] entschlossen, die mitteleuropäische Position unter allen Umständen zu halten. Er würde auch vor den energischsten Massnahmen nicht zurückschrecken.

Hitler was assisted in realizing his plans for Southeastern Europe by the constant quarrels between the small countries in the region. Diplomatically it was simple enough to exploit those differences. Germany could pose either as an upholder of order and justice, or as a protector of one country against another, as the circumstances demanded. It was the classic policy of divide and rule, by no means the newest or most repellent constituent of Hitler's barbarous mix of policy. Almost all the countries in the region were willing to compete for Germany's favors, whether overtly or tacitly, either with demeaning flattery or with a plain resignation that stemmed from a realistic acknowledgement of the unequal power relations. While stressing their own merits and fidelity, the competitors indulged in denunciations of their rivals. One can speculate on the political worth of a Croatian diplomat who could bring himself to utter these words:

> Der Führer sich nicht vorstellen könne, mit welcher Angänglichkeit das kroatische Volk zu ihm stünde. Man spreche dort nicht vom Führer und auch nicht von Adolf Hitler, sondern überall höre man nur den Ausdruck 'unser lieber Adolf.' Auch in einem Briefe, den er kürzlich von seinem Bruder bekommen habe, sei ihm diese Bezeichnung aufgefallen (February 14, 1942).

Hungary's Regent, Nicholas Horthy, whose negotiating manner was far more dignified, expressed his complaint during the highly critical discussions of 1943 as follows: "Ungarn nicht mehr das 'lieb Schosskind Deutschlands sei."

Let us consider briefly the series of occasions upon which conscious use was made of the quarrels and the flood of mutual accusations.

At talks with the Slovak ambassador in October 1939, Hitler deliberately reinforced Slovak awareness of the threat from Hungary by remarking that he himself had considered for a long time that Slovakia was part of the thousand-year-old kingdom of Hungary. Although his comments concerning Hungary's alleged oppression of her national minorities and about the evils of the system of large estates contained elements of truth, there were undoubtedly some foreign policy considerations behind his reference to the dangers of friendship between Hungary and Poland.

In his negotiations with the Hungarians Hitler said little about Slovakia, since he knew that in this case Romania was the main concern. In his talks with Tiso, however, he constantly pointed to the Hungarian danger that hangs like the sword of Damocles over the head of the Slovak politicians, who lacked political self-confidence and showed an obvious feeling of inferiority vis-à-vis the Hungarian leaders.

In 1943 Hitler declared that Germany would defend Slovakia against the Hungarians, and as such the Slovaks need have no fear of them so long as Germany existed. When Hitler was scolding the Hungarian leaders for failing to meet his demands in solving the Jewish question as the Slovaks had done, Tiso added to their problems by complaining to the German Chancellor about Hungary's treatment of the Slovaks. He was particularly upset about the number of Slovak soldiers in the Hungarian front lines, which, in his view, was disproportionately high.

Hitler came to the real point of his discussions with Tiso when he brought up the idea that a few German bayonets should be stationed in the Little Carpathians. This was simply a way of trying to justify the extention of the Slovak territories under German military occupation by pointing to the alleged dangers from Hungary.

In 1944 Tiso was extremely pleased to see Hungary occupied by the Germans. He declared it was an important strategic move that would bring Hungary political and social relief. He recalled that Hungary had sent no troops to the eastern front, or when she had, they had mainly been units recruited from her national minorities. The motive was Hungary's desire to save her strong army for the reconquest of former Hungarian territories. Now they would be forced by the Führer's measures to send real Hungarian divisions to the front.

Tiso also referred to the corruption of the Hungarian ruling classes, the Jews and the magnates, who, according to him, lived off the people. In Hitler's opinion,

> Ungarn sei dabei besonders anfällig für den Kommunismus. Dort unterjoche eine Oberschicht das Volk, das Horthy selbst gesprächsweise als "Zugvieh" bezeichnet habe. . . .
> Es sei kaum glaublich, wie viele Engländer, Amerikaner, Polen und sogar deutsche Emigranten wir in Ungarn jetzt verhaftet hätten. . . .
> Im übrigen übersähe Horthy ja die Lage selbst gar nicht, da er vollkommen in jüdische Interessen verstrickt sei.

Hitler was convinced that through Hungary's occupation he had produced a new situation, wherein the reluctant Hungarians would be forced to contribute more to the war effort. Or as he expressed it, "Jedenfalls müssten die Ungarn jetzt mehr leisten als im Ersten Weltkrieg, wo sie sehr wenig zu den gemeinsamen Anstrengungen Deutschlands und der österriechischen Reichshälfte beigetragen hätten."

Nonetheless, Slovakia was so much Hitler's own creation and so insignificant as an independent factor in the politics of the region that she could only play the part of a mere pawn on Hitler's chessboard in Southeastern Europe. He pursued the classic policy of divide and rule also in connection with the more significant Romanian-Hungarian relationship. But there the puppets—and both these countries had been more or less reduced to the role of puppets by the grip of German policy—at least struggled against being handled as puppets. They tried to retain as much of their independence and freedom for manoeuvre as they could.

In order to appreciate the historical significance of the Second Vienna Award, one has to realize that Hitler knew that a resolution of the Romanian-Hungarian tensions was indispensable, for these two countries were almost reaching the point of an open warfare. Hitler's aim was certainly not to find some kind of a just solution to the original problem, and he knew of the complex ethnic relations of the region. The Second Vienna Award, for example, failed to satisfy two-thirds of Hungary's claims to Transylvania, which, if carried through, would have raised disproportionately the Romanian population under Hungarian rule. But it did ensure the continuance of a policy fully loyal to Germany, both by Hungary and by Romania. The former, the territorial gainer, hoped for German support in defending her gains and in acquiring still more; while the latter, the territorial loser, feared further losses and hoped to regain what has been lost.

Although Hitler's sympathy for Hungary's claims was minimal, there were two reasons why he could not ignore them. For one thing, he could not appear as a defender of any border created by the Versailles Peace Treaty system, which had just been crushed; for another, despite his rapidly growing dissatisfaction with Hungarian policy and his utter lack of any political sentiment, he could not ignore the fact that Hungary had been politically cooperative ever since 1933, while the Romanians had only renounced the British guarantee of their borders on July 1, 1940. Moreover, not until the end of that July did the Romanians signal their readiness for a 180-degree turn towards Germany, both in their domestic and in their foreign policy. And, even though this Romanian action was far more than what the Hungarians had promised, Hitler was justifiably afraid that the importance his Hungarian ally attached to territorial revisions might mean that, in case of need, she would be prepared to act independently. Furthermore, this action may be implemented in spite of his stern warning to Hungary of the serious international consequences and dubious military outcome of any such deed.

The Second Vienna Award itself and the concomitant annexation to Hungary of a million Romanians (while about half a million Hungarians remained in Romanian territory) created a hotbed of constant tensions and the chance for Hitler to continue to play one country off against the other and also interfere into their affairs. A few days later, the narrow-minded vengefulness of the licentious Hungarian soldiery made matters even worse. To the surprise and dismay of Prime Minister Teleki and his government, the Hungarian army units committed a number of atrocities during their march into northern Transylvania.

Germany's attitude to the Second Vienna Award was expressed most clearly by Ribbentrop's remark to the Bulgarian Prime Minister Bossilov. The conflict between Romania and Hungary was naturally discussed during their talks, with particular attention to the mutual accusations the representatives of the two countries kept making to the Germans. Hitler scornfully described their policy in an old Viennese saying: "Hold me back, or I'll do something that'll lead to a calamity." The Bulgarian foreign minister poked fun at the Romanian and Hungarian ambassadors in Sofia, who watched like hawks, lest the foreign minister's talks with one should last a minute longer than his talks with the other. Ribbentrop's response to this was the following witty remark; "Der Schiedsspruch sei beiden Parteien gerecht geworden. Dies habe sich bei seiner Verkündung ergeben, bei der der rumänische Aussenminister in Ohnmacht fiel und der ungarische Aussenminister seinen Rücktritt erklären wollte."

The Romanian question was not so dominant in the minutes of Hitler's talks with Hungarian politicians as the Hungarian question was in his talks with Romania. This was so in part because fewer minutes of the former have survived, and in part because the Hungarian politicians appear to have behaved with more circumspection, at least until 1944. Altogether one finds only two Hungarian remarks that definitely denounce Romania; and only one of them—the remark made by Bárdossy at talks on March 21, 1941—give expression to Hungary's hopes for further territorial gains:

> Der ungarische Aussenminister versicherte, dass für die ganze ungarische Nation die Treue zu Deutschland eine ganz besondere Bedeutung habe. Ungarns Platz sei an der Seite Deutschlands, im jetzigen Kriege sowie in der Zukunft, und zwar aus geopolitischen gefühlsmässigen, geistigen und wirtschaftlichen Gründen. Besonders dankbar sei er für die Zusicherung des Führers, dass sich Ungarn, wenn es in eine schwierige Lage geriete, um Hilfe an das Reich wenden könne.
> Bezüglich des Wiener Schiedsspruchs sagte Herr von Bárdossy, dass man in Ungarn wohl begreife, dass eine Kompromisslösung nötig war. Ungarn wolle jetzt nicht daran rütteln, hoffe aber, das später einmal eine Änderung zugunsten Ungarns eintreten werde, die auch aus wirtschaftlichen Gründen für Deutschland von Interesse sein dürfte. Im übrigen betonte er mehrfach, dass Ungarn eine nützliche Rolle für Deutschland als "Vermittlerland nach Süden" spielen könne.

With this statement Bárdossy confirmed the political aim Hungary had been pursuing since the autumn of 1940. He defined Hungary's part in the German system of alliances in Southeastern Europe as one of *primus inter pares*.

Whereas Bárdossy made his remarks at a time when Germany was victorious, Horthy expressed his views on April 16, 1943, when the Germans were already in retreat. As such, Horthy's remarks are much more cautious:

> ...es ihm fern läge, gegen Rumänien bohren zu wollen, dass er aber doch im Verlauf dieses Gesprächs etwas "in die Hinterland" geraten sei und daher ein Schreiben eines pensionierten Rittmeisters aus Siebenbürgen verlesen wolle, das immerhin interessante Aufschlüsse über die Zustände in Rumänien gebe.—In dem dann verlesenen Brief wurde ein Äusserung des rumänischen Königs wiedergegeben, wonach dieser erklärt habe, dass alles was bisher geschehen sei und noch geschehen würde, auf Rechnung Antonescus gehe. Der König bleibe im Hintertreffen. Es würde jedoch der Augenblick kommen, wo er das Land in Richtung seiner natürlichen Gefühle führen würde.

Horthy had just heard a long tirade from Hitler on the unreliability of Hungarian foreign policy and of her peace feelers towards the West, and undoubtedly he wanted to divert the suspicion of unreliability from

Hungary onto Romania. The aged Regent was not to know that a few days earlier Hitler had presented a similar list of grievances to Antonescu, although in a milder tone. In his discussions with Horthy Hitler laid the blame on Prime Minister Kállay, while in his talks with Antonescu he accused the latter's deputy, Mihai Antonescu. In fact the main theme of the negotiations with the Romanians was the threat from Hungary—the purpose being to strengthen the Romanian leader's belief that the war they were fighting on the German side would bring its rewards. Hitler tried to impress upon Antonescu that Germany increasingly regarded Romania as a good and reliable ally, and that on the Transylvanian question her sympathies were more and more on Romania's side and not on Hungary's.

The Romanian leaders, in the person of Antonescu, fought with blind eagerness for the position of being Germany's "Number One Satellite." They made enormous military sacrifices on the Soviet front, never losing an opportunity to refer to the truly amazing number of their troops, and to remark on the far less significant Hungarian contribution. In one way or another they blamed Hungary for her relative leniency to the Jews and her secret talks with the western powers, and also urged Hitler openly to occupy that country, and even offered assistance for this occupation. In spite of all these efforts, however, all the Romanians could achieve toward their longed-for goal was to get Hitler to declare—at least verbally—that the Second Vienna Award was invalid. Hitler also fed them with fond hopes of the return of the territories they sought.

This is a sad and astonishing story indeed. During discussions with Gigurtu, a Romanian politician considered less reliable than Antonescu, Hitler explained that the territorial concessions by Romania could not have been avoided. Alluding to a possible German guarantee of Romania's borders, Hitler distanced himself from the exaggerated Hungarian references to the thousand-year-old borders of the Kingdom of St. Stephen, and declared that "Derartige Dinge natürlich unmöglich seien, da Deutschland bei Anlegung eines ähnlichen Massstabes z.B. erklären könne, es habe einmal bis nach Sizilien gereicht, während die Ansprüche Italiens auf Grund des Römischen Reiches noch weitere sein würden."

After the Vienna Awards the right-wing turn in Romania and Antonescu's introduction of a fascist military dictatorship, the tone quickly changed.

When the introductory visit had been made and the difficulties of making acquaintance had been overcome, Antonescu became the ally Hitler estimated most highly. His esteem was shown in the support he gave in January 1941 to Antonescu and the army, rather than to the Fascist Party, when the Iron Guard rebelled. (By and large Germany's policy was similar in the other allied countries as well. In Hungary for instance German support was transferred to Szálasi only when Horthy became thoroughly difficult to deal with.) The same esteem was demonstrated in the growing frequency of visits and the increasing length of discussions. Antonescu was the first foreigner to receive Germany's highest military decoration from Hitler and to be put in supreme command of German army units. Of course, once Antonescu had assured Hitler of his admiration and his faith, and explained how all the aspects of the Romanian policy previously unsatisfactory to Berlin had been the work of the Bolsheviks and the Jews, he always brought the conversation back to his grievances against Hungary. The brutality and undeniable atrocities by the Hungarian Army, which had driven many Romanians out of Northern Transylvania, provided a good basis for complaints, but he handled the figures absolutely arbitrarily. His historical justification consisted of the well-known arguments of Romanian chauvinism. He talked of the Romanians' 2000-year long fight against the Slavs, Tatars and Hungarians, and stressed that Hungary's claims lacked both ethnic and historical foundations. In Antonescu's view, Transylvania had only been part of Hungary for 50 years (i.e., from the Austro-Hungarian Compromise of 1867 to the end of the empire in 1918), and the Seklers (Székelys) were not Hungarians at all.

Hitler paid no particular attention to the arguments, remarking that not long since he had listened to a similar lengthy presentation of the Hungarian case. But he was an astute enough politician to add that he could understand Antonescu's anger and sorrow, and that history would not after all come to an end in 1940. The next discussion, in February 1941, was mainly concerned, from Antonescu's point of view, with events at home. Hitler was presumably concerned largely with his Barbarossa Plan, and therefore Hungary was relegated into the background. But Antonescu still complained about the way the Romanian minority was being handled and about the expulsion of Romanians from

Northern Transylvania. Hitler on his part took note of the strange Hungarian behavior and said that he was glad he had managed to get Hungary to allow German military transports through the country. But he also added that within the given circumstances he still lacked the necessary means to influence the Hungarians on matters of interest to Romania. It seems that at the next two rounds of negotiations, which took place right before the attack on the Soviet Union and in the flush of the first victories after the reoccupation of Bessarabia, Hungary was not on the agenda, at least not to an extent that would show up in the summary minutes.

All the more important, therefore, was an element in the talks with the Romanian Deputy Prime Minister Mihai Antonescu on November 28, 1941. Referring to the Hungarian attacks and frontier violations, Mihai Antonescu declared that they might disturb Romania's internal security and ability to resist. Then, as summarized by the protocoll officer, "Er spielte...auf die Möglichkeit einer engeren Verbindung zwischen Rumänien, Bulgarien, der Slowakei und Kroatien an und bat den Führer, Rumänien zu raten, ob er eine solche Verbindung eingehen solle oder nicht."

So the idea of restoring the old Little Entente under German patronage was clearly raised. But at the time Hitler was too preoccupied with the Soviet Union to wish to concentrate on the Romanian-Hungarian differences. It appeared he would rather have defused the matter by offering further Russian territories at a time when, in Ribbentrop's phrase, Hungarian-German relations were "enjoying their honeymoon".[2] Then he added:

> Im Osten jedoch hätten sowohl Rumänien als auch Deutschland riesige Gebiete zu besiedeln. Rumänische und deutsche Interessen träfen sich hier und zwängen zu biologischen Entschlüssen, d.h. auch Rumänien müsse im Interesse der Erhaltung dieser neuerworbenen Gebiete möglichst viel eines Volkstum hineingeben, und zwar bis an die äusserste Grenze dieser neuen Gebiete.

But Hitler went even further in his hints to Romania. As noted in the protocoll book, "der Führer würde es durchaus verstehen, wenn ausser der Wiederherstellung seiner alten Grenze Rumänien noch ein entsprechendes, zur Sicherung notwendiges Vorland und Odessa beansprüchte."

After the first serious German defeats, the tone in which relations with Hungary were discussed in Romanian-German negotiations were also altered. In February 1942 Antonescu became more and more aggressive towards Hungary. In most instances he cited similar Hungarian measures, and demanded that Germany should take sides officially. To buttress his arguments, he pointed out that "Rumänien für den gemeinsamen Krieg bisher 200 Milliarden Lei ausgegeben und 700 000 Mann mobilisiert habe."

Antonescu described the Romanian losses as follows: 5,400 officers, i.e., 25% of the staff, and 130,000 men, i.e., 23% of all those serving in the ranks; and given the "correct" German attitude on Transylvania, he was even willing to offer more: "Mit der wieder aufgefüllten und neu ausgerüsteten rumänischen Armee stehe er [Antonescu] dem Führer jederzeit zur Verfügung, und er sei bereit, bis zum Kaukasus und auch bis zum Ural zu marschieren."

But what was Hungary doing in the meantime? While the Romanians were increasing their wheat and oil deliveries, Hungary—so claimed Antonescu—was constantly threatening Romania. Speaking on behalf of the Romanian people, he demanded that Hungary be made to contribute her share to the efforts in the common war; and if she did not, then the proper conclusions should be drawn. He was willing to place a million men at the disposal of the Germans, but he wanted guarantees that neither then, nor after the war, would Hungary be favored over Romania.

Hitler tried to soothe Antonescu by giving the desired historical interpretation to the events, by shelving his critical remarks about earlier Romanian policy, and by stressing the prime importance of the war against the Soviet Union. He said the purpose of Ribbentrop's and Keitel's recent visit to Budapest had been to persuade the Hungarians to make greater sacrifices of manpower to the war, and it would seem they had succeeded. Quite clearly that did not satisfy Antonescu, because he continued to press his point by summarizing once more Romania's sacrifices in the war:

> Er sprach von 40 000 Toten, von denen 2000 Offiziere gewesen seien und von 110 000 Verletzten, von der Inflationsgefahr und

> Staatsausgaben von insgesamt 34 000 000 Lei sowie davon, dass von einer Gesamtproduktion von 5 3000 000 Tonnen Petroleum 3 900 000 Tonnen an die "Achsenländer" exportiert worden seien, und behauptete, dass 80% der gesamten Petroleumausfuhr nach Deutschland und den Achsenländern gegangen seien. Ebenso seien 90% des Aussenhandels in dieser Richtung verlaufen... Das Volk habe jedes Opfer auf sich genommen, um den Sieg über die Russen zu erringen:
>
> Die Tatsache, dass sich Ungarn so bei seiner Mitwirkung im Kriege zurückhielte, erfülle Rumänien mit ernster Sorge für die Zeit nach dem Kriege, besonders, da auch Bulgarien militärisch vom Kriege unberührt sei.

Hitler tried to calm him down by promising that "was in seiner [des Führers] Macht stehe, die Ungarn dazu zu bewegen, sich ganz anders als bisher am Krieg zu beteiligen, würde geschehen." He also assured Antonescu that he would be sending Bulgarian troops for occupation duties to Serbia, and thereby lessen the threat to Romania.

The conversation after dinner centered around the same problem. Antonescu again claimed that Hungary was taking too small a part in the war, and requested guarantees from Hitler that the Hungarians would not be permitted to do anything against Romania. Hitler repeated several times that Hungary would be taking a full part in the war in the future, and that if she did not fulfill her promise, which he could scarcely believe, he would warn them that there would be serious consequences.

A good six months later, in September 1942, Antonescu was again given an audience by Hitler at the latter's headquarters. It seemed the star of Hitler's forces was in the ascendancy once more. The latest offensive had proved successful. German soldiers were fighting in the streets of Stalingrad, and the fall of the city appeared imminent. In light of this expectation a German-Romanian agreement had been prepared for the period after the occupation of the city. Under this agreement the German and Romanian troops stationed between the river Volga and Astrakhan would be consolidated into a single army command, which would be assigned as a special token of Hitler's confidence to Antonescu himself. During those days Antonescu again mentioned the huge military efforts being expanded by the Romanians and the sacrifices they were making for the common cause. It seemed the investment was yielding a profit. Moreover, the Hungarian Army was now stationed along the river Don, not far from the Romanians.

The next discussion took place in an atmosphere of greater tension than ever before. It was the time of the Stalingrad débacle, after the collapse of the 3rd and 4th Romanian armies. The Romanian leader was in a state of shock from the military defeat when Hitler began applying new pressures on him to allow the former Iron Guard leader Horia Sima—who received asylum in Germany after the failed coup of January 1941—to escape to Italy. Antonescu took that to be an indication that Hitler intended to give his future support to the Iron Guard. Having cleared up that anxiety, Hitler went on to criticize the attitude of the Romanian troops. Antonescu replied in kind by criticizing Germany's command and troops, who quite probably treated the withdrawing Romanian soldiers at least as badly as they did the remnants of the 2nd Hungarian Army. At the following meeting Hitler hardly let Antonescu get in a word and monopolized the entire conversation.

On April 12 and 13, 1943, two very critical conversations took place. Hitler brought up the same subject he had broached with Horthy a few days later, i.e. peace feelers and talks aimed at pulling out of the war. He gave a lengthy and detailed list of the German secret service's reports on the subject, against which Antonescu defended himself at length, declaring the reports false and attempting to prove his loyalty by citing again Romania's many sacrifices. According to the minutes no mention was made of Hungary, but it certainly was not fortuitous that Hitler's historical summary contained remarks concerning Germany's earlier exertions on behalf of European Civilization against such eastern invaders as the Huns, the Hungarians and the Turks. The word "Hungarian" was, of course, omitted from the otherwise almost verbatim version addressed to Horthy a week or so later.

Alongside the military events on the eastern front, the fall of Mussolini and the death of King Boris of Bulgaria were the dominant themes at the talks on September 7, 1943. These events dominated the discussion to such a degree that Hungary was not dealt with at all. Moreover, Antonescu used the occasion to lay a few traps for his southern neighbor, saying that if Russian troops landed, the Bulgarians would change sides immediately. Moreover, as far as he knew it had been stated by a high ranking official that the Bulgarian Army would not fight either if the British landed in the Balkans.

One would expect that in the war's final phase, when almost each one of Germany's allies saw its sole hope of avoding a national catastrophe by means of a separate peace with the Western powers (in pursuit of which they continued their endeavors to score points off each other), Hitler would no longer be able to consolidate his hold on the region by exploiting the differences between Hungary and Romania. But he managed to do so nonetheless. In fact, the carrot of Northern Transylvania proved effective in keeping Antonescu on his side, and turning him from a mere supporter into the direct instigator of Hungary's occupation by Germany. Antonescu was even prepared to take part in that occupation. Hitler, however, wanted no actual Romanian participation (which would clearly have been counterproductive), but only a promise to participate. He was certain that such a promise alone would be an effective enough threat with which to blackmail the Hungarians. On February 26, 1944, in contradiction to his previous practice, Hitler was the one to raise the Hungarian issue. At the end of their conversation, he casually mentioned that he had received a letter from Horthy requesting that Hungary's troops be withdrawn from the Soviet front.

Antonescu latched onto the topic eagerly. The Hungarians, he said, were wholly unreliable and Hitler should handle them more severely. That Hitler promised to do.

Afterwards Antonescu barraged Ribbentrop with a flood of complaints against the Hungarians. As summarized in the minutes:

> Er wies darauf hin, dass die Ungarn nach 1919 sofort auf die englische Seite übergeschwenkt seien, um auf diese Weise ihre Revisionsforderungen durchzusetzen, und dann 1935 wieder auf die deutsche Seite zurückgegangen seien. Wenn Ungarn als kleines Land es jetzt wage, in einem Schreiben des Reichsverwesers an den Führer offen die Zurückziehung sämtlicher ungarischer Truppen in das Mutterland zu verlangen, so bedeute dies nach seiner Ansicht, dass Ungarn von der Gegenseite bereits irgendwelche Zusicherungen erhalten haben müsse. Die Forderung der Feinde, die Truppen von der Front zurückzuberufen, sei auch ihm, Antonescu, zugeleitet worden. Er habe sie mit einer glatten Ablehnung und einem schriftlichen "Niemals" beantwortet.... Die Forderung nach Zurückziehung ihrer Truppen käme doch eigentlich einer Aufkündigung des Bündnisses gleich.
>
> Daher müsse man gegen Ungarn einschreiten, und zwar möglichst bald, da bei einer etwaigen Verschlimmerung der Lage an der Ostfront ein unsicheres Ungarn im Rücken zu einer ausserordentlichen Gefahr werden könne.

Urging the occupation of Hungary, Antonescu again promised "eine Million rumänischer Soldaten für den Kampf zur Verfügung stünden, wenn einmal die ungarische Gefahr beseitigt sei."

Unfortunately the minutes of the meeting between Hitler and Horthy at Klessheim on March 18, 1944 have not survived. Most of what we know about the meeting comes from indirect sources, such as the four versions of Horthy's report, the notes he made at Szombathely, Ribbentrop's testimony at the Nuremberg trial, the memoires of Paul Schmidt, Hitler's interpreter, the war diary of the German Army and the German Foreign Ministry's documents on the direct preparation and execution of the occupation of Hungary.

What occurred is clear. Horthy finally submitted to the fact of the occupation, remained in office and appointed the puppet government the Germans demanded. He stated that a major fact in his decision was his assumption that he would be able to retain command of the Hungarian Army and prevent Antonescu's troops from taking part in the occupation.

So the Hungarians and the Romanians seem to have been played off against each other in a masterly fashion once again. Yet Antonescu's narrow-mindedness had still not reached the ultimate. On March 23, partly because of the new military successes by the Red Army, and partly because of the changed situation in Hungary, Hitler summoned the Romanian general to still more talks. He briefed Antonescu about events in Hungary, and said it was still unclear what direction the occupation of Hungary would take. But in all events, he asserted, "es liege im gemeinsamen Interesse Deutschlands und seiner Verbündeten, wenn mit einem Minimum an eigenem Einsatz ein Maximum an Wirksamkeit erzielt werde."

Then in a private conversation Hitler told Antonescu:

> Nach der illoyalen Haltung der ungarischen Regierung und nachdem sowohl Rumänien als auch Ungarn sich den Wiener Schiedsspruch innerlich nie zu eigen gemacht hätten und nachdem Italien jetzt ausgefallen sei, halte es Deutschland nich für angebracht, weiterhin als Signator des Wiener Schiedsspruches zu fungieren. Er [der Führer] bäte Antonescu, die vorgenannte Erklärung zunächst niemandem gegenüber zu erwähnen; im gegebenen Augenblick würde er [der Führer] sie öffentlich abgeben. Zunächst aber liege es im deutschen wie in rumänischen Interesse zu versuchen, einen Partisanenkrieg in

Ungarn zu vermeiden; denn es sei jede deutsche Division wertvoll, die in Ungarn nicht gebraucht würde und an die Front geschickt werden könne.

Aontonescu grasped the opportunity to vent his anger against Hungary. He delivered a lengthy speech on disloyalty, which he himself as a man of war despised. He commented that even though Hungary owed everything to Germany, her disloyalty was something to be expected; for as he (Antonescu) always asserted: "er zu Ungarn auch nicht das geringste Vertrauen habe, weil dort nicht das ungarische Volk die Geschicke des Landes bestimme, sondern die Politik von den Juden gemacht werde. Das sei früher wie heute so gewesen und würde auch in Zukunft so bleiben."

Antonescu warned Hitler against leaving an armed enemy intact, for at any given moment such an enemy might attack from the rear. So in his view the sooner the Hungarian Army was disarmed, the better for Germany and her allies. Having repeatedly expressed his gratitude for the announcement about Northern Transylvania, he stressed once again how unreliable the Hungarian leadership was, attributing this to the Hungarian nobility's intermarriage with Jews and Anglo-Saxons. In his words: "Die ungarischen Adligen seien grösstenteils mit Jüdinnen oder reichen Engländerinnen und Amerikanerinnen verheiratet; sie würden nur für ihren persönlichen Besitz kämpfen. Dabei sie zu allem fähig."

Hitler mentioned his own reservations about the new Hungarian Government, but he pointed out that:

> der Vorteil, den das Bestehen einer solchen Regierung jedoch mit sich brächte, läge darin, dass die Ungarn selbst im Lande ihre eigene Verwaltung weiterarbeiten liessen und dass nicht etwa Deutschland als Besatzungsmacht gezwungen sei, einen ganz neuen Verwaltungsapparat aufzuziehen, wozu im natürlich schon rein personalmässig die Kräfte fehlen würden. Ausserdem sei es wichtig, dass die ungarische Wirtschaft weitergehe. Mehr erwarte er nicht von der jetzigen Regierung. An einen Einsatz der ungarischen Armee glaube er [der Führer], wie gesagt, nicht.[3]

Antonescu, in turn, informed Hitler that according to reliable sources Hungary had concluded a secret agreement with the Russians that as soon as the Soviet Army had reached the Carpathians and Galicia, the Hungarian forces would allow them to cross the country, thus enabling them to link up with Tito's forces. He then began denouncing the Bulgarians, saying that they were Slavs too, and so could not be relied on. Moreover the Bolsheviks exerted a great influence in the country. They had diplomatic relations with the Russians and were on good terms with the Hungarians as well. In the course of the next few days' talks Antonescu pointed out again that Romania would be able to carry out a total mobilization of her forces against the Soviet Union once she had received proper guarantees against Hungary.

Hiter announced that Transylvania was to be declared a field of operations and that all Hungarian troops would be withdrawn. Antonescu was very pleased to hear so and reaffirmed the willingness of his troops to fight on Hitler's side against the Hungarians. He made certain anti-Hungarian suggestions concerning Transylvania:

> Ausserdem machte er den Vorschlag, die rumänischen Flüchtlinge aus Ungarisch-Siebenbürgen, die sich jetzt in Rumänien aufhielten wieder nach Ungarisch-Siebenbürgen zurückkehren zu lassen, da sie bei einem etwaigen Ausbruch eines Partisanenkrieges wirksam als rumänische Partisanen gegen ungarische Partisanenbanden eingesetzt werden könnten.

He urged that the Hungarian troops be compelled at all costs to withdraw from Northern Transylvania so as to prevent them from retreating into the mountains and becoming free troops that would endanger the communication lines of the Romanian Army.

But the new circumstances—the continued existence of the Hungarian Army and the deployment of Hungarian troops on the Soviet front—meant that Hitler only kept his promise in part. Although the majority of the troops of the 1st Hungarian Army sent to the front had been stationed in Transylvania, the withdrawal of the entire Hungarian armed forces from Northern Transylvania never took place.

Afterwards events speeded up and the subject was never broached again. At Antonescu's next and all but last meeting with Hitler (August 5, 1944) pressing military considerations pushed the Hungarian problem well into the background, although a short remark of Antonescu's is not without interest. The Romanian head of state again expressed his reservations about Hungary's willingness to continue the fight against Russia: "Sollten dort die Russen einbrechen und über Siebenbürgen nach Rumänien vorstossen, läge ihnen das Land völlig offen, da die gesamte rumänische Armee im Osten stünde." He also reassured Hitler once more about his and Romania's loyalty to the Reich: "Im übrigen sei kein Verbündeter Deutschlands so loyal wie Rumänien. Es würde an Deutschlands Seite bleiben und das letzte Land sein was das Reich verliesse."

Within scarcely three weeks after this meeting, events belied Antonescu. On August 23 Romania successfully extricated herself from the war and by and large the Hungarian Army was the one that found itself in the sort of situation Antonescu had warned against in the event of a pull-out by the Hungarians.

Contrary to the Romanians, Croatian political leaders were far too engaged in combating their internal problems and the growing partisan movement to make much of their relations with Hungary and of the territorial disputes during their talks with Hitler.

Croatia was the only country against which Horthy and his government did not press Hungary's territorial claims. On March 27, 1941, when Hitler suddenly decided to launch military operations against Yugoslavia, he wanted to gain Hungary's support. Obliquely he had promised Croatia to Hungary, and all he was thinking of was to give Croatia a measure of autonomy. At the same time he also promised Hungary some kind of corridor to the sea. But when two days later Sztójay deliverd Horthy's assent to the attack against Yugoslavia, he also pointed out that: "Ungarn kein Interesse an Kroatien habe und dieses Land nicht innerhalb seiner Grenzen aufnehmen wolle." Hitler on his part was intent on abolishing Yugoslavia and had no intention of setting up a sovereign Croatian state. Thus, he continued to urge the two states to establish at least some kind of fraternal union, involving a measure of economic cooperation. But Sztójay only repeated his government's lack of interest in Croatia, while at the same time emphasizing Hungary's wish for an outlet to the Adriatic Sea. He then pointed out that there were no real conflicts between Hungary and Croatia, or if there were any these could only stem from machinations by Belgrade.

The German troops soon occupied Belgrade, and Yugoslavia—with which Hungary had just signed an agreement of eternal friendship—ceased to exist. The leader of the Croatian fascist movement, Ante Pavelić, whom Hitler had chosen to head the "independent" Croatian state, seemed to have little sympathy for Hungary. This was true even though a few years earlier several *ustasha* terrorists had received asylum in Hungary. Moreover, in the critical hours in the spring of 1941, it was the Hungarians who had proposed the establishment of an independent Croatia to be headed by Pavelić. The reasoning behind this was the Hungarian political leaders' belief that this would release Hungary from her obligations embodied in the agreement of eternal friendship with Yugoslavia.

But Pavelić, at his first audience with Hitler, announced he had territorial differences with Hungary over the Muraköz region, and he did not omit to identify the Hungarian territorial claims with the Jews: "Von jüdischer ungarischer Seite würde alles in Bewegung gesetzt, damit dieses Gebiet an Ungarn falle."

Finally, what did Hitler really think of Hungary, the Hungarians and of Horthy himself? It is instructive to reread the text of the talks with this question in mind, even though the story is incomplete. After all, the links between Germany and Hungary were not produced solely by the war years. Indeed Hungary between 1933 and 1938 was one of the countries upon which Hitler could most rely. This was true mostly for reasons of foreign policy. Hungary's policy of revisionism was closest to Hitler's own policy, and Hungary often gave significant assistance to him in the pursuance of Germany's plan for Southeastern Europe. But a similarity in policy does not necessarily mean an agreement on its implementation. One can hardly describe German-Hungarian relationships as altruistic. Even though ideological affinity and similarities in the two political systems did play a part in it, the actual momentum was provided primarily by the identity of foreign policy interests—whether putative or real, short or long-term.

By 1938 the honeymoon was over. In the summer of 1938 the Hungarians were unwillikng to commit themselves unconditionally to a military attack upon Czechoslovakia, which annoyed Hitler extremely. He also took it amiss that, although Hungary had realized before the Munich talks that she had nothing to fear from Britain and quickly ranged herself on Germany's side, she was disinclined to bear the brunt by risking the first attack when Hitler proposed she should do so. In the same year two other matters fouled an already worsening atmosphere. The Hungarians were far from satisfied with the results of the First Vienna Award and said so openly in the press, in parliamentary speeches, and on various other public occasions. Moreover, in November 1938 they prepared an unexpected and secret military plan for the occupation of Carpatho-Ruthenia (Sub-Carpathian Ukraine), and only abandoned it at the last minute under strong pressure from Germany.

In January 1939 the Hungarian Foreign Minister Csáky tried to remedy everything at the German-Hungarian discussions, and his words were soon followed up by actions. These included a new anti-Jewish law, adherence to the Anti-Comintern Pact, withdrawal from the League of Nations, and fulfillment of Germany's economic demands. The Germans then declared their readiness to open a new page in the history of German-Hungarian relations, but it was not long before the Hungarian Government managed to collect a few more black marks on the new page. One of the gravest matters was Prime Minister Teleki's letter informing Hitler that, although Hungary stood by Germany and the Axis for moral reasons, she was disinclined to partake in the campaign against Poland, which had friendly relations with Hungary. While this letter was subsequently withdrawn, and once the Second World War had broken out Hungary—at Germany's request—declared herself a "non-belligerent" rather than a "neutral" country, the affair was never forgotten. This was all the more so, as Germany was collecting additional black marks against Hungary in connection with the Polish campaign. On September 7 Ribbentrop unexpectedly asked his Hungarian counterpart on the phone to allow German troops to pass along one of the northern rail lines so as to be able to attack the withdrawing Polish forces in the rear. After consulting Mussolini and gaining his support, the Hungarian Government refused. It later became clear that the move would have brought no military advantage to Germany, and one cannot help thinking the request was only made in order to exert pressure on the Hungarian Government. Yet, the refusal could not just be swallowed. Nor could the fact that, in spite of vehement German protest, about 150,000 defeated Polish soldiers were granted refuge in Hungary. Some of them actually stayed in the country throughout the war, although the majority did flee to the West and formed the core of the Free Polish Army there.

In light of the above, one can understand Hitler's unusually critical and unfriendly attitude toward Hungarian policies. To Hungarian politicians he made scarcely any remarks about Romanian policy (after 1940), nor about Bulgarian, Croatian or Slovak politicians. At the same time, criticism of Hungarian policy and Hungarian politicians was a constant subject at his conversations with Antonescu, Tiso and Pavelić.

As early as October 21, 1939 he told the Slovak Ambassador Černak that Polish-Hungarian friendship derived from the relations of the ruling magnates in the two nations. The ruling classes in both countries ruthlessly exploited their fellow countrymen and had no sense of social responsibility whatsoever. This interpretation of Polish-Hungarian relations, in which there was a grain of somewhat distorted truth, appeared time and again in Hitler's statements.

In the summer of 1941 he expressed criticism of the Hungarian feudal system to Kvaternik and concluded that it formed the basis of the strong Hungarian sympathy for the Poles and the British. In both those countries the land and the economy were in the hands of a small ruling class.

> The Hungarians have always been *poseurs*. In war they are like the British and the Poles; war to them is an affair which concerns the Government and to which they go like oxen to slaughter. They all wear swords, but have none of the earnest chivalry which the bearing of a sword should imply.[4]

That Hitler's views about the Hungarians did not change during the war, is evident from his remarks to Tiso on May 12, 1944:

> Bemerkenswert sei auch, dass England, Polen und Ungarn eine führende Schicht mit grossen Ambitionen besässen, die aber durchaus asozial sei. Horthy habe Sympathien für die Engländer und Polen, aber nicht etwa für das Volk, sondern nur für die gleiche Gesellschaftsschicht. Alle hätten ihr Geld aus dem Volke gesogen und in Paris verjubelt.

In the same vein he informed Gigurtu that it was the Hungarian Jews who were backing the endeavors of the wildest Transylvanian revisionists. Almost simultaneously, in his discussions with Filov in the summer of 1940 he emphasized Hungary's apparent lack of gratitude after the First Vienna Award.

After the Second Vienna Award Hitler immediately criticized Hungary's policy toward the national minorities to Sztójay, with particular attention to the Germans. He also warned the Hungarian ambassador, with obvious references to the future: "Behandeln Sie die Deutschen gut!"

When trying to persuade Cincar-Marković, the Yugoslav Foreign Minister, to subscribe to the Three Powers Pact, Hitler reassured him that there was no danger of any territorial claims by Hungary. In Hitler's view, Hungary's latest territorial gains (the Second Vienna Award) had already given her indigestion, and she resembled a sated pithon that was unable to swallow and digest what it had just bolted down.

To Pavelić, in the summer of 1941, Hitler likewise criticized Hungary's national minority policy, and once more in connection with the Germans; while in his talks with Kvaternik he condemned the Hungarians for their attitude on the Jewish question. After that, the Hungarian Army's participation in the operations against the Soviet Union led Hitler to forget his antipathies for a while.

From the end of 1942 onwards, Hitler's remarks against Hungary became frequent and increasingly critical. He viewed the collapse of the Second Hungarian Army on the Don more or less as a proven failure by the Hungarian soldiers. There was a long and unpleasant discussion with Horthy in April 1943. Then at talks with Tiso, Hitler did not confine himself to sporadic remarks, but launched into a detailed critique of the whole country. He attacked the Hungarian press, which, in his view lacked discipline and was wont to blurt out secrets; he complained against Hungary's lack of action against the Jews, which allegedly increased the Bolshevik danger in the country; and he fumigated against the Hungarian ruling classes for treating both Hungarian and Slovak peasants as inferiors—in accordance with their anachronistic social values.

At these unofficial talks Hitler again and again unbridled his passions against Hungary and the Hungarians:

> The Hungarian is as lazy as the Russian. He's by nature a man of the steppe.[5] From a social point of view, the sickest communities of the New Europe are: first, Hungary, then Italy.[6] The Hungarians are wild nationalists. They assimilate the Germans at extraordinary speed, and they know how to select the best of them for posts of command. We shan't succeed in preserving the German minorities in Hungary except by taking over control of the State—or else we shall have to withdraw our minorities from Hungary.[7] We shall only be repaying the Hungarians in their own coin, once the war is over, for having everywhere and so promptly taken advantage of circumstances and pulled their chestnuts out of the fire.[8]

About his discussions with Miklós Kállay in the summer of 1942 (of which no official minutes have survived), Hitler had this to say to his associates:

Kállay, the new Prime Minister of Hungary, came to me with two "little requests" from Regent Horthy—namely, that firstly the Lord God and secondly I myself should turn a benevolent blind eye if the Hungarians started a fight with the Rumanians. From the Hungarian point of view, said Kállay, such a fight would be a struggle against Asia, for the frontier between Europe and Asia was, in Hungarian eyes, the line where the Orthodox Church ceased to hold sway. It was, after all, he said, only the countries on this side of that frontier which had played their part in European cultural developments and all its great accomplishments such as the Reformation, the Renaissance and the like.[9]

Hitler's response was anything but positive: "The day will come," he said on August 9, 1942,

> when the Viennese idea will be proved to be right. In the ten thousand cafés of Vienna this is how the Hungarian problem is envisaged: 'Hungary belongs to us and the people in Berlin know nothing about it. It is we who liberated the Hungarians from the Turks, and order will not be restored to Hungary until we liberate the country again. So why on earth don't we take it over and have done with it!'[10]

As Hitler's dissatisfaction with Hungarian policy rose, his criticisms of Hungarian internal affairs grew proportionately. On March 2, 1944, for example, he told Antonescu that "Sollten morgen die Sowjets an die Tür Ungarns klopfen, so würde ohne eine deutsche Besetzung des Landes sofort die Revolution von Juden and Proletariern entfacht werden." In the same vein, on May 12, he informed Tiso:

> Seit einem Jahr habe die ungarische Regierungsclique laufend Verrat getrieben, obwohl doch das heutige Ungarn ein Produkt sei, das nicht aus eigener Kraft, sondern nur durch den deutschen Kräfteeinsatz aus seiner Bedeutungslosigkeit herausgehoben worden sei.

In general Hitler liked to speak about Hungary as a land of corruption and national and social oppression, which, for these very reasons, is a good soil for communism:

> Alles strebe danach, schnell reich zu werden und das Geld in Budapest zu vergeuden.

> Es herrsche in Ungarn eine schreckliche Korruption. Horthy ihm einmal gesagt habe, die Ungarn liebten das Geld nicht, das sei schmutzig. Man habe die Geldgeschäfte immer den Juden überlassen; in Wirklichkeit aber sei—so meinte der Führer—nich das Geld schmutzig, sondern die Methode, wie man in Ungarn das Geld verdient habe.

As recorded in the minutes, in the summer of 1944, Hitler also expressed his low opinion about Hungary and the Hungarians to General Béla Miklós:

> Er [der Führer] sehe Ungarn anders an als der Reichsverweser. Er betrachte es als ein völlig unkonsolidiertes, rassisch zerrissenes Land, dessen Minderheiten sowieso keine Lust hätten, für seinen Bestand zu kämpfen. Zu der grossen Gefahr, die von dem starken jüdischen Bevölkerungsteil ausgehe, komme die völlig unausgeglichene soziale Struktur des Landes hinzu, die Ungarn zu einer leichten Beute für den Bolschewismus machen könne. Bei irgendeiner Krise würde der Staat in Ungarn angesichts dieser Lage zusammenbrechen.

Finally, having surveyed Europe, Hitler also recited his complaints about the Hungarians to the Hungarian Arrow Cross leader Szálasi. Enumerating how all his allies had played him false, Hitler went on to say,

> In Ungarn endlich habe der Reichsverweser geherrscht, ein Grandseigneur, der vielleicht nicht in seiner Weltanschauung, aber doch in seiner Lebensanschauung mehr mit England als mit seinem eigenen Lande übereinstimmte und dem Volke völlig fremd gegenüberstand, der immer den leichteren Weg suchte und ihn [den Führer] in geradezu schamloser Weise belogen habe . . . .

Szálasi was the last politician with whom Hitler negotiated. Six weeks after his talks with the Arrow Cross leader, the Führer retired to his Berlin bunker, where he spent his last 105 days. There he attempted to perform his last great act in the twilight of the gods. His talks with Szálasi constitute a kind of symbolic end to the chapter that Nazi Germany's policy had begun in Southeastern Europe. They show what the Nazi system of alliances had degenerated into; how it had become a system that could have no allies, only satellites, and then not even satellites, only puppets it had created itself. It was this system that raised and kept these puppets in power briefly. By Szálasi's days, however, no more alliances could be conceived of, and—as in the adventures of Baron Münchausen, where he lifts himself out of the bog by his own hair—Hitler signed and adhered to alliances only with himself. But the decline was a failure not only of Nazi Germany, but also of her allies, most of whom sat paralyzed, awaiting the end, unable to shrug off Hitler's deadly embrace. Who was to blame? Fate? Circumstances? Misfortune? Human frailty? Germany's mistaken policies, backed up by her military superiority? Or all of these together? There were perceptible differences among Hitler's puppets and allies. Horthy, the old admiral, was absolutely delighted at Hitler's rise to power, and for a while Hitler too had shown him some kind of regard. Yet, contrary to Hitler's most other puppets, Horthy could blush with shame when speaking of the death of 30,000 unarmed Jews forced into labor camps. Moreover, concern for the fate of his country had time and again awakened in him a need for sober calculation and reflection—irrespective of his distorted view of the internal social and political conditions of his country. Then there was the darling, the disciplined Romanian soldier Antonescu, whose leitmotif, besides hatred of Bolshevism, was thirst for vengeance against Hungary and reacquisition of Transylvania. There was Tiso, the Slovak village priest, whom Hitler had turned into a head of state, and in whom all he had learned and taught about Christ and Christian charity has been washed away by the pursuit of an illusory Slovak independence. There was the Croatian lawyer Pavelić, corrupt through and through, who had lived for a decade under the spell of violence. He murdered *en masse* all who sought to save things of real value, instead of running after the independence declared under Germany's auspices, and did so with an unparalleled brutality immortalized by Malaparte. And Pavelić did all this under the pretext of gaining Croatia's independence. Finally, there was the rational Professor Filov, whom clear socio-political and power considerations, plus some territorial concessions, could persuade to take his country into the Nazi camp.

Were they all pieces on a chessboard? Or were they characters in a tragedy—sometimes tragic, sometimes comic? Were they power-crazed maniacs or victims? Or were they simply bystanders when a lunatic ran amok, when a great historical scene was being played, when there came the twilight of the gods? Indeed they were. But behind their names were countries, and the lives, fates and sufferings of millions. The flatterers, the cringers, and even the retainers of a certain degree of dignity while in power—all bowed to the will of this lunatic. But each of them was the leader of a country, and each spoke on behalf of the ruling classes of his country. Although now and then they may have appeared helpless and defenseless before Hitler, at home in their own countries—whether legitimate leaders or Hitler's stooges—their word was the law of the land, and upon their mercy depended the lives of many millions.

NOTES

* All quotations, unless specifically stated otherwise, are from Andreas Hillgruber, *Staatsmänner und Diplomaten bei Hitler* (Frankfurt am Main: Bernard und Graefe Verlag für Wehrwesen, 1970).

1. The English translation of Hitler's *Tischgeschpräche* (Bonn: Athenäum-Verlag, 1951) first appeared under the title *Table Talk, 1941-1944* (London: Weidenfeld and Nicolson, 1953). Its American edition, introduced by H. R. Trevor-Roper, was published under the title: *Hitler's Secret Conversations, 1941-1944* (New York: Farrar, Straus and Young, 1953). The quotations are from this edition. See the entry for July 25, 1941, p. 12.

2. *A Wilhelmstrasse és Magyarország. Német diplomáciai iratok Magyarországról, 1933-1944* [Wilhelmstrasse and Hungary, German Diplomatic Documents on Hungary, 1933-1944], edited by Gy. Ránki, E. Pamlényi, Gy. Juhász and L. Tilkovszky (Budapest: Kossuth Kiadó, 1968).

3. As is well known, a few days later Hitler changed his view and succeeded in gaining the assistance of the majority of the Hungarian staff of generals and officers to pressure Hungary's entry into the war.

4. *Hitler's Secret Conversations,* August 22, 1942, p. 531.
5. Ibid., September 17, 1931, p. 28.
6. Ibid., November 5, 1941, p. 96.
7. Ibid., February 26, 1942, pp. 274-275.
8. Ibid., April 28, 1942, pp. 362-363.
9. Ibid., June 7, 1942, pp. 418-419.
10. Ibid., August 9, 1942, p. 506.

CONTRIBUTORS

ACZÉL, TAMÁS, D.Lit., is professor of English at the University of Massachusetts, Amherst. He was a member of Imre Nagy's circle both before and during the Hungarian Revolution of 1956. He is the author (with Tibor Méray) of *The Revolt of the Mind* (1959), *The Ice Age* (novel, 1965), and *Illuminations* (novel, 1981); the editor and co-author of *Ten Years After: The Hungarian Revolution in the Perspective of History* (1966); and the co-editor and translator of *Poetry from the Russian Underground* (1973), and *The Literature of Eastern Europe: An Introduction with an Anthology* (1978).

BAK, JÁNOS M., Dr. Phil., is Professor of Medieval History at the University of British Columbia. His publications include: *Königtum und Stände in Ungarn im 14-16. Jahrhundert* (1973); and *The German Peasant War of 1526*, ed. (1977).

BENECKE, GERHARD, Ph.D., is Senior Lecturer in History at the University of Kent at Canterbury. Born in war-time Berlin, he was educated in Britain and West Germany. He has previously taught at Aberdeen University and at the University of British Columbia. He is the author of *Society and Politics in Germany, 1500-1750* (1974); and *Maximilian I, 1459-1519: An Analytical Biography* (1982).

BOBA, IMRE, Ph.D., studied Slavic philology and history at the Pázmány Péter University in Budapest, and received his Ph.D. in history from the University of Washington. Currently he is Professor of Medieval History and of East European Studies at the latter institution. Professor Boba is interested in the study of medieval societies in Europe and Central Asia. His publications include: *Nomads, Northmen and Slavs: Eastern Europe in the Ninth Century* (1967); and *Moravia's History Reconsidered* (1971).

BORSODY, STEPHEN [ISTVÁN], J.U.Dr. (Prague), *Privatdozent* (Budapest), Professor Emeritus at Chatham College (Pittsburgh) has served Hungary's postwar coalition government as a diplomat in Washington. He is the author of *Beneš* (in Hungarian, 1943); *The Hungarian-Slovak Compromise* (in Hungarian, 1945); *The Triumph of Tyranny* (1960); *The Tragedy of Central Europe: Nazi and Soviet Conquest and Aftermath* (1980); the editor of *Hungarians in Czechoslovakia, 1918-1938* (in Hungarian, 1938); and the co-author of several other major works in East Central European History.

BRISCH, HANS, Ph.D., is Associate Vice President and Provost and Executive Assistant to the President of the University of Nebraska. He holds academic appointments in management and public administration, where he has published extensively. He has also co-edited (with Ivan Volgyes) *Czechoslovakia: The Heritage of Ages Past* (1979).

CLARKE, JAMES F. (1906-1982), Ph.D., born into an American missionary family in European Turkey, was one of the pioneers of Balkan (especially Bulgarian) studies in the United States. Educated at Amherst and Harvard, during World War II he was Chief of the Balkan Section, Office of Strategic Services. Following the war he taught at Indiana University (Director of the University's East European Institute) and at the University of Pittsburgh. His books include *Bible Societies, American Missionaries and the National Revival of Bulgaria* (1971); and his forthcoming *Bulgaria Past and Present: Studies in Bulgarian History*.

COPPA, FRANK J., Ph.D., is Professor of History at St. John's University (Jamaica), and a member of the Columbia Seminar on Studies on Modern Italy. He is the author of *Planning, Protectionism and Politics in Liberal Italy* (1971); and *Pope Pius IX: Crusader in a Secular Age* (1979). He has edited or co-edited *From Vienna to Vietnam: War and Peace in the Modern World* (1969); *Cities in Transition from the Ancient World to Urban America* (1974); *Religion in the Making of Western Man* (1975); *The Immigrant Experience in America* (1977); and *Screen and Society: The Impact of Television upon Aspects of Contemporary Civilization* (1979).

DEAK, ISTVAN, Ph.D., is Professor of History at Columbia University and the former Director of the University's Institute on East Central Europe (1967-1978). Educated in his native Hungary, the Sorbonne, Maryland and Columbia Universities, Professor Deak's research interests include the modern history of Germany and East Central Europe. He is the author of *Weimar Germany's Left-Wing Intellectuals* (1968); and *The Lawful Revolution: Louis Kossuth and the Hungarians, 1848-1849* (1979). He has also co-edited *Eastern Europe in the 1970s* (1972); and the two-volume work *Everyman in Europe: Essays in Social History* (1974; 2nd ed. 1981).

Contributors

DECSY, JÁNOS, Ph.D., is a former aide-de-camp of General Béla K. Király. A graduate of the Hungarian Military Academy, the Hungarian War College and Columbia University, Professor Decsy has taught at Rhode Island College, Providence College, Rutgers University and Brooklyn College. Currently he is Professor of History at Greater Hartford Community College. He is the author of a number of articles on modern Hungarian history and of the monograph *Prime Minister Gyula Andrássy's Influence on Habsburg Foreign Policy* (1979).

DOMONKOS, LESLIE S., Ph.D., is a Professor of Medieval History and Renaissance Studies at Youngstown State University. A graduate of the Mediaeval Institute of the University of Notre Dame, Professor Domonkos has been a recipient of a number of Ford Foundation, Fulbright and IREX Fellowships. He is the co-author of *Studium Generale: Studies in Honor of A. L. Gabriel* (1967), and the author of a number of articles on late medieval and Renaissance education, as well as of the forthcoming *The Political and Cultural History of Hungary in the Age of Matthias Corvinus*.

DREISZIGER, N. F., Ph.D., is Associate Professor of History at the Royal Military College of Canada, and the founding editor of the *Hungarian Studies Review* (formerly *The Canadian-American Review of Hungarian Studies*). His publications include *Hungary's Way to World War II* (1968); and *Struggle and Hope: The Hungarian-Canadian Experience* (1982). He has also edited *The Hungarian Revolution Twenty Years After* (1976); and *Mobilization for Total War* (1981).

ELTETO, LOUIS J., Ph.D., is Associate Professor of German and Hungarian, and Chairman of the Department of Foreign Languages at Portland State University. He is also the founding editor (with Andrew Ludanyi) of the bilingual periodical *ITT-OTT*, and the co-editor of the forthcoming *Transylvania: The Roots of Ethnic Conflict*.

FENYO, MARIO D., Ph.D., is currently on the faculty of the University of Calabar, Nigeria. A graduate of Virginia, Yale and American Universities, Professor Fenyo has taught at several universities in the United States, Puerto Rico, Asia and Africa. He is the author of *Hitler, Horthy and Hungary* (1972), and a number of scholarly articles on various aspects of contemporary history. He also dabbles in not-so-contemporary history, sociology, literature and journalism.

FICHTNER, PAULA SUTTER, Ph.D., is a Professor of History at Brooklyn College and the Graduate Center of the City University of New York. She is the author of *Ferdinand I of Austria: The Politics of Dynasticism in the Age of the Reformation* (1982).

FISCHER-GALATI, STEPHEN, Ph.D., is Professor of History at the University of Colorado and the Editor and Publisher of the *East European Quarterly* and of the *East European Monographs*. He is the author of numerous books and articles on the history of Eastern Europe including, among others, *Ottoman Imperialism and German Protestantism* (1959); *Twentieth-Century Romania* (1970); *Man, State, and Society in East European History* (1970); and *The Balkans Revolutionary Tradition* (with D. Djorjevic, 1981).

HELD, JOSEPH, Ph.D., is Associate Dean at Rutgers University's University College, Camden. In addition to a dozen articles and chapters, Professor Held is the author of *A History of Eastern Europe* (1978); and of the forthcoming *János Hunyadi: The Life and Times of a Fifteenth-Century Soldier-Statesman*. He has also edited and co-edited *Social and Intellectual History in the Habsburg Empire from Maria Theresa to World War I* (1975); and *The Modernization of Agriculture: Rural Transformation in Hungary, 1848-1975* (1980).

HUPCHIK, DENNIS P., is a candidate for the Ph.D. in history at the University of Pittsburgh. In addition to writing his dissertation entitled "Bulgaria in the Seventeenth Century: A Slavic Christian Culture under Foreign Domination," Mr. Hupchik is also involved in the co-editing of the collected studies of James F. Clarke (his Ph.D. mentor until his recent death), as well as a *Festschrift* in honor of Professor Clarke.

KRAMÁR, ZOLTÁN, Ph.D., is a Professor of History at Central Washington University, where he specializes in military history with an emphasis on the problems of combat command style. Born in Hungary, and educated in Hungary, Germany and the United States, Professor Kramár is the author of articles on military history, and the editor of *From the Danube to the Hudson: U.S. Ministerial and Consular Dispatches on Immigration from the Habsburg Monarchy, 1850-1900* (1978).

LOWENTHAL, MARK M., Ph.D., is currently Specialist in National Defense at the Congressional Research Services, Library Congress, where he heads the Defense Policy/Arms Control Section. Having studied under Béla

K. Király at Brooklyn College, he received his Ph.D. in history at Harvard University. In addition to numerous reports in the area of intelligence, national security and arms control, and articles on U.S. foreign policy in the period between 1937-1942, he is also the author of the novel *Crispan Magicker*.

LUDANYI, ANDREW, Ph.D., is Professor of Political Science at Ohio Northern University, and the founding editor (with Louis J. Elteto) of the bilingual periodical *ITT-OTT*. His research interest centers on international relations and comparative politics with particular emphasis on inter-ethnic relations in East Central Europe and the United States. In addition to authoring a number of articles on these topics, he is also the co-editor of the forthcoming *Transylvania: The Roots of Ethnic Conflict*.

NAGY, KÁROLY, Ph.D., is Professor and Chairman of the Social and Rehabilitation Services Curriculum at Middlesex County College, and Coadjutant Associate Professor of Sociology at Rutgers University. His studies, articles, and essays on sociology, literature, human services, and pedagogy have been published in various periodicals and books in the United States, Hungary, West Germany, Canada, and France.

PALUMBO, MICHAEL, Ph.D., is a graduate of the City University of New York. He is the author of *Human Rights: Meaning and History* (1982); and the co-editor of *Naturalism: Essays in Honor of Louis L. Snyder* (1981). He has also published a number of scholarly articles. Currently he is working on "Legions of Infamy," which tells the story of Italian Fascist atrocities and British and American governmental efforts to protect war criminals.

PASTOR, PETER, Ph.D., is Professor of History at Montclair State College, where he teaches Russian, East European and diplomatic history. He is the author of *Hungary between Wilson and Lenin: The Hungarian Revolution of 1918-1919 and the Big Three* (1976); and the co-editor of *Essays on World War I: Origins and Prisoners of War* (1983), and *Essays on World War I: Total War and Peacemaking. A Case Study of Trianon* (1983), Professor Pastor has also contributed widely to books and scholarly periodicals.

PERJÉS, GÉZA, Dr. Phil., is a Senior Fellow at the Institute of History, Hungarian Academy of Sciences, Budapest. Being one of Hungary's most noted military historians, Dr. Perjés's interest centers on military strategy in the sixteenth and seventeenth centuries. His publications include *Agricultural Production, Population, Military Food Supplies, and Strategy in* the Second Half of the Seventeenth Century (1963); *Nicholas Zrínyi and his Age* (1965); *The Country that had been Cast to the Wayside* (1975); and *Mohács* (1979). He has also edited *Nicholas Zrínyi's Writings on the Art of War* (1957).

RÁNKI, GYÖRGY, Ph.D., D.Sc., is a full member of the Hungarian Academy of Sciences, the Deputy Director of the Academy's Institute of History, and currently the Hungarian Chair Professor at Indiana University, Bloomington. Professor Ránki has authored or co-authored over two dozen volumes, among them the following: *Hungary: A Century of Economic Development* (1974); *History of the Second World War* (1976, 3rd ed., 1982); *Economic Development of East-Central Europe in the 19th and 20th Centuries* (1977); *East-Central Europe in the 19th and 20th Centuries* (1978); *Underdevelopment and Economic Growth. Studies in Hungarian Economic and Social History* (1979); and *Industrialization and the European Periphery* (1982).

SANDERS, IVAN, Ph.D., is Professor of English at Suffolk County Community College. In recent years he has also taught modern Hungarian literature at Columbia University. His articles on East European literature have appeared in both American and European journals, and his translations of George Konrád's novel, *The Loser*, has just appeared in print (1982). He is also co-editor of *Essays on World War I: Total War and Peacemaking. A Case Study of Trianon* (1983).

SNYDER, LOUIS, L., Dr.Phil., is Emeritus Professor of History at the City University of New York. He is the author of sixty books, including *The War, 1939-1945*, translated into many languages, and is co-editor of Simon & Schuster's best-seller, *A Treasury of Great Reporting*. He is a general editor of the 123-volume Anvil original paperbacks in history. Holder of Rockefeller, Ford, and von Humbolt Fellowships, his latest assignment was Fulbright Visiting Professor at the University of Cologne, West Germany. He represents authors on the board of directors of the Copyright Clearance Center, and is an author-panelist for the American Arbitration Association.

SOZAN, MICHAEL, Ph.D., is an Associate Professor of Sociology and Anthropology at Slippery Rock University, and a specialist in the comparative study of East and West European social systems. A recipient of many fellowships (e.g. Woodrow Wilson, IREX, National Academy of Sciences), Professor Sozan is the author of *The History of Hungarian Ethnography* (1977); and of the forthcoming work *Peasants in Two Political Systems: Village Life in Austria and Hungary*.

SUGAR, PETER F., Ph.D., is Professor of History and International Studies at the University of Washington, and a former Director of the Russian and East European Studies program at the same institution. He is also past President of the American Association for the Study of Hungarian History, the Western Slavic Association, the Conference on Slavic and East European Studies of the American Historical Association, and the current Vice-President of the Slavic Conference of the International Historical Association. He is the author, editor, or co-editor of a half a dozen books, and the co-editor of the eleven-volume *A History of East Central Europe* series.

SZENDREY, THOMAS, Ph.D., is Associate Professor of History at Gannon University. Before going to Gannon, he taught at Walsh College and at Duquesne University. His area of specialization is European intellectual and cultural history and the philosophy of history, where he has published a number of articles, as well as a text on the general councils of the Catholic Church. He has also translated a number of studies from Hungarian, including E. C. Mályusz's *The Theater and National Awakening: East Central Europe* (1980).

TREFOUSSE, HANS L., Ph.D., is Professor of History at Brooklyn College and at the Graduate Center of the City University of New York. Professor Trefousse is the author and editor of well over a dozen books. His authored works include: *Germany and American Neutrality, 1939-1941* (1951); *Ben Butler: The South Called him Beast* (1957); *Benjamin Franklin Wade: Radical Republican from Ohio* (1963); *The Radical Republicans: Lincoln's Vanguard for Racial Justice* (1969); *Impeachment of a President: Andrew Johnson, the Blacks, and Reconstruction* (1975); and *Carl Schurz: A Biography*. Among many other honors, in 1977-1978 Professor Trefousse was also the recipient of the Guggenheim Fellowship.

VARDY, AGNES HUSZAR, Ph.D., is Associate Professor of Literature at Robert Morris College, while also teaching Hungarian language and culture at the University of Pittsburgh. Her areas of interest include Hungarian-American immigrant literature, Germanistics and comparative literature, with particular attention to German, Austrian and Hungarian Romanticism. Her books include *A Study of Austrian Romanticism: Hungarian Influences on Lenau's Poetry* (1974); and *The Life and Times of Karl Beck* (1983). She has co-edited *The Folk Arts of Hungary* (1981), and is one of the editors of the present volume.

VARDY, STEVEN BELA, Ph.D., is Professor of East European History and Director of the Duquesne University History Forum, and an Adjunct

Professor of History at the University of Pittsburgh. He is also the current President of the American Association for the Study of Hungarian History. Professor Vardy's books include *Hungarian Historiography and the Geistesgeschichte School* (1974); *Modern Hungarian Historiography* (1976); and his forthcoming *Clio's Art in Hungary*. He is also completing a book on Hungarian immigration to the United States. He is one of the editors of the present volume.

VERMES, GÁBOR, Ph.D., is an Associate Professor of History at Rutgers University, Newark. A specialist in modern East Central European and Hungarian history, Professor Vermes's studies have appeared in a number of well-known periodicals and collective volumes. He is also the author of the forthcoming *Count István Tisza: A Political Biography*.

VOLGYES, IVAN, Ph.D., is Professor of Political Science and Director of the Slavic and East European Area Studies Program at the University of Nebraska. Author or co-editor of more than twenty books and several scores of scholarly articles dealing with Eastern Europe, the USSR and the Warsaw Pact, Professor Volgyes has also been a frequent consultant of the Department of State and the Department of Defense.